AN
ENCYCLOPEDIA
OF
COMPELLING
QUOTATIONS

AN
ENCYCLOPEDIA
OF
COMPELLING
QUOTATIONS

Quotes From
Over 3200 Sources

R. DANIEL WATKINS

HENDRICKSON
PUBLISHERS

An Encyclopedia of Compelling Quotations

Printed in the United States of America

ISBN 1-56563-645-7

First printing — July 2001

Cover design by Richmond & Williams, Nashville, Tennessee
Interior design and typesetting by Booksetters, White House, Tennessee

Library of Congress Cataloging-in-Publication Data

An encyclopedia of compelling quotations / [compiled by] R. Daniel Watkins.
p. cm.
Includes index.
ISBN 1-56563-645-7 (cloth)
1. Quotations, English. I. Watkins, R. Daniel 1951-

PN6081 .E55 2001
082--dc21

2001039006

To my wife and best friend,
Bonnie,
without whom this book
would not exist.

ACKNOWLEDGMENT:

My warm thanks go to my editor at Hendrickson Publishers, Dan Penwell, for his kindness and patient guidance. My extreme appreciation go to Bob Bubnis for his work in developing the distinctive page layout and typesetting of this book.

Additionally, I am indebted to the reference librarians at the Austin Public Library for their consistent, cheerful willingness to help. Finally, I thank my many friends and relatives for the numerous quotations that they have routed my way.

CONTENTS

INTRODUCTION

Speakers, writers, pastors, and teachers are constantly on the lookout for pertinent quotations to illustrate specific points. Some writers, speakers, and even pastors hire people to be their eyes and ears when it comes to finding good quotations.

An Encyclopedia of Compelling Quotations is such a compilation. Quotations have been gathered from over 3200 different sources. You will find almost 1000 topics arranged alphabetically from Ability to Zeal.

Included in the back of the book is a CD-ROM providing convenient cut-and-paste opportunities to move quotes directly from the CD-ROM into actual manuscripts, talks, sermons, and lessons. The CD-ROM is designed as a database to help you develop your own electronic reference file wherein you can add additional quotations, quips, illustrations, and stories.

One additional note: The slashes (/) interjected throughout the text of many of the quotations are simply indicators within a free verse quotation or poetry that a new line is beginning.

My hope and prayer is that this collection will both excite you and bless you.

— A —

ABILITY

We are not all able to do all things.　　—Virgil, *Eclogues*, VIII, line 63

Ability is a poor man's wealth.　　　　　　　　—Matthew Wren

ABSENCE

Absence makes the heart grow fonder,
　Isle of Beauty, Fare thee well!　—Thomas H. Bayly, "Isle of Beauty"

Absence is to love what wind is to fire; it extinguishes the small, it
　enkindles the great.　　　　　　　　—Comte de Bussy-Rabutin

It takes time for the absent to assume their true shape in our thoughts.
　After death they take on a firmer outline and then cease to change.
　　—Colette, in Robert Phelps, editor, "*Earthly Paradise*, The Captain"

The absent are never without fault. Nor the present without excuse.
　　　　　　　　　　　　　　　　　—Benjamin Franklin

The absent are always in the wrong.
　　　　　　　　　—George Herbert, *Outlandish Proverbs*

Achilles absent, was Achilles still.　　　　　　—Homer, *Iliad*

The joy of life is variety; the tenderest love requires to be renewed by
　intervals of absence.　　　　　　　　　　—Samuel Johnson

Absence diminishes little passions and increases great ones.
　　　　　　　　　　　—François de La Rochefoucauld

Short absence quickens love.　　　　　　　　　—Mirabeau

Is not absence death to those who love?　　　　—Alexander Pope

Out of sight, out of mind.　　　　—Proverb (13th century English)

Far from eye, far from heart.　　　　　—Proverb (14th century)

Speak not Evil of the absent for it is unjust.
　　　　　　　—George Washington, copybook, 1748, at age 16

ABSTINENCE

Abstinence is as easy to me, as temperance would be difficult.
—Samuel Johnson, in William Roberts, editor,
Memoirs of the Life and Correspondence of Mrs. Hannah More

It is easier to abstain than restrain. —Proverb (French)

When in doubt, do without. —Proverb (Vermont)

ABSURDITY

I have too much respect for the idea of God to make it responsible for
such an absurd world. —Georges Duhamel,
Chronique des Pasquier, V, "Le désert de Bièvres"

ABUNDANCE

Not what we have, but what we enjoy, constitutes our abundance.
—J. Petit-Senn

Too much sunshine in life makes a desert. —Gustav J. White

ACCEPTANCE

Accept the place the divine providence has found for you.
—Ralph Waldo Emerson, *Essays, First Series*, "Self-Reliance"

. . . what is forbidden to put right becomes lighter by acceptance.
—Horace, *Odes*

Where there is no choice, we do well to make no difficulty.
—George Macdonald

ACCIDENT

Receive the accidents that befall you as good, knowing that nothing
happens without God. —Anonymous (2nd century A.D.)

What men call accident is God's own part. —Gamaliel Bailey

Accidents will occur in the best of regulated families.
—Charles Dickens, *David Copperfield*

There is an ambush everywhere from the army of accidents; therefore
the rider of life runs with loosened reins. —Hafez, *Divan*

Men's accidents are God's purposes. —Sophia A. Hawthorne, in
Nathaniel Hawthorne, 1 June 1842,
Claude M. Simpson, editor, *The American Notebooks*

Nothing with God can be accidental. —Henry Wadsworth Longfellow

What happened was no accident. Everything was preordained. True,
the will was free, but heaven also made its ordinances.
—Isaac Beshevis Singer, *The Slave*

There is no such thing as an accident. What we call by that name is
the effect of some cause which we do not see. —Voltaire

ACCOMPLISHMENT

Everyone is trying to accomplish something big, not realizing that
life is made up of little things. —Frank A. Clark

I long to accomplish a great and noble task, but it is my chief duty to
accomplish small tasks as if they were great and noble.
—Helen Keller

All my life I wanted to accomplish something worthwhile—a thing
people will say took a little something . . .
—Bernard Malamud, *The Assistant*

ACCUMULATION

Many littles make a much. —Miguel de Cervantes,
Don Quixote, Part ii, Ch. 7

If you should put even a little on a little, and should do this often,
soon this too would become big. —Hesiod

Let this be an example for the acquisition of all knowledge, virtue,
and riches. By the fall of drops of water, by degrees, a pot is filled.
—*The Hitopadesa*

There will grow from straws a mighty heap. —Ovid, *Amores*

Little and often fills the purse. —Proverb (17th century)

ACTING

Five stages of an actor . . . 1. Who's Mary Astor? 2. Get me Mary
Astor. 3. Get me a Mary Astor type. 4. Get me a young Mary Astor.
5. Who's Mary Astor? —Mary Astor, *A Life on Film*

An actor is a sculptor who carves in snow.   —Lawrence Barrett

Remember that you are but an actor, acting whatever part the Master has ordained. It may be short or it may be long. If he wishes you to represent a poor man, do so heartily; if a cripple, or a magistrate, or a private man, in each case act your part with honor.   —Epictetus

We all have a contract with the public—in us they see themselves or what they would like to be.   —Clark Gable

Acting is happy agony.   —Alec Guinness

The whole essence of learning lines is to forget them so you can make them sound like you thought of them that instant.
                                            —Glenda Jackson,
                in *Sunday Telegraph* (a British newspaper), 26 Jul 1992

The drama's laws, the drama's patrons give.
For we that live to please, must please to live.   —Samuel Johnson

In really good acting we should be able to believe that what we hear and see is of our own imagining; it should seem to be to us as a charming dream.   —Joseph Joubert

By acting as you wish yourself to be, in due course you will become as you act.   —Norman Vincent Peale

Each man has some part to play. —Adelaide Procter, *Legends and Lyrics*

Just learn your lines and don't bump into the furniture.
                                                    —Spencer Tracy

Every now and then, when you're on stage, you hear the best sound a player can hear . . . It is the sound of a wonderful, deep silence that means you've hit them where they live.
                        —Shelley Winters, *That Wonderful, Deep Silence*

ACTION

Action is the antidote to despair.   —Joan Baez, *Rolling Stone*, 1983

Action may not always bring happiness; but there is no happiness without action.   —Beaconsfield

Be slow in considering, but resolute in action.   —Bias

Active natures are rarely melancholy—activity and sadness are incompatible.   —Christian Nestell Bovée

A contemplative life has more the appearance of a life of piety than any other; but it is the divine plan to bring faith into activity and exercise.   —Cecil

Every action of our lives touches on some chord that will vibrate in eternity.   —Edwin Hubbel Chapin

A man's most open actions have a secret side to them.
                                  —Joseph Conrad, *Under Western Eyes*

A true history of human events would show that a far larger proportion of our acts are the results of sudden impulses and accidents than of that reason of which we so much boast.   —Cooper

We must not, in trying to think about how we can make a big difference, ignore the small daily differences we can make which, over time, add up to big differences that we often cannot foresee.
                                            —Marian Wright Edelman

A man's action is only a picture book of his creed.
                                            —Ralph Waldo Emerson

Be active first thyself,
     Then seek the aid of heaven;
     For to the worker God Himself lends aid.   —Euripides

Action is the proper fruit of knowledge.
                    —Thomas Fuller, M. D., *Gnomologia*, No. 760

Give me the ready hand rather than the ready tongue.
                                            —Giuseppe Garibaldi

The highest cannot be spoken; it can only be acted.
                                    —Johann Wolfgang von Goethe

Be content to act, and leave the talking to others.
                                    —Baltasar Gracián, *The Oracle*

Invariably, we act first and think later.   —Lars Gustaffson,
                                            Stories of Happy People,
             "The Fugitives Discover That They Knew Nothing"

The road to holiness necessarily passes through the world of action.
—Dag Hammarskjöld, *Markings*

Our acts make or mar us,—we are the children of our own deeds.
—Victor Hugo

Make up your mind to act decidedly and take the consequences. No good is ever done in this world by hesitation.
—Thomas Henry Huxley

The great end of life is not knowledge but action.
—Thomas Henry Huxley,
Science and Culture, "Technical Education"

Act, and God will act.
—Joan of Arc (1430),
in Edward Lucie-Smith, *Joan of Arc*

It is not enough to have ideals. We must translate them into action. We must clear our own little corner of creation.
—Toyohiko Kagawa, *Meditation on the Cross*

The greatest pleasure I know is to do a good action by stealth, and to have it found out by accident.
—Charles Lamb,
"Table Talk by the late Elia"

Act well at the moment, and you have performed a good action to all eternity.
—Johann Kaspar Lavater

The smallest good act today is the capture of a strategic point from which, a few months later, you may be able to go on to victories you never dreamed of.
—C. S. Lewis, *Mere Christianity*

I have always thought the actions of men the best interpreters of their thoughts.
—John Locke,
An Essay Concerning Human Understanding, I, 3

Every man feels instinctively that all the beautiful sentiments in the world weigh less than a single lovely action.
—James Russell Lowell,
Among My Books, "Rousseau and the Sentimentalists"

It is well to think well: it is divine to act well.
—Horace Mann

Act quickly, think slowly.
—Proverb (Greek), in Aristotle,
Nichomachean Ethics

The conviction: I will not tolerate this age. The freedom: the freedom
  to act on my conviction. And I will act. No one else has both the conviction and the freedom. Many agree with me, have the conviction,
  but will not act. Some act, assassinate, bomb, burn, etc., but they are
  the crazies. Crazy acts by crazy people. But what if one, sober, reasonable, and honorable man should act, and act with perfect sobriety,
  reason, and honor? Then you have the beginning of a new age. We
  shall start a new order of things.   —Walker Percy, *Lancelot*

To do two things at once is to do neither.   —Publilius Syrus,
                                                          Sententioe, No. 7

Above all, try something.   —Franklin D. Roosevelt

Action is eloquence . . .   —William Shakespeare,
                                                Coriolanus, Act III, Sc. ii

I myself must mix with action, lest I wither by despair.
                                  —Alfred, Lord Tennyson, *Locksey Hall*

If you have built castles in the air, your work need not be lost; that is
  where they should be. Now put foundations under them.
                                                  —Henry David Thoreau

People rarely do what they don't want to.   —Peter de Vries,
                                                          Forever Panting

[Action] is the last resource of those who know not how to dream.
                    —Oscar Wilde, *Intentions*, "The Critic as Artist"

Thought and learning are of small value unless translated into action.
                                                      —Wang Yang-ming

ADAM AND EVE

In Adam's fall
  We sinned all.   —Anonymous, in Benjamin Harris,
                          compiler and publisher, *The New England Primer*,
                                                                      1690

Adam
  Had 'em.   —Strickland Gillilan, "On the Antiquity of Microbes"

Lord, forgive Adam, for Adam is me.   —Richard G. Jones,
                                                      100 Hymns for Today

In Adam's fall
  We sinned all.
  In the new Adam's rise,
  We shall all reach the skies.
                    —Henry David Thoreau, "In Adam's Fall"

ADAPTATION

Man is a pliable animal, a being who gets accustomed to everything!
                    —Fyodor Dostoyevsky

Slowly we adjust, but only if we have to.   —Ellen Goodman

Even in slight things the experience of the new is rarely without
  some stirring of foreboding.   —Eric Hoffer, *The Ordeal of Change*

Every new adjustment is a crisis in self-esteem.   —Eric Hoffer,
                                        The Ordeal of Change

Adapt yourself to the things among which your lot has been cast and
  love sincerely the fellow creatures with whom destiny has ordained
  that you shall live.   —Marcus Aurelius Antoninus

Who keeps company with the wolf will learn to howl.   —Proverb
                                        (16th century)

It's an ill plan that cannot be changed.   —Proverb (Latin)

We do our best that we know how at the moment, and if it doesn't
  turn out, we modify it.   —Franklin D. Roosevelt

Suit your manner to the man.   —Terence, *Adelphi*

He adapted to what there was to adapt to.   —Kurt Vonnegut, Jr.,
                                        Breakfast of Champions

ADMIRATION

It is good discretion not to make too much of any man at first;
  because one cannot hold out that proportion.   —Francis Bacon

We always like those who admire us. —François de La Rochefoucauld

If a man thinks well of you, make his thought come true.
                    —Proverb (Arab)

Season your admiration for a while. —William Shakespeare,
Hamlet, Act I, Sc. ii

. . . the people she admired . . . had this in common: they gazed at
the world from a distance.
—Anne Tyler, *Dinner at the Homesick Restaurant*

ADULTERY

Do not adultery commit;
Advantage rarely comes of it.
—Arthur Hugh Clough, "The Latest Decalogue"

He and I had an office so tiny that an inch smaller and it would have
been adultery. —Dorothy Parker, on sharing space
with Robert Benchley at Vanity Fair

ADVENTURE

Some men are by nature explorers; my nature is to stay under the
same moon and stars, and if the weather is wet, under the same
roof. It's a strange world, why make it stranger?
—Bernard Malamud, *The Fixer*

Adventure is the result of poor planning. —Col. Blatchford Snell

ADVERSITY

Sometimes life has a way of putting us on our backs in order to force
us to look up. —Charles L. Allen

Luctor et Emergo—I struggle and I come through. —Anonymous,
motto of Notre Dame College of Saskatchewan

He that has never known adversity is but half acquainted with others
or himself. —Aughey

All rising to great place is by a winding stair.
—Francis Bacon, *Essays II*, "Of Great Place"

He knows not his own strength that hath not met adversity.
—Francis Bacon, "Of Fortune"

Prosperity doth best discover vice; but adversity doth best discover
virtue. —Francis Bacon, *Essays*, "Of Adversity"

Prosperity is not without many fears and distastes; and adversity is not without comforts and hopes.

—Francis Bacon, *Essays*, "Of Adversity"

Prosperity is the blessing of the Old Testament, adversity is the blessing of the New.   —Francis Bacon, *Essays*, "Of Adversity"

. . . I was brought low, and he helped me.

—*The Bible* (KJV): Psalms 116:6

Adversity has the same effect on a man that severe training has on the pugilist—it reduces him to his fighting weight.   —Josh Billings

It is a great thing, when our Gethsemane hours come, when the cup of bitterness is pressed to our lips . . . to feel that it is not fate, that it is not necessity, but divine love for good ends working upon us.

—Edwin Hubbel Chapin

You may not realize it when it happens, but a kick in the teeth may be the best thing in the world for you.   —Walt Disney

Bad times have a scientific value. These are occasions a good learner would not miss.   —Ralph Waldo Emerson, *The Conduct of Life*, "Considerations by the Way"

Adversity is a trial of principle. Without it a man hardly knows whether he is honest or not.   —Henry Fielding

One day in retrospect the years of struggle will strike you as the most beautiful.   —Sigmund Freud

Almost anything can be dealt with if people are of good will and light hearts and strong values.   —Robert Fulghum, *Uh-Oh*

The worse the passage the more welcome the port.

—Thomas Fuller, M. D., *Gnomologia*, No. 4848

Learn how to appropriate the bad days.   —Dr. Bill Glover

Prosperity is a great teacher; adversity is a greater. Possession pampers the mind; privation trains and strengthens it.   —William Hazlitt

Adversity has the effect of eliciting talents which in prosperous circumstances would have lain dormant.   —Horace

Remember to be calm in adversity.   —Horace

God will not look you over for medals, degrees or diplomas, but for
    scars.   —Elbert Hubbard, *A Thousand and One Epigrams*

Remember that there is nothing stable in human affairs; therefore
    avoid undue elation in prosperity, or undue depression in adversity.
        —Isocrates

Adversity has ever been considered as the state in which a man most
    easily becomes acquainted with himself, being free from flatterers.
        —Samuel Johnson

It's a good thing to have all the props pulled out from under us occa-
    sionally. It gives us some sense of what is rock under our feet, and
    what is sand.   —Madeleine L'Engle,
        The Summer of the Great-Grandmother

Adversity reminds men of religion.   —Livy, *Annales*, V

Mishaps are like knives, that either serve us or cut us, as we grasp
    them by the blade or the handle.   —James Russell Lowell,
        Fireside Travels, "Cambridge Thirty Years Ago"

Outward attacks and troubles rather fix than unsettle the Christian,
    as tempests from without only serve to root the oak faster.
        —Hannah More

That which does not kill me makes me stronger.
        —Friedrich Nietzsche, *Twilight of the Idols* (1888)

But since . . . it was fun to struggle why complain?
    —Flannery O'Connor, "Everything That Rises Must Converge"

Unless the clay be well pounded, no pitcher can be made.
        —Proverb (Latin)

The good are better made by ill,
    As odors crushed are sweeter still.
        —Samuel Rogers, "Jacqueline," Stanza 3

Genuine morality is preserved only in the school of adversity, and a
    state of continuous prosperity may easily prove a quicksand to
    virtue.   —Friedrich Schiller

Adversity's sweet milk, philosophy.
    —William Shakespeare, *Romeo and Juliet*, Act III, Sc. iii

Sweet are the uses of adversity;
    Which, like the toad, ugly and venomous,
    Wears yet a precious jewel in his head.
                —William Shakespeare, *As You Like It*, Act II, Sc. i

. . . the worst is not
    So long as we can say, "This is the worst."
                —William Shakespeare, *King Lear*, Act IV, Sc. i

If a bird is flying for pleasure it flies with the wind, but if it meets
    danger it turns and faces the wind, in order that it may rise higher.
                —Corrie ten Boom

How should thy patience be crowned in heaven if none adversity
    should befall to thee in earth? If thou wilt suffer none adversity
    how mayest thou be the friend of Christ?   —Thomas à Kempis

It is easy enough to be pleasant
    When life flows along like a song,
    But the man worth while is the man who can smile
    When everything goes dead wrong.   —Ella Wheeler Wilcox

ADVERTISING

Good times, bad times, there will always be advertising. In good
    times, people want to advertise; in bad times, they have to.
                —Bruce Barton

Doing business without advertising is like winking at a girl in the
    dark. You know what you are doing, but nobody else does.
                —Steuart Henderson Britt

Half the money I spend on advertising is wasted, and the trouble is I
    don't know which half.
                —Viscount Leverhulme, in David Ogilvy,
                Confessions of an Advertising Man

(A b o u t)   A D V I C E

Distrust interested advice.   —Aesop, *Fables*, "The Fox Without a Tail"

We give advice by the bucket, but we take it by the grain.
                —William R. Alger

Most people, when they come to you for advice, come to have their
    own opinions strengthened, not corrected.   —Josh Billings

When a man comes to me for advice, I find out the kind of advice he
wants and I give it to him. —Josh Billings

When a man seeks your advice he generally wants your praise.
—Earl of Chesterfield

To profit from good advice requires more wisdom than to give it.
—Churton Collins

We seek advice, but we mean approbation.
—Charles Caleb Colton, *Lacon*

Perhaps one of the only positive pieces of advice that I was ever given
was that supplied by an old courtier who observed: Only two rules
really count. Never miss an opportunity to relieve yourself; never
miss a chance to sit down and rest your feet.
—Edward VIII, later Duke of Windsor, *A King's Story*

Unasked advice is a trespass on sacred privacy. —Henry S. Haskins

Advise none to marry or go to war.
—George Herbert, *Outlandish Proverbs*

Whatever advice you give, be short. —Horace, *Ars Poetica*

A good scare is worth more to a man than good advice.
—Edgar Watson Howe, *Country Town Sayings*

When a man asks your advice, he usually tells you just how he
expects you to decide. —Edgar Watson Howe, *Country Town Sayings*

Advice is what we ask for when we already know the answer but wish
we didn't. —Erica Jong, *How to Save Your Own Life*

Most people who ask advice of others have already resolved to act as
it pleases them. —Knigge

When we ask advice, we are usually looking for an accomplice.
—Marquis de La Grange

You will always find a few Eskimos ready to tell the Congolese how to
cope with the heat. —Stanislaw Lec, *Unkempt Thoughts*

What a difficult thing it is to ask someone's advice on a matter without coloring his judgment by the way in which we present our
problem. —Blaise Pascal, *Pensées*

He who builds to every man's advice will have a crooked house.
—Proverb (Danish)

Never give advice unless asked.
—Proverb (German)

Be slow of giving advice, ready to do a service.
—Proverb (Italian)

Bread is the best advice to the hungry.
—Proverb (Russian)

When the rabbit has escaped comes advice.
—Proverb (Spanish)

Ask advice, but use your common sense.
—Proverb (Yiddish)

Many receive advice, only the wise profit by it.
—Publilius Syrus, *Maxims*

The true secret of giving advice is, after you have honestly given it, to
be perfectly indifferent whether it is taken or not and never persist
in trying to set people right. —Hannah Whitall Smith

In giving advice, seek to help, not to please, your friend. —Solon

No one wants advice—only corroboration.
—John Steinbeck, *The Winter of Our Discontent*

It is easy for a man in good health to offer advice to the sick.
—Terence, *Andria*

I have found the best way to give advice to your children is to find
out what they want and then advise them to do it.
—Harry S. Truman,
interview with Edward R. Morrow, *Person to Person*, 27 May 1955

But I don't think people take bad advice. They've got intuition too,
you know. In fact I'd be surprised if they take any advice at all.
—Anne Tyler, *Searching for Caleb*

Generosity gives help rather than advice.
—Luc de Clapiers Vauvenargues

The only thing to do with good advice is to pass it on. It is never of
any use to oneself. —Oscar Wilde

ADVICE

Follow your bliss.
—Joseph Campbell

Hope for the best, get ready for the worst, and then take what God chooses to send. —Matthew Henry

Don't let other people tell you what you want. —Pat Riley

Have more than thou showest, / Speak less than thou knowest, / Lend less than thou owest . . .—William Shakespeare, *King Lear*, Act I, Sc. iv

Do what you love. —Henry David Thoreau

Never laugh at live dragons. —J. R. R. Tolkien, *The Hobbit*

Twenty years from now you will be more disappointed by the things that you didn't do than by the ones you did do. So throw off the bowlines. Sail away from the safe harbor. Catch the trade winds in your sails. Explore. Dream. Discover. —Mark Twain

Arrange whatever pieces come your way. —Virginia Woolf

Ask for what you want; take what you get; work on the difference. —Tom Zimmermann

AFFAIRS

Every man's affairs, however little, are important to himself. —Samuel Johnson, letter to the Earl of Bute, 3 Nov 1762, in James Boswell, *Life of Samuel Johnson*

Affairs, . . . , like everything else, ask too much. —John Updike

AFFECTION

The hardest of all is learning to be a well of affection, and not a fountain, to show them that we love them, not when we feel like it, but when they do. —Nan Fairbrother

Talk not of wasted affection, affection never was wasted, / If it enrich not the heart of another, its waters, returning / Back to their springs, like the rain, shall fill them full of refreshment; / That which the fountain sends forth returns again to the fountain. —Henry Wadsworth Longfellow

He liked to like people, therefore people liked him. —Mark Twain

AFFLICTION

It is not affliction itself, but affliction rightly borne, that does us good. —Aughey

The wisdom of God appears in afflictions. By these He separates the sin which He hates, from the son whom He loves. By these thorns He keeps him from breaking over into Satan's pleasant pastures, which fatten him indeed, but only to the slaughter. —Aughey

Affliction comes to us all, not to make us sad, but sober; not to make us worry, but wise . . . It is a trial that proves one thing weak and another strong . . . A cobweb is as good as the mightiest cable when there is no strain upon it. —Henry Ward Beecher

It is good for me that I have been afflicted, that I might learn thy statutes. —*The Bible* (KJV): Psalms 119: 71

Behold, I have refined thee, but not with silver; I have chosen thee in the furnace of affliction. —*The Bible* (KJV): Isaiah 48:10

. . . in their affliction they will seek me early. —*The Bible* (KJV): Hosea 5:15

For our light affliction, which is but for a moment, worketh for us a far more exceeding and eternal weight of glory. —*The Bible* (KJV): 2 Corinthians 4:17

Affliction, like the iron-smith, shapes as it smites. —Christian Nestell Bovée

Now let us thank th' eternal power, convinced / That Heaven but tries our virtue by affliction: / That oft the cloud that wraps the present hour / Serves but to brighten all our future days. —John Brown, *Barbarossa*, Act V, Sc. iii

If you would not have affliction visit you twice, listen at once to what it teaches. —James Burgh

The agony of a man's affliction is often necessary to put him into the right mood to face the fundamental things of life. The Psalmist says: "Before I was afflicted I went astray, but now have I kept Thy Word." —Oswald Chambers

God measures out affliction to our need. —John Chrysostom, *Homily IV*

Count each affliction, whether light or grave, God's messenger sent down to thee. —Aubrey Thomas De Vere, *Sorrow*

Affliction is a treasure, and scarce any man hath enough of it. No
man hath affliction enough that is not matured and ripened by it
and made fit for God. —John Donne

To bear other people's afflictions, every one has courage and enough
to spare. —Benjamin Franklin, *Poor Richard's Almanack*, 1740

Our afflictions would trouble us much less if we knew God's reason
for sending them. —Billy Graham, *Facing Death and the Life After*

Whatever affliction comes in our life, our Lord goes into the valley
with us, leading us by the hand, even carrying us when it is necessary. —Billy Graham, *Till Armageddon*

We should be more anxious that our afflictions should benefit us
than they should be speedily removed from us. —Robert Hall

Sanctified afflictions are spiritual promotions. —Matthew Henry

Affliction is but the shadow of God's wing. —George Macdonald

Affliction is the wholesome soil of virtue, where patience, honor,
sweet humanity, calm fortitude, take root and strongly flourish.
—Mallet

Are afflictions aught / But mercies in disguise? / Th' alternate cup,
/ Medicinal though bitter, and prepared / By Love's own hand for
salutary ends. —Mallet

By afflictions God is spoiling us of what otherwise might have spoiled
us. When he makes the world too hot for us to hold, we let it go.
—John Powell

Afflictions clarify the soul. —Francis Quarles

The very afflictions of our earthly pilgrimage are presages of our
future glory, as shadows indicate the sun. —Jean Paul Richter

Through many afflictions we must enter into the kingdom of God . . .
It is folly to think to steal to heaven with a whole skin.
—Samuel Rutherford

Afflictions are the steps to heaven. —Elizabeth Seton

There is healing in the bitter cup. —Robert Southey

The Lord gets his best soldiers out of the highlands of affliction.
—Charles H. Spurgeon

The afflictions of earth exalt the spirit and lift the soul to God. —Tiedge

AFRICA

Most people have a Tarzan view of Africa, as if there's something
more savage about a spear than a howitzer.   —Warren M. Robbins

AFTERLIFE

. . . He that heareth my word, and believeth on him that sent me,
hath everlasting life, and shall not come into judgment, but is
passed from death unto life.   —*The Bible* (KJV): John 5:24

. . . be faithful unto death, and I will give thee a crown of life.
—*The Bible* (KJV): Revelation 2:10

Must in death your daylight finish? My sun sets to rise again.
—Robert Browning, "At the 'Mermaid'"

Reason speaketh to my soul: Fret not Soul, Thou hast a better goal.
—Jane Cavendish

The thought of being nothing after death is a burden insupportable
to a virtuous man.   —John Dryden

This world is the land of the dying; the next is the land of the living.
—Tryon Edwards

The average man, who does not know what to do with his life, wants
another one which will last forever.
—Anatole France, *The Revolt of the Angels*

The question whether our conscious personality survives after death
has been answered by almost all races of men in the affirmative.
—James Frazer

Is there another life? Shall I awake and find all this a dream? There
must be, we cannot be created for this sort of suffering.
—John Keats

Belief in the future life is the appetite of reason.
—Walter Savage Landor, *Imaginary Conversations*,
"Marcos Tullius and Quinctus Cicero"

Age is not all decay; it is the ripening, the swelling, of the fresh life within, that withers and bursts the husk.
—George Macdonald, *The Marquis of Lossie*, Ch. 40

They say a man is as old as the women he feels.   —Groucho Marx

The best years of a man's life are after he is forty. A man at forty has ceased to hunt the moon.   —George du Maurier

I would be twenty before I learned how to be fifteen, thirty before I knew what it meant to be twenty, and now at seventy-two I have to stop myself from thinking like a man of fifty who has plenty of time ahead.   —Arthur Miller, *Timebends*

Age does not protect you from love. But love, to some extent, protects you from age.   —Jeanne Moreau

People expect old men to die, / They do not really mourn old men. / Old men are different. People look / At them with eyes that wonder when . . . / People watch with unshocked eyes; / But the old men know when an old man dies.
—Ogden Nash, *Verses From 1929 On*, "Old Men"

In youth the absence of pleasure is pain; in old age the absence of pain is pleasure.   —*Old Farmer's Almanac* (1892)

How old would you be if you didn't know how old you was?
—Leroy "Satchel" Paige, in Morrie Goldfischer, *New York Times*, "Ruminations Inspired by a Medicare Card," 8 Jun 1984

One of the delights known to age, and beyond the grasp of youth, is that of "not going."   —J. B. Priestley

Two things doth prolong thy life: A quiet heart and a loving wife.
—Proverb (17th century)

The older the fiddle the sweeter the tune.   —Proverb (English)

The young have aspirations that never come to pass; the old have reminiscences of what never happened.   —Saki

The closing years of life are like the end of a masquerade party, when the masks are dropped.   —Arthur Schopenhauer

The first forty years of life give us the text; the next thirty supply the
commentary on it. —Arthur Schopenhauer

Life is most delightful on the downward slope. —Seneca

. . . an old man is twice a child.
—William Shakespeare, *Hamlet*, Act II, Sc. ii

You can have your face lifted but there comes a time when you are
still going to be offered the Nurse, not Juliet. —Sylvia Sims

When you're young, you haven't the experience, when you're old
you haven't the strength. —Alexander Solzhenitsyn, *Cancer Ward*

Nobody loves life like him that's growing old. —Sophocles, *Acrisius*

In the days of my youth I remembered my God!
And He hath not forgotten my age. —Robert Southey,
"The Old Man's Comforts, and How He Gained Them"

We are always the same age inside. —Gertrude Stein

Growing old—it's not nice, but it's interesting.
—Johan August Strindberg

Every man desires to live long, but no man would be old.
—Jonathan Swift, *Thoughts on Various Subjects*

No wise man ever wished to be younger. —Jonathan Swift

For the unlearned, old age is a winter; for the learned it is the season
of the harvest. —*The Talmud*

Do not go gentle into that good night, / Old age should burn and
rave at close of day; / Rage, rage against the dying of the light.
—Dylan Thomas, *Collected Poems*,
"Do Not Go Gentle into that Good Night"

I shall grow old, but never lose life's zest, / Because the road's last turn
will be the best. —Henry Van Dyke, "The Zest of Life"

An inherent kindness exists in the process of aging . . . we are allowed
to move along gradually.
—Robert James Waller, *Old Songs in a New Cafe*

I'm very pleased with each advancing year. It stems back to when I was forty. I was a bit upset about reaching that milestone, but an older friend consoled me. "Don't complain about growing old—many, many people do not have that privilege." —Earl Warren

At thirty man suspects himself a fool; / Knows it at forty, and reforms his plan; / At fifty chides his infamous delay, Pushes his prudent purpose to resolve, / Resolves—and reresolves; then dies the same.
—Young

AGNOSTICISM

Agnosticism simply means that a man shall not say he knows or believes that for which he has no grounds for professing to believe.
—Thomas Henry Huxley

Agnosticism is the everlasting perhaps.
—Francis Thompson, *Paganism Old and New*

We need to be agnostics first and then there is some chance at arriving at a sensible system of belief.
—David Elton Trueblood, *The Logic of Belief*

AGREEMENT

Can two walk together, except they be agreed?
—*The Bible* (KJV): Amos 3:3

You can always spot a well-informed man—his views are the same as yours.
— Ilka Chase

My idea of an agreeable person . . . is a person who agrees with me.
—Benjamin Disraeli, *Lothair*, XLI

Men are much more apt to agree in what they do than in what they think.
—Johann Wolfgang von Goethe

Oh, how sweet it is to hear our own conviction from another's lips!
—Johann Wolfgang von Goethe

One can be very happy without demanding that others should agree with one.
—Johann Wolfgang von Goethe

Even savage bears agree among themselves.
—Juvenal

We rarely think that people have good sense unless they agree with us.
—François de La Rochefoucauld

If you want people to think you are wise, agree with them.

—Proverb (Yiddish)

A I M

The aim, if reached or not, makes great the life;
  Try to be Shakespeare, leave the rest to fate.   —Robert Browning

Whither should we aim if not towards God?   —André Gide, *Thésée*

As the arrow, loosed from the bow by the hand of the practiced
  archer, does not rest till it has reached the mark, so men pass from
  God to God. He is the mark for which they have been created, and
  they do not rest till they find their rest in him. —Sören Kierkegaard

If you would hit the mark, you must aim a little above it;
  Every arrow that flies feels the attraction of the earth.
              —Henry Wadsworth Longfellow, "Elegaic Verse"

A good archer is not known by his arrows, but his aim.
                    —Proverb (16th century)

An aim in life is the only fortune worth the finding; and it is not to
  be found in foreign lands but in the heart itself.
                    —Robert Louis Stevenson

In the long run, men hit only what they aim at. Therefore . . . they
  had better aim high. —Henry David Thoreau, *Walden*, "Economy"

A L C O H O L

One reason I don't drink is that I want to know when I am having a
  good time.   —Nancy Astor

The innkeeper loves the drunkard, but not for a son-in-law.
                    —Proverb (Jewish)

To dispute with a drunkard is to debate with an empty house.
                —Publilius Syrus, *Moral Sayings*

Drunkenness is nothing else but voluntary madness.
          —Seneca, *Epistuloe ad Lucilium*, Epistle lxxxiii, 18

A M B I G U I T I E S

. . . I am much better now at ambiguities.   —Saul Bellow, *Herzog*

In our sad condition, our only consolation is the expectancy of
another life. Here below all is incomprehensible.
—Martin Luther, *Table Talk*

I have good hope that there is something after death. —Plato, *Phaedo*

Those who live in the Lord never see each other for the last time.
—Proverb (German)

Every natural longing has its natural satisfaction. If we thirst, God
has created liquids to gratify thirst. If we are susceptible of attach-
ment, there are beings to gratify that love. If we thirst for life and
love eternal, it is likely that there are eternal life and eternal love to
satisfy that craving.   —F. W. Robertson

I have suffered too much in this world not to hope to another.
—Jean Jacques Rousseau

It may be that after this life we shall perish utterly, but if that is our
fate, let us so live that annihilation will be unjust.
—Etienne de Sénancour

For years he had been curious about what lay on the other side of
flesh and blood.   —Isaac Bashevis Singer, *The Slave*

It's what we weave in this world that we shall wear in the next.
—Bishop Taylor Smith

Our restlessness in this world seems to indicate that we are intended
for a better. We have all of us a longing after happiness; and surely
the Creator will gratify all the natural desires He has implanted in
us.   —Robert Southey

Divine Wisdom, intending to detain us some time on earth, has done
well to cover with a veil the prospect of the life to come; for if our
sight could clearly distinguish the opposite bank, who would
remain on this tempestuous coast of time?   —Madame de Staël

I have never seen what to me seemed an atom of proof that there is a
future life. And yet—I am strongly inclined to expect one.
—Mark Twain

He sins against this life, who slights the next.
—Edward Young, *Night Thoughts*, "Night 3"

AGING

To know how to grow old is the master-work of wisdom, and one of the most difficult chapters in the great art of living.
—Henri Frédéric Amiel, *The Private Journal of Henri Frédéric Amiel*, 21 Sep 1874

You're never too old to do goofy stuff.
—Anonymous, line delivered by the character Ward Cleaver on the TV show "Leave It to Beaver"

Years ago I thought old age would be dreadful, because I should not be able to do things I would want to do. Now I find there is nothing I want to do.
—Nancy Astor

To me, old age is always fifteen years older than I am.
—Bernard Baruch, on his 85th birthday

We grow neither better nor worse as we get old, but more like ourselves.
—May Lamberton Becker

. . . there is no old age of the soul.
—Saul Bellow, *More Die of Heartbreak*

At 82, I feel like a 20-year-old but, unfortunately, there's never one around.
—Milton Berle

If I'd known I was gonna live this long, I'd have taken better care of myself.
—Eubie Blake, American jazz performer and songwriter who lived to be a hundred

Grow old along with me! The best is yet to be, / The last of life for which the first was made.   —Robert Browning, *Dramatis Personae*, opening lines of "Rabbi ben Ezra"

When the waitress puts the dinner on the table, the old men look at the dinner. The young men look at the waitress.   —Gelett Burgess

By the time you're eighty years old you've learned everything. You only have to remember it.
—George Burns

There's many a good tune played on an old fiddle.
—Samuel Butler (1835-1902), *The Way of All Flesh*, Ch. 61

An aged man is but a paltry thing, a tattered coat upon a stick
  [William Butler Yeats], unless he sees the bright plumage of the
  bird called courage . . .
                        —John Cheever, *Oh What a Paradise It Seems*

Old age isn't so bad when you consider the alternative.
                        —Maurice Chevalier, in *New York Times*, 9 Oct 1960

No man is so old as not to think he can live one year more.
                        —Cicero, *De Senectute*, 7, 24

Eighty years old! No eyes left, no ears, no teeth, no legs, no wind!
  And when all is said and done, how astonishingly well one does
  without them.
                        —Paul Claudel, in Malcom Cowley,
                        The View from 80, "Vices and Pleasures"

I have often thought what a melancholy world this would be without
  children, and what an inhuman world without the aged.
                        —Samuel Taylor Coleridge

Old age ain't for sissies.
                        —Bette Davis, quoted by Paul Newman in a James Lipton
                        television interview, *Inside the Actors Studio*, 31 May 1995

It's not how old you are but how you are old.   —Marie Dressler

Old as I am, for ladies' love unfit, / The power of beauty I remember
  yet.   —John Dryden, *Cymon and Iphigenia*, line 1

In youth we learn; in age we understand.   —Marie Ebner-Eschenbach

It is time to be old, / To take in sail.   —Ralph Waldo Emerson,
                        May-Day and Other Poems, opening lines of "Terminus"

If youth but knew; if age could!
                        —Henri Estienne, *Les Prémices*, Épigramme cxci

All would live long, but none would be old.
                        —Benjamin Franklin, *Poor Richard's Almanack*, 1749

At 20 years of age the will reigns, at 30 the wit, at 40 the judgment.
                        —Benjamin Franklin, *Poor Richard's Almanack*

The great thing about being 30 is that there are a great deal more available women. The young ones look younger and the old ones don't look nearly as old. —Glenn Frey

Some things, of course, one had to accept without whimpering, such as old age. —John Gardner, *October Light*, Ch. 6

If you survive long enough, you're revered rather like an old building. —Katharine Hepburn

About the time we get old enough to be as wicked as we want to be, we don't want to be so very wicked after all. —Don Herold, *There Ought to Be a Law*

Oh to be seventy again. —Oliver Wendell Holmes, Jr., on seeing an attractive woman on his 90th birthday

The riders in a race do not stop short when they reach the goal. There is a little finishing canter before coming to a standstill. There is time to hear the kind voice of friends and to say to one's self: "The work is done." —Oliver Wendell Holmes, Jr., in a radio broadcast on his 90th birthday, 8 Mar 1931

The young man knows the rules but the old man knows the exceptions. —Oliver Wendell Holmes, Sr.

Youth longs and manhood strives, but age remembers. —Oliver Wendell Holmes, Sr.

Forty is the old age of youth; fifty the youth of old age. —Victor Hugo

Few people know how to be old. —François de La Rochefoucauld

The great thing about getting older is that you don't lose all the other ages you've been. —Madeleine L'Engle, in *The New York Times*, 1985

For age is opportunity no less / Than youth itself, though in another dress, And as the evening twilight fades away / The sky is filled with stars, invisible by day. —Henry Wadsworth Longfellow, "Morituri Salutamus"

The best thing about getting old is that all those things you couldn't have when you were young you no longer want. —L. S. McCandless

Age is not all decay; it is the ripening, the swelling, of the fresh life within, that withers and bursts the husk.
—George Macdonald, *The Marquis of Lossie*, Ch. 40

They say a man is as old as the women he feels. —Groucho Marx

The best years of a man's life are after he is forty. A man at forty has ceased to hunt the moon. —George du Maurier

I would be twenty before I learned how to be fifteen, thirty before I knew what it meant to be twenty, and now at seventy-two I have to stop myself from thinking like a man of fifty who has plenty of time ahead. —Arthur Miller, *Timebends*

Age does not protect you from love. But love, to some extent, protects you from age. —Jeanne Moreau

People expect old men to die, / They do not really mourn old men. / Old men are different. People look / At them with eyes that wonder when . . . / People watch with unshocked eyes; / But the old men know when an old man dies.
—Ogden Nash, *Verses From 1929 On*, "Old Men"

In youth the absence of pleasure is pain; in old age the absence of pain is pleasure. —*Old Farmer's Almanac* (1892)

How old would you be if you didn't know how old you was?
—Leroy "Satchel" Paige, in Morrie Goldfischer, *New York Times*, "Ruminations Inspired by a Medicare Card," 8 Jun 1984

One of the delights known to age, and beyond the grasp of youth, is that of "not going." —J. B. Priestley

Two things doth prolong thy life: A quiet heart and a loving wife.
—Proverb (17th century)

The older the fiddle the sweeter the tune. —Proverb (English)

The young have aspirations that never come to pass; the old have reminiscences of what never happened. —Saki

The closing years of life are like the end of a masquerade party, when the masks are dropped. —Arthur Schopenhauer

The first forty years of life give us the text; the next thirty supply the
   commentary on it.   —Arthur Schopenhauer

Life is most delightful on the downward slope.   —Seneca

. . . an old man is twice a child.
                        —William Shakespeare, *Hamlet*, Act II, Sc. ii

You can have your face lifted but there comes a time when you are
   still going to be offered the Nurse, not Juliet.   —Sylvia Sims

When you're young, you haven't the experience, when you're old
   you haven't the strength.   —Alexander Solzhenitsyn, *Cancer Ward*

Nobody loves life like him that's growing old.   —Sophocles, *Acrisius*

In the days of my youth I remembered my God!
      And He hath not forgotten my age.   —Robert Southey,
           "The Old Man's Comforts, and How He Gained Them"

We are always the same age inside.   —Gertrude Stein

Growing old—it's not nice, but it's interesting.
                                        —Johan August Strindberg

Every man desires to live long, but no man would be old.
                        —Jonathan Swift, *Thoughts on Various Subjects*

No wise man ever wished to be younger.   —Jonathan Swift

For the unlearned, old age is a winter; for the learned it is the season
   of the harvest.   —*The Talmud*

Do not go gentle into that good night, / Old age should burn and
   rave at close of day; / Rage, rage against the dying of the light.
                                    —Dylan Thomas, *Collected Poems*,
                        "Do Not Go Gentle into that Good Night"

I shall grow old, but never lose life's zest, / Because the road's last turn
   will be the best.   —Henry Van Dyke, "The Zest of Life"

An inherent kindness exists in the process of aging . . . we are allowed
   to move along gradually.
                        —Robert James Waller, *Old Songs in a New Cafe*

I'm very pleased with each advancing year. It stems back to when I was forty. I was a bit upset about reaching that milestone, but an older friend consoled me. "Don't complain about growing old— many, many people do not have that privilege."   —Earl Warren

At thirty man suspects himself a fool; / Knows it at forty, and reforms his plan; / At fifty chides his infamous delay, Pushes his prudent purpose to resolve, / Resolves—and reresolves; then dies the same.
—Young

AGNOSTICISM

Agnosticism simply means that a man shall not say he knows or believes that for which he has no grounds for professing to believe.
—Thomas Henry Huxley

Agnosticism is the everlasting perhaps.
—Francis Thompson, *Paganism Old and New*

We need to be agnostics first and then there is some chance at arriving at a sensible system of belief.
—David Elton Trueblood, *The Logic of Belief*

AGREEMENT

Can two walk together, except they be agreed?
—*The Bible* (KJV): Amos 3:3

You can always spot a well-informed man—his views are the same as yours.
— Ilka Chase

My idea of an agreeable person . . . is a person who agrees with me.
—Benjamin Disraeli, *Lothair*, XLI

Men are much more apt to agree in what they do than in what they think.
—Johann Wolfgang von Goethe

Oh, how sweet it is to hear our own conviction from another's lips!
—Johann Wolfgang von Goethe

One can be very happy without demanding that others should agree with one.
—Johann Wolfgang von Goethe

Even savage bears agree among themselves.
—Juvenal

We rarely think that people have good sense unless they agree with us.
—François de La Rochefoucauld

If you want people to think you are wise, agree with them.
—Proverb (Yiddish)

A I M

The aim, if reached or not, makes great the life;
  Try to be Shakespeare, leave the rest to fate.   —Robert Browning

Whither should we aim if not towards God?   —André Gide, *Thésée*

As the arrow, loosed from the bow by the hand of the practiced
  archer, does not rest till it has reached the mark, so men pass from
  God to God. He is the mark for which they have been created, and
  they do not rest till they find their rest in him. —Sören Kierkegaard

If you would hit the mark, you must aim a little above it;
  Every arrow that flies feels the attraction of the earth.
              —Henry Wadsworth Longfellow, "Elegaic Verse"

A good archer is not known by his arrows, but his aim.
                    —Proverb (16th century)

An aim in life is the only fortune worth the finding; and it is not to
  be found in foreign lands but in the heart itself.
                    —Robert Louis Stevenson

In the long run, men hit only what they aim at. Therefore . . . they
  had better aim high. —Henry David Thoreau, *Walden*, "Economy"

A L C O H O L

One reason I don't drink is that I want to know when I am having a
  good time.   —Nancy Astor

The innkeeper loves the drunkard, but not for a son-in-law.
                    —Proverb (Jewish)

To dispute with a drunkard is to debate with an empty house.
              —Publilius Syrus, *Moral Sayings*

Drunkenness is nothing else but voluntary madness.
        —Seneca, *Epistuloe ad Lucilium*, Epistle lxxxiii, 18

A M B I G U I T I E S

. . . I am much better now at ambiguities.   —Saul Bellow, *Herzog*

The awareness of the ambiguity of one's highest achievements . . . is a
definite symptom of maturity.   —Paul Tillich

A M B I T I O N

How like a mounting devil in the heart
Rules the unreined ambition.   —Anonymous

Ye looked for much, and lo, it came to little . . .
                    —*The Bible* (KJV): Haggai 1:9

Ambition has no rest.
          —Edward Bulwer-Lytton (1803-1873), *Richelieu*, Act III, Sc. i

I have found some of the best reasons I ever had for remaining at the
bottom simply by looking at the men at the top.
                    —Frank Colby, *The Colby Essays*

Nothing is so common-place as to wish to be remarkable.
          —Oliver Wendell Holmes, Sr., *The Autocrat of the Breakfast Table*

Ambition is only vanity ennobled.
          —Jerome K. Jerome, *The Idle Thoughts of an Idle Fellow*,
                    "On Vanity and Vanities"

We grow small trying to be great.   —E. Stanley Jones

Ambition makes more trusty slaves than need.
                    —Ben Jonson, *Sejanus His Fall*, I, i

A slave has but one master; the ambitious man has as many as can
help in making his fortune.   —Jean de La Bruyère, *Characters*, 8.70

Every man is said to have his peculiar ambition.   —Abraham Lincoln

Most people would succeed in small things if they were not troubled
with great ambitions.   —Henry Wadsworth Longfellow

Beware ambition; Heaven is not reached with pride, but with submission.   —Middleton

If ye would go up high, then use your own legs! Do not get yourselves
carried aloft; do not seat yourselves on other people's backs and
heads.   —Friedrich Nietzsche, *Thus Spake Zarathustra*, Part IV

The tallest trees are most in the power of the winds, and ambitious
men of the blasts of fortune.
—William Penn, *Some Fruits of Solitude*, 2, 97

But there is much to be said for giving up . . . grand ambitions and
living the most ordinary life imaginable.
—Walker Percy, *The Moviegoer*

Hew not too high,
Lest the chips fall in thine eye.   —Proverb (14th century)

Ambition destroys its possessor.   —Proverb (Hebrew)

Though ambition in itself is a vice, yet it is often the parent of
virtues.   —Quintilian, *De Institutio Oratoria*

Cromwell, I charge thee, fling away ambition: / By that sin fell the
angels . . .   —William Shakespeare, *King Henry VIII*, Act III, Sc. ii

There is a loftier ambition than merely to stand high in the world. It
is to stoop down and lift mankind a little higher.
—Henry Van Dyke

Ambition has but one reward for all: / A little power, a little transient
fame, / A grave to rest in, and a fading name!
—William Winter, "The Queen's Domain"

The vague torment of . . . ambition.   —Émile Zola

AMERICA

America—half-brother of the world; / With something good and bad
of every land.   —Philip James Bailey, *Festus*, x.

America! America!   God shed His grace on thee.
—Katharine L. Bates, "America the Beautiful"

Our nation was founded as an experiment in human liberty. Its institutions reflect the belief of our founders that men had their origin
and destiny in God; that they were endowed by Him with inalienable rights and had duties prescribed by moral law, and that
human institutions ought primarily to help men develop their
God-given possibilities.   —John Foster Dulles

. . . America didn't have to fight scarcity and we all felt guilty before people who still had to struggle for bread and freedom in the old way . . . We weren't starving, we weren't bugged by the police, locked up in madhouses for our ideas, arrested, deported, slave laborers sent to die in concentration camps. We were spared the holocausts and nights of terror. With our advantages we should be formulating the new basic questions for mankind. But instead we sleep. Just sleep and sleep, and eat and play and fuss and sleep again. —Saul Bellow, *Humboldt's Gift*

Americans can be counted on to do the right thing after they have exhausted all other options. —Winston Churchill

The thing that impresses me most about America is the way parents obey their children.
—Edward VIII, Duke of Windsor, *Look*, 5 Mar 1957

We go forth all to seek America. And in the seeking we create her. In the quality of the search shall be the nature of the America that we created. —Waldo Frank, *Our America* (1919)

. . . the American system of rugged individualism.
—Herbert Hoover, speech, 22 Oct 1928

My fellow Americans, ask not what your country can do for you—ask what you can do for your country.
—John F. Kennedy, Inaugural Address, 20 Jan 1961

Give me your tired, your poor, / Your huddled masses yearning to breathe free, / The wretched refuse of your teeming shore, / Send these, the homeless, tempest-tossed, to me: / I lift my lamp beside the golden door. —Emma Lazarus, "The New Collosus," lines inscribed on the Statue of Liberty

Abandon your animosities and make your sons Americans.
—Gen. Robert E. Lee

Sail on, O Ship of State! Sail on, O Union, strong and great.
—Henry Wadsworth Longfellow

We on this continent should never forget that men first crossed the Atlantic not to find soil for their ploughs but to secure liberty for their souls. —Robert J. McCracken

The trouble with us is that we are ever looking for a princely chance of acquiring riches, or fame, or worth. We are dazzled by what Emerson calls the "shallow Americanism" of the day. We are expecting mastery without apprenticeship, knowledge without study, and riches by credit.   —O. S. Marden, *Pushing to the Front*

The United States has the power to destroy the world, but not the power to save it alone.   —Margaret Mead

These are times that try men's souls.
    —Thomas Paine, "The American Crisis,"
        in *Pennsylvania Magazine*, 1776

The United States never lost a war or won a conference. —Will Rogers

We are the first nation in the history of the world to go to the poor-house in an automobile.
    —Will Rogers, 1931, in Lois and Alan Gordon,
        American Chronicle (1987)

I pledge you—I pledge myself—to a new deal for the American people.
    —Franklin D. Roosevelt, speech at convention,
        Chicago, 2 Jul 1932

There is no room in this country for hyphenated Americanism.
    —Theodore Roosevelt, speech, New York City, 12 Oct 1915

This country will not be a good place for any of us to live in unless we make it a good place for all of us to live in.   —Theodore Roosevelt

America is the only matriarchy where women are fighting for equality.
    —A. Roth

. . . Americans are forever searching for love in forms it never takes, in places it can never be. It must have something to do with the vanished frontier.   —Kurt Vonnegut, Jr., *The Cat's Cradle*

. . . Americans couldn't imagine about what it was like to be some-thing else and be proud of it. —Kurt Vonnegut, Jr., *The Cat's Cradle*

. . . a national anthem . . . sprinkled with question marks.
    —Kurt Vonnegut, Jr., *Breakfast of Champions*

The Constitution does not provide for first and second class citizens.
    —Wendell Willkie, *An American Programme*

Some Americans need hyphens in their names, because only part of them has come over; but when the whole man has come over, heart and thought and all, the hyphen drops of its own weight out of his name.
—Woodrow Wilson, speech, Washington, D.C., 16 May 1914

The American people are not cowardly. But, living in prosperous isolation, they have been the spoiled children of modern history.
—Herman Wouk, *The Winds of War*

America is God's Crucible, the great Melting-Pot where all the races of Europe are melting and reforming . . .
—Israel Zangwill, *The Melting-Pot*, I.

AMUSEMENT

If you would rule the world quietly, you must keep it amused.
Ralph Waldo Emerson, *Essays, Second Series*,
"New England Reformers"

The mind ought to be amused, that it may the better return to thought, and to itself.
—Phaedrus

The real character of a man is found out by his amusements.
—Joshua Reynolds

We are not amused.
—Queen Victoria, *Notebooks of a Spinster Lady*, 2 Jan 1900

ANALOGIES

Analogies prove nothing, that is quite true, but they can make one feel more at home.
—Sigmund Freud

ANCESTORS

All blood is alike ancient.
—Anonymous

The man without a navel still lives in me.
—Sir Thomas Browne

Although we have it easier than our forefathers, we have more uneasiness.
—Billy Graham, *World Aflame*

Walking, I am listening to a deeper way. Suddenly all my ancestors are behind me. Be still, they say. Watch and listen. You are the result of the love of thousands.
—Linda Hogan

It is of no consequence of what parents any man is born, so that he be a man of merit.
—Horace

There is no king who has not had a slave among his ancestors, and no slave who has not had a king among his.
—Helen Keller, *Story of My Life*

I don't know who my grandfather was; I am much more concerned to know what his grandson will be.
—Abraham Lincoln

Noble ancestry makes a poor dish at table.
—Proverb (Italian)

I am no herald to inquire into men's pedigree; it sufficeth me if I know their virtues.
—Sir Philip Sidney

From yon blue heaven above us bent, the grand old gardener and his wife smile at the claims of long descent.
—Alfred, Lord Tennyson

Those who depend on the merits of their ancestors may be said to search in the roots of the tree for those fruits which the branches ought to produce.
—Alfred, Lord Tennyson

ANGELS

How many angels can dance on the point of a needle?
—Anonymous, attributed to various medieval theologians

Be not forgetful to entertain strangers: for thereby some have entertained angels unawares.
—*The Bible* (KJV): Hebrews 13:2

Hold the fleet angel until he bless thee.
—Nathaniel Cotton, "To-morrow," line 36

Every blade of grass has its Angel that bends over it and whispers, "Grow, grow."
—*The Talmud*

ANGER

Anger manages everything badly.
—Anonymous

Oppose not rage while rage is in its force, but give it way awhile and let it waste.
—Anonymous

It is easy to fly into a passion—anybody can do that—but to be angry with the right person to the right extent and at the right time and with the right object and in the right way—that is not easy, and it is not everyone who can do it.
—Aristotle, *Nicomachean Ethics*, 2.9

Never forget what a man says to you when he is angry.
—Henry Ward Beecher

He that is soon angry dealeth foolishly . . .
—*The Bible* (KJV): Proverbs 14:17

Be ye angry, and sin not; let not the sun go down upon your wrath.
—*The Bible* (KJV): Ephesians 4:26

. . . let every man be swift to hear, slow to speak, slow to wrath.
—*The Bible* (KJV): James 1:19

Few men can afford to be angry.
—Augustine Birrell, *Obiter Dicta*, "Edmund Burke"

Anger is self-immolation.
—Phillips Brooks

He that strives not to stem his anger's tide, / Does a wild horse without a bridle ride.
—Colley Cibber, *Love's Last Shift*, Act III

. . . to be wroth with one we love / Doth work like madness in the brain.
—Samuel Taylor Coleridge, *Christabel*, 2.410

Beware the fury of a patient man.
—John Dryden, *Absalom and Achitophel*, l. 1005

We boil at different degrees.
—Ralph Waldo Emerson, *Society and Solitude*, "Eloquence"

Act nothing in furious passion; it's putting to sea in a storm.
—Thomas Fuller, *Introductio ad Prudentiam*

A man in a passion rides a horse that runs away with him.
—Thomas Fuller, M. D., *Gnomologia*, No. 283

Anger punishes itself.   —Thomas Fuller, M. D., *Gnomologia*, No. 799

The proud man hath no God; the envious man hath no neighbor; the angry man hath not himself.
—Bishop Hall

Anger is a momentary madness.   —Horace, *Epistles*, Book I, epistle ii

My life is in the hands of any fool who makes me lose my temper.
—Dr. John Hunter

Anger blows out the lamp of the mind. In the examination of a great
and important question, every one should be serene, slow-pulsed,
and calm.
—Robert G. Ingersoll

No use fanning up hot coals when you have to walk across them.
—Bernard Malamud, *The Fixer*

Anger helps straighten out a problem like a fan helps straighten out a
pile of papers.
—Susan Marcotte

Consider how much more you often suffer from your anger and grief,
than from those for which you are angry and grieved.
—Marcus Aurelius Antoninus

How much more grievous are the consequences of anger than the
causes of it.
—Marcus Aurelius Antoninus

When thou art above measure angry, bethink thee how momentary is
man's life.
—Marcus Aurelius Antoninus,
Meditations, Book XI, Ch. 18, Sec. 8

Be ye angry, and sin not; therefore all anger is not sinful, because
some degree of it, and on some occasions, is inevitable. But it
becomes sinful and contradicts the rule of Scripture when it is conceived upon slight and inadequate provocation, and when it con-
tinues long.
—William Paley

Every stroke our fury strikes is sure to hit ourselves at last.
—William Penn, *Fruits of Solitude*

Anger turns the mind out of doors and bolts the entrance. —Plutarch

To be angry is to revenge the faults of others on ourselves.
—Alexander Pope

Anger is often more hurtful than the injury that caused it.
—Proverb (American)

Wrath begins in madness and ends in repentance.   —Proverb (Arab)

In the good man anger quickly dies.   —Proverb (Latin)

Anger is a stone cast into a wasp's nest.   —Proverb (Malabar)

Arrows pierce the body, but harsh words pierce the soul.
—Proverb (Spanish)

People hardly ever do anything in anger, of which they do not
repent. —Richardson

The greatest remedy for anger is delay. —Seneca

Think, when you are enraged at anyone, what would probably
become your sentiments should he die during the dispute.
—William Shenstone

Though very troublesome to others, anger is most so to him that
has it. —Sir Richard Steele

Keep cool; anger is not an argument. —Daniel Webster

ANIMALS

When you see a snake, never mind where he came from.
—W. G. Benham

The question is not, Can they reason? nor, Can they talk? but, Can
they suffer? —Jeremy Bentham

Animals are such agreeable friends—they ask no questions, they pass
no criticisms. —George Eliot, *Scenes of Clerical Life*,
"Mr. Gilfil's Love-Story," Ch. 7

Brutality to an animal is cruelty to mankind—it is only the difference
in the victim. —Alphonse de Lamartine

I never saw a wild thing / Sorry for itself.—D. H. Lawrence, "Self-Pity"

God in His wisdom made the fly / And then forgot to tell us why.
—Ogden Nash, *Good Intentions*, "The Fly"

The turtle lives 'twixt plated decks / Which practically conceal its sex.
/ I think it clever of the turtle In such a fix to be so fertile.
—Ogden Nash, *Hard Lines*, "Autres Bêtes, Autres Moeurs"

He who rides the tiger can never dismount. —Proverb (Chinese)

Even the lion has to defend himself against flies. —Proverb (German)

One, but that one a lion. —Proverb (Greek)

One must accept the cow's kick as well as her milk and butter.
—Proverb (Indian)

Don't call a wolf to help you against the dogs.　　—Proverb (Russian)

The wolf will hire himself out very cheaply as a shepherd.
　　　　　　　　　　　　　　　　　—Proverb (Russian)

A lot of baa-ing and not much wool.　　—Proverbial phrase (Russian)

A cow must graze where he is tied.　　　—Proverb (West African)

When the snake is in the house, one need not discuss the matter at
　　length.　　　　　　　　　　　—Proverb (West African)

I like animals who trust people.
　　　　　　　　—Andrew A. Rooney, *Word for Word*, "Lady"

We aren't consistent in our treatment of animals.
　　　　　　　—Andrew A. Rooney, *Word for Word*, "Spent Hens"

There is in every animal's eye a dim image and gleam of humanity, a
　　flash of strange light through which their life looks out and up to
　　our great mystery of command over them, and claims the fellow-
　　ship of the creature if not of the soul.　　　　—John Ruskin

The best thing about animals is that they don't talk much.
　　　　　　　　　　　　　　　　　—Thornton Wilder

ANIMOSITY

Life appears to me to be too short to be spent in nursing animosity or
　　registering wrongs.　　　　　　　　　—Charlotte Brontë

ANTI-SEMITISM

Since my little daughter is only half Jewish, would it be all right if she
　　went into the pool only up to her waist?
　　　　　—Groucho Marx, letter to a country club after it barred his
　　daughter as Jewish, in his obituary in *New York Times*, 20 Aug 1977

It is disgraceful that people are being barred from neighborhoods and
　　clubs on a basis that would have barred Jesus Himself.
　　　　　　　　　　　　　　　　　—James A. Pike

ANXIETY

Nothing in the affairs of men is worthy of great anxiety.　　—Plato

It has been well said that our anxiety does not empty tomorrow of its sorrows, but only empties today of its strength.
—Charles H. Spurgeon

APOLOGY

Never make a defense or apology before you be accused.
—Charles I of Great Britain,
letter to Lord Wentworth, September, 1636

We have in my country [Russia] a quotation: "It is impossible to make out of apology a fur coat."
—Bernard Malamud, *Rembrandt's Hat*, "Man in the Drawer"

When you have to apologize, it is well, I suppose, to get the thing over quickly . . .
—Dorothy Parker, *Constant Reader*, "Excuse It, Please"

The APOSTLES

The apostles suffered incredible persecution and died horrible deaths in the Christian cause. The only possible explanation for their zeal was that they had actually seen, talked with and eaten with the resurrected Lord Jesus Christ. If Christ had not really risen and had not appeared to the apostles, would they all have died for a lie?
—Fritz Ridenour, *So What's the Difference*

APPEARANCES

. . . man looketh on the outward appearance, but the Lord looketh on the heart.   —*The Bible* (KJV), 1 Samuel 16:7

God Almighty never created a man half as wise as he looks.
—Thomas Carlyle

Habit maketh no monk, ne wearing of gilt spurs maketh no knight.
—Geoffrey Chaucer

Be and not seem.   —Ralph Waldo Emerson

Things are seldom what they seem,
   Skim milk masquerades as cream.
—W. S. Gilbert, "H. M. S. Pinafore"

No man, for any considerable period, can wear one face to himself, and another to the multitude, without finally getting bewildered as to which may be the true.
—Nathaniel Hawthorne, *The Scarlet Letter*, 20.

The world more frequently recompenses the appearance of merit, than merit itself.
—François da La Rochefoucauld

Be content to seem what you really are.   —Martial, *Epigrams*, 10.83

All that glitters is sold as gold.   —Ogden Nash, *Verses from 1929 On*, "Look What You Did, Christopher!"

A fine cage won't feed the bird.   —Proverb (French)

All are not hunters that blow the horn.   —Proverb (French)

It is not the beard that makes the philosopher.   —Proverb (Italian)

All that glisters is not gold.
—William Shakespeare, *The Merchant of Venice*, Act II, Sc. vii

APPETITE

Eat when you're hungry, love when you're young.   —Anonymous

Appetite, n. An instinct thoughtfully implanted by Providence as a solution to the labor question.
—Ambrose Bierce, *The Devil's Dictionary*

She laughed. "You never think about anything but sex, do you?"
"Not so. Sometimes I think about eating."
—Judith Guest, *Second Heaven*

. . . appetite turns common food into the fare of kings.
—Laurel Lee, *Godspeed: Hitchhiking Home*

One should eat to live, not live to eat. —Molière, *L'Avare*, Act III, Sc. ii

The appetite grows by eating.
—François Rabelais, *Gargantua*, Act I., Sc. v

APPLAUSE

Every ear is tickled with the sweet music of applause.   —Barrow

He who seeks only for applause from without has all his happiness in another's keeping. —Oliver Goldsmith

My advice to you concerning applause is this: enjoy it but never quite believe it. —Robert Montgomery

APPRECIATION

Wise men appreciate all men, for they see the good in each and know how hard it is to make anything good.
—Baltasar Gracián, *The Art of Worldly Wisdom*

. . . the deepest principle in Human Nature is the craving to be appreciated. —William James, *Letters*, Vol. 2, 6 Apr 1896

ARCHITECTURE

It is the task of the architect to give life a gentler structure.
—Aalto Alvar, in *Connoisseur*, June, 1987

Architecture is inhabited sculpture. —Constantin Brancusi, in Igor Stravinsky and Robert Craft, *Themes and Episodes*

We shape our buildings; thereafter they shape us.
—Winston Churchill

[Architecture is] the flowering of geometry. —Ralph Waldo Emerson

Light, God's eldest daughter, is a principal beauty in a building.
—Thomas Fuller, *The Holy State and the Profane State*, "Of Building"

Pay attention only to the form; emotion will come spontaneously to inhabit it. A perfect dwelling place always finds an inhabitant.
—André Gide, *Pretexts*, "Portraits and Aphorisms"

Small rooms or dwellings discipline the mind, large ones weaken it.
—Leonardo da Vinci, *Notebooks*

If an architect wants to strengthen a decrepit arch, he increases the load laid upon it, for thereby the parts are joined more firmly together. —Friedrich Nietzsche

[Architecture] is music in space, as it were a frozen music.
—Friedrich von Schelling, *Philosophie der Kunst*

The frightening thought that what you draw may become a building makes for reasoned lines. —Saul Steinberg

Form ever follows function.
—Louis Henri Sullivan, *Lippincott's Magazine*,
"The Tall Office Building Artistically Considered," March, 1896

The physician can bury his mistakes, but the architect can only
advise the client to plant vines. —Frank Lloyd Wright

ARGUMENT

Arguments out of a pretty mouth are unanswerable.
—Joseph Addison, *Women and Liberty*

How many a dispute could have been deflated into a single paragraph
if the disputants had dared to define their terms? —Aristotle

Use soft words in hard arguments. —H. G. Bohn

Avoid wrangling with the contentious . . . —Dionysius Cato

Neither irony nor sarcasm is argument. —Rufus Choate

Strong and bitter words indicate a weak cause. —Victor Hugo

The aim of argument, or of discussion, should not be victory, but
progress. —Joseph Joubert, *Pensées*, 7, 31

Religious contention is the devil's harvest. —Jean de La Fontaine

Argument should be polite as well as logical.
—Alphonse de Lamartine

He who strikes the first blow admits he's lost the argument.
—Proverb (Chinese)

In excess altercation, truth is lost. —Publilius Syrus

ART

Good art is not what it looks like, but what it does to us. —Roy Adzak

The great artist is the simplifier. —Henri Frédéric Amiel,
The Private Journal of Henri Frédéric Amiel, 25 Nov 1861

An artist is at home everywhere. —Anonymous

One great artist was asked which of all his productions was the greatest. His prompt answer was: "The next." —Anonymous

The little dissatisfaction which every artist feels at the completion of
a work forms the germ of a new work.   —Anonymous

Life is very nice, but it lacks form. It's the aim of art to give it some.
                              —Jean Anouilh, *The Rehearsal*

The object of art is to give life a shape.   —Jean Anouilh, *The Rehearsal*

The aim of art is not the outward appearance of things, but their
inward significance.   —Aristotle

Art is man added to nature.   —Francis Bacon

The essence of all art is to have pleasure in giving pleasure.
                              —Mikhail Baryshnikov

The sincerity of an artist is . . . letting himself be led without knowing
where.   —Jean Bazaine

Art and Religion are two roads by which men escape from circumstance to ecstasy.   —Clive Bell

Art has something to do with the achievement of stillness in the
midst of chaos. A stillness which characterizes prayer, too, and
the eye of the storm. . . . an arrest of attention in the midst of
distraction.   —Saul Bellow, in George Plimpton, editor,
                              Writers at Work: Third Series

The ultimate justification of the work of art is to help the spectator to
become a work of art himself.   —Bernard Berenson,
                              Essays in Appreciation

Art is I; science is we.   —Claude Bernard

The great work of art is great because it creates a special world of its
own. It revives and readapts time and space, and the measure of its
success is the extent to which it makes you an inhabitant of that
world—the extent to which it invites you in and lets you breathe
its strange, special air.   —Leonard Bernstein

Art upsets, science reassures.   —Georges Braque, *Pensées sur l'Art*

Artistry's haunting curse, the Incomplete!   —Robert Browning

. . . a product of the untalented, sold by the unprincipled to the
utterly bewildered.   —Al Capp, definition of abstract art

What was any art but a mold in which to imprison for a moment the shining elusive element which is life itself—life hurrying past us and running away, too strong to stop, too sweet to lose.
—Willa Cather, *The Song of the Lark*

See in nature the cylinder, the sphere, the cone.　　—Paul Cézanne

Art, we are told, is a criterion of one's taste. How humiliating, should our taste turn out to be bad. Rather as though we were caught stark naked with a poor figure.　　—Ilka Chase

Art is limitation; the essence of every picture is the frame!
—G. K. Chesterton, *Orthodoxy*

Every work of art has one indispensable mark . . . the center of it is simple, however much the fulfillment may be complicated.
—G. K. Chesterton, *The Innocence of Father Brown*, "The Queer Feet"

An artist cannot speak about his art any more than a plant can discuss horticulture.　　—Jean Cocteau

But the artist appeals to that part of our being which is not dependent on wisdom; to that in us which is a gift and not an acquisition—and therefore, more permanently enduring. He speaks to our capacity for delight and wonder, to the sense of mystery surrounding our lives: to our sense of pity, and beauty, and pain.
—Joseph Conrad

Art is a wholly physical language whose words are all the visible objects.　　—Gustave Courbet

Art for art's sake.　　—Victor Cousin, lecture, Sorbonne, 1818

The object of art is to crystallize emotion into thought and then to fix it in form.　　—François Delsarte

The greatest danger in art is too much knowledge.　　—André Derain

First move me, astonish me, break my heart, let me tremble, weep, stare, be enraged—only then regale my eyes.　　—Denis Diderot

Art is the stored honey of the human soul, gathered on wings of misery and travail.　　—Theodore Dreiser, *Life, Art and America* (1917)

Art is the expression of the profoundest thoughts in the simplest way.
—Albert Einstein

Every artist writes his own autobiography.
—Havelock Ellis, *The New Spirit*

Art is a jealous mistress . . .
—Ralph Waldo Emerson, *The Conduct of Life*, "Wealth"

Every artist was at first an amateur.
—Ralph Waldo Emerson, *Letters and Social Aims*,
"Progress of Culture"

'Tis the privilege of Art / Thus to play its cheerful part, / Man on earth
to acclimate / And bend the exile to his fate.
—Ralph Waldo Emerson, *Essays, First Series*, "Art"

In art, as in love, instinct is enough.
—Anatole France,
Le Jardin d'Epicure

Art is significant deformity.
—Roger Fry, in Virginia Woolf, *Roger Fry*, Ch. 8

Art is either a plagiarist or a revolutionist.
—Paul Gauguin

Art is 90% sex.
—Barry Gealt

Art is a collaboration between God and the artist, and the less the
artist does the better.
—André Gide

The scholar seeks, the artist finds.
—André Gide

The work of art is a part of nature seen through a temperament.
—André Gide, *Pretexts*, "The Limits of Art"

The highest problem in every art is, by means of appearances, to produce the illusion of a loftier reality.—Johann Wolfgang von Goethe

Art is partly communication but only partly. The rest is discovery.
—William Golding, *Free Fall*

Aesthetic emotion puts man in a state favorable to the reception of
erotic emotion. Art is the accomplice of love. Take love away and
there is no longer art.
—Rémy de Gourmont

The contemplation of truth and beauty is the proper object for which
we were created, which calls forth the most intense desires of the
soul, and of which it never tires.
—William Hazlitt, *Criticisms on Art*, Vol. I

Art . . . is a force which blows the roof off the cave where we crouch imprisoned. —Ernest Hello, *Life, Science, and Art*

The real artist's work is a surprise to himself. —Robert Henri

Life is short and art is long. —Hippocrates, *Aphorisms*

A picture is a poem without words. —Horace

Art is not a thing; it is a way. —Elbert Hubbard, *Epigrams*

Money and art are far apart.
—Langston Hughes, in Arnold Rampersad and David Roessel, editors, *The Complete Poems of Langston Hughes*, "Plaint" (whole poem)

If art is to nourish the roots of our culture, society must set the artist free to follow his vision wherever it takes him.
—John F. Kennedy, speech at Amherst College, 26 Oct 1963

The artist, . . . faithful to his personal vision of reality, becomes the last champion of the individual mind and sensibility against an intrusive society and an offensive state. —John F. Kennedy

It's clever, but is it Art?
—Rudyard Kipling, "The Conundrum of the Workshops"

Art does not reproduce the visible; rather, it makes visible.
—Paul Klee, *The Inward Vision*

Science is spectrum analysis; art is photosynthesis. —Kraus

When a work lifts your spirits and inspires bold and noble thoughts in you, do not look for any other standard to judge by: the work is good, the product of a master craftsman. —Jean de La Bruyère

Art is objectification of feeling.
—Susanne K. Langer, *Mind, An Essay on Human Feeling*

The artist is like a hunter who must be on his toes at all times, with eyes and ears fully open to respond to the anxious signals the world sends out. —Les Levine

Art enlarges experience by admitting us to the inner life of others.
—Walter Lippmann, *A Preface to Politics*,
"The Golden Rule and After"

O thou sculptor, painter, poet! / Take this lesson to thy heart: / That is best which lieth nearest; / Shape from that thy work of art.
—Henry Wadsworth Longfellow, "Gaspar Becerra," Stanza 7

Art is the conveyance of spirit by means of matter.
—Salvador de Madariaga, *Americans Are Boys*

Art is a revolt against man's fate. —André Malraux, *Voices of Silence*

Who will deliver us from the overelaborate?
—Édouard Manet, to Proust

Arrival = Prison, and the artist must never be a prisoner.
—Henri Matisse

Exactitude is not truth. —Henri Matisse

Beauty is something wonderful and strange that the artist fashions out of the chaos of the world in the torment of his soul.
—W. Somerset Maugham, *The Moon and Sixpence*

Art is an effort to create, beside the real world, a more human world.
—André Maurois

Art is not a mirror to reflect the world, but a hammer with which to shape it. —Vladimir Mayakovsky

Art is man's refuge from adversity. —Menander

Nothing can come out of an artist that is not in the man.
—H. L. Mencken, *Prejudices: Fifth Series*

Art is a shadow of Divine perfection. —Michelangelo

It is the treating of the commonplace with the feeling of the sublime that gives to art its true power. —J. F. Millet

One puts into one's art what one has not been capable of putting into one's existence. It is because he was unhappy that God created the world. —Henri de Montherlant

Great artists have no country. —Alfred de Musset, *Lorenzaccio*

Art is not an end in itself, but a means of addressing humanity.
—Modeste Petrovich Mussorgsky

Art is the sex of the imagination.
> —George Jean Nathan, *American Mercury*, "Art," July, 1926

Great art is as irrational as great music. It is mad with its own loveliness.
> —George Jean Nathan, *The House of Satan* (1926)

A fine artist is one who makes familiar things new and new things familiar.
> —Louis Nizer

Art is the difference between seeing and just identifying.
> —Jean Mary Norman, *Art: Of Wonder and the World*

The artist belongs to his work, not the work to the artist.   —Novalis

Art is the communication of ecstasy.
> —Peter Ouspensky, *A New Model of the Universe*

To be instructed in the arts softens the manners and makes men gentle.
> —Ovid

A picture has been said to be something between a thing and a thought.
> —Samuel Palmer

Art is a form of catharsis.   —Dorothy Parker, *Sunset Gun* (1928)

Art is the lie that enables us to realize the truth.   —Pablo Picasso

Art washes away from the soul the dust of everyday life.
> —Pablo Picasso

Every child is an artist. The problem is how to remain an artist once he grows up.
> —Pablo Picasso

. . . nature and art are two different things. Through art we express our conception of what nature is not.
> —Pablo Picasso

There is no abstract art. You must always begin with something.
> —Pablo Picasso

To draw, you must close your eyes and sing.   —Pablo Picasso

A work should convey its entire meaning by itself, imposing it on the spectator even before he knows what the subject is.
> —Marcel Proust, *Within a Budding Grove*

Every young artist has to do it one way, his way, and the hell with patterns. Remember who you are and where you are and what you're doing. Nobody else can do anything for you and you really wouldn't want them to anyway. And never take advice, including this.   —Katherine Anne Porter

The supreme goal of art—and ever forgotten—is to help man endure reality better.   —Reverdy, *En vrac*

[Art is] the reasoned derangement of the senses.   —Kenneth Rexroth

A room hung with pictures is a room hung with thoughts.
                                     —Joshua Reynolds

Art is indeed not the bread but the wine of life.   —Jean Paul Richter

One must work, nothing but work, and one must have patience.
                                     —Auguste Rodin

Fine art is that in which the hand, the head and the heart go together.   —John Ruskin, *The Two Paths*, Lecture ii.

When love and skill work together expect a masterpiece.
                                     —John Ruskin

Art must take reality by surprise.   —Françoise Sagan

I say that the true artist-seer, the heavenly fool who can and does produce beauty, is mainly dazzled to death by his own scruples, the blinding shapes and colors of his own sacred human conscience.
                         —J. D. Salinger, *Seymour, an Introduction*

An artist is a dreamer consenting to dream of the actual world.
      —George Santayana, *The Life of Reason: Reason in Common Sense*

We should comfort ourselves with the masterpieces of art as with exalted personages—stand quietly before them and wait till they speak to us.   —Arthur Schopenhauer

That which achieves its effect by accident is not art.   —Seneca

All art is based on non-conformity.   —Ben Shahn

God made the world as an artist and that is why the world must learn from its artists.   —George Bernard Shaw

You use a glass mirror to see your face: you use works of art to see
  your soul.   —George Bernard Shaw, *Back to Methuselah*, 5

Art is the signature of civilizations.   —Beverly Sills

An artist has been defined as a neurotic who continually cures himself with his art.   —Lee Simonson

By means of art we are sometimes sent—dimly, briefly—revelations
  unattainable by reason.   —Alexander Solzhenitsyn, *Nobel Lecture*

Human nature is full of riddles and contradictions; its very com-
  plexity engenders art—and by art I mean the search for something more than simple linear formulations, flat solutions,
  oversimplified explanations.
                —Alexander Solzhenitsyn, *Warning to the West*

". . . It's not what but how that matters in art." K-123 jumped up and
  banged his fist on the table. "No! Your how can go to hell if it does-
  n't raise the right feelings in me!"
        —Alexander Solzhenitsyn, *One Day in the Life of Ivan Denisovich*

The task of the artist is to sense more keenly than others the harmony of the world, the beauty and the outrage of what man has
  done to it, and poignantly to let people know.
                    —Alexander Solzhenitsyn, *Nobel Lecture*

Too much art was no art at all. Like candy instead of bread!
    —Alexander Solzhenitsyn, *One Day in the Life of Ivan Denisovich*

We will die, but art will remain.
                    —Alexander Solzhenitsyn, *Nobel Lecture*

Who has the skill to make a narrow, obstinate human being aware of
  others' far-off grief and joy, to make him understand dimensions
  and delusions he himself has never lived through? Propaganda,
  coercion, and scientific proofs are powerless. But happily, in our
  world there is a way. It is art, and it is literature.
                    —Alexander Solzhenitsyn, *Nobel Lecture*

Who will dare say he has defined art?
                    —Alexander Solzhenitsyn, *Nobel Lecture*

Interpretation is the revenge of the intellect upon art.
                    —Susan Sontag, "Against Interpretation"

. . . blinded by the creative pride of the parent.
—Irving Stone, *Lust for Life*

. . . that horrible moment of suspense when the artist shows one of his creations to strange eyes for the first time.
—Irving Stone, *Lust for Life*

Art postulates communion, and the artist has an imperative need to make others share the joy which he experiences himself.
—Igor Stravinsky, *An Autobiography*, 10.

To have read the greatest works of any great poet, to have beheld or heard the greatest works of any great painter or musician, is a possession added to the best things of life.
—Algernon Charles Swinburne

Art is the only way to run away without leaving home.
—Twyla Tharp, *Push Comes to Shove*

Statues and pictures and verse may be grand, / But they are not the Life for which they stand.   —James Thomson, "Sunday Up the River"

All art has this characteristic—it unites people.   —Leo Tolstoy

Art is a human activity having for its purpose the transmission to others of the highest and best feeling to which men have risen.
—Leo Tolstoy, *What is Art?*, Ch. 8

If that's art, I'm a Hottentot!   —Harry S. Truman

The artist brings something into the world that didn't exist before, and . . . he does it without destroying something else.
—John Updike

An artist never really finishes his work, he merely abandons it.
—Paul Valéry

. . . such distortions, such aberrations, deformations, alterations of reality that, if you will, they must end up as lies—but as lies that have more truth in them than literal truth.   —Vincent van Gogh

All the arts are brothers; each one is a light to the others.   —Voltaire

Murals in restaurants are on a par with the food in museums.
—Peter de Vries, *Madder Music*

It's not a question of liking. One is moved or not moved.
— David Weiss, *Naked Came I*

Fertilization of the soul is the reason for the necessity of art.
— Alfred North Whitehead, *Science and the Modern World*

Art is communication spoken by man for humanity in a language raised above the everyday happening.   — Mary Wigman

Strong and convincing art has never arisen from theories.
— Mary Wigman

The morality of art consists in the perfect use of an imperfect medium.   — Oscar Wilde, *The Picture of Dorian Gray*, Preface

Art is the daughter of pleasure.   — J. J. Winckelmann

A work of art is a corner of creation seen through a temperament.
— Émile Zola, *Mes Haines*, "M. H. Taine, Artist"

ASKING

To ask well is to know much.   — Proverb (African)

He who asks a question is a fool for five minutes; he who does not ask a question remains a fool forever.   — Proverb (Chinese)

He who is afraid of asking is ashamed of learning. — Proverb (Danish)

Many things are lost for want of asking.   — Proverb (English)

Better ask twice than go wrong once.   — Proverb (German)

Asking costs little.   — Proverb (Italian)

He who wants a great deal must not ask for a little. — Proverb (Italian)

He that asketh faintly beggeth a denial.   — Proverb (Latin)

To ask is no sin, and to be refused is no calamity. — Proverb (Russian)

It don't cost money to ask.   — John Steinbeck, *The Grapes of Wrath*

ASPIRATIONS

Ah, but a man's reach should exceed his grasp, Or what's a heaven for?   — Robert Browning, *Men and Women*, "Andrea del Sarto"

Our aspirations are our possibilities. —Robert Browning

'Tis not what man Does which exalts him, but what man Would do.
—Robert Browning, *Men and Women*, "Saul," Stanza 18

What I aspired to be / And was not, comforts me.
—Robert Browning, *Dramatis Personae*, "Rabbi ben Ezra"

When you are aspiring to the highest place, it is honorable to reach
the second or even the third rank. —Cicero, *De Oratore*

Hitch your wagon to a star.
—Ralph Waldo Emerson, *Society and Solitude*, "Civilization"

First, say to yourself what you would be; and then do what you have
to do. —Epictetus, *Discourses*

Slight not what's near by aiming at what's far. —Euripides, *Rhesus*

The significance of man is not in what he attains, but rather in what
he longs to attain. —Kahlil Gibran

Whoever aspiring, struggles on, for him there is salvation.
—Johann Wolfgang von Goethe

This world has too low a ceiling for aspiring man.
—J. Wallace Hamilton

What we truly and earnestly aspire to be, that in some sense we are.
The mere aspiration, by changing the frame and spirit of the mind,
for the moment realizes itself. —Anna Jameson

Indeed, everybody wants to be a wow, / But not everybody knows
exactly how. —Ogden Nash, *Verses From 1929 On*,
"Kindly Unhitch That Star, Buddy"

What would you attempt to do if you knew you could not fail?
—Robert H. Schuller

Reach high, for stars lie hidden in your soul. Dream deep, for every
dream precedes the goal. —Starr

An aspiration is a joy forever, a possession as solid as a landed estate,
a fortune which we can never exhaust and which gives us year by
year a revenue of pleasurable activity.
—Robert Louis Stevenson, *Virginibus Puerisque*

ASSOCIATION

The Sun visits cesspools without being defiled. —Diogenes the Cynic

If you sleep with a dog you will rise full of fleas.   —Proverb (Greek)

Know a horse by riding him; a person by associating with him.
—Proverb (Japanese)

Whoever runs with the wolf is no sheep.   —Proverb (Russian)

ASTONISHMENT

The wise man is astonished by anything.   —André Gide

ATHEISM

Seems as unfounded . . . to say there isn't a God as to say there is.
—James Agee, *A Death in the Family*

A good reply to an atheist is to give him an excellent dinner and then
ask if he believes there is a cook.   —Anonymous

There has never been a race of atheists.   —Anonymous

A little philosophy inclineth men's minds to atheism; but depth in
philosophy bringeth men's minds about to religion.
—Francis Bacon, *Essays*, "Of Atheism"

Atheism is rather in the lip than in the heart of man.
—Francis Bacon, *Essays*, "Of Atheism"

God never wrought miracle to convince atheism, because His ordinary works convince it.   —Francis Bacon, *Essays*, "Of Atheism"

Those who deny the existence of God are hard put to explain the
existence of man.   —Harold Berry

I can see how it might be possible for a man to look down upon the
earth and be an atheist, but I cannot conceive how he could look
up into the heavens and say there is no God.   —Abraham Lincoln

Absolute atheism starts in an act of faith in reverse gear and is a full-
blown religious commitment. Here we have the first internal
inconsistency of contemporary atheism: it proclaims that all religion must necessarily vanish away, and it is itself a religious phenomenon.   —Jacques Maritain, *The Range of Reason*

No one is so much alone in the universe as a denier of God.
—Jean Paul Richter

My atheism, like that of Spinoza, is true piety towards the universe
and denies only gods fashioned by men in their own image, to be
servants of their human interests.
—George Santayana, *Soliloquies in England*

Who denies God, denies himself.
—*The Upanishads*, "Taittiriya Upanishad"

The atheist's most embarrassing moment is when he feels profoundly
thankful for something but can't think of anybody to thank for it.
—Mary Ann Vincent

The religion of the atheist has a God-shaped blank at its heart.
—H. G. Wells

By night an atheist half believes a God.
—Edward Young, *Night Thoughts*, "Night 5"

ATTITUDE

Things turn out best for people who make the best of the way things
turn out.   —Anonymous

A lost battle is a battle one thinks one has lost.
—Marshal Ferdinand Foch

The last of human freedoms is to choose one's attitude in any given
circumstance.   —Victor Frankl

No life is so hard that you can't make it easier by the way you take it.
—Ellen Glasgow

. . . human beings can alter their lives by altering the attitudes of the
mind.   —William James

God often comforts us, not by changing the circumstances of our
lives, but by changing our attitude towards them.
—S. H. B. Masterman

If you looked for things to make you feel hurt and wretched and
unnecessary, you were certain to find them . . .
—Dorothy Parker, "The Lovely Leave"

The meaning of things lies not in the things themselves but in our
attitude towards them.
—Antoine de Saint-Exupéry, *The Wisdom of Sands*

Anything too far out of tune with our attitude is lost, either in the
ears themselves or somewhere beyond, but it is lost.
—Alexander Solzhenitsyn, *The Gulag Archipelago*

If you can't change your fate, change your attitude. —Amy Tan

. . . if you catalogue grudges, anything looks bad.
—Anne Tyler, *Dinner at the Homesick Restaurant*

They can because they think they can. —Virgil, *Aeneid*

ATTRACTIVENESS

A handsome woman is soon dressed. —Anonymous

We all love a pretty girl. —Anonymous

Life belongs to the pretty woman. —Lady Isobel Barnett

A pretty girl is like a melody / That haunts you night and day.
—Irving Berlin, "A Pretty Girl is like a Melody" (1919 song)

We discovered the existence of a strong physical attractiveness stereo-
type: Attractive people are assumed to be kinder, more genuine,
sincere, warm, sexually responsive, poised, modest, sociable, sensitive, interesting, strong, more exciting, more nurturant, and of better character than the less attractive.
—Dr. Ellen Berscheid (psychologist)

A pretty woman's worth some pains to see. —Robert Browning

A pretty woman is a welcome guest. —Lord Byron

She that is fair hath half her portion. —Thomas Drake

Are you not scared by seeing that the gypsies are more attractive to us
than the apostles? —Ralph Waldo Emerson

None but the brave can live with the fair.
—Frank McKinney ("Kin") Hubbard

Poor brain! How helplessly it dissolves when willing eyes meet and
the nose warms to those old jungle scents.
—Arthur Miller, *Timebends*

A handsome woman is always right. —Proverb (German)

A handsome man is not quite poor. —Proverb (Spanish)

A fair exterior is a silent recommendation. —Publilius Syrus, *Maxims*

Every pretty girl one sees is a reminiscence of the Garden of Eden.
—Sheldon

It is no sin to look at a nice girl. —Leo Tolstoy, *The Cossacks*, Ch. 12

What, when drunk, one sees in other women, one sees in Garbo
sober. —Kenneth Tynan, *Curtains*

Even virtue is fairer in a fair body. —Virgil, *Aeneid*, Book V, line 344

AUTHORITY

. . . I [Paul] appeal unto Caesar. —*The Bible* (KJV): The Acts 25:11

If you wish to know what a man is, place him in authority.
—Proverb (Yugoslav)

AUTOBIOGRAPHY

Autobiography is the outcome of a struggle in the author's brain
between the desire to be truthful and the desire to be interesting.
—Vernon Bartlett, *I Know What I Liked*

AWE

The highest point a man can attain is not knowledge . . . but something even greater, more heroic . . . sacred awe!
—Nikos Kazantzakic

— B —

BABIES

A perfect example of minority rule is a baby in the house.
—Anonymous

Babies are such a nice way to start people. —Don Herold

What instruction the baby brings to the mother! —T. W. Higginson

Families with babies and families without babies are sorry for each
other. —Edgar Watson Howe

A loud noise at one end and no sense of responsibility at the other.
—Ronald Knox, definition of a baby

Where did you come from, baby dear? Out of the everywhere into
here? —George Macdonald, *At the Back of the North Wind*, 33

If you please ma'am, it was a very little one.
—Frederick Marryat, *Midshipman Easy*, Ch. 3,
the nurse on her illegitimate baby

A bit of talcum Is always walcum.
—Ogden Nash, *Many Long Years Ago*, "Reflection of Babies"

Of all the joys that brighten suffering earth, / What joy is welcom'd
like a new-born child? —Caroline Norton

Whatever a child babbles, its mother will understand.
—Proverb (Yiddish)

A baby is God's opinion that life should go on.
—Carl Sandburg, *Remembrance Rock*

A little child born yesterday, / A thing on mother's milk and kisses
fed.
—Percy Shelley, *Homer's Hymn to Mercury*, Stanza 69

Sweetes' li'l feller, / Everybody knows; / Dunno what to call him,
/ But he's mighty lak'a rose; / Lookin' at his mammy / Wid eyes so
shiny blue / Mek' you think that Heav'n / Is comin' clost ter you.
—Frank L. Stanton, "Mighty Lak'a Rose" (1901 song)

A babe in a house is a well-spring of pleasure, as messenger of peace and love, a resting place for innocence on earth; a link between angels and men. —Martin Farquhar Tupper

A baby is an inestimable blessing and bother.
—Mark Twain, letter to Annie Webster, 1 Sep 1876

I remember leaving the hospital . . . thinking, "Wait, are they going to let me just walk off with him? I don't know beans about babies!"
—Anne Tyler

BABY SITTERS

A baby sitter is someone to watch your television while your kids cry themselves to sleep. —Anonymous

BAIT

One catches more flies with a spoonful of honey that with twenty casks of vinegar. —King Henry IV of France

More flies are caught with honey than vinegar. —Proverb (French)

We must lose a minnow to catch a salmon. —Proverb (French)

BANKS

A bank is a place that will lend you money if you can prove that you don't need it. —Bob Hope, in Alan Harrington, *Life in the Crystal Palace*, "The Tyranny of Forms"

Most banks will gladly grant a loan; / In fact, they often speed it; / The only thing that they require / Is proof that you don't need it.
—F. G. Kernan

BAPTISM

Then Peter said unto them, Repent, and be baptized, every one of you, in the name of Jesus Christ for the remission of sins, and ye shall receive the gift of the Holy Spirit.
—*The Bible* (KJV): The Acts 2:38

What is baptism but a declaration of our misery by sin, our need of Christ, and a badge of our belonging to Him? —W. D. Paden

Baptism does not save you. It identifies you. —Lewis Timberlake

BARGAINS

A bad thing is dear at any price. —Anonymous

At a great bargain make a pause. —Anonymous

Cheap is dear in the long run. —Anonymous

Make every bargain clear and plain, / That none may afterwards complain. —Anonymous

Nothing is cheap if you don't want it. —Anonymous

On a good bargain think twice. —George Herbert, *Jacula Prudentum*

Don't buy everything that's cheap. —Proverb (Chinese)

Bad wares are never cheap. —Proverb (French)

Forever is a long bargain. —Proverb (German)

Good bargains empty our pockets. —Proverb (German)

BASEBALL

Didn't come up here to read. —Hank Aaron, to Casey Stengel, who told him to hold the bat so that he could read the label

Trying to sneak a pitch past Hank Aaron is like trying to sneak the sunrise past a rooster. —Joe Adcock

Baseball isn't statistics, it's Joe DiMaggio rounding second base. —Anonymous

It ain't over 'til it's over.
—Yogi Berra, *The Yogi Book*, said in 1973 to a reporter when the Yankees trailed by nine games. They subsequently won their division.

If people don't want to come to the ballpark, how are you going to stop them? —Yogi Berra, *The Yogi Book*, to baseball commissioner Bud Selig about lagging baseball attendance

Ninety percent of the game is half mental. —Yogi Berra, *The Yogi Book*

Swing at the strikes.   —Yogi Berra, advice to a batter in a slump

You can observe a lot by watching.
> —Yogi Berra, *The Yogi Book*, in 1964 while managing
> the New York Yankees, to inattentive players

You can't think and hit at the same time.   —Yogi Berra, *The Yogi Book*

More than any other American sport, baseball creates the magnetic, addictive illusion that it can be almost understood.
> —Thomas Boswell

A curve ball that doesn't give a damn.
> —Jimmy Cannon, definition of a knuckleball

Reporter: What do you think you'd hit if you were playing today? Cobb: About .320. Reporter: Why so low? Cobb: You have to remember. I'm sixty-two years old.
> —Ty Cobb (1886-1961), in David James Duncan, *The Brothers K*

You don't save a pitcher for tomorrow. Tomorrow it may rain.
> —Leo Durocher

There is no defense against a base on balls.
> —Joe Garagiola, sportscasting commentary, 1989

Joe McCarthy (baseball manager): Lefty, I don't think you are throwing as hard as you used to. Gomez (pitcher): You're wrong, Joe. I'm throwing twice as hard, but the ball isn't going as fast.
> —Vernon "Lefty" Gomez, in Joseph Durso,
> "Vernon (Lefty) Gomez, 80, Dies; Starred as
> Pitcher for the Yankees," *New York Times*, 18 Feb 1989

Every ball player arrives some time at his last pitch . . .
> —Mark Harris, *It Looked Like For Ever*, Ch. 12

It ain't nothin' till I call it.
> —Bill Klem, baseball umpire, to those who argued close calls

Sure, I have muffed a few in my time. But I never called one wrong in my heart.   —Bill Klem, baseball umpire

Pitching is . . . the art of instilling fear.
> —Sandy Koufax, Los Angeles Dodger pitcher

There are two theories on hitting the knuckleball. Unfortunately, neither of them work.   —Charlie Lau

It ain't getting it that hurts them, it's staying up all night looking for it. They got to learn that if you don't get it by midnight, you ain't gonna get it, and if you do, it ain't worth it.
—Charles Dillon "Casey" Stengel, in Robert Creamer's *Stengel*, on baseball players who break curfew

Oh, somewhere in this favored land the sun is shining bright; / The band is playing somewhere, and somewhere hearts are light, / And somewhere men are laughing, and little children shout; / But there is no joy in Mudville—mighty Casey has struck out.
—Ernest Lawrence Thayer, "Casey at the Bat"

Baseball was the only sport that made sense, she said: clear as Parcheesi, clever as chess.
—Anne Tyler, *Dinner at the Homesick Restaurant*

The way to catch a knuckleball is to wait until the ball stops rolling and then pick it up. —Bob Uecker, baseball catcher and broadcaster

For the parent of a Little Leaguer, a baseball game is simply a nervous breakdown divided into innings. —Earl Wilson

BASHFULNESS

To get thine ends, lays bashfulness aside; / Who fears to ask, doth teach to be deny'd. —Robert Herrick, "No Bashfulness in Begging"

Bashfulness is of no use to the needy. —Proverb (Dutch)

If you are bashful, you'll have no children. —Proverb (Yiddish)

BATHING

. . . most of its lifetime a cake of soap is too small.
—Andrew A. Rooney, *A Few Minutes with Andy Rooney*, "Soap"

Soap, like people, shouldn't smell like anything.
—Andrew A. Rooney, *A Few Minutes with Andy Rooney*, "Soap"

BEAUTY

Beauty is more important to a woman than brains because most men can see better than they can think. —Anonymous

Beauty, real beauty, is something very grave. If there is a God, He must be partly that. —Jean Anouilh, *The Rehearsal*, 2

Things are beautiful if you love them.
—Jean Anouilh, *Mademoiselle Colombe*, 2.2

Beauty is a gift of God.
—Aristotle, in Diogenes Laertius, *Aristotle*, Book V, Sec. 19

Personal beauty is a greater recommendation than any letter of intro-duction. —Aristotle, in Diogenes Laertius, *Aristotle*, Book V, Sec. 18

A beautiful face is a silent recommendation. —Francis Bacon

There is no excellent beauty that hath not some strangeness in the proportion. —Francis Bacon, *Essays*, "Of Beauty"

Rugged the breast that beauty cannot tame.
—John Codrington Bampfylde, "Sonnet in Praise of Delia"

The beauty seen is partly in him who sees it. —Christian Nestell Bovée

To cultivate the sense of the beautiful is one of the most effectual ways of cultivating an appreciation of the divine goodness.
— Christian Nestell Bovée

All that is beautiful shall abide, / All that is base shall die.
—Robert W. Buchanan

In life, as in art, the beauty moves in curves. —Edward Bulwer-Lytton

She walks in beauty, like the night / Of cloudless climes and starry skies; / And all that's best of dark and bright / Meet in her aspect and her eyes. —Lord Byron

"She Walks in Beauty" / . . . the beauty of strange women.
—John Cheever, *Bullet Park*

I have not yet met the man who loves virtue as he loves beauty.
—Confucius

Oh no, it wasn't the aeroplanes. It was Beauty killed the Beast.
—James Creelman and Ruth Rose,
King Kong (1933 movie), closing words

That which is striking and beautiful is not always good, but that which is good is always beautiful. —Ninon De l'Enclos

Nothing so truly becomes feminine beauty as simplicity.
—Madame Deluzy

Beauty in woman is power.

—De Rotrou

The beauty of a lovely woman is like music.

—George Eliot

Beauty is the child of love.

—Havelock Ellis, *The New Spirit*

If eyes were made for seeing, / Then Beauty is its own excuse for being.
—Ralph Waldo Emerson, *May Day and Other Pieces*, "The Rhodora"

Never lose an opportunity of seeing anything beautiful; for beauty is
God's handwriting.

—Ralph Waldo Emerson

Though we travel the world over to find the beautiful, we must carry
it with us or we find it not.

—Ralph Waldo Emerson, *Essays, First Series*, "Art"

Beauty when most unclothed is clothed best.

—Phineas Fletcher, *Sicelides*, Act II, Sc. iv

A beautiful woman is the hell of the soul, the purgatory of the purse,
and the paradise of the eyes.   —Bernard le Bovier de Fontenelle

In beauty, faults conspicuous grow; / The smallest speck is seen on
snow.

—John Gay

If a man hears much that a woman says, she is not beautiful.

—Henry S. Haskins

Nothing's beautiful from every point of view.

—Horace

Beauty is only skin deep, but it's a valuable asset if you're poor and
haven't any sense.   —Frank McKinney ("Kin") Hubbard

Beauty is altogether in the eye of the beholder.

—Margaret Wolfe Hungerford, *Molly Bawn*

Beauty, the smile of God, Music, His voice.

—Robert Underwood Johnson, *Goethals of Panama*

'Beauty is truth, truth beauty,'—that is all / Ye know on earth, and all
ye need to know.   —John Keats, "Ode on a Grecian Urn"

A thing of beauty is a joy for ever: Its loveliness increases; it will never
/ Pass into nothingness.

—John Keats

I'm tired of all this nonsense about beauty being only skin-deep.
That's deep enough. What do you want—an adorable pancreas?
—Jean Kerr, *The Snake Has All the Lines*, "Mirror, Mirror,
on the Wall, I Don't Want to Hear One Word Out of You"

The strongest evidence to prove God exists is a beautiful woman.
—Giovanni Leone

The most beautiful object in the world, it will be allowed, is a beautiful woman. —Thomas Babington Macaulay,
Criticisms on Italian Writers, "Dante"

I want to help you to grow as beautiful as God meant you to be when
he thought of you first.
—George Macdonald, *The Marquis of Lossie*, Ch. 22

Such as ne'er saw swans / May think crows beautiful.
—Philip Massinger, *Great Duke of Florence*, III

I am waylaid by beauty. —Edna St. Vincent Millay, "Assault," Stanza 2

Beauty is God's handwriting—a wayside sacrament. —John Milton

Beauty is everlasting and dust is for a time.
—Marianne Moore, *Collected Poems*, "In Distrust of Merits"

In every man's heart there is a secret nerve that answers to the vibrations of beauty. —Christopher Morley

There is certainly no beauty on earth which exceeds the natural loveliness of woman. —J. Petit-Senn

Fair tresses man's imperial race insnare, / And beauty draws us with
a single hair.
—Alexander Pope, *The Rape of the Lock*, Canto 2, line 27

Nothing so well becomes true feminine beauty as simplicity.
—George D. Prentice

Beauty is power. —Proverb (Arab)

Beauty is a good letter of introduction. —Proverb (German)

Beauty is as good as ready money. —Proverb (German)

Beauty without grace is a rose without scent. —Proverb (Swedish)

What is really beautiful needs no adorning. We do not grind down
the pearl upon a polishing stone. —Sataka

True beauty is in the mind; and the expression of the features
depends more upon the moral nature than most persons are accustomed to think. —Frederic Saunders

Beauty itself doth of itself persuade / The eyes of men without an orator.
—William Shakespeare, *The Rape of Lucrece, Part I*

For where is any author in the world / Teaches such beauty as a
woman's eye?
—William Shakespeare, *Love's Labour's Lost*, Act IV, Sc. iii

If I could write the beauty of your eyes / And in fresh numbers number all your graces, / The age to come would say, "This poet lies . . ."
—William Shakespeare, Sonnet XVII

Every good picture is the best of sermons and lectures. The sense
informs the soul. Whatever you have, have beauty. —Sydney Smith

I insist on believing that beauty elevates human beings.
—Alexander Solzhenitsyn, *The Love-Girl and the Innocent*

. . . beauty, like truth, never is so glorious as when it goes the
plainest. —Laurence Sterne

From out of pain, beauty. —Irving Stone, *Lust for Life*

Oh who can tell the range of joy / Or set the bounds of beauty.
—Sara Teasdale, *Rivers to the Sea*, "A Winter Blue Jay"

Loveliness / Needs not the foreign aid of ornament, / But is when
unadorned adorned the most.
—James Thomson, *The Seasons*, "Autumn"

The soul, by an instinct stronger than reason, ever associates beauty
with truth. —Tuckerman

Nothing beautiful can be summarized. —Paul Valéry, *Tel Quel*

Most works are most beautiful without ornament. —Walt Whitman

What is beautiful is a joy for all seasons . . . —Oscar Wilde

Beauty is worse than wine, it intoxicates both the holder and the
beholder.   —Zimmermann

BED

Bed is a bundle of paradoxes: we go to it with reluctance, yet we quit
it with regret.   —Charles Caleb Colton, *Lacon*, 2.262

In bed we laugh, in bed we cry; / And born in bed, in bed we die; /
The near approach the bed doth show, / Of human bliss to human
woe.   —Isaac De Benserade

O bed! O bed! delicious bed! / That heaven upon earth to the weary
head.   —Hood

The happiest part of a man's life is what he passes lying awake in bed
in the morning.   —Samuel Johnson

And so to bed.   —Samuel Pepys, *Diary*, 6 May 1660

I have so much to do that I am going to bed.   —Proverb (Savoyard)

'Tis very warm weather when one's in bed.   —Jonathan Swift

BEGGING

Beggars should be no choosers.   —John Heywood

He buys very dear who begs.   —Proverb (Portuguese)

BEGINNING(s)

Begin—to begin is half the work, let half remain; again begin this,
and thou wilt have finished.   —Ausonius

The beginnings of all things are small.
                          —Cicero, *De Finibus*, Book V, Ch. 21, Sec. 58

The great majority of men are bundles of beginnings.
                                —Ralph Waldo Emerson, *Journals*

The first blow is half the battle.   —Oliver Goldsmith

He has half the deed done who has made a beginning.   —Horace

Well begun is half done.   —Horace, *Epistles*, I, ii.

Know ye not, each thing we prize / Does from small beginnings rise?
—Mary Anne Lamb

The journey of a thousand miles starts from beneath one's feet.
—Lao Tzu, *Tao Te Ching*, Ch. LXIV

The beginning is the most important part of the work.
—Plato, *The Republic*, Book I, 377

The man who removes a mountain begins by carrying away small stones.
—Proverb (Chinese)

You won't win if you don't begin.
—Robert H. Schuller, *Tough Times Never Last, But Tough People Do!*

He that climbs a ladder must begin at the first round.
—Kenilworth Scott

Only the first swath cut by the scythe is difficult.
—Alexander Solzhenitsyn, *The Gulag Archipelago*

BEHAVIOR

To really know a man, observe his behavior with a woman, a flat tire, and a child.
—Anonymous

Things that happen, however painful they are at the time, do not matter very much for long. Only how we behave to them matters.
—Phyllis Bottome

Society always has a share of responsibility in the bad behavior of its members.
—Delore, *L'Homme dans la nature et la societé*

For the most part I do the thing which my own nature drives me to do.
—Albert Einstein

If you treat men the way they are you never improve them. If you treat them the way you want them to be, you do.
—Johann Wolfgang von Goethe

Considering how bad men are, it is wonderful how well they behave.
—Salvador de Madriaga

A man's acts are partly determined by spontaneous impulse, partly by the conscious and unconscious effects of the various groups to which he belongs.
—Bertrand Russell, *The Future of Science*

Every attempt to explain human behavior, especially the irrational,
must as a matter of course end in simplification.
—Morton Irving Seiden,
The Paradox of Hate: A Study in Ritual Murder, 14

Every human act can be disguised with a coating of gilt.
—Alexander Solzhenitsyn, *August 1914*

I love you always, but sometimes I do not love your behavior.
—Amy Vanderbilt

The way we behave toward people indicates what we really believe
about God.
—Warren Wiersbe

BELIEF

A belief is not true because it is useful.
—Henri Frédéric Amiel, *The Private Journal of Henri Frédéric Amiel*

If life is a comedy to him who thinks and a tragedy to him who feels,
it is a victory to him who believes.
—Anonymous

I believe in order that I may understand.   —Saint Anselm, *Proslogion*

Believe not every tale.
—Apocrypha, "Ecclesiasticus"

. . . it is how we choose to assess the unique experiences of our life
that ultimately determines what we believe.
—Phillip L. Berman, *The Courage of Conviction*, Introduction

Jesus saith unto him, Thomas, because thou hast seen me, thou hast
believed: blessed are they that have not seen, and yet have
believed.
—*The Bible* (KJV): John 20:29

A man lives by believing something.
—Thomas Carlyle

Man is what he believes.
—Anton Chekhov

Believe only half of what you see and nothing that you hear.
—Dinah Mulock Craik

The easiest thing of all is to deceive one's self; for what a man wishes
he generally believes to be true.   —Demosthenes, *Olynthiaca*, 3

For they can conquer who believe they can.   —John Dryden

We are all apt to believe what the world believes about us.

—George Eliot

We are born believing. A man bears beliefs as a tree bears apples.

—Ralph Waldo Emerson

The practical effect of a belief is the real test of its soundness.

—James Anthony Froude

He does not believe that does not live according to belief.

—Thomas Fuller, M. D., *Gnomologia*, No. 1838

Maturity of mind is best shown in slow belief.   —Baltasar Gracián

Some things have to be believed to be seen.   —Ralph Hodgson

Believe that life is worth living, and your belief will help create the fact.   —William James, *The Will to Believe: And Other Essays in Popular Philosophy*, "Is Life Worth Living?"

We are inclined to believe those whom we do not know, because they have never deceived us.   —Samuel Johnson, *The Idler*

We can never finally know. I simply believe that some part of the human Self or Soul is not subject to the laws of space and time.

—Carl Jung

The victory's in believing.   —James Russell Lowell, "To ———"

You're not free until you've been made captive by supreme belief.
—Marianne Moore, *Collected Poems*, "Spenser's Ireland"

Do not believe hastily.   —Ovid, *Ars Amatoria*, Book III, line 685

To believe is to be strong. Doubt cramps energy. Belief is power.
—Frederick W. Robertson

You believe that easily which you hope for earnestly.   —Terence

I believe because it is impossible.   —Tertullian, *De Carne Christi*

What we believe about God is the most important thing about us.
—A. W. Tozer

I firmly believe in Divine Providence. Without belief in Providence I think I should go crazy. Without God the world would be a maze without a clue. —Woodrow Wilson, speech, 1919

What we ardently wish we soon believe. —Young

The BIBLE

The lion and the calf shall lie down together but the calf won't get much sleep. —Woody Allen, *Without Feathers*, "The Scrolls"

As in Paradise, God walks in the Holy Scriptures, seeking man. —Saint Ambrose

A man is not educated who does not know the basic truths of the Bible. —Anonymous

Other books were given for our information; the Bible was given for our transformation. —Anonymous

Read thou; but first thyself prepare / To read with zeal and mark with care . . . / And, when thou has read what here is writ, / Let thy best practice second it. / So twice each precept read shall be— / First in the Book and next in thee. —Anonymous

The Bible, as a revelation from God, was not designed to give us all the information we might desire, nor to solve all the questions about which the human soul is perplexed, but to impart enough to be a safe guide to the haven of eternal rest. —Albert Barnes

Coming [to the Bible] through commentaries is much like looking at a landscape through garret windows, over which generations of unmolested spiders have spun their webs. —Henry Ward Beecher

Men can make an idol of the Bible. —Henry Ward Beecher

. . . Man shall not live by bread alone, but by every word that proceedeth out of the mouth of God. —*The Bible* (KJV): Matthew 4:4

Heaven and earth shall pass away, but my words shall not pass away. —*The Bible* (KJV): Matthew 24:35

All scripture is given by inspiration of God . . . —*The Bible* (KJV): 2 Timothy 3:16

For the word of God is quick, and powerful, and sharper than any
    two-edged sword . . .   —*The Bible* (KJV): Hebrews 4:12

There is not a single pessimistic note anywhere in the New Testament
    after the resurrection.   —Andrew W. Blackwood

The Bible is like a telescope. If a man looks through his telescope,
    then he sees worlds beyond; but if he looks at his telescope, then
    he does not see anything but that. The Bible is a thing to be looked
    through, to see that which is beyond.   —Phillips Brooks

I know the Bible is inspired because it finds me at greater depths of
    my being than any other book.   —Samuel Taylor Coleridge

It [the Bible] seems to portray a struggle between our mental inclina-
    tions and our actions.   —Gary R. Collins, *The Magnificent Mind*

Whence but from Heaven, could men unskill'd in arts, / In several
    ages born, in several parts, / Weave such agreeing truths? or how,
    or why / Should all conspire to cheat us with a lie? —John Dryden

The Bible is a window in this prison-world, through which we may
    look into eternity.   —Timothy Dwight

I believe that the intention of Holy Writ was to persuade men of the
    truths necessary to salvation; such as neither science nor other
    means could render credible, but only the voice of the Holy Spirit.
        —Galileo Galilei, letter to Father Benedetto Castelli, 1613

The doctrine of the moveity of the sun is condemned on the ground
    that the Scriptures speak in many places of the sun moving and the
    earth standing still . . .
        It is piously spoken that the Scriptures cannot lie. But none will
    deny that they are frequently abstruse and their true meaning diffi-
    cult to discover, and more than the bare words signify. One taking
    the sense too literally might pervert the truth and conceive blas-
    phemies, and give God feet, and hands, and eyes, and human
    affections, such as anger, repentance, forgetfulness, ignorance,
    whereas these expressions are employed merely to accommodate
    the truth to the mental capacity of the unlearned.
                                        —Galileo Galilei,
        "The Authority of Scripture in Philosophical Controversies"

It is impossible mentally or socially to enslave a Bible-reading people.
                                        —Horace Greeley

I have an implicit faith . . . that mankind can only be saved through non-violence, which is the central teaching of the Bible, as I have understood the Bible.　　　　　—Mahatma Gandhi, in S. Hobhouse, editor, *True Patriotism: Some Sayings of Mahatma Gandhi*

It [the Bible] has never bowed its head before the discoveries of science.　　　　　—Billy Graham, *World Aflame*

Like Joseph storing up grain during the years of plenty to be used during the years of famine that lay ahead, may we store up the truth of God's Word in our hearts as much as possible, so that we are prepared for whatever suffering we are called upon to endure.　　　　　—Billy Graham, *Till Armageddon*

Jacob's ladder is short.　　　　　—Steve Hawthorne, guest sermon, Hope Chapel, Austin, Texas, 11 Jan 1991

The best evidence of the Bible's being the word of God is to be found between its covers. It proves itself.　　　　　—Charles Hodge

The difference between the Old and the New Testament is the difference between a man who said "There is nothing new under the sun" and a God who says "Behold, I make all things new."　　　　　—Ronald A. Knox, *Stimuli*

Honey and locusts were his food, / And he was most severely good.　　　　　—Mary Anne Lamb, about John the Baptist, "Salome"

This great Book . . . is the best gift God has given to man . . . But for it we could not know right from wrong.　　　　　—Abraham Lincoln

It is not our comment on the Word that saves, but the Word itself.　　　　　—Robert Murray McCheyne

When you are reading a book in a dark room, and come to a difficult part, you take it to a window to get more light. So take your Bibles to Christ.　　　　　—Robert Murray McCheyne

It is a fallacy to suppose that by omitting a subject you teach nothing about it. On the contrary, you teach that it is to be omitted.　　　　　—Walter Moberly, on the Bible in the curriculum

The central conception of Man in the Gospels is that he is an unfinished creation capable of reaching a higher level by a definite evolution which must begin by his own efforts.　　　　　—Maurice Nicoll, *The New Man*

The best way to know God's will is to be familiar with the Bible.
—Pat Robertson, *Answers to 200 of Life's Most Probing Questions*

The Bible, and the peace that comes about through a continuous relationship with God are the best ways of knowing His will.
—Pat Robertson, *Answers to 200 of Life's Most Probing Questions*

The only way to understand the difficult parts of the Bible is first to read and obey the easy ones.
—John Ruskin

Nobody ever outgrows Scripture; the book widens and deepens with our years.
—Charles H. Spurgeon

Be careful how you live, you may be the only Bible some person ever reads.
—W. J. Toms, *Detroit News*

The Bible does not profess to make men omniscient, but simply to tell them enough to make them happy and good, if they will believe it and live up to it.
—Henry Van Dyke

A man may read the figures on the dial, but he cannot tell how the day goes unless the sun is shining on it; so we may read the Bible over, but we cannot learn to purpose till the spirit of God shine upon it and into our hearts.
—T. Watson

The Bible is a harp with a thousand strings. Play on one to the exclusion of its relationship to the others, and you will develop discord. Play on all of them, keeping them in their places in the divine scale, and you will hear heavenly music all the time.
—William P. White

We search the world for truth; we cull / The good, the pure, the beautiful, / From all old flower fields of the soul; / And, weary seekers of the best, / We come back laden from our quest, / To find that all the sages said / Is in the Book our mothers read.
—John Greenleaf Whittier, "Miriam"

BIOGRAPHY

Biography is the best form of history.
—Josh Billings

Biography is the only true history.
—Thomas Carlyle

Nobody can write the life of a man but those who have eaten and drunk and lived in social intercourse with him.
—Samuel Johnson, in James Boswell, *Life of Samuel Johnson*

Just how difficult it is to write biography can be reckoned by anybody who sits down and considers just how many people know the real truth about his or her love affairs.
—Rebecca West, "The Art of Skepticism," *Vogue*, 1 Nov 1952

BIRDS

Because the road is rough and long, / Should we despise the skylark's song?
—Anne Brontë, "Views of Life"'

Be thou like the bird perched upon some frail thing, although he feels the branch bending beneath him, yet loudly sings, knowing full well that he has wings.
—Madame de Gasparin

The idea of the nest in the bird's mind, where does it come from?
—Joseph Joubert, *Pensées*

Even when the bird walks we see that it has wings.
—Antoine-Marin Lemierre

A bird flies to its own.
—Proverb (Latin)

The smallest bird cannot light upon the greatest tree without sending a shock to its most distant fiber.
—Gen. Lew Wallace

BIRTH

When I was born I was so surprised I didn't talk for a year and a half.
—Gracie Allen

Having a baby is like taking your lower lip and forcing it over your head.
—Carol Burnett

The birth of every new baby is God's vote of confidence in the future of man.
—Imogene Fey

Man's main task in life is to give birth to himself.
—Erich Fromm, *Man for Himself*

God one morning, glad of heaven, / Laughed—and that was you!
—Brian Hooker, "A Little Person"

Somewhere on this globe every 10 seconds, there is a woman giving birth to a child. She must be found and stopped.
—Sam Levenson

Love set you going like a fat gold watch. / The midwife slapped your
footsoles, and your bald cry / Took its place among the elements.
—Sylvia Plath, *Ariel*, "Morning Song"

God makes the world all over again, whenever a little child is born.
—Jean Paul Richter

In the early days of the Indian Territory, there were no such things as
birth certificates. You being there was certificate enough.
—Will Rogers

When we are born, we cry that we are come / To this great stage of
fools.
—William Shakespeare, *King Lear*, Act IV, Sc. vi

I am still not clear how I got here.
—Kurt Vonnegut, Jr., *Slapstick*, Prologue

Our birth is but a sleep and a forgetting.
—William Wordsworth, "Intimations of Immortality"

BIRTHDAYS

The first fact about the celebration of a birthday is that it is a way of
affirming defiantly, and even flamboyantly, that it is a good thing
to be alive.
—G. K. Chesterton

BITTERNESS

Never succumb to the temptation of bitterness.
—Martin Luther King, Jr., *The Strength to Love*

BLACK AMERICA

A young white boy's badness is simply the overflowing of young ani-
mal spirits; the black boy's badness is badness, pure and simple.
—Anonymous, letter from a Negro mother,
The Independent, 18 Sep 1902

To be black and conscious in America is to be in a constant state of
rage.

—James Baldwin, in *Time*,
"Negro Leaders on Violence," 20 Aug 1965

It is not healthy when a nation lives within a nation, as colored
Americans are living inside America. A nation cannot live confi-
dent of its tomorrow if its refugees are among its own citizens.
—Pearl S. Buck, *What America Means to Me*

Black is beautiful.
—Stokely Carmichael, at a Mississippi civil rights rally, 6 Jun 1966

Black men built the railroads, not blue eyes.
—Ralph Waldo Emerson, *Journals*, 1845

The Negro's primary aim is to be the white man's brother, not his
brother-in-law.   —Martin Luther King, Jr., *Stride Toward Freedom*

I have one criticism about the Negro troops who fought under my
command in the Korean War. They didn't send me enough of
them.   —Gen. Douglas MacArthur

White society has crippled the Negro for over three centuries, then
we self-righteously blame them for limping. —Rabbi Judea B. Miller

The haughty American nation . . . makes the Negro clean its boots
and then proves the moral and physical inferiority of the Negro by
the fact that he is a bootblack.   —George Bernard Shaw

BLAME

The fox condemns the trap, not himself.   —William Blake

I praise loudly, I blame softly.   —Catherine II of Russia

Let us no more contend, nor blame / Each other, blamed enough elsewhere, but strive / In offices of love, how we may lighten / Each
other's burden, in our share of woe.   —John Milton

The fault, dear Brutus, is not in our stars, / But in ourselves . . .
—William Shakespeare, *Julius Caesar*, Act I, Sc. ii

BLESSINGS

When you count your blessings, do not forget to reckon in a lot of
things you have not got.   —Anonymous

'Tis not for mortals always to be blest.
—John Armstrong, *Art of Preserving Health*, Book IV

Yet everyone grapples, each in his awkward muffled way, with a
power, a Jacob's angel, to get a final satisfaction or glory that is
withheld. —Saul Bellow, *Mr. Sammler's Planet*, Ch. 3

I have been blessed to be a blessing. —Scott Wesley Brown

Come what may, I have been blest. —Lord Byron,
The Giaour, line 1115

It is only when we have lost them that we fully appreciate our blessings.
—Plautus, *Captivi*

Not blessedness itself, but to be worthy of it, / That is the blossom of
this earthly vale. —Tiedge

I dimly guess, from blessings known, of greater out of sight.
—John Greenleaf Whittier

Amid my list of blessings infinite,
Stands this the foremost, "That my heart has bled." —Young

BLONDES

It is possible that blondes also prefer gentlemen. —Mamie Van Doren

BLOOD

The blood of the lamb applied over the doorpost on the night of
Israel's deliverance from Egypt distinguished the obedient from the
disobedient. Just so today the applied blood of the Lamb of God is
the distinguishing mark of God's called out ones, the church . . .
—Billy Graham, *Till Armageddon*

There's no getting blood out of a turnip.
—Frederick Marryat, *Japhet in Search of a Father*, Ch. 4

I see His blood upon the rose / And in the stars the glory of His eyes.
—Joseph Plunkett, "I See His Blood"

The BLUES

The blues ain't nothin' but a good man feelin' bad.
—Anonymous, line from the movie *Crossroads*

BOLDNESS

... fling yourself straight into life, without deliberation; don't be
afraid—the flood will bear you to the bank and set you safe on your
feet again.   —Fyodor Dostoyevsky, *Crime and Punishment*

There is only one thing, one thing needful: one has only to dare.
        —Fyodor Dostoyevsky, *Crime and Punishment*

Better hazard once than always be in fear.
        —Thomas Fuller, M. D., *Gnomologia*, No. 906

Where Necessity pinches, Boldness is Prudence.
        —Thomas Fuller, M. D., *Gnomologia*, No. 5650

A bold onset is half the battle.   —Giuseppe Garibaldi

What you can do, or dream you can, begin it; / Boldness has genius,
power and magic in it.   —Johann Wolfgang von Goethe

Be bold—and mighty forces will come to your aid.   —Basil King

In difficult and desperate situations, the boldest plans are safest.
        —Lucius Marcius, Roman commander,
3rd century B.C., in Livy, *The History of Rome*

Even God lends a hand to honest boldness.
        —Menander, Fragments, No. 572

Fortune and Love befriend the bold.   —Ovid

Venus favors the bold.   —Ovid

BOOKS

Of gifts, there seems none more becoming to offer a friend than a
beautiful book.   —Bronson Alcott

Some books are undeservedly forgotten; none are undeservedly
remembered.   —W. H. Auden, *The Dyer's Hand*, "Reading"

Some books are to be tasted, others to be swallowed, and some few to
be chewed and digested.   —Francis Bacon, *Essays*, "Of Studies"

'Tis pleasant, sure, to see one's name in print; / A book's a book,
although there's nothing in't.
        —Lord Byron, *English Bards and Scotch Reviewers*

You think your pain and your heartbreak are unprecedented in the history of the world, but then you read. It was books that taught me that the things which tormented me most were the very things that connected me with all the people who were alive, or who had ever been alive.
—James Baldwin

A book is good company. It is full of conversation without loquacity. It comes to your longing with full instruction, but pursues you never.
—Henry Ward Beecher, in William Drysdale, editor, *Proverbs from Plymouth Pulpit*

Books are not men and yet they are alive.   —Stephen Vincent Benét

The covers of this book are too far apart.
—Ambrose Bierce, in C. H. Grattan, *Bitter Bierce* (1929)

When you find that a book is poor . . . waste no more time upon it.
—James Bryce

Of all the things which man can do or make here below, by far the most momentous, wonderful, and worthy are the things we call books.
—Thomas Carlyle

The best effect of any book is that it excites the reader to self-activity.
—Thomas Carlyle

The true university of these days is a collection of books.
—Thomas Carlyle, *On Heroes, Hero-Worship and the Heroic in History* (1841), "The Hero as Man of Letters"

What one knows best is . . . what one has learned not from books but as a result of books, through the reflections to which they have given rise.   —Nicolas Chamfort, *Maximes et pensées*

It is chiefly through books that we enjoy intercourse with superior minds. In the best books, great men talk to us, and give us their most precious thoughts. —William Ellery Channing, "Self-Culture"

Let every man, if possible, gather some good books under his roof, and obtain access for himself and family to some social library.
—William Ellery Channing

The easiest books are generally the best; for, whatever author is obscure and difficult in his own language, certainly does not think clearly.   —Earl of Chesterfield, letter to his son, 8 Feb 1750

A room without books is a body without a soul. —Cicero

Books support us in solitude, and keep us from being a burden to ourselves. —Jeremy Collier

Next to acquiring good friends, the best acquisition is that of good books. —Charles Caleb Colton

A good book has no ending. —R. D. Cumming

There are still a few of us booklovers around despite the awful warnings of Marshall McLuhan with his TV era and his pending farewell to Gutenberg. —Frank Davies

If I were going to tell one of my sons how to possess the world, I would simply bring him into my house, show him that solid wall of books, and say to him: "The secret is in there somewhere, and even if you never find out what it is, you will still have come closer than if you had never read these." —James Dickey, *Sorties*

It is a marvelous thing, this having a house full of books. Something crosses the mind—a flash of light, some connection, some recognition—and one simply rises from one's chair and goes, as though by predestination, to that book, to that poem. —James Dickey, *Sorties*

A book may be as great a thing as a battle. —Benjamin Disraeli

Beware of the man of one book. —Isaac D'Israeli, *Curiosities of Literature*

Books are the beehives of thought; laconics the honey taken from them. —James Ellis

It is a tie between men to have read the same book. —Ralph Waldo Emerson, *Journals*

We are too civil to books. For a few golden sentences we will turn over and actually read a volume of four or five hundred pages. —Ralph Waldo Emerson, *Journals*

I suggest that the only books that influence us are those for which we are ready, and which have gone a little farther down our particular path than we have yet got ourselves. —E. M. Forster, *Two Cheers for Democracy*, "A Book That Influenced Me"

One always tends to overpraise a long book because one has got
through it.   —E. M. Forster, *Aspects of the Novel*

The book is the world's most patient medium.
              —Northrop Frye, in NFB documentary film,
                  The Scholar in Society, 1984

Books, like friends, should be few, and well chosen.   —Thomas Fuller

What a convenient and delightful world is this world of books!—If
you bring to it not the obligations of the student, or look upon it as
an opiate for idleness, but enter it rather with enthusiasm of the
adventurer.   —David Grayson, *Adventures in Contentment*, 12

Books give not wisdom where was none before, / But where some is,
there reading makes it more.   —Sir John Harington, *Epigrams*

From your parents you learn love and laughter and how to put one
foot in front of the other. But when books are opened you discover
that you have wings.   —Helen Hayes

Be as careful of the books you read as of the company you keep, for
your habits and character will be as much influenced by the former
as the latter.   —Paxton Hood

Books have their destinies.   —Horace

No book is of much importance; the vital thing is, What do you yourself think?   —Elbert Hubbard, *The Philistine*

This will never be a civilized country until we expend more money
for books than we do for chewing-gum.
                  —Elbert Hubbard, *The Philistine*, Vol. xxv.

It is from books that wise men derive consolation in the troubles of
life.   —Victor Hugo

It is with books as with women, where a certain plainness of manner
and of dress is more engaging than that glare of paint and airs and
apparel which may dazzle the eye, but reaches not the affections.
                          —David Hume

A book should teach us to enjoy life, or to endure it.
                          —Samuel Johnson

Books go out into the world, travel mysteriously from hand to hand, and somehow find their way to the people who need them at the times when they need them . . . Cosmic forces guide such passings-along.   —Erica Jong, *How to Save Your Life*

A book must be the ax for the frozen sea within us.
                              —Franz Kafka, letter to Oskar Pollak, 27 Jan 1904

Except a living man there is nothing more wonderful than a book . . .
                                                —Charles Kingsley

You can send in tanks against armed insurgents—but what weapon is there against a book?   —*Kölnische Rundschau* (newspaper),
                        in Alexander Solzhenitsyn, *The Oak and the Calf*

Wear the old coat and buy the new book.   —Austin Phelps

Books have always been to me like a kind of embalmed mind. The dead may be scattered, and who can find them, but their voices live in the library.   —Laurel Lee, *Godspeed: Hitchhiking Home*

Even at her loneliest she liked being among books, although she was sometimes depressed to see how much there was to read that she hadn't.   —Bernard Malamud, *The Assistant*

The greatest advantage of books does not always come from what we remember of them, but from their suggestiveness, their character-building power.   —O. S. Marden

It is astonishing how many books I find there is no need for me to read at all.   —W. Somerset Maugham

Nevertheless, one learned very early that books had to be respected; they were all putative Bibles and to some small degree had a share in holiness.   —Arthur Miller, *Timebends*

The real purpose of books is to trap the mind into doing its own thinking.   —Christopher Morley

We visit bookshops not so often to buy any one special book, but rather to rediscover, in the happier and more expressive words of others, our own encumbered soul.
                —Christopher Morley, *44 Essays*, "On Visiting Bookshops"

Just the knowledge that a good book is awaiting one at the end of a long day makes that day happier.
—Kathleen Norris, *Hands Full of Living*

No man understands a deep book until he has seen and lived at least part of its contents.
—Ezra Pound

Books do furnish a room.
—Anthony Powell

A book is like a garden carried in the pocket.
—Proverb (Chinese)

Every book must be chewed to get out its juice.
—Proverb (Chinese)

Books are nourishment to the mind.
—Proverb (Italian)

There is no worse robber than a bad book.
—Proverb (Italian)

In the futile attempts we all make to tidy up our lives and our surroundings, nothing is more difficult than throwing out a book.
—Andrew A. Rooney, *Pieces of My Mind*, "Casting Out Books"

You can't tell a book by its movie.
—Louis A. Safian, compiler, *The Book of Updated Proverbs*

What really knocks me out is a book that, when you're all done reading it, you wish the author that writes it was a terrific friend of yours and you could call him up on the phone whenever you felt like it.
—J. D. Salinger, *The Catcher in the Rye*

A bookstore is one of the only pieces of physical evidence we have that people are still thinking.
—Jerry Seinfeld, *SeinLanguage*, Introduction

The big advantage of a book is it's very easy to rewind. Close it and you're right back at the beginning.
—Jerry Seinfeld, *SeinLanguage*, Introduction

Men often discover their affinity to each other by the mutual love they have for a book.
—Samuel Smiles

Books are a finer world within the world.
—Alexander Smith

No furniture so charming as books.
—Sydney Smith, in *Lady S. Holland's Memoir*

Man builds no structure which outlives a book.
—E. F. Ware

Hard-covered books break up friendships. You loan a hard-covered book
to a friend and when he doesn't return it you get mad at him. It
makes you mean and petty. But twenty-five-cent books are different.
—John Steinbeck

Books are good enough in their own way, but they are a mighty
bloodless substitute for life.
—Robert Louis Stevenson, *Virginibus Puerisque*,
"An Apology for Idlers"

Everywhere I have sought rest and found it not except sitting apart in
a nook with a little book. —Thomas à Kempis

The man who does not read good books has no advantage over the
man who can't read them. —Mark Twain

In a way, the main fault of all books is that they are too long.
—Luc de Clapiers Vauvenargues

Books are lighthouses erected in the great sea of time. —E. P. Whipple

Never read a book through merely because you have begun it.
—John Witherspoon

To me the charm of an encyclopedia is that it knows—and I needn't.
—Francis Yeats-Brown

BOREDOM

When a thing bores you, do not do it. —Eugène Delacroix

Down with boredom. It has to go. —Elsa Maxwell

Boredom is the midwife of creativity. —Talia Shire

The life of the creative man is led, directed and controlled by boredom. Avoiding boredom is one of our most important purposes.
—Saul Steinberg

Somebody's boring me. I think it's me.
—Dylan Thomas, in Rayner Heppenstall, *Four Absentees*, Ch. 16

BORROWING

Give to him that asketh thee, and from him that would borrow of
thee turn not thou away. —*The Bible* (KJV): Matthew 5:42

Borrowing from Peter to pay Paul.

—Cicero

He who borrows sells his freedom.

—Proverb (German)

An old loan repaid is like finding something new. —Proverb (Russian)

Have a horse of your own and you may borrow another's.

—Proverb (Welsh)

Neither a borrower nor a lender be; / For loan oft loses both itself and friend, / And borrowing dulls the edge of husbandry. / This above all: to thine own self be true, / And it must follow as the night the day, / Thou canst not then be false to any man.

—William Shakespeare, *Hamlet*, Act I, Sc. iii

I not only use all the brains I have, but all I can borrow.

—Woodrow Wilson, 1914, *New York Times Magazine*, 10 Jun 1956, "Woodrow Wilson in His Own Words"

B O X I N G

Float like a butterfly, / Sting like a bee, / Your hands can't hit / What your eyes can't see!

—Drew "Bundini" Brown, Muhammad Ali's trainer, catch phrase for Ali

We was robbed!

—Joe Jacobs, boxing manager, shouted when his fighter, Max Schmeling, lost a heavyweight title match to Jack Sharkey on a decision

B R A V E R Y

Tell a man he is brave, and you help him to become so.

—Thomas Carlyle

None but the brave deserves the fair.

—John Dryden, "Alexander's Feast," 15

. . . it's you who stands to lose if you're not brave enough to state your case.

—Garsenda de Forcalquier

Some have been thought brave because they were afraid to run away.

—Thomas Fuller, M.D., *Gnomologia*, No. 4214

The bravest sight in all this world is a man fighting against odds.

—Franklin K. Lane, *The Unconquerable Soul*

True bravery is shown by performing, without witnesses, what one
might be capable of doing before all the world.
—François de La Rochefoucauld

You can't be brave if you've only had wonderful things happen to
you. —Mary Tyler Moore

God himself favors the brave. —Ovid, *Metamorphoses*, X, 586

All are brave when the enemy flies. —Proverb (Italian)

God helps the brave. —Friedrich Schiller

. . . nothing is so entirely admirable as a man bravely wretched.
—Seneca

BREVITY

Be brief, for no discourse can please when too long.
—Miguel de Cervantes

Never be so brief as to become obscure. —Tryon Edwards

Good things, when short, are twice as good.
—Baltasar Gracián, *The Art of Worldly Wisdom*

The most valuable of all talents is that of never using two words
when one will do. —Thomas Jefferson

. . . brevity is the soul of wit . . .
—William Shakespeare, *Hamlet*, Act II, Sc. ii

BROTHERHOOD

I sought my soul—but my soul eluded me; I sought my God—but my
God eluded me; I sought my brother—and found all three.
—Anonymous

Of a truth, men are mystically united: a mystic bond of brotherhood
makes all men one. —Thomas Carlyle, *Essays*

The world is now too dangerous for anything but the truth, too small
for anything but brotherhood.
—Arthur Powell Davies, *Ethical Outlook*

While there is a lower class I am in it, while there is a criminal element I am of it; while there is a soul in prison, I am not free.
—Eugene V. Debs, speech at trial in Cleveland, Ohio, 14 Sep 1918, in *Liberator*, Nov 1918

I want to realize brotherhood or identity not merely with the beings called human, but I want to realize identity with all life, even with such beings as crawl on earth.   —Mahatma Gandhi

We are all gathered to the same fold.   —Horace, *Odes*

We seek not the worldwide victory of one nation or system but a worldwide victory of men.
—John F. Kennedy, State of the Union Message, 14 Jan 1963

We must learn to live together as brothers or perish together as fools.
—Martin Luther King, Jr.

If God is thy father, man is thy brother.   —Alphonse de Lamartine

Adapt yourself to the environment in which your lot has been cast, and show true love to the fellow-mortals with whom destiny has surrounded you.   —Marcus Aurelius Antoninus, *Meditations*, 6.39

The universal brotherhood of man is our most precious possession, what there is of it.   —Mark Twain, *Following the Equator*, "Pudd'n Wilson's New Calendar"

BUILDING

Rome was not built in a day.   —John Heywood

To build is to dwell.   —Maxine Kumine, *The Designated Heir*, Ch. 1

Ah, to build, to build! That is the noblest of all the arts.
—Henry Wadsworth Longfellow

All the wood for the temple does not come from one tree.
—Proverb (Chinese)

When we build, let us think we build forever.
—John Ruskin, *The Seven Lamps of Architecture*, 6.10

The foundation stones of a great building are destined to groan and be pressed upon; it is not for them to crown the edifice.
—Alexander Solzhenitsyn, *The Gulag Archipelago*

Too low they build, who build beneath the stars.
                                —Edward Young, *Night Thoughts*

BURDENS

When the load feels heavy, it's a sign you're climbing. —Anonymous

Take your burdens, and troubles, and losses, and wrongs, if come they
    must and will, as your opportunities, knowing that God has girded
    you for greater things than these.   —Horace Bushnell

Heaven suits the back to the burden.   —Charles Dickens,
        The Life and Adventures of Nicholas Nickleby, Ch. 18

None knows the weight of another's burden.
                        —Thomas Fuller, M. D., *Gnomologia*

Thank God when He lays a burden on thee, and thank Him when He
    takes it off.   —Johann Wolfgang von Goethe

None knows the weight of another's burden.
                        —George Herbert, *Outlandish Proverbs*

Weigh well what your shoulders can and cannot bear.   —Horace

It is when tomorrow's burden is added to the burden of today that
    the weight is more than a man can bear.   —George Macdonald

The burden becomes light which is cheerfully borne.   —Ovid

Every one thinks his own burden heavy.   —Proverb (French)

God burdens no man beyond his powers.   —Proverb (Indian)

A burden which one chooses is not felt.   —Proverb (Italian)

When the ass bears too light a load, he wants to lie down.
                                —Proverb (Russian)

Shoulders are from God and burdens too.
                —Isaac Bashevis Singer, "Gimpel the Fool"

Not few nor light are the burdens of life; then load it not with heavi-
    ness of spirit.   —Martin Farquhar Tupper

O you who have borne even heavier things, to these too, God will
    grant an end!   —Virgil, *Aeneid*, Book I, line 199

What we are assigned to bear is in a sense a measure of our stature.
—Peter de Vries, *Forever Panting*

BUREAUCRACY

. . . the sort of compromise one has to strike in dealing with a
bureaucracy.   —John Cheever, *Bullet Park*

The only thing that saves us from bureaucracy is its inefficiency.
—Eugene McCarthy

Bureaucracy defends the status quo long past the time when the quo
has lost its status.   —Laurence J. Peter, *The Peter Prescription*

In any bureaucracy, one soon learns that an error is never admitted. It
is corrected as discreetly as possible.
—Lawrence Sanders, *The Tomorrow File*

BUSINESS

Always let the man you are doing business with make some money.
—Jarvis Astaire, in *Tactics: The Art and Science of Success*,
edited by Edward de Bono

Whenever you see a successful business, someone once made a courageous decision.   —Peter Drucker

A small Shop may have a good Trade.—Thomas Fuller, M.D., *Gnomologia*

Great businesses turn on a little pin.
—George Herbert, *Jacula Prudentum*

We shall build good ships here—at a profit if we can, at a loss if we
must—but always good ships.
—motto of the Newport News Shipbuilding
and Drydock Company

In discussing business matters with others . . . it is better to discreetly
let them do most of the talking. When you are talking, they are
learning about you and your affairs . . . When they are talking, you
are learning about them and it is a pretty shrewd man who can talk
very long without disclosing to you a great deal that he does not
intend for you to know.   —William Nickerson

Keep your shop and your shop will keep you.
—Proverb (17th century)

Live together like brothers and do business like strangers.
—Proverb (Arab)

A man without a smiling face must not open shop.
—Proverb (Chinese)

It is easy to open a shop, but hard to keep it open. —Proverb (Chinese)

For every man hath business and desire, / Such as it is . . .
—William Shakespeare, *Hamlet*, Act I, Sc. v

To business that we love we rise betime, / And go to 't with delight.
—William Shakespeare, *Antony and Cleopatra*, Act IV, Sc. iv

It is an excessive price if our business costs us our home life.
—Roy L. Smith

Profits are part of the mechanism by which society decides what it
wants to see produced.   —Henry C. Wallich

The BUSY

When the devil can't make you bad, he makes you too busy.
—Anonymous

The busy have no time for tears.   —Lord Byron

If the enemy can keep us occupied, we don't present much opposition.
—Dan Davis, sermon, Hope Chapel, Austin, Texas, 28 Sep 1991

. . . too busy with the crowded hour to fear to live or die.
—Ralph Waldo Emerson, *Quatrains*, "Nature"

If you want work well done, select a busy man—the other kind has no
time.   —Elbert Hubbard, *A Thousand and One Epigrams*

A bee is never as busy as it seems; it's just that it can't buzz any
slower.   —Frank McKinney ("Kin") Hubbard

He that has too much to do will do something wrong.
—Samuel Johnson, *Rasselas*, Ch. 27

Beware of the barrenness of a busy life.   —Socrates

BUYING / SELLING

Cheat me in the price but not in the goods.   —Anonymous

He who decries wants to buy. —Anonymous

If you buy a bad thing you will soon buy again. —Anonymous

If you sell the cow, you sell her milk too. —Anonymous

It is no sin to sell dear, but a sin to give ill measure. —Anonymous

It is naught, it is naught, saith the buyer; but when he is gone his
way, then he boasteth. —*The Bible* (KJV): Proverbs 20:14

If the deal isn't good for the other party, it isn't good for you.
—B. C. Forbes

He who findeth Fault meaneth to buy.
—Thomas Fuller, M.D., *Gnomologia*, No. 2383

Weigh right and sell dear. —Thomas Fuller, M.D., *Gnomologia*, No. 5467

Ill ware is never cheap. Pleasing ware is half sold.
—George Herbert, *Jacula Prudentum*

Don't a fellow feel good after he gets out of a store where he nearly
bought something. —Frank McKinney ("Kin") Hubbard

The worth of a thing is what it will bring. —Proverb (17th century)

Fuel is not sold in a forest, nor fish on a lake. —Proverb (Chinese)

When the market is brisk, the seller does not stop to wash the mud
from his turnips. —Proverb (Chinese)

When you buy, use your ears and your mind, not your ears.
—Proverb (Czechoslavakian)

He is no merchant who always gains. —Proverb (Dutch)

Good ware makes quick markets. —Proverb (Latin)

Let the buyer beware. —Proverb (Latin)

Everything is worth what its purchaser will pay for it.
—Publilius Syrus, *Sententioe*, No. 847

He has an advantage in any deal whose merchandise will stand
inspection. —Roy L. Smith

The best things are not bought and sold.   —Walter Smith

How many things I can do without.
                    —Socrates, remark in a marketplace, in Diogenes Laertius,
                                        Lives of Eminent Philosophers

Everyone lives by selling something.
                    —Robert Louis Stevenson, *Across the Plains*, "Beggars"

Never buy a thing you don't want merely because it is dear.
                                        —Oscar Wilde

— C —

CAGES

You can cage the singer but not the song.
> —Harry Belafonte, on the arts in South Africa,
> in *International Herald Tribune*, 3 Oct 1988

A Robin Red breast in a Cage
  Puts all Heaven in a Rage.
> —William Blake, "Auguries of Innocence"

I know why the caged bird sings!
> —Paul Lawrence Dunbar, "Sympathy"

Nightingales do not sing well in cages.   —Pierre Schneider

CALAMITY

Every calamity is a spur and valuable hint.
> —Ralph Waldo Emerson, *The Conduct of Life*, "Fate"

Calamity is virtue's opportunity.   —Seneca

CALLING

The world is to be cleaned by somebody, and you are not called of
  God if you are ashamed to scrub.   —Henry Ward Beecher

The place God calls you to is the place where your deep gladness and
  the world's deep hunger meet.
> —Frederick Buechner, *Wishful Thinking*: *A Theological ABC*

Only the individual knows to what God is calling him.
> —Joseph F. Girzone, *Joshua*, Ch. 9

Every calling is great when greatly pursued.
> —Oliver Wendell Holmes, Jr., speech,
> Suffolk Bar Association, 5 Feb 1885

CANDLES

A candle loses nothing by lighting another candle.   —Anonymous

Many candles can be kindled from one candle without diminishing
  it.   —*The Midrash*

My candle burns at both ends; / It will not last the night; / But ah, my
  foes, and oh my friends— / It gives a lovely light!
      —Edna St. Vincent Millay, *A Few Figs from Thistles*, "First Fig"

CAPITAL

Capital is only the fruit of labor, and could never have existed had
  not labor first existed.
  —Abraham Lincoln, First Annual Message to Congress, 8 Dec 1861

CAPITAL PUNISHMENT

It is fairly obvious that those who are in favor of the death penalty
  have more affinity with murderers than those who are not.
                  —Rémy de Gourmont, *Pensées inédites*

Why do we kill people who are killing people to show that killing
  people is wrong?   —Holly Near, "Foolish Notion"

CAREERS

Keep interested in your own career, however humble; it is a real possession in the changing fortunes of time.
                          —Max Ehrman, "Desiderata"

Nothing is more boring than a man with a career.
      —Alexander Solzhenitsyn, *The Gulag Archipelago Three*

CARES

How many cares one loses when one decides not to be something,
  but to be someone.   —Gabrielle (Coco) Chanel

Cast all your cares on God; that anchor holds.
            —Alfred, Lord Tennyson, "Enoch Arden"

Care to our coffin adds a nail, no doubt; / And every grin, so merry,
  draws one out.   —John Wolcot, *Expostulatory Odes*, Ode 15

CARPENTERS

He's not the best carpenter that makes the most chips. —Anonymous

The house praises the carpenter.   —Ralph Waldo Emerson, *Journals*

CARS

The automobile changed our dress, manners, social customs, vacation habits, the shape of our cities, consumer purchasing patterns, common tastes and positions in intercourse.
                    —John Keats, *The Insolent Chariots*, 1958

The car has become a secular sanctuary for the individual, his shrine to the self, his mobile Walden Pond.   —Edward McDonagh

The car has become an article of dress without which we feel uncertain, unclad, and incomplete in the urban compound..
                    —Marshall McLuhan, *Understanding Media*

I think one of the reasons Americans are so reluctant to carpool is that, for many, the commute is their Walden Pond—their only quiet time alone.   —Katherine Sands

A Ford will run whenever a quorum of its parts is present.
                    —F. L. Warner, in *Reader's Digest*, Oct 1927

CATS

When I play with my cat, who knows whether she is not amusing herself with me more than I with her.
                    —Michel de Montaigne, *Essays*,
                    "Apology for Raimond de Sebonde"

The trouble with a kitten is THAT / Eventually it becomes a CAT.
                    —Ogden Nash, "The Kitten"

When the mouse laughs at the cat, there is a hole nearby.
                    —Proverb (Nigerian)

CAUSE and EFFECT

The connection between cause and effect is empirical and not necessary . . . The pattern of experience is not, as mathematics is, held together by logical and necessary relations.
—J. Bronowski and Bruce Mazlish, *The Western Intellectual Tradition*

CAUTION

Open your mouth and purse cautiously . . .   —Anonymous

Where the road bends abruptly take short steps.
—Ernest Bramah, *Kai Lung's Golden Hours*

He that will not sail till all dangers are over must never put to sea.
—Thomas Fuller, M. D., *Gnomologia*, No. 2353

The dry reed does not seek the company of the fire.   —Proverb (Arab)

Though the snake be small, it is wise to hit it with a big stick.
—Proverb (Indian)

Look the other way when the girl at the teahouse smiles.
—Proverb (Japanese)

He that counts all cost will never put plough in the earth.   —John Ray

Of all forms of caution, caution in love is perhaps the most fatal to
true happiness.   —Bertrand Russell, *The Conquest of Happiness*

If one is forever cautious, can one remain a human being?
—Alexander Solzhenitsyn, *The First Circle*

CENSORSHIP

Books won't stay banned. They won't burn. Ideas won't go to jail.
—A. Whitney Griswold, *Essays on Education*

Who kills a man kills a reasonable creature, God's image; but he
who destroys a good book kills reason itself.
—John Milton, *Areopagitica*

A book is somehow sacred. A dictator can kill and maim people, can
sink to any kind of tyranny and only be hated, but when books are
burned the ultimate in tyranny has happened. This we cannot forgive.   —John Steinbeck

CERTAINTIES

A bird in the hand is worth two in the bush.
—Miguel de Cervantes, *Don Quixote*

What a dusty answer gets the soul
When hot for certainties in this our life!
—George Meredith, *Modern Love*, Stanza 50

CHAINS

Why should a man be in love with his fetters, though of gold?
—Francis Bacon

My very chains and I grew friends.
—Lord Byron

No man loveth his fetters, be they made of gold.
—John Heywood, *Proverbs*

Man was born free, and everywhere he is in chains.
—Jean Jacques Rousseau, *The Social Contract*

CHALLENGES

It is not the mountain we conquer but ourselves.
—Sir Edmund Hillary

CHANCE

Chance is not.
—James Allen, *As a Man Thinketh*

They . . . who await / No gifts from Chance, have conquered Fate.
—Matthew Arnold, "Resignation"

How slight a chance may raise or sink a soul!   —Philip James Bailey

Surely there are in everyone's life certain connections, twists and
turns which pass awhile under the category of Chance, but at the
last, well examined, prove to be the very Hand of God.
—Sir Thomas Browne, *Religio Medici*

Chance is a nickname for Providence.
—Nicolas Chamfort

A consistent man believes in destiny, a capricious man in chance.
—Benjamin Disraeli

. . . chance may do anything.
—Fyodor Dostoyevsky, *Crime and Punishment*

At any rate, I am convinced that He [God] does not play dice.
—Albert Einstein, letter to Max Born, 4 Dec 1926,
in *Einstein un Born Briefwechsel*

God casts the die, not the dice.
—Albert Einstein

Chance is perhaps the pseudonym of God when He did not want to
  sign.   —Anatole France, *The Garden of Epicurus*

The laws of probability, so true in general, so fallacious in particular.
                              —Edward Gibbon, *Autobiography*

Under the bludgeonings of Chance / My head is bloody, but unbowed.
                              —William Ernest Henley, "Invictus"

Chance usually favors the prudent man.   —Joseph Joubert

Only God can make a random selection.   —Marion L. Levy, Sr.

That power which erring men call Chance.   —John Milton, *Comus*

Chance is always powerful—let your hook be always cast; in the pool
  where you least expect it, there will be a fish.   —Ovid

Chance favors the prepared mind.   —Louis Pasteur, speech, 1854

All Nature is but Art, unknown to thee; / All Chance, Direction,
  which thou canst not see.   —Alexander Pope, *An Essay on Man*, I

Chance is a name for our ignorance.
              —Leslie Stephen, *English Thought in the 18th Century*

How often things occur by mere chance which we dared not even
  hope for.   —Terence, *Phormio*, V, I

Chance is a word that does not make sense. Nothing happens without a cause.   —Voltaire

. . . all you can do is play the cards they deal you.
                              —Kurt Vonnegut, Jr., *Hocus Pocus*

CHANGE

Great cultural changes begin in affectation and end in routine.
                              —Jacques Barzun, *The House of Intellect*

Nought endures but change.   —Ludwig Boerne, speech, 2 Dec 1825

All that is, at all, / Lasts ever, past recall; / Earth changes, but thy soul
  and God stand sure.
  —Robert Browning, *Dramatis Personae*, "Rabbi ben Ezra," Stanza 27

Things don't change. You change your way of looking, that's all.
—Carlos Castaneda

All is change; all yields its place and goes. —Euripides, *Heracles*

Christians are supposed not merely to endure change, nor even to
profit by it, but to cause it. —Harry Emerson Fosdick

Most of the change we think we see in life / Is due to truths being in
and out of favor.
—Robert Frost, *North of Boston*, "The Black Cottage"

You must be the change you wish to see in the world.
—Mahatma Gandhi

People change and forget to tell each other.
—Lillian Hellman, *Toys in the Attic*

All things flow, nothing abides. —Heraclitus

Nothing endures but change.
—Heraclitus, in Diogenes Laertius, *Lives of Imminent Philosophers*

You cannot step twice into the same river, for other waters are continually flowing in. —Heraclitus, Fragments

If matters go badly now, they will not always be so. —Horace

When one life is changed, the world is changed. —Thomas L. Johns

We must change to master change.
—Lyndon B. Johnson, State of the Union Message, 12 Jan 1966

The more things change, the more they are the same.
—Alphonse Karr, *Les Guêpes*, Jan 1849

Nothing that is can pause or stay. —Henry Wadsworth Longfellow

Tomorrow the world is not the same as today, though God listens
with the same ear.
—Bernard Malamud, *Rembrandt's Hat*, "The Silver Crown"

We never know beforehand how new posts or new work will change us.
—Alexander Solzhenitsyn, *The Oak and the Calf*

All things human change. —Alfred, Lord Tennyson

Things do not change; we change. —Henry David Thoreau

The only way to make sense out of change is to plunge into it, move with it, and join the dance. —Alan Watts

Too many things are occurring for even a big heart to hold. —William Butler Yeats

But life's changes are nothing to a sage's heart. —Yü Hsüan-chi

CHAOS

. . . chaos doesn't run the whole show. —Saul Bellow, *Henderson the Rain King*

CHARACTER

Personality has the power to open many doors, but character must keep them open. —Anonymous

Happiness is not the end of life: character is. —Henry Ward Beecher, *Life Thoughts*

Character is higher than intellect. / Thinking is the function; living is the functionary. —Ralph Waldo Emerson

Character is that which can do without success. —Ralph Waldo Emerson, *Uncollected Lectures*, "Character"

Our character is but the stamp on our souls of the free choices we have made through life. —J. C. Geikie

Only what we have wrought into our character during life can we take away with us. —Humboldt

The measure of a man's real character is what he would do if he knew he would never be found out. —Thomas Babington Macaulay

Character is what you are in the dark. —Dwight L. Moody, *Sermons*, "Character"

Reputation is what men and women think of us; character is what God and angels know of us. —Thomas Paine

A man never shows his own character so plainly as by the way he portrays another's. —Jean Paul Richter

It is in the trifles, and when he is off his guard, that a man best shows his character. —Arthur Schopenhauer

CHARITY

The poor man's charity is to wish the rich man well.   —Anonymous

In charity there is no excess. —Francis Bacon, *Essays*, 13, "Of Goodness and Goodness of Nature"

In necessary things, unity; in doubtful things, liberty; in all things, charity. —Richard Baxter, motto

Though I speak with the tongues of men and of angels, and have not charity, I am become as sounding brass, or a tinkling cymbal. —*The Bible* (KJV): 1 Corinthians 13:1

Charity suffereth long, and is kind; charity envieth not; charity vaunteth not itself, is not puffed up, doth not behave itself unseemly, seeketh not her own, is not easily provoked, thinketh no evil; rejoiceth not in iniquity, but rejoiceth in the truth; beareth all things, believeth all things, hopeth all things, endureth all things. Charity never faileth . . .   —*The Bible* (KJV): 1 Corinthians 13:4-8

And now abideth faith, hope, charity, these three; but the greatest of these is charity. —*The Bible* (KJV): 1 Corinthians 13:13

And above all things have fervent charity among yourselves: for charity shall cover the multitude of sins.   —*The Bible* (KJV): 1 Peter 4:8

The highest exercise of charity is charity towards the uncharitable. —Buckminster

First daughter to the love of God is charity to man.   —Drennan

The charity that hastens to proclaim its good deeds ceases to be charity, and is only pride and ostentation.   —William Hutton

With malice toward none; with charity toward all. —Abraham Lincoln, 2nd Inaugural Address, 4 Mar 1865

The organized charity, scrimped and iced, / In the name of a cautious, statistical Christ. —John Boyle O'Reilly, "In Bohemia"

Charity gives itself rich; covetousness hoards itself poor. —Proverb (German)

Charity is a naked child, giving honey to a bee without wings.
—Francis Quarles, *Enchiridion*

Charity begins at home. —Terence, *Andria*, line 635

CHARM

Charm is . . . a way of getting the answer yes without having asked
   any clear question. —Albert Camus, *The Fall*

A beauty is a woman you notice; a charmer is one who notices you.
   —Adlai Stevenson, speech, Radcliffe College, 1963

CHASTENING

Thou shalt also consider in thine heart, that, as a man chasteneth his
   son, so the Lord thy God chasteneth thee.
   —*The Bible* (KJV): Deuteronomy 8:5

My son, despise not the chastening of the Lord; neither be weary of
   his correction: for whom the Lord loveth he correcteth; even as a
   father the son in whom he delighteth.
   —*The Bible* (KJV): Proverbs 3:11–12

He that spareth his rod hateth his son: but he that loveth him chasteneth him betimes. —*The Bible* (KJV): Proverbs 13:24

Chasten thy son while there is hope, and let not thy soul spare for his
   crying. —*The Bible* (KJV): Proverbs 19:18

He who truly loves will chastise well. —Proverb (French)

CHEATING

Who purposely cheats his friend, would cheat his God.
   —Johann Kaspar Lavater

CHEERFULNESS

Cheerfulness smooths the road of life. —Anonymous

A merry heart maketh a cheerful countenance.
   —*The Bible* (KJV): Proverbs 15:13

. . . he that is of a merry heart hath a continual feast.
   —*The Bible* (KJV): Proverbs 15:15

A merry heart doeth good like a medicine . . .
—*The Bible* (KJV): Proverbs 17:22

Oh, give us the man who sings at his work.   —Thomas Carlyle

You find yourself refreshed by the presence of cheerful people. Why not make an honest effort to confer that pleasure on others?
—Lydia M. Child

My religion of life is always to be cheerful.   —George Meredith

. . . a light heart lives long.
—William Shakespeare, *Love's Labour's Lost*, Act V, Sc. ii

I can't be happy every day but I can be cheerful.   —Beverly Sills

I'm not happy, I'm cheerful. There's a difference. A happy woman has no cares at all. A cheerful woman has cares but has learned how to deal with them.   —Beverly Sills

All succeeds with people who are sweet and cheerful.
—Voltaire, *Le Depositaire*

'Tis easy enough to be pleasant, / When life flows along like a song; But the man worth while is the one who will smile / When everything goes dead wrong.   —Ella Wheeler Wilcox, "Worth While"

CHEMISTRY

. . . is the carbon molecule lined with thought? —Saul Bellow, *Herzog*

Life exists in the universe only because the carbon atom possesses certain exceptional properties.
—Sir James Jeans, *The Mysterious Universe*, Ch. 1

Immensity is made up of atoms.   —Gottfried Wilhelm Leibniz

CHILDREN

God I bring each wounded child to Thee.
—Sarah Adams, "Prayer for the Wounded Child" (song)

Every new generation is a fresh invasion of savages.   —H. Allen

. . . thou shalt not neglect . . . thy son as long as he cannot take care of himself.   —Anonymous

Blessed be childhood, which brings down something of heaven into the midst of our rough earthliness. —Henri Frédéric Amiel, *The Private Journal of Henri Frédéric Amiel*, 26 Jan 1868

Happy is he that is happy in his children. —Anonymous

The parent's life is the child's copy-book. —Anonymous

Children have never been very good at listening to their elders, but they have never failed to imitate them.
—James Baldwin, *Nobody Knows My Name*, "Fifth Avenue, Uptown"

That energy which makes a child hard to manage is the energy which afterward makes him a manager of life.
—Henry Ward Beecher, in William Drysdale, editor, *Proverbs from Plymouth Pulpit*

. . . Suffer little children, and forbid them not, to come unto me: for of such is the kingdom of heaven.—*The Bible* (KJV): Matthew 19:14

As arrows are in the hand of a mighty man; so are the children of the youth. —*The Bible* (KJV): Psalms 127:4

When I was a child, I spake as a child, I understood as a child, I thought as a child; but when I became a man, I put away childish things. —*The Bible* (KJV): 1 Corinthians 13:11

You can do anything with children if you only play with them.
—Bismarck

It goes without saying that you should never have more children than you have car windows. —Erma Bombeck

If, in instructing a child, you are vexed with it for want of adroitness, try, if you have never tried before, to write with your left hand, and then remember that a child is all left hand. —J. F. Boyse

Yes, you [children] are a marvel. And when you grow up, can you then harm another who is, like you, a marvel? You must work—we must all work—to make this world worthy of its children.
—Pablo Casals

What gift has Providence bestowed on man that is so dear to him as his children? —Cicero

I am convinced that every boy, in his heart, would rather steal second base than an automobile. —Thomas C. Clark

Praise the child, and you make love to the mother. —William Cobbett

Better to be driven out from among men than to be disliked of children.
　　　　　　　　　　　　　　　　　　　　—Richard Henry Dana

It occurred to him that one never ceased to be taken unawares by
　boys.　　　　　　　　—R. F. Delderfield, *To Serve Them All My Days*

I love these little people; and it is not a slight thing when they, who
　are so fresh from God, love us.
　　　　　　　　　　　—Charles Dickens, *The Old Curiosity Shop*

If you want to see what children can do, you must stop giving them
　things.　　　　　　　　　　　　　　　　—Norman Douglas

In the man whose childhood has known caresses and kindness, there
　is always a fiber of memory that can be touched to gentle issues.
　　　　　　　　　　　　　　　　　　　　　—George Eliot

There never was child so lovely but his mother was glad to get him to
　sleep.　　　　　　　　　　—Ralph Waldo Emerson, *Journals*

It is the childlike mind that finds the kingdom.　　—Charles Fillmore

Every child is born a genius.　　　　　　—R. Buckminster Fuller

Children are poor men's riches.　　　　　　　—Thomas Fuller

What children hear at home soon flies abroad.
　　　　　　　　—Thomas Fuller, M. D., *Gnomologia*, No. 5482

If children grew up according to early indications, we should have
　nothing but geniuses.　　　　—Johann Wolfgang von Goethe

Nothing is more dependable than a child's digestive juices.
　—Renee Hawkley, *Welcome Home*, Nov 1987, "Feeding the Family"

Do not handicap your children by making their lives easy.
　　　　　　　　　　　　　　　　　　　—Robert Heinlein

Pretty much all the honest truth telling there is in the world is done
　by children.　　　　　　　　—Oliver Wendell Holmes, Sr.

A boy has two jobs. One is just being a boy. The other is growing up
　to be a man.　　　　　　—Herbert Hoover, speech, 21 May 1956
　　　　　　　　　　　　　(50th anniversary of the Boys' Club)

Children are our most valuable natural resource.　—Herbert Hoover

Boys will be boys.   —Anthony Hope, *The Dolly Dialogues*, 16

Children need love, especially when they do not deserve it.
                                    —Harold S. Hulbert

Your children need your presence more than your presents.
                                    —Rev. Jesse Jackson

Children need models rather than critics.   —Joseph Joubert, *Pensées*

Children are the true connoisseurs. What's precious to them has no
    price—only value.   —Bel Kaufman, television interview, 1967

Each child comes to us with a message from God and it is our job to
    help them deliver that message.   —Jim Kern

Children enjoy the present because they have neither a past nor a
    future.   —Jean de La Bruyère

A child is fed with milk and praise.   —Mary Anne Lamb

. . . in all our efforts to provide "advantages" we have actually pro-
    duced the busiest, most competitive, highly pressured and over-
    organized generation of youngsters in our history—and possibly
    the unhappiest. We seem hell-bent on eliminating much of child-
    hood.   —Eda J. Le Shan, *The Conspiracy Against Childhood*, Ch. 1

We have kept our children so busy with "useful" and "improving"
    activities that we are in danger of raising a generation of young
    people who are terrified of silence, of being alone with their own
    thoughts . . .
              —Eda J. Le Shan, *The Conspiracy Against Childhood*, Ch. 11

He [God] can be revealed only to the child; perfectly, to the pure
    child only. All the discipline of the world is to make men children,
    that God may be revealed to them.
                            —George Macdonald, *Life Essential*

The best teacher of children . . . is one who is essentially childlike.
            —H. L. Mencken, from *New York Evening Mail*, 23 Jan 1918

The childhood shows the man, / As morning shows the day.
                —John Milton, *Paradise Regained*, Book IV, 220

Within the child lies the fate of the future.   —Maria Montessori

We've had bad luck with our kids—they've all grown up.
—Christopher Morley

If a child lives with approval, he learns to live with himself.
—Dorothy Law Nolte

Nature makes boys and girls lovely to look upon so they can be tolerated until they acquire some sense.
—William Lyon Phelps, *Essays on Things*

What is so real as the cry of a child?   —Sylvia Plath, *Ariel*, "Kindness"

Of all the animals, the boy is the most unmanageable.
—Plato, *Theaetetus*

You know children are growing up when they start asking questions that have answers.
—John J. Plomp

Many kiss the child for the nurse's sake.   —Proverb (13th century)

A growing youth has a wolf in his belly.   —Proverb (17th century)

Who takes the child by the hand, takes the mother by the heart.
—Proverb (Danish)

What is learned in the cradle lasts till the grave.   —Proverb (French)

It is not easy to straighten in the oak the crook that grew in the sapling.
—Proverb (Gaelic)

Treat your neighbors' children as your own.   —Proverb (Spanish)

Children act in the village as they have learned at home.
—Proverb (Swedish)

Small children don't let you sleep; big children don't let you rest.
—Proverb (Yiddish)

Children pick up words as pigeons peas / And utter them again as God shall please.   —John Ray, *English Proverbs* (1670)

It's never too late to have a happy childhood.   —Tom Robbins

Give a little love to a child, and you get a great deal back.
—John Ruskin

Our children are the gift we give the world we'll never see.   —Lee Salk

While we try to teach our children all about life, our children teach
us what life is all about. —Angela Schwindt

There's a time when you have to explain to your children why they're
born, and it's a marvelous thing if you know the reason by then.
—Hazel Scott, in *Ms.*, "Great (Hazel) Scott," Nov 1974

Children are the anchors that hold a mother to life.
—Sophocles, *Phaedra*

Call not that man wretched, who, whatever ills he suffers, has a child
to love. —Robert Southey

Every child comes with the message that God is not yet discouraged
of man. —Rabindranath Tagore, *Stray Birds*

The most influential of all educational factors is the conversation in a
child's home. —William Temple

A son is like a lopped off branch. As a falcon he comes when he wills
and goes where he lists. —Ivan Turgenev, *Fathers and Sons*

But children, you should never let / Such angry passions rise; / Your
little hands were never made / To tear each other's eyes.
—Isaac Watts, *Divine Songs for Children*, "Against Quarreling"

Every child born into the world is a new thought of God, an ever-
fresh and radiant possibility. —Kate Douglas Wiggin

The Child is father of the Man.
—William Wordsworth, "My Heart Leaps Up When I Behold"

There are no illegitimate children—only illegitimate parents.
—Judge Leon R. Yankwich, Zipkin vs. Mozon, Jun 1928

The lost child cries, but still he catches fireflies. —Ryushui Yoshida

CHOICE

You're always free to change your mind and choose a different future.
—Richard Bach

. . . choose you this day whom ye will serve . . . but as for me and my
house, we will serve the Lord. —*The Bible* (KJV), Joshua 24:15

The strongest principle of growth lies in human choice.
　　　　　　　　　　　　　　　　　　　—George Eliot

When you have to make a choice and don't make it, that is in itself a
　choice.　　　　　　　　　　　—William James, *Memories and Studies*

It becomes essential to choose one's path. Life consists in making
　these choices. One develops by choosing. It requires strength to
　become a child of God . . .
　　　　　　　　　　　—Toyohiko Kagawa, *Meditations on the Cross*

I discovered I always have choices, and sometimes it's only a choice
　of attitude.　　　　　　　　　　　　　　　—Judith Knowlton

And the choice goes by forever 'twixt that darkness and that light.
　　　　　　　　　—James Russell Lowell, "The Present Crisis"

Once to every man and nation comes the moment to decide, / In the
　strife of Truth with Falsehood, for the good or evil side.
　　　　　　　　　—James Russell Lowell, "The Present Crisis"

I [God] will leave man to make the fateful guess, / Will leave him torn
　between the no and yes, / Leave him unresting till he rests in me,
　/ Drawn upward by the choice that makes him free, / Leave him in
　tragic loneliness to choose, / With all in life to win or all to lose.
　　　　　　　　　　　　　　　　　　　—Edwin Markham

Sometimes it is a good choice not to choose at all.
　　　　　　　　　　　—Michel de Montaigne, *Essays*, III, ix

The difficulty in life is the choice.
　　　　　　　　—George Moore, *The Bending of the Bough*, 4

The power of choosing good and evil is within the reach of all.
　　　　　　　　　　　—Origen, *De Principiis*, Proem 5

. . . there's small choice in rotten apples.
　　　　　—William Shakespeare, *The Taming of the Shrew*, Act I, Sc. i

All is foreseen but the choice is given.
　　　　　　　　　　—Isaac Bashevis Singer, *The Slave*

We are the choices we have made.
　　　　　　　—Meryl Streep, in a Katie Couric television interview,
　　　　　　　　　　　　The Today Show, NBC, 2 June 1995

CHRISTIANITY

The ten commandments and the sermon on the mount contain my
    religion.   —John Adams, to Thomas Jefferson, 4 Nov 1816

The Christian is not one who had gone all the way with Christ. None
    of us has. The Christian is one who has found the right road.
        —Charles L. Allen, *When the Heart is Hungry*

A young RAF pilot said to a Christian, "Don't try to help me or tell
    me what I ought to think yet. Don't work for my salvation—show
    me yours, show me it is possible, and the knowledge that some-
    thing works will give me courage and belief."   —Florence Allshorn

If you are a Christian, remember that men judge your Lord by you.
        —Anonymous

The Christian life doesn't get easier; it gets better.   —Anonymous

The distinction between Christianity and all other systems of religion
    consists largely in this, that in these other men are found seeking
    after God, while Christianity is God seeking after man.
        —Thomas Arnold

Too many clergymen have become keepers of an aquarium instead of
    fishers of men—and often they are just swiping each other's fish.
        —M. S. Augsburger

There was never law, or sect, or opinion, did so magnify goodness as
    the Christian religion doth.   —Francis Bacon

Christianity is completed Judaism, or it is nothing.   —Beaconsfield

If a man cannot be a Christian in the place where he is, he cannot be
    a Christian anywhere.   —Henry Ward Beecher, *Life Thoughts*

To be a Christian is to obey Christ no matter how you feel.
        —Henry Ward Beecher

Christians and camels receive their burdens kneeling.
        —Ambrose Bierce

The glory of Christianity is to conquer by forgiveness.
        —William Blake, *Jerusalem*, "To the Deists"

A Christian is one who rejoices in the superiority of a rival.
—Edwin Booth

Dear friends, the life is more than meat, / The soul excels the clay; / O labor then for gospel food, / Which never shall decay.
—Martha Brewster, "A Farewell to Some of My Christian Friends at Goshen, Lebanon"

You ask what you can do? You can furnish one Christian life.
—Phillips Brooks

How very hard it is to be a Christian!—Robert Browning, "Easter Day"

Christians have burnt each other, quite persuaded / That all the Apostles would have done as they did.
—Lord Byron, *Don Juan*, Canto I, 83

These Christians love each other even before they are acquainted.
—Saint Celsus

Carlyle said that men were mostly fools. Christianity, with a surer and more reverend realism, says that they are all fools.
—G. K. Chesterton, *Heretics*, Ch. 12

The Christian ideal has not been tried and found wanting. It has been found difficult and left untried.
—G. K. Chesterton, *What's Wrong with the World*, Part 1, Ch. 5

What Christianity in her antagonism with every form of unbelief most needs is holy living.
—Christlieb

To feel sorry for the needy is not the mark of a Christian—to help them is.
—Frank A. Clark

He who begins by loving Christianity better than Truth, will proceed by loving his sect or church better than Christianity, and end in loving himself better than all.
—Samuel Taylor Coleridge

A Christian should always remember that the value of his good works is not based on their number and excellence, but on the love of God which prompts him to do these things.
—Juan De La Cruz

The Christian life is not hearing nor knowing, but doing.
—Rev. S. L. Dickey

The greatest proof of Christianity for others is not how far a man can logically analyze his reasons for believing, but how far in practice he will stake his life on his belief. —T. S. Eliot

If you were arrested for being a Christian, would there be enough evidence to convict you? —David Otis Fuller

A Christian is the keyhole through which other folk see God.
—Robert E. Gibson

A Christian is not one who withdraws but one who infiltrates.
—Bill Glass

Being a Christian is more than just an instantaneous conversion—it is a daily process whereby you grow to be more and more like Christ. —Billy Graham

Something larger is happening than just going to heaven.
—Steve Hawthorne, guest sermon,
Hope Chapel, Austin, Texas, 21 Sep 1991

. . . Christianity is a system of radical optimism.
—William R. Inge, obituary editorial,
Manchester Guardian, 27 Feb 1954

Christians are made, not born. —Saint Jerome

He said not, "thou shalt not be troubled, thou shalt not be travailed, thou shalt not be diseased;" but He said, "Thou shalt not be overcome." —Juliana of Norwich

Preparation for becoming attentive to Christianity does not consist in reading many books . . . but in fuller immersion in existence.
—Sören Kierkegaard

We as Christians have a mandate to be nonconformists.
—Martin Luther King, Jr., *The Strength to Love*

Christianity taught men that love is worth more than intelligence.
—Jacques Maritain, *I Believe*

Christianity is one beggar telling another beggar where he found bread. —D. T. Niles

Each and every one of us has one obligation, during the bewildered
days of our pilgrimage here: the saving of his own soul, and secon-
darily and incidentally thereby affecting for good such other souls
as come under our influence. —Kathleen Norris

The Christian religion teaches me two points—that there is a God
whom men can know, and that their nature is so corrupt that they
are unworthy of Him. —Blaise Pascal, *Pensées*

Christianity is a battle, not a dream. —Wendell Phillips

Most Christians do not have fellowship with God; they have fellowship with each other about God. —Paris Reidhead

The goal of the Christian is to grow up into Christ.
—Pat Robertson, *Answers to 200 of Life's Most Probing Questions*

Christianity might be a good thing if anyone ever tried it.
—George Bernard Shaw

A good Christian is a velvet-covered brick. —Fred Smith

Christianity is a religion of the open tomb.
—Roy L. Smith, *The Methodist Story*

When Christ came into my life, I came about like a well-handled ship.
—Robert Louis Stevenson

The life of a Christian is an education for higher service.
—Corrie ten Boom, *Tramp for the Lord*,
with Jamie Buckingham, Introduction

A man becomes a Christian; he is not born one.
—Tertullian, *The Testimony of the Christian Soul*

Christianity is not a religion, it is a relationship. —Dr. Thieme

Christianity, with its doctrine of humility, of forgiveness, of love, is
incompatible with the state, with its haughtiness, its violence, its
punishment, its wars.
—Leo Tolstoy, *The Kingdom of God Is Within You*

The primary declaration of Christianity is not "This do!" but "This
happened!" —Evelyn Underhill

Whatever makes men good Christians makes them good citizens.
—Daniel Webster

Much in sorrow, oft in woe, Onward, Christians, onward go.
—Henry Kirke White, hymn

Christianity can be condensed into four words: Admit, Submit, Commit and Transmit.
—Samuel Wilberforce

What Christ is saying always . . . is this: "I am my Father's son, and you are my brothers." And the unity that binds us all together, that makes this earth a family, and all men brothers and so the sons of God, is love. —Thomas Wolfe, "The Anatomy of Loneliness"

CHRISTMAS

Christmas began in the heart of God. It is complete only when it reaches the heart of man.
—Anonymous

Christmas is coming, the geese are getting fat, / Please put a penny in the old man's hat; / If you haven't got a penny, a ha' penny will do, / If you haven't got a ha' penny, God bless you!
—Anonymous, "Beggar's Rhyme"

It is good to be children sometimes, and never better than at Christmas, when its mighty Founder was a child Himself. —Charles Dickens

I heard the bells on Christmas Day / Their old, familiar carols play, / And wild and sweet / The words repeat, / Of peace on earth, / Good-will to men! —Henry Wadsworth Longfellow, "Christmas Bells"

And when we give each other Christmas gifts in His name, let us remember that He has given us the sun and the moon and the stars, and the earth with its forests and mountains and oceans— and all that lives and moves upon them. He has given us all green things and everything that blossoms and bears fruit—and all that we quarrel about and all that we have misused—and to save us from all our sins, he came down to earth and gave us himself.
—Sigrid Undset

CHURCH

A church is a hospital for sinners, not a club for saints. —Anonymous

Some families think church is like a convention where you send a delegate—and it's usually Mother.
—Anonymous

This was posted on a Bronx, New York, church bulletin board: "Do come in—Trespassers will be forgiven." —Anonymous

I have no objection to churches so long as they do not interfere with God's work. —Brooks Atkinson, *Once Around the Sun*

. . . upon this rock I will build my church, and the gates of hades shall not prevail against it. —*The Bible* (KJV): Matthew 16:18

The Church is a house with a hundred gates, and no two men enter at exactly the same angle. —G. K. Chesterton

We don't achieve a church for God; rather we receive a church from God. —Kenny Crosswhite

I like the silent church before the service begins, better than any preaching.
—Ralph Waldo Emerson, *Essays, First Series*, "Self-Reliance"

The church is the only institution in the world that has lower entrance requirements than those for getting on a bus.
—Wilbur Laroe

The Christian church is the only society in the world in which membership is based upon the qualification that the candidate shall be unworthy of membership. —Charles Clayton Morrison

Having church can be a substitute for being the church.
—Charles Patterson, guest sermon,
Hope Chapel, Austin, Texas, 28 Oct 1990

The only trouble was, Church . . . didn't take up the whole of your life. No matter how much you knelt and prayed, you still had to eat three meals a day and have a job and live in the world.
—Sylvia Plath, *The Bell Jar*

A beautiful church is a sermon in stone . . . —Schaft

The Christian church is not a congregation of righteous people. It is a society of those who know they are not good.
—Dwight E. Stevenson

It does not take a perfect church to introduce a man to the perfect Christ. —Richard Woodsome

CIRCUMSTANCES

A man cannot directly choose his circumstances, but he can choose his thoughts, and so indirectly, yet surely, shape his circumstances.
—James Allen, *As a Man Thinketh*

Nothing splendid has ever been achieved except by those who dared believe that something inside of them was superior to circumstances.
—Anonymous

It's not the situation . . . It's your reaction to the situation.
—Bob Comblin

Circumstances are beyond the control of man, but his conduct is in his own power.
—Benjamin Disraeli

. . . Every circumstance in life, no matter how crooked and distorted and ugly it appears to be, if it is reacted to in love and forgiveness and obedience to your will can be transformed.
—Hannah Hurnard, *Hinds' Feet on High Places*

A great point is gained when we have learned not to struggle against the circumstances God has appointed for us.
—H. L. Sidney Lear

I am I plus my circumstances.
—Jose Ortega y Gasset

What we are, and where we are, is God's providential arrangement . . . and the manly and wise way is to look your disadvantages in the face, and see what can be made of them.
—Frederick W. Robertson

People are always blaming their circumstances for what they are. I don't believe in circumstances. The people who get on in this world are the people who get up and look for the circumstances they want, and, if they can't find them, make them.
—George Bernard Shaw, *Mrs. Warren's Profession*, Act II

There are no conditions to which a man cannot get accustomed, especially if he sees that everyone around him lives in the same way.
—Leo Tolstoy, *Anna Karenina*

There's a way out of every situation.
—Leo Tolstoy, *Anna Karenina*

CITIES

I like the rough impersonality of New York . . . Human relations are oiled by jokes, complaints, and confessions—all made with the assumption of never seeing the other person again.
—Bill Bradley

God the first garden made, and the first city Cain.
> —Abraham Cowley, "The Garden"

God made the country, and man made the town.
> —William Cowper, *The Task*, "The Sofa"

In small settlements everyone knows your affairs. In the city everyone does not—only those you choose to tell will know about
you. This is one of the attributes of cities that is precious to most
city people.
> —Jane Jacobs, *The Death and Life of Great American Cities*

The planner's problem is to find ways of creating, within the urban
environment, the sense of belonging.
> —Leo Marx

All cities are mad: but the madness is gallant. All cities are beautiful:
but the beauty is grim. —Christopher Morley, *Where the Blue Begins*

The slum is the measure of civilization.
> —Jacob Riis

CITIZENSHIP

I am a citizen of the world.
> —Diogenes the Cynic, in Diogenes Laertius,
> *Lives and Opinions of Eminent Philosophers*

My country is the world; my countrymen are mankind.
> —William Lloyd Garrison, Prospectus for *The Liberator*

I am a citizen, not of Athens or Greece, but of the world.
> —Socrates, in Plutarch, *De Exilio*

CIVIL DISOBEDIENCE

. . . true civil disobedience . . . compels the state to resort to power.
> —Archibald Cox, *Civil Rights, the Constitution and the Courts*

The only safe and honorable course for a self-respecting man is to do
what I have decided to do, that is, to submit without protest to the
penalty of disobedience . . . not for want of respect for lawful
authority, but in obedience to the higher law of our being, the
voice of conscience. —Mahatma Gandhi

If however the law is so promulgated that it of necessity makes you
an agent of injustices against another, then I say to you . . . break
the law. —Henry David Thoreau

An individual who breaks a law that conscience tells him is unjust, and who willingly accepts the penalty of imprisonment in order to arouse the conscience of the community over its injustice, is in reality expressing the highest respect for the law.
—Martin Luther King, Jr., letter from Birmingham Jail, 1963

CIVILITY

Be civil to all; sociable to many; familiar with few; friend to one; enemy to none.—Benjamin Franklin, *Poor Richard's Almanack*, 1756

Fair words cost nothing.   —John Gay

He was so generally civil that nobody thanked him for it.
—Samuel Johnson

Civility costs nothing and buys everything.
—Lady Mary Wortley Montagu, letter, 1756

CIVILIZATION

The test of civilization is the estimate of woman.
—George William Curtis

Not until the creation and maintenance of decent conditions of life for all men are recognized and accepted as a common obligation of all men . . . shall we be able to speak of mankind as civilized.
—Albert Einstein

The civilized man has built a coach, but has lost the use of his feet.
—Ralph Waldo Emerson, *Essays, First Series*, "Self-Reliance"

The true test of civilization is, not the census, nor the size of cities, nor the crops,—no, but the kind of man the country turns out.
—Ralph Waldo Emerson, *Society and Solitude*, "Civilization"

What is civilization? I answer, the power of good women.
—Ralph Waldo Emerson, *Miscellanies*, "Woman"

A decent provision for the poor is the true test of civilization.
—Samuel Johnson, in James Boswell, *Life of Samuel Johnson*

Civilization is just a slow process of learning to be kind.
—Charles L. Lucas

Civilization is nothing else but the attempt to reduce force to being the last resort. —Jose Ortega y Gasset

If there hadn't been women we'd still be squatting in a cave eating raw meat because we made civilization in order to impress our girl-friends. —Orson Welles

Civilization is a race between education and catastrophe.
—H. G. Wells

I do not think that any civilization can be called complete until it has progressed from sophistication to unsophistication, and made a conscious return to simplicity of thinking and living.
—Lin Yutang, *The Importance of Living*

CIVIL RIGHTS

We Shall Overcome.
—Zilphia Horton, Pete Seeger, Frank Hamilton, and Guy Carawan, title and refrain of a civil rights anthem popular in the 1960's

I swear to the Lord I still can't see / Why democracy means / Everybody but me.
—Langston Hughes, *Jim Crow's Last Stand*, "The Black Man Speaks"

I have a dream . . . It is a dream deeply rooted in the American dream . . . I have a dream that one day in the red hills of Georgia, sons of former slaves and sons of former slave-owners will be able to sit down together at the table of brotherhood.
—Martin Luther King, Jr., address delivered at the foot of the Lincoln Memorial, Washington, D.C., 28 Aug 1963

CLARITY

When things are too clear, they are no longer interesting.
—Alexander Solzhenitsyn, *August 1914*

Clearness is the ornament of profound thought.
—Luc de Clapiers Vauvenargues

Everything that can be thought at all can be thought clearly. Everything that can be said can be said clearly. —Ludwig Wittgenstein

CLASSIFICATIONS

Classes? Categories? Was that what we had come to?
—Walker Percy, *Lancelot*

All classifications in this world lack sharp boundaries, and all transitions are gradual.
—Alexander Solzhenitsyn, *The Gulag Archipelago Two*

CLEANLINESS

Cleanliness is indeed next to godliness. —John Wesley, sermon

CLEVERNESS

Cleverness is not wisdom. —Euripides

When cleverness emerges
There is great hypocrisy. —Lao Tzu, *Tao Te Ching*, Ch. XVIII

Here's a good rule of thumb: / Too clever is dumb.
—Ogden Nash, *Verses From 1929 On*, "Reflection on Ingenuity"

CLOCKS

Seek not to reform every one's dial by your own watch. —Anonymous

Clock, n. A machine of great moral value to man, allaying his concern for the future by reminding him what a lot of time remains to him. —Ambrose Bierce, *The Devil's Dictionary*

CLOTHING

A fine woman can do without fine clothes. —Anonymous

A sweater is a garment worn by a child when his mother feels chilly.
—Anonymous

Cut your coat according to your cloth. —Anonymous

I spent a weekend at the beach and couldn't decide whether bikinis are getting smaller of girls are getting bigger. —Anonymous

What if my shirt is shabby and worn, it covers a warm heart.
—Anonymous

You cannot strip a garment off a naked man. —Anonymous

It's OK to wear the same thing every day.
—Suzy Becker, *All I Need to Know I Learned From My Cat*

It is not every man that can afford to wear a shabby coat.
—Charles Caleb Colton

Probably every new and eagerly expected garment ever put on since clothes came in, fell a trifle short of the wearer's expectation.
—Charles Dickens, *Great Expectations*, 19

To most people a savage nation is wan that doesn't wear oncomf'rtable clothes.
—Finley Peter Dunne, *Mr. Dooley's Philosophy*, "Casual Observations"

If a woman's young and pretty, I think you can see her good looks all the better for her being plainly dressed.
—George Eliot

I want to know why, if men rule the world, they don't stop wearing neckties.
—Linda Ellerbee, *Move On*

When a woman wears a low-cut gown, what does she expect you to do: look or not look?
—William Feather, *The Business of Life*

What a man most enjoys about a woman's clothes are his fantasies of how she would look without them.
—Brendan Francis

Good clothes open all doors.
—Thomas Fuller, M. D., *Gnomologia*, No. 1705

'Tis not the habit that makes the monk.
—Thomas Fuller

A sweet disorder in the dress / Kindles in clothes a wantonness.
—Robert Herrick, *Hesperides*, "Delight in Disorder"

[Clothes] cannot change a man's nature. He's either kind or he isn't, with or without clothes.
—Bernard Malamud, *The Fixer*

Silk was invented so that woman could go naked in clothes.
—Proverb (Arab)

Anything will fit a naked man.
—Proverb (Irish)

God will listen to you whatever cloak you wear.
—Proverb (Spanish)

. . . clothes sometimes gave one more of a lift than any philosophic comforting.
—Erich Maria Remarque, *Heaven Has No Favorites*

I never expected to see the day when the girls would get sunburned in the places they do now.
—Will Rogers

American closets are filled with once-worn clothes that got a bad
  review from a friend on their first appearance.
  —Andrew A. Rooney, *Word for Word*, "Decisions, Decisions"

If you put on an item of clothing that hurts just because you have an
  idea it looks better or conforms to what other people are wearing,
  it's dumb.   —Andrew A. Rooney, *Word for Word*, "Dress Sneakers"

Costly thy habit as thy purse can buy, / But not express'd in fancy;
  rich, not gaudy; / For the apparel oft proclaims the man . . .
  —William Shakespeare, *Hamlet*, Act I, Sc. iii

Beware of all enterprises that require new clothes.
  —Henry David Thoreau, *Walden*

Clothes make the man. Naked people have little or no influence on
  society.   —Mark Twain

Modesty died when clothes were born.   —Mark Twain

. . . neckties strangle clear thinking.   —Lin Yutang

COACHING

A successful coach is one who is still coaching.
  —Ben Schwartzwalder, speech to a gathering of coaches
  in San Francisco, 19 Dec 1963

COINCIDENCE

Coincidence is when God works a miracle and chooses to remain
  anonymous.   —Anonymous

The COLD WAR

Let us not be deceived—we are today in the midst of a cold war.
  —Bernard Baruch,
  speech to South Carolina Legislature, 16 Apr 1947

An iron curtain has descended across the Continent.
  —Winston Churchill, address at Westminster College, 5 Mar 1946

COLLECTING

One cannot collect all the beautiful shells on the beach.
  —Anne Morrow Lindbergh, *A Gift from the Sea*

COLOR

Colors speak all languages. —Joseph Addison, *The Spectator*

All colors will agree in the dark.
—Francis Bacon, *Essays*, "Of Unity in Religion"

All colors are the friends of their neighbors and the lovers of their opposites. —Chazal

People can have the Model T in any color—so long as it's black.
—Henry Ford, in Allan Nevins, *Ford*, Vol. 2, Ch. 15

Color was not given to us in order that we imitate Nature. It was given to us so that we can express our emotions. —Henri Matisse

A good horse cannot be of a bad color. —Proverb (17th century)

I use color in a completely arbitrary way in order to express myself powerfully. —Vincent van Gogh

There are colors which cause each other to shine brilliantly, which form a couple, which complete each other like man and woman.
—Vincent van Gogh, letter to his sister Wilhelmina

It doesn't matter if the cat is black or white, so long as it catches mice. —Deng Xiaoping, 6 Jun 1986

COMFORT

[God] comforteth us in all our tribulation, that we may be able to comfort them which are in any trouble, by the comfort wherewith we ourselves are comforted of God.
—*The Bible* (KJV): 2 Corinthians 1:4

Them as ha' never had a cushion don't miss it.
—George Eliot, *Adam Bede*, Ch. 49

God does not comfort us to make us comfortable, but to make us comforters. —John Henry Jowett

To ease another's heartache is to forget one's own.—Abraham Lincoln

COMMERCE

Commerce is the great civilizer. We exchange ideas when we exchange fabrics. —Robert G. Ingersoll

Treat the little customer as if he was a big customer, and he will stay
with you when he grows up.   —Roy L. Smith

COMMITMENT

With regard to ham and eggs: The chicken is involved; the pig, committed.   —Anonymous

COMMON SENSE

Common sense is the collection of prejudices acquired by age 18.
                                                        —Albert Einstein

Common sense is genius in homespun.   —Alfred North Whitehead

COMMUNICATION

Think like a wise man, but communicate in the language of the people.
                                                            —Aristotle

Ninety percent of the friction of daily life is caused by tone of voice.
                                                        —Arnold Bennett

Communication of all kinds is like painting—a compromise with
impossibilities.   —Samuel Butler (1835-1902)

Put the hay down where the sheep can reach it.   —Clovis Chappell

An orator or an author is never successful till he has learned to make
his words smaller than his ideas.   —Ralph Waldo Emerson

What an argument in favor of social connections is the observation
that by communicating our grief we have less, and by communicating our pleasure we have more.   —Greville

Unless one is a genius, it is best to aim at being intelligible.
                                —Anthony Hope, *The Dolly Dialogues*

Word gets around when the circus comes to town, don't it?
                        —Cormac McCarthy, *All the Pretty Horses*, Ch. 2

We seek pitifully to convey to others the treasures of our heart, but
they have not the power to accept them, and so we go lonely, side
by side but not together, unable to know our fellows and unknown
by them.   —W. Somerset Maugham, *The Moon and Sixpence*, 41

"The medium is the message" because it is the medium that shapes and controls the search and form of human associations and action.
—Marshal McLuhan

Never throw mud. You may miss your mark; but you must have dirty hands.
—Joseph Parker

Examine what is said, not him who speaks.
—Proverb (Arab)

No answer is also an answer.
—Proverb (Danish)

Not all words require an answer.
—Proverb (Italian)

If it takes a lot of words to say what you have in mind, give it more thought.
—Dennis Roch

. . . it is a major responsibility . . . of all communication for each of us to help everyone else discover the best that is in him.
—Alexander Solzhenitsyn, *The First Circle*

Look around you—there are people around you. Maybe you will remember one of them all your life and later eat your heart out because you didn't make use of the opportunity to ask him questions. And the less you talk, the more you'll hear.
—Alexander Solzhenitsyn, *The Gulag Archipelago*

This is a grave danger: the stoppage of information between the parts of the planet. Contemporary science knows that such stoppage is the way of entropy, of universal destruction.
—Alexander Solzhenitsyn, *Nobel Lecture*

Learn to say "No"; it will be of more use to you than to be able to read Latin.
—Charles H. Spurgeon

C O M M U N I O N

He was the Word, that spake it: / He took the bread and brake it; / And what that Word did make it, / I do believe and take it.
—John Donne, *Divine Poems*, "On the Sacrament"

C O M M U N I S M

Communism is like one big phone company.
—Lenny Bruce

What is a communist? One who hath yearnings / For equal division of unequal earnings.
—Ebenezer Elliot, *Poetical Works*, "Epigram"

The Communist is a Socialist in a violent hurry.
> —G. W. Gough, "The Economic Consequence of Socialism"

COMMUNITY

Rain does not fall on one roof alone. —Proverb (Cameroon)

COMPANY

For a single woman, preparing for company means wiping the lipstick off the milk carton. —Elayne Boosler

The more the merrier. —John Heywood

The company makes the feast. —Proverb (17th century)

A guy goes nuts if he ain't got nobody.
> —John Steinbeck, *Of Mice and Men*

But a man needs company.
> —John Steinbeck, *The Long Valley*, "The Red Pony"

COMPARISON

It is comparison that makes men miserable. —Anonymous

There is no such thing as "best" in the world of individuals.
> —Hosea Ballou

Enjoy your life without comparing it with that of others.
> —Marquis de Condorcet

When you see a worthy person, endeavor to emulate him. When you see an unworthy person, then examine your inner self.—Confucius

Comparisons are odious. —Sir John Fortescue, (1385–1479)
> *De laudibus legum Angliae*, "In Praise of the Laws of England"

You're a better man than I am, Gunga Din.
> —Rudyard Kipling, *Gunga Din*

Better is an enemy to well. —Proverb (Italian)

The best is enemy of the good.
> —Voltaire, *Dictionaire philosophique*, "Art dramatique"

Brothers naturally invite comparison . . .
—Larry Watson, *Montana 1948*

COMPASSION

One man starving puts a crimp in my evening.
—Woody Allen, line from the movie *Annie Hall*

Compassion will cure more sins than condemnation.
—Henry Ward Beecher, in William Drysdale, editor,
Proverbs from Plymouth Pulpit

Can a sparrow know how a stork feels?
—Johann Wolfgang von Goethe

COMPETITION

The only competition worthy of a wise man is with himself.
—Washington Allston

If you can't win, make the fellow ahead of you break the record.
—Anonymous

Our business in life is not to get ahead of other people, but to get
ahead of ourselves.   —Maltbie Davenport Babcock

Competitions are for horses, not artists.   —Béla Bartók

Desire for approval and recognition is a healthy motive; but the
desire to be acknowledged as better, stronger, or more intelligent
than a fellow being or fellow scholar easily leads to an excessively
egoistic psychological adjustment, which may become injurious
for the individual and for the community. Therefore, the school
and the teacher must guard against employing the easy method of
creating individual ambition, in order to induce the pupils to diligent work . . . The most important motive for work in the school
and in life is the pleasure in work, pleasure in its result, and the
knowledge of the value of the result to the community. In the
awakening and strengthening of these psychological forces in the
young man, I see the most important task given by the school.
—Albert Einstein, *Ideas and Opinions*

I'm for each and against none.   —Dwight D. Eisenhower

Never compete.   —Baltasar Gracián

The way of the sage is to act but not compete. —Lao Tzu

The wise man doesn't compete; therefore nobody can compete with
   him. —Lao Tzu

COMPLAINT

Those who do not complain are never pitied. —Jane Austen

I hate to be a kicker, I always long for peace, / But the wheel that does
   the squeaking, is the one that gets the grease. —Josh Billings

Complain to one who can help you. —Proverb (Yugoslav)

He who complains, sins. —Saint Francis de Sales

COMPLIMENTS

A compliment is a gift, not to be thrown away carelessly unless you
   want to hurt the giver. —Eleanor Hamilton

Anyone who likes to compliment finds ready listeners. —Alan Harris

Compliments cost nothing, yet many pay dear for them.
   —Proverb (German)

I can live for two months on a good compliment. —Mark Twain

COMPROMISE

Truth is the glue that holds governments together. Compromise is
   the oil that makes governments go. —Gerald Ford

COMPUTERS

. . . the familiar phenomenon of GIGO (Garbage In—Garbage Out).
   —Anonymous

If you put tomfoolery into a computer, nothing comes out but tomfoolery. But this tomfoolery, having passed through a very expensive
   machine, is somehow ennobled, and no one dares to criticize it.
   —Pierre Gallois

Software suppliers are trying to make their software more "user
   friendly" . . . Their best approach, so far, has been to take all the
   old brochures, and stamp the words "user friendly" on the cover.
   —Bill Gates

The real danger is not that computers will begin to think like men, but that men will begin to think like computers. —Sydney J. Harris

One of the best things to come out of the home computer revolution could be the general and widespread understanding of how severely limited logic really is. —Frank Herbert

From then on, when anything went wrong with a computer, we said it had bugs in it. —Grace Murray Hopper, in *Time*, 16 Apr 1984, on the removal of a 2-inch long moth from an experimental computer at Harvard in 1945

Man is still the most extraordinary computer of all.—John F. Kennedy

Computers can figure out all kinds of problems, except the things in the world that just don't add up. —James Magary

Computers are useless. They can only give you answers. —Pablo Picasso

Any sufficiently crisp question can be answered by a single binary digit—0 or 1, yes or no. —Carl Sagan, *The Dragons of Eden*

The real question is not whether machines think but whether men do. —B. F. Skinner, *Contingencies of Reinforcement*

. . . hummings and clickings could be heard—the sounds attendant to the flow of electrons, now augmenting one maze of electromagnetic crises to a condition that was translatable from electrical qualities and quantities to a high grade of truth. —Kurt Vonnegut, Jr., *Player Piano*

A computer will do what you tell it to do, but that may be much different from what you had in mind. —Joseph Weizenbaum

CONDEMNATION

They condemn what they do not understand. —Edgar Quinet

CONFESSION

A man who has broken with his past feels a different man. He will not feel it a shame to confess his past wrongs, for the simple reason that these wrongs do not touch him at all. —Mahatma Gandhi

He's half absolv'd
  Who has confess'd. —Matthew Prior, *Alma*, Canto II, line 22

Confession is good for the soul.   —Proverb (Scottish)

It is the confession, not the priest, that gives absolution.—Oscar Wilde

CONFIDENCE

Confidence is a plant of slow growth.   —Proverb (English)

CONFIDING

Open not thine heart to every man.
                          —Apocrypha, "Ecclesiasticus," 8, 19

But there are things you can't consult anybody about.
                          —Saul Bellow, *More Die of Heartbreak*

You confided in people, you had to.
                          —Saul Bellow, *The Dean's December*

A fool uttereth all his mind . . .   —*The Bible* (KJV): Proverbs 29:11

. . . people get confidential at midnight.
                          —Maxine Kumin, *The Designated Heir*, Ch. 4

God save me from those I confide in.   —Proverb (French)

Be courteous to all, but intimate with few; and let those few be well
    tried before you give them your confidence. —George Washington

CONFLICT

No, when the fight begins within himself, / A man's worth something.
          —Robert Browning, *Bishop Blougram's Apology*, line 693

Pick battles big enough to matter, small enough to win.
                          —Jonathan Kozol, *On Being a Teacher*

CONFORMITY

Thou shalt not follow a multitude to do evil . . .
                          —*The Bible* (KJV): Exodus 23:2

If fifty million people say a foolish thing, it is still a foolish thing.
                          —Anatole France

In matters of principle, stand like a rock; in matters of taste, swim
    with the current.   —Thomas Jefferson

Is uniformity of opinion desirable? No more than that of face and
stature. —Thomas Jefferson, *Notes on the State of Virginia*

Where all think alike, no one thinks very much. —Walter Lippmann

When a dove begins to associate with crows its feathers remain white
but its heart grows black. —Proverb (German)

Some of the roads most used lead nowhere. —Proverb (Jewish)

If you always live with those who are lame, you will yourself learn to
limp. —Proverb (Latin)

Orthodoxy is my doxy; heterodoxy is another man's doxy.
—Bishop William Warburton,
remark to Lord Sandwich, in Priestley's *Memoirs*

CONFUSION

. . . an era of turmoil and ideological confusion, the principal phenomenon of the present age. —Saul Bellow, *Humboldt's Gift*

For God is not the author of confusion, but of peace . . .
—*The Bible* (KJV): 1 Corinthians 14:33

It is easy enough to praise men for the courage of their convictions. I
wish I could teach the sad young of this mealy generation the
courage of their confusions. —John Ciardi

Today, if you are not confused, you are just not thinking clearly.
—Irene Peter

CONSCIENCE

A man's first care should be to avoid the reproaches of his own heart.
—Joseph Addison, *Sir Roger de Coverley Papers*,
"Sir Roger on the Bench"

A guilty conscience needs no accuser. —Anonymous

The world has achieved brilliance without conscience. Ours is a world
of nuclear giants and ethical infants.
—Gen. Omar Bradley, speech, Armistice Day, 1948

The great beacon light God sets in all, the conscience of each bosom.
—Robert Browning, *Strafford*, Act IV, Sc. ii

A good conscience is a continual feast.
—Robert Burton, *The Anatomy of Melancholy*, II

Whatever creed be taught or land be trod, / Man's conscience is the
oracle of God. —Lord Byron

No hell like a bad conscience.
—John Crowne, *The Ambitious Statesman*, Act V, Sc. iii

Never do anything against conscience, even if the state demands it.
—Albert Einstein,
remark to Virgil G. Hinshaw, Jr., in Paul Arthur Schilpp, editor,
Albert Einstein Philosopher-Scientist, "Einstein's Social Philosophy"

A good conscience is a continual Christmas. —Benjamin Franklin

A clear conscience can bear any trouble.
—Thomas Fuller, M. D., *Gnomologia*, No. 374

Don't listen to friends when the Friend inside you says, "Do this!"
—Mahatma Gandhi

In matters of conscience, the law of majority has no place.
—Mahatma Gandhi, in *Young India*, 4 Aug 1920

The still small voice within you must always be the final arbiter when
there is a conflict of duty.
—Mahatma Gandhi, in *Young India*, 4 Aug 1920

I cannot and will not cut my conscience to fit this year's fashions.
—Lillian Hellman,
refusal to discuss political opinions and activities of others, letter
to the Honorable John S. Wood, Chairman of the House
Committee on un-American Activities, 19 May 1952

The one thing that doesn't abide by majority rule is a person's conscience. —Harper Lee, *To Kill a Mockingbird*

Conscience warns us as a friend before it punishes as a judge.
—Stanislaus Leszcynski

I am more afraid of my own heart, than of the Pope and all his cardi-
nals.—I have within me the great Pope, self. —Martin Luther

Perhaps the challenge is to invent the political structure that will give
conscience a better chance against authority. —Stanley Milgram

A good conscience is a soft pillow. —Proverb (German)

. . . I feel within me / A peace above all earthly dignities, / A still and quiet conscience.
—William Shakespeare, *King Henry VIII*, Act III, Sc. ii

Thus conscience does make cowards of us all.
—William Shakespeare, *Hamlet*, Act III, Sc. i

People who are at ease with their consciences always look happy.
—Alexander Solzhenitsyn, *Stories and Prose Poems*,
"Matryona's House"

Conscience is God's presence in man.
—Emanuel Swedenborg, *Arcana Coelesta*

Conscience is, in most men, an anticipation of the opinion of others.
—Sir Henry Taylor

A twinge of conscience is a glimpse of God. —Peter Ustinov

In the midst of all the doubts which we have discussed for 4000 years in 4000 ways, the safest course is to do nothing against one's conscience. With this secret, we can enjoy life and have no fear from death. —Voltaire, letter to Frederick the Great, 6 Apr 1767

Labor to keep alive in your breast that little spark of celestial fire, called Conscience. —George Washington, *Moral Maxims*,
Virtue and Vice, "Conscience"

Conscience is the soft whispers of the God in man. —Young

CONSCIENTIOUS OBJECTION

[Reply when asked by a Tribunal what he, as a conscientious objector, would do if he saw a German soldier trying to rape his sister:] I should try to come between them.
—Lytton Strachey, in Michael Holroyd,
Lytton Strachey: A Critical Biography

CONSCRIPTION

I believe the most important mission of the state is to protect the individual and make it possible for him to develop into a creative personality . . . The state violates this principle when it compels us to do military service. —Albert Einstein

I have made no secret, either privately or publicly, of any sense of
    outrage over officially enforced military and war service. I regard it
    as a duty of conscience to fight against such barbarous enslave-
    ment of the individual with every means available.
                        —Albert Einstein, statement made to the
                        Danish newspaper *Politiken*, 5 Aug 1930

While the State may respectfully require obedience on many matters,
    it cannot violate the moral nature of a man, convert him into a ser-
    viceable criminal, and expect his loyalty and devotion.
                    —Liane Norman, "Selective/Conscientious Objection"

C O N S E Q U E N C E S

It was the saying of Bion that though boys throw stones at frogs in
    sport, the frogs do not die in sport but in earnest.
                    —Plutarch, "Which are the Most Crafty, Water or Land
    Animals." Bion was a Greek poet who flourished about 280 B.C.

There is no act, however trivial, but has its train of consequences.
                                            —Samuel Smiles

C O N S E R V A T I S M

The very word conservative means that we conserve all that is good,
    that we reject all that is bad, and we must use our intelligence, our
    intellect, our training for the purpose of determining what we shall
    reject and what we shall conserve and retain.   —R. B. Bennett

Conservative, n. A statesman who is enamored of existing evils, as
    distinguished from the Liberal, who wishes to replace them with
    others.   —Ambrose Bierce

A man who is not a Liberal at sixteen has no heart; a man who is not
    a Conservative at sixty has no head.   —Benjamin Disraeli

The highest function of conservatism is to keep what progressiveness
    has accomplished.   —R. H. Fulton

The radical invents the views. When he has worn them out the con-
    servative adopts them.   —Mark Twain, *Notebooks*

C O N S I S T E N C Y

It's not up to me . . . to make the world consistent.   —Saul Bellow,
                                        Henderson the Rain King

A foolish consistency is the hobgoblin of little minds . . .
—Ralph Waldo Emerson, *Essays, First Series*, "Self-Reliance"

CONTENTEDNESS

A contented mind is the greatest blessing a man can enjoy in this
world.
—Joseph Addison

A contented heart is an even sea in the midst of all storms.
—Anonymous

A little bird is content with a little nest.
—Anonymous

Content is better than riches.
—Anonymous

He has enough who is content.
—Anonymous

He who is content in his poverty, is wonderfully rich.   —Anonymous

The contented man is never poor.
—Anonymous

The secret of contentment is the realization that life is a gift, not a
right.
—Anonymous

Contentment opes the source of every joy.
—Beattie

. . . for I have learned, in whatsoever state I am, therewith to be content.
—*The Bible* (KJV): Philippians 4:11

And having food and raiment let us be therewith content.
—*The Bible* (KJV): 1 Timothy 6:8

But if I'm content with a little,
  Enough is as good as a feast.
—Isaac Bickerstaffe, *Love in a Village*, Act III, Sc. i

Who lives content with little possesses everything. —Nicolas Boileau

My riches consist not in the extent of my possessions but in the few-
ness of my wants.
—J. Brotherton

True contentment is a real, even an active virtue—not only affirmative but creative. It is the power of getting out of any situation all
there is in it.
—G. K. Chesterton, *A Miscellany of Men*

To be content with what we possess is the greatest and most secure of
riches.
—Cicero

If you would know contentment, let your deeds be few.
—Democritus, in Marcus Aurelius Antoninus, *Meditations*

To be content with little is difficult; to be content with much, impossible.
—Marie Ebner-Eschenbach

Fortify yourself with contentment, for this is an impregnable fortress.
—Epictetus

I am always content with what happens; for I know that what God chooses is better than what I choose.
—Epictetus

Contentment gives a crown where fortune hath denied it.
—Ford

He that's content hath enough.
—Benjamin Franklin, *Poor Richard's Almanack*, 1758

Content lodges oftener in cottages than palaces.
—Thomas Fuller, M. D., *Gnomologia*, No. 1155

Contentment consists not in adding more fuel, but in taking away some of the fire; not in multiplying of wealth, but in subtracting men's desires.
—Thomas Fuller, M. D.

It is not given to the world to be contented.
—Johann Wolfgang von Goethe

A wise man cares not for what he cannot have.
—George Herbert

That best of blessings, a contented mind.
—Horace, *Epistolae*, i., 18, 111

It is right to be contented with what we have, never with what we are.
—James Mackintosh

All fortune belongs to him who has a contented mind. Is not the whole earth covered with leather for him whose feet are encased in shoes?
—*Panchatantra*

Learn to be pleased with everything; with wealth, so far as it makes us beneficial to others; with poverty, for not having much to care for; and with obscurity, for being unenvied.
—Plutarch

They that desire but a few things can be crossed but in a few.
—Proverb (German)

Enjoy your little while the fool is seeking for more.

—Proverb (Spanish)

He who is contented is not always rich.

—Proverb (Spanish)

And you have the right to arrange your own life under the blue sky and the hot sun, to get a drink of water, to stretch, to travel wherever you like without a convoy. So what's this about unwiped feet? And what's this about a mother-in-law? What about the main thing in life, all its riddles? . . . Do not pursue what is illusory—property and position: all that is gained at the expense of your nerves decade after decade . . . Live with a steady superiority over life—don't be afraid of misfortune, and do not yearn after happiness; it is, after all, all the same: the bitter doesn't last forever, and the sweet never fills the cup to overflowing. It is enough if you don't freeze in the cold and if thirst and hunger don't claw at your insides. If your back isn't broken, if your feet can walk, if both arms can bend, if both eyes see, and if both ears hear, then whom should you envy? And why? . . . and prize above all else in the world those who love you and wish you well.

—Alexander Solzhenitsyn, *The Gulag Archipelago*

As the old proverb says: "Well-fed horses don't rampage."

—Alexander Solzhenitsyn, *The Gulag Archipelago*

He who knows how to be content will be content with little.

—Alexander Solzhenitsyn

Want of desire is the greatest riches.

—Vigée

Lord of himself, though not of lands, / And having nothing, yet hath all.   —Sir Henry Wotton, "The Character of a Happy Life"

. . . he who wants little always has enough.   —Zimmermann

CONTRADICTION

We cannot possibly imagine the variety of contradictions in every heart.   —François de La Rochefoucauld

Do I contradict myself? / Very well then I contradict myself, / (I am large, I contain multitudes).

—Walt Whitman, *Leaves of Grass*, "Song of Myself"

Often care of the soul means not taking sides when there is conflict at a deep level. It may be necessary to stretch the heart wide enough to embrace contradiction and paradox.
—Thomas Moore, *Care of the Soul*

CONTROVERSY

No great advance has ever been made in science, politics, or religion, without controversy.
—Lyman Beecher

. . . religious controversy does only harm. It destroys humble inquiry after truth, and throws all the energies into an attempt to prove ourselves right—a spirit in which no man gets at truth.
—Frederick W. Robertson

CONVERSATION

Education begins a gentleman, conversation completes him.
—Anonymous

Please, Lord, fill my mouth with worthwhile stuff, and nudge me when I've said enough.
—Anonymous

Take as many half minutes as you can get, but never talk more than half a minute without pausing and giving others an opportunity to strike in.
—Anonymous

The best guide to conversation is to ask questions.
—Anonymous

The secret of success in conversation is to be able to disagree without being disagreeable.
—Anonymous

Never miss a good chance to shut up.
—Scott Beach's grandfather

Unless Sammler had private thoughts to occupy him, he couldn't sit through these talks with Margotte.
—Saul Bellow, *Mr. Sammler's Planet*, Ch. 1

Drawing on my fine command of language, I said nothing.
—Robert Benchley, *Chips off the Old Benchley*

Hear much, speak little.
—Bias

Bore, n. A person who talks when you wish him to listen.
—Ambrose Bierce, *The Devil's Dictionary*

Conversation, n. A fair for the display of the minor mental commodities, each exhibitor being too intent upon the arrangement of his own wares to observe those of his neighbor.
—Ambrose Bierce, *The Devil's Dictionary*

The true spirit of conversation consists in building on another man's observation, not overturning it.   —Edward Bulwer-Lytton

But stories somehow lengthen when begun.   —Lord Byron

Look in the face of the person to whom you are speaking if you wish to know his real sentiments, for he can command his words more easily than his countenance.   —Earl of Chesterfield

Never seem wiser or more learned than the people you are with.
—Earl of Chesterfield, *Letters*, 22 Feb 1748

Take the tone of the company you are in.
—Earl of Chesterfield, *Letters*, 9 Oct 1747

Talk often, but never long: in that case, if you do not please, at least you are sure not to tire your hearers.
—Earl of Chesterfield, *Letters*, 19 Oct 1748

Be swift to hear, slow to speak.   —Cleobulus

When we are in the company of sensible men, we ought to be doubly cautious of talking too much, lest we lose two good things, their good opinion and our own improvement; for what we have to say we know, but what they have to say we know not.
—Charles Caleb Colton

When you have nothing to say, say nothing.
—Charles Caleb Colton, *Lacon*, Vol. I, no 183

We have two ears and one tongue in order that we may hear more and speak less.   —Diogenes the Cynic

. . . you simply can't imagine what men will say!
—Fyodor Dostoyevsky, *Crime and Punishment*

Conversation is the laboratory and workshop of the student.
—Ralph Waldo Emerson, *Society and Solitude*, "Blubs"

How can I tell what I think till I see what I say?   —E. M. Forster

Education begins a gentleman; conversation completes him.
—Thomas Fuller, M. D.

It is by speech that many of our best gains are made. A large part of
the good we receive comes to us in conversation.
—Washington Gladden

The older I grow, the more I listen to people who don't say much.
—Germain G. Glidden

The time to stop talking is when the other person nods his head affir-
matively but says nothing.   —Henry S. Haskins

The soul of conversation is sympathy.   —William Hazlitt

We talk little if we do not talk about ourselves.   —William Hazlitt

Wit is the salt of conversation, not the food.   —William Hazlitt

A civil guest / Will no more talk all, than eat all the feast.
—George Herbert, *The Church-Porch*, Stanza 51

Speak clearly, if you speak at all; / Carve every word before you let it fall.
—Oliver Wendell Holmes, Sr., *A Rhymed Lesson*, line 408

The flowering moments of the mind
    Drop half their petals in our speech.
—Oliver Wendell Holmes, Sr., "To My Readers," Stanza 11

No man would listen to you talk if he didn't know it was his turn
next.   —Edgar Watson Howe

That is the happiest conversation where there is no competition, no
vanity, but a calm quiet interchange of sentiments.
—Samuel Johnson, in James Boswell, *Life of Samuel Johnson*

Conversation is the art of telling people a little less than they want to
know.   —Franklin P. Jones

A gossip is one who talks to you about others; a bore is one who talks
to you about himself; a brilliant conversationalist is one who talks
to you about yourself.   —Lisa Kirk

One thing which makes us find so few people who appear reasonable and agreeable in conversation is, that there is scarcely any one who does not think more of what he is about to say than of answering precisely what is said to him.   —François de La Rochefoucauld

The opposite of talking is not listening. The opposite of talking is waiting.   —Fran Lebowitz

It's not necessary to tell all you know.
                              —Harper Lee, *To Kill a Mockingbird*

Would you like to be a brilliant conversationalist? Just give your natural enthusiasm free reign and say whatever comes into your head. Your rashness will be taken for extraordinary courage.
                              —Alain René Lesage, *Gil Blas*

A single conversation across the table with a wise man is better than ten years' study of books.
                              —Henry Wadsworth Longfellow, *Hyperion*, Ch. 7

Avoid witticisms at the expense of others.   —Horace Mann

The fullest instruction, and the fullest enjoyment are never derived from books, till we have ventilated the ideas thus obtained in free and easy chat with others.   —William Matthews

In a discussion, the difficulty lies, not in being able to defend your opinion, but to know it.   —André Maurois

Conversation opens our views, and gives our faculties a more vigorous play; it puts us upon turning our notions on every side, and holds them up to a light that discovers those latent flaws which would probably have lain concealed in the gloom of unagitated abstraction.   —Melmoth

Most conversations are simply monologues delivered in the presence of a witness.   —Margaret Millar, *The Weak-Eyed Bat*

It is good to rub and polish our brain against that of others.
                              —Michel de Montaigne, *Essays*, Book I, Ch. 24

A gentleman never heard the story before.   —Austin O'Malley

The more the pleasures of the body fade away, the greater to me is the pleasure and charm of conversation.   —Plato, *The Republic*

Examine what is said, not him who speaks.   —Proverb (Arab)

Who speaks, sows; who keeps silence, reaps.   —Proverb (Italian)

Witticisms never are agreeable which are injurious to others.
    —Proverb (Latin)

What a strange scene if the surge of conversation could suddenly ebb
like the tide, and show us the real state of people's minds.
    —Sir Walter Scott

One of the greatest pleasures in life is conversation.
    —Sydney Smith, *Essays*, "Female Education"

It is a secret known but to few, yet of no small use in the conduct of
life, that when you fall into a man's conversation, the first thing
you should consider is, whether he has a greater inclination to
hear you, or that you should hear him.
    —Sir Richard Steele, *The Spectator*, 49

Perhaps the best conversationalist in the world is the man who helps
others to talk.   —John Steinbeck, *East of Eden*

Show me the man who isn't interested in discussing himself.
    —John Steinbeck, *East of Eden*

If you wish to appear agreeable in society, you must consent to be
taught many things you know already.
    —Charles Talleygrand-Perigord

The secret of being a bore is to tell everything.
    —Voltaire, *Sept discours en verse sur l'homme*, "De la nature"

Much of the conversation in the country consisted of lines from television shows, both present and past.
    —Kurt Vonnegut, Jr., *Breakfast of Champions*

There is no such thing as conversation. It is an illusion. There are
intersecting monologues, that is all.
    —Rebecca West, *The Harsh Voice*, "There is No Conversation"

CONVERSION

Kindness has converted more sinners that zeal, eloquence or learning.
    —Frederick William Faber

Charming women can true converts make, / We love the precepts for the teacher's sake.
— George Farquhar, *The Constant Couple*, Act V, Sc. iii

Every story of conversion is the story of blessed defeat. — C. S. Lewis

You have not converted a man because you have silenced him.
— John Morley, *On Compromise*

CONVICTION

Be true to your own highest convictions. — William Ellery Channing

Convictions are more dangerous foes of truth than lies.
— Friedrich Nietzsche

The best lack all conviction while the worst are full of passionate intensity. — William Butler Yeats, *Michael Robartes and the Dancer* (1921), "The Second Coming"

COOKING

Many a good drop of broth may come out of an old pot.
— Anonymous

The discovery of a new dish does more for the happiness of mankind than the discovery of a star.
— Anthelme Brillat-Savarin, *Physiologie du goût*

To make an omelette we have to break eggs. — Proverb (French)

The most remarkable thing about my mother is that for thirty years she served the family nothing but leftovers. The original meal has never been found. — Calvin Trillin

Cooking is like love. It should be entered into with abandon or not at all. — Harriet Van Horne

COOPERATION

One hand washes another. — Anonymous

Let everyone sweep in front of his own door, and the whole world will be clean. — Johann Wolfgang von Goethe

We can play to each other's strengths. — Karen Hale

By mutual confidence and mutual aid / Great deeds are done, and great discoveries made.
—Homer

Light is the task when many share the toil.
—Homer, *Iliad*

We are born for cooperation, as are the feet, the hands, the eyelids, and the upper and lower jaws.
—Marcus Aurelius Antoninus, *Meditations*

Many hands make light work.
—William Patten, *Expedition into Scotland* (1547)

Permit a man to light his fire from yours.
—Proverb (Latin), in Cicero, *De officiis*

What is impossible for one, many may yet accomplish.
—Paula Underwood, "Who Speaks for Wolf: A Native American Learning Story"

COPING

She liked to see people manage, somehow.
—Anne Tyler, *Searching for Caleb*

CORRECTION

Behold, happy is the man whom God correcteth . . .
—*The Bible* (KJV): Job 5:17

See everything; overlook a great deal; correct a little.
—Pope John XXIII

CORRESPONDENCE

I would have answered your letter sooner, but you didn't send one.
—Goodman Ace, in *The Groucho Letters*

The test of a good letter is a very simple one. If one seems to hear the other person talking as one reads, it is a good letter.
—A. C. Benson

Letters should be easy and natural.
—Earl of Chesterfield

Letters are largely written to get things out of your system.
—John Dos Passos, in Townsend Ludington, editor, *The Fourteenth Chronicle*

In a man's letters his soul lies naked. —Samuel Johnson

I have made this letter longer than usual, only because I have not had the time to make it shorter. —Blaise Pascal, *Lettres provinciales*

If you want to discover your true opinion of anybody, observe the impression made on you by the first sight of a letter from him. —Arthur Schopenhauer

But what can you say in a letter? —Alexander Solzhenitsyn, *One Day in the Life of Ivan Denisovich*

A man who gets few letters does not open one lightly. —John Steinbeck, *East of Eden*

A pleasant letter I hold to be the pleasantest thing that this world has to give. —Anthony Trollope

COUNSEL

The greatest trust between man and man is trust of giving counsel. —Francis Bacon

Let no man value at a little price / A virtuous woman's counsel; her winged spirit / Is feathered often times with heavenly words, / And, like her beauty, ravishing and pure. —George Chapman

He that will not be counseled cannot be helped. —Thomas Fuller, M. D., *Gnomologia*, No. 2350

No man is so foolish but he may sometimes give another good counsel, and no man so wise that he may not easily err if he takes no other counsel than his own. He that is taught only by himself has a fool for a master. —Ben Jonson

Better counsel comes overnight. —Gotthold Ephraim Lessing, *Emilia Galotti*, IV, iii

Come not to counsel uncalled. —Proverb (16th century)

A determined heart will not be counseled. —Proverb (Spanish)

Get good counsel before you begin; and when you have decided, act promptly. —Sallust, *Catalina*, I.

Do not give thy friends the most agreeable counsels, but the most
advantageous.   —Tuckerman

COUNTENANCE

Where the countenance is fair, there need no colors.
                                    —John Lyly, *Euphues*

A pleasing countenance is no light advantage.   —Ovid

A troubled countenance oft discloses much.   —Seneca, *Thyestes*

COURAGE

To live we must conquer incessantly, we must have the courage to be
happy.   —Henri Frédéric Amiel

Courage—fear that has said its prayers.   —Dorothy Bernard

Courage is like love; it must have hope for nourishment.
                                    —Napoleon Bonaparte, *Maxims*

I beg you to take courage; the brave soul can mend even disaster.
                                    —Catherine of Russia

A great part of courage is the courage of having done the thing before.
                —Ralph Waldo Emerson, *The Conduct of Life*, "Culture"

This is the courage in a man: To bear unflinchingly what heaven
sends.   —Euripides, *Heracles*

Dorothy Parker: Exactly what do you mean by "guts"?
                Ernest Hemingway: I mean grace under pressure.
                        —interview, *New Yorker*, 30 Nov 1929

The greatest test of courage on earth is to bear defeat without losing
heart.   —Robert G. Ingersoll

One man with courage makes a majority.   —Andrew Jackson

. . . I wanted you to see what real courage is, instead of getting the
idea that courage is a man with a gun in his hand. It's when you
know you're licked before you begin but you begin anyway and
you see it through no matter what.
                —Harper Lee, *To Kill a Mockingbird*, said by the character
                                Atticus Finch to his son Jem

Courage is the ladder on which all the other virtues mount.
—Clare Booth Luce

Being a man, ne'er ask the gods for a life set free from grief, but ask for courage that endureth long.
—Menander

Courage is fear holding on a minute longer.   —Gen. George S. Patton

Courage consists not in blindly overlooking danger, but in seeing it and conquering it.
—Jean Paul Richter

Courage is doing what you're afraid to do. There can be no courage unless you're scared.
—Eddie Rickenbacker

Courage does not always march to airs blown by a bugle . . .
—Frances Rodman, "For a Six-Year-Old"

There is nothing in the world so much admired as a man who knows how to bear unhappiness with courage.
—Seneca

. . . For courage mounteth with occasion.
—William Shakespeare, *King John*, Act II, Sc. I

. . . that's a valiant flea that dare eat his breakfast on the lip of a lion.
—William Shakespeare, *King Henry V*, Act III, Sc. vii

Keep your fears to yourself, but share your courage with others.
—Robert Louis Stevenson

'Tisn't life that matters! 'Tis the courage you bring to it.
—Sir Hugh Walpole, *Fortitude*

Have the courage to try something once, and you could enjoy it for years to come.
—Brian Alexander Watkins (age 9)

COURTESY

It's nice to be important, but it's more important to be nice.
—Anonymous

The mark of a man is how he treats a person who can be of no possible use to him.
—Anonymous

If a man be gracious and courteous to strangers, it shows he is a citizen of the world.
—Francis Bacon, *Essays*, "Goodness, and Goodness of Nature"

Creative activity could be described as a type of learning process
where teacher and pupil are located in the same individual.
—Arthur Koestler

By the creative act, we are able to reach beyond our own death.
—Rollo May

Creativity is so delicate a flower that praise tends to make it bloom,
while discouragement often nips it in the bud. Any of us will put
out more and better ideas if our efforts are appreciated.
—Alex F. Osborn

To live a creative life, we must lose our fear of being wrong.
—Joseph Chilton Pearce

The deepest experience of the creator is feminine, for it is the experience of receiving and bearing. —Rainer Maria Rilke

The very essence of the creative is its novelty, and hence we have no
standard by which to judge it. —Carl Rogers

Continuity does not rule out fresh approaches to fresh situations.
—Dean Rusk

It hinders the creative work of the mind if the intellect examines too
closely the ideas as they pour in. —Friedrich Schiller

Creativity can be described as letting go of certainties.
—Gail Sheehy, *Pathfinders*

Every creator painfully experiences the chasm between his inner
vision and its ultimate expression. —Isaac Bashevis Singer

CREEDS

Doubt that creed which you cannot reduce to practice.—Hosea Ballou

Creeds grow so thick along the way their boughs hide God. —Reese

CRIME

Bad judgment and carelessness are not punishable by rape.
—Pearl Cleage, *Deals With the Devil*, "The Other Facts of Life"

The real significance of crime is in its being a breach of faith with the
community of mankind. —Joseph Conrad

A thief believes everybody steals. —Edgar Watson Howe

CRISES

Try to relax and enjoy the crisis.   —Ashleigh Brilliant

We learn geology the morning after the earthquake.
                    —Ralph Waldo Emerson, *The Conduct of Life*

Crises in themselves are highly educational.   —Henry Arthur Jones

It's real hard to schedule a crisis.   —Mildred Vuris

Force the moment to its crisis.
                    —Eileen Walkenstein, M. D., *Don't Shrink To Fit!*

CRITICISM

To belittle is to be little.   —Anonymous

You may scold a carpenter who has made you a bad table, though you
    cannot make a table. It is not your trade to make tables.
                    —Samuel Johnson, in James Boswell, *Life of Samuel Johnson*

Few persons have sufficient wisdom to prefer censure which is useful
    to them, to praise which deceives them.
                    —François de La Rochefoucauld

People ask you for criticism but they only want praise.
                    —W. Somerset Maugham, *Of Human Bondage*

All looks yellow to the Jaundic'd Eye.
                    —Alexander Pope, *An Essay on Criticism*

The sieve with a thousand holes finds fault with the basket.
                    —Proverb (Indian)

Find fault, when you must find fault, in private if possible, and some-
    time after the offense, rather than at the time.   —Sydney Smith

CROSSES

To repel one's cross is to make it heavier.   —Henri Frédéric Amiel

Every man is crucified upon the cross of himself.
                    —Whittaker Chambers

The cross cannot be defeated for it is defeat.   —G. K. Chesterton

No Cross, no Crown.   —Thomas Fuller, M. D., *Gnomologia*

My only boast: The cross of Christ.
    —Kathy Kanewske, "Higher and Higher" (song)

Everyone bears his cross.   —Proverb (French)

The way to bliss lies not on beds of down, / And he that had no cross
    deserves no crown.   —Francis Quarles

If you bear the cross gladly, it will bear you.
    —Thomas à Kempis, *The Imitation of Christ*

CRUELTY

. . . 't is a cruelty / To load a falling man.
    —William Shakespeare, *King Henry VIII*, Act V, Sc. iii

CULTS

The quickest way to recognize a cult is its treatment of Jesus.
    —Pat Robertson, *Answers to 200 of Life's Most Probing Questions*

CULTURE

Culture, the acquainting ourselves with the best that has been known
and said in the world, and thus with the history of the human
spirit.
    —Matthew Arnold, *Literature and Dogma*, Preface

The acquiring of culture is the developing of an avid hunger for
    knowledge and beauty.   —Jess Lee Bennet, "On Culture"

CURES

A good laugh and a long sleep are the two best cures.   —Anonymous

It is part of the cure to wish to be cured.   —Seneca, *Hippolytus*

Diseases desperate grown / By desperate appliances are relieved, / Or
    not at all.   —William Shakespeare, *Hamlet*, Act IV, Sc. iii

CURIOSITY

Curiosity is the reason why most of us haven't committed suicide
    long ago.   —Anonymous

A free curiosity is more effective in learning than a rigid discipline.
—Saint Augustine

He was in a rage to know.
—J. Bronowski and Bruce Mazlish, about Leonardo da Vinci,
The Western Intellectual Tradition

The secret of happiness is curiosity. —Norman Douglas

The important thing is not to stop questioning. Curiosity has its own reason for existing. One cannot help but be in awe when he contemplates the mysteries of eternity, of life, of the marvelous structure of reality. It is enough if one tries merely to comprehend a little of this mystery every day. Never lose a holy curiosity.
—Albert Einstein

As long as you are curious, you will never be bored. —Lillian Gish

Curiosity is one of the permanent and certain characteristics of a vigorous intellect. —Samuel Johnson

Curiosity is the thirst of the soul. —Samuel Johnson

As long as you are curious, you defeat age. —Burt Lancaster

With us, the infantile inquisitiveness is strengthened and stretched out into our mature years. We never stop investigation. We are never satisfied that we know enough to get by. Every question we answer leads on the another question. This has become the greatest survival trick of our species. —Desmond Morris, *The Naked Ape*

If we lacked curiosity, we should do less for the good of our neighbor. But, under the name of duty or pity, curiosity steals into the home of the unhappy and the needy. Perhaps even in the famous mother-love there is a good deal of curiosity. —Friedrich Nietzsche

Curiosity and the urge to solve problems are the emotional hallmarks of our species . . . —Carl Sagan, *The Dragons of Eden*

What had made me move through so many dead and pointless years was curiosity. —Kurt Vonnegut, Jr., *Mother Night*

Seize the moment of excited curiosity on any subject, to solve your doubts; for if you let it pass, the desire may never return, and you may remain in ignorance. —W. Wirt

CURSING

His heart cannot be pure whose tongue is not clean.   —Anonymous

Diogenes struck the father when the son swore.
     —Robert Burton, *The Anatomy of Melancholy*, Part III, Sect. ii

Everybody swears everywhere . . . Shakespeare and all the rest, all up
     and down the years they swore at life. Plain old mother talk ain't
     nowheres near strong enough to describe such a terrible mixup as
     life . . .   —Mark Harris, *Bang the Drum Slowly*

Cussin' de weather is mighty po' farming.   —Proverb (American Negro)

To curse is to pray to the Devil.   —Proverb (German)

CUSTOM

When in Rome, live as the Romans do; when elsewhere, live as they
     live elsewhere.
          —Saint Ambrose, in Bishop Jeremy Taylor, *Ductor Dubitantium*,
                    "When in Rome, do as the Romans do"

The way of the world is to make laws, but follow customs.
                    —Michel de Montaigne

Custom is a second law.   —Proverb (Latin)

How many things, just and unjust, have no higher sanction than
     custom!   —Terence

Be not so bigoted to any custom as to worship it at the expense of
     truth.   —Zimmermann

CYCLES

That which the fountain sends forth returns again to the fountain.
                    —Henry Wadsworth Longfellow

The wheel is come full circle.
                    —William Shakespeare, *King Lear*, Act V, Sc. iii

CYNICISM

Cynic:—A blackguard whose faulty visions see things as they are, and
     not as they ought to be.   —Ambrose Bierce, *The Devil's Dictionary*

What is a cynic? A man who knows the price of everything, and the
     value of nothing.   —Oscar Wilde, *Lady Windermere's Fan*

— D —

DANCING

I have no desire to prove anything by dancing . . . I just dance.
—Fred Astaire

Dancing is the body made poetic.   —Ernst Bacon, *Notes on the Piano*

How inimitably graceful children are before they learn to dance.
—Samuel Taylor Coleridge

[Dance is] the poetry of the foot.   —John Dryden, *The Rival Ladies*

Dance is a song of the body.   —Martha Graham

Dancers aren't pompous; they're too tired.
—José Limón, *New York Times*, 31 Jul 1966

I dance to the tune that is played.   —Proverb (Spanish)

The girl who can't dance says the band can't play. —Proverb (Yiddish)

[Dancing is] a perpendicular expression of a horizontal desire.
—George Bernard Shaw

Dance is the only art of which we ourselves are the stuff of which it is made.   —Ted Shawn

DANGER

For danger levels man and brute
And all are fellows in their need.   —John Dryden

DARING

Bravely dared is half done.   —Proverb (German)

Who bravely dares must sometimes risk a fall. —Tobias George Smollett

It is better to err on the side of daring than of the side of caution.
—Alvin Toffler

DARKNESS

When it is dark enough, men see the stars.   —Ralph Waldo Emerson

The stars are constantly shining, but often we do not see them until the dark hours. —Earl Riney

Everyone is a moon and has a dark side which he never shows to anybody. —Mark Twain, *Notebook*

DEATH

Whatever thou lovest, man, that, too, become thou must— / God, if thou lovest God; dust if thou lovest dust.
—Angelus Silesius, "The Cherubic Pilgrim"

Death is a swift rider. —Anonymous

Death is nature's way of telling you to slow down. —Anonymous

Man, forget not death, for death certainly forgets not thee.
—Anonymous

Where death finds you, there eternity will keep you. —Anonymous

God made no Death: neither hath he pleasure in the destruction of the living. —Apocrypha, "Wisdom of Solomon," 1, 13

Life for the living, and rest for the dead!
—George Arnold, "The Jolly Old Pedagogue," Stanza 2

Death is the sound of distant thunder at a picnic.
—W. H. Auden, *The Dyer's Hand*

To a father, when his child dies, the future dies; to a child when his parents die, the past dies. —Auerbach

Death is but a sharp corner near the beginning of life's procession down eternity. —John Ayscough

It is as natural to die as to be born; and to a little infant, perhaps, the one is as painful as the other. —Francis Bacon, *Essays*, "Of Death"

Men fear death as children fear to go into the dark. —Francis Bacon

To die will be an awfully big adventure.
—Sir James Matthew Barrie, *Peter Pan*, Act III

Let no man fear to die, we love to sleep all, / And death is but the sounder sleep. —Francis Beaumont

Now comes the mystery.   —Henry Ward Beecher, on his deathbed

Only those who are prepared to die are really prepared to live.
                                        —Dr. L. Nelson Bell

Death deserves dignity.   —Saul Bellow, *Humboldt's Gift*

. . . for dust thou art, and unto dust shalt thou return.
                                        —*The Bible* (KJV): Genesis 3:19

. . . the Lord gave, and the Lord hath taken away; blessed be the name
    of the Lord.   —*The Bible* (KJV): Job 1:21

Precious in the sight of the Lord is the death of his saints.
                                        —*The Bible* (KJV): Psalms 116:15

For to me to live is Christ, and to die is gain.
                                        —*The Bible* (KJV): Philippians 1:21

. . . it is appointed unto men once to die, but after this the judgment.
                                        —*The Bible* (KJV): Hebrews 9:27

A long life or a short life are of equal importance to God. —Jack Black

God has reserved to Himself the right to determine the end of life,
    because He alone knows the goal to which it is His will to lead it. It
    is for Him alone to justify a life or to cast it away.
                                        —Dietrich Bonhoeffer

Earth to earth, ashes to ashes, dust to dust, in sure and certain hope
    of the resurrection.   —*The Book of Common Prayer*

In the midst of life we are in death.
    —*The Book of Common Prayer*, "The Order of the Burial of the Dead"

The loss of a beloved connection awakens an interest in Heaven
    before unfelt.   —Christian Nestell Bovée

Proud, then, clear-eyed and laughing, go to greet Death as a friend!
                                        —Rupert Brooke, "Second Best"

[Death is] A leap into the dark.
                                        —Sir Thomas Browne, *Letters from the Dead*

The long habit of living indisposeth us for dying.
                                        —Sir Thomas Browne, *Hydriotaphia: Urn Burial*

The small courtesies sweeten life; the great ennoble it.
—Christian Nestel Bovée

Fair and softly goes far.
—Miguel de Cervantes, *Don Quixote*, Part I, Ch. 2

Fair words never hurt the tongue.
—George Chapman, *Eastward Hoe*, Act IV, Sc. i

Life is not so short but that there is always time for courtesy.
—Ralph Waldo Emerson, *Letters and Social Aims*, "Social Aims"

All doors open to courtesy.
—Thomas Fuller, M. D., *Gnomologia*, No. 512

There is great force hidden in a sweet command.
—George Herbert, *Jacula Prudentum*

Courtesy which oft is found in lowly sheds, with smoky rafters, than in tapestry halls and courts of princes, where it first was named.
—John Milton

Be nice to people on your way up because you'll meet 'em on your way down.
—Wilson Mizner, in Alva Johnston, *The Legendary Mizners*, Ch. 4

Lip courtesy pleases much and costs little.   —Proverb (Spanish)

Hail! the small courtesies of life, for smooth do ye make the road of it, like grace and beauty, which beget inclinations to love at first sight; it is ye who open the door and let the stranger in.
—Laurence Sterne

Nothing is more valuable to a man than courtesy.
—Terence, *Adelphi*, Act V, Sc. iv

Love may fail, but courtesy will prevail.   —Kurt Vonnegut, Jr., *Jailbird*

Nothing is ever lost by courtesy. It is the cheapest of pleasures; costs nothing and conveys much. It pleases the one who gives and him who receives, and thus, like mercy, is twice blessed.
—Erastus Winman

COVETOUSNESS

The man who covets is always poor.   —Claudian

Let's live with that small pittance we have: / Who covets more is evermore a slave.
—Thomas Herrick

COWARDICE

A coward's fear can make a coward valiant.
—Owen Feltham

Many would be cowards if they had courage enough.
—Thomas Fuller, M. D.

Strange that cowards cannot see that their greatest safety lies in
dauntless courage.
—Johann Kaspar Lavater

The coward regards himself as cautious; the miser, as thrifty.
—Publilius Syrus, *Maxims*

Cowards die many times before their deaths;
The valiant never taste of death but once.
—William Shakespeare, *Julius Caesar*, Act II, Sc. ii

The better part of valour is discretion.
—William Shakespeare, *King Henry IV, Part I*, Act V, Sc. iv

The human race is a race of cowards, and I am not only marching in
that procession but carrying a banner.
—Mark Twain, *Mark Twain in Eruption: Hitherto Unpublished Pages
About Men and Events*

CREATION

All things bright and beautiful, / All creatures great and small, / All
things wise and wonderful, / The Lord God made them all.
—Cecil Frances Alexander, "All Things Bright and Beautiful"

It is not difficult for one seal to make many impressions exactly alike,
but to vary shapes almost infinitely, which is what God has done
in creation, this is in truth a divine work.   —Robert Bellarmine,
De ascensione mentis in Deum per scalas creaturarum

And the Lord God formed man of the dust of the ground, and
breathed into his nostrils the breath of life; and man became a living soul.
—*The Bible* (KJV): Genesis 2:7

We are the miracle of force and matter making itself over into imagination and will. Incredible. The Life Force experimenting with
forms. You for one. Me for another. The Universe shouted itself
alive. We are the shouts.   —Ray Bradbury, "G. B. S.—Mark V"

Although the creationist . . . must of necessity hold that there was a
"first man," it is of no consequence whether he looked like a
Pithecanthropoid or a Caucasoid.   —James D. Buswell III,
                    in R. L. Mixter, editor, *Evolution and Christian Thought*

Creation proceeds from moment to moment.
                              —N. M. Chatterjee, *Letters from Earth*

The probability of life originating from accident is comparable to the
probability of the unabridged dictionary resulting from an explo-
sion in a printing shop.   —Edwin Conklin

Eternal love made me.   —Dante Alighieri

I want to know how God created the world. I'm not interested in this
or that phenomenon. I want to know his thoughts, the rest are
details.   —Albert Einstein

He created us because He wanted other creatures in His image in the
universe upon whom He could pour out His love, and who, in
turn, would voluntarily love Him. —Billy Graham, *Till Armageddon*

Man, like Deity, creates in his own image.
                              —Elbert Hubbard, *The Note Book*

From the intrinsic evidence of his creation, the Great Architect of the
Universe now begins to appear as a pure mathematician.
                        —Sir James Jeans, *Mysterious Universe*, Ch. 5

In creating, the only hard thing's to begin; / A grass blade's no easier
to make than an oak.   —James Russell Lowell, *A Fable for Critics*

We live at a time when man believes himself fabulously capable of
creation, but he does not know what to create.
                        —Jose Ortega y Gasset, *The Revolt of the Masses*, 4

God creates the world anew in each moment.   —Jan van Ruysbroeck

In order to create there must be a dynamic force, and what force is
more potent than love?   —Igor Stravinsky, *An Autobiography*, 5

That the universe was formed by a fortuitous concourse of atoms, I
will no more believe than that the accidental jumbling of the
alphabet would fall into a most ingenious treatise of philosophy.
                                          —Jonathan Swift

What can be more foolish than to think that all this rare fabric of heaven and earth could come by chance, when all the skill of art is not able to make an oyster!
—Jeremy Taylor

In the beginning, the Creator longed for the joy of creation.
—*The Upanishads*, "Prasna Upanishad," translated by Juan Mascary

The art of creation / Is older than the art of killing.
—Andrey Voznesensky, *The New York Times Review of Books*, "Poem with a Footnote," 19 May 1967

I believe a leaf of grass is no less than the journey-work of the stars.
—Walt Whitman, *Leaves of Grass*, "Song of Myself"

CREATIVITY

A capacity for childlike wonder, carried into adult life, typifies the creative person.
—Anonymous

The essence of the creative act is to see the familiar as strange.
—Anonymous

A person either creates or destroys. There is no neutrality.
—Saul Bellow, *Seize the Day*

Every production must resemble its author.
—Miguel de Cervantes, *Don Quixote*, Preface

It is the creative potential itself in human beings that is the image of God.
—Mary Daly, *Beyond God the Father*, Ch. 1

The monotony of a quiet life stimulates the creative mind.
—Albert Einstein, from a speech, "Civilization and Science," at Royal Albert Hall, London, 3 Oct 1933

No great thing is created suddenly.
—Epictetus

In the creative state a man is taken out of himself. He lets down as it were a bucket into his subconscious, and draws up something which is normally beyond his reach. He mixes this thing with his normal experiences, and out of this mixture he makes a work of art.
—E. M. Forster

Institutions are essential in order to preserve the achievement of the past, but the original creative impulse in every age comes from the amateur, the rebel, the breaker of idols.
—Robert Gordis, *A Faith for Moderns*

Creative activity could be described as a type of learning process
where teacher and pupil are located in the same individual.
—Arthur Koestler

By the creative act, we are able to reach beyond our own death.
—Rollo May

Creativity is so delicate a flower that praise tends to make it bloom,
while discouragement often nips it in the bud. Any of us will put
out more and better ideas if our efforts are appreciated.
—Alex F. Osborn

To live a creative life, we must lose our fear of being wrong.
—Joseph Chilton Pearce

The deepest experience of the creator is feminine, for it is the experience of receiving and bearing.   —Rainer Maria Rilke

The very essence of the creative is its novelty, and hence we have no
standard by which to judge it.   —Carl Rogers

Continuity does not rule out fresh approaches to fresh situations.
—Dean Rusk

It hinders the creative work of the mind if the intellect examines too
closely the ideas as they pour in.   —Friedrich Schiller

Creativity can be described as letting go of certainties.
—Gail Sheehy, *Pathfinders*

Every creator painfully experiences the chasm between his inner
vision and its ultimate expression.   —Isaac Bashevis Singer

CREEDS

Doubt that creed which you cannot reduce to practice.—Hosea Ballou

Creeds grow so thick along the way their boughs hide God.   —Reese

CRIME

Bad judgment and carelessness are not punishable by rape.
—Pearl Cleage, *Deals With the Devil*, "The Other Facts of Life"

The real significance of crime is in its being a breach of faith with the
community of mankind.   —Joseph Conrad

A thief believes everybody steals.   —Edgar Watson Howe

CRISES

Try to relax and enjoy the crisis.   —Ashleigh Brilliant

We learn geology the morning after the earthquake.
—Ralph Waldo Emerson, *The Conduct of Life*

Crises in themselves are highly educational.   —Henry Arthur Jones

It's real hard to schedule a crisis.   —Mildred Vuris

Force the moment to its crisis.
—Eileen Walkenstein, M. D., *Don't Shrink To Fit!*

CRITICISM

To belittle is to be little.   —Anonymous

You may scold a carpenter who has made you a bad table, though you
cannot make a table. It is not your trade to make tables.
—Samuel Johnson, in James Boswell, *Life of Samuel Johnson*

Few persons have sufficient wisdom to prefer censure which is useful
to them, to praise which deceives them.
—François de La Rochefoucauld

People ask you for criticism but they only want praise.
—W. Somerset Maugham, *Of Human Bondage*

All looks yellow to the Jaundic'd Eye.
—Alexander Pope, *An Essay on Criticism*

The sieve with a thousand holes finds fault with the basket.
—Proverb (Indian)

Find fault, when you must find fault, in private if possible, and sometime after the offense, rather than at the time.   —Sydney Smith

CROSSES

To repel one's cross is to make it heavier.   —Henri Frédéric Amiel

Every man is crucified upon the cross of himself.
—Whittaker Chambers

The cross cannot be defeated for it is defeat.   —G. K. Chesterton

No Cross, no Crown. —Thomas Fuller, M. D., *Gnomologia*

My only boast: The cross of Christ.
—Kathy Kanewske, "Higher and Higher" (song)

Everyone bears his cross. —Proverb (French)

The way to bliss lies not on beds of down, / And he that had no cross
deserves no crown. —Francis Quarles

If you bear the cross gladly, it will bear you.
—Thomas à Kempis, *The Imitation of Christ*

C R U E L T Y

... 't is a cruelty / To load a falling man.
—William Shakespeare, *King Henry VIII*, Act V, Sc. iii

C U L T S

The quickest way to recognize a cult is its treatment of Jesus.
—Pat Robertson, *Answers to 200 of Life's Most Probing Questions*

C U L T U R E

Culture, the acquainting ourselves with the best that has been known
and said in the world, and thus with the history of the human
spirit.
—Matthew Arnold, *Literature and Dogma*, Preface

The acquiring of culture is the developing of an avid hunger for
knowledge and beauty. —Jess Lee Bennet, "On Culture"

C U R E S

A good laugh and a long sleep are the two best cures. —Anonymous

It is part of the cure to wish to be cured. —Seneca, *Hippolytus*

Diseases desperate grown / By desperate appliances are relieved, / Or
not at all. —William Shakespeare, *Hamlet*, Act IV, Sc. iii

C U R I O S I T Y

Curiosity is the reason why most of us haven't committed suicide
long ago. —Anonymous

A free curiosity is more effective in learning than a rigid discipline.
—Saint Augustine

He was in a rage to know.
—J. Bronowski and Bruce Mazlish, about Leonardo da Vinci,
The Western Intellectual Tradition

The secret of happiness is curiosity.   —Norman Douglas

The important thing is not to stop questioning. Curiosity has its own
reason for existing. One cannot help but be in awe when he contemplates the mysteries of eternity, of life, of the marvelous structure of reality. It is enough if one tries merely to comprehend a
little of this mystery every day. Never lose a holy curiosity.
—Albert Einstein

As long as you are curious, you will never be bored.   —Lillian Gish

Curiosity is one of the permanent and certain characteristics of a vigorous intellect.   —Samuel Johnson

Curiosity is the thirst of the soul.   —Samuel Johnson

As long as you are curious, you defeat age.   —Burt Lancaster

With us, the infantile inquisitiveness is strengthened and stretched
out into our mature years. We never stop investigation. We are
never satisfied that we know enough to get by. Every question we
answer leads on the another question. This has become the greatest survival trick of our species. —Desmond Morris, *The Naked Ape*

If we lacked curiosity, we should do less for the good of our neighbor.
But, under the name of duty or pity, curiosity steals into the home
of the unhappy and the needy. Perhaps even in the famous
mother-love there is a good deal of curiosity. —Friedrich Nietzsche

Curiosity and the urge to solve problems are the emotional hallmarks
of our species . . .   —Carl Sagan, *The Dragons of Eden*

What had made me move through so many dead and pointless years
was curiosity.   —Kurt Vonnegut, Jr., *Mother Night*

Seize the moment of excited curiosity on any subject, to solve your
doubts; for if you let it pass, the desire may never return, and you
may remain in ignorance.   —W. Wirt

CURSING

His heart cannot be pure whose tongue is not clean.   —Anonymous

Diogenes struck the father when the son swore.
> —Robert Burton, *The Anatomy of Melancholy*, Part III, Sect. ii

Everybody swears everywhere . . . Shakespeare and all the rest, all up
and down the years they swore at life. Plain old mother talk ain't
nowheres near strong enough to describe such a terrible mixup as
life . . .   —Mark Harris, *Bang the Drum Slowly*

Cussin' de weather is mighty po' farming.   —Proverb (American Negro)

To curse is to pray to the Devil.   —Proverb (German)

CUSTOM

When in Rome, live as the Romans do; when elsewhere, live as they
live elsewhere.
> —Saint Ambrose, in Bishop Jeremy Taylor, *Ductor Dubitantium*,
> "When in Rome, do as the Romans do"

The way of the world is to make laws, but follow customs.
> —Michel de Montaigne

Custom is a second law.   —Proverb (Latin)

How many things, just and unjust, have no higher sanction than
custom!   —Terence

Be not so bigoted to any custom as to worship it at the expense of
truth.   —Zimmermann

CYCLES

That which the fountain sends forth returns again to the fountain.
> —Henry Wadsworth Longfellow

The wheel is come full circle.
> —William Shakespeare, *King Lear*, Act V, Sc. iii

CYNICISM

Cynic:—A blackguard whose faulty visions see things as they are, and
not as they ought to be.   —Ambrose Bierce, *The Devil's Dictionary*

What is a cynic? A man who knows the price of everything, and the
value of nothing.   —Oscar Wilde, *Lady Windermere's Fan*

— D —

DANCING

I have no desire to prove anything by dancing . . . I just dance.
—Fred Astaire

Dancing is the body made poetic. —Ernst Bacon, *Notes on the Piano*

How inimitably graceful children are before they learn to dance.
—Samuel Taylor Coleridge

[Dance is] the poetry of the foot. —John Dryden, *The Rival Ladies*

Dance is a song of the body. —Martha Graham

Dancers aren't pompous; they're too tired.
—José Limón, *New York Times*, 31 Jul 1966

I dance to the tune that is played. —Proverb (Spanish)

The girl who can't dance says the band can't play. —Proverb (Yiddish)

[Dancing is] a perpendicular expression of a horizontal desire.
—George Bernard Shaw

Dance is the only art of which we ourselves are the stuff of which it is
made. —Ted Shawn

DANGER

For danger levels man and brute
And all are fellows in their need. —John Dryden

DARING

Bravely dared is half done. —Proverb (German)

Who bravely dares must sometimes risk a fall. —Tobias George Smollett

It is better to err on the side of daring than of the side of caution.
—Alvin Toffler

DARKNESS

When it is dark enough, men see the stars. —Ralph Waldo Emerson

The stars are constantly shining, but often we do not see them until the dark hours. —Earl Riney

Everyone is a moon and has a dark side which he never shows to any-body. —Mark Twain, *Notebook*

DEATH

Whatever thou lovest, man, that, too, become thou must— / God, if thou lovest God; dust if thou lovest dust.
—Angelus Silesius, "The Cherubic Pilgrim"

Death is a swift rider. —Anonymous

Death is nature's way of telling you to slow down. —Anonymous

Man, forget not death, for death certainly forgets not thee.
—Anonymous

Where death finds you, there eternity will keep you. —Anonymous

God made no Death: neither hath he pleasure in the destruction of the living. —Apocrypha, "Wisdom of Solomon," 1, 13

Life for the living, and rest for the dead!
—George Arnold, "The Jolly Old Pedagogue," Stanza 2

Death is the sound of distant thunder at a picnic.
—W. H. Auden, *The Dyer's Hand*

To a father, when his child dies, the future dies; to a child when his parents die, the past dies. —Auerbach

Death is but a sharp corner near the beginning of life's procession down eternity. —John Ayscough

It is as natural to die as to be born; and to a little infant, perhaps, the one is as painful as the other. —Francis Bacon, *Essays*, "Of Death"

Men fear death as children fear to go into the dark. —Francis Bacon

To die will be an awfully big adventure.
—Sir James Matthew Barrie, *Peter Pan*, Act III

Let no man fear to die, we love to sleep all, / And death is but the sounder sleep. —Francis Beaumont

Now comes the mystery.　　　—Henry Ward Beecher, on his deathbed

Only those who are prepared to die are really prepared to live.
　　　　　　　　　　　　　　　　　　—Dr. L. Nelson Bell

Death deserves dignity.　　　　　　　—Saul Bellow, *Humboldt's Gift*

. . . for dust thou art, and unto dust shalt thou return.
　　　　　　　　　　　　　　—*The Bible* (KJV): Genesis 3:19

. . . the Lord gave, and the Lord hath taken away; blessed be the name
　　of the Lord.　　　　　　　　—*The Bible* (KJV): Job 1:21

Precious in the sight of the Lord is the death of his saints.
　　　　　　　　　　　　　—*The Bible* (KJV): Psalms 116:15

For to me to live is Christ, and to die is gain.
　　　　　　　　　　　　—*The Bible* (KJV): Philippians 1:21

. . . it is appointed unto men once to die, but after this the judgment.
　　　　　　　　　　　　　—*The Bible* (KJV): Hebrews 9:27

A long life or a short life are of equal importance to God.　—Jack Black

God has reserved to Himself the right to determine the end of life,
　　because He alone knows the goal to which it is His will to lead it. It
　　is for Him alone to justify a life or to cast it away.
　　　　　　　　　　　　　　　　　　—Dietrich Bonhoeffer

Earth to earth, ashes to ashes, dust to dust, in sure and certain hope
　　of the resurrection.　　　　　　—*The Book of Common Prayer*

In the midst of life we are in death.
　—*The Book of Common Prayer*, "The Order of the Burial of the Dead"

The loss of a beloved connection awakens an interest in Heaven
　　before unfelt.　　　　　　　　—Christian Nestell Bovée

Proud, then, clear-eyed and laughing, go to greet Death as a friend!
　　　　　　　　　　　　　　—Rupert Brooke, "Second Best"

[Death is] A leap into the dark.
　　　　　　　　　—Sir Thomas Browne, *Letters from the Dead*

The long habit of living indisposeth us for dying.
　　　　　　　—Sir Thomas Browne, *Hydriotaphia: Urn Burial*

Knowledge by suffering entereth, / And life is perfected by death.
—Elizabeth Barrett Browning, *Lady Geraldine's Courtship*

The grand Perhaps!   —Robert Browning, *Bishop Blougram's Apology*

. . . the kind earth waited without haste until he came to it.
—Pearl S. Buck, *The Good Earth*, Ch. 34

. . . to die on a kitchen floor at 7 o'clock in the morning while other people are frying eggs is not so rough unless it happens to you.
—Charles Bukowski, "The Twins"

How can I die? I'm booked.   —George Burns, in Garson Kanin,
It Takes a Long Time to Become Old

Because I have loved life, I shall have no sorrow to die.
—Amelia Burr, *Life and Living*, "A Song of Living," Stanza 3

It is death, and not what comes after death, that men are generally afraid of.   —Samuel Butler (1835-1902)

To live in the hearts we leave behind / Is not to die.
—Thomas Campbell, "Hallowed Ground"

The character wherewith we sink into the grave at death is the very character wherewith we shall reappear at the resurrection.
—Thomas Chalmers

We don't know yet about life, how can we know about death?
—Confucius

The miserablest day we live there is many a better thing to do than die.   —Darley

Isn't death the boundary we need?   —Don DeLillo, *White Noise*

The dead have a presence.   —Don DeLillo, *White Noise*

Because I could not stop for Death / He kindly stopped for me— / The Carriage held but just Ourselves— / And Immortality.
—Emily Dickinson, "Because I could not stop for Death"

I was afraid of the pain of dying and terribly reluctant to leave the world behind because I liked life a lot, even if it had been pretty tough sometimes.   —Alexander Dolgun, *Alexander Dolgun's Story*

All mankind is of one Author, and in one volume; when one Man dies, one chapter is not torn out of the book, but translated into a better language; and every Chapter must be so translated.
—John Donne, *Devotions upon Emergent Occasions*

Any man's death diminishes me, because I am involved in mankind; and therefore never send to know for whom the bell tolls; it tolls for thee.
—John Donne, *Devotions upon Emergent Occasions*

One short sleep past, we wake eternally, / And death shall be no more; Death thou shalt die.
—John Donne, *Holy Sonnets*, II, xiii

Death ends our woes, and the kind grave shuts up the mournful scene.
—John Dryden

Death in itself is nothing; but we fear / To be we know not what, we know not where.
—John Dryden, *Aureng-Zebe*, IV, i

Of no distemper, of no blast he died / But fell like autumn fruit that mellow'd long.
—John Dryden

This is the way the world ends / Not with a bang but a whimper.
—T.S. Eliot, "The Hollow Men"

Good-bye, proud world! I'm going home; / Thou art not my friend, and I'm not thine.
—Ralph Waldo Emerson, *Poems*, "Good-bye"

Never say about anything, "I have lost it," but only "I have given it back." Is your child dead? It has been given back. Is your wife dead? She has been returned.
—Epictetus, *Discourses*

Death is a debt we all must pay.   —Euripides, *Alcestis*, "Andromache"

When good men die their goodness does not perish.   —Euripides

Death is my neighbor now.
—Dame Edith Evans, in an interview a week before her death

He who waits upon God, is ready whenever he calls.—He is a happy man who so lives that death at all times may find him at leisure to die.
—Owen Feltham

When our parents are living we feel that they stand between us and death; when they go, we move to the edge of the unknown.
—Robert I. Fitzhenry

But it is the will of God and nature, that these mortal bodies be laid
aside, when the soul is to enter into real life . . . A man is not completely born until he be dead.
—Benjamin Franklin, letter, 23 Feb 1756

Life is rather a state of embryo,—a preparation for life. A man is not
completely born until he has passed through death.
—Benjamin Franklin

Death is the grand leveler.　　　　—Thomas Fuller, M. D., *Gnomologia*

. . . in the midst of death life persists . . .　　　　—Mahatma Gandhi

The wise are unaffected either by death or life. These are but faces of
the same coin.　　　—Mahatma Gandhi, in *Young India*, 25 Oct 1928

To die quickly in one's eighth decade at the very top of one's powers
is an enviable end, and not an occasion for mourning.
—Brendan Gill, *Here at the New Yorker*

He only half dies who leaves an image of himself in his sons.
—Goldoni

All will fall.　　　　　　　　　　　　—Francisco de Goya

Although we may trust God's promises for life after death and the certainty of a heavenly home, we must still face the reality of death.
—Billy Graham, *Till Armageddon*

Death is robbed of much of its terror for the true believer.
—Billy Graham, *Angels: God's Secret Agents*

One of the primary goals in life . . . should be to prepare for death.
Everything else should be secondary.
—Billy Graham, *Till Armageddon*

Someday a loving Hand will be laid upon our shoulder and this brief
message will be given: "Come home."
—Billy Graham, *Till Armageddon*

. . . the way we view death determines, to a surprising degree, the way
we live our lives.　　　—Billy Graham, *Facing Death and the Life After*

To the Christian death is the exchanging of a tent for a building.
—Billy Graham, *Till Armageddon*

Do not seek death. Death will find you. But seek the road which
  makes death a fulfillment.   —Dag Hammarskjöld

In the last analysis, it is our conception of death which decides our
  answers to all the questions that life puts to us.
                                        —Dag Hammarskjöld, *Diaries*

Death quickens us for love for living friends.
                                        —Mark Harris, *Wake Up Stupid*

Everybody knows everybody is dying. That's why people are as good
  as they are.
            —Mark Harris, from his screenplay *Bang the Drum Slowly*,
                          based on his book by the same name

He will not die . . . He will only pass on.
                              —Mark Harris, *Bang the Drum Slowly*

You all die soon enough, so why not be nice to each other?
                              —Mark Harris, *Bang the Drum Slowly*

We sometimes congratulate ourselves at the moment of waking from
  a troubled dream; it may be so the moment after death.
              —Nathaniel Hawthorne, journal entry, 25 Oct 1835

No young man believes he shall ever die.
                            —William Hazlitt, *Literary Remains*,
                    "On the Feeling of Immortality in Youth"

. . . someday the silver cord will break.
                          —Ernest Hemingway, quoting a hymn,
                      The Nick Adams Stories, "Three Shots"

And death makes equal the high and low.
                  —John Heywood, "Be Merry, Friends" (c. 1557)

Now I am about to take my last voyage, a frightful leap in the dark.
                    —Thomas Hobbes, on his deathbed, 4 Dec 1679

Unbody me—I'm tired—and get me home. —Ralph Hodgson, *The Moor*

Death ends a life. But it doesn't end a relationship.
                    —Hal Holbrook, *I Never Sang for My Father*

Life has given me of its best— / Laughter and weeping, labor and rest,
  / Little of gold, but lots of fun; / Shall I then sigh that all is done?
                              —Norah M. Holland, "Life"

... death crowns the Christian. —Hopfner

I shall not altogether die. —Horace, *Odes*, xxx. 6

Death belongs to God alone; by what right do men touch that
unknown thing? —Victor Hugo

My day's work will begin again the next morning. The tomb is not a
blind alley. —Victor Hugo

Death is the only thing we haven't succeeded in completely vulgarizing.
—Aldous Huxley, *Eyeless in Gaza*, XXXI

Death is only perfect rest. —Robert G. Ingersoll

Oh, write of me not "Died in bitter pains," / But "Emigrated to
another star!" —Helen Hunt Jackson, "Emigravit"

Let us pass over the river and rest under the shade of the trees.
—Gen. Stonewall Jackson, last words

When a man dies they who survive him ask what property he has left
behind. The angel who bends over the dying man asks what good
deeds he has sent before him. —*The Koran*

The wise man is never surprised by death: he is always ready to
depart. —Jean de La Fontaine, *Fables*, "La Mort et le Mourant"

When you're dead, you stay a long time dead.
—Ring Lardner, *Zone of Quiet*

Death is the only pure, beautiful conclusion of a great passion.
—D. H. Lawrence, *Fantasia of the Unconscious*, Ch. 15

Let the tent be struck. —Gen. Robert E. Lee, last words

As a well-spent day brings happy sleep, so a life well used brings a
happy death. —Leonardo da Vinci

Death is not a foe, but an inevitable adventure.
—Sir Oliver Joseph Lodge

Art is long, and Time is fleeting. / And our hearts, though stout and
brave, / Still, like muffled drums, are beating / Funeral marches to
the grave.
—Henry Wadsworth Longfellow, "A Psalm of Life"

Death is the chillness that precedes the dawn; / We shudder for a
moment, then awake / In the broad sunshine of the other life.
—Henry Wadsworth Longfellow, "Michael Angelo"

There is no Death! What seems so is a transition; / This life of mortal
breath / Is but a suburb of the life Elysian, / Whose portal we call
Death.   —Henry Wadsworth Longfellow,
The Seaside and the Fireside, "Resignation"

The gods conceal from men the happiness of death, that they may
endure life.   —Lucan

Dying ain't in people's plans, is it?
—Cormac McCarthy, *All the Pretty Horses*, Ch. 3

In Flanders fields the poppies blow / Between the crosses, row on row.
—John Macrae, "In Flanders Fields"

You died alone.   —Bernard Malamud, *The Natural*

A man's dying is more the survivors' affair than his own.
—Thomas Mann, *The Magic Mountain*

Death is a release from the impressions of sense, and from the
impulses that make us their puppets; from the vagaries of mind,
and from the hard service of the flesh.
—Marcus Aurelius Antoninus, *Meditations*

The act of dying is also one of the acts of life.
—Marcus Aurelius Antoninus, *Meditations*

A little while with grief and laughter, / And then the day will close;
The shadows gather . . . what comes after / No man knows.
—Don Marquis, "A Little While"

Death hath a thousand doors to let out life.
—Philip Massinger, *A Very Woman*, Act V, Sc. iv

Life must go on, / Though good men die.
—Edna St. Vincent Millay, "Lament"

Death cannot come untimely to him who is fit to die.   —Milman

Death be not proud! A short sleep, and I will wake again, eternally. A
short voyage, and I will meet my Maker face to face. —John Milton

So may'st thou live, till like ripe fruit thou drop / Into thy mother's lap, or be with ease / Gather'd, not harshly pluck'd, for death mature.
—John Milton

Like a full-fed guest, depart to rest . . .   —Michel de Montaigne

No man dies before his hour. The time you leave behind was no more yours, than that which was before your birth, and concerneth you no more.   —Michel de Montaigne, *Essays*, xix

The Dead are like the stars by day; / Withdrawn from mortal eye, / But not extinct, they hold their way / In glory through the sky.
—James Montgomery

Brief life is here our portion.
—John Mason Neale, hymn, a translation from Latin of St. Bernard of Cluny (c. 1145)

When death gives us a long lease of life, it takes as hostages all those whom we have loved.   —Madame Suzanne Necker

Men after death . . . are understood worse than men of the moment, but heard better.   —Friedrich Nietzsche

The dead don't bother with particulars.
—Flannery O'Connor, *The Complete Stories*, "You Can't Be Any Poorer Than Dead"

Well blest is he who has a dear one dead; / A friend he has whose face will never change— / A dear communion that will not grow strange; / The anchor of a love is death.
—John Boyle O'Reilly, "Forever," Stanza 3

Death's but a path that must be trod, / If man would ever pass to God.   —Thomas Parnell, "A Night-Piece on Death"

Dying / Is an art, like everything else.   —Sylvia Plath, "Lady Lazarus"

Vital spark of heav'nly flame! / Quit, oh quit this mortal frame: / Trembling, hoping, ling'ring, flying, / Oh the pain, the bliss of dying.   —Alexander Pope, "The Dying Christian to His Soul"

He who must die must die in the dark, even though he sells candles.
—Proverb (Colombian)

Dead men tell no tales.   —Proverb (English)

When one is dead, it is for a long time.   —Proverb (French)

Our last garment is made with no pockets.   —Proverb (Italian)

Flowers and buds fall, and the old and ripe fall.   —Proverb (Malay)

Not all of me shall die.
                    —Pushkin, in Alexander Solzhenitsyn, *Cancer Ward*

I go to seek a great perhaps.   —François Rabelais, on his deathbed

Life is eternal; and love is immortal; and death is only a horizon; and
    a horizon is nothing save the limit of our sight.
            —Rossiter Worthington Raymond, "A Commendatory Prayer"

Death squares all accounts.
                    —Charles Reade, *The Cloister and the Hearth*, XCII

Remember me when I am gone away, / Gone far away into the silent
    land. / Better by far you should forget and smile / Than you should
    remember and be sad.   —Christina Rossetti, "Remember"

When I am dead, my dearest, / Sing no sad songs for me; / Plant thou
    no roses at my head, / Nor shady cypress tree: / Be the green grass
    above me / With showers and dewdrops wet; / And if thou wilt,
    remember, / And if thou wilt, forget.   —Christina Rossetti

There is no cure for birth and death save to enjoy the interval. The
    dark background which death supplies brings out the tender colors
    of life in all their purity.   —George Santayana,
        Soliloquies in England and Later Soliloquies (1922), "War Shrines"

Is death the last sleep? No, it is the last final awakening.
                                            —Sir Walter Scott

Is life a pregnancy? That would make death a birth.
                                            —Florida Scott-Maxwell

I have a rendezvous with Death / At some disputed barricade.
                    —Alan Seeger, "I Have a Rendezvous with Death"

Death's the discharge of our debt of sorrow.   —Seneca

Not lost, but gone before.   —Seneca

That day which you fear as being the end of all things is the birthday
   of your eternity.   —Seneca

After life's fitful fever he sleeps well.
                    —William Shakespeare, *Macbeth*, Act III, Sc. ii

. . . all that lives must die, / Passing through nature to eternity.
                    —William Shakespeare, *Hamlet*, Act I, Sc. ii

. . . a man can die but once: we owe God a death.
                    —William Shakespeare, *King Henry IV, Part II*, Act III, Sc. ii

. . . And death unloads thee.
                    —William Shakespeare, *Measure for Measure*, Act III, Sc. i

. . . and death will have his day.
                    —William Shakespeare, *King Richard II*, Act III, Sc. ii

. . . gave . . . his pure soul unto his captain Christ.
                    —William Shakespeare, *King Richard II*, Act IV., Sc. i

If I must die,
   I will encounter darkness as a bride, / And hug it in mine arms.
                    —William Shakespeare, *Measure for Measure*, Act III, Sc. i

It seems to me most strange that men should fear, / Seeing that death,
   a necessary end, / Will come, when it will come.
                    —William Shakespeare, *Julius Caesar*, Act II, Sc. ii

Nothing in his life / Became him like the leaving of it.
                    —William Shakespeare, *Macbeth*, Act I, Sc. iv

The sense of death is most in apprehension, / And the poor beetle,
   that we tread upon, / In corporal sufferance finds a pang as great /
   As when a giant dies.
                    —William Shakespeare, *Measure for Measure*, Act III, Sc. i

This fell sergeant, death, / Is strict in his arrest.
                    —William Shakespeare, *Hamlet*, Act V, Sc. ii

We are such stuff / As dreams are made on, and our little life / Is rounded
   with a sleep.   —William Shakespeare, *The Tempest*, Act IV, Sc. i

. . . what's brave, what's noble, / Let's do it after the high Roman fashion, / And make death proud to take us.
                    —William Shakespeare, *Antony and Cleopatra*, Act IV, Sc. xiii

Dust to the dust! but the pure spirit shall flow / Back to the burning
    fountain whence it came, / A portion of the Eternal.
—Percy Shelley, Adonais

How wonderful is Death, / Death and his brother sleep!
—Percy Shelley, "The Daemon of the World"

Peace, Peace! He is not dead, he doth not sleep—He hath awakened
    from the dream of life.   —Percy Shelley, Adonais

If we were to live here always, with no other care than how to feed,
    clothe, and house ourselves, life would be a very sorry business. It
    is immeasurably heightened by the solemnity of death.
—Alexander Smith

I cannot forgive my friends for dying; I do not find these vanishing
    acts of theirs at all amusing.
—Logan Pearsall Smith, Afterthoughts, "Age and Death"

Be of good cheer about death, and know this of a truth, that no evil
    can happen to a good man, either in life or after death.   —Socrates

Death is one of two things. Either it is annihilation, and the dead
    have no consciousness of anything; or, as we are told, it is really a
    change: a migration of the soul from one place to another.
—Socrates

The hour of departure has arrived and we go our ways—I to die, and
    you to live. Which is the better, God only knows.   —Socrates

Say nothing but good of the dead.   —Solon

If there were no executioners, there would be no executions.
—Alexander Solzhenitsyn, The Gulag Archipelago Three

Not death itself, but only the moral preparation for it, holds terrors.
—Alexander Solzhenitsyn, The Gulag Archipelago Three

My name is Death: the last best friend am I.
—Robert Southey, Carmen Nuptiale,
"The Lay of the Laureate: the Dream"

We understand death for the first time when he puts his hand upon
    one whom we love.   —Madame de Staël

Old and young, we are all on our last cruise.
—Robert Louis Stevenson, *Virginibus Puerisque*,
"Crabbed Age and Youth"

There is no death—the thing that we call death / Is but another, sadder name for life, / Which is itself an insufficient name, / Faint recognition of that unknown life— / That Power whose shadow is the Universe. —Richard Henry Stoddard

It is impossible that anything so natural, so necessary, and so universal as death should ever have been designed by Providence as an evil to mankind. —Jonathan Swift

When we must go—then go, And make as little fuss as you can.
—T'ao Ch'ien

You must overcome death by finding God in it.
—Pierre Teilhard de Chardin, *The Divine Milieu*

God's finger touched him, and he slept.
—Alfred, Lord Tennyson, *In Memoriam A. H. H.*

I hope to see my Pilot face to face / When I have crost the bar.
—Alfred, Lord Tennyson, "Crossing the Bar"

Old men must die, or the world would grow mouldy, would only breed the past again. —Alfred, Lord Tennyson, *Becket*, Prologue

Trust that those we call the dead / Are breathers of an ampler day.
—Alfred, Lord Tennyson, *In Memoriam A. H. H.*, cxviii

Though they go mad they shall be sane, / Though they sink through the sea they shall rise again; / Though lovers be lost love shall not; / And death shall have no dominion. —Dylan Thomas, *25 Poems*,
"And Death Shall Have No Dominion"

Love is God, and to die means that I, a particle of love, shall return to the general eternal source. —Leo Tolstoy, *War and Peace*

Well, so it isn't time yet to die, is it? —Leo Tolstoy, *Anna Karenina*

Let us endeavor so to live that when we come to die even the undertaker will be sorry. —Mark Twain, *Pudd'nhead Wilson*

Odd how clear it suddenly became, once a person had died, that the body was the very least of him. —Anne Tyler, *The Accidental Tourist*

Something was wrong with a world where people came and went so easily. —Anne Tyler, *Saint Maybe*, Ch. 3

Is it then so sad a thing to die? —Virgil, *Aeneid*, Book XII, 646

These passions of soul, these conflicts so fierce, will cease, and be repressed by the casting of a little dust. —Virgil

To learn to die is an heroic work. —Mercy Otis Warren

Two months ago my mother died. She made, as the expression goes, a good death. —Larry Watson, *Montana 1948*

The tall, the wise, the reverend head, / Must lie as low as ours. —Isaac Watts

Take care of your life and the Lord will take care of your death. —George Whitefield

God gives quietness at last. —John Greenleaf Whittier

Death is the quiet haven of us all. —William Wordsworth

DEBTS

Happy is he who owes nothing. —Anonymous

Wilt thou seal up the avenues of ill? / Pay every debt as if God wrote the bill. —Ralph Waldo Emerson

Getting into debt, is getting into a tanglesome net. —Benjamin Franklin

My father taught me that a bill is like a crying baby and has to be attended to at once. —Anne Morrow Lindbergh

And looks the whole world in the face, / For he owes not any man. —Henry Wadsworth Longfellow, "The Village Blacksmith"

He that dies pays all debts. —William Shakespeare, *The Tempest*, Act III, Sc. ii

DECENCY

Decency is like gold, the same in all countries. —Li Hung-chang

I believe in an ultimate decency of things.
—Robert Louis Stevenson, letter, 23 Aug 1893

DECEPTION

Deceive not thy physician, confessor, nor lawyer.
—George Herbert, *Jacula Prudentum*

You can fool some of the people all of the time, and all of the people some of the time, but you cannot fool all of the people all of the time.
—Abraham Lincoln, speech in Bloomington, Illinois, 29 May 1856

We are easily duped by those we love.
—Molière

O what a tangled web we weave, / When first we practice to deceive!
—Sir Walter Scott, "Marmion"

DECISIONS

The man who insists upon seeing with perfect clearness before he decides, never decides.
—Henri Frédéric Amiel

All important decisions must be made on the basis of insufficient data.
—Anonymous

Decisions can take you out of God's will but never out of His reach.
—Anonymous

No one learns to make right decisions without being free to make wrong ones.
—Anonymous

If you come to a fork in the road, take it.
—Yogi Berra

Decide, v. i. To succumb to the preponderance of one set of influences over another set.
—Ambrose Bierce, *The Devil's Dictionary*

Wait, and thy soul shall speak.
—Ralph Waldo Emerson

It does not take much strength to do things, but it requires great strength to decide on what to do.
—Elbert Hubbard

The absence of alternatives clears the mind marvelously.
—Henry Kissinger

Caution always, but when a man acts he should act suddenly and with decision.
—Louis L'Amour, *The Walking Drum*

Decide promptly, but never give your reasons. Your decisions may be
    right, but your reasons are sure to be wrong.   —Lord Mansfield

. . . so many tremendous decisions in life are made because it is five
    o'clock.   —Arthur Miller

Deliberate often—decide once!   —Proverb (Latin)

That should be long considered which can be decided but once.
     —Publilius Syrus

Somewhere along the line of our development we discover what we
    really are, and then we make our decision for which we are respon-
    sible. Make that decision primarily for yourself because you can
    never really live anyone else's life.   —Eleanor Roosevelt

DEEDS

A tree is known by its fruit; a man by his deeds.   —Anonymous

Better do it than wish it done.   —Anonymous

Deeds are fruits, words are but leaves.   —Anonymous

Deeds are love and not fine phrases.   —Anonymous

He does much who does a little well.   —Anonymous

I am only one, but I am one; I cannot do everything, but I can do
    something. What I can do, I ought to do. And what I ought to do,
    by God's grace, I will do.   —Anonymous

It is a great thing to do little things well.   —Anonymous

Our deeds follow us, and what we have been makes us what we are.
     —Anonymous

People may doubt what you say, but they will always believe what
    you do.   —Anonymous

Nothing is eternal but that which is done for God and others. That
    which is done for self dies.   —Aughey

The search is in the doing.   —Joan Baez, television interview

We live in deeds, not years; in thoughts, not breaths; / In feelings, not in figures on a dial. / We should count time by heart-throbs. He most lives / Who thinks most—feels the noblest—acts the best.
—Philip James Bailey, *Festus*, v.

A good deed is never lost; he who sows courtesy reaps friendship, and he who plants kindness gathers love.
—Basil

Deeds not words.
—Francis Beaumont and John Fletcher

Not what I Have, but what I Do is my Kingdom.
—Thomas Carlyle, *Sartor Resartus*

Our grand business undoubtedly is not to see what lies dimly at a distance, but to do what lies clearly at hand.
—Thomas Carlyle, *Essays*, "Signs of the Times"

As I grow older, I pay less attention to what men say. I just watch what they do.
—Andrew Carnegie

Whatever is worth doing at all, is worth doing well.
—Earl of Chesterfield, letter to his son, 10 Mar 1746

Our deeds determine us . . . as much as we determine our deeds.
—George Eliot, *Adam Bede*, 29

Our deeds still travel with us from afar, / And what we have been makes us what we are.
—George Eliot, *Middlemarch*, heading of Ch. 70

The reward of a thing well done is to have done it.
—Ralph Waldo Emerson, *Essays*, "New England Reformers"

What you do speaks so loud that I cannot hear what you say.
—Ralph Waldo Emerson

Well done is better than well said.
—Benjamin Franklin, *Poor Richard's Almanack*, 1737

Whatever you can no longer bear, you do.
—Alan Harris

The shortest answer is doing.
—George Herbert, *Jacula Prudentum*

A noble deed is a step toward God.
—Josiah Gilbert Holland

We are the children of our own deeds.
—Victor Hugo

To do something is in every man's power. —Samuel Johnson

The greatest pleasure I know is to do a good action by stealth, and to
have it found out by accident. —Charles Lamb, "The Athenaeum"

Let us, then, be up and doing, / With a heart for any fate.
—Henry Wadsworth Longfellow, "A Psalm of Life"

. . . by doing you shall know / What it is you have to do.
—Thomas Lynch

Trust in God and do something. —Mary Lyon

I find that doing of the will of God leaves me no time for disputing
about His plans. —George Macdonald

There are thousands willing to do great things for one willing to do a
small thing. —George Macdonald

Deeds survive the doers. —Horace Mann

The only measure of what you believe is what you do.
—Ashley Montagu

You do what you can, and you do it because you should. But all you
can do is all you can do. —Dorothy Parker, "Song of the Shirt"

Do little things as if they were great, because of the majesty of the
Lord Jesus Christ who dwells in thee. —Blaise Pascal

Good deeds, when concealed, are the most admirable.
—Blaise Pascal, *Pensées*

One good turn deserves another. —Proverb (15th century)

Better to do a good deed near at home than go far away to burn
incense. —Proverb (Chinese)

It is not the knowing that is difficult, but the doing. —Proverb (Chinese)

The shortest answer is doing. —Proverb (English)

It is the deed that matters, not the fame. —Proverb (German)

From saying to doing is a long stride. —Proverb (Italian)

The deed is forgotten but its results remain.　　　—Proverb (Latin)

Rest satisfied with doing well, and leave others to talk of you as they please.　　　—Pythagoras

God does not want us to do extraordinary things; he wants us to do ordinary things extraordinarily well.　　　—Rabbi Bernard S. Raskas

Not a day passes over the earth, but men and women of no note do great deeds, speak great words and suffer noble sorrows.
　　　—Charles Reade, *The Cloister and the Hearth*, opening words

It is not the deed we do / Though the deed be never so fair, / But the love that the dear Lord looketh for, / Hidden with lovely care / In the heart of the deed so fair.　　　—Christina Rossetti

If it's going to be it's up to me. Better to do something imperfectly than to do nothing flawlessly.
　　　—Robert H. Schuller, *Winning Starts with Beginning*

A man can do only what he can do. But if he does that each day he can sleep at night and do it again the next day. —Albert Schweitzer

How far that little candle throws his beams! So shines a good deed in a naughty world.
　　　—William Shakespeare, *The Merchant of Venice*, Act V, Sc. i

It is the greatest of all mistakes to do nothing because you can only do a little. Do what you can.　　　—Sydney Smith

To do anything in this world worth doing, we must not stand back shivering and thinking of the cold and danger, but jump in, and scramble through as well as we can.　　　—Sydney Smith

Only one life, 'twill soon be past; / Only what's done for Christ will last.　　　—C. T. Studd

Good deeds are better than wise sayings.　　　—*The Talmud*

The point is not to do remarkable things, but to do ordinary things with the conviction of their immense importance.
　　　—Pierre Teilhard de Chardin

We can do no great things—only small things with great love.
　　　—Mother Teresa

Verily, when the day of judgment comes, we shall not be asked what we have read, but what we have done.
— Thomas à Kempis, *The Imitation of Christ*, 1

We're here to do something, not everything. —Henry David Thoreau

But with every deed you are sowing a seed, / Though the harvest you may not see.
— Ella Wheeler Wilcox, "You Never Can Tell," Stanza 2

Who does the best his circumstances allows / Does well, acts nobly; angels could do no more.
— Edward Young, *Night Thoughts*, "Night 2"

Doing good to others is not a duty. It is a joy, for it increases your own health and happiness. —Zoroaster

DEFEAT

Yet there is a dignity in the human spirit which can become most clearly visible in the moment of defeat and disaster. —Bruce Catton

Victory has a hundred fathers, but defeat is an orphan.
— Count Galeazzo Ciano, *Diary*, Vol. 2, 9 Sep 1942

We may be personally defeated, but our principles never.
— William Lloyd Garrison

Man is not made for defeat.
— Ernest Hemingway, *The Old Man and the Sea*

The only really fatal element in defeat is the resolution not to try again. —John Henry Jowett

Defeat may be victory in disguise. —Henry Wadsworth Longfellow

Do not despair. In every defeat are found the seeds of victory.
— Walter Mondale, speech after losing
U. S. Presidential election, 6 Nov 1984

There are some defeats more triumphant than victories.
— Michel de Montaigne

A man is not finished when he's defeated; he's finished when he quits. —Richard Nixon

Never talk defeat. Use words like hope, belief, faith, victory.
—Norman Vincent Peale

Every man meets his Waterloo at last.
—Wendell Phillips, speech in Brooklyn, 1 Nov 1859

What is defeat? Nothing but education, nothing but the first step to something better.
—Wendell Phillips

The purpose of life is to be defeated by greater and greater things.
—Rainier Maria Rilke

He had an idea that even when beaten he could steal a little victory by laughing at defeat.
—John Steinbeck, *East of Eden*

Defeat comes not so much from physical effects, as from a state of mind which makes men reduce or cease from their efforts.
—Gen. Charles P. Summerall

DEFENSE

The best armor is to keep out of range.
—Proverb (Italian)

DEGRADATION

Whoever degrades another degrades me.
—Walt Whitman, *Leaves of Grass*, "Song of Myself"

DÉJÀ VU

It's déjà vu all over again.
—Yogi Berra

DELAY

Delay is preferable to error.
—Thomas Jefferson, letter to George Washington, 16 May 1792

Every man has something to do which he neglects, every man has faults to conquer which he delays to combat.
—Samuel Johnson

Delays are dangerous.
—Proverb (14th century)

Delays have dangerous ends.
—William Shakespeare, *King Henry VI, Part I*, Act II, Sc. ii

. . . delay is itself a decision.
—Theodore Sorenson

DELIBERATION

He who considers too much will accomplish little.—Friedrich Schiller

DELUSIONS

No man is happy without a delusion of some kind. Delusions are as necessary to our happiness as realities. —Christian Nestell Bovée

DEMOCRACY

Democracy is the worst system devised by the wit of man, except for all the others. —Winston Churchill

My political ideal is democracy. Let every man be respected as an individual and no man idolized.
—Albert Einstein, *Forum and Century*

Democracy is based upon the conviction that there are extraordinary possibilities in ordinary people. —Harry Emerson Fosdick

Democracy is not simply a political system; it is a moral movement and it springs from adventurous faith in human possibilities.
—Harry Emerson Fosdick, *Adventurous Religion*

Democracy is measured not by its leaders doing extraordinary things, but by its citizens doing ordinary things extraordinarily well.
—John Gardner

Democracy depends on information circulating freely in society.
—Katherine Graham

Even though counting heads is not an ideal way to govern, at least it is better than breaking them.
—Learned Hand, speech, Federal Bar Association, 8 Mar 1932

Democracy does not necessarily result from majority rule, but rather from the forged compromise of the majority with the minority . . . The philosophy of the Constitution . . . is not simply to grant the majority the power to rule but is also to set limitation after limitation upon that power . . . —Senator Daniel Ken Inouye

We can be so democratic that nothing gets done. —Nadine Jay

Democracy is the government of the people, by the people, for the people. —Abraham Lincoln

No man is good enough to govern another man without that other's consent.   —Abraham Lincoln, speech, 16 Oct 1854

Man's capacity for evil makes democracy necessary and man's capacity for good makes democracy possible.   —Reinhold Niebuhr

Democracy means not "I am as good as you are," but "you are as good as I am."   —Theodore Parker

Although Christianity has never been the guarantee of a democratic state anywhere in the world, no democracy has ever thrived successfully for any period of time outside of Christian influence.
—Theodore H. White

DENOMINATIONS

I do not want the walls of separation between different orders of Christians to be destroyed, but only lowered, that we may shake hands a little easier over them.   —Rowland Hill

DENUNCIATION

It is better to go to prison for life rather than denounce someone.
—Pio Baroja, *La Dama Errante*

DEPENDABILITY

The greatest ability is dependability.   —Curt Bergwall

DEPRESSION

It is important for depressed people to remember that most get better—especially when there is counseling and the support of friends.
—Gary R. Collins, *The Magnificent Mind*

While each of us . . . has depressed hours, none of us needs to be a depressed person.   —Harry Emerson Fosdick

Depression is a partial surrender to death.   —Arnold A. Hutschnecker

Depression is the inability to construct a future.   —Rollo May

Awake, arise, or be forever fall'n!
—John Milton, *Paradise Lost*, Book I, line 330

Depression is such a waste of valuable time.
—Frank B. Minirth and Paul D. Meier, *Happiness is a Choice*

Having been depressed, I am exalted.
—Proverb (Latin)

Becoming active is the key remedy for depression.
—Pat Robertson, *Answers to 200 of Life's Most Probing Questions*

Depression is melancholy minus its charms.
—Susan Sontag

DESERVING

'Tis not in mortals to command success, / But we'll do more,
Sempronius; we'll deserve it.
—Joseph Addison, *Cato*, I, ii.

To well deserve is somewhat, in spite of ill success.
—Martin Farquhar Tupper

DESIRE

Discontents do arise from our desires oftener than from our needs.
—Anonymous

Three basic desires of man—to be loved, to be secure, to be valuable.
—Anonymous

I count him braver who conquers his desires than him who conquers
his enemies; for the hardest victory is the victory over self.
—Aristotle

Where desire doth bear the sway, / The heart must rule, the head obey.
—Francis Davison

Freedom is obtained not by the enjoyment of what is desired but by
controlling desire itself.
—Epictetus, *Discourses*

Two things only the people anxiously desire—bread and circuses.
—Juvenal, *Satires*, X

DESPAIR

You may not know it, but at the far end of despair, there is a white
clearing where one is almost happy.
—Jean Anouilh, *Restless Heart*

I learned to love despair.
—Lord Byron, *The Prisoner of Chillon*

He that despairs degrades the Deity, and seems to intimate that he is insufficient, or not just to his word; in vain hath he read the Scriptures, the world, and man.   —Owen Feltham

In a real dark night of the soul it is always three o'clock in the morning, day after day.   —F. Scott Fitzgerald, "The Crack-Up"

I have plumbed the depths of despair and have found them not bottomless.   —Thomas Hardy

Despair lames most people, but it wakes others fully up.
    —William James

Manhood is the ability to outlast despair.   —James Jones

So long as one does not despair, so long as one doesn't look upon life bitterly, things work out fairly well in the end.   —George Moore

Despair is the only genuine atheism.   —Jean Paul

Human life begins on the other side of despair.
    —Jean-Paul Sartre, *The Flies*

. . . from the heights of worldly glory I am astonished by the path through despair You have provided me.
    —Alexander Solzhenitsyn, 1962, in *Vogue*, Christmas issue, 1971

It is impossible for that man to despair who remembers that his Helper is omnipotent.   —Jeremy Taylor

Never despair, but if you do, work on in despair.   —Terence

DESPERATION

Beware of desperate steps; the darkest day, lived till tomorrow, will have passed away.   —William Cowper

. . . tempt not a desperate man.
    —William Shakespeare, *Romeo and Juliet*, Act V, Sc. iii

In all probability an outburst of desperation in the midst of general submissiveness will always help.
    —Alexander Solzhenitsyn, *The Gulag Archipelago*

The mass of men lead lives of quiet desperation.
    —Henry David Thoreau, *Walden*, "Economy"

Nowadays most men lead lives of noisy desperation. —James Thurber

D E S T I N Y

Riddle of destiny, who can show / What thy short visit meant, or
know / What thy errand here below?   —Charles Lamb

One meets his destiny often in the road he takes to avoid it.
—Proverb (French)

This generation of Americans has a rendezvous with destiny.
—Franklin D. Roosevelt, speech, 1936

. . . there is this feeling that I have a destiny far away from the shallow and preposterous posing that is our life . . .
—Kurt Vonnegut, Jr., *God Bless You, Mr. Rosewater*

D E T A I L S

Exactness in little things is a wonderful source of cheerfulness.
—Frederick William Faber

Less is more. God is in the details.   —Mies van der Rohe

We think in generalities, but we live in detail.
—Alfred North Whitehead

D E T E R M I N A T I O N

The longer I live, the more deeply am I convinced that that which
makes the difference between one man and another—between the
weak and powerful, the great and insignificant is energy—invincible determination—a purpose once formed, and then death or victory.   —Fowell Buxton

The DEVIL

The devil's snare does not catch you, unless you are first caught by
the devil's bait.   —Saint Ambrose

Few may play with the devil and win.   —Anonymous

Open not your door when the devil knocks.   —Anonymous

Prince of darkness, begone.   —Anonymous

Satan keeps school for neglected children. —Anonymous

The devil will promise you the whole world, but he doesn't own a
    grain of sand. —Anonymous

When the devil is called the god of this world, it is not because he
    made it, but because we serve him with our worldliness.
                  —Saint Thomas Aquinas

Is Satan omnipresent? No, but he is very spry. Is he bound? Yes, but
    with a rather loose rope. —William Ashmore

The Devil's best ruse is to persuade us that he does not exist.
               —Charles Baudelaire, *Petis Poèmes*

. . . Get thee behind me, Satan . . .   —*The Bible* (KJV): Matthew 16:23

Rage on, Satan.
   —Jim Brannon, sermon, Hope Chapel, Austin, Texas, 16 Nov 1991

The heart of man is the place the devil dwells in: I feel sometimes a
    hell within myself.
           —Sir Thomas Browne, *Religio Medici*, Part I, sec 51

The devil's most devilish when respectable.
   —Elizabeth Barrett Browning, *Aurora Leigh*, Book VII, line 105

There is a battle going on for the minds of people. We do need to be
    alert to the devil's schemes and subtle teachings that masquerade
    as truth in our society. But the way to resist such mental error is
    not with emotional diatribes. Instead there needs to be a clear
    understanding of the Bible's teaching about demonic error, accom-
    panied by a committed submission to the commands of scripture.
           —Gary R. Collins, *The Magnificent Mind*

. . . even the devil works for God.   —Judy Collins, *Shameless*, Ch. 62

Better sit still, than rise to meet the devil.   —Michael Drayton

Better keep the devil at the door than turn him out of the house.
            —Thomas Fuller, M. D., *Gnomologia*

They who play with the devil's rattles will be brought by degrees to
    wield his sword. —Thomas Fuller

Whenever I am conscious of satan's presence, I try to follow the formula once offered by a little girl: "When satan knocks, I just send Christ to the door."
—Billy Graham

The devil has got to be resisted, not merely deprecated.
—Michael Green

Keep doing something, so that the devil may always find you occupied.
—Saint Jerome

It is Lucifer, / The son of mystery; / And since God suffers him to be, / He too, is God's minister, / And labors for some good / By us not understood.
—Henry Wadsworth Longfellow

I believe Satan to exist for two reasons: first, the Bible says so, and second, I've done business with him.
—Dwight L. Moody

Better not read books in which you make acquaintance of the devil.
—Reinhold Niebuhr

Better the devil you know than the devil you don't know.
—Proverb (19th century)

He that takes the Devil into his boat must carry him over the sound.
—Proverb (English)

When the Devil finds the door is shut, he goes away.
—Proverb (French)

The devil catches most souls in a golden net.
—Proverb (German)

The Devil and me, we don't agree;
I hate him, and he hates me.
—Salvation Army hymn

. . . the devil can cite Scripture for his purpose.
—William Shakespeare, *The Merchant of Venice*, Act I, Sc. iii

. . . the devil hath power / To assume a pleasing shape.
—William Shakespeare, *Hamlet*, Act II, Sc. ii

Since the Lord wasn't in charge of my life, Satan was.
—Warren Walden, from his testimony at Hope Chapel, Austin, Texas, 13 Jun 1992

The devil protects his own, as long as they are serving him.
—Kathleen Watkins, 1 May 1992

The Devil never tempts us with more success than when he tempts us with a sight of our own good actions. —Bishop Wilson

DICTATORS

Dictators ride to and fro on tigers from which they dare not dismount. —Proverb (Hindustani)

DICTIONARIES

Dictionaries are like watches; the worst is better than none, and the best cannot be expected to go quite true.
—Samuel Johnson, in Jester Lynch Piozzi,
Anecdotes of Samuel Johnson

DIETS

I'm on a seafood diet. I see food and I eat it. —Anonymous

At the end of every diet, the path curves back toward the trough.
—Mason Cooley

Diets are for those who are thick and tired of it. —Mary Tyler Moore

The waist is a terrible thing to mind. —Tom Wilson, "Ziggy"

The DIFFICULT

Not everything that is more difficult is more meritorious.
—Saint Thomas Aquinas

What is difficult? To keep a secret, to employ leisure well, to be able to bear an injury. —Chilon

DIFFICULTIES

When difficulties are overcome they become blessings. —Anonymous

In the middle of difficulty lies opportunity. —Albert Einstein

It is difficulties that show what men are. —Epictetus

A man's worst difficulties begin when he is able to do as he likes.
—Thomas Henry Huxley

Out of difficulties grow miracles. —Jean de La Bruyère

Don't dodge difficulties; meet them, greet them, beat them. All great men have been through the wringer. —Alfred Armand Montapert

When you encounter difficulties and contradictions, do not try to break them, but bend them with gentleness and time.
—Saint Francis de Sales

To overcome difficulties is to experience the full delight of existence.
—Arthur Schopenhauer

Difficulties strengthen the mind, as labor does the body. —Seneca

Many men owe the grandeur of their lives to their tremendous difficulties. —Charles H. Spurgeon

DIGNITY

A man can dignify his rank; no rank
  Can dignify a man. —Lucius Accius

Dignity does not consist in possessing honors, but in deserving them.
—Aristotle

The dignity of man lies in his ability to face reality in all its meaninglessness. —Martin Esslin

No race can prosper till it learns that there is as much dignity in tilling a field as in writing a poem.
—Booker T. Washington, *Up From Slavery*

DIPLOMACY

Diplomacy is the art of letting someone else have your way.
—Anonymous

Diplomacy is the art of saying "Nice doggie" until you can find a rock. —Will Rogers

Diplomacy has rarely been able to gain at the conference table what cannot be gained or held on the battlefield.
—Gen. Walter Bedell Smith

A diplomat is a person who can tell you to go to hell in such a way that you actually look forward to the trip.
—Caskie Stinnet, *Out of the Red*

DIRECTION

The great thing in the world is not so much where we stand, as in
what direction we are moving.
—Oliver Wendell Holmes, Sr., *The Autocrat of the Breakfast Table*

Whichever way you point a wagon tongue, that's the way it goes.
—Proverb (Russian)

DISAPPOINTMENT

Disappointments are His appointments.   —Anonymous

I've had a lot to do with glue and the experiences have almost always
been disappointing.
—Andrew A. Rooney, *And More by Andy Rooney*, "Glue"

DISARMAMENT

People will not disarm step by step; they will disarm at one blow or
not at all.   —Albert Einstein, *Ideas and Opinions*

Let there be more corn and more meat and let there be no hydrogen
bombs at all.   —Nikita Kruschchev

In disarming Peter, Christ disarmed every soldier.   —Tertullian

DISASTER

Any disaster you can survive is an improvement in your character,
your stature, and your life. What a privilege!   —Joseph Campbell

DISCIPLINE

Discipline is the refining fire by which talent becomes ability.
—Roy L. Smith

DISCOMFORT

Even our discomfort has meaning in God's plan.   —Anonymous

DISCONTENT

He that is discontented in one place will seldom be happy in another.
—Aesop, *Fables*, "The Ass and His Masters"

Discontent is the first step in the progress of a man or a nation. Bad will be the day for every man when he becomes absolutely contented with the life that he is living, with the thoughts that he is thinking, and with the deeds that he is doing.   —Phillips Brooks

Intelligent discontent is the mainspring of civilization.
                                                            —Eugene V. Debs

To the discontented man no chair is easy.   —Benjamin Franklin

What makes us discontented with our condition is the absurdly exaggerated idea we have of the happiness of others. —Proverb (French)

The splendid discontent of God with Chaos, made the world; and from the discontent of man the world's best progress springs.
                                        —Ella Wheeler Wilcox, "Discontent"

DISCOURAGEMENT

Don't discourage the other man's plans unless you have better ones to offer.   —Anonymous

More people fail through discouragement than for any other reason.
                                                            —Anonymous

DISCOVERY

First doubt, then inquire, then discover. This has been the process with all our great thinkers.   —Anonymous

Eureka! [I have found it!]
            —Archimedes, upon his discovery of the law of buoyancy

The great obstacle to discovery is not ignorance; it is the illusion of knowledge.   —Daniel J. Boorstein

One doesn't discover new lands without consenting to lose sight of the shore.   —André Gide

It is a profound mistake to think that every thing has been discovered; as well think the horizon the boundary of the world.
                                            —Antoine-Marin Lemierre

All great discoveries are made by men whose feelings run ahead of their thinkings.   —Charles H. Parkhurst

The real voyage of discovery consists not in seeking new landscapes
but in having new eyes. —Marcel Proust

Discovery consists in seeing what everybody has seen and thinking
what nobody has thought. —Albert von Szent-Györgyi

DISCRETION

Thy friend has a friend, and thy friend's friend has a friend; be discreet.
—*The Talmud*

DISCRIMINATION

"In the end, antiblack, antifemale, and all forms of discrimination are
equivalent to the same thing-antihumanism."
—Shirley Chisholm, *Unbought and Unbossed*

DISEASE

A disease known is half cured.
—Thomas Fuller, M. D., *Gnomologia*, No. 75

. . . this long Disease, my Life.
—Alexander Pope, *Epistles and Satires of Horace Imitated*,
"An Epistle to Dr. Arbuthnot"

He who conceals his disease cannot expect to be cured.
—Proverb (Ethiopian)

Where there is sunshine the doctor starves. —Proverb (Flemish)

A disease is farther on the road to being cured when it breaks forth
from concealment and manifests its power.
—Seneca, *Epistuloe ad Lucilium*, Epistle lvi, Sec. 10

DISORDERLINESS

One of the advantages of being disorderly is that one is constantly
making exciting discoveries. —A. A. Milne

DISPOSITION

A sweet temper is to the household what sunshine is to trees and
flowers. —Anonymous

Good temper oils the wheels of life. —Anonymous

You are not responsible for the disposition you are born with, but you
  are responsible for the one you die with.
> —Maltbie Davenport Babcock

Good-humor makes all things tolerable. —Henry Ward Beecher

Good humor is the sunshine of the mind. —Edward Bulwer-Lytton

From suffering God alone can shield thee, ill-humor thou canst spare
  thyself.
> —Giebel

Good temper is an estate for life.
> —William Hazlitt, *Plain Speaker*, "On Personal Character"

The wearer of smiles and the bearer of a kindly disposition needs no
  introduction, but is welcome anywhere. —O. S. Marden

Even if you put a snake in a bamboo tube, you cannot change its
  wriggling disposition. —Proverb (Japanese)

. . . the greater part of our happiness or misery depends on our dispositions and not on our circumstances. —Martha Washington

DISTRESS

Distress is virtue's opportunity: we only live to teach us to die.
> —Southern

DIVINITY

Our humanity were a poor thing were it not for the divinity that stirs
  within us. —Francis Bacon

There is surely a piece of Divinity in us, something that was before
  the elements, and owes no homage to the sun.
> —Sir Thomas Browne, *Religio Medici*, II

There is a divinity within our breast.
> —Ovid, *Epistuloe ex Ponto*, Book III

The soul has this proof of divinity: that divine things delight it.
> —Seneca, *Quoestionum Naturalium*

. . . There's a divinity that shapes our ends,
  Rough-hew them how we will.
> —William Shakespeare, *Hamlet*, Act VI, Sc. ii

DIVISION

Division has done more to hide Christ from the view of men than all the infidelity that has ever been spoken.　　—George Macdonald

DIVORCE

. . . Whosoever shall put away his wife, except it be for fornication, and shall marry another, committeth adultery . . .
　　　　　　　　—*The Bible* (KJV): Matthew 19:9

DOCTRINE

There is one sure criterion of judgment as to religious faith in doctrinal matters; can you reduce it to practice? If not, have none of it.
　　　　　　　　—Hosea Ballou

False doctrine does not necessarily make a man a heretic, but an evil heart can make any doctrine heretical.　　—Samuel Taylor Coleridge

The conduct of our lives is the true mirror of our doctrine.
　　—Michel de Montaigne, *Essays*, "Of the Education of the Children"

Live to explain thy doctrine by thy life.　　　　　—Matthew Prior

DOGS

The great pleasure of a dog is that you may make a fool of yourself with him and not only will he not scold you, he will make a fool of himself too.　　　　—Samuel Butler (1835-1902), *Note-books*

To his dog, every man is Napoleon, hence the constant popularity of dogs.　　　　　　　—Aldous Huxley

A dog in a kennel barks at his fleas; a dog hunting does not notice them.　　　　　　　—Proverb (Chinese)

One dog barks at something; the rest bark at him.—Proverb (Chinese)

DOORS

Don't ever slam the door; you might want to go back.　—Don Herold

Not many sounds in life, and I include all urban and all rural sounds, exceed in interest a knock at the door.
　　　　　—Charles Lamb, *Essays of Elia*, "Valentine's Day"

... a door is what a dog is perpetually on the wrong side of.
　　　　　—Ogden Nash, "A Dog's Best Friend is His Illiteracy"

D O U B T

Doubt makes the mountain which faith can move.
　　　　　—Anonymous, from the *Toledo* (Ohio) *Blade,* Jan 1931

If a man will begin with certainties, he shall end in doubts; but if he
will be content to begin with doubts, he shall end in certainties.
　　　　　—Francis Bacon, *The Advancement of Learning*

Who never doubted never half believed; / Where doubt, there truth
is,—'tis her shadow.
　　　　　—Philip James Bailey, *Festus*, "A Country Town"

Doubt is an incentive to truth and patient inquiry leadeth the way.
　　　　　—Hosea Ballou

If the sun and moon should doubt / They'd immediately go out.
　　　　　—William Blake, *The Marriage of Heaven and Hell*

We reach the rock of thought when we can no longer doubt; and
therefore we reach it only by doubting.
　　　　　—J. Bronowski and Bruce Mazlish, *The Western Intellectual Tradition*

The more of doubt, the stronger faith, I say, / If faith o'ercomes doubt.
　　　　　—Robert Browning, *Bishop Blougram's Apology*

Through doubt we arrive at the truth.　　　　　　　　—Cicero

If you would be a real seeker after truth, it is necessary that at least
once in your life you doubt, as far as possible, all things.
　　　　　—René Descartes, *Principles of Philosophy*

For right is right, since God is God, / And right the day must win; / To
doubt would be disloyalty, / To falter would be sin.
　　　　　—Frederick William Faber

To have doubted one's own first principles, is the mark of a civilized
man.　　　　　　　　　　　　　　—Oliver Wendell Holmes, Jr.

Question with boldness even the existence of God; because, if there
be one, he must more approve of the homage of reason than that
of blindfolded fear.
　　　　　—Thomas Jefferson, letter to Peter Carr, 10 Aug 1787

Doubts we all have.
> —Bernard Malamud, *Rembrandt's Hat*, "The Silver Crown"

I respect faith, but doubt is what gets you an education.
> —Wilson Mizner, in Alva Johnston, *The Legendary Mizners*

The trouble with the world is that the stupid are cocksure and the intelligent full of doubt.
> —Bertrand Russell

. . . modest doubt is call'd / The beacon of the wise.
> —William Shakespeare, *Troilus and Cressida*, Act II, Sc. ii

Our doubts are traitors / And make us lose the good we oft might win / By fearing to attempt.
> —William Shakespeare, *Measure for Measure*, Act I, Sc. iv

Faith and doubt both are needed—not as antagonists but working side by side—to take us around the unknown curve.
> —Lillian Smith, *The Journey*

. . . that maxim of Descartes: "Question everything!" Question everything!
> —Alexander Solzhenitsyn, *The Gulag Archipelago*

To believe with certainty we must begin with doubting.
> —King Stanislaw II

Cleave ever to the sunnier side of doubt.
> —Alfred, Lord Tennyson, *The Ancient Sage*, 68

There lives more faith in honest doubt,
Believe me, than in half the creeds.
> —Alfred, Lord Tennyson, *In Memoriam A. H. H.*, lxcvi

When you are in doubt abstain.
> —Zoroaster

DRAMA

My life has a superb cast but I can't figure out the plot.
> —Ashleigh Brilliant

Drama is life with the dull bits cut out.
> —Alfred Hitchcock

True tragedy may be defined as a dramatic work in which the outward failure of the principal personage is compensated for by the dignity and greatness of his character.
> —Joseph Wood Krutch, *Nine Plays by Eugene O'Neill*, Introduction

The real object of the drama is the exhibition of human character.
—Thomas Babington Macaulay

Drama—what literature does at night.
—George Jean Nathan, *The Testament of a Critic* (1931)

All the world's a stage and most of us are desperately unrehearsed.
—Sean O'Casey

A novel is a static thing that one moves through; a play is a dynamic thing that moves past one. —Kenneth Tynan

DREAMS

Plan your castle in the air, / Then build a ship to take you there.
—Anonymous

If there were dreams to sell, / What would you buy?
—Thomas Lovell Beddoes, "Dream-Pedlary"

I've always believed that dreams were both the love letters and the hate mail of the subconscious.
—Pat Conroy, *The Prince of Tides*, Ch. 7

Dreaming permits each and every one of us to be quietly and safely insane every night of our lives. —William Dement

To accomplish great things, we must dream as well as act.
—Anatole France

. . . but a dream is nothing more than reality shorn of cynicism.
—Joseph F. Girzone, *Joshua in the Holy Land*, Ch. 19

Dream no small dreams for they have no power to move the hearts of men. —Johann Wolfgang von Goethe

We only stay alive by pipe dreams.
—Mark Harris, *It Looked Life For Ever*

Did anyone ever have a boring dream? —Ralph Hodgson

Dreams are sent by God. —Homer, *The Iliad*

There is nothing like a dream to create the future. —Victor Hugo

The poor man is not he who is without cent, but he who is without a dream. —Harry Kemp

. . . if you have nothing, you are free to choose among dreams and
    fantasies.   —Doris Lessing, *The Memoirs of a Survivor*

And what they dare to dream of, dare to do.
                —James Russell Lowell, "Ode Recited at the Harvard
                                   Commemoration," 1865

All that we see or seem / Is but a dream within a dream.
                —Edgar Allan Poe, "A Dream Within a Dream"

The future belongs to those who believe in the beauty of their
    dreams.   —Eleanor Roosevelt

It's unfulfilled dreams that keep you alive.   —Robert H. Schuller

You see things; and you say, "Why?" But I dream things that never
    were; and I say, "Why not?"
                —George Bernard Shaw, *Back to Methuselah*

In the drowsy dark cave of the mind dreams build their nest with
    fragments dropped from day's caravan.
                      —Rabindranath Tagore, *Fireflies*

If one advances confidently in the direction of his dreams, and
    endeavors to live the life he has imagined, he will meet with a suc-
    cess unexpected in common hours.   —Henry David Thoreau

I wonder how many times we dream that kind of dream—something
    strange and illogical—and fail to realize God is trying to tell us
    something.   —Anne Tyler, *Saint Maybe*, Ch. 7

D U T Y

The best way to get rid of unpleasant duties is to discharge them
    faithfully.   —Anonymous

What is thy duty? To accept the challenge of the passing day.
                              —Anonymous

We are supposed to do something for our kind.
                  —Saul Bellow, *Humboldt's Gift*

Do what you have in hand, and God will show what thing is next to
    do.   —Beneke

You have not fulfilled every duty unless you have fulfilled that of
    being pleasant.   —Charles Buxton

"Do the duty which lies nearest thee," which thou knowest to be thy
duty. Thy second duty will already have become clear.
—Thomas Carlyle, *Sartor Resartus*

This little life has its duties that are great—that are alone great, and
that go up to heaven and down to hell.   —Thomas Carlyle

Do the duty which lies nearest to thee.
—Johann Wolfgang von Goethe

I do not have to make over the universe; I have only to do my job,
great or small, and to look often at the trees and the hills and the
sky, and be friendly with all men.   —David Grayson

God obligeth no man to more than he hath given him ability to perform.   —*The Koran*

For truth and duty it is ever the fitting time; who waits until circumstances completely favor his undertaking will never accomplish
anything.   —Martin Luther

England expects every man to do his duty.
—Admiral Horatio Nelson, signaled to the fleet before the Battle of
Trafalgar, in Robert Southey, *The Life of Nelson*

Do well the duty that lies before you.   —Pittacus

Learn to commend thy daily acts to God, so shall the dry every-day
duties of common life be steps to heaven, and lift they heart
hither.   —Edward B. Pusey

God never imposes a duty without giving time to do it.
—John Ruskin, *Lectures on Architecture*, No. 2

There is no duty we so much underrate as the duty of being happy.
—Robert Louis Stevenson

— E —

EARTH

Give me but one firm spot on which to stand, and I will move the
earth. —Archimedes, about the lever

Earth's crammed with heaven, / And every common bush afire with
God. —Elizabeth Barrett Browning, *Aurora Leigh*

Right now I am a passenger on space vehicle Earth zooming about the
Sun at 60,000 miles per hour somewhere in the solar system.
—R. Buckminster Fuller, in Gene Youngblood, *Expanded Cinema*

Yet it does move.
—Galileo Galilei, traditional words after being forced to
recant his doctrine that the earth moves around the sun

The earth is like the breasts of a woman: useful as well as pleasing.
—Friedrich Nietzsche, *Thus Spake Zarathustra*,
"On Old and New Tablets"

. . . the earth weeps as it turns.
—Louis M. Savary and Maureen P. Collins, *Peace, War & Youth*

. . . man is eating the earth up like a candy bar.
—Anne Sexton, *The Awful Rowing Toward God*,
"The Earth Falls Down"

We are so attached to the earth, and yet we are incapable of holding
onto it. —Alexander Solzhenitsyn, *Cancer Ward*

We are pilgrims, not settlers; this earth is our inn, not our home.
—J. H. Vincent

ECCENTRICITY

That so few dare to be eccentric marks the chief danger of the time.
—John Stuart Mill, *On Liberty*, Ch. 3

Psychiatrists were presumed to be more entitled to eccentricities than
ordinary folks. —Craig Stafford, *The Walk of the Penguins*

ECOLOGY

The first law of ecology is that everything is related to everything
else. —Barry Commoner

ECONOMY

Economy is of itself a great revenue. —Cicero

Inflation: when nobody has enough money because everybody has
too much. —Harold Coffin

Upper classes are a nation's past; the middle class is its future.
—Ayn Rand

Economy is too late at the bottom of the purse.
—Seneca, *Epistulie ad Lucilium*, Epistle I, Sec. 5

Economy is half the battle of life; it is not so hard to earn money as to
spend it well. —Charles H. Spurgeon

It's a recession when your neighbor loses his job; it's a depression
when you lose your own. —Harry S. Truman

The economy is a thoughtless weather system.
—Kurt Vonnegut, Jr., *Jailbird*

EDUCATION

What sculpture is to a block of marble, education is to the soul.
—Joseph Addison

Education is the sum total of one's experience, and the purpose of
higher education is to widen our experiences beyond the circum-
scribed existence or our own daily lives. —Mortimer Adler

A child promoted to a new class said to a dearly beloved teacher: "I
wish you knew enough to teach me next year." —Anonymous

Education covers a lot of ground, but it doesn't cultivate it.
—Anonymous

Education is not received. It is achieved. —Anonymous

It is the mark of an educated mind to be able to entertain a thought
without accepting it. —Aristotle

It takes most men five years to recover from a college education, and to learn that poetry is as vital to thinking as knowledge.
—Brooks Atkinson, *Once Around the Sun*, "August 31"

Education commences at the mother's knee, and every word spoken within the hearing of little children tends towards the formation of character.
—Hosea Ballou

There are three schoolmasters for everybody that will employ them—the senses, intelligent companions, and books.
—Henry Ward Beecher

A good education is not so much one which prepares a man to succeed in the world, as one which enables him to sustain failure.
—Bernard Iddings Bell

The moment the little boy is concerned with which is a jay and which is a sparrow, he can no longer see the birds or hear them sing.
—Eric Berne

If you think education is expensive, try ignorance.   —Derek Bok

Public instruction should be the first object of government.
—Napoleon Bonaparte

Education makes people easy to lead, but difficult to drive; easy to govern, but impossible to enslave.
—Henry Peter Brougham, speech, House of Commons, 29 Jan 1828

I question whether we can afford to teach mother macramé when Johnny still can't read. —Jerry Brown, when governor of California

Without education we are in a horrible and deadly danger of taking educated people seriously.   —G. K. Chesterton

What greater work is there than training the mind and forming the habits of the young?   —John Chrysostom

I wrote my name at the top of the page. I wrote down the number of the question "1". After much reflection I put a bracket round it thus "(1)". But thereafter I could not think of anything connected with it that was either relevant or true.
—Winston Churchill, *My Early Life*

A university is what a college becomes when the faculty loses interest.
—John Ciardi

Cultivation to the mind is as necessary as food to the body.   —Cicero

Every person has two educations: one which he receives from others, and one more important, which he gives himself.
—Charles Caleb Colton

Teachers open the door . . . you enter by yourself.   —Confucius

The school is not the end but only the beginning of education.
—Calvin Coolidge

The aim of education should be to teach the child to think, not what to think.   —John Dewey

The average Ph.D. thesis is nothing but the transference of bones from one graveyard to another.—J. Frank Dobie, *A Texan in England*

How is it that little children are so intelligent and men are so stupid? It must be education that does it.
—Alexandre Dumas, in L. Treich, *L'Esprit Francais*

You can lade a man up to th' university, but ye can't make him think.
—Finley Peter Dunne, *Mr. Carnegie's Gift*

Education is progressive discovery of our ignorance.   —Will Durant

Education is that which remains, if one has forgotten everything he learned in school.   —Albert Einstein, *Ideas and Opinions*

Knowledge is dead; the school, however, serves the living.
—Albert Einstein, *Ideas and Opinions*

The development of general ability for independent thinking and judgment should always be placed foremost, not the acquisition of special knowledge.   —Albert Einstein, *Ideas and Opinions*

The most important method of education always has consisted of that in which the pupil was urged to actual performance.
—Albert Einstein

Everything is prospective, and man is to live hereafter. That the world is for his education is the only sane solution of the enigma.
—Ralph Waldo Emerson

Meek young men grow up in colleges and believe it is their duty to accept the views which books have given, and grow up slaves.
—Ralph Waldo Emerson, *Journals*

The office of the scholar is to cheer, to raise, and to guide men by
   showing them facts amidst appearances.   —Ralph Waldo Emerson

The secret of education lies in respecting the pupil.
                                             —Ralph Waldo Emerson

The things taught in schools are not an education but the means of
   an education.   —Ralph Waldo Emerson, *Journals*

Only the educated are free.
                        —Epictetus, *Discourses*, Book II, Ch. 1, Sec. 23

An education isn't how much we have committed to memory, or
   even how much we know. It's being able to differentiate between
   what you do know and what you don't. It's knowing where to go to
   find out what you need to know; and it's knowing how to use the
   information once you get it.   —William Feather

What did you ask at school today?   —Richard Fenyman

Genius without education is like silver in the mine.
               —Benjamin Franklin, *Poor Richard's Almanack*, 1750

If a man empties his purse into his head, no one can take it from him.
                                             —Benjamin Franklin

Education doesn't change life much. It just lifts trouble to a higher
   plane of regard . . . College is a refuge from hasty judgment.
                                             —Robert Frost

All I ever needed to know I learned in kindergarten. Share everything
   . . . Don't hit people . . . Clean up your own mess . . .
               —Robert Fulghum, *All I Really Need to Know I Learned in
                                                      Kindergarten*

The ultimate goal of the educational system is to shift to the individual the burden of pursuing his education.   —John W. Gardner

If you feel that you have both feet planted on level ground, then the
   university has failed you.
               —Robert Goheen, when president of Princeton University

A college education shows a man how little other people know.
                                   —Thomas Chandler Haliburton

Our educational system gives the children neat answers long before
   they care about the questions.   —Alan Harris

Fathers send their sons to college either because they went to college
or because they didn't. —L. L. Hendren

The main part of intellectual education is not the acquisition of facts
but learning how to make facts live.
—Oliver Wendell Holmes, Jr., speech, Harvard Law School
Association, 5 Nov 1886

I never saw the man that couldn't teach me something.
—Oliver Wendell Holmes, Sr.

Every man should have a college education in order to show him
how little the thing is really worth. —Elbert Hubbard

He who opens a school door closes a prison. —Victor Hugo

The object of education is to prepare the young to educate themselves throughout their lives. —Robert Maynard Hutchens

The true purpose of education is to cherish and unfold the seed of
immortality already sown within us. —Anna Jameson

This institution will be based on the illimitable freedom of the
human mind. For here we are not afraid to follow truth wherever it
may lead, nor to tolerate error so long as reason is free to combat it.
—Thomas Jefferson, to prospective teachers
of the University of Virginia

Education is not a product: mark, diploma, job, money—in that
order; it is a process, a never-ending one.
—Bel Kaufman, television interview, 1967

I find the three major administrative problems on a campus are sex
for the students, athletics for the alumni, and parking for the faculty. —Clark Kerr

The basis of all education is to learn by doing. —Donald Laird

Nothing is small in the great business of education.
—Legouvé, *L'Art de la lecture*

Too often we give children answers to remember rather than problems to solve. —Roger Lewin

Education without religion, as useful as it is, seems rather to make
man a more clever devil. —C. S. Lewis

The freshmen bring a little knowledge in and the seniors take none
out, so it accumulates through the years.
　　　　　　　　　—A. Lawrence Lowell, when president of Harvard

The mark of an educated man is the ability to make a reasoned guess
on the basis of insufficient information.　　　—A. Lawrence Lowell

The better part of every man's education is that which he gives
himself.
　　　　—James Russell Lowell, *My Study Windows*, "Abraham Lincoln"

There are three great questions which in life we have over and over
again to answer: Is it right or wrong? Is it true or false? Is it beautiful or ugly? Our education ought to help us answer these questions.　　　　　　　　　　　　　　　　　　　　　—John Lubbock

Those who have not distinguished themselves at school need not on
that account be discouraged. The greatest minds do not necessarily
ripen the quickest.　　　　　　　　　　　　　　—John Lubbock

The goal of education is not the pursuit of knowledge for the glorification of the mind, but for the purification of the heart.
　　　　　　　　　　　　　　　—Rabbi Bernard Mandelbaum

Women, like men, must be educated with a view to action, or their
studies cannot be called education.　　　　—Harriet Martineau

A whale ship was my Yale College and my Harvard.
　　　　　　　　　　　　　　　—Herman Melville, *Moby Dick*

The aim of college, for the individual student, is to eliminate the
need in his life for the college; the task is to help him become a
self-educating man.　　　—C. Wright Mills, *Power, Politics and People*,
　　　　　　　　　　　　　　"Mass Society and Liberal Education"

To be instructed in the arts softens the manners and makes men gentle.
　　　　　　　　　　　　　　　　　　　　　　　　　—Ovid

To elevate above the spirit of the age must be regarded as the end of
education.　　　　　　　　　　　　　　　　　　—Jean Paul

The best education in the world is that got by struggling to get a living.
　　　　　　　　　　　　　　　　　　　—Wendell Phillips

Knowledge which is acquired under compulsion has no hold on the mind. Therefore do not use compulsion, but let early education be rather a sort of amusement; this will better enable you to find out the natural bent of the child.   —Plato, *The Republic*, Section 536

The direction in which education starts a man, will determine his future life.   —Plato, *The Republic*

'Tis education forms the common mind,
   Just as the twig is bent the tree's inclined.
      —Alexander Pope, *Epistles to Several Persons*, "To Lord Cobham"

Real education must ultimately be limited to one who *insists* on knowing, the rest is mere sheep-herding.
                              —Ezra Pound, *The ABC of Reading*

If you are planning for a year, sow rice; if you are planning for a decade, plant trees; if you are planning for a lifetime, educate people.   —Proverb (Chinese)

A child is being properly educated only when he is learning to become independent of his parents.   —Admiral H. G. Rickover

Instruction ends in the schoolroom, but education ends only with life. A child is given to the universe to be educated.
                              —Frederick W. Robertson

There is nothing so stupid as an educated man, if you get off the thing that he was educated in.   —Will Rogers

When it comes to educating all of us about the most basic things in life, it seems to me we need more kindergartens and fewer graduate schools.   —Andrew A. Rooney, *Word for Word*, "Back to Basics"

The entire object of true education is to make people not merely do the right things, but enjoy them—not merely industrious, but to love industry—not merely learned, but to love knowledge—not merely pure, but love purity—not merely just, but to hunger and thirst after justice.   —John Ruskin

To make your children capable of honesty is the beginning of education.   —John Ruskin, *Time and Tide*, letter 8

The great difficulty in education is to get experience out of ideas.
      —George Santayana, *The Life of Reason: Reason in Common Sense*

All men who have turned out worth anything have had the chief
    hand in their own education.
                    —Sir Walter Scott, letter to J. G. Lockhart, 1830

He is educated who knows how to find out what he doesn't know.
                                —Georg Simmel

Education is what survives when what has been learnt has been for-
    gotten.   —B. F. Skinner

Indeed one of the ultimate advantages of an education is simply com-
    ing to the end of it.   —B. F. Skinner, *The Technology of Teaching*

The problem of education is twofold: first to know, and then to utter.
    Everyone who lives any semblance of an inner life thinks more
    nobly and profoundly than he speaks.
                    —Robert Louis Stevenson, *Lay Morals*

Teach thy tongue to say, "I do not know."   —*The Talmud*

Education is only a ladder to gather fruit from the tree of knowledge,
    not the fruit itself.   —Voltaire

We all missed a lot. We'd all do well to start again, preferably with
    kindergarten.   —Kurt Vonnegut, Jr., *The Cat's Cradle*

If we work upon marble, it will perish. If we work upon brass, time
    will efface it. If we rear temples, they will crumble to dust. But if we
    work upon men's immortal minds, if we imbue them with high
    principles, with the just fear of God and love of their fellow men,
    we engrave on those tablets something which no time can efface,
    and which will brighten and brighten to all eternity.
              —Daniel Webster, speech in Faneuil Hall, 1852

Educate children without religion and you make a race of clever dev-
    ils out of them.   —Arthur Wellesley, 1st Duke of Wellington

Education is not the filling of a pail, but the lighting of a fire.
                          —William Butler Yeats

EFFORT

Doing your best is more important than being the best.—Anonymous

I have done what I could—let those who can, do better.
          —Anonymous, in Alexander Solzhenitsyn, *August 1914*

In joy or sorrow, health or sickness, prosperity or the reverse, the effort must still continue. One must rise after every fall and gradually acquire courage, faith, the will to succeed and the capacity to love.
—Alexis Carrel

Your own efforts "did not bring it to pass," only God—but rejoice if God found a use for your efforts in His work.
—Meister Eckhart

He that would have the fruit must climb the tree.
—Thomas Fuller, M. D., *Gnomologia*, No. 2366

It is for us to make the effort. The result is always in God's hands.
—Mahatma Gandhi

The mode by which the inevitable comes to pass is effort.
—Oliver Wendell Holmes, Jr.

I go at what I have to do as if there were nothing else in the world for me to do.
—Charles Kingsley

He who limps is still walking.
—Stanislaw Lec, *Unkempt Thoughts*

No man fails who does his best . . .
—O. S. Marden

Whether our efforts are, or not, favored by life, let us be able to say, when we come near the great goal, "I have done what I could."
—Louis Pasteur

Always do more than is required of you.
—Gen. George S. Patton

Perhaps only when human effort had done its best and failed, would God's power alone be free to work.
—Corrie ten Boom, *The Hiding Place*,
with John and Elizabeth Sherrill

You must not only aim aright, / But draw the bow with all your might.
—Henry David Thoreau, "You Must Not Only Aim Aright"

An honest try is better than success.
—Brian Alexander Watkins (age 9)

The truth is I'm doing the best I can with the world as I see it.
—Sloan Wilson, *The Man in the Gray Flannel Suit*

EGOTISM

Egotism is the opiate that the devil administers to dull the pains of mediocrity.
—Anonymous

Egotist, n. A person of low taste, more interested in himself than in me. —Ambrose Bierce, *The Devil's Dictionary*

ELDERS

Miss not the discourse of the elders. —Apocrypha, "Ecclesiasticus," 8, 9

A man is not an elder because his hair is gray. —Buddhist saying

ELOQUENCE

Eloquence is the power to translate a truth into language perfectly intelligible to the person to whom you speak.
—Ralph Waldo Emerson, *Letters and Social Aims*, "Eloquence"

Eloquence lies as much in the tone of the voice, in the eyes, and in the speaker's manner, as in his choice of words.
—François de La Rochefoucauld, *Maximes*

Eloquence is the painting of thought . . . —Blaise Pascal

It is the heart which inspires eloquence. —Quintilian

EMOTIONS

Emotion is always new. —Victor Hugo

Probably one of the most important lessons man has to learn is how to guide by his reason the great driving force of his emotions.
—William Ross

At certain periods of life, we live years of emotion in a few weeks, and look back on those times as on great gaps between the old life and the new. —William Makepeace Thackeray

EMPLOYMENT

The crowning fortune of a man is to be born to some pursuit which finds him employment and happiness, whether it be to make baskets, or broadswords, or canals, or statues, or songs.
—Ralph Waldo Emerson

You who help to employ other people fruitfully, and help families to live, are in a sense heroic. —Richard L. Evans

It is all one to me if a man comes from Sing Sing or Harvard. We hire a man, not his history. —Henry Ford

Employment is nature's physician, and is essential to human happiness.
—Galen

If you suspect a man don't employ him, and if you employ him, don't suspect him. —Proverb (Chinese)

When looking for a job, tell the man what you can do for him, not how good you are. —Martin Vanbee

Employment gives health, sobriety, and morals. —Daniel Webster

Find out what you like doing best and get someone to pay you for doing it. —Katherine Whitehorn

ENCOURAGEMENT

There are high spots in all of our lives and most of them have come through encouragement from someone else. I don't care how great, how famous or how successful a man or woman may be, each hungers for applause. —George M. Adams

We should seize every opportunity to give encouragement. Encouragement is oxygen to the soul. The days are always dark enough. There is no need for us to emphasize the fact by spreading further gloom. —George M. Adams

Our focus must always be on building people up.
—Dan Davis, sermon, Hope Chapel, Austin, Texas, 12 Oct 1991

Correction does much, but encouragement does more. Encouragement after censure is as the sun after a shower.
—Johann Wolfgang von Goethe

END

But all things earthly have an end.
—Matilda Greathouse Alexander, *Going West*

In the end / Things will mend. —Anonymous

In everything we ought to look at the end. —Jean de La Fontaine

The weariest nights, the longest days, sooner or later must perforce come to an end. —Baroness Orczy, *The Scarlet Pimpernel*

All is well that ends well. —Proverb (14th century)

The end crowns the work. —Proverb (Latin)

ENDURANCE

Learn to endure. —Anonymous

Mend your clothes and you may hold out this year. —Anonymous

. . . but he that endureth to the end shall be saved.
—*The Bible* (KJV): Matthew 10:22

Whether it be to failure or success, the first need of being is
endurance—to endure with gladness if we can, with fortitude in
any event. —Bliss Carman

Nothing great was ever done without much enduring.
—Catherine of Siena

One simply goes on. —John Gardner, *The Resurrection*

Enjoy when you can, and endure when you must.
—Johann Wolfgang von Goethe

This greatest mortal consolation, which we derive from the transitori-
ness of all things—from the right of saying, in every conjuncture,
"This, too, will pass away."
—Nathaniel Hawthorne, *The Marble Faun*, Preface

Everything passes. (That's what makes it endurable.)
—Joseph Heller, *Something Happened*

'Tis sweet to think on what was hard t'endure. —Robert Herrick

Bear, O my heart; thou hast borne a yet harder thing.
—Homer, *The Odyssey*, XX. 18

Nothing befalls any man which he is not fitted to endure.
—Marcus Aurelius Antoninus, *Meditations*, Book V, Sec. 18

Bear and endure: this trouble will one day prove to have been for
your good. —Ovid, *Amores*

I knew that I would live another day.
—Dimitri Panin, *The Notebooks of Sologdin*

He conquers who endures. —Persius

Even this shall pass away. —Proverb (Arab)

One can go a long way after one is tired. —Proverb (French)

Even a good horse can't keep running. —Proverb (Irish)

. . . that's all we ask for, isn't it? Just to hold out until next morning.
—Erich Maria Remarque, *Heaven Has No Favorites*

Who speaks of conquering? To endure is everything.
—Rainer Maria Rilke

To endure is the first and most necessary lesson a child has to learn.
—Jean Jacques Rousseau

. . . what cannot be cured must be endured. —Ignatius Sancho

Tough Times Never Last, But Tough People Do!
—Robert H. Schuller, book title

You cannot imagine yourself enduring so much.
—Alexander Solzhenitsyn, *The Oak and the Calf*

Illegimati non carborundum. (Don't let the bastards grind you
down.) —Gen. Joseph W. Stillwell

He went on enduring because there was nothing else he could do . . .
—Leo Tolstoy, *Anna Karenina*

Endure, and keep yourselves for days of happiness.
—Virgil, *Aeneid*, Book I, line 207

I'll not willingly offend, / Nor be easily offended; / What's amiss I'll
strive to mend, / And endure what can't be mended.
—Isaac Watts, "Good Resolutions"

To bear is to conquer our fate.
—William Wordsworth, "On Visiting a Scene in Argyleshire"

ENEMIES

God makes servants of His enemies. —Anonymous

No enemy can come so near that God is not nearer. —Anonymous

Let necessity, and not your will, slay the enemy who fights against
you. —Saint Augustine

Rejoice not when thine enemy falleth, and let not thine heart be glad
when he stumbleth. —*The Bible* (KJV): Proverbs 24:17

If thine enemy be hungry, give him bread to eat; and if he be thirsty,
give him water to drink. —*The Bible* (KJV): Proverbs 25:21

. . . I say unto you that ye resist not evil, but whosoever shall smite
thee on thy right cheek, turn to him the other also.
—*The Bible* (KJV): Matthew 5:39

. . . I say unto you, Love your enemies, bless them that curse you, do
good to them that hate you, and pray for them who despitefully
use you, and persecute you. —*The Bible* (KJV): Matthew 5:44

And unto him that smiteth thee on the one cheek, offer also the
other . . . —*The Bible* (KJV): Luke 6:29

Dearly beloved, avenge not yourselves but, rather, give place unto
wrath; for it is written, Vengeance is mine; I will repay, saith the
Lord. Therefore, if thine enemy hunger, feed him; if he thirst, give
him drink; for in so doing thou shalt heap coals of fire on his head.
—*The Bible* (KJV): Romans 12:19-20

The truly civilized man has no enemies. —Charles Fletcher Dole

I own no enemy on earth. That is my creed.
—Mahatma Gandhi, *Bombay Statesman*, 8 Aug 1942

Wherever you are confronted with an opponent, conquer him with
love. —Mahatma Gandhi

One enemy is too much. —George Herbert, *Jacula Prudentum*

We has met the enemy, and he is us.
—Walt Kelly, from his cartoon strip *Pogo*, 22 Apr 1971

I destroy my enemy when I make him my friend. —Abraham Lincoln

If we could read the secret history of our enemies, we should find in
each man's life sorrow and suffering enough to disarm all hostility.
—Henry Wadsworth Longfellow, "Driftwood"

We should ever conduct ourselves towards our enemy as if he were
one day to be our friend. —John Henry Newman

Man has not a greater enemy than himself. —Petrarch

Get your enemy to read your works in order to mend them, for your friend is so much your second self that he will judge too like you.
—Alexander Pope

It is better that my enemy see good in me than that I see bad in him.
—Proverb (Jewish)

What can the enemy do when the friend is cordial?
—Proverb (Persian)

The only safe and sure way to destroy an enemy is to make him your friend.
—Mark Twain

A merely fallen enemy may rise again, but the reconciled one is truly vanquished.
—Friedrich Schiller

God loves everyone, even his enemies.
—Phillip Daniel Watkins (age 7)

A foe to God ne'er was true friend to man, / Some sinister intent taints all he does.   —Edward Young, *Night Thoughts*, "Night 8," line 704

ENERGY

When men are young, they want experience and when they have gained experience, they want energy.   —Benjamin Disraeli

This world belongs to the energetic.   —Ralph Waldo Emerson

The energy within you is stronger than ever for being held back, compressed, and said No to . . .   —Henri Matisse

The more you lose yourself in something bigger than yourself, the more energy you will have.   —Norman Vincent Peale

To be energetic, act energetic.   —Clement Stone

Energy is based on love.   —Leo Tolstoy, *Anna Karenina*

ENGINEERING

. . . immersed in the notational chaos which is engineering practice.
—Holt Ashley, *Engineering Analysis of Flight Vehicles*

. . . engineering is a basic instinct in man, the expression of which is existentially fulfilling.
—Samuel C. Florman, *The Existential Pleasures of Engineering*

... man cannot help but transcend himself as soon as he begins to design and construct.
—Samuel C. Florman, *The Existential Pleasures of Engineering*

... the ancient joy of helping the tribe to survive is constantly rekindled in the engineer's heart.
—Samuel C. Florman, *The Existential Pleasures of Engineering*

... the elementary pleasure of solving technical problems.
—Samuel C. Florman, *The Existential Pleasures of Engineering*

The engineer's power was usually limited to a refusal to endorse a given plan, or to the tender of his resignation.
—Samuel C. Florman, *The Existential Pleasures of Engineering*

... mechanics is the paradise of the mathematical sciences because by means of it one comes to the fruits of mathematics.
—Leonardo da Vinci

One has to look out for engineers—they begin with sewing machines and end up with the atomic bomb.
—Marcel Pagnol, *Critique des critiques*

An engineer cannot participate in irrationality ...
—Alexander Solzhenitsyn, *The Gulag Archipelago*

To his and everybody else's way of thinking, you should build a house with your own hands before you start talking about being an engineer.
—Alexander Solzhenitsyn, *One Day in the Life of Ivan Denisovich*

To define it rudely but not inaptly, engineering is the art of doing that well with one dollar which any bungler can do with two after a fashion.
—Arthur M. Wellington,
The Economic Theory of Railway Location, Introduction

... singing the strong light works of engineers.
—Walt Whitman

ENJOYMENT

Not what we have, but what we enjoy, constitutes our abundance.
—Anonymous

Do not miss a day's enjoyment or forgo your share of innocent pleasure.
—Apocrypha, "Ecclesiasticus"

All animals, except man, know that the principal business of life is to enjoy it.　　　—Samuel Butler (1835-1902), *The Way of All Flesh*

If I don't enjoy myself now, when shall I?　　　—Omar Khayyám

He scatters enjoyment who can enjoy much. —Johann Kaspar Lavater

The world is his who enjoys it.　　　—Proverb (18th century)

Sleep, riches, and health, to be truly enjoyed, must be interrupted.
　　　—Jean Paul Richter, *Flower, Fruit, and Thorn*

The test of an enjoyment is the remembrance which it leaves behind.
　　　—Jean Paul Richter

Be absolutely determined to enjoy what you do.　　　—Gerry Sikorski

My advice to you is not to inquire why or whither, but just enjoy the ice cream while it's on your plate—that's my philosophy.
　　　—Thornton Wilder, *The Skin of Our Teeth*

ENTERTAINMENT

In general, children, like men, and men, like children, prefer entertainment to education.　　　—Denis Diderot, *Le Neveu de Rameau*

ENTHUSIASM

Enthusiasm is the breath of genius.　　　—Beaconsfield

In things pertaining to enthusiasm no man is sane who does not know how to be insane on proper occasion. —Henry Ward Beecher

Enthusiasm is the leaping lightning, not to be measured by the horsepower of the understanding.　　　—Ralph Waldo Emerson

Enthusiasm is the mother of effort, and without it nothing great was ever accomplished.　　　—Ralph Waldo Emerson

Every great and commanding moment in the annals of the world is the triumph of some enthusiasm.　　　—Ralph Waldo Emerson,
　　　"The Reformer," lecture, Boston, 25 Jan 1841

Nothing great was ever achieved without enthusiasm.
　　　—Ralph Waldo Emerson, *Essays, First Series*, "Circles"

Enthusiasm is the fever of reason.   —Victor Hugo

We act as though comfort and luxury were the chief requirements of life, when all that we need to make us really happy is something to be enthusiastic about.   —Charles Kingsley

Enthusiasm begets enthusiasm.   —Henry Wadsworth Longfellow

The sense of this word among the Greeks affords the noblest definition of it: enthusiasm signifies God in us.   —Madame de Staël

Enthusiasm for a cause sometimes warps judgment.
    —William Howard Taft

The successful man has enthusiasm: Good work is never done in cold blood, heat is needed to forge anything. Every great achievement is the story of a flaming heart.   —A. B. Zu Tavern

ENVIRONMENT

We should seek the atmosphere and the surrounding which call forth the best that is in us.   —Councillor

The environment is everything that isn't me.   —Albert Einstein

It is a common habit to blame life upon the environment. Environment modifies life but does not govern life. The soul is stronger than its surroundings.   —William James

There's an old saying which goes: Once the last tree is cut and the last river poisoned, you will find you cannot eat your money.
    —Joyce McLean, *The Globe and the Mail*

No one should voluntarily remain in an environment which prevents his development.   —O. S. Marden

Scientific research shows that, under identical environment, one man will go forward while another goes backward.   —William Ross

ENVY

Enjoy your own life without comparing it with that of another.
    —Marquis de Condorcet

Envy shooteth at others, but hitteth and woundeth herself.
    —Gabriel Harvey, *Marginalia*

Envy is littleness of soul. —William Hazlitt

Do not speak of your happiness to a man less fortunate than yourself.
—Plutarch

There is a strong disposition in youth, from which some individuals never escape, to suppose that everyone else is having a more enjoyable time than we are ourselves.
—Anthony Powell, *A Buyer's Market*

. . . set not your heart on another's possession.
—*The Upanishads*, "Isa Upanishad," translated by Juan Mascarsi

EPITAPHS

And were an epitaph to be my story I'd have a short one ready for my own. I would have written of me on my stone: I had a lover's quarrel with the world.
—Robert Frost, *Witness Tree*, "Lesson for Today"

Here lies one whose name was writ in water.
—epitaph on the tombstone of Keats

Excuse my dust. —Dorothy Parker, "Her Own Epitaph"

EQUALITY

For religion all men are equal, as all pennies are equal, because the only value of any of them is that they bear the image of the king.
—G. K. Chesterton, *Charles Dickens*

The best way to prove to yourself that you're not superior to a brother man of different color or creed is to get acquainted with him.
—*Mason City* (Iowa) *Globe Gazette*

All men are by nature equal, made, all, of the same earth by the same Creator, and however we deceive ourselves, as dear to God is the poor peasant as the mighty prince. —Plato

The rain does not recognize anyone as a friend; it drenches all equally. —Proverb (Ibo)

The poorest he that is in England hath a life to live as the greatest he.
—Thomas Rainborowe, in the army debates at Putney, 29 Oct 1647

The Constitution does not provide for first and second class citizens.
—Wendell Willkie, *An American Programme*, Ch. 2

ERROR

The best may err.   —Joseph Addison, *Cato*, Act V, Sc. iv

An error is the more dangerous in proportion to the degree of truth
    which it contains.   —Henri Frédéric Amiel,
            The Private Journal of Henri Frédéric Amiel, 26 Dec 1852

Sometimes the best way to convince a man he is wrong is to let him
    have his own way.   —Anonymous

There is precious instruction to be got by finding we were wrong.
                               —Thomas Carlyle

Error is the discipline through which we advance.
                 —William Ellery Channing, *The Present Age*

Ignorance of God's Word and failure to obey his teachings are among
    the major reasons that people's minds fall into error.
                  —Gary R. Collins, *The Magnificent Mind*

Ignorance is a blank sheet, on which we may write; but error is a
    scribbled one, on which we must first erase.
                     —Charles Caleb Colton, *Lacon*

Errors, like straws, upon the surface flow; / He who would search for
    pearls must dive below.   —John Dryden, *All for Love*, Prologue

Freedom is not worth having if it does not connote freedom to err.
                            —Mahatma Gandhi

An error gracefully acknowledged is a victory won.
                      —Caroline L. Gascoigne

It is no disgrace to acknowledge an error.   —R. Gutzkov

The road to wisdom? Well, it's plain / And simple to express: Err / and
    err / and err again / but less / and less / and less.
              —Piet Hein, *Grooks*, "The Road to Wisdom"

He errs as other men do, but errs with integrity.
           —Thomas Jefferson, about George Washington,
                       in a letter to W. B. Giles, 1795

Ignorance is preferable to error.   —Thomas Jefferson

Sometimes we may learn more from a man's errors than from his
   virtues.   —Henry Wadsworth Longfellow

A man should never be ashamed to own he has been in the wrong,
   which is but saying in other words that he is wiser today than he
   was yesterday.   —Alexander Pope, *Thoughts on Various Subjects*

From the errors of others a wise man corrects his own. —Publilius Syrus

Love truth, but pardon error.   —Voltaire, *Discours sur l'homme*, No. 3

Error itself may be happy chance.   —Alfred North Whitehead

E S T E E M

We particularly like people who value us highly.
                         —Alexander Solzhenitsyn, *The First Circle*

E T E R N I T Y

Eternity looks grander and kinder if Time grow meaner and more
   hostile.   —Thomas Carlyle

All great men find eternity affirmed in the very promise of their faculties.   —Ralph Waldo Emerson

I delight in the feeling that I am in eternity, that I can serve God now
   fully and effectively, that the next piece of the road will come in
   sight when I am ready to walk in it.   —Forbes Robinson

Eternal life does not begin with death; it begins with faith.
                                              —Samuel Shoemaker

Eternity's a terrible thought. I mean, where's it all going to end?
   —Tom Stoppard, *Rosencrantz and Guildenstern Are Dead*

He who provides for this life, but takes no care for eternity, is wise for
   a moment, but a fool forever.   —Tillotson

Time's violence rends the soul, by the rent eternity enters.
                                                 —Simone Weil

E T H I C S

The world has achieved brilliance without conscience. Ours is a world
   of nuclear giants and ethical infants.
                    —Gen. Omar Bradley, speech, Armistice Day, 1948

We have grasped the mystery of the atom and rejected the Sermon on the Mount.   —Gen. Omar Bradley, speech, Boston, Massachusetts, Armistice Day, 1948

The real problem is in the hearts and minds of men. It is not a problem of physics but of ethics. It is easier to denature plutonium than to denature the evil spirit of man.   —Albert Einstein

I am not sure whether ethical absolutes exist. But I am sure that we have to act as if they existed or civilization perishes.   —Arthur Koestler

EVANGELISM

I just want to lobby for God.   —Billy Graham

EVENTS

Events are never absolute, their outcome depends entirely upon the individual.   —Honoré de Balzac

Nothing ever happens but once in all this world. What I do now I do once for all. It is over and gone, with all its eternity of solemn meaning.   —Thomas Carlyle

Often do the spirits / Of great events stride on before the events, / And in to-day already walks to-morrow.   —Samuel Taylor Coleridge, "Death of Wallenstein," translated from Schiller

Events of all sorts creep or fly exactly as God pleases.   —William Cowper

Learn to wish that everything should come to pass exactly as it does.   —Epictetus

Nothing happens to man without the permission of God . . .   —Euripides

When I can't handle events, I let them handle themselves.   —Henry Ford

Events are less important than our responses to them.   —John Hersey

I have always believed, and I still believe, that whatever good or bad may come our way we can always give it meaning and transform it into something of value.   —Hermann Hesse

What really matters is what happens in us, not to us.
> —Rev. James W. Kennedy, *Minister's Shop-Talk*

What happens to a man is less significant than what happens within him.
> —Louis Mann

Nothing happens to any man which he is not formed by nature to bear.
> —Marcus Aurelius Antoninus

A man is not hurt so much by what happens, as by his opinion of what happens.
> —Michel de Montaigne

All the events of our life are materials of which we can make what we will.
> —Novalis

In every life there is one particular event that is decisive for the entire person—for his fate, his convictions, his passions.
> —Alexander Solzhenitsyn, *The Gulag Archipelago*

The only true hope for civilization—the conviction of the individual that his inner life can affect outward events and that, whether or not he does so he is responsible for them.
> —Stephen Spender

EVIDENCE

Some circumstantial evidence is very strong, as when you find a trout in the milk.
> —Henry David Thoreau, *Journal*, 11 Nov 1854

EVIL

Bear with evil, and expect good.
> —Anonymous

Let evil not come through me.
> —Anonymous

Do good, and evil shall not find you.
> —Apocrypha, "Tobit," 12, 7

God himself would not permit evil in this world if good did not come of it for the benefit and harmony of the universe.
> —Saint Thomas Aquinas, *On Princely Government*

God judged it better to bring good out of evil than to suffer no evil to exist.
> —Saint Augustine, *Enchiridion*, XXVII, 421

Woe unto them that call evil good, and good evil.
> —*The Bible* (KJV): Isaiah 5:20

Recompense to no man evil for evil. Provide things honest in the
sight of all men. If it be possible, as much as lieth in you, live
peaceably with all men. —*The Bible* (KJV): Romans 12:17–18

. . . I would have you wise unto that which is good, and simple concerning evil. —*The Bible* (KJV): Romans 16:19

Put on the whole armor of God, that ye may be able to stand against
the wiles of the devil. For we wrestle not against flesh and blood,
but against principalities, against powers, against the rulers of the
darkness of this world, against spiritual wickedness in high places.
  —*The Bible* (KJV): Ephesians 6:11–12

None are all evil. —Lord Byron

Men's hearts ought not to be set against one another, but against evil
only. —Thomas Carlyle

When God sends us evil, he sends with it the weapon to conquer it.
  —Paul Vincent Carroll, *Irish Stories and Plays*,
  "Shadow and Substance"

. . . moral evil is its own curse. —Thomas Chalmers

In the history of man it has been very generally the case that when
evils have grown insufferable they have touched the point of cure.
  —Edwin Hubbel Chapin

We cannot do evil to others without doing it to ourselves.
  —Joseph Francois Eduard Desmahis

How much have cost us the evils that never happened!
  —Thomas Jefferson, letter, 1825

No one ever became thoroughly bad in one step.
  —Juvenal, *Satires*, 2, 83

God uses evil to educate His children for a place in His kingdom.
  —Kaufmann Kohler, *Jewish Theology*

You are not to do evil that good may come of it. —law maxim

There are two equal and opposite errors into which our race can fall
about the devils. One is to disbelieve in their existence, the other is
to believe and to feel an unhealthy interest in them!
  —C. S. Lewis, *Screwtape Letters*

Evil springs up, and flowers, and bears no seed, / And feeds the green
  earth with its swift decay, / Leaving it richer for the growth of truth.
  —James Russell Lowell, *Prometheus*

Evil on itself shall back recoil.   —John Milton, *Comus*

. . . under a steady attack from men of good will, evil will always
  retreat.   —Dimitri Panin

All human evil comes from a single cause, man's inability to sit still
  in a room.   —Blaise Pascal, *Pensées*

Men never do evil so completely and cheerfully as when they do it
  from religious conviction.   —Blaise Pascal, *Pensées*

To a good man nothing that happens is evil.
                    —Plato, *Apology of Socrates*, Ch. 33, Sec. 41

Avoid the evil and it will avoid thee.   —Proverb (Gaelic)

Thinking evil is much the same as doing it.   —Proverb (Greek)

An evil deed remains with the evil-doer.   —Proverb (Japanese)

An evil life is a kind of death.   —Proverb (Spanish)

No man is justified in doing evil on the ground of expediency.
                    —Theodore Roosevelt, *The Strenuous Life*

Evil often triumphs, but never conquers.   —Joseph Roux

The doing evil to avoid an evil / Cannot be good.
                    —Friedrich Schiller, *Wallenstein*, Act IV, 6

But the line dividing good and evil cuts through the heart of every
  human being.   —Alexander Solzhenitsyn, *The Gulag Archipelago*

As sure as God is good, so surely there is no such thing as necessary
  evil.   —Robert Southey

He who accepts evil without protesting against it is really cooperating
  with it.   —Henry David Thoreau

Take the good with the evil, for ye all are pensioners of God, and
  none may choose or refuse the cup His wisdom mixeth.
                    —Martin Farquhar Tupper

Good has but one enemy, the evil; but the evil has two enemies, the
good and itself.   —J. Von Muller

E V O L U T I O N

Some call it Evolution,   And others call it God.
                    —William Herbert Carruth, "Each in His Own Tongue"

I have called this principle, by which each slight variation, if useful,
is preserved, by the term of Natural Selection.
                              —Charles Darwin, *Origin of Species*

In itself the theory of evolution, which asserts the variability of
species of animals and plants, is by no means opposed to religious
truths. It neither includes a necessity of assuming the origin of the
human soul from the essentially lower animal soul, nor is it an
atheistic theory.   —J. Donat, *The Freedom of Science*

Survival of the fittest.   —Herbert Spencer, *Principles of Biology*

E X A G G E R A T I O N

Exaggeration is a branch of lying.   —Baltasar Gracián

We always weaken whatever we exaggerate.
                              —La Harpe, *Mélanie*, Act I, Sc. i

To exaggerate invariably weakens the point of what we have to say.
                                          —Proverb (French)

E X A M P L E

Example is the best precept.   —Aesop, *Fables*, "The Two Crabs"

Many people will not read a Bible but will read a Christian.
                                              —Anonymous

Others follow in your footsteps quicker than they follow your advice.
                                              —Anonymous

Preaching is of much avail, but practice is far more effective. A godly
life is the strongest argument that you can offer to the skeptic.
                                              —Hosea Ballou

. . . As is the mother, so is her daughter.
                              —*The Bible* (KJV): Ezekiel 16:44

... The Son can do nothing of himself, but what he seeth the Father
do ...   —*The Bible* (KJV): John 5:19

For I [Jesus] have given you an example, that ye should do as I have
done to you.   —*The Bible* (KJV): John 13:15

Advice may be wrong, but examples prove themselves. —Josh Billings

Example has more followers than reason.   —Christian Nestell Bovée

Example is the school of mankind, and they will learn at no other.
                                —Edmund Burke, *Letters on a Regicide Peace*

We are, in truth, more than half what we are by imitation. The great
point is, to choose good models and to study them with care.
                                —Earl of Chesterfield, *Letters*, 18 Jan 1750

No man is so insignificant as to be sure his example can do no hurt.
                                                    —Lord Clarendon

A good example is the best sermon.
                                —Thomas Fuller, M. D., *Gnomologia*

He teaches me to be good that does me good.
                                —Thomas Fuller, M. D., *Gnomologia*, No. 2034

I have learned silence from the talkative; tolerance from the intolerant; and kindness from the unkind.   —Kahlil Gibran

One example is worth a thousand arguments.   —William Gladstone

You can preach a better sermon with your life than with your lips.
                                                    —Oliver Goldsmith

Example is always more efficacious than precept.
                                —Samuel Johnson, *Rasselas*, Ch. 29

So act that your principle of action might safely be made a law for the
whole world.   —Immanuel Kant

Nothing is so contagious as example. —François de La Rochefoucauld

Be noble! and the nobleness that lies / In other men, sleeping, but
never dead Will rise in majesty to meet thine own.   —Lowell

Example moves the world more than doctrine.
—Henry Miller, *The Cosmological Eye*

The conduct of our lives is the true mirror of our doctrine.
—Michel de Montaigne, *Essays*, "Of the Education of Children"

Not the cry, but the flight of the wild duck, leads the flock to fly and
follow. —Proverb (Chinese)

"For example" is not proof. —Proverb (Yiddish)

There is a transcendent power in example. —Madame Swetchine

Somebody is looking at God through you. —Lewis Timberlake

You become like those you spend time with. —Lewis Timberlake

Our task as laymen is to live our personal communion with Christ
with such intensity as to make it contagious. —Paul Tournier

Few things are harder to put up with than the annoyance of a good
example. —Mark Twain, *Pudd'nhead Wilson*,
"Pudd'nhead Wilson's Calendar"

EXCELLENCE

I May Not Be Totally Perfect, But Parts of Me Are Excellent
—Ashleigh Brilliant, book title

Whoever I am or whatever I am doing, some kind of excellence is
within my reach. —John W. Gardner

Whatever you are, be a good one. —Abraham Lincoln

There is no excellence uncoupled with difficulties. —Ovid

EXCESSES

We pay in old age the penalty of excesses in youth. —Proverb (Latin)

EXCUSES

Bad excuses are worse than none. —Anonymous

You don't have to make excuses for God.
—Dan Davis, sermon, Hope Chapel, Austin, Texas, 25 Jul 1992

Several excuses are always less convincing than one.
—Aldous Huxley, *Point Counter Point*

EXERCISE

Our minds are rendered buoyant by exercise. —Cicero

My grandmother started walking five miles a day when she was sixty. She's ninety-five now, and we don't know where the hell she is.
—Ellen DeGeneres

Exercise is bunk. If you are healthy you don't need it: if you are sick you shouldn't take it. —Henry Ford

Whenever I feel like exercise, I lie down until the feeling passes.
—Robert Maynard Hutchins

Exercise is an unnatural act. —Peter de Vries, *Forever Panting*

EXISTENCE

The material universe exists only in the mind. —Jonathan Edwards

As long as any man exists, there is some need of him.
—Ralph Waldo Emerson

No power of genius has ever yet had the smallest success in explaining existence. The perfect enigma remains.
—Ralph Waldo Emerson, *Representative Men*, "Plato"

Man is the only animal for whom his own existence is a problem which he has to solve. —Erich Fromm, *Man for Himself*

Every life is its own excuse for being. —Elbert Hubbard, *The Note Book*

. . . our existence is but a crack of light between two eternities of darkness. —Vladimir Nabokov, *Speak, Memory*, Ch. 1

All known existence points beyond itself. —Reinhold Niebuhr

Everything that is incomprehensible does not cease to exist.
—Blaise Pascal, *Pensées*

We are because God is. —Proverb (Yiddish)

Existence is a miracle, and, morally considered, a free gift from moment to moment. —George Santayana

That I exist is a perpetual surprise which is life.
—Rabindranath Tagore, *Stray Birds*

EXPECTATIONS

It is a great obstacle to happiness to expect too much.
—Bernard le Bovier de Fontenelle

I believe you rarely achieve more than you expect.   —Carol Grosse

Occasionally necessity takes its jackhammer to our expectations to make way for what the chief architect really wants.   —Alan Harris

There would be few enterprises of great labor or hazard undertaken, if we had not the power of magnifying the advantages which we persuade ourselves to expect from them.   —Samuel Johnson

We ought not to raise expectations which it is not in our power to satisfy.—It is more pleasing to see smoke brightening into flame, than flame sinking into smoke.   —Samuel Johnson

Even the best things are not equal to their fame.
—Henry David Thoreau

High expectations are the key to everything.   —Sam Walton

EXPERIENCE

All experience is an arch, to build upon.
—Henry Adams, *The Education of Henry Adams* (1907)

Our bravest lessons are not learned through success, but misadventure.   —Alcott

By experience we find out a short way by long wandering.
—Roger Ascham

Experience is retrospect knowledge.   —Hosea Ballou

Oh, who can tell, save he whose heart has tried?   —Lord Byron

A little experience often upsets a lot of theory.   —Cadman

Bad times have a scientific value. These are occasions a good learner would not miss.   —Ralph Waldo Emerson

Only so much do I know, as I have lived. —Ralph Waldo Emerson,
Nature Addresses, "The American Scholar"

No amount of reading and intelligent deduction could supplant the
direct experience. —John Fowles, *The Ebony Tower*

After crosses and losses, men grow humbler and wiser.
—Benjamin Franklin

Experience keeps a dear school, but fools will learn in no other.
—Benjamin Franklin, *Poor Richard's Almanack*, 1743

The things which hurt, instruct. —Benjamin Franklin

Forget the times of your distress, but never forget what they taught
you. —Gasser

A good scare is worth more to a man than good advice.
—Edgar Watson Howe, *Howe's Monthly*

Experience is not what happens to a man; it is what a man does with
what happens to him. —Aldous Huxley, *Texts and Pretexts*

Experience, as we know, has a way of boiling over, and making us correct our present formulas. —William James

Experience enables you to recognize a mistake when you make it
again. —Franklin P. Jones

No man's knowledge here can go beyond his experience.
—John Locke, "Essay Concerning Human Understanding"

One thorn of experience is worth a whole wilderness of warning.
—James Russell Lowell

A man is not hurt so much by what happens, as by his opinion of
what happens. —Michel de Montaigne

The experience may have been costly, but it was also priceless.
—Peter G. Peterson, former U. S. Secretary of Commerce,
on his term in the Cabinet

He who has not tasted bitter does not know what sweet is.
—Proverb (German)

He who has once burnt his mouth always blows his soup.
—Proverb (German)

A new broom sweeps clean, but the old brush knows the corners.
—Proverb (Irish)

When it happens to you, you'll know it's true.   —Proverb (Russian)

Experience is what we call the accumulation of our mistakes.
—Proverb (Yiddish)

Each succeeding day is the scholar of that which went before it.
—Publilius Syrus

We must be broken into life.   —Charles E. Raven

Education is when you read the fine print. Experience is what you get
if you don't.   —Pete Seeger

. . . by indirections find directions out.
—William Shakespeare, *Hamlet*, Act II, Sc. i

And thus it is that we have to keep getting banged on flank and snout
again and again so as to become, in time at least, human beings,
yes, human beings . . .
—Alexander Solzhenitsyn, *The Gulag Archipelago*

I know that the experiences of our lives, when we let God use them,
become the mysterious and perfect preparation for the work He
will give us to do.   —Corrie ten Boom, *The Hiding Place*,
with John and Elizabeth Sherrill

I am a part of all that I have met.   —Alfred, Lord Tennyson

Trust one who has gone through it.   —Virgil

Experience is the name everyone gives to their mistakes.
—Oscar Wilde, *Lady Windermere's Fan*

If you have faced pain and disappointment, you not only value your
happiness more highly, but you are prepared for unpredictable exigencies.   —W. Beran Wolfe

EXPERTS

An expert is one who knows more and more about less and less.
—Nicolas Murray Butler

An expert is someone who knows some of the worst mistakes that can be made in his subject and how to avoid them.
—Werner Heisenberg, *The Part and the Whole*

Even when experts all agree, they may be mistaken.—Bertrand Russell

EXTREMISM

I would remind you that extremism in the defense of liberty is no vice. And let me remind you also that moderation in the pursuit of justice is no virtue. —Barry Goldwater,
acceptance speech for Presidential nomination, 16 Jul 1964

What is objectionable, what is dangerous about extremists is not that they are extreme, but that they are intolerant. The evil is not what they say about their cause, but what they say about their opponents. —Robert F. Kennedy, *The Pursuit of Justice*,
"Extremism, Left and Right"

The world acquires value only through its extremes and endures only through moderation; extremists make the world great, the moderates give it stability. —Paul Valéry

EYES

The eye is inlet to the soul. —Hosea Ballou

The countenance is the portrait of the soul, and the eyes mark its intentions. —Cicero

In one soft look what language lies! —Dibdin

These lovely lamps, these windows of the soul. —Du Bartas

The eye of a master will do more work than both his hands.
—Benjamin Franklin, *Poor Richard's Almanack*, 1758

The eyes have one language everywhere.
—George Herbert, *Outlandish Proverbs*

The balls of sight are so formed, that one man's eyes are spectacles to another, to read his heart with. —Samuel Johnson

The eye is the window of the soul; even an animal looks for a man's intentions right into his eyes. —Hiram Powers

The eyes are the pioneers that first announce the soft tale of love.
—Propertius

For where is any author in the world / Teaches such beauty as a
woman's eye?
—William Shakespeare, *Love's Labour's Lost*, Act IV, Sc. iii

Women bring conquerors to their feet with the magic of their eyes.
—Dr. J. V. C. Smith

The eye is the jewel of the body.   —Henry David Thoreau

— F —

The FACE

The God we worship writes his name upon our faces. —Roger Babson

It is the common wonder of all men how, among so many millions of
faces, there should be none alike.
—Sir Thomas Browne, *Religio Medici*, Part ii, Sec. 2

The magic of a face.　　　—Thomas Carew, *The Epitaph on the Lady S—*

A good face is the best letter of recommendation. —Queen Elizabeth I

But most he loved a happy human face.
—L. Hunt, *The Story of Rimini*, Canto III, line 110

How various a face . . .
—Erich Maria Remarque, *All Quiet on the Western Front*

God has given you one face, and you make yourself another.
—William Shakespeare, *Hamlet*, Act III, Sc. i

There's no art / To find the mind's construction in the face . . .
—William Shakespeare, *Macbeth*, Act I, Sc. iv

How rich is anyone who can simply see human faces.
—Corrie ten Boom, *The Hiding Place*,
with John and Elizabeth Sherrill

Trust not too much to an enchanting face.　　　　　　—Virgil

She knew now to look slowly and carefully at a face; she was convinced that it was impossible to see it all at once.
—Eudora Welty, *Selected Stories of Eudora Welty*, "Clyte"

In the faces of men and women I see God.
—Walt Whitman, *Leaves of Grass*, "Song of Myself"

FACTS

Every man has a right to his opinion, but no man has a right to be
wrong in his facts.
—Bernard Baruch

There is nothing I know of so sublime as a fact.   —George Canning

What are facts but compromises? A fact merely marks the point
  where we have agreed to let investigation cease.   —Bliss Carman

The trouble with facts is that there are so many of them.
                    —Samuel McChord Crothers, *The Gentle Reader*

Facts are stubborn things.   —Ebenezer Elliott, *Field Husbandry*

Facts do not cease to exist because they are ignored.
                    —Aldous Huxley, *Proper Studies*, "Note on Dogma"

Comment is free but facts are sacred.   —Charles Prestwich Scott

FAILURE

We mount to heaven mostly on the ruins of our cherished schemes,
  finding our failures were successes.
                    —Bronson Alcott, *Concord Days*, "June"

They fail, and they alone, who have not striven.
        —Thomas Bailey Aldrich, *Enamored Architect of Airy Rhyme*

A man can fail many times but he isn't a failure until he begins to
  blame somebody else.   —Anonymous

Failure is not sweet, but it need not be bitter.   —Anonymous

Look at the bright side of a failure as well as the dark.   —Anonymous

Man takes account of our failures but God of our striving.
                                    —Anonymous

There is much to be said for failure. It is more interesting than success.   —Max Beerbohm, *Mainly on the Air*

All that is necessary to break the spell of inertia and frustration is
  this: act as if it were impossible to fail.   —Dorothea Brande

A first failure is often a blessing.   —A. L. Brown

In great attempts it is glorious even to fail.   —Cassius

Failure sometimes enlarges the spirit. You have to fall back upon
  humanity and God.   —Charles Horton Cooley

Every failure teaches a man something, if he will but learn.
—Charles Dickens

Success isn't permanent, and failure isn't fatal. —Mike Ditka

Sometimes a noble failure serves the world as faithfully as a distinguished success. —Dowden

There is only one real failure in life that is possible, and that is, not to be true to the best one knows. —Farrar

No man is a failure who is enjoying life. —William Feather

Failure is simply the opportunity to begin again only more intelligently. —Henry Ford

But success and failure are of no account. They are God's concern, not mine. —Mahatma Gandhi

Apparent failure may hold in its rough shell the germs of a success that will blossom in time, and bear fruit throughout eternity.
—Frances Ellen Watkins Harper

It is often the failure who is the pioneer in new lands, new undertakings, and new forms of expression. —Eric Hoffer

There is the greatest practical benefit in making a few failures early in life. —Thomas Henry Huxley, *On Medical Education*

Only those who dare to fail greatly can ever achieve greatly.
—Robert F. Kennedy

We need to teach the highly educated person that it is not a disgrace to fail and that he must analyze every failure to find its cause. He must learn how to fail intelligently, for failing is one of the greatest arts in the world. —Charles F. Kettering

The probability that we may fail in the struggle ought not to deter us from the support of a cause we believe to be just.
—Abraham Lincoln

There is always another chance . . . This thing that we call "failure" is not the falling down, but the staying down. —Mary Pickford

The great question is not whether you have failed, but whether you are content with failure. —Proverb (Chinese)

You always pass failure on the way to success.   —Mickey Rooney

Men do not fail; they give up trying.   —Elihu Root

Our business in this world is not to succeed, but to continue to fail, in
    good spirits.   —Robert Louis Stevenson

Failure is more frequently from want of energy than want of capital.
        —Daniel Webster

Every failure is a step to success; every detection of what is false
    directs us toward what is true; every trial exhausts some tempting
    form of error.   —Whewell

FAITH

Faith is the continuation of reason.   —William Adams

Faith is not a possession; it's a decision.
        —Alcoholics Anonymous saying

Every life is a profession of faith . . .   —Henri Frédéric Amiel

Faith is certitude without proofs . . . Faith is a sentiment, for it is a
    hope; it is an instinct, for it precedes all outward instruction.
        —Henri Frédéric Amiel, *The Private Journal of Henri Frédéric Amiel*

Faith makes things possible—it does not make them easy.
        —Anonymous

Feed your faith and your doubts will starve to death.   —Anonymous

The final criterion that will be used by God to judge us is not success
    but faithfulness.   —Anonymous

Weave in faith and God will find thread.   —Anonymous

God does not expect us to submit our faith to him without reason,
    but the very limits of reason make faith a necessity.
        —Saint Augustine

[Faith is] an inner conviction of being overwhelmed by God.
        —Gustaf Aulén

. . . If ye have faith as a grain of mustard seed, ye shall say unto this mountain, Move from here to yonder place; and it shall move; and nothing shall be impossible unto you.
                                    —*The Bible* (KJV): Matthew 17:20

. . . The just shall live by faith.   —*The Bible* (KJV): Romans 1:17

So, then, faith cometh by hearing, and hearing by the word of God.
                                    —*The Bible* (KJV): Romans 10:17

Fight the good fight of faith . . .   —*The Bible* (KJV): 1 Timothy 6:12

Now faith is the substance of things hoped for, the evidence of things not seen.   —*The Bible* (KJV): Hebrews 11:1

For whatever is born of God overcometh the world, and this is the victory that overcometh the world, even our faith.
                                    —*The Bible* (KJV): 1 John 5:4

Infidel, n. In New York, one who does not believe in the Christian religion; in Constantinople, one who does.   —Ambrose Bierce

Live by faith until you have faith.   —Peter Boehler, to John Wesley

If you desire faith, then you've faith enough.   —Robert Browning

You can do very little with faith, but you can do nothing without it.
        —Samuel Butler (1835-1902), *Note-books*, "On Rebelliousness"

Pin thy faith to no man's sleeve. Hast thou not two eyes of thy own?
                                    —Thomas Carlyle

The celestial order and the beauty of the universe compel me to admit that there is some excellent and eternal Being, who deserves the respect and homage of men.
        —Cicero, *De Divinatione*, Book II, Ch. 72, Sec. 148

And almost every one when age, / Disease, or sorrows strike him, / Inclines to think there is a God, / Or something very like Him.
                        —Arthur Hugh Clough, *Dipsychus*, I. v

Faith lights us through the dark to Deity.   —W. Davenant

To me, faith means not worrying.   —John Dewey

Reason saw not, till Faith sprung the Light.
—John Dryden, *Religio Laici*

All I have seen teaches me to trust the Creator for all I have not seen.
—Ralph Waldo Emerson

There are subjects where reason cannot take us far and we have to accept things on faith. Faith then does not contradict reason but transcends it. Faith is a kind of sixth sense which works in cases which are without the purview of reason. —Mahatma Gandhi

The school of faith teaches us to trust God to solve our problems. And then, for a graduate course, it teaches us to trust God when He chooses not to solve our problems. —Stephen Goard

If you have any faith, give me, for heaven's sake, a share of it! Your doubts you may keep to yourself, for I have plenty of my own.
—Johann Wolfgang von Goethe

Faith in order, which is the basis of science, cannot reasonably be separated from faith in an Ordainer, which is the basis of religion.
—Asa Gray

Treat the other man's faith gently; it is all he has to believe with. His mind was created for his own thoughts, not yours or mine.
—Henry S. Haskins

Faith in God is synonymous with the brave hope that the universe is friendly to the ideals of man. —A. E. Haydon

Human misery is too great for men to do without faith.
—Heinrich Heine

The great act of faith is when man decides that he is not God.
—Oliver Wendell Holmes, Jr., letter to William James, 1907

We are wrong when we say that we must verify God and then we will have faith in him. Faith throws a bridge toward God and finds the divine Reality. —Hugh Thomson Kerr

We are called not to be successful but to be faithful. —Ellwood Kieser

My faith in man is, at bottom, a faith in God.
—Martin Luther King, Jr., sermon, 26 Feb 1956

Faith is the capacity to trust God while not being able to make sense
out of everything.
—James Kok

There are things that must be done in faith, else they never have
being.
—George Macdonald, *The Flight of the Shadow*, Ch. 12

Faith is the sight of the inward eye.
—Alexander Maclaren

There can be no faith so feeble that Christ does not respond to it.
—Alexander Maclaren

A little faith will bring your soul to heaven, but a lot of faith will
bring heaven to your soul.
—Dwight L. Moody

Belief is a truth held in the mind; faith is a fire in the heart.
—Joseph Fort Newton

If I didn't have faith, I'd be worried about this world.
—W. Jack Noble, from a sermon, Canyon Creek
Presbyterian Church, Richardson, Texas, 4 Sep 1994

Faith is the heroism of intellect.
—Charles H. Parkhurst

Faith affirms what the senses do not affirm, but not the contrary of
what they perceive. It is above, and not contrary to.
—Blaise Pascal, *Pensées*

Anybody who has been seriously engaged in scientific work of any
kind realizes that over the entrance to the gates of the temple of
science are written the words: Ye must have faith. It is a quality
which the scientist cannot dispense with.
—Max Planck, *Where is Science Going?*

Faith is not jumping to conclusions. It is concluding to jump.
—W. T. Purkiser

The faith that acts not, is it truly faith? —Jean Baptiste Racine, *Athalie*

It is at night that faith in light is admirable.
—Edmond Rostand, *Chantecler*, Act II, Sc. iii

In actual life every great enterprise begins with and takes its first forward step in faith.
—Schlegel

Faith is like love: it cannot be forced.
—Arthur Schopenhauer, *Parerga und Paralipomena*

Have faith in your faith—and doubt your doubts.
  —Robert H. Schuller, *Tough Times Never Last, But Tough People Do*

Faith creates the virtues in which it believes.   —Madame de Sévigné

There are no tricks in plain and simple faith.
  —William Shakespeare, *Julius Caesar*, Act IV, Sc. ii

Most people are brought to faith in Christ not by argument for it but
  by exposure to it.   —Samuel M. Shoemaker

Faith is the subtle chain / Which binds us to the infinite.
  —Elizabeth Oakes Smith

. . . because they believed thoroughly in a just, moral God they could
  put their faith there and let the smaller securities take care of
  themselves.   —John Steinbeck, *East of Eden*

Faith is the bird that feels the light and sings when the dawn is still
  dark.   —Rabindranath Tagore

Faith is not believing God can; it's believing God will.
  —Lewis Timberlake

What I admire in Columbus is not his having discovered a world, but
  his having gone to search for it on the faith of an opinion.—Turgot

. . . As the most beautiful light is born of darkness, so the faith that
  springs from conflict is often the strongest and best.   —R. Turnbull

The world embarrasses me, and I cannot dream that this watch exists
  and has no watchmaker.   —Voltaire

The steps of faith fall on the seeming void, but find the rock beneath.
  —John Greenleaf Whittier

Our life must answer for our faith.   —Thomas Wilson

Faith builds a bridge across the gulf of death, / To break the shock
  blind nature cannot shun, / And lands Thought smoothly on the
  further shore.   —Young

FALLS

By falling we learn to go safely.   —Anonymous

We fall the way we lean.   —Anonymous

The desire of power in excess caused the angels to fall; the desire of knowledge in excess caused man to fall.　　—Francis Bacon

For a just man falleth seven times, and riseth up again . . .
　　　　　　　　　　　—*The Bible* (KJV): Proverbs 24:16

He that is down needs fear no fall; / He that is low, no pride.
　　—John Bunyan, *Pilgrim's Progress*, Part 2, "Shepherd Boy's Song"

Our very walking is an incessant falling; a falling and a catching of ourselves before we come actually to the pavement. It is emblematic of all things a man does.　　—Thomas Carlyle

Our greatest glory is not in never falling, but in rising every time we fall.　　　　　　　　　　　　—Confucius

A stumble may prevent a fall.
　　　　　　—Thomas Fuller, M. D., *Gnomologia*, No. 424

Our greatest glory consists not in never falling, but in rising every time we fall.　　　　　　　—Oliver Goldsmith

Who falls for love of God shall rise a star.　　—Ben Jonson, *Underwoods*

He who falls obstinate in his courage, if he falls he fights from his knees.　　　　—Michel de Montaigne, "Des Cannibales"

He who climbs too high is near a fall.　　　　—Proverb (Italian)

The apple falls not far from the tree.　　　　—Proverb (Yiddish)

Be cheerful; wipe thine eyes: / Some falls are means the happier to arise　　　　—William Shakespeare, *Cymbeline*, Act IV, Sc. ii

Who bravely dares must sometimes risk a fall.
　　　　　　—Tobias George Smollett, *Advice*, l. 208

FAME

Those who write books on despising fame inscribe their own name on the title-page.　　　　　　　—Anonymous

Fame has eagle wings, and yet she mounts not so high as man's desire.　　　　　　　　—Beaconsfield

Fame is the thirst of youth.　　　　　　—Lord Byron

Fame is a powerful aphrodisiac.　　　　　　　　　—Graham Greene

Who would not rather have the fame of Archimedes than that of his
　　conqueror Marcellus?　　　　　—Sir William Rowan Hamilton

There are names on her immortal scroll at which Fame blushes.
　　　　　　　　　　　—William Hazlitt, *Characteristics*

Seven cities warred for Homer, being dead,
　　Who, living, had no roof to shroud his head.
　　　　　　　　—Thomas Heywood, "On Homer's Birthplace"

Every man has a lurking wish to appear considerable in his native
　　place.　　　　　　　　　　　　　　—Samuel Johnson

On stage I make love to twenty-five thousand people; then I go home
　　alone.　　　　　　　　　　　　　　　—Janis Joplin

The fame of great men ought always to be estimated by the means
　　used to acquire it.　　　　　—François de La Rochefoucauld

Every society honors its live conformists and its dead troublemakers.
　　　　　　　　　　　　　　　—Mignon McLaughlin

The famous are balloons far up in the sky, to be envied for their quiet
　　freedom or shot down as enemies.　　—Arthur Miller, *Timebends*

She [fame] comes unlooked for if she comes at all.　—Alexander Pope

Seven wealthy towns contend for Homer dead, / Through which the
　　living Homer begg'd his bread.　　　　—Thomas Seward

I have learned to praise the quiet, lightning deed, not the applauding
　　thunder at its heels that men call fame.　　　　—A. Smith

Thus it is that weeds get into the harvest of fame.
　　　　　　—Alexander Solzhenitsyn, *The Gulag Archipelago*

The lust of fame is the last that a wise man shakes off.　　—Tacitus

What a heavy burden is a name that has become too soon famous.
　　　　　　　　　　　　　　　　　　—Voltaire

In the future everyone will be world famous for fifteen minutes.
　　　　　　　　—Andy Warhol, in a catalogue for his
　　　　　　exhibition of photographs, Stockholm, 1968

FAMILIARITY

Familiarity breeds contempt. —Aesop, *Fables*, "The Fox and the Lion"

Familiarity breeds.   —Mary Pettibone Poole, *A Glass Eye at a Keyhole*,
"Beggars Can't Be Choosers"

Familiar things are a comfort to us all.
—Andrew A. Rooney, *Pieces of My Mind*

FAMILY

. . . wife and children are a kind of discipline of humanity.
—Francis Bacon, *Essays*, "Of Marriage and Single Life"

A brother is a friend that nature provides us with.
—Baudoin, *Demetrius*

Good family life is never an accident but always an achievement by
those who share it.   —James H. S. Bossard

A happy family is but an earlier heaven.   —John Bowring

'Tis sweet to know there is an eye will mark our coming, and look
brighter when we come.   —Lord Byron

Our kindred first.   —Nicolas Chamfort

Domestic happiness, thou only bliss / Of paradise that has surviv'd
the fall!
—William Cowper, *The Task*, "The Garden"

The family is the nucleus of civilization.   —Will Durant

To an old father, nothing is more sweet / Than a daughter. / Boys are
more spirited, but their ways / Are not so tender.
—Euripides, *The Suppliant Women*

. . . the mysteries and complexities of a family were really too much
for the dryness and pseudoscience of books and theories to handle.
—Janet and Paul Gotkin, *Too Much Anger, Too Many Tears*

You have to live your life according to what comforts you, not what
the rest of your family thinks you ought to be doing.
—Judith Guest, *Errands*, Ch. 5

The happiest moments of my life have been the few which I have
passed at home in the bosom of my family.   —Thomas Jefferson

For millions of men and women the family is the one and only setting in which human relationships are not governed predomi-
nantly by considerations of bargaining.   —Mascall

No matter how many communes anybody invents, the family always
creeps back.   —Margaret Mead

The family is more sacred than the state.   —Pope Pius XI

That man will never be unwelcome to others who makes himself
agreeable to his own family.   —Plautus

A large family, quick help.   —Proverb (Serbian)

The family—that dear octopus from whose tentacles we never quite
escape.   —Dodie Smith, "Dear Octopus"

All happy families resemble one another, each unhappy family is
unhappy in its own way.
—Leo Tolstoy, *Anna Karenina*, opening words

We flatter those we scarcely know, / We please the fleeting guest,
/ And deal full many a thoughtless blow / To those who love us best.
—Ella Wheeler Wilcox, "Life's Scars"

FANATICISM

There is no doubt that religious fanatics have done more to prejudice
the cause they affect to advocate than have its opponents.
—Hosea Ballou

A fanatic is one who can't change his mind and won't change the
subject.   —Winston Churchill

A fanatic is a man that does what he thinks th' Lord wud do if He
knew th' facts iv th' case.
—Finley Peter Dunne, *Mr. Dooley's Opinions*

There is no strong performance without a little fanaticism in the performer.   —Ralph Waldo Emerson, *Journals*

It is easier to tame a fanatic than to put life into a corpse.
—Walter Marshal Horton

A religious fanatic is somebody who knows Jesus Christ better than
you do.   —Jim Kaat, Chicago White Sox pitcher, 1975

Fanaticism consists in redoubling your effort when you have forgotten your aim.   —George Santayana,
The Life of Reason: Reason in Common Sense, Introduction

FARMING

He that would reap well must sow well.   —Anonymous

He who skimps on the seed will raise a poor harvest.   —Anonymous

Let gleaners glean, though crops be lean.   —Anonymous

You may grow good corn in a little field.   —Anonymous

. . . for whatsoever a man soweth, that shall he also reap.
—*The Bible* (KJV): Galatians 6:7

As you have sown, so shall you reap.   —Cicero, *De Oratore*

The diligent farmer plants trees, of which he himself will never see
the fruit.   —Cicero, *Tusculanarum Disputationum*

Even if a farmer intends to loaf, he gets up in time to get an early
start.   —Edgar Watson Howe, *Country Town Sayings*

Earth is here so kind, that just tickle her with a hoe and she laughs
with a harvest.
—Douglas William Jerrold, about Australia, *A Land of Plenty*

You've a darned long row to hoe.
—James Russell Lowell, *The Biglow Papers, First Series*

Better reap two days too soon than one day too late.
—Proverb (English)

You must plough with such oxen as you have.   —Proverb (English)

Praise the ripe field not the green corn.   —Proverb (Irish)

Farmers are patient men. They got to be. Got to see those seeds come
up week by week, fraction by fraction, and sweat it out for some
days not knowing yet is it weeds or vegetables . . .
—Anne Tyler, *If Morning Ever Comes*

Whoever could make two ears of corn or two blades of grass to grow
upon a spot of ground where only one grew before would deserve
better of mankind and do more essential service to his country
than the whole race of politicians put together.
—Jonathan Swift, *Gulliver's Travels*, Ch. 7

F A S H I O N

. . . the fashion of this world passeth away.
—*The Bible* (KJV): 1 Corinthians 7:31

Change of fashions is the tax which industry imposes on the vanity
of the rich.   —Nicolas Chamfort

Beauty too often sacrifices to fashion.   —Leigh Hunt

Other times, other fashions.   —Proverb (French)

Fashion is more powerful than any tyrant.   —Proverb (Latin)

The empire of fashion is mighty.   —Proverb (Latin)

I base most of my fashion taste on what doesn't itch. —Gilda Radner

. . . the fashion wears out more apparel than the man.
—William Shakespeare, *Much Ado About Nothing*, Act III, Sc. iii

Fashions, after all, are only induced epidemics.
—George Bernard Shaw, *The Doctor's Dilemma*, Preface

Every generation laughs at the old fashions, but follows religiously
the new.   —Henry David Thoreau, *Walden*, Ch. 1

Fashion is a form of ugliness so intolerable that we have to alter it
every six months.   —Oscar Wilde

F A S T I N G

Fasting is a medicine.   —John Chrysostom

F A T E

Fulfill thy fate! Be—do—bear—and thank God.   —Philip James Bailey

I want to seize fate by the throat.
—Ludwig van Beethoven, letter to Dr. Franz Wegeler, 16 Nov 1801

The die is cast.
> —Julius Caesar, as he crossed the Rubicon, quoted by Suetonius

Whatever limits us we call Fate.
> —Ralph Waldo Emerson, *The Conduct of Life*, "Fate"

'Tis writ on Paradise's gate, "Woe to the dupe that yields to Fate!"
> —Hafez

. . . with a heart for any fate.
> —Henry Wadsworth Longfellow, "A Psalm of Life"

I believe in fate, never in chance.
> —George Macdonald, *The Flight of the Shadow*, Ch. 12

Whatever may happen to thee, it was prepared for thee from all eternity . . .
> —Marcus Aurelius Antoninus

Heaven from all creatures hides the book of fate.
> —Alexander Pope, *An Essay on Man*, Epis. I, l. 77

It is God's giving if we laugh or weep.
> —Sophocles

FATHERS

A wise son maketh a glad father.
> —Anonymous

I've an idea that when he [my father] gets to heaven, he won't just sit on a cloud and wait for the woman he's loved and the children she bore. He'll be busy there, too, repairing the stairs, oiling the gates, improving the streets, smoothing the way.
> —Anonymous

The most important thing a father can do for his children is to love their mother.
> —Anonymous

And ye fathers, provoke not your children to wrath, but bring them up in the nurture and admonition of the Lord.
> —*The Bible* (KJV): Ephesians 6:4

The night you were born, I ceased being my father's boy and became my son's father. That night I began a new life.
> —Henry Grogor Felsen, *Letters to a Teen-Age Son*

One father is more than a hundred schoolmasters.
> —George Herbert, *Jacula Prudentum*

My father didn't tell me how to live; he lived, and let me watch him
do it. —Clarence Buddington Kelland

From his [George Macdonald's] own father, he first learned that
Fatherhood must be at the core of the universe.
—C. S. Lewis, in his introduction
to *Phantastes*, by George Macdonald

He that will have his son have a respect for him and his orders, must
himself have a great reverence for his son. —John Locke

From father to son, so it goes on. —Proverb (Ashanti)

A father is a banker provided by nature. —Proverb (French)

Every father who ever lived has a dream for his son. —Grantland Rice

What a father says to his children is not heard by the world, but it
will be heard by posterity. —Jean Paul Richter

. . . it is a wise father that knows his own child.
—William Shakespeare, *The Merchant of Venice*, Act II, Sc. ii

As the fathers live, so the children play.
—Alexander Solzhenitsyn, *The Gulag Archipelago Three*

A child is not likely to find a father in God unless he finds something
of God in his father. —Austin L. Sorenson

It is a father's duty to accustom his son to act rightly of his own
freewill rather than from fear of the consequences. —Terence

When I was a boy of fourteen, my father was so ignorant I could
hardly stand to have the old man around. But when I got to be
twenty-one, I was astonished at how much the old man had
learned in seven years. —Mark Twain

Fathers Day is very nice especially if you have a father that is.
—Phillip Daniel Watkins (age 7)

Perhaps host and guest is really the happiest relation for father and
son. —Evelyn Waugh

FAULTS

A fault confessed is half redressed. —Anonymous

He looked beyond my fault and saw my need.
                    —Anonymous, "He Looked Beyond My Fault" (song)

It is defective oysters that produce the pearls.   —Anonymous

The cardinal method with faults is to overgrow them and choke them
    out with virtues.   —John Bascom

No man can tell another his faults so as to benefit him, unless he
    loves him.   —Henry Ward Beecher, in William Drysdale, eidtor,
                              Proverbs from Plymouth Pulpit, (1887)

The greatest of faults, I should say, is to be conscious of none.
    —Thomas Carlyle, *On Heroes, Hero-Worship, and the Heroic in History*
                              (1841), "The Hero as Prophet"

Excuse small faults.   —Confucius

I'm not perfect, but those flaws make an interesting person.
                                                —Mary Frann

A good garden may have some weeds.   —Thomas Fuller, M. D.

Wink at small faults; for thou hast great ones.
                    —Thomas Fuller, *Introductio and Prudentiam*

E'en his failings lean'd to Virtue's side.
                    —Oliver Goldsmith, *The Deserted Village*

Everybody has something wrong with them.
                    —Ernest Hemingway, *A Moveable Feast*

Deal with the faults of others as gently as with your own. —Henrichs

Faults are thick where love is thin.   —James Howell, *Proverbs*, Part ii.

Bad men excuse their faults, good men will leave them. —Ben Jonson

We only confess our little faults to persuade people that we have no
    large ones.   —François de La Rochefoucauld, *Maximes*

The fault of another is a good teacher.   —Proverb (German)

Make peace with men and quarrel with your faults.
                                          —Proverb (Russian)

And oftentimes excusing of a fault / Doth make the fault the worse by
    excuse . . .   —William Shakespeare, *King John*, Act IV, Sc. ii

They say best men are moulded out of faults, / And, for the most,
    become much more the better / For being a little bad . . .
          —William Shakespeare, *Measure for Measure*, Act V, Sc. i

What you dislike in another, take care to correct in yourself.
          —Thomas Sprat

If you want a person's faults, go to those who love him. They will not
    tell you, but they know.
          —Robert Louis Stevenson, *Familiar Studies of Men and Books*

Misfortunes one can endure—they come from outside, they are acci-
    dents. But to suffer for one's own faults—ah! there is the sting of
    life.   —Oscar Wilde, *Lady Windermere's Fan*

FAVORS

If you can't return a favor, pass it on.   —Louise Brown

A favor loses its grace by publishing it too loudly. —Thomas Corneille

FEAR

Fear that man who fears not God.   —Abdl-El-Kader

Fear is unbelief parading in disguise.   —Anonymous

God assisting, there is nothing to be feared.   —Anonymous

It is only the fear of God that can deliver us from the fear of men.
          —Anonymous

Nothing is to be feared but fear.   —Francis Bacon

The vain waste of fear.   —Saul Bellow, *Henderson the Rain King*

. . . the Lord is the strength of my life; of whom shall I be afraid?
          —*The Bible* (KJV): Psalm 27:1

The fear of the Lord is the beginning of wisdom.
          —*The Bible* (KJV): Psalms 111:10

The fear of the Lord is the beginning of knowledge . . .
          —*The Bible* (KJV): Proverbs 1:7

. . . by the fear of the Lord men depart from evil.
—*The Bible* (KJV): Proverbs 16:6

. . . Be not afraid, only believe. —*The Bible* (KJV): Mark 5:36

There is no fear in love; but perfect love casteth out fear . . .
—*The Bible* (KJV): 1 John 4:18

The fear of God kills all other fears. —Hugh Black

The first and great commandment is, Don't let them scare you.
—Elmer Davis, *But We Were Born Free*

Too busy with the crowded hour to fear to live or die.
—Ralph Waldo Emerson, *Quatrains*, "Nature"

Better hazard once than always be in fear.
—Thomas Fuller, M. D., *Gnomologia*, No. 906

It's all right to have butterflies in your stomach. Just get them to fly
in formation. —Dr. Rob Gilbert

The greatest fear comes when God is a stranger . . . —Billy Graham,
Facing Death and the Life After

Fear kills more than disease. —George Herbert, *Jacula Prudentum*

I, a stranger and afraid / In a world I never made.
—A. E. Houseman, "The laws of God, the laws of man"

A good scare is worth more to a man than good advice.
—Edgar Watson Howe, *Country Town Sayings*

. . . nothing is as terrible when it is actually happening to us as when
we are dreading, fearing and anticipating it.
—Lara Jefferson, "These Are My Sisters"

Fear is the sand in the machinery of life. —E. Stanley Jones

It is better . . . to fear a little. One is cautious then.
—Louis L'Amour, *The Warrior's Path*

Keep fear out of your child's mind, as you would keep poison out of
his body; for fear is the deadliest of mental poisons.
—O. S. Marden, *Conquest of Worry*

We lend power to the things we fear!
—O. S. Marden, *Conquest of Worry*

He who fears he shall suffer, already suffers what he fears.
—Michel de Montaigne, *Essays*

Fear makes the wolf bigger than he is. —Proverb (German)

You gain strength, courage and confidence by every experience in which you really stop to look fear in the face. You are able to say to yourself, "I lived through this horror. I can take the next thing that comes along." . . . You must do the thing you think you cannot do.
—Eleanor Roosevelt, *You Learn by Living*

The only thing we have to fear is fear itself.
—Franklin D. Roosevelt, First Inaugural Address, 4 Mar 1933

Never let the fear of striking out get in your way. —Babe Ruth

I fear God, and next to God I chiefly fear him who fears him not.
—Saadi

There is so much coldness in the world because we are afraid to be as cordial as we really are. —Albert Schweitzer

Keep your fears to yourself, but share your courage with others.
—Robert Louis Stevenson

A great fear, when it is ill-managed, is the parent of superstition; but a discreet and well-guided fear produces religion.
—Jeremy Taylor, *The Rule and Exercises of Holy Living*

Fear follows crime, and is its punishment. —Voltaire

I am not afraid of tomorrow, for I have seen yesterday and I love today. —William Allen White

It is only the fear of God that can deliver us from the fear of man.
—John Witherspoon

FEELING

What unknown seas of feeling lie in man, and will from time to time break through! —Thomas Carlyle

Every human feeling is greater and larger than its exciting cause—a
proof, I think, that man is designed for a higher state of existence.
—Samuel Taylor Coleridge

I do not wish you to act from these truths; no, still and always act
from your feelings; only meditate often on these truths that sometime or other they may become your feelings.
—Samuel Taylor Coleridge

I am not responsible for my feelings—only for what I do with them.
—Ceophus Martin

What we feel matters much more than what we know.
—George Moore

Man's feelings are always purest and most glowing in the hour of
meeting and of farewell.   —Jean Paul Richter

People can live through hardship, but from hard feelings they perish.
—Alexander Solzhenitsyn, *The Oak and the Calf*

Which of us can control his feelings?
—Alexander Solzhenitsyn, *Victory Celebrations*

FELLOWSHIP

The business at hand is to lift one another up.
—Dwayne Adams, bass singer for the singing group Acappella

You need to be in fellowship of a church . . . If you separate a live coal
from the others, it will soon die out. However, if you put a live coal
in with other live coals, it will be a glow that will last for hours.
—Billy Graham, *World Aflame*

Today there's more fellowship among snakes than among mankind.
Wild beasts spare those with similar markings.   —Juvenal, *Satires*

You do not have to be in a church to be saved, but to continue in the
things of God, you must be in some type of fellowship with other
Christian people.
—Pat Robertson, *Answers to 200 of Life's Most Probing Questions*

FENCES

Good fences make good neighbors.   —Robert Frost, "Mending Wall"

Do not protect yourself by a fence, but rather by your friends.
—Proverb (Czechoslavakian)

Love your neighbor; but don't tear down the fence.
—Proverb (German)

FICTION

Fiction is not a dream. Nor is it guesswork. It is imagining based on facts, and the facts must be accurate or the work of imagining will not stand up.　　　　—Margaret Culkin Banning

The truth is, we've not really developed a fiction that can accommodate the full tumult, the zaniness and crazed quality of modern experience.　　　　—Saul Bellow

Fiction may be said to be the caricature of history.
—Edward Bulwer-Lytton

All novels are experimental.　　　　—Anthony Burgess

My novels point out that the world consists entirely of exceptions.
—Joyce Carey

With me, a story usually begins with a single idea or mental picture. The writing of the story is simply a matter of working up to that moment, to explain why it happened or what caused it to follow.
—William Faulkner

I have often maintained that fiction may be much more instructive than real history.　　　　—John Foster

There are many reasons why novelists write, but they all have one thing in common—a need to create an alternative world.
—John Fowles

History is a novel which did take place; a novel is history that could take place.　　　　—Edmond and Jules de Goncourt, *Idées et sensations*

If you would understand your own age, read the works of fiction produced in it. People in disguise speak freely.　　　　—Arthur Helps

Journalism allows its readers to witness history; fiction gives its readers an opportunity to live it.　　　　—John Hersey

All that non-fiction can do is answer questions. It's fiction's business
to ask them.   —Richard Hughes

Fiction is the microscope of truth.   —Alphonse de Lamartine

Some things can only be said in fiction, but that doesn't mean they
aren't true.   —Aaron Latham

The few really great—the major novelists . . . are significant in terms
of the human awareness they promote; awareness of the possibilities of life.   —F. R. Leavis, *The Great Tradition*

Wondrous strong are the spells of fiction.
                                —Henry Wadsworth Longfellow

In any work that is truly creative, I believe, the writer cannot be
omniscient in advance about the effects that he proposes to produce. The suspense of a novel is not only in the reader, but in the
novelist, who is intensely curious about what will happen to the
hero.   —Mary McCarthy

What I really do is take real plums and put them in an imaginary
cake.   —Mary McCarthy, in Elisabeth Niebuhr, *The Paris Review*,
                                        "The Art of Fiction XXVIII"

There are three rules for writing the novel. Unfortunately, no one
knows what they are.   —W. Somerset Maugham

One should be able to return to the first sentence of a novel and find
the resonances of the entire work.   —Gloria Naylor

Everybody else is working to change, persuade, tempt and control
them. The best readers come to fiction to be free of all that noise.
                                                      —Philip Roth

A good science fiction story is a story with a human problem, and a
human solution, which would not have happened without its science content.   —Theodore Sturgeon

Fiction gives us a second chance that life denies us.   —Paul Theroux

Why shouldn't truth be stranger than fiction? Fiction, after all, has to
make sense.   —Mark Twain

My family can always tell when I'm well into a novel because the
meals get very crummy.   —Anne Tyler

Long before I wrote stories, I listened for stories.
                        —Eudora Welty, *One Writer's Beginnings*

Fiction reveals truths that reality obscures.
                        —Jessamyn West, *To See the Dream*

FIGHTING

When elephants fight it is the grass that suffers.   —Proverb (African)

Once the fight is on—strike quickly and often.
                —Alexander Solzhenitsyn, *The Oak and the Calf*

Life isn't about fighting.   —Tom Zimmermann

FIRE

In the coldest flint there is a hot fire.   —Anonymous

Let him that is cold blow at the coal.   —Anonymous

Violent fires soon burn out.   —Anonymous

From little spark may burst a mighty flame.   —Dante Alighieri

The most tangible of all mysteries—fire.   —Leigh Hunt

Kindle not a fire that you cannot extinguish.—Proverb (16th century)

Since the house is on fire let us warm ourselves.   —Proverb (Italian)

A little fire is quickly trodden out, / Which, being suffer'd, rivers cannot quench.
            —William Shakespeare, *King Henry VI*, *Part III*, Act IV, Sc. viii

If the world is cold, make it your business to build fires.
                                            —Horace Traubel

FISHING

All men are equal before fish.   —Herbert Hoover, 1951

If you cannot catch a fish, do not blame the sea.   —Proverb (Greek)

FLATTERY

Imitation is the sincerest form of flattery.
—Charles Caleb Colton, *Lacon*

We love flattery even though we are not deceived by it, because it shows that we are of importance enough to be courted.
—Ralph Waldo Emerson, *Essays, Second Series*, "Gifts"

Self-love is the greatest of flatterers.   —François de La Rochefoucauld

We sometimes think we hate flattery, when we only hate the manner in which we have been flattered.   —François de La Rochefoucauld

Flattery is like wine, which exhilarates a man for a moment, but usually ends by going to his head and making him act foolishly.
—Helen Rowland

Lay not that flattering unction to your soul . . .
—William Shakespeare, *Hamlet*, Act III, Sc. iv

What really flatters a man is that you think him worth flattering.
—George Bernard Shaw, *John Bull's Other Island*, Act IV

Though flattery blossoms like friendship, yet there is a vast difference in the fruit.   —Socrates

More people are flattered into virtue than bullied out of vice.
—Surtees

'Tis an old maxim in the schools, / That flattery's the food of fools; / Yet now and then your men of wit / Will condescend to take a bit.
—Jonathan Swift, "Cadenus and Vanessa"

FLEXIBILITY

A wise man altereth his purpose, but a fool persevereth in his folly.
—James Mabbe, *Celestina*

FLIRTATION

Women do not know all their powers of flirtation.
—François de La Rochefoucauld

FLOWERS

Flowers are the sweetest things that God ever made and forgot to put a soul into. —Henry Ward Beecher, *Life Thoughts*

The flower in the vase still smiles, but no longer laughs. —Chazal

Earth laughs in flowers. —Ralph Waldo Emerson, *Poems*, "Hamatreya"

Many eyes go through the meadow, but few see the flowers in it. —Ralph Waldo Emerson, *Journals*

Flowers are the beautiful hieroglyphics of nature with which she indicates how much she loves us. —Johann Wolfgang von Goethe

Full many a flower is born to blush unseen, / And waste its sweetness on the desert air. —Thomas Gray, *Elegy Written in a Country Churchyard*

Gather ye rosebuds while ye may, / Old Time is still a-flying; / And this same flower that smiles today, / Tomorrow will be dying. —Robert Herrick, *Hesperides*, "To the Virgins, To Make Much of Time"

Lovely flowers have been known to grow out of trash heaps. —Elizabeth Kata, *A Patch of Blue*

I will be the gladdest thing under the sun / I will touch a hundred flowers and not pick one. —Edna St. Vincent Millay

Where, unwilling, dies the rose Buds / the new, another year. —Dorothy Parker, *Enough Rope*, "Recurrence"

When you have only two pennies left in the world, buy a loaf of bread with one, and a lily with the other. —Proverb (Chinese)

FLYING

"Come to the edge," he said. / They said, "We are afraid." / "Come to the edge," he said. / They came. / He pushed them / And they flew. —Guillaume Apollinaire

Surely no child, and few adults, have ever watched a bird in flight without envy.
—Isaac Asimov, *Isaac Asimov's Book of Science and Nature Quotations*, compiled by Isaac Asimov and Jason A. Shulman

Flying is hours and hours of boredom sprinkled with a few seconds of
  sheer terror.   —Gen. Gregory "Pappy" Boyington

Flight is the only truly new sensation that men have achieved in
  modern history.   —James Dickey

At the end of the first half-century of engine-driven flight, we are
  confronted with the stark fact that the historical significance of aircraft has been primarily military and destructive.
                                              —Charles A. Lindbergh

I have seen the science I worshiped, and the aircraft I loved, destroying the civilization I expected them to serve.
                          —Charles A. Lindbergh, in *Time*, 26 May 1967

FOLLOWING

You are to follow no man further than he follows Christ.
    —John Collins, from *The Golden Treasury of Puritan Quotations*

FOLLY

No one is wise but has a little folly to spare.   —Anonymous

Mingle a little folly with your wisdom.   —Horace

FONDNESS

Kindness is in our power, but fondness is not.   —Samuel Johnson

FOOD

Eaten bread is forgotten.   —Anonymous

Grumbling makes the loaf no larger.   —Anonymous

Never fall out with your bread and butter.   —Anonymous

Surprised as a sardine that went to sleep in the ocean and woke up in
  a delicatessen store.   —Anonymous

They that have good store of butter, may lay it thick on their bread.
                                                         —Anonymous

Your request for no MSG was ignored. —Anonymous, fortune cookie

. . . reluctance to cause pain coupled with the necessity to devour . . . a peculiar human trick is the result, which consists in admitting and denying evils at the same time. To have human life, and also an inhuman life . . . To bite, to swallow. At the same time to pity your food.
—Saul Bellow, *Herzog*

Nobody goes there anymore. It's too crowded.
—Yogi Berra, *The Yogi Book*, to Stan Musial and Joe Garagiola about Ruggeri's Restaurant in St. Louis

Chili's a lot like sex: When it's good it's great, and even when it's bad, it's not so bad.
—Bill Boldenweck, in *American Way* magazine, Jun 1982

I doubt whether the world holds for any one a more soul-stirring surprise than the first adventure with ice-cream.
—Heywood Broun, *Seeing Things at Night* (1921), "Holding a Baby"

Man is the only animal that can remain on friendly terms with the victims he intends to eat until he eats them.
—Samuel Butler (1835-1902), *Note-Books*, "Mind and Matter"

Since we have a good loaf, let us not look for cheesecakes.
—Miguel de Cervantes

The proof of the pudding is in the eating.   —Miguel de Cervantes

With bread all sorrows are less.   —Miguel de Cervantes, *Don Quixote*

Cheese—milk's leap toward immortality.
—Clifton Fadiman, *Any Number Can Play*

The way to a man's heart is through his stomach.
—Fanny Fern, *Willis Parton*

A fat kitchen, a lean will.
—Benjamin Franklin, *Poor Richard's Almanack*, 1733

He was a very valiant man who first ventured on eating of oysters.
—Thomas Fuller (1608-1661),
The History of the Worthies of England (1662)

I want every peasant to have a chicken in his pot on Sundays.
—King Henry IV of France

Better is half a loaf than no bread.   —John Heywood, *Proverbs*

I know on which side my bread is buttered. —John Heywood, *Proverbs*

Man should not be over-anxious for a subsistence, for it is provided
by the Creator. The infant no sooner droppeth from the womb
than the breasts of the mother begin to stream. —*The Hitopadesa*

Oh! God! that bread should be so dear, / And flesh and blood so
cheap! —Thomas Hood, "The Song of the Shirt"

He is rich enough who does not want bread.
—Saint Jerome, *Epistles*, Ep. 125

Till somebody touches your mush, you never grasp anything.
—Petya Kishkin, in Alexander Solzhenitsyn,
The Gulag Archipelago Three

That's something I've noticed about food: whenever there's a crisis if
you can get people to eating normally things get better.
—Madeleine L'Engle, *The Moon by Night*

Everything you see I owe to spaghetti. —Sophia Loren

It's a very odd thing— / As odd as can be— / That whatever Miss T
eats / Turns into Miss T. —Walter de la Mare, *Peacock Pie*, "Miss T"

The trouble with eating Italian food is that five or six days later
you're hungry again. —George Miller

No man is lonely while eating spaghetti; it requires too much attention. —Robert Morley

When I ponder my mind / I consistently find / It is glued / On food.
—Ogden Nash, *Many Long Years Ago*, "The Clean Platter"

Strange to see how a good dinner and feasting reconcile everybody.
—Samuel Pepys, *Diary*, 9 Nov 1665

Never eat more than you can lift.
—"Miss Piggy" (a Jim Henson puppet)

You cannot unscramble eggs. —Proverb (American)

Can one start a fast with baklava in one's hand?—Proverb (Armenian)

When eating bamboo shoots, remember the man who planted them.
—Proverb (Chinese)

Even crumbs are bread. —Proverb (Danish)

Bread is the staff of life. —Proverb (English)

A little gall spoils a great deal of honey. —Proverb (French)

Whose bread I eat, his song I sing. —Proverb (German)

He that will eat the kernel must crack the nut. —Proverb (Latin)

The rich would have to eat money, but luckily the poor provide food.
—Proverb (Russian)

Coffee—black as hell, strong as death, sweet as love.
—Proverb (Turkish)

If you want the meat, you have to take the bones.
—Proverb (Viennese)

Worries go down better with soup than without. —Proverb (Yiddish)

There is no love sincerer than the love of food.
—George Bernard Shaw, *Man and Superman*

He who feasts every day, feasts no day. —Charles Simmons

In Mexico we have a word for sushi: bait. —Jose Simon

I eat merely to put food out of my mind. —N. F. Simpson

Serenely full, the epicure would say, / Fate cannot harm me, I have
dined to-day. —Sydney Smith, "Receipt for a Salad"

. . . but food eaten quickly isn't food.
—Alexander Solzhenitsyn, *One Day in the Life of Ivan Denisovich*

It [soup] hadn't been ladled from the top of the caldron, but it wasn't
the stuff from the bottom either.
—Alexander Solzhenitsyn, *One Day in the Life of Ivan Denisovich*

He was a bold man that first ate an oyster. —Jonathan Swift

I don't care where I sit as long as I get fed. —Calvin Trillin

Part of the secret of success in life is to eat what you like and let the
food fight it out inside. —Mark Twain

It is harder to be unhappy when you are eating.
—Kurt Vonnegut, Jr., *Breakfast of Champions*

I saw him even now going the way of all flesh, that is to say towards
the kitchen.   —John Webster, *Westward Hoe*, Act II, Sc. ii

Gluttony is not a secret vice.   —Orson Welles

You'll be hungry again in an hour.
—Tom Wilson, fortune cookie opened by
his cartoon character Ziggy

FOOLISHNESS

The best way to convince a fool that he is wrong is to let him have his
own way.   —Josh Billings

Foolproof systems don't take into account the ingenuity of fools.
—Gene Brown

You will do foolish things, but do them with enthusiasm.   —Colette

When in doubt, make a fool of yourself. There is a microscopically
thin line between being brilliantly creative and acting like the
most gigantic idiot on earth. So what the hell, leap.
—Cynthia Heimel, in *Village Voice* (1982),
"Lower Manhattan Survival Tactics"

People are never so near playing the fool as when they think themselves wise.   —Mary Wortley Montagu, letter to her daughter,
Countess of Bute, 1 Mar 1755

For fools rush in where angels fear to tread.
—Alexander Pope, *An Essay on Criticism*

. . . there are no fools . . .   —J. D. Salinger, *Seymour an Introduction*

Lord, what fools these mortals be!
—William Shakespeare, *A Midsummer-Night's Dream*, Act III, Sc. ii

Give me the young man who has brains enough to make a fool of
himself.   —Robert Louis Stevenson,
Virginibus Puerisque, "Crabbed Age and Youth"

If thou hast never been a fool, be sure thou wilt never be a wise man.
—William Makepeace Thackeray

One way in which fools succeed where wise men fail is that through ignorance of the danger they sometimes go coolly about a hazardous business. —Richard Whately

FOOTBALL

Pro football is like nuclear warfare. There are no winners, only survivors. —Frank Gifford

Coach, some day when the going gets rough, tell the boys to win one for the Gipper. —George Gipp, on the authority of Knute Rockne

The way to succeed at quarterback is to call the unexpected consistently. —John Hadl, Los Angeles Ram quarterback

Football players, like prostitutes, are in the business of ruining their bodies for the pleasure of strangers. —Merle Kessler

Probably the Beatles' white album.
—Steve Largent, Seattle Seahawks receiver, 1987 comment when asked what record he would treasure most

The offense sells tickets and the defense wins the games.
—Lindsey Nelson, sportscaster, CBS-TV, about football, 1982

Sport is a product of human culture. America seems to need football at this state of our social development. When you get ninety million people watching a single game on television, it . . . shows you that people need something to identify with. —Joe Paterno

Momma always told me never to wear a hat indoors. When it can't rain on you, you're indoors. —Bum Phillips, former NFL coach, on why he didn't wear a hat in the Astrodome

Thinking . . . is what gets you caught from behind. —O. J. Simpson

It's a lonesome walk to the sidelines, especially when thousands of people are cheering your replacement.
—Fran Tarkenton, NFL quarterback

When everything else breaks down, I don't hesitate to roam out of the pocket and do the boogaloo. —Frank Tarkenton, NFL quarterback

FORBEARANCE

There is a limit at which forbearance ceases to be a virtue.
—Edmund Burke, *Observations on a Late State of the Nation*

FORCE

Force is not a remedy.
—John Bright, speech, Birmingham, England, 16 Nov 1880

The use of force alone is but temporary. It may subdue for a moment;
but it does not remove the necessity of subduing again: and a
nation is not governed, which is perpetually to be conquered.
—Edmund Burke,
speech on conciliation with America, 22 Mar 1775

Force is of brutes.   —John Dryden, *Palamon and Arcite*, Book III

. . . force always attracts men of low morality . . .
—Albert Einstein, *Ideas and Opinions*

Force without reason falls of its own weight.   —Horace, *Odes*

The power that is supported by force alone will have cause often to
tremble.   —Kossuth

Force is all-conquering, but its victories are short-lived.
—Abraham Lincoln

May the Force be with you.
—George Lucas, running line in the move Star Wars

Force is never more operative than when it is known to exist but is
not brandished.   —Alfred Thayer Mahan

Who overcomes / By force, hath overcome but half his foe.
—John Milton, *Paradise Lost*, Book 1

Force rules the world—not opinion; but it is opinion that makes use
of force.   —Blaise Pascal

All of the nations of the world, for realistic as well as spiritual rea-
sons, must come to the abandonment of the use of force.
—Franklin D. Roosevelt and Winston Churchill,
The Atlantic Charter, 14 Aug 1941

Even in a righteous cause force is a fearful thing.   —Friedrich Schiller

Men must reap the things they sow, / Force from force must ever flow.
—Percy Shelley, "Lines Written Among the Euganean Hills"

FOREIGN LANGUAGES

When you start a sentence in German, you have to know in the
beginning what the end will be. —Otto Friedrich, *Before the Deluge*

Who does not know another language, does not know his own.
—Johann Wolfgang von Goethe, *Sprüche in Prosa*

In Paris they simply stared when I spoke to them in French; I never
did succeed in making those idiots understand their own language.
—Mark Twain

They spell it Vinci and pronounce it Vinchy; foreigners always spell
better than they pronounce.
—Mark Twain, *Innocents Abroad*, Ch. 19

FORESIGHT

A stitch in time saves nine. —Thomas Fuller, M. D., *Gnomologia*

The time to repair the roof is when the sun is shining.
—John F. Kennedy, State of the Union Message, 11 Jan 1962

Dig a well before you are thirsty. —Proverb (Chinese)

FORETHOUGHT

In life, as in chess, forethought wins. —Charles Buxton

FOREWARNING

Forewarned is forearmed. —Proverb (Latin)

FORGETTING

Life cannot go on without much forgetting. —Honoré de Balzac

Good to forgive; / Best to forget! —Robert Browning

We have all forgot more than we remember.
—Thomas Fuller, M. D., *Gnomologia*, No. 5442

All of us forget more than we remember . . .
—Kevin Goldstein-Jackson

Though the past haunt me as a spirit, I do not ask to forget.
—Felicia Dorothea Browne Hemans

But now I see well the old proverb is true: That parish priest forget-
teth that ever he was a clerk! —John Heywood

But men are men: the best sometimes forget.
—William Shakespeare, *Othello*, Act II, Sc. iii

FORGIVENESS

Doing an injury puts you below your enemy; revenging one makes
you but even with him; forgiving it sets you above him.
—Anonymous

They who forgive most shall be most forgiven.
—Philip James Bailey, *Festus*

But if ye forgive not men their trespasses, neither will your Father forgive your trespasses. —*The Bible* (KJV): Matthew 6:15

And when ye stand praying, forgive, if ye have anything against any:
that your Father also which is in heaven may forgive you your trespasses. —*The Bible* (KJV): Mark 11:25

Judge not, and ye shall not be judged: condemn not, and ye shall not
be condemned: forgive, and ye shall be forgiven.
—*The Bible* (KJV): Luke 6:37

Take heed to yourselves: If thy brother trespass against thee, rebuke
him; and if he repent, forgive him. —*The Bible* (KJV): Luke 17:3

Then said Jesus, Father, forgive them; for they know not what they
do . . . —*The Bible* (KJV): Luke 23:34

And be ye kind one to another, tenderhearted, forgiving one another,
even as God, for Christ's sake, hath forgiven you.
—*The Bible* (KJV): Ephesians 4:32

The noblest vengeance is to forgive.
—H. G. Bohn, *Hand-Book of Proverbs*

He who cannot forgive others breaks the bridge over which he himself must pass. —Confucius

Life is an adventure in forgiveness. —Norman Cousins

The kindest and happiest pair / Will find occasion to forbear; / And something, every day they live, / To pity, and perhaps forgive.
—William Cowper, "Mutual Forbearance Necessary to the Happiness of the Married State"

Forgive, son; men are men, they needs must err.
—Euripides, *Hippolytus*

A man must learn to forgive himself.   —Arthur Davison Ficke

But forgiveness must not only be given but received also.
—William Golding, *Free Fall*, Ch. 14

If you forgive people enough you belong to them, and they to you, whether either person likes it or not—squatter's rights of the heart.
—James Hilton, *Time and Time Again*

It is easier to get forgiveness than permission.   —Grace Hopper

If you hug to yourself any resentment against somebody else, you destroy the bridge by which God would come to you.
—Peter Marshall

To err is human, to forgive divine.
—Alexander Pope, *An Essay on Criticism*

Forgive and forget.   —Proverb (14th century)

He that forgives gains the victory.   —Proverb (African)

He who forgives ends the quarrel.   —Proverb (African)

The more a man knows, the more he forgives.   —Proverb (Italian)

Forgiving the unrepentant is like drawing pictures on water.
—Proverb (Japanese)

The remedy for wrongs is to forget them.   —Publilius Syrus

We win by tenderness; we conquer by forgiveness.
—Frederick W. Robertson

Forgiveness is the divinest of victories.   —Friedrich Schiller

Forgive that you may be forgiven.
—Seneca, *De Beneficiis*, Book VII, Sec. 28

Who needs forgiveness, should the same extend with readiness.
                                                —Seneca, *Agememnon*

There is a noble forgetfulness—that which does not remember
    injuries.   —Charles Simmons

The more we know, the better we forgive; / Whoe'er feels deeply, feels
    for all who live.   —Madame de Staël

God forgave us without any merit on our part; therefore we must for-
    give others, whether or not we think they merit it.
                    —Lehman Strauss, *Sense and Nonsense About Prayer*

We Christians cannot refuse to forgive anyone, no matter what the
    circumstances.   —Lehman Strauss, *Sense and Nonsense About Prayer*

What every Christian owes to every other Christian is forgiveness.
                    —Lehman Strauss, *Sense and Nonsense About Prayer*

You must forgive those who transgress against you before you can
    look to forgiveness from Above.   —*The Talmud*

But forgiveness is not an emotion . . . Forgiveness is an act of will,
    and the will can function regardless of the temperature of the
    heart.
          —Corrie ten Boom, *Tramp for the Lord*, with Jamie Buckingham

If we forgive other people, our hearts are made fit to receive forgive-
    ness.
          —Corrie ten Boom, *Tramp for the Lord*, with Jamie Buckingham

It is by forgiving that one is forgiven.
                    —Mother Teresa, *For the Brotherhood of Man*

Forgiveness is the fragrance the violet sheds on the heel that has
    crushed it.   —Mark Twain

F O R T U N E

Bear good fortune modestly.   —Ausonius, *Epigrams*

Fortune befriends the bold.   —John Dryden

He that courts fortune boldly, makes her kind.   —John Dryden

Fortune favors the audacious.   —Erasmus

One is never as fortunate or as unfortunate as one imagines.
—François de La Rochefoucauld

We need greater virtues to sustain good than evil fortune.
—François de La Rochefoucauld

A true philosopher is beyond the reach of fortune.
—Walter Savage Landor

But Fortune, who never forgets her duty, turns her wheel suddenly.
—Marie de France, *The Lais of Marie de France*

Fortune gives too much to many, enough to none.
—Martial, *Epigrams*, Book XII, epig. 10.

Hath fortune dealt thee ill cards? Let wisdom make thee a good
gamester. —Francis Quarles

Fortune brings in some boats that are not steer'd.
—William Shakespeare, *Cymbeline*, Act IV, Sc. iii

Fortune favors the brave. —Terence, *Phormio*

Fortune sides with him who dares. —Virgil, *The Aeneid*

A man is never so on trial as in the moment of excessive good fortune. —Gen. Lew Wallace, *Ben Hur*, Book V, Ch. 7

FRANCE

It's impossible in normal times to rally a nation that has 265 kinds of
cheese. —Charles de Gaulle, in *Newsweek*, 13 Nov 1967

Boy those French, they have a different word for everything.
—Steve Martin

FRANKNESS

Frankness invites frankness.
—Ralph Waldo Emerson, *Essays, First Series*, "Prudence"

Be yourself and speak your mind today, though it contradict all you
have said before. —Elbert Hubbard, *The Note Book*

It's important to our friends to believe that we are unreservedly frank with them, and important to friendship that we are not.
—Mignon McLaughlin, *The Neurotic's Notebook*

FREEDOM

The most certain test by which we judge whether a country is really free is the amount of the security enjoyed by minorities.
—Lord Acton, *The History of Freedom in Antiquity*

The clash of ideas is the sound of freedom.   —Anonymous, graffiti

If the Son, therefore, shall make you free, ye shall be free indeed.
—*The Bible* (KJV): John 8:36

Who would be free, themselves must strike the blow.   —Lord Byron

For what avail the plough or sail, / Or land or life, if freedom fail?
—Ralph Waldo Emerson

The story of man is the history, first, of the acceptance and imposition of restraints necessary to permit communal life; and second, of the emancipation of the individual within that system of necessary restraints.   —Justice Abe Fortas

Freedom is not worth having if it does not include the freedom to make mistakes.   —Mahatma Gandhi

Martin Luther King [Jr.] during the civil rights movement used to exclaim that he looked forward to heaven where he would be "Free at last." That is the inscription on his tomb in Atlanta.
—Billy Graham, *Till Armageddon*

The greatest glory of a free-born people
Is to transmit that freedom to their children.   —Havard

. . . he was jeopardizing his traditional rights of freedom and independence by daring to exercise them.   —Joseph Heller, *Catch-22*

There can be no real freedom without the freedom to fail.
—Eric Hoffer, *The Ordeal of Change*

The price of freedom of religion or of the press is that we must put up with, and even pay for, a good deal of rubbish.
—Justice Robert Jackson

What stands if freedom fall? —Rudyard Kipling

Those who deny freedom to others deserve it not for themselves, and, under a just God, cannot long retain it.
—Abraham Lincoln, letter to H. L. Pierce

How bad was bad if you were free? —Bernard Malamud

Free men set themselves free. —James Oppenheim

If the body is enslaved, at least the mind is free. —Proverb (Greek)

Man is born free; and everywhere he is in chains.
—Jean Jacques Rousseau, *The Social Contract*

It is only when a man is alone that he is really free.
—Arthur Schopenhauer

My definition of a free society is a society where it is safe to be unpopular. —Adlai Stevenson, speech, Detroit, 1952

The sound of tireless voices is the price we pay for the right to hear the music of our own opinions.
—Adlai Stevenson, speech, New York City, 28 Aug 1952

FRIENDS

Friends are born, not made.
—Henry Adams, *The Education of Henry Adams* (1907)

One friend in a lifetime is much; two are many; three are barely possible.
—Henry Adams

Friends are family you choose for yourself. —Jane Adams

Friendship improves happiness, and abates misery, by doubling our joy, and dividing our grief. —Joseph Addison

Stay is a charming word in a friend's vocabulary.
—Bronson Alcott, *Concord Days*, "June"

A friend is a person who goes around saying nice things about you behind your back. —Anonymous

Friendships multiply joys and divide griefs. —Anonymous

God send me a friend that will tell me of my faults.   —Anonymous

If you were another person, would you like to be a friend of yours?
—Anonymous

Real friends are those who, when you've made a fool of yourself,
   don't think you've done a permanent job.   —Anonymous

To suspect a friend is worse than to be deceived by him.
—Anonymous

When a friend deals with a friend, / Let the bargain be clear and well-
   penned, / That they may continue friends to the end. —Anonymous

A faithful friend is the medicine of life.
—Apocrypha, "Ecclesiasticus," 6:16

A friend is a second self.   —Aristotle, *Nichomachean Ethics*

Friends are much better tried in bad fortune than in good. —Aristotle

Friendship is a single soul dwelling in two bodies.
—Aristotle, in Diogenes Laertius,
Lives and Opinions of Eminent Philosophers

Without friends, the world is but a wilderness.   —Francis Bacon

Friendships last when each friend thinks he has a slight superiority
   over the other.   —Honoré de Balzac

One sees much more in a friend.
—Saul Bellow, *Henderson the Rain King*

A friend loveth at all time, and a brother is born for adversity.
—*The Bible* (KJV): Proverbs 17:17

Our friends see the best in us, and by that very fact call forth the best
   from us.   —Black

A companion loves some agreeable qualities which a man may possess, but a friend loves the man himself.
—James Boswell, *London Journal*, 7 Jul 1763

Friends are the family we choose for ourselves.
—Edna Buchanan, *Suitable for Framing*

A real friend is somewhat like a ghost or apparition; much talked of,
but rarely seen. —Charles N. Buck

Friendship is a strong and habitual inclination in two persons to promote the good and happiness of one another. —Eustace Budgell

You can make more friends in two months by becoming interested in
other people than you can in two years by trying to get other people interested in you. —Dale Carnegie

A man must eat a peck of salt with his friend before he knows him.
—Miguel de Cervantes, *Don Quixote*

A true friend is a sort of second self. —Cicero, *De Amicitia*

Friends are proved by adversity. —Cicero

Friendship is a sheltering tree.
—Samuel Taylor Coleridge, *Youth and Age*

The friendships which last are those wherein each friend respects the
other's dignity to the point of not really wanting anything from
him. —Cyril Connolly, *The Unquiet Grave*

Plenty, as well as Want, can separate friends. —Abraham Cowley

What is a friend? I will tell you. It is a person with whom you dare to
be yourself. —Frank Crane, "A Definition of Friendship"

Friends, those relations that one makes for oneself. —Delille, *Pitié*

It is the friends you can call up at 4 a.m. that matter.
—Marlene Dietrich

Friendships which are born in misfortune are more firm and lasting
than those which are formed in happiness. —D'Urfrey

Oh, the comfort, the inexpressible comfort of feeling safe with a person; having neither to weigh thoughts nor measure words, but to
pour them all out, just as they are, chaff and grain together, knowing that a faithful hand will take and sift them, keep what is worth
keeping, and then, with the breath of kindness, blow the rest away.
—George Eliot

A friend is a person with whom I may be sincere.
—Ralph Waldo Emerson

A friend is one before whom I may think aloud.
—Ralph Waldo Emerson, *Essays, First Series*, "Friendship"

A friend may well be reckoned the masterpiece of nature.
—Ralph Waldo Emerson

God evidently does not intend us all to be rich, or powerful or great,
but He does intend us all to be friends.   —Ralph Waldo Emerson

Go oft to the house of thy friend, for weeds choke the unused path.
—Ralph Waldo Emerson

Happy is the house that shelters a friend.   —Ralph Waldo Emerson

I didn't find my friends; the good God gave them to me.
—Ralph Waldo Emerson

I do with my friends as I do with books. I would have them where I
can find them but seldom use them.   —Ralph Waldo Emerson

It is one of the blessings of old friends that you can afford to be stupid with them.   —Ralph Waldo Emerson

The only reward of virtue is virtue; the only way to have a friend is to
be one.   —Ralph Waldo Emerson, *Essays, First Series*, "Friendship"

It is not so much our friends' help that helps us as the confident
knowledge that they will help us.   —Epicurus

He does good to himself who does good to his friend.
—Erasmus, *Familiar Colloquies*

Take heed of a speedy professing friend; love is never lasting which
flames before it burns.   —Owen Feltham

Let me live in my house by the side of the road
And be a friend to man.   —Sam Walter Foss, in Hazel Felleman,
editor, *Best Loved Poems of the American People*,
"The House by the Side of the Road"

Be slow in choosing a friend, slower in changing.
—Benjamin Franklin

If you have one true friend you have more than your share.
—Thomas Fuller

Let friendship creep gently to a height; if it rush to it, it may soon run itself out of breath. —Thomas Fuller

Be a friend to thyself, and others will be too.
—Thomas Fuller, M. D., *Gnomologia*, No. 847

We shall never have friends, if we expect to find them without fault.
—Thomas Fuller, M. D., *Gnomologia*, No. 5456

To friendship every burden's light. —John Gay

True friendship comes when silence between two people is comfortable. —Dave Tyson Gentry

Friends are a second existence. —Baltasar Gracián

Find some friends you like, or be stuck with the friends who like you.
—Alan Harris

Friendship is blessed, not so much for the friends it makes for us, which has an element of gain, but the friend it makes of us, which has the element of giving. —Henry S. Haskins

The discussing the characters and foibles of common friends is a great sweetness and cement of friendship. —William Hazlitt

Choose thy friends like thy books, few but choice. —James Howell

Your friend is the man who knows all about you, and still likes you.
—Elbert Hubbard, *The Roycroft Dictionary and Book of Epigrams*

A man, Sir, should keep his friendships in constant repair.
—Samuel Johnson, in James Boswell, *Life of Samuel Johnson*

The endearing elegance of female friendship.
—Samuel Johnson, *Rasselas*, Ch. 45

Nothing is more dangerous than a friend without discretion; even a prudent enemy is preferable. —Jean de La Fontaine

It is more shameful to distrust our friends than to be deceived by them. —François de La Rochefoucauld

The better part of one's life consists of his friendships.
—Abraham Lincoln

A friend gives us confidence for life, a friend makes us outdo ourselves. —Anna Lindsay

Friendships, like marriages, are dependent on avoiding the unforgiv-
able. —John D. MacDonald

To lose an old friend is as the loss of a bead from life's rosary; or to
drop a jewel into the depths of a turbulent sea. —Douglas Meador

. . . you can't have theories about friends. If you can't take friends
largely, and without suspicion—then they are not friends at all.
—Sara Murphy, *Living Well is the Best Revenge*

In life you throw a ball. You hope it will reach a wall and bounce back
so you can throw it again. You hope your friends will provide that
wall. —Pablo Picasso

Honest men esteem and value nothing so much in this world as a real
friend. Such a one is, as it were, another self. —Pilpay

Prosperity is no just scale; adversity is the only balance to weigh
friends. —Plutarch

Friends are lost by calling often and calling seldom.—Proverb (Gaelic)

A hedge between keeps friendship green. —Proverb (German)

Friendship is a plant which one must water often.
—Proverb (German)

A friend's eye is a good mirror. —Proverb (Irish)

Love your friend with all his faults. —Proverb (Italian)

Hold a true friend with both your hands. —Proverb (Nigerian)

Be a friend to yourself, and others will. —Proverb (Scottish)

Books and friends should be few and good. —Proverb (Spanish)

Sooner or later you've heard about all your best friends have to say.
Then comes the tolerance of real love. —Ned Rorem

What is love? two souls and one flesh; friendship? two bodies and
one soul.
—Joseph Roux, *Meditations of a Parish Priest*, Part XX, no 31

The friends thou hast, and their adoption tried, / Grapple them to
thy soul with hoops of steel . . .
—William Shakespeare, *Hamlet*, Act I, Sc. iii

A real friendship is a light thing. A real friend holds you loosely.
—Anne Rivers Siddons

Be slow to fall into friendship, but when thou art in, continue firm
and constant.   —Socrates

Reprove thy friend privately; commend him publicly.   —Solon

The heart senses who is friend and who is no friend.
—Alexander Solzhenitsyn, *The Gulag Archipelago Three*

The best friends in the world may differ sometimes.—Laurence Sterne

True friends visit us in prosperity only when invited, but in adversity
they come without invitation.   —Theophrastus

. . . one friend was all that a man needed in order to be well-supplied
with friendship.   —Kurt Vonnegut, Jr., *The Sirens of Titan*

Friendship is the wine of life.   —Young

FRUGALITY

By sowing frugality we reap liberty, a golden harvest.   —Agesilaus

Frugality is an estate.   —Anonymous

Eat it up, make it do, wear it out.   —Calvin Coolidge

I am strongly drawn to a frugal life and am often oppressively aware
that I am engrossing an undue amount of the labor of my fellow
men.   —Albert Einstein, *Ideas and Opinions*

Frugality is a handsome income.   —Erasmus, *Familiar Colloquies*

Mend your clothes and you may hold out this year.
—George Herbert, *Jacula Prudentum*

Ask your purse what you should buy.   —Proverb (English)

Live within your harvest.   —Proverb (Latin)

... frugality makes a poor man rich. —Seneca

FUN

I've taken my fun where I've found it. —Rudyard Kipling, *The Ladies*

FUNERALS

Always go to other people's funerals, otherwise they won't go to
yours. —Yogi Berra, to Mickey Mantle, *The Yogi Book*

Few occasions are as joyous to small children as funerals, almost better than the big wedding blowouts that take place at night when
it's hard to stay awake. A small boy will never be harshly criticized
at a funeral; he is more treasured as death comes close and all his
wickedness vanishes before the inescapable fact that thank God, he
is healthy. —Arthur Miller, *Timebends*

Isn't a memorial service meant to comfort the living?
—Anne Tyler, *Breathing Lessons*

The FUTURE

The future ain't what it used to be. —Yogi Berra, *The Yogi Book*

Boast not thyself of tomorrow; for thou knowest not what a day may
bring forth. —*The Bible* (KJV): Proverbs 27:1

When all else is lost, the future still remains.
—Christian Nestell Bovée

Light tomorrow with today. —Elizabeth Barrett Browning

Coming events cast their shadows before.
—Thomas Campbell, "Lochliel's Warning"

Often do the spirits of great events stride on before the events / And
in today already walks tomorrow. —Samuel Taylor Coleridge

Only mothers can think of the future—because they give birth to it in
their children. —Maxim Gorky, *Vassa Zheleznova*

A wise God shrouds the future in obscure darkness. —Horace

The future is purchased by the present. —Samuel Johnson

We have the power to make this the best generation of mankind in
the history of the world—or to make it the last. —John F. Kennedy

The best thing about the future is that it comes only one day at a
time.   —Abraham Lincoln

No man ever sank under the burden of the day. It is when tomorrow's
burden is added to the burden of today that the weight is more
than a man can bear. Never load yourself so. If you find yourself so
loaded, at least remember this: it is your own doing, not God's. He
begs you to leave the future to him, and mind the present.
—George Macdonald

After all, tomorrow is another day.
—Margaret Mitchell, *Gone with the Wind*

It is my invincible belief that science and peace will triumph over
ignorance and war; that the nations will come to an understanding, not for destruction but for construction, and that the future
will be to those who have done the most for suffering humanity.
—Louis Pasteur

The afternoon knows what the morning never suspected.
—Proverb (Swedish)

The future belongs to those who believe in the beauty of their
dreams.   —Eleanor Roosevelt

Lord! we know what we are, but know not what we may be.
—William Shakespeare, *Hamlet*, Act IV, Sc. v

Future shock: the shattering stress and disorientation that we induce
in individuals by subjecting them to too much change in too short
a time.   —Alvin Toffler, *Future Shock*

— G —

GAMBLING

A lottery is a tax on people who are bad at math.
—Anonymous bumper sticker

He who gambles picks his own pocket. —Anonymous

The best throw with the dice is to throw them away. —Anonymous

Keep flax from fire, and youth from gaming. —Benjamin Franklin

A pack of cards is the devil's prayer book. —Proverb (German)

GAMES

As in a game of cards, so in the game of life, we must play what is dealt to us, and the glory consists, not so much in winning as in playing a poor hand well. —Josh Billings

Life's too short for chess. —Henry James Byron, *Our Boys*, Act I

Games lubricate the body and the mind. —Benjamin Franklin

When in doubt, win the trick. —Edmond Hoyle, *Hoyle's Games*

Once the game is over, the king and the pawn go back into the same box. —Proverb (Italian)

Mahatma GANDHI

As Gandhi stepped aboard a train one day, one of his shoes slipped off and landed on the track. He was unable to retrieve it as the train was moving. To the amazement of his companions, Gandhi calmly took off his other shoe and threw it back along the track to land close to the first. Asked by a fellow passenger why he did so, Gandhi smiled. "The poor man who finds the shoe lying on the track," he replied, "will now have a pair he can use." —Anonymous

Generations to come will scarce believe that such a one as this ever in flesh and blood walked upon this earth.
—Albert Einstein, in Richard Attenborough, compiler, *The Words of Gandhi*

We should strive to do things in his [Gandhi's] spirit . . . not to use violence in fighting for our cause, but by non-participation in what we believe is evil.   —Albert Einstein, *Ideas and Opinions*

I have nothing new to teach the world. Truth and nonviolence are as old as the hills. All I have done is to try experiments in both on as vast a scale as I could. In doing so, I have sometimes erred and learnt by my errors. Life and its problems have thus become to me so many experiments in the practice of truth and nonviolence . . .
          —Mahatma Gandhi, in Richard Attenborough, compiler, *The Words of Gandhi*

[It was] the poet Rabindranath Tagore who . . . dubbed Gandhi "Mahatma," or Great Soul, a traditional Indian honorary title.
          —Gerald Gold, *Gandhi, A Pictorial Biography*

GARDENS

God Almighty first planted a garden; and, indeed, it is the purest of human pleasures.   —Francis Bacon, *Essays*, "Of Gardens"

To cultivate a garden is to walk with God.   —Christian Nestell Bovée

What is a weed? A plant whose virtues have not been discovered.
          —Ralph Waldo Emerson, *Fortune of the Republic*

One is nearer God's Heart in a garden
Than anywhere else on earth.   —Dorothy Frances Gurney, *Poems*, "The Lord God Planted a Garden"

He who makes a garden / Works hand in hand with God.
          —Douglas Malloch, "Who Makes a Garden"

The bad gardener quarrels with his rake.   —Proverb (American)

GENERALIZATION

Given a thimbleful of facts we rush to make generalizations as large as a tub.   —Gordon W. Allport

All generalizations are false, including this one.
          —Alexander Chase, *Perspectives*

Intellectuals . . . regard over-simplification as the original sin of the
  mind and have no use for the slogans, the unqualified assertions
  and sweeping generalizations.   —Aldous Huxley

General notions are generally wrong.
      —Mary Wortley Montagu, letter to her husband, 28 Mar 1710

GENERATIONS

The generations of living things pass in a short time, and like runners
  hand on the torch of life.   —Lucretius, *De Rerum Natura*

Every generation revolts against its fathers and makes friends with its
  grandfathers.   —Lewis Mumford, *The Brown Decade*

GENEROSITY

The generous man enriches himself by giving, the miser hoards himself poor.   —Anonymous

As a rule, only the poor are generous.   —Honoré de Balzac

The secret pleasure of a generous act is the great mind's great bribe.
      —John Dryden

Generosity, to be perfect, should always be accompanied by a dash of
  humor.   —Marie Ebner-Eschenbach

. . . do it now.—it is not safe to leave a generous feeling to the cooling
  influences of a cold world.   —Guthrie

The quickest generosity is the best.   —Proverb (Arab)

Generosity gives help rather than advice.
      —Luc de Clapiers Vauvenargues

GENIUS

Doing easily what others find difficult is talent; doing what is impossible is genius.   —Henri Frédéric Amiel

Genius is mainly an affair of energy.
      —Matthew Arnold, *Essays in Criticism,*
      "Literary Influence of Academies"

We define genius as the capacity for productive reaction against one's
   training.   —Bernard Berenson

Genius learns from nature; talent learns from books.   —Josh Billings

... where a man's wound is, that is where his genius will be.
                                          —Robert Bly, *Iron John*

Passion holds up the bottom of the universe and genius paints up its
   roof.   —Chang Ch'ao

Genius is of no country.   —Charles Churchill, *The Rosciad*

Mediocrity can talk; but it is for genius to observe.
                                          —Benjamin Disraeli

When nature has work to do, she creates a genius to do it.
                     —Ralph Waldo Emerson, lecture, Waterville
               (now Colby) College, 1841, "Method of Nature"

The first and last thing which is required of genius is the love of
   truth.   —Johann Wolfgang von Goethe

Men of genius do not excel in any profession because they labor in it,
   but they labor in it because they excel.   —William Hazlitt,
            Characteristics in the Manner of Rochefoucauld's Maxims

It is for truth that God created genius.   —Alphonse de Lamartine

Many a genius has been slow of growth. Oaks that flourish for a thousand years do not spring up into beauty like a reed.
                     —George Henry Lewes, *Spanish Drama*, Ch. 2

To genius life never grows commonplace.   —James Russell Lowell

It is a mark of genius not to astonish but to be astonished.
                                          —Aubrey Menen

Genius does what it must, and Talent does what it can.
      —Owen Meredith, "Last Words of a Sensitive Second-Rate Poet"

There is no great genius without some touch of madness.
                          —Seneca, *On Tranquility of the Mind*

A man possesses talent; genius possesses the man.   — Isaac Stern

I have nothing to declare but my genius.
—Oscar Wilde, remark at the New York Customs House,
Jan 1882, in Frank Harris, *Oscar Wilde*

Genius lights its own fire, but it is constantly collecting materials to keep alive the flame. —Wilmott

GENTLEMEN

Education begins the gentleman, but reading, good company, and reflection must finish him. —John Locke

This is the final test of a gentleman: his respect for those who can be of no possible service to him. —William Lyon Phelps

GENTLENESS

Speak gently! 'Tis a little thing / Dropp'd in the heart's deep well; / The good, the joy which it may bring / Eternity shall tell. —David Bates

'Tis merry when gentle-folks meet. —Antony Brewer, "Countrie Girl"

The great mind knows the power of gentleness, / Only tries force because persuasion fails. —Robert Browning, "Herakles"

Throw away thy rod, / Throw away thy wrath; / O my God, / Take the gentle path. —George Herbert, "Discipline"

But curb thou the high spirit in thy breast, / For gentle ways are best, and keep aloof / From sharp contentions.
—Homer, *The Iliad*, Book IX, line 317

Gentleness succeeds better than violence. —Jean de La Fontaine

The power of gentleness is irresistible. —H. Martyn

The true problem of living is to keep our hearts sweet and gentle in the hardest conditions and experiences. —J. R. Miller

He who goes gently, goes safely and will go far. —Proverb (Italian)

Nothing is so strong as gentleness, / Nothing so gentle as real strength. —Saint Francis de Sales

His life was gentle, and the elements / So mix'd in him that / Nature
might stand up / And say to all the world, / 'This was a man!'
—William Shakespeare, *Julius Caesar*, Act V, Sc. v

Gentleness and affability conquer at last. —Terence

GEOGRAPHY

Oh, East is East, and West is West, and never the twain shall meet,
/ Till Earth and Sky stand presently at God's Judgment Seat.
—Rudyard Kipling, "The Ballad of East and West"

GIFTS

God's gifts put man's best dreams to shame.
—Elizabeth Barrett Browning, *Sonnets from the Portuguese*, 26

The only true gift is a portion of yourself. —Ralph Waldo Emerson

Accept that well-meant gift happily, for taking is giving too.
—Marion Flood French

Never look a gift horse in the mouth. —Saint Jerome

It isn't as important to name one of God's gifts as to use it.
—Ron Parrish, sermon, Hope Chapel, Austin, Texas, 13 Nov 1994

Whatever a man has is only a gift. —Proverb (German)

. . . the weakest among us has a gift, however seemingly trivial, which
is peculiar to him, and which, worthily used, will be a gift also to
his race forever. —John Ruskin

God has given some gifts to the whole human race, from which no
one is excluded. —Seneca, *De Beneficiis*, IV, 28

The excellence of a gift lies in its appropriateness rather than in its
value. —Charles Dudley Warner, *Backlog Studies*, "Eleventh Study"

GIVING

Ceasing to give we cease to have, / Such is the law of love.
—Anonymous

You can't out give God. —Anonymous

If thou hast abundance, give alms accordingly: if thou have but a little, be not afraid to give according to that little.

—Apocrypha, "Tobit," 4, 8

From what we get we can make a living; what we give, however, makes a life.

—Arthur Ashe

Blessed are those who can give without remembering and take without forgetting.

—Elizabeth Bibesco

. . . freely ye have received, freely give.

—*The Bible* (KJV): Matthew 10:8

Give, and it shall be given unto you . . . For with the same measure that ye measure it shall be measured to you again.

—*The Bible* (KJV): Luke 6:38

Then Peter said, Silver and gold have I none; but such as I have give I thee: In the name of Jesus Christ of Nazareth rise up and walk.

—*The Bible* (KJV): Acts 3:6

. . . It is more blessed to give than to receive.

—*The Bible* (KJV): The Acts 20:35

Every man according as he purposeth in his heart, so let him give, not grudgingly, or of necessity; for God loveth a cheerful giver.

—*The Bible* (KJV): 2 Corinthians 9:7

Give and spend / And God will send.

—H. G. Bohn, *Hand-Book of Proverbs*

. . . give to the world / The best that you have, / And the best will come back to you.

—Madeline Bridges

He that gives quickly gives twice. —Miguel de Cervantes, *Don Quixote*

To receive everything, one must simply open one's hands and give.

—Taisen Deshimaru

Give, but, if possible, spare the poor man the shame of begging.

—Denis Diderot

One must be poor to know the luxury of giving.

—George Eliot, *Middlemarch*

A beneficent person is like a fountain watering the earth, and spreading fertility; it is, therefore, more delightful to give than to receive.
—Epicurus

. . . it is in giving that we receive, it is in pardoning that we are pardoned, and it is in dying that we are born to eternal life.
—Saint Francis of Assisi

It is well to give when asked, but it is better to give unasked, through understanding.
—Kahlil Gibran

You give but little when you give of your possessions. It is when you give of yourself that you truly give.
—Kahlil Gibran

The only things we ever keep / Are what we give away.
—Louis Ginzberg

What we frankly give, forever is our own.
—Granville

The more we give to others, the more we are increased.
—Lao Tzu

Give what you have. To someone it may be better than you dare to think.
—Henry Wadsworth Longfellow

Giving is most blessed and most acceptable when the donor remains completely anonymous.
—Moses Maimonides

We can give our smiles, our encouragement, our sympathy to someone who needs them every day of the year.
—O. S. Marden

The world asks, How much does he give? Christ asks why does he give?
—John Raleigh Mott

If you have much give of your wealth, if you have little give of your heart.
—Proverb (Arab)

A bit of fragrance clings to the hand that gives the flower.
—Proverb (Chinese)

Who gives to me teaches me to give.
—Proverb (Dutch)

He who lends to the poor gets his interest from God.
—Proverb (German)

What I kept, I lost, / What I spent, I had, / What I gave, I have.
—Proverb (Persian)

All we can hold in our cold dead hands is what we have given away.
—Proverb (Sanskrit)

He gives twice who gives promptly.   —Publilius Syrus, *Moral Sayings*

Giving is true having.   —Charles H. Spurgeon

The hand that gives, gathers.   —Eugene Sue

Behold, I do not give lectures or a little charity, / When I give I give myself.   —Walt Whitman, *Leaves of Grass*, "Song of Myself"

Give all thou canst; high Heaven rejects the lore / Of nicely-calculated less or more.   —William Wordsworth, *Ecclesiasticals*, "Tax Not the Royal Saint"

GLADNESS

One can bear grief, but it takes two to be glad.   —Elbert Hubbard

GLORY

All glory is fleeting.   —Anonymous

The paths of glory lead but to the grave.
—Thomas Gray, *Elegy Written in a Country Churchyard*

GOALS

Forget goals. Value the process.   —Jim Bouton

If you want to live a happy life, tie it to a goal, not to people or things.
—Albert Einstein, in Ernst Straus, in French, *Einstein: A Centenary Volume*

Perfection of means and confusion of goals characterize our age.
—Albert Einstein, *Out of My Later Years*

Now everybody has some secret goals in life.   —Robert Fulghum, *All I Really Need to Know I Learned in Kindergarten*

Every healthy person must have a goal in life and that life must have content.   —Hermann Hesse, *Beneath the Wheel*, Ch. 6

Fail not for sorrow, falter not for sin,
   But onward, upward, till the goal ye win.   —Francis Anne Kemble

We, whoever we are, must have a daily goal in our lives, no matter
   how small or great, to make that day mean something.
                                             —Maxwell Maltz

It is more important to know where you are going than to get there
   quickly.   —Mabel Newcomber

You must have long-range goals to keep you from being frustrated by
   short-range failures.   —Charles C. Noble

Nothing can add more power to your life than concentrating all your
   energies on a limited set of targets.   —Nido Quibein

And set his heart upon the goal, / Not on the prize. —William Watson

G O D

He sendeth sun, he sendeth shower, / Alike they're needful to the
   flower; / And joys and tears alike are sent / To give the soul fit nourishment.   —Sarah Flower Adams,
                         "He Sendeth Sun, He Sendeth Shower"

God-doesn't-believe-in-the-easy-way.
                         —James Agee, *A Death in the Family*

God does not pay at the end of every week, but He pays.
                                             —Anne of Austria

Call on God, but row away from the rocks.   —Anonymous

Does God seem far away? Guess who moved.   —Anonymous

God does not ask about our ability or our inability, but our availability.
                                             —Anonymous

God has a tender reason for everything we face.   —Anonymous

God intervenes in the affairs of men by invitation only. —Anonymous

God is dead   —Nietzsche

Nietzsche is dead—God   —Anonymous, graffiti, in Robert Reisner,
                                        *Graffito: Two Thousand
                                        Years of Wall Writing*

God is the aggressive lover. —Anonymous

God loves us, not for what we are, but for what He can make us. —Anonymous

God never closes one door without opening another. He didn't deliver you this far to desert you now. —Anonymous

God permits, but not forever. —Anonymous

God, the great pursuer of our hearts. —Anonymous

Happy the man who sees God employ'd / In all the good and ill that checker life! —Anonymous

He always wins who sides with God. —Anonymous

If God abides in my home, His presence cannot be hidden. —Anonymous

If God does not give us what we want, he gives us what we need. —Anonymous

Most men forget God all day and ask Him at night to remember them. —Anonymous

Practice the presence of God. —Anonymous

Sometimes the Lord calms the storm; sometimes He lets the storm rage and calms His child. —Anonymous

We have come from somewhere and we are going somewhere. The Great Architect of the universe never built a stairway that leads nowhere. —Anonymous

Wherever God has placed a period, don't try to change it to a question mark. —Anonymous

Whoever walks toward God one cubit, God runs toward him twain. —Anonymous

You are a child of God. Please call home.   —Anonymous

God is that, the greater than which cannot be conceived.
                              —Saint Anselm, *Proslogion*, Ch. 3

God strikes not as an enemy, to destroy; but as a father, to correct.
                                                          —Aughey

We can know what God is not, but we cannot know what He is.
                                          —Saint Augustine

We are all dangerous folk without God's controlling hand.
                                          —William Ward Ayer

God must have something to do with joy . . . and with sadness.
                 Joan Baez, in Paul Rifkin, editor, *The God Letters*

People see God every day, they just don't recognize Him.
                                          —Pearl Bailey

Naught but God / Can satisfy the soul.
                    —Philip James Bailey, *Festus*, "Heaven"

Walk boldly and wisely . . . There is a hand above that will help thee
  on.   —Philip James Bailey

I nothing lack if I am His, / And He is mine forever.
                    —H. W. Baker, "The King of Love" (hymn, 1868)

God reveals himself unfailingly to the thoughtful seeker.
                                          —Honoré de Balzac

I believe in the incomprehensibility of God.
                 —Honoré de Balzac, letter to Madame de Hanska, 1837

God's glory is His goodness.   —Henry Ward Beecher

Is anything too hard for the Lord? . . .—*The Bible* (KJV): Genesis 18:14

God is our refuge and strength, a very present help in trouble.
                              —*The Bible* (KJV): Psalms 46:1

A man's heart deviseth his way, but the Lord directeth his steps.
                              —*The Bible* (KJV): Proverbs 16:9

For I am the Lord, I change not . . .   —*The Bible* (KJV): Malachi 3:6

. . . he maketh his sun to rise on the evil and on the good, and
sendeth rain on the just and on the unjust.
—*The Bible* (KJV): Matthew 5:45

. . . With men it is impossible, but not with God; for with God all
things are possible. —*The Bible* (KJV): Mark 10:27

And he [Jesus] said, The things which are impossible with men are
possible with God. —*The Bible* (KJV): Luke 18:27

In the beginning was the Word, and the Word was with God, and the
Word was God. —*The Bible* (KJV): John 1:1

. . . If God be for us, who can be against us?
—*The Bible* (KJV): Romans 8:31

I [Paul] have planted, Apollos watered, but God gave the increase.
—*The Bible* (KJV): 1 Corinthians 3:6

There is one body, and one Spirit, even as ye are called in one hope of
your calling; one Lord, one faith, one baptism, one God and Father
of all, who is above all, and through all, and in you all.
—*The Bible* (KJV): Ephesians 4:4–6

All things proclaim the existence of God. —Napoleon Bonaparte

God! Thou art love! I build my faith on that.
—Robert Browning, *Paracelsus*, Part v, line 52

God's in His heaven—/ All's right with the world!
—Robert Browning, *Pippa Passes*, 1, "Morning"

I have lived, / And seen God's hand thro a life time, / And all was for
the best. —Robert Browning

The everlasting Yea.
—Thomas Carlyle, *Past and Present*, Book III, Ch. 9, title

Human beings cannot probe the mind of God by asking themselves
what they would do if they were God. They are men and not God.
And if they are virtuous men, they will wait for God to reveal himself under conditions of his own choosing. —Edward John Carnell

God who gives the wound gives the salve.
—Miguel de Cervantes, *Don Quixote*, Part II, Ch. 4

We ought to love our Maker for His own sake, without either hope of
good or fear of pain.   —Miguel de Cervantes

When God sends the dawn, he sends it for all. —Miguel de Cervantes

We always keep God waiting while we admit more importunate suitors.
—Chazal

All things are full of God.   —Cicero

The beauty of the world and the orderly arrangement of everything
celestial makes us confess that there is an excellent and eternal
nature, which ought to be worshiped and admired by all mankind.
—Cicero

God is as great in minuteness as He is in magnitude.
—Charles Caleb Colton

Even bein' Gawd ain't a bed of roses.
—Marc Connelly, "The Green Pastures"

. . . the wing of a fly is proof enough of the existence of God for me.
—Pat Conroy, *Beach Music*, Ch. 6

God moves in a mysterious way His wonders to perform.
—William Cowper, "Light Shining Out of Darkness"

Trust in God and keep your powder dry.
—Oliver Cromwell, to troops preparing to cross a stream to attack

God bless us every one.   —Charles Dickens, *A Christmas Carol*

God is a fountain flowing into itself.   —Saint Dionysius

If we seek God for our own good and profit, we are not seeking God.
—Johannes Eckhart

God expects only one thing of you: that you come out of yourself as
far as you are a created being, and let God be God within you.
—Meister Eckhart

Some people want to see God with their eyes as they see a cow, and
love Him as they love a cow—for the milk and cheese and profit it
brings them.   —Meister Eckhart

I know this world is ruled by Infinite Intelligence. It required Infinite
   Intelligence to create it and it requires Infinite Intelligence to keep
   it on its course . . . It is mathematical in its precision.
                                                        —Thomas A. Edison

He [God] is never surprised.
              —Sandy Edmonson, *God's Faithfulness in Trials & Testings*

God is a scientist, not a magician.   —Albert Einstein

God is subtle but he is not malicious.
                     —Albert Einstein, remark at Princeton University,
                            May 1921, in R. W. Clark, *Einstein*, Ch. 14

God is our name for the last generalization to which we can arrive.
                               —Ralph Waldo Emerson, *Journals*

I am a part and parcel of God.   —Ralph Waldo Emerson

Try first thyself, and after call in God; / For to the worker God himself
   lends aid.   —Euripides, *Hippolytus*, Fragment 435

God tempers the wind to the shorn lamb.
              —Henri Estienne, *Le Livre des Proverbes Epigrammatiques*

A state of mind that sees God in everything is evidence of growth in
   grace and a thankful heart.   —Charles G. Finney

God loves us the way we are but He loves us too much to leave us that
   way.   —Leighton Ford

God is not a cosmic bell-boy for whom we can press a button to get
   things.   —Harry Emerson Fosdick

Let us walk joyfully over this earth answering to that of God in every
   man.   —George Fox

Having abandoned God why should we whimper, "Where is God?"
                               —Rabbi Benjamin Friedman

. . . for God, to me, it seems, is a verb not a noun, proper or improper.
   —R. Buckminster Fuller, "No More Secondhand God" (1940 poem)

I implicitly believe in the truth of the saying that not a blade of grass
   moves but by His will. He will save it [my life] if He needs it for further service in this body. None can save it against His will.
                                              —Mahatma Gandhi

But God is never cruel.
                    —Joseph F. Girzone, *Joshua in the Holy Land*, Ch. 15

God has no favorites.   —Joseph F. Girzone, *Joshua*, Ch. 8

Down inside we have a longing for God—what Pascal called "the vacuum which God left behind."
                    —Billy Graham, in Phillip L. Berman, editor,
                                          The Courage of Conviction

Even if we may not always understand why God allows certain things to happen to us, we can know He is able to bring good out of evil, and triumph out of suffering.   —Billy Graham, *Till Armageddon*

God's hand never slips.   —Billy Graham

. . . our little things are all big to God's love; our big things are all small to His power.   —Billy Graham, *Till Armageddon*

God wants us along for the victory, but it is His fight.
                    —Steve Hawthorne, guest sermon, Hope Chapel, 11 Aug 1991

He doesn't want to give you anything less than Himself.
                    —Steve Hawthorne, guest sermon, Hope Chapel, Austin,
                                          Texas, 21 Mar 1992

God strikes with his finger, and not with all his arm.—George Herbert

God's mill grinds slow, but sure.   —George Herbert, *Jacula Prudentum*

God gives every bird its food, but he does not throw it into the nest.
                    —Josiah Gilbert Holland

God reigneth. All is well!   —Oliver Wendell Holmes, Sr., hymn
                                          at the funeral service of Charles Sumner

Mine eyes have seen the glory of the coming of the Lord; / He is trampling out the vintage where the grapes of wrath are stored; / He hath loosed the fateful lightning of his terrible swift sword; / His truth is marching on.
                    —Julia Ward Howe, "Battle Hymn of the Republic"

Have courage for the great sorrows of life, and patience for the small ones. And when you have finished your daily tasks, go to sleep and have peace knowing that God is awake.   —Victor Hugo

For the word is the Verb, and the Verb is God.
—Victor Hugo, *Contemplations*, I, 8

I myself believe that the evidence for God lies primarily in inner personal experiences. —William James, *Pragmatism*, Lecture 3 (1907)

We know God easily, if we do not constrain ourselves to define him.
—Joseph Joubert

God plays a lot of jokes on us to get our attention. —Garrison Keillor

God creates out of nothing. Wonderful, you say. Yes, to be sure, but He does what is till more wonderful: He makes saints out of sinners.
—Sören Kierkegaard

And God hath spread the earth as a carpet for you, that ye may walk therein through spacious paths.
—*The Koran*

Give God Time.
—*The Koran*

God taketh an account of all things.
—*The Koran*

What God does, He does well.
—Jean de La Fontaine, *Fables*, "Le gland et la citrouille"

The finger of God never leaves identical fingerprints.
—Stanislaw J. Lec

For He [God] seems to do nothing of himself which He can possibly delegate to His creatures.
—C. S. Lewis, *The World's Last Night and Other Essays*,
"The Efficacy of Prayer"

After all, is our idea of God anything more than personified incomprehensibility?   —Georg Christoph Lichtenberg

. . . if God strikes you with one hand, he consoles us with another.
—Marie de L'Incarnation, letter to her son, 1665

I am satisfied that when the Almighty wants me to do or not to do any particular thing, He finds a way of letting me know it.
—Abraham Lincoln

Though the mills of God grind slowly, yet they grind exceeding small; / Though with patience He stands waiting, with exactness grinds He all.
—Friedrich von Logau, *Sinngedichte*, III. ii. 24, translated by Henry Wadsworth Longfellow

'Tis heaven alone that is given away, / 'Tis only God may be had for the asking.   —James Russell Lowell, "The Vision of Sir Launfal"

Why seek the Deity further? Whatever we see is God, and wherever we go.   —Lucan, *De Bello Civili*, Book IX

God doesn't always smooth the path, but sometimes he puts springs in the wagon.   —Marshall Lucas

A mighty fortress is our God, / A bulwark never failing.
—Martin Luther, "Ein' feste Burg"

You think God looks out for people? said Rawlins.   Yeah. I guess He does. You?   Yeah. I do. Way the world is. Somebody can wake up and sneeze in Arkansas or some damn place and before you're done there's wars and ruination and all hell. You don't know what's going to happen. I'd say He's just about got to. I don't believe we'd make it a day otherwise.
—Cormac McCarthy, *All the Pretty Horses*, Ch. 1

By and by / God caught his eye.
—David McCord, *Bay Window Ballads*, "Remainders" (epitaph for a waiter)

Do not measure God's mind by your own.   —George Macdonald

The Almighty can hardly be such a fool as the churches make out.
—W. Somerset Maugham, *Of Human Bondage*

Even those who resist Him carry out His will without realizing that they are doing so.   —Thomas Merton, *No Man Is an Island*

An idol tells people exactly what to believe, God presents them with choices they have to make for themselves. The difference is far from insignificant; before the idol men remain dependent children, before God they are burdened and at the same time liberated to participate in the decisions of endless creation.
—Arthur Miller, *Timebends*

By humble experience man has learned that there are very few things in this world worth getting upset about. He knows that if he does his best, God will do the rest. —John Miller

God has not promised us an easy journey, but he has promised us a safe journey. —William C. Miller

By steps we may ascend to God. —John Milton

For wonderful indeed are all his works, / Pleasant to know, and worthiest to be all / Had in remembrance always with delight; / But what created mind can comprehend / Their number, or the wisdom infinite / That brought them forth, but hid their causes deep? —John Milton

Deep within each human is a God-vacuum—an inner emptiness that can be filled only by a personal relationship with God through Jesus Christ.
—Frank B. Minirth and Paul D. Meier, *Happiness is a Choice*

God sends the cold according to the coat.
—Michel de Montaigne, *Essays*, III, vi

To know God is to be adjusted to daily living.
—Alfred Armand Montapert

There is a very good saying that if the triangles invented a god, they would make him three-sided. —Montesquieu, *Lettres persanes*

Give your life to God; he can do more with it than you can!
—Dwight L. Moody

God not only orders our steps. He orders our stops. —George Müller

Our heavenly Father never takes anything from his children unless he plans to give them something better. —George Müller

I sought to hear the voice of God / And climbed the topmost steeple, / But God declared: "Go down again— / I dwell among the people."
—John Henry Newman

Nothing is going to thwart God's purpose in our lives.
—W. Jack Noble, from a sermon,
Canyon Creek Presbyterian Church, Richardson, Texas, 4 Sep 1994

If God be my friend, I cannot be wretched. —Ovid, *Tristia*, I, Ch. 10

God and the doctor we alike adore / But only when in danger, not before; / The danger o'er, both are alike requited, / God is forgotten, and the Doctor slighted.　　　　　　　　　　—John Owen

Two men please God—who serves Him with all his heart because he knows Him; who seeks Him with all his heart because he knows Him not.　　　　　　　　　　—Nikita Ivanovich Panin

Discern what God is doing and be a part of it.
　　—Ron Parrish, sermon, Hope Chapel, Austin, Texas, 26 Nov 1994

God often has a different mission than we have.
　　—Ron Parrish, sermon, Hope Chapel, Austin, Texas 26 Nov 1994

Let go and let God. Let Him take over your life and run it. He knows how.　　　　　　　　　　—Norman Vincent Peale

Remind yourself that God is with you and nothing can defeat him.
　　　　　　　　　　—Norman Vincent Peale

Sometimes God doesn't tell us His plan because we wouldn't believe it anyway.　　　　　　　　　　—Carlton Pearson

I praise God because he not only guides my directions but overrules my mistakes.　　　　　　　　　　—H. Norman Pell

Man proposes, God disposes.　　　　　　　　　　—Plautus

All are but parts of one stupendous whole, / Whose body Nature is, and God the soul.　　　　—Alexander Pope, *An Essay on Man*

Thou Great First Cause, least Understood!
　　　　　　　—Alexander Pope, "Universal Prayer"

God promises a safe landing but not a calm passage.
　　　　　　　　　　—Proverb (Bulgarian)

Father and mother are fine, but God is kinder.　　—Proverb (Danish)

God does not pay weekly, but he pays at the end.　　—Proverb (Dutch)

God gives the nuts, but he does not crack them.　—Proverb (German)

God giveth the shoulder according to the burden.
　　　　　　　　　　—Proverb (German)

God never shuts one door but he opens another.　　—Proverb (Irish)

God sends nothing but what can be borne.　　—Proverb (Italian)

He who leaves God out of his reckoning does not know how to count.
　　—Proverb (Italian)

God will be present, whether asked or not.　　—Proverb (Latin)

We do nothing without the leave of God.　　—Proverb (Latin)

Whom God will help nae man can hinder.　　—Proverb (Scottish)

Many millions search for God and find Him in their hearts.
　　—Proverb (Sikh)

No leaf moves but as God wills it.　　—Proverb (Spanish)

In a small house God has His corner, in a big house He has to stand in
　　the hall.　　—Proverb (Swedish)

God knows what He does.　　—Proverb (Yiddish)

I am afraid I shall not find Him [God]; but I shall still look for Him, if
　　He exists. He may be appreciative of my efforts.
　　—Jules Renard, *Journal*, Sep 1903

God is an unutterable sigh, planted in the depths of the soul.
　　—Jean Paul Richter

When God wounds from on high he will follow with the remedy.
　　—Fernando de Rojas, *La Celestina*, Act X

God could have kept Daniel out of the lion's den . . . But God has
　　never promised to keep us out of hard places . . . What he
　　promised is to go with us through every hard place, and bring us
　　through victoriously.　　—Merv Rosell

Of myself I can only say that I am an unprofitable servant; but I serve
　　a good Master.　　—Richard Rothe, *Still Hours*

If there wasn't a God we would have to invent one to keep people
　　sane.　　—Jean Jacques Rousseau

God often visits us, but most of the time we are not at home.
　　—Joseph Roux

Provided that God be glorified, we must not care by whom.
—Saint Francis de Sales

When you cannot stand, He will bear you in His arms.
—Saint Francis de Sales

God has his dwelling within every good man.   —Seneca

The heavens are still: no sound. / Where then shall God be found?
/ Seek not in distant skies; / In man's own heart he lies. —Shao Yung

I don't know much, but what I do know has changed my life.
—George Beverly Shea, when asked how much he knew about God

All that God does is for the good.   —Isaac Bashevis Singer, *The Slave*

In God's mill even chaff becomes flour.
—Isaac Bashevis Singer, *The Slave*

One has to trust that God knows how to manage the world.
—Isaac Bashevis Singer, *The Slave*

Our love for God is tested by the question of whether we seek Him or
His gifts.   —Ralph W. Sockman, interview, 1961

I looked at God and he looked at me, and we were one forever.
—Charles H. Spurgeon

No one could ever wrong you as much as we have wronged God.
—Lehman Strauss, *Sense and Nonsense About Prayer*

We cannot be right with God when we are wrong with others.
—Lehman Strauss, *Sense and Nonsense About Prayer*

I am able to love my God / because He gives me freedom to deny
Him.
—Rabindranath Tagore, *Fireflies*

God says to man: "With thy very wounds I will heal thee."
—*The Talmud*

I think there's probably a God-shaped hole in everybody's being.
Even if God only exists in people's minds, He's still a force.
—James Taylor

Modern engineers, after having erected a viaduct, insist upon subjecting it to a severe strain by a formal trial trip before allowing it to be opened for public traffic, and it would almost seem that God, in employing moral agents for the carrying out of His purposes, secures that they shall be tested by some dreadful ordeal before He fully commits to them the work which He wishes them to perform.
—William M. Taylor

As the flower turns to the sun, or the dog to his master, so the soul turns to God.
—William Temple

God can give a straight blow with a crooked stick.
—Corrie ten Boom, *In My Father's House*, with C. C. Carlson

. . . God uses such seemingly insignificant ways to prepare us for the plan He has for our lives.
—Corrie ten Boom, *In My Father's House*, with C. C. Carlson

If God sends us on stony paths, he provides strong shoes.
—Corrie ten Boom

What a sad mistake we sometimes make when we think that God only cares about Christians.
—Corrie ten Boom, *Tramp for the Lord*, with Jamie Buckingham

When the Lord does it, He does a thorough job.
—Corrie ten Boom, in Pamela Rosewell,
The Five Silent Years of Corrie ten Boom

Closer is He than breathing, and nearer than hands and feet.
—Alfred, Lord Tennyson, "The Higher Pantheism"

Alas, O Lord, to what a state dost Thou bring those who love Thee!
—Saint Teresa of Ávila, *Interior Castles*

. . . whoever has God needs nothing else. God alone suffices.
—Saint Teresa of Ávila

I did not know we had quarreled, Aunt.
—Henry David Thoreau, responding to his Aunt Louisa after she asked whether he had made his peace with God

Don't be ashamed to belong to God.
—Lewis Timberlake

Even though life is not easy, God is good.
—Lewis Timberlake

God does everything right.   —Lewis Timberlake

Little is much if God is in it.   —Lewis Timberlake

There is nothing that you and God can't do.   —Lewis Timberlake

He who serves God hath a good master.
                              —Torriano, *Piazza Universale*, LXIX

None but God can satisfy the longings of an immortal soul; that as
    the heart was made for Him, so He only can fill it.   —Trench

God has put something noble and good into every heart which his
    hand has created.   —Mark Twain

He is rich indeed whom God loves.
                      —J. de la Veprie, *Les Proverbes Commun*

Reach up as far as you can, and God will reach down all the way.
                                      —Bishop Vincent

If God did not exist, it would be necessary to invent him.
    —Voltaire, "Epitre à l'auteur du nouveau livre des trois imposteurs"

If God made us in his own image, we have more than reciprocated.
                                      —Voltaire, *Le sottisier*

Love God and laugh at the devil . . .   —Chad Walsh, *Behold the Glory*

God has two dwellings: one in heaven, and the other in a meek and
    thankful heart.   —Izaak Walton

The only things you have to remember about God are that there is
    one and you're not him.   —Michael G. Watkins

God rules in the realms to which he is admitted.   —Mary Welch

God is and all is well.   —John Greenleaf Whittier, "My Birthday"

I only know I cannot drift / Beyond His love and care.
        —John Greenleaf Whittier, "The Eternal Goodness," xxii.

All roads that lead to God are good.   —Ella Wheeler Wilcox

I don't care what other people say about God. He has been very sweet
    to me.   —Godfrey Winn

He [Job] did not seek the Giver because of His gifts; when all gifts were removed he still sought the Giver.
—Philip Yancey, *Where is God When It Hurts*

The GOLDEN RULE

What thou thyself hatest, do to no man. —Apocrypha, "Tobit"

And as ye would that men should to do you, do ye also to them likewise. —*The Bible* (KJV): Luke 6:31

What you do not wish done to yourself, do not do to others.
—Confucius, *Analects*

What is hateful to you, do not to your fellowman. That is the whole Torah; all the rest is commentary. —Rabbi Hillel

This is the sum of all true righteousness: deal with others as thou wouldst thyself be dealt by. Do nothing to thy neighbor which thou wouldst not have him do to thee hereafter.—*The Mahabharata*

Do as you would be done by. —Proverb (14th century)

GOLF

If a ball comes to rest in dangerous proximity to a hippopotamus or crocodile, another ball may be dropped at a safe distance.
—Anonymous, local golf rule, Nyanza Club, British East Africa

Golf is an awkward set of bodily contortions designed to produce a graceful result. —Tommy Armour

Cow-pasture pool. —O. K. Bovard, description of golf

Golf is a game whose aim is to hit a very small ball into a very small hole, with weapons singularly ill designed for the purpose.
—Winston Churchill

The game of golf consists of a lot of walking, broken up by disappointment and bad arithmetic. —Earl Wilson

GOOD

But let the good prevail. —Aeschylus, *Agememnon*

All is good that God sends us. —Anonymous

The good you do is not lost, though you forget it.   —Anonymous

As often as we do good, we offer sacrifices to God.   —Aristotle

What I wanted was to do good.   —Saul Bellow, *Humboldt's Gift*

Good things, when short, are twice as good.
        —Baltasar Gracián, *The Art of Worldly Wisdom*

Every person is responsible for all the good within the scope of his
    abilities, and for no more.   —Gail Hamilton

He who waits to do a great deal of good at once, will never do any-
    thing.   —Samuel Johnson

The greatest pleasure I have known is to do a good action by stealth,
    and to have it found out by accident.
        —Charles Lamb, *The Athenaeum*, "Table Talk by the Late Elia"

What is not good for the swarm is not good for the bee.
        —Marcus Aurelius Antoninus, *Meditations*, VI

He that does good for good's sake seeks neither paradise nor reward,
    but he is sure of both in the end.   —William Penn

Do good by stealth, and blush to find it fame.
        —Alexander Pope, Epilogue to *Satires*, Dialogue 1, line 136

Rather be called good than fortunate.   —Proverb (Latin)

There is nothing so bad that good may not come of it.
        —Proverb (Spanish)

Do good and ask not for whom.   —Proverb (Yiddish)

There is not a single ill-doer who could not be turned to some good.
        —Jean Jacques Rousseau, *The Social Contract*

He that does good to another, does good also to himself, not only in
    the consequences, but in the very act; for the consciousness of well
    doing is, in itself, ample reward.   —Seneca

Find the good and celebrate it.   —Betty Shabazz

For naught so vile that on the earth doth live / But to the earth some special good doth give . . .
—William Shakespeare, *Romeo and Juliet*, Act II, Sc. iii

By strengthening the good, we progressively get rid of the evil.
—Szekely

The best is enemy of the good.
—Voltaire, *Dictionaire Philosophique*, "Art Dramatique"

Do all the good you can, / In all the ways you can, / In all the places you can, / At all the times you can, / To all the people you can, / As long as ever you can.
—John Wesley, "Rules of Conduct"

GOOD NATURE

God bless the good-natured, for they bless everybody else.
—Henry Ward Beecher

Good nature is stronger than tomahawks.
—Ralph Waldo Emerson

GOODNESS

Content thyself to be obscurely good. / When vice prevails, and impious men bear sway, / The post of honor is a private station.
—Joseph Addison

No man or woman of the humblest sort can really be strong, gentle, pure and good without the world being better for it, without somebody being helped and comforted by the very existence of that goodness.
—Phillips Brooks

He cannot long be good that knows not why he is good.
—Richard Carew, *Survey of Cornwall*

You Can't Keep a Good Man Down.
—M. F. Carey, title and refrain of song

If good men were only better, Would the wicked be so bad?
—J. W. Chadwick

Goodness consists not in outward things we do, but in the inward thing we are.
—Edwin Hubbel Chapin

Good and bad men are each less so than they seem.
—Samuel Taylor Coleridge, *Table Talk*

Be good and leave the rest to Heaven.
—William Combe, *Dr. Syntax in Search of the Picturesque*

Look round the habitable world, how few / Know their own good, or, knowing it, pursue.   —John Dryden

It is very hard to be simple enough to be good.
—Ralph Waldo Emerson, *Journals*

I once liked clever people. Now I like good people.
—Rabbi Solomon B. Freehof

Few persons have courage enough to appear as good as they really are.
—Julius Charles Hare and Augustus William Hare, *Guesses at Truth*

No matter how good or great a man may be, there is yet a better and a greater man within him.   —Karl Humboldt

As I know more of mankind I expect less of them, and am ready now to call a man a good man, upon easier terms than I was formerly.
—Samuel Johnson, in James Boswell, *Life of Samuel Johnson*

Be good, sweet maid, and let who will be clever; / Do noble things, not dream them, all day long; / And so make Life, and Death, and that For Ever / One grand, sweet song.   —Charles Kingsley,
"A Farewell"

When I think of those who have influenced my life the most, I think not of the great but of the good.   —John Knox

Those who are good I treat as good. Those who are not good I also treat as good.   —Lao Tzu, *Tao Te Ching*, Ch. XLIX

The life of a good man is a continual prayer.
—Charlotte Lennox, *Euphemia*, Vol. IV

A good man doubles the length of his existence; to have lived so as to look back with pleasure on our past life is to live twice.
—Martial

The good man makes others good.
—Menander, *The Charioteer* (Fragment)

There is no man so good, who, were he to submit all his thoughts and actions to the laws, would not deserve hanging ten times in his life.   —Michel de Montaigne

How goodness heightens beauty! —Hannah More

Be good, and let heaven answer for the rest. —Pollok

The good must merit God's peculiar care; / But who but God can tell us who they are? —Alexander Pope, *An Essay on Man*, Epis. iv, l. 135

It is his good nature, not his standing, that makes the good man.
—Publilius Syrus, *Moral Sayings*

The worst sinner has a future, even as the greatest saint has had a past. No one is so good or bad as he imagines.
—Sarvepalli Radhakrishnan

Most of the people in the world are good and decent if you give them a chance to be . . .
—Andrew A. Rooney, *Word for Word*, "Strangers on a Train"

The best way to do good to ourselves is to do it to others; the right way to gather is to scatter. —Seneca

The hand that hath made you fair hath made you good . . .
—William Shakespeare, *Measure for Measure*, Act III, Sc. i

Nothing can harm a good man, either in life or after death.
—Socrates, in Plato's *Apology*

There is an idea abroad among moral people that they should make their neighbors good . . . One person I have to make good: myself.
—Robert Louis Stevenson

God made thee good as thou art beautiful.
—Alfred, Lord Tennyson, "The Holy Grail"

Be not simply good; be good for something. —Henry David Thoreau

GOOD WILL

Good will is the mightiest practical force in the universe.
—Charles Fletcher Dole

Good will, like a good name, is got by many actions, and lost by one.
—Francis Jeffrey

GOSPEL

If you believe in the Gospel what you like, and reject what you don't like, it is not the Gospel you believe, but yourself.
—Saint Augustine

It's not that we have to give to support the gospel. Giving *is* the gospel.
—Dan Davis, sermon, Hope Chapel, Austin, Texas, 6 Oct 1991

Preach the Gospel at all times. If necessary, use words.
—Saint Francis of Assisi

It was a common saying among the Puritans, "Brown bread and the Gospel is good fare." —Matthew Henry, *Commentaries*, Isaiah XXX

God writes the gospel, not in the Bible alone, but on trees and flowers and clouds and stars.
—Martin Luther

GOSSIP

There is so much good in the worst of us, and so much bad in the best of us, that it's rather hard to tell which of us ought to reform the rest of us.
—Alain-Fournier, *Le Grand Meaulnes*

Gossip is the devil's radio.
—Anonymous

Hear no ill of a friend, nor speak any of an enemy.
—Anonymous

If anyone speaks evil of you, so live that none will believe it.
—Anonymous

The only fair way to talk about somebody is to speak as though you know he was listening in.
—Anonymous

There is so much good in the worst of us, / And so much bad in the best of us, / That it hardly becomes any of us / To talk about the rest of us.
—Anonymous, in the *Marion* (Kansas) *Record*

Hast thou heard a word against thy neighbor? Let it die within thee, trusting that it will not burst thee.
—Apocrypha, "Ecclesiasticus," 19, 10

There are male as well as female gossips.
—Charles Caleb Colton

Make it pass, before you speak, three gates of gold; Is it true? Is it
    needful? Is it kind?   —Beth Day, "Three Gates of Gold"

I will speak ill of no man, not even in matters of truth; but rather
    excuse the faults I hear charged upon others, and upon proper
    occasion speak all the good I know of everybody.
                              —Benjamin Franklin

To listen to gossip both creates and encourages gossip. No listeners,
    no gossip. It is as simple as that.   —A. P. Gouthey

When will talkers refrain from evil speaking?—When listeners refrain
    from evil hearing.   —Hare

What people say behind your back is your standing in the commu-
    nity in which you live.
            —Edgar Watson Howe, *Sinner Sermons* (1926)

Never tell evil of a man if you do not know it for a certainty; and if
    you do know it for a certainty, then ask yourself: "Why should I
    tell it?"   —Johann Kaspar Lavater

Never believe anything bad about anybody unless you positively
    know it to be true; never tell even that unless you feel that it is
    absolutely necessary—and that God is listening while you tell it.
                                —William Penn

Leave the bad tale where you found it.   —Proverb (Irish)

Whoever gossips to you will gossip of you.   —Proverb (Spanish)

Gossip is spreading other people's misery.   —Lewis Timberlake

GOVERNMENT

States, as great engines, move slowly.
    —Francis Bacon, *Advancement of Learning*, Book II

The king's heart is in the hand of the Lord, as the rivers of water: He
    turneth it withersoever he will.   —*The Bible* (KJV): Proverbs 21:1

The point to remember is that what the government gives it must
    first take away.   —John S. Coleman,
            speech to the Detroit Chamber of Commerce, 1956

Nothing is easier than spending the public money. It does not appear to belong to anybody. The temptation is overwhelming to bestow it on somebody. —Calvin Coolidge

Everyone is always in favor of general economy and specific expenditure. —Anthony Eden

As quickly as you start spending federal money in large amounts, it looks like free money. —Dwight D. Eisenhower

Every actual state is corrupt. Good men must not obey laws too well. —Ralph Waldo Emerson

The less government we have, the better. —Ralph Waldo Emerson

The proper function of government is to make it easy for people to do good, and difficult for them to do evil. —William Gladstone

What is the best government? That which teaches us to govern ourselves. —Johann Wolfgang von Goethe

A government that is big enough to give you all you want is big enough to take it all away. —Barry Goldwater, speech in West Chester, Pennsylvania, 21 Oct 1964

The impersonal hand of government can never replace the helping hand of a neighbor. —Hubert Humphrey, speech in Washington, D.C., 10 Feb 1965

Were we directed from Washington when to sow and when to reap, we should soon want bread. —Thomas Jefferson, *Autobiography*

. . . the state is not absolute, and loyalty to the state cannot be absolute. —Petra K. Kelly, in Phillip L. Berman, editor, *The Courage of Conviction*

A government is free in proportion to the rights it guarantees to the minority. —Alfred Landon

Govern a great nation as you would fry small fish. —Lao Tzu

No man is good enough to govern another man without that other's consent. —Abraham Lincoln, speech, 1854

A state which dwarfs its men, in order that they may be more docile instruments in its hands—even for beneficial purposes—will find that with small men no great thing can really be accomplished.
—John Stuart Mill

How different the new order would be if we could consult the veteran instead of the politician.
—Henry Miller, *The Wisdom of the Heart* (1941), "The Alcoholic Veteran with the Washboard Cranium"

Big Brother is watching you.
—George Orwell, *1984*

The best government is that which governs least.
—John L. O'Sullivan, introduction to *United States Magazine and Democratic Review*, Oct 1837

Do you not know with how very little wisdom the world is governed?
—A. Oxenstierna, Swedish statesman

Governments exist to protect the rights of minorities. The loved and the rich need no protection,—they have many friends and few enemies.
—Wendell Phillips

Thank heavens we don't get all the government we pay for.
—Will Rogers, in *Will Rogers U.S.A.*, CBS-TV, 9 Mar 1972

The function of Government must be to favor no small group at the expense of its duty to protect the rights of personal freedom and of private property of all its citizens.
—Franklin D. Roosevelt

The Vice Presidency is sort of like the last cookie on the plate. Everybody insists he won't take it, but somebody always does.
—Bill Vaughan

GRACE

Grace is everything for nothing to those who don't deserve anything.
—Anonymous

For by grace are ye saved through faith; and that not of yourselves: it is the gift of God.
—*The Bible* (KJV): Ephesians 2:8

But for the grace of God there goes John Bradford.
—John Bradford, on seeing criminals taken to execution

We can be certain that God will give us the strength and resources we need to live through any situation in life that he ordains. The will of God will never take us where the grace of God cannot sustain us.
—Billy Graham, *Till Armageddon*

Grace is God's unmerited, free spontaneous love for sinful man, revealed and made effective in Jesus Christ. —C. L. Mitton

Amazing grace! how sweet the sound / That saved a wretch like me! / I once was lost, but now am found, / Was blind, but now I see.
—John Newton, "Amazing Grace" (hymn)

This is Daddy's little secret for today; man is born broken. He lives by mending. The grace of God is glue.
—Eugene O'Neill, *The Great God Brown*

Grace cannot forgive unconfessed sin. —Rod Parsley

Grace cannot wipe out the law of sewing and reaping. —Rod Parsley

Lambs have the grace to kneel while nursing. —Proverb (Chinese)

God does not refuse grace to one who does what he can.
—Proverb (Medieval Latin)

Grace grows best in the winter. —Samuel Rutherford

. . . use every man after his deserts, and who should 'scape whipping!
—William Shakespeare, *Hamlet*, Act II, Sc. ii

GRADUALNESS

Step by step one goes far. —Anonymous

A falling drop at last will carve a stone. —Lucretius

Feather by feather the goose is plucked. —John Ray

GRAMMAR

A double negative is a no-no. —Anonymous

Grammar, which knows how to control even kings. —Molière

A period is a stop sign. A semicolon is a rolling stop sign; a comma is merely an amber light. —Andrew J. Offut

No matter what any of the grammar teachers say, punctuation is an arbitrary matter. It should be used to make sentences clear.
—Andrew A. Rooney, *Word for Word*, "Notes on the English Language"

GRANDPARENTS

Everybody should try to have a grandmother, 'cause grandmothers are the only grownups who seem to have time for us kids.
—Anonymous, excerpt from a child's essay called "What is a Grandmother?"

Grandchildren don't make a man feel old; it's the knowledge that he's married to a grandmother.
—G. Norman Collie

If you would civilize a man, begin with his grandmother.
—Victor Hugo

GRATEFULNESS

Don't grumble because you don't have what you want . . . rather be exceedingly grateful you don't get what you deserve!—Anonymous

Unless you are utterly exploded, there is always something to be grateful for.
—Saul Bellow, *Herzog*

Gratefulness is the poor man's payment.
—Proverb (English)

A favor is to a grateful man delightful always; to an ungrateful man only once.
—Seneca

He who is not grateful for the things he has will not be happy with what he wishes he had.
—Rabbi Saul I. Teplitz

GRATITUDE

A blind man will not thank you for a looking-glass.
—Anonymous

Gratitude is like credit; it is the backbone of our relations; frequently we pay our debts not because equity demands that we should, but to facilitate future loans.
—François de La Rochefoucauld

One can never pay in gratitude; one can only pay "in kind" somewhere else in life.
—Anne Morrow Lindbergh

Gratitude is the memory of the heart.
—Jean Baptiste Massieu, letter to Abbe Sicard

Gratitude is a duty which ought to be paid, but which none have a
  right to expect.   —Jean Jacques Rousseau

A dog will never forget the crumb thou gavest him, though thou
  mayest afterwards throw a hundred stones at his head.
                                              —Saadi, *Gulistan*

The GRAVE

Up, sluggard, and waste not life; in the grave will be sleeping enough.
                                              —Anonymous

We shall lie all alike in our graves.   —Anonymous

We go to the grave of a friend saying, "A man is dead"; but angels
  throng about him, saying, "A man is born." —Henry Ward Beecher

O death, where is thy sting? O grave, where is thy victory?
                    —*The Bible* (KJV): 1 Corinthians 15:55

And if there be no meeting past the grave, / If all is darkness, silence,
  yet 'tis rest. / Be not afraid, ye waiting hearts that weep, / For still
  He giveth His beloved sleep, / And if an endless sleep He will, 'tis
  best.   —Henrietta Anne Heathorn, on the grave of
                                her husband Thomas Henry Huxley

The impartial earth opens alike for the child of the pauper and the
  king.   —Horace

Life is real! Life is earnest! / And the grave is not its goal. / Dust thou
  art, to dust returnest, / Was not spoken of the soul.
              —Henry Wadsworth Longfellow, "A Psalm of Life"

Who's a prince or a beggar in the grave?   —Otway

GREAT BRITAIN

Let us therefore brace ourselves to our duties, and so bear ourselves
  that, if the British Empire and its Commonwealth last for a thousand years, men will still say, "This was their finest hour."
                    —Winston Churchill, speech, Jun 1940

In the end it may well be that Britain will be honoured by historians
  more for the way she disposed of an empire than for the way in
  which she acquired it.
                    —Lord Harlech, in *New York Times*, 28 Oct 1962

When Britain first, at Heaven's command, / Arose from out the azure
main, / This was the charter of the land, / And guardian angels
sung this strain: / "Rule, Britannia, rule the waves; / Britons never
will be slaves."   —James Thomson, *Alfred: A Masque*, Act II, Sc. v

G R E A T N E S S

You don't have to be big to be great.   —Shalom Aleichem

A person who is truly great is one who will take more than his share
of the blame and less than his share of the credit.   —Anonymous

The less people speak of their greatness the more we think of it.
—Francis Bacon

Greatness lies, not in being strong, but in the right using of strength.
—Henry Ward Beecher

Greatness, after all, in spite of its name, appears to be not so much a
certain size as a certain quality in human lives. It may be present in
lives whose range is very small.   —Phillips Brooks

What millions died—that Caesar might be great!
—Thomas Campbell, *Pleasures of Hope*, II, line 174

They're only great who are truly good.
—George Chapman, *Revenge for Honour*

There is a great man who makes every man feel small. But the really
great man is the man who makes every man feel great.
—G. K. Chesterton, *Charles Dickens*

If I cannot do great things, I can do small things in a great way.
—James Freeman Clarke

Times of great calamity and confusion have ever been productive of
the greatest minds. The purest ore is produced from the hottest furnace, and the brightest thunderbolt is elicited from the darkest
storm.   —Charles Caleb Colton

Each reckons greatness to consist / In that in which he heads the list . . .
—Arion Spurl Doke

A great man is always willing to be little.   —Ralph Waldo Emerson

Immortality will come to such as are fit for it; and he who would be a
  great soul in the future must be a great soul now.
                                        —Ralph Waldo Emerson

The essence of greatness is the perception that virtue is enough.
                  —Ralph Waldo Emerson, *Essays, First Series*, "Heroism"

To be great is to be misunderstood.
            —Ralph Waldo Emerson, *Essays, First Series*, "Self Reliance"

Trust men and they will be true to you; treat them greatly, and they
  will show themselves great.
                  —Ralph Waldo Emerson, *Essays*, "On Prudence"

No life ever grows great until it is focused, dedicated, and disciplined.
                                        —Harry Emerson Fosdick

Gathered at the Passover feast . . . Jesus took a towel and basin and
  redefined greatness.
                  —Richard C. Foster, *The Celebration of Discipline*

Few great men could pass Personnel.
            —Paul Goodman, *Growing Up Absurd: Problems of Youth in
                                        the Organized Society*

Little minds are interested in the extraordinary; great minds in the
  commonplace.
            —Elbert Hubbard, *The Roycroft Dictionary and Book of Epigrams*

Nothing can be truly great which is not right.   —Samuel Johnson

Everybody can be great because anybody can serve.
                                        —Martin Luther King, Jr.

If a man is called to be street sweeper, he should sweep streets even as
  Michelangelo painted, or Beethoven composed music, or
  Shakespeare wrote poetry. He should sweep streets so well that all
  the host of heaven and earth will pause to say, here lived a great
  street sweeper who did his job well.
                  —Martin Luther King, Jr., *The Strength to Love*

Neither genius, fame, nor love show the greatness of the soul. Only
  kindness can do that.   —Jean Baptiste Henri Lacordaire

Lives of great men all remind us / We can make our lives sublime,
/ And, departing, leave behind us / Footprints on the sands of time.
—Henry Wadsworth Longfellow, "A Psalm of Life"

The heights by great men reached and kept, / Were not attained by
sudden flights. —Henry Wadsworth Longfellow

The wisest man could ask no more of Fate / Than to be simple, modest,
manly, true, / Safe from the many, honored by the few; / To count as
naught in world, or church, or state; / But inwardly in secret to be
great. —James Russell Lowell, Sonnet, "Jeffries Wyman"

One of the marks of true greatness is the ability to develop greatness
in others. —J. C. Macaulay

That man is great, and he alone, / Who serves a greatness not his
own, / For neither praise nor self: / Content to know and be
unknown: / Whole in himself. —Owen Meredith, "A Great Man"

To love one that is great is almost to be great one's self.
—Madame Suzanne Necker

You can be greater than anything that can happen to you.
—Norman Vincent Peale

The great doing of little things makes the great life. —Eugenia Price

The great are only great because we are on our knees. Let us rise!
—P. J. Proudhon

Seem not greater than thou art. —Proverb (Latin)

Do not despise the bottom rungs in the ascent to greatness.
—Publilius Syrus

Not a day passes over this earth, but men and women of no note do
great deeds, speak great words and suffer noble sorrows.
—Charles Reade, *The Cloister and the Hearth*

It's great to be great, but it's greater to be human. —Will Rogers

. . . some are born great, some achieve greatness, and some have
greatness thrust upon 'em.
—William Shakespeare, *Twelfth Night*, Act II, Sc. v

The world knows nothing of its greatest men.
—Sir Henry Taylor, *Philip Van Artevelde*, I, v

I am greater than the stars for I know that they are up there and they
do not know that I am down here.
—William Temple, Archbishop of Canterbury

Is a man one whit the better because he is grown great in other men's
esteem?　　　　　　　　　　　　　　　—Thomas à Kempis

G R E E D

There is enough in the world for everyone's need, but not enough for
everyone's greed.　　　　　—Frank Buchman, *Remaking the World*

Much would have more.
—John Clarke, *Proverbs*: *English and Latine* (1639)

Those who want much are always much in need.　　　—Horace

Avarice is always poor.　　　　　　　　　　—Samuel Johnson

As the farmer said, "I'm not greedy, all I want is the land next to
mine."　　　　　　　　　—Laurence J. Peter, compiler,
Peter's Quotations: *Ideas for Our Time*

Poverty is in want of much, but avarice of everything.
—Publilius Syrus

G R I E F

Great griefs are mute.　　　　　　　　　　　—Anonymous

Grief hallows hearts, even while it ages heads.　　—Philip James Bailey

Time will cure you, but now is your grief still young.
—Euripides, *Alcestis*

Memory is the only friend of grief.　　—Rumer Godden, *China Court*

Great grief makes sacred those upon whom its hand is laid. Joy may
elevate, ambition glorify, but sorrow alone can consecrate.
—Horace Greeley

Grief is a stone that bears one down but two bear it lightly.—W. Hauff

Grief knits two hearts in closer bonds than happiness ever can; and common sufferings are far stronger links than common joys.
—Alphonse de Lamartine

The only cure for grief is action.   —George Henry Lewes,
The Spanish Drama: Life of Lope De Vega, Ch. 2

Well has it been said that there is no grief like the grief which does not speak.   —Henry Wadsworth Longfellow

The closest bonds we will ever know are bonds of grief. The deepest community, one of sorrow.
—Cormac McCarthy, *All the Pretty Horses*, Ch. 4

The sad relief / That misery loves—the fellowship of grief.
—Montgomery, *The West Indies*, Part iii.

Grief won't kill you, but it will knock you off your feet.
—Proverb (Russian), in Alexander Solzhenitsyn,
The Oak and the Calf

He that conceals his grief finds no remedy for it.   —Proverb (Turkish)

Light griefs can speak; but deeper ones are dumb.—Seneca, *Hippolytus*

. . . everyone can master a grief but he that has it.
—William Shakespeare, *Much Ado About Nothing*, Act III, Sc. ii

Give sorrow words: the grief that does not speak / Whispers the o'er-fraught heart and bids it break.
—William Shakespeare, *Macbeth*, Act IV, Sc. iii

Grief best is pleased with grief's society . . .
—William Shakespeare, *The Rape of Lucrece*, Part II

Honest plain words best pierce the ear of grief . . .
—William Shakespeare, *Love's Labour's Lost*, Act V, Sc. ii

What's gone and past help / Should be past grief . . .
—William Shakespeare, *The Winter's Tale*, Act III, Sc. ii

. . . if you live in a graveyard, you can't weep for everyone.
—Alexander Solzhenitsyn, *The Gulag Archipelago*

There is no grief which time does not lessen.
—Servius Sulpicius Rufus, in Cicero's *Epistles*

Time effaces grief. —Terence, *The Self-Tormentor*

GROWTH

Unless you try to do something beyond what you have already mastered, you will never grow. —Anonymous

The spirit knows that its growth is the real aim of existence.
—Saul Bellow, *Mr. Sammler's Planet*, Ch. 5

Why stay you on the earth except to grow? —Robert Browning

Bloom where you are planted. —Nancy Reader Campion

Love not what you are, but what you may become.
—Miguel de Cervantes

The lofty oak from a small acorn grows. —Lewis Duncombe

Remember the little seed in the Styrofoam cup. The roots go down and the plant goes up and nobody really knows how or why, but we are all like that. —Robert Fulghum,
All I Really Need to Know I Learned in Kindergarten

Nothing is lost upon a man who is bent upon growth; nothing is wasted on one who is always preparing for his work and his life by keeping eyes, mind, and heart open to nature, men, books, experience. Such a man finds ministers to his education on all sides; everything cooperates with his passion for growth. —H. Mabie

And so all growth that is not towards God / Is growing towards decay.
—George Macdonald

He [God] loves what I shall be. —George Macdonald

All growth is a leap in the dark, a spontaneous, unpremeditated act without benefit of experience. —Henry Miller

The biggest dog has been a pup. —Joaquin Miller

Every man must do his own growing, no matter how tall his grandfather was.
—Laurence J. Peter, compiler, *Peter's Quotations*: *Ideas for Our Time*

You don't grow up; you just keep growing. —Tom Zimmermann

GRUDGES

Grudges are too heavy a load to bear.   —Anonymous

GUESTS

If you want to become the perfect guest, then try to make your host
feel at home.   —W. A. "Dub" Nance

A guest sees more in an hour than the host in a year.
                                          —Proverb (Polish)

GUILT

Guilt has very quick ears to an accusation.   —Henry Fielding

Nobody becomes guilty by fate.   —Seneca, *Oedipus*

Every man is guilty of all the good he didn't do.   —Voltaire

— H —

HABIT

Habits are at first cobwebs, at last cables.   —Anonymous

Habit, if not resisted, soon becomes necessity.   —Saint Augustine

It is easy to assume a habit; but when you try to cast it off, it will take skin and all.   —Josh Billings

Habits are soon assumed; but when we strive to strip them off, 'tis being flayed alive.   —William Cowper

We first make our habits, and then our habits make us.—John Dryden

My problem lies in reconciling my gross habits with my net income.   —Errol Flynn

The chains of habit are generally too small to be felt till they are too strong to be broken.   —Samuel Johnson

Habit is a cable; we weave a thread of it every day, and at last we cannot break it.   —Horace Mann

A large part of Christian virtue consists in right habits.   —William Paley

The strength of a man's virtue should not be measured by his special exertions, but by his habitual acts.   —Blaise Pascal

Habit is a shirt made of iron.   —Proverb (Czechoslavakian)

Sow an act, and you reap a habit. Sow a habit, and you reap a character. Sow a character, and you reap a destiny.   —Charles Reade

Habit is overcome by habit.   —Thomas à Kempis, *The Imitation of Christ*

Habit is habit, and not to be flung out of the window by any man, but coaxed downstairs a step at a time.   —Mark Twain, *Pudd'nhead Wilson*, "Pudd'nhead Wilson's Calendar"

HAIR

Her hair / In ringlets rather dark than fair, / Does down her ivory
    bosom roll, And hiding half adorns the whole.   —Matthew Prior

Hair is another name for sex.

                                      —Vidal Sassoon

HANDICAPS

Rebellion against your handicaps gets you nowhere. Self-pity gets you
    nowhere. One must have the adventurous daring to accept oneself
    as a bundle of possibilities and undertake the most interesting
    game in the world—making the most of one's best.
                              —Harry Emerson Fosdisk

Mock not at those who are misshapen by nature.   —Thomas Fuller

Scoff not at the natural defects of any which are not in their power to
    amend. Oh, it is cruel to beat a cripple with his own crutches.
              —Thomas Fuller, *The Holy State*, "Of Testing"

I thank God for my handicaps, for, through them, I have found
    myself, my work, and my God.   —Helen Keller

So much has been given to me, I have no time to ponder over that
    which has been denied.   —Helen Keller

The best things in life are not seen or heard . . . but felt with the
    heart.   —Helen Keller

They took away what should have been my eyes, / (But I remembered
    Milton's Paradise). / They took away what should have been my ears,
/ (Beethoven came and wiped away my tears). / They took away what
    should have been my tongue, / (But I had talked with God when I
    was young). / He would not let them take away my soul—
/ Possessing that, I still possess the whole.   —Helen Keller

It is not miserable to be blind; it is miserable to be incapable of
    enduring blindness.   —John Milton

HAPPINESS

If we are not happy and joyous at this season, for what shall we wait
    and for what other time shall we look?   —Abdu'l-Bah

The grand essentials to happiness in this life are something to do, something to love, and something to hope for.   —Joseph Addison

Happiness is a butterfly, which, when pursued, is always just beyond your grasp but which, if you sit down quietly, may alight on you.
—Anonymous

Happy is the man who has learned to hold the things of this world with a loose hand.   —Anonymous

There is only one way to be happy, and that is to make somebody else so.   —Anonymous

The thing that counts most in the pursuit of happiness is choosing the right traveling companion.   —Anonymous

Happy persons seldom think of happiness. They are too busy losing their lives in the meaningful sacrifices of service.
—David Augsburger

Real happiness is cheap enough, yet how dearly we pay for its counterfeit.   —Hosea Ballou

Happiness sneaks in through a door you didn't know you left open.
—John Barrymore

Happiness is good health and a bad memory.   —Ingrid Bergman

There is no cosmetic for beauty like happiness.   —Lady Blessington

It is only possible to live happily ever after on a day-to-day basis.
—Margaret Bonnano

The secret of happiness is something to do.   —John Burroughs

All who joy would win / Must share it,— / Happiness was born a twin.
—Lord Byron, *Don Juan*

The only happiness a brave man ever troubled himself with asking much about, was happiness enough to get his work done.
—Thomas Carlyle

Remember happiness doesn't depend upon who you are or what you have; it depends solely upon what you think.   —Dale Carnegie

People don't notice whether it's winter or summer when they're
    happy.   —Anton Chekhov

Happiness can be built only on virtue, and must of necessity have
    truth for its foundation.   —Samuel Taylor Coleridge

Happiness is a delicate balance between what one is and what one
    has.   —J. H. Denison

To fill the hour,—that is happiness.
    —Ralph Waldo Emerson, *Essays, Second Series*, "Experience"

There is only one way to happiness and that is to cease worrying
    about things which are beyond the power of our will.   —Epictetus

No one is happy all his life long.   —Euripides

If we cannot live so as to be happy, let us at least live so as to deserve it.
    —Immanuel Hermann von Fichte

Happiness Makes Up in Height for What It Lacks in Length.
    —Robert Frost, title of a poem in *Witness Tree*

To be happy is not the purpose for which you are placed in this
    world.   —James Anthony Froude

He is happiest, be he king or peasant, who finds peace in his home.
    —Johann Wolfgang von Goethe

If we do not find happiness in the present moment, in what shall we
    find it?   —Oliver Goldsmith

Happiness consists in activity; it is a running stream, and not a stag-
    nant pool.   —J. M. Good

I am more and more convinced that our happiness depends far more
    on the way we meet the events of life than on the nature of those
    events themselves.   —Frederich H. Humboldt

Happy people are those who are producing something.
    —William R. Inge

The happiest people seem to be those who have no particular reason
    for being happy except that they are so.   —William R. Inge

My creed is this: / Happiness is the only good. / The place to be happy
is here. / The time to be happy is now. / The way to be happy is to
help make others so.
—Robert G. Ingersoll, motto on the title page of *Works*, Vol. xii

Happiness is a form of courage. —Holbrook Jackson

Rules for Happiness: / Something to do, / Someone to love,
/ Something to hope for. —Immanuel Kant

I remember when I switched from Christmas to sex as the secret of
happiness . . . —Garrison Keillor, *We Are Still Married*

We are no longer happy as soon as we wish to be happier.
—Walter Savage Landor

Happy people rarely correct their faults; they consider themselves
vindicated, since fortune endorses their evil ways.
—François de La Rochefoucauld

The happiness or unhappiness of men depends no less upon their dispositions than their fortunes. —François de La Rochefoucauld

A man's happiness or unhappiness depends as much on his temperament as on his destiny. —François de La Rochefoucauld

Most people are about as happy as they choose to be.
—Abraham Lincoln

Happiness is a thing to be practiced, like the violin. —John Lubbock

Our own happiness ought not to be our main objective in life.
—John Lubbock

The world would be better and brighter if people were taught the
duty of being happy as well as the happiness of doing their duty.
—John Lubbock

To be happy ourselves is a most effectual contribution to the happiness of others. —John Lubbock

We cannot be happy if we expect to live all the time at the highest
peak of intensity. Happiness is not a matter of intensity, but of balance and order and rhythm and harmony. —Thomas Merton

If we only wanted to be happy it would be easy; but we want to be happier than other people, which is almost always difficult, since we think them happier than they are. —Montesquieu

Happiness comes from within, and rests most securely on simple goodness and clear conscience. —William S. Ogdon

The foolish man seeks happiness in the distance; / The wise grows it under his feet. —James Oppenheim, "The Wise"

Happiness is neither within us only, or without us; it is the union of ourselves with God. —Blaise Pascal

Happiness does not depend upon a full pocketbook, but upon a mind full of rich thoughts and a heart full of rich emotions. —Wilferd Peterson

True happiness consists in being considered deserving of it. —Pliny

Happiness is a way-station between too little and too much. —Channing Pollock, *Mr. Moneypenny*

It is ever thus with happiness; / It is the gay to-morrow of the mind, / That never comes. —Proctor

From contentment with little comes happiness. —Proverb (African)

Make happy those who are near, and those who are far will come. —Proverb (Chinese)

Only he is happy who thinks he is. —Proverb (French)

When a man is happy he does not hear the clock strike. —Proverb (German)

Be happy while y'er leevin, for y'er a lang time deid. —Proverb (Scottish)

Happiness depends more on how life strikes you than on what happens. —Andrew A. Rooney, *And More by Andy Rooney*, "Rules of Life"

Happiness is not a station you arrive at, but a manner of traveling. —Margaret Lee Runbeck

To be without some of the things you want is an indispensable part of happiness. —Bertrand Russell

The greatest happiness you can have is knowing that you do not necessarily require happiness. —William Saroyan

We have no more right to consume happiness without producing it than to consume wealth without producing it.
—George Bernard Shaw, *Candida*, Act I

The doors of happiness open outward. —Natalie Sleeth

We are never happy: we can only remember that we were so once.
—Alexander Smith

A man is happy so long as he chooses to be happy and nothing can stop him. —Alexander Solzhenitsyn, *Cancer Ward*

The habit of being happy enables one to be freed, or largely freed, from the domination of outward conditions.
—Robert Louis Stevenson

There is no duty we so much underrate as the duty of being happy.
—Robert Louis Stevenson

Happy the heart where love has come to birth. —Saint Teresa of Ávila

. . . happiness enough has fallen to our lot.
—Leo Tolstoy, *The Death of Ivan Ilych and Other Stories*,
"Family Happiness"

A man must seek his happiness and inward peace from objects which cannot be taken away from him. —Wilhelm von Humboldt

. . . the greater part of our happiness or misery depends on our dispositions and not our circumstances. —Martha Washington

If you make children happy now, you will make them happy twenty years hence by the memory of it. —Kate Douglas Wiggin

Talk happiness. The world is sad enough / Without your woe. No path is wholly rough. —Ella Wheeler Wilcox

Much happiness is overlooked because it doesn't cost anything.
—Oscar Wilde

HARASSMENT

From here on I rag nobody.
> —Mark Harris, closing words of *Bang the Drum Slowly*

HARDSHIP

People had no tolerance for your particular hardship unless you knew
how to entertain them with it.   —Don DeLillo, *White Noise*

It is the north wind that made the Vikings. —Proverb (Scandinavian)

I believe that all we go through here must have some value.
> —Eleanor Roosevelt

A hard life improves the vision.   —Alexander Solzhenitsyn

HASTE

Make haste slowly.
> —Augustus Caesar, in Suetonius, *Divus Augustus*, XXV

Hasty climbers have sudden falls.
> —John Clarke, *Proverbs*: *English and Latine* (1639)

Haste makes waste.   —Benjamin Franklin

Good and quickly seldom meet. —George Herbert, *Outlandish Proverbs*

Haste is of the devil.   —*The Koran*

The hasty and the slow meet at the ferry.   —Proverb (Arab)

In haste there is error.   —Proverb (Chinese)

God made time, but man made haste.   —Proverb (Irish)

Haste is not speed.   —Proverb (Latin)

Haste is slow.   —Proverb (Latin)

Wisely, and slow; they stumble that run fast.
> —William Shakespeare, *Romeo and Juliet*, Act II, Sc. iii

Raw Haste, half-sister to Delay.   —Alfred, Lord Tennyson

HATRED

Hate is a prolonged manner of suicide.   —Anonymous

Hate is a two-edged sword. Hate cuts the one who uses it more than
    the one against whom it is used.   —Anonymous

Hatred can be an acid that does more damage to the vessel in which it
    is stored than to the object on which it's poured.   —Anonymous

Hatred is self-punishment.   —Hosea Ballou

Hatred like love feeds on the merest trifles.   —Honoré de Balzac

A true man hates no one.   —Napoleon Bonaparte

Hate no one; hate their vices, not themselves.   —J. G. C. Brainard

Hatred is not diminished by hatred at any time. Hatred is diminished
    by love—that is the eternal law.   —Buddhist saying

Hatred is the madness of the heart.   —Lord Byron

Standing, as I do, in the view of God and eternity, I realize that patri-
    otism is not enough. I must have no hatred or bitterness toward
    anyone.
      —Edith Cavell, an English nurse, spoken in prison to a chaplain
        before her execution by the Germans on 12 Oct 1915

The price of hating other human beings is loving oneself less.
      —Eldridge Cleaver, *Soul on Ice*, "On Becoming"

Heaven has no rage like love to hatred turned.   —William Congreve

Hating people is like burning down your own house to get rid of a rat.
      —Harry Emerson Fosdick

We can scarcely hate anyone that we know.
      —William Hazlitt, *Table-Talk*, "Why Distant Objects Please"

Don't hate, it's too big a burden to bear.   —Martin Luther King, Sr.

When our hatred is too keen, it places us beneath those we hate.
      —François de La Rochefoucauld

I do not hate the man, but his vices.   —Martial

Our hatred of someone does not affect their peace of mind, but it certainly can ruin ours. —W. A. "Dub" Nance

The hatred we bear our enemies injures their happiness less than our own. —J. Petit-Senn

Take care that no one hates you justly. —Publilius Syrus, *Sententioe*

I shall allow no man to belittle my soul by making me hate him.
—Booker T. Washington

Let no man pull you so low as to make you hate him.
—Booker T. Washington, in Martin Luther King, Jr.,
Stride Toward Freedom

HEALING

. . . Daughter, thy faith hath made thee whole.
—*The Bible* (KJV): Mark 5:34

Every day, in every way, I am getting better and better.
—Émile Coué, *De la suggestion et de ses application*; Coué advised his patients to repeat this phrase 15 to 20 times, morning and evening

We must learn never to underestimate the capacity of the human mind and body to regenerate—even when the prospects seem most wretched . . . What the patient expects to happen . . . can be as potent in touching off biochemical processes as any medication.
—Norman Cousins, *Human Options*

Love cures people. Both the ones who give it, and the ones who receive it. —Karl Menninger

'Tis half the cure to be willing to be cured. —Seneca, *Hippolytus*, 249

What wound did ever heal but by degrees?
—William Shakespeare, *Othello*, Act II, Sc. iii

. . . I discovered that it is not on our forgiveness any more than on our goodness that the world's healing hinges, but on His.
—Corrie ten Boom, *The Hiding Place*,
with John and Elizabeth Sherrill

It makes the whole world better when one person gets better.
—Tom Zimmermann

HEALTH

Health is not valued till sickness come. —Anonymous

He who hath good health is young.
—H. G. Bohn, *Hand-Book of Proverbs*

The best promoter of health is something to do. —John Burroughs

The first wealth is health.
—Ralph Waldo Emerson, *The Conduct of Life*, "Power"

Sickness is felt, but health not at all.
—Thomas Fuller, M. D., *Gnomologia*, No. 4160

He who has health has hope, and he who has hope has everything.
—Proverb (Arab)

A man too busy to take care of his health is like a mechanic too busy
to take care of his tools. —Proverb (Spanish)

Good thoughts are half of good health. —Proverb (Yugoslav)

Take care of your health, that it may serve you to serve God.
—Saint Francis de Sales

Look to your health; and if you have it, praise God, and value it next
to a good conscience. —Izaak Walton

HEART

God can do wonders with a broken heart if you give him all the
pieces. —Victor Alfsen

Every heart hath its own ache. —Anonymous

I don't believe in quantum physics when it comes to matters of the
heart. —Anonymous, Kevin Kostner line in the movie *Bull Durham*

The heart has its arguments with which understanding is not
acquainted. —Anonymous

The same heart beats in every human breast.
—Matthew Arnold, *The Buried Life*

Thou hast created us for thyself, and our heart cannot be quieted till it may find repose in thee.
—Saint Augustine, *Confessions*, Book I, Ch. 1

What the heart has once owned and had, it shall never lose.
—Henry Ward Beecher

Only God can fully satisfy the hungry heart of man.   —Hugh Black

The heart must be beaten or bruised, and then the sweet scent will come out.
—John Bunyan

The heart will break, yet brokenly live on.   —Lord Byron

Feel it in thy heart and then say whether it is of God!
—Thomas Carlyle

If seed in the black earth can turn into such beautiful roses, what might not the heart of man become in its long journey towards the stars?
—G. K. Chesterton

Be persuaded that your only treasures are those which you carry in your heart.
—Demophilus

God always fills in all hearts all the room which is left Him there.
—Frederick William Faber

Nobody has ever measured, not even poets, how much the heart can hold.
—Zelda Fitzgerald

In the small matters trust the mind; in the large ones the heart.
—Sigmund Freud

All the knowledge I possess everyone else can acquire, but my heart is all my own.
—Johann Wolfgang von Goethe, *The Sorrows of Young Werther*

Every time a man unburdens his heart to a stranger he reaffirms the love that unites humanity.
—Germaine Greer

Don't put anyone out of your heart, there's room for all.
—Judith Guest, *Errands*, Ch. 38

Let us knock gently at each other's heart, / Glad of a chance to look within.
—Carol Haynes

My heart resembles the ocean; has storm, and ebb, and flow; / And many a beautiful pearl / Lies hid in its depths below. —Heine

There is strength deep bedded in our hearts, of which we reck but little till the shafts of heaven have pierced its fragile dwelling. Must not earth be rent before her gems are found?
—Felicia Dorothea Browne Hemans

There is no exercise better for the heart than reaching down and lifting people up. —John Andrew Holmes

It is better to break one's heart than to do nothing with it.
—Margaret Kennedy

The finest victory is to conquer one's own heart.
—Jean de La Fontaine, *Nymphes de Vaux*

What can the will do when the heart commands?
—Louis L'Amour, *The Walking Drum*

Perhaps pure reason without heart would never have thought of God.
—G. C. Lichtenberg

My heart is a lonely hunter that hunts on a lonely hill.
—Fiona Macleod, *The Lonely Hunter*

The Heart is a Lonely Hunter. —Carson McCullers, title of novel

The heart of a good man is the sanctuary of God in this world.
—Madame Suzanne Necker

The heart has eyes that the brain knows nothing of.
—Charles H. Parkhurst, *Sermons*, "Coming to the Truth"

The heart has its reasons which reason does not know.
—Blaise Pascal, *Pensées*, 4, 277

Keep a green tree in your heart and perhaps the singing bird will come. —Proverb (Chinese)

The heart that loves is always young. —Proverb (Greek)

The deep sea can be fathomed, but who knows the hearts of men?
—Proverb (Malay)

Science is no substitute for virtue; the heart is as necessary for a good
life as the head.   —Bertrand Russell, *The Future of Science*

... the solitary pain that gnaws the heart.
          —Bertrand Russell, *The Autobiography of Bertrand Russell*

O heart! love is thy bane and thy antidote.   —George Sand

A merry heart goes all the day, / Your sad tires in a mile.
          —William Shakespeare, *The Winter's Tale*, Act IV, Sc. iii

Go to your bosom; / Knock there, and ask your heart what it doth
know ...   —William Shakespeare, *Measure for Measure*, Act II, Sc. ii

What stronger breastplate than a heart untainted! / Thrice is he
arm'd, that hath his quarrel just ...
          —William Shakespeare, *King Henry VI, Part II*, Act III, Sc. ii

God wants the heart.   —*The Talmud*

We say that money talks, but it speaks a broken, poverty-stricken language. Hearts talk better, clearer, and with wider intelligence.
          —William Allen White

Hearts live by being wounded.
          —Oscar Wilde, *A Woman of No Importance*

HEARTBREAK

More Die of Heartbreak.   —Saul Bellow, title of a novel

You know, a heart can be broken, but it keeps on beating just the
same.   —Fannie Flagg, *Fried Green Tomatoes at the Whistle Stop Cafe*

Never morning wore
To evening but some heart did break.   —Alfred, Lord Tennyson

HEAVEN

There is no coming to heaven with dry eyes.   —Thomas Adams

From every spot on earth we are equally near heaven and the infinite.
          —Henri Frédéric Amiel

He will never go to heaven who is content to go alone. —Anonymous

Heaven often smites in mercy, even when the blow is severest.
—Joanna Baillie

There is a blessed home / Beyond this land of woe.
—Henry W. Baker, "There is a Blessed Home"

The gates of heaven are so easily found when we are little, and they
are always standing open to let children wander in.
—Sir James Matthew Barrie, *Sentimental Tommy*

Heaven will be the endless portion of every man who has heaven in
his soul. —Henry Ward Beecher

. . . Whatsoever ye shall bind on earth shall be bound in heaven; and
whatsoever ye shall loose on earth shall be loosed in heaven.
—*The Bible* (KJV): Matthew 18:18

But many that are first shall be last; and the last first.
—*The Bible* (KJV): Mark 10:31

In my Father's house are many mansions; if it were not so, I would
have told you. I go to prepare a place for you.
—*The Bible* (KJV): John 14:2

The world no longer lets me love, / My hope and treasure are above.
—Anne Bradstreet, "Upon the Burning of Our House," 10 Jul 1666

All places are distant from heaven alike.
—Robert Burton, *The Anatomy of Melancholy*

One sweetly solemn thought / Comes to me o'er and o'er; / I am
nearer home to-day / Than I ever have been before.
—Phoebe Car, "Nearer Home"

Does Heaven ever speak? The four seasons come and go, and all creatures thrive and grow. Does Heaven ever speak! —Confucius

Whatever heaven ordains is best. —Confucius

To get to heaven we must take it with us. —Henry Drummond

Heaven always bears some proportion to earth. The god of the cannibal will be a cannibal, of the crusaders a crusader, and of the mer-
chants a merchant.
—Ralph Waldo Emerson, *The Conduct of Life*, "Worship"

No man can ever enter heaven until he is first convinced he deserves
  hell. —John W. Everett

Both heaven and hell are within us.
  —Mahatma Gandhi, in *Young India*, 25 Oct 1928

. . . the same hand that made trees and fields and flowers, the seas
  and hills, the clouds and sky, has been making a home for us called
  heaven. —Billy Graham, *Till Armageddon*

Think of working forever at something you love to do, for one you
  love with all your heart, and never getting tired! We will never
  know weariness in heaven. —Billy Graham, *Till Armageddon*

Everybody talking 'bout heaven ain't going there!
  —Lorraine Hansberry, *A Raisin in the Sun*

Heaven appears to have ordained a great many things which it is supposed to disapprove of. —Henry S. Haskins

All this, and Heaven too!
  —Philip Henry, in Matthew Henry, *Life of Philip Henry*

Heaven is not reached at a single bound; / But we build the ladder by
  which we rise / From the lowly earth to the vaulted skies, / And we
  mount to its summit round by round.
  —Josiah Gilbert Holland, "Graditim"

Heaven is for those who think of it. —Joseph Joubert

You think that the only thing that counts is the bottom line! What a
  presumptuous thing to say. The bottom line is in heaven.
  —Edwin Herbert Land, at a Polaroid Corporation shareholders'
  meeting, 26 Apr 1977

Aim at heaven and you will get earth thrown in. Aim at earth and
  you will get neither. —C. S. Lewis

'Tis heaven alone that is given away, / 'Tis only God may be had for
  the asking. —Lowell

How blind men are to Heaven's gifts!
  —Lucan, *De Bello Civili*, Book V, line 528

Beyond this vale of tears / There is a life above, / Unmeasured by the flight of years; / And all that life is love.
—James Montgomery, "The Issues of Life and Death"

Heaven is equally distant everywhere.   —Petronius, *Satyricon*

All things are from above.   —Proverb (Latin)

Heav'n is not always got by running.   —Francis Quarles

Heaven Has No Favorites   —Erich Maria Remarque, title of a novel

We must bear what Heaven sends.   —Friedrich Schiller

Every man is received in heaven who receives heaven in himself while in the world, and he is excluded who does not.
—Emanuel Swedenborg

Heaven must be in thee before thou canst be in heaven.
—George Swinnock, from *The Golden Treasury of Puritan Quotations*

Short arms needs man to reach to Heaven / So ready is Heaven to stoop to him.   —Francis Thompson, "Grace of the Way," Stanza 6

There are no step children in heaven.   —Lewis Timberlake

Entrance into Heaven is not at the hour of death, but at the moment of conversion.
—Benjamin Whichcote, *Moral and Religious Aphorisms*

As much of heaven is visible as we have eyes to see.
—William Winter, *The Actor and His Duty*

Heaven wills our happiness, allows our doom.
—Edward Young, *Night Thoughts*, "Night 7"

H E L L

God will never send anybody to hell. If man goes to hell, he goes by his own free choice.   —Billy Graham

The safest road to Hell is the gradual one—the gentle slope, soft underfoot, without sudden turnings, without milestones, without signposts.   —C. S. Lewis

. . . when all the world dissolves, / And every creature shall be puri-
fied, / All places shall be hell that are not heaven.
—Christopher Marlowe, *Doctor Faustus*, Act II, Sc. i

Hell is wherever heaven is not. —Proverb (17th century)

The Lord casts no one down in Hell, but the spirit casts himself
hither. —Emanuel Swedenborg

H E L P

God loves to help him who strives to help himself.
—Aeschylus, Fragments

The gods help them that help themselves.
—Aesop, *Fables*, "Hercules and the Waggoner"

God will help thee bear what comes. —Anonymous

Help yourself and your friends will help you. —Anonymous

He that does good to another does good also to himself, not only in
the consequence but in the very act. For the consciousness of well-
doing is in itself ample reward. —Anonymous

It is the best thing for a stricken heart to be helping others.
—Anonymous

The Lord helps those that help others. —Anonymous

When you help someone else up the hill, you reach the top yourself.
—Anonymous

God's help is nearer than the door. —Gurney Benham

Be brave enough to accept the help of others.
—Melba Colgreve, Harold H. Bloomfield,
and Peter McWilliams, *How to Survive the Loss of a Love*

If you believe in the Lord, He will do half the work—but the last half.
He helps those who help themselves. —Cyrus K. Curtis

Nature's stern discipline enjoins mutual help at least as often as warfare. The fittest may also be the gentlest.
—Theodosius Dobzhansky, *Mankind Evolving*

Better to expose ourselves to ingratitude than fail in assisting the
  unfortunate.   —Du Coeur

It is one of the most beautiful compensations of this life that no man
  can sincerely try to help another without helping himself.
                                          —Ralph Waldo Emerson

It is not so much our friends help that helps us as the confidence of
  their help.   —Epicurus

He helps others most, who shows them how to help themselves.
                                                  —A. P. Gouthey

To oblige persons often costs little and helps much.—Baltasar Gracián

God helps them that help themselves.
                          —George Herbert, *Outlandish Proverbs*

Help thyself, and God will help thee.   —George Herbert

Help thy brother's boat across, / And lo! thine own has reached the
  shore.   —Hindu saying

The pleasure we derive from doing favors is partly in the feeling it
  gives us that we are not altogether worthless.
                          —Eric Hoffer, *The Passionate State of Mind*

When a friend is in trouble, don't annoy him by asking if there is any
  thing you can do. Think up something appropriate and do it.
                                          —Edgar Watson Howe

The hands that help are holier than the lips that pray.
              —Robert G. Ingersoll, *The Children of the Stage*

Great opportunities to help others seldom come, but small ones sur-
  round us every day.   —Sally Koch

Help yourself, and heaven will help you.
        —Jean de La Fontaine, *Fables*, vi. 18, "Le Chartier Embourbé"

No one is so rich that he does not need another's help; no one so
  poor as not to be useful in some way to his fellow man; and the disposition to ask assistance from others with confidence and to grant
  it with kindness is part of our very nature.   —Pope Leo XIII

I'm going your way, so let us go hand in hand. You help me and I'll
help you. We shall not be here very long, for soon death, the kind
old nurse, will come back and rock us all to sleep. Let us help one
another while we may.   —William Morris

Help other people to cope with their problems, and your own will be
easier to cope with.   —Norman Vincent Peale

One good turn deserves another.   —Proverb (15th century)

God is a good worker, but He loves to be helped.   —Proverb (Basque)

A willing helper does not wait to be called.   —Proverb (Danish)

Mutual help is the law of nature.   —Proverb (French)

God likes help when helping people.   —Proverb (Irish)

We cannot exist without mutual help. All therefore that need aid
have a right to ask it from their fellow men; and no one who has
the power of granting can refuse it without guilt. —Sir Walter Scott

If someone asked you, why not help him out?
—Alexander Solzhenitsyn, *One Day in the Life of Ivan Denisovich*

My friends! Let us try to be helpful, if we are worth anything.
—Alexander Solzhenitsyn, *Nobel Lecture*

If you're in trouble or hurt or need—go to poor people. They're the
only ones that'll help—the only ones.
—John Steinbeck, *The Grapes of Wrath*, Ch. 26

Let us help one another to bear our burdens.
—Voltaire, *Réligion Naturelle*, Part 2

It is one of the beautiful compensations of this life that no one can
sincerely try to help another without helping himself.
—Charles Dudley Warner, *Backlog Studies*, "Fifth Study"

HEREDITY

Heredity is nothing but stored environment.   —Burbank

Heredity sets limits; environment decides the exact portion within
these limits.   —Edwin Carleton MacDowell

HEROES

The world's battlefields have been in the heart chiefly, and there the greatest heroism has been secretly exercised.—Henry Ward Beecher

Everyone who does the best he can is a hero. —Josh Billings

The hero saves us. Praise the hero! Now, who will save us from the hero?
—Cato the Elder, Roman Senate speech, in David Schoenbrun, *The Three Lives of Charles de Gaulle*, pt. 2

No man is a hero to his valet.
—Anne Bigot de Cornuel, letter, 13 Aug 1728

He who does his duty is a hero, whether anyone rewards him for it or not. —George Failing

Too much has been said of the heroes of history—the strong men, the troublesome men; too little of the amiable, the kindly, the tolerant.
—Stephen Leacock, *Essays and Literary Studies*

Some men are heroes by nature in that they will give all that is in them without regard to the effort or to the personal returns.
—Carson McCullers, *The Mortgaged Heart*, "Author's Outline of 'The Mute'"

I hate to see a hero fail. There are so few of them . . . Without heroes we're all plain people and don't know how far we can go.
—Bernard Malamud, *The Natural*

Heroes: Fanatics who succeed.
—David A. Modell, *Smart Set*, Sep 1914, "A Modernist's Lexicon"

The grandest of heroic deeds are those which are performed within four walls and in domestic privacy. —Jean Paul Richter

A hero is one who does what he can. —Romain Rolland

There is more heroism in self-denial than in deeds of arms. —Seneca

God is preparing his heroes; and when the opportunity comes, he can fit them into their places in a moment, and the world will wonder where they came from. —A. B. Simpson

In real life the greatest heroes are often found among the plainest people.   —Roy L. Smith

But in the hero ne'er forget the man.
                —Mercy Otis Warren, *The Ladies of Castile*, Act I, Sc. ii

To go against the dominant thinking of your friends, of most of the people you see every day, is perhaps the most difficult act of heroism you can have.   —Theodore H. White

HILLS

If the hill will not come to Mahomet, Mahomet will go to the hill.
                        —Francis Bacon, *Essays*, "Of Boldness"

To make a mountain out of a mole-hill.   —Havelock Ellis

Do not climb the hill until you get to it.   —Proverb (English)

Set a stout heart to a steep hillside.   —Proverb (Scottish)

Does the road wind up-hill all the way? / Yes, to the very end. / Will the day's journey take the whole long day? / From morn to night, my friend.   —Christina Rossetti, "Up-Hill"

HINDSIGHT

After the event, even a fool is wise.   —Homer

It is easy to be wise after the event.   —Proverb (17th century)

Hindsight is always twenty-twenty.   —Billy Wilder

. . . the wisdom of hindsight.   —Herman Wouk, *The Winds of War*

HISTORY

History is always repeating itself, but each time the price goes up.
                                            —Anonymous

History is His story.   —Anonymous

The highways of history are strewn with the wreckage of the nations that forgot God.   —Anonymous

We learn from history that we don't learn from history.—Anonymous

Well, everybody has a history.
—Saul Bellow, *Mr. Sammler's Planet*, Ch. 4

History is but a fable agreed upon.   —Napoleon Bonaparte

History is but the polemics of the victor.   —William F. Buckley

A thousand years scarce serve to form a state; / An hour may lay it in
the dust.   —Lord Byron

Not to know what has been transacted in former times is to be always
a child. If no use is made of the labors of past ages, the world must
remain always in the infancy of knowledge.   —Cicero

History is philosophy teaching by examples.
—Dionysius of Halicarnassus, *Ars rhetorica*

History teaches us that men and nations behave wisely once they
have exhausted all other alternatives.
—Abba Eban, speech in London, 16 Dec 1970

There is properly no history; only biography.
—Ralph Waldo Emerson, *Essays*, "History"

The pyramids themselves, doting with age, have forgotten the names
of their founders.   —Thomas Fuller

Sin writes histories, goodness is silent.
—Johann Wolfgang von Goethe

The best benefit we derive from history is the enthusiasm it excites.
—Johann Wolfgang von Goethe

That men do not learn very much from the lessons of history is the
most important of all the lessons that history has to teach.
—Aldous Huxley, *Collected Essays*, "Case of Voluntary Ignorance"

It is history that teaches us to hope.
—Gen. Robert E. Lee, in a letter to Charles Marshall, circa 1866

Perhaps in time the so-called Dark Ages will be thought of as including our own.   —G. C. Lichtenberg

Not a stone but has its history.   —Lucan, said of the ruins of Troy

Had Cleopatra's nose been shorter, the whole history of the world
would have been different. —Blaise Pascal, *Pensées*

Until lions have their historians, tales of the hunt shall always glorify
the hunter. —Proverb (African)

The history of humanity is not the history of its wars, but the history
of its households. —John Ruskin

Those who cannot remember the past are condemned to repeat it.
—George Santayana

History is too slow for our life, for our hearts.
—Alexander Solzhenitsyn

It only needed two or three such defeats in succession for the backbone of a country to be put out of joint forever and for a thousand-
year-old nation to be utterly destroyed.
—Alexander Solzhenitsyn, *August 1914*

If you want the present to be different from the past, study the past.
—Benedict de Spinoza

History! Read it and weep! —Kurt Vonnegut, Jr., *The Cat's Cradle*

We are still in the Dark Ages. The Dark Ages—they haven't ended yet.
—Kurt Vonnegut, Jr., *Deadeye Dick*, closing words

Human history becomes more and more a race between education
and catastrophe. —H. G. Wells, *The Outline of History*, Vol. 2, Ch. 41

HOBBIES

Everyone should have a deep-seated interest or hobby to enrich his
mind, add zest to living, and perhaps, depending upon what it is,
result in a service to his country. —Dale Carnegie

No man is really happy or safe without a hobby . . .
—Sir William Osler

A fascinating and creative interest apart from your work is an
absolute essential for happy living. —John Schindler, M. D.

HOCKEY

You miss 100 percent of the shots you never take. —Wayne Gretzky

HOLDING

He that grasps at too much holds nothing fast.   —Anonymous

Learn to hold loosely all that is not eternal.   —A. Maude Royden

HOLINESS

It is a great deal better to live a holy life than to talk about it.
Lighthouses do not ring bells and fire cannon to call attention to
their shining—they just shine.   —Dwight L. Moody

HOLY SPIRIT

If a son shall ask bread of any of you that is a father, will he give him
a stone? Or if he ask a fish, will he for a fish give him a serpent? Or
if he shall ask an egg, will he offer him a scorpion? If ye then, being
evil, know how to give good gifts unto your children, how much
more shall your heavenly Father give the Holy Spirit to them that
ask him?   —*The Bible* (KJV): Luke 11:11–13

. . . the Spirit also helpeth our infirmities; for we know not what we
should pray for as we ought; but the Spirit himself maketh interces-
sion for us with groanings which cannot be uttered.
    —*The Bible* (KJV): Romans 8:26

To the one who remembers the Spirit there is always a way out, even
in the wilderness with the devil.   —Herbert F. Brokering

We must not be content to be cleansed from sin; we must be filled
with the Spirit.   —John Fletcher

The Holy Spirit is a helper, not a doer.   —Karen Huybrechts

HOME

A hundred men can make an encampment, but it requires a woman
to make a home.   —Anonymous

Love makes a house a home.   —Anonymous

Men make houses, but women make homes.   —Anonymous

The duties of home are discipline for the ministries of heaven.
    —Anonymous

Home is the chief school of human virtue.—William Ellery Channing

There is no place more delightful than home.   —Cicero

Home is the sacred refuge of our life.   —John Dryden

Home is the place where, when you have to go there, / They have to
    take you in.
                    —Robert Frost, *North of Boston*, "Death of the Hired Man"

A home is no home unless it contains food and fire for the mind as
    well as for the body.   —Margaret Fuller

It takes a heap o' livin' in a house t' make it home.
                    —Edgar A. Guest, "Home"

If you travel you see people in variety. But if you stay home you see
    them in development.   —Joseph Washington Hall

The fellow that owns his own home is always just coming out of a
    hardware store.
            —Frank McKinney ("Kin") Hubbard, in Charles McCabe, "The
                    Fearless Spectator," *San Francisco Chronicle*, 23 Sep 1971

A man's home is his wife.   —Jewish saying

In violent and chaotic times such as these, our only chance for sur-
    vival lies in creating our own little islands of sanity and order, in
    making little havens of our homes.   —Sue Kaufman, *Falling Bodies*

A Christian home! What a power it is to the child when he is far away
    in the cold, tempting world, and voices of sin are filling his ears,
    and his feet stand on slippery places.   —A. E. Kittreage

[Home] is you in things.   —Laurel Lee, *Walking Through the Fire*

No other success can compensate for failure in the home.
                    —David O. McKay

A man travels the world over in search of what he needs, and returns
    home to find it.   —George Moore, *Brook Kerith*, Ch. 11

Home interprets heaven. Home is heaven for beginners.
                    —Charles H. Parkhurst

Be it ever so humble, / There's no place like home.
—John Howard Payne, "Home, Sweet Home" (song)

Home is where the heart is. —Pliny

East or west, home is best. —Proverb (19th century)

Every bird likes its own nest best. —Proverb (French)

To every bird his nest is fair. —Proverb (Latin)

Home after all is the best place when life begins to wobble.
—Lady Russell

The strength of a nation, especially of a republican nation, is in the intelligent and well-ordered homes of the people.
—Lydia Sigourney

Domestic happiness depends upon the ability to overlook.
—Roy L. Smith

Whatever brawls disturb the street, / There should be peace at home.
—Isaac Watts, *Divine Songs for Children*, xvii, "Love between Brothers and Sisters"

You Can't Go Home Again. —Thomas Wolfe, book title

HONESTY

Make yourself an honest man, and then you may be sure that there is one rascal less in the world. —Thomas Carlyle

Honesty's the best policy. —Miguel de Cervantes

Honesty is one part of eloquence. We persuade others by being in earnest ourselves. —William Hazlitt

Honesty is praised and starves. —Juvenal, *Satires*

Honesty needs no disguise or ornament. —Thomas Otway

An honest man's the noblest work of God.
—Alexander Pope, *An Essay on Man*, IV.

Person-to-person, most people are honest.
—Andrew A. Rooney, *Word for Word*, "Dishonesty"

I hold the maxim no less applicable to public than to private affairs,
that honesty is always the best policy.   —George Washington

He's an honest man—you could shoot craps with him over the telephone.   —Earl Wilson

H O N O R

Honor and shame from no condition rise; / Act well your part, there
all the honor lies.   —Alexander Pope, *An Essay on Man*

H O P E

While I breathe, I hope.   —Anonymous

Despondency is ingratitude; hope is God's worship.
                                        —Henry Ward Beecher

My hope is built on nothing less / Than Jesus' blood and righteousness.   —William Bradbury

Man is, properly speaking, based upon Hope; he has no other possession but Hope.   —Thomas Carlyle, *Sartor Resartus*

Hope means expectancy when things are otherwise hopeless.
                                          —G. K. Chesterton

There is no medicine like hope, no incentive so great, and no tonic so
powerful as expectation of something better tomorrow.
                                          —G. K. Chesterton

Hope is a thing with feathers, / That perches in the soul.
                                          —Emily Dickinson

Hopeful men do not die so easily . . .
                    —Alexander Dolgun, *Alexander Dolgun's Story*

One must not tie a ship to a single anchor, nor life to a single hope.
                                              —Epictetus

If it were not for hopes, the heart would break.
                    —Thomas Fuller, M. D., *Gnomologia*, No. 2689

Of all delusions perhaps none is so great as the thought that our past
has ruined our present, that the evils we have done, the mistakes
we have committed, have made all further Hope impossible.
                                        —Archbishop Goodier

It is silly not to hope . . . Besides I believe it is a sin.
—Ernest Hemingway, *The Old Man and the Sea*

Hope is itself a species of happiness, and perhaps, the chief happiness which this world affords.
—Samuel Johnson

The natural flights of the human mind are not from pleasure to pleasure, but from hope to hope.
—Samuel Johnson, in James Boswell, *Life of Samuel Johnson*

Hope is the mother of faith.
—Walter Savage Landor

Everything that is done in the world is done by hope.—Martin Luther

There is no medicine like hope . . .
—O. S. Marden

Hope proves man deathless. It is the struggle of the soul, breaking loose from what is perishable, and attesting her eternity.
—Henry Melvill

Hope is the dream of a waking man.
—Pliny the Elder

Hope springs eternal in the human breast: / Man never is, but always to be blest.
—Alexander Pope, *An Essay on Man*, Epistle 1, lines 95-96

For hope is but the dream of those that wake.
—Matthew Prior

If hope were not, heart would break.
—Proverb (13th century)

I live in hope.
—Proverb (French)

Love will subsist on wonderfully little hope, but not altogether without it.
—Scott

The miserable have no other medicine / But only hope . . .
—William Shakespeare, *Measure for Measure*, Act III, Sc. i

To travel hopefully is a better thing than to arrive.
—Robert Louis Stevenson, *Virginibus Puerisque*, "El Dorado"

While there's life, there's hope.
—Terence, *Heauton Timoroumenos*

Hope is the poor man's bread.
—Thales

Hope ever urges on and tells us tomorrow will be better.
—Tibillus

Hope and be happy that all's for the best!
—Martin Farquhar Tupper, "All's for the Best," Stanza 3

Arise, why look behind, / When Hope is all before?
—John Greenleaf Whittier

Whether we be young or old, / Our destiny, our being's heart and home, / Is with infinitude, and only there; / With hope it is, hope that can never die, / Effort, and expectation, and desire, / And something evermore about to be. —William Wordsworth, *The Prelude*, VI, 603

HOPELESSNESS

When you say a situation or a person is hopeless, you are slamming the door in the face of God. —Charles A. Allen

There are no hopeless situations; there are only men who have grown hopeless about them. —Clare Booth Luce, *Europe in the Spring*

HORSES

From a hundred rabbits you can't make a horse.
—Fyodor Dostoyevsky, *Crime and Punishment*

The ear of the bridled horse is in the mouth. —Horace

It is not best to swap horses while crossing a river.
—Abraham Lincoln, reply to
the National Union League, 9 Jun 1864

One cannot shoe a running horse. —Proverb (Dutch)

There is no horse so sure-footed as never to trip. —Proverb (French)

Better ride a lame horse than go afoot. —Proverb (German)

A good horse never lacks a saddle. —Proverb (Latin)

HOUSES

As you build, such your house. —Anonymous

Your house is your larger self. —Anonymous

Houses are built to live in, and not to look on.
—Francis Bacon, *Essays*, "Of Building"

Whom God loves, his house is sweet to him.
> —Miguel de Cervantes, *Don Quixote*, Part II, Ch. 43

A man builds a fine house; and now he has a master, and a task for life; he is to furnish, watch, show it, and keep it in repair the rest of his life.
> —Ralph Waldo Emerson, *Society and Solitude*, "Works and Days"

The houses people live in reflect their opinions of themselves.
> —Joseph F. Girzone, *Joshua*, Ch. 19

I want a house that has got over all its troubles; I don't want to spend the rest of my life bringing up a young and inexperienced house.
> —Jerome K. Jerome, *They and I*, Ch. 11

A house is a machine for living in.
> —Le Corbusier, "Vers une architecture"

A house is a machine for loving in.
> —Craig McGregor, in Ian McKay et al., *Living and Partly Living*

If you want a golden rule that will fit everybody, this is it: Have nothing in your houses that you do not know to be useful, or believe to be beautiful.
> —William Morris, *The Beauty of Life*

... the kitchen, where all the fair prospects of life were centered.
> —Katherine Anne Porter, *Noon Wine*

A house that is built according to every man's advice seldom gets a roof.
> —Proverb (Swedish)

The national sport of England is obstacle-racing. People fill their rooms with useless and cumbersome furniture, and spend the rest of their lives in trying to dodge it.
> —Herbert Beerbohm Tree

Oh, this wasn't a very organized house ... The counters seemed to collect stray objects on their own.
> —Anne Tyler, *Breathing Lessons*

Early relative—things relatives gave me.
> —Shelley Winters, when asked how her house was furnished

HOUSEWORK

Housework is something you do that nobody notices unless you don't do it.
> —Anonymous

Dust is a protective coating for the furniture.
—Mario Buatta, in "Fringe Lunatic," by John Taylor

There was no need to do any housework at all. After the first four
years the dirt doesn't get any worse.
—Quentin Crisp, *The Naked Civil Servant*, Ch. 15

Cleaning your house while your children are still growing
Is like shoveling the walk before it stops snowing.   —Phyllis Diller

The worst thing about work in the house or home is that whatever
you do is destroyed, laid waste or eaten within twenty-four hours.
—Lady Hasluck, in Michèle Brown
and Ann O'Connor, *Woman Talk*, vol. 1

Dirt is matter in the wrong place.   —Lord Palmerston

The fingers of the housewife do more than a yoke of oxen.
—Proverb (German)

There is no such thing as a self-cleaning oven.   —Wes Smith

The HUMAN BODY

. . . the movements of the body reveal the movements of the soul.
—Leon Battista Alberti

A man's head is his castle.   —Anonymous

Modesty is the conscience of the body.   —Honoré de Balzac

God made the human body, and it is by far the most exquisite and
wonderful organization which has come to us form the Divine
hand.   —Henry Ward Beecher

Brain, n. An apparatus with which we think we think . . .
—Ambrose Bierce, *The Devil's Dictionary*

Lap, n. One of the most important organs of the female system—an
admirable provision for the repose of infancy, but chiefly useful in
rural festivities to support plates of cold chicken and heads of adult
males.   —Ambrose Bierce, *The Devil's Dictionary*

The more you use your brain, the more brain you will have to use.
—George R. Dorsey

Life itself is the real and most miraculous miracle of all. If one had
never before seen a human hand and were suddenly presented for
the first time with this strange and wonderful thing, what a miracle, what a magnificently shocking and inexplicable and mysterious thing it would be.   —Christopher Fry

Your body is the harp of the soul.   —Kahlil Gibran

The body says what words cannot.   —Martha Graham

The most highly prized curve of all is that of the bosom . . .
                              —Germaine Greer, *The Female Eunuch*

Whoever considers the study of anatomy I believe will never be an
atheist; the frame of man's body and coherence of his parts being
so strange and paradoxical that I hold it to be the greatest miracle
of Nature.   —Herbert of Cherbury

We should teach our children to think no more of their bodies when
dead than they do of their hair when cut off, or of their old clothes
when they have done with them.
                    —George Macdonald, *Annals of a Quiet Neighborhood*

. . . if it were the fashion to go naked, the face would be hardly
observed.   —Mary Wortley Montagu, letter to Lady Rich, 1717

A human being: an ingenious assembly of portable plumbing.
                          —Christopher Morley, *Human Being* (1932)

The human brain is the highest bloom of the whole organic meta-
morphosis of the earth.   —Friedrich von Schelling

The human brain is a most unusual instrument of elegant and as yet
unknown capacity.
                    —Stuart Luman Seaton, speech to the American Institute of
                              Electrical Engineers, in *Time*, 17 Feb 1958

Poor creature though I be, I am the hand and foot of Christ. I move
my hand and my hand is wholly Christ's hand, for deity is become
inseparably one with me. I move my foot, and it is aglow with
God.   —Saint Symeon the New Theologian

If anything is sacred the human body is sacred.
                    —Walt Whitman, *Leaves of Grass*, "I Sing the Body Electric"

We think in youth that our bodies are identical to ourselves and have the same interests, but discover later in life that they are heartless companions who have been accidentally yoked with us, and who are as likely as not, in our extreme sickness or old age, to treat us with less mercy than we would have received at the hands of the worst bandits. —Rebecca West

HUMANISM

There is nothing new about humanism. It is the yielding to Satan's first temptation of Adam and Eve: "Ye shall be as gods." (Gen. 3:5) —Billy Graham, *World Aflame*

HUMANITY

Our humanity were a poor thing but for the divinity that stirs within us. —Francis Bacon

We know better than we do. We do not yet possess ourselves, and we know at the same time that we are much more. —Ralph Waldo Emerson, *Essays*, *First Series*, "The Over-Soul"

I believe in the absolute oneness of God and, therefore, also of humanity. What though we have many bodies? We have but one soul. The rays of the sun are many through refraction. But they have the same source. I cannot, therefore, detach myself from the wickedest soul (nor may I be denied identity with the most virtuous). —Mahatma Gandhi

The ingratitude of the world can never deprive us of the conscious happiness of having acted with humanity ourselves. —Oliver Goldsmith

Wise men appreciate all men, for they see the good in each and know how hard it is to make anything good. —Baltasar Gracián, *The Art of Worldly Wisdom*

Humanity is outraged in me and with me. —George Sand

Humanity is composed but of two categories, the invalids and the nurses. —Walter Sickert

The human is the only guilty animal. —John Steinbeck, *East of Eden*

Everybody thinks of changing humanity and nobody thinks of changing himself. —Leo Tolstoy

How embarrassing to be human.   —Kurt Vonnegut, Jr., *Hocus Pocus*

. . . humanity deserved to die horribly, since it had behaved so cruelly
and wastefully on a planet so sweet.
—Kurt Vonnegut, Jr., *Breakfast of Champions*

The still, sad music of humanity.   —John Greenleaf Whittier

We're all of us guinea pigs in the laboratory of God. Humanity is just
a work in progress.   —Tennessee Williams, *Camino Real*

HUMAN NATURE

It's easy to understand human nature when we bear in mind that
almost everybody thinks he's an exception to most rules.
—Anonymous

. . . perhaps a moratorium on definitions of human nature is now
best.   —Saul Bellow, *Herzog*

What we do we must, and call it by the best names.
—Ralph Waldo Emerson

God showers upon us his gifts—more than enough for all; / But like
swine scrambling for food, we tread them in the mire, and rend
each other.   —Henry George

One of the worst things about life is not how nasty the nasty people
are. You know that already. It is how nasty the nice people can be.
—Anthony Powell, *The Kindly Ones*, Ch. 4

We forfeit three-fourths of ourselves in order to be liked by other people.
—Arthur Schopenhauer

People always get tired of one another. I grow tired of myself whenever I am left alone for ten minutes, and I am certain that I am
fonder of myself than anyone can be of another person.
—George Bernard Shaw

. . . human beings are better and lazier than their rules and instructions . . .   —Alexander Solzhenitsyn, *The Gulag Archipelago*

Human nature, if it changes at all, changes not much faster than the
geological face of the earth.
—Alexander Solzhenitsyn, *The Gulag Archipelago*

No man thinks there is much ado about nothing when the ado is
about himself. —Anthony Trollope, *The Bertrams*

HUMILIATION

It has always been a mystery to me how men can feel themselves
honored by the humiliation of their fellow beings.
—Mahatma Gandhi

HUMILITY

Humility is a strange thing: The moment you think you have it, you
have lost it. —Anonymous

Humility is not the belittling of self; it is the forgetting of self.
—Anonymous

It is the laden bough that hangs low, and the most fruitful Christian
is the most humble. —Anonymous

Many would be scantily clad if clothed in their humility.
—Anonymous

Life is a long lesson in humility.
—Sir James Matthew Barrie, *The Little Minister*

It's no disgrace to be a private, you know. Socrates was a plain foot
soldier, a hoplite. —Saul Bellow, *Dangling Man*

I ate 'umble pie with an appetite. —Charles Dickens, *David Copperfield*

Nothing sets a person so much out of the devil's reach as humility.
—Jonathan Edwards

There is no true holiness without humility.
—Thomas Fuller, M. D., *Gnomologia*

You can have no greater sign of a confirmed pride than when you
think you are humble enough. —William Law

Soar not too high to fall; but stoop to rise.
—Philip Massinger, *The Duke of Milan*, I. ii

Humility, that low, sweet root, / From which all heavenly virtues
shoot. —Thomas Moore, *Loves of the Angels*

Humility is pride in God. —Austin O'Malley

Sense shines with double lustre when set in humility. —William Penn

If sun thou canst not be, then be the humble planet.
—Proverb (Tibetan)

I believe the first test of a truly great man is his humility.
—John Ruskin

He who stays not in his own littleness loses his greatness.
—Saint Francis de Sales, *Letters to Persons in Religion*

The mark of the immature man is that he wants to die nobly for a
cause, while the mark of the mature man is that he wants to live
humbly for one. —Wilhelm Stekel

Humility like darkness reveals the heavenly lights.
—Henry David Thoreau, *Walden*

HUMOR

A sense of humor is the lubricant of life's machinery. —Anonymous

Mirth is God's medicine. —Henry Ward Beecher

Humor is just another defense against the universe. —Mel Brooks

The great humorist forgets himself in his delighted contemplations of
other people. —Douglas Bush

Jests that give pain are no jests.
—Miguel de Cervantes, *Don Quixote*, Part ii, Ch. 62

In the end, everything is a gag. —Charlie Chaplin

Humor is the instinct for taking pain playfully. —Max Eastman

The man who tells me an indelicate story does me an injury.
—J. T. Fields

Humor is an affirmation of dignity, a declaration of man's superiority
to all that befalls him. —Romain Gary, *Promise at Dawn*

Men show their characters in nothing more clearly than in what they
think laughable.
—Johann Wolfgang von Goethe, *Maxims and Reflections*

Of all the griefs that harass the distress'd, / Sure the most bitter is a
scornful jest. —Samuel Johnson, "London"

Nothing reveals a man's character better than the kind of joke at
which he takes offense. —G. C. Lichtenberg

Humor is really laughing off a hurt, grinning at misery.—Bill Mauldin

A clown is a poet in action. —Henry Miller

Pointing out the comic elements of a situation can bring a sense of
proportion and perspective to what might otherwise seem an overwhelming problem. —Harvey Mindess

There are things of deadly earnest that can only be safely mentioned
under cover of a joke. —J. J. Procter

Many a true word is spoken in jest. —Proverb (14th century)

He who does not like you will defame you in jest. —Richard Schickel

To smile at the jest which plants a thorn in another's breast is to
become a principal in the mischief. —Sheridan

Humor is an excellent path to enlightenment. —Tama Starr

If there's anything I hate it's the word humorist—I feel like counter-
ing with the word seriousist. —Peter de Vries

Whenever you find Humor, you find Pathos by its side.
—E. P. Whipple

Imagination was given a man to compensate him for what he is not,
and a sense of humor was provided to console him for what he is.
—Oscar Wilde

Being a comedian is like being a con man. You have to make 'em like
you before you can fool 'em. —Flip Wilson

HUNGER

Hunger makes everything sweet. —Antiphanes

Hunger makes a thief of any man.
—Pearl S. Buck, *The Good Earth*, Ch. 15

Hunger is the best sauce. —Cicero, *De finibus*, II

Hunger never saw bad bread.
　　　　　　　　—Benjamin Franklin, *Poor Richard's Almanack*

It is a hell of a thing to be hungry in your own house.
　　　　　　　　—Ernest Hemingway, *Islands in the Stream*

Hunger makes hard beans sweet.
　　　　　　　　—John Heywood, *Proverbs*, Part I, Ch. 10

Bread to a man with a hungry family comes first—before his union,
　before his citizenship, before his church affiliation. Bread!
　　　　　　　　—John L. Lewis

Stop short of your appetite; eat less than you are able.
　　　　　　　　—Ovid, *Ars Amatoria*, Book III

All her life she saw no point in doing anything that was not her
　heart's hunger.　　　—Reynolds Price, *The Tongues of Angels*, Ch. 1

The man who is not hungry says that the coconut has a hard shell.
　　　　　　　　—Proverb (African)

Appetite grows with eating.　　　　　　　—Proverb (French)

Hunger drives the wolf out of the wood.　　　—Proverb (French)

Hunger is a good cook.　　　　　　　　—Proverb (Gaelic)

If you ask the hungry man how much is two and two, he replies four
　loaves.　　　　　　　　—Proverb (Hindu)

If there is no apple one eats a little carrot.　　—Proverb (Russian)

A hungry monkey will not dance.　　　　　—Proverb (Turkish)

. . . a starving man doesn't ask what the meal is.
　　　　　　—Anne Sexton, *The Awful Rowing Toward God*, "Is It True?"

Still, everybody wants to eat.
　　　　　　　—Alexander Solzhenitsyn, *Stories and Prose Poems*,
　　　　　　　　"An Incident at Krechetovka Station"

You get no thanks from your belly—it always forgets what you've just
　done for it and comes begging again the next day.
　　　　　　—Alexander Solzhenitsyn, *One Day in the Life of Ivan Denisovich*

A hungry man is not a free man.
—Adlai Stevenson, speech, 6 Sep 1952

Make hunger thy sauce, as a medicine for health.
—Thomas Tusser, *Five Hundred Points of Good Husbandry*, 10.

. . . eating his bread with the appetite which laborious industry alone can give. —Mark Twain, *Life on the Mississippi*

HUNTING

Detested sport, / That owes its pleasures to another's pain.
—William Cowper, of hunting,
The Task, Book III, "The Garden," line 326

It is easy to shoot a skylark, but it is not so easy to produce its song.
—Lionel B. Fletcher

If you run after two hares, you will catch neither.
—Thomas Fuller, M. D., *Gnomologia*, No. 2782

With foxes we must play the fox.
—Thomas Fuller, M. D., *Gnomologia*, No. 5797

When a man wantonly destroys a work of man we call him a vandal; when a man destroys one of the works of God, we call him a sportsman. —Joseph Wood Krutch

Shoot all the bluejays you want, if you can hit 'em, but remember it's a sin to kill a mockingbird.
—Harper Lee, *To Kill a Mockingbird*, Ch. 10

When its time has come, the prey goes to the hunter.
—Proverb (Persian)

When a man wants to murder a tiger he calls it sport: when a tiger wants to murder him he calls it ferocity. —George Bernard Shaw

HURRY

He is invariably in a hurry. Being in a hurry is one of the tributes he pays to life. —Elizabeth Bibesco, *Balloons*

One of the great disadvantages of hurry is that it takes such a long time. —G. K. Chesterton

No man who is in a hurry is quite civilized.
—Will Durant, *The Life of Greece*

The great soul that sits on the throne of the universe is not, never
was, and never will be, in a hurry.   —Josiah Gilbert Holland

Good things are not done in a hurry.   —Proverb (German)

Christ never was in a hurry. There was no rushing forward, no anticipating, no fretting over what might be. Each day's duties were
done as each day brought them, and the rest was left with God.
—Mary Slessor

He had schooled himself against hurry. —John Steinbeck, *East of Eden*

HURTS

. . . when we are hurt it is important to remember that God Himself
has allowed it for a purpose.   —Billy Graham, *Till Armageddon*

I wonder if—if God lets us be hurt—so we can learn to transcend the
pain.   —Jerome Lawrence and Robert E. Lee,
The Night Thoreau Spent in Jail

We ought not to keep score of the number of times others have hurt
us. God keeps records, and vengeance belongs to him.
—Lehman Strauss, *Sense and Nonsense About Prayer*

HUSTLE

It takes no talent to hustle.   —Anonymous

Everything comes to him who hustles while he waits.
—Thomas A. Edison

Hustle is another word for survival.
—Whitney Reiner, coach at Canarsie High School

HYPOCRISY

Great hypocrites are the real atheists.   —Francis Bacon

It must be a good thing to be good or ivrybody wudden't be pre-
tendin' he was.
—Finley Peter Dunne, *Observations by Mr. Dooley*, "Hypocrisy"

What hypocrites we seem to be whenever we talk of ourselves!—our words sound so humble while our hearts are so proud.   —Hare

It is no fault of Christianity that a hypocrite falls into sin.
—Saint Jerome

Hypocrisy is a sort of homage that vice pays to virtue.
—François de La Rochefoucauld, *Maximes*, ccxvii.

— I —

IDEALS

Our ideals are our better selves. —Bronson Alcott, *Table Talk*, "Habits"

Our ideals are our possibilities. —Anonymous

. . . many persons strive for high ideals, and everywhere life is full of heroism. —Max Ehrman, "Desiderata"

It is only in marriage with the world that our ideals can bear fruit: divorced from it, they remain barren. —Bertrand Russell

Ideals are like the stars—we never reach them, but like the mariners of the sea, we chart our course by them. —Carl Schurz

Our ideals are the blueprints of our lives. —Roy L. Smith

IDEAS

. . . the right way to present an idea is in the speech of the men to whom it came as a revelation.
—J. Bronowski and Bruce Mazlish, *The Western Intellectual Tradition*

A new idea is delicate. It can be killed by a sneer or a yawn; it can be stabbed to death by a quip and worried to death by a frown on the right man's brow. —Charles Brower

No fathers or mothers think their own children ugly; and this self-deceit is yet stronger with respect to the offspring of the mind.
—Miguel de Cervantes

When we are exalted by ideas, we do not owe this to Plato, but to the idea, to which also Plato was debtor. —Ralph Waldo Emerson

You can kill a man but you can't kill an idea. —Medgar Evers

Daring ideas are like chessmen moved forward; they may be beaten, but they may start a winning game.
—Johann Wolfgang von Goethe

The only sure weapon against bad ideas is better ideas.
—A. Whitney Griswold, *Essays on Education*

Ideas move fast when their time comes.   —Carolyn Heilbrun

Man's mind stretched to a new idea never goes back to its original
  dimensions.   —Oliver Wendell Holmes, Sr.

Many ideas grow better when transplanted into another mind than
  in the one where they sprang up.   —Oliver Wendell Holmes, Jr.

There is one thing stronger than all the armies in the world, and that
  is an idea whose time has come.   —Victor Hugo

. . . there is nothing more precious in life than the idea one serves.
                    —Zhora Ingal, in Alexander Solzhenitsyn,
                                        The Gulag Archipelago Two

You do not destroy an idea by killing people; you replace it with a
  better one.   —Edward Keating

An idea isn't responsible for the people who believe in it.
            —Don Marquis, *The Sun Dial* column, *New York Sun*, 1918

The best way to have a good idea is to have lots of ideas.
                                            —Linus Pauling

All great ideas are controversial, or have been at one time.
                                            —George Seldes

The man with a new idea is a crank until the idea succeeds.
                                            —Mark Twain

Ideas on Earth were badges of friendship or enmity. Their content did
  not matter. Friends agreed with friends, in order to express friendli-
  ness. Enemies disagreed with enemies, in order to express enmity.
                —Kurt Vonnegut, Jr., *Breakfast of Champions*

We are healthy only to the extent that our ideas are humane.
                —Kurt Vonnegut, Jr., *Breakfast of Champions*

I D L E N E S S

An idle man's brain is the devil's workshop.   —John Bunyan

To do great work a man must be very idle as well as very industrious.
                                —Samuel Butler (1835-1902)

The outlook for our country lies in the quality of its idleness.
                                            —Irwin Edman

Idleness is the Dead Sea that swallows all virtues. Be active in business, that temptation may miss her aim; the bird that sits is easily shot. —Benjamin Franklin

If the devil catch a man idle, he'll set him at work.
—Thomas Fuller, M. D., *Gnomologia*

Be always employed about some rational thing, that the devil find thee not idle. —Saint Jerome

Certainly work is not always required of a man. There is such a thing as a sacred idleness—the cultivation of which is now fearfully neglected. —George Macdonald

Sweet idleness. —Proverb (Italian)

He is not only idle who does nothing but he is idle who might be better employed. —Socrates

Untilled soil, however fertile it may be, will bear thistles and thorns; so it is with man's mind. —Saint Teresa of Ávila

For Satan finds some mischief still / For idle hands to do.
—Isaac Watts, *Divine Songs for Children*, "Against Idleness"

IGNORANCE

I have tried to know absolutely nothing about a great many things, and I have succeeded fairly well. —Robert Benchley

It is better to know nothing than to know what ain't so.
—Josh Billings

The first step to knowledge is to know that we are ignorant.
—Cecil

One part of knowledge consists in being ignorant of such things as are not worthy to be known. —Crates

I do not pretend to know what many ignorant men are sure of.
—Clarence Darrow

To be conscious that you are ignorant is a great step to knowledge.
—Benjamin Disraeli

In order to have wisdom we must have ignorance. —Theodore Dreiser

There are many things of which a wise man might wish to be ignorant.   —Ralph Waldo Emerson, *Demonology*

. . . where ignorance is bliss, / 'Tis folly to be wise.
              —Thomas Gray, "Ode on a Distant Prospect of Eton College"

Ignorance is preferable to error; and he is less remote from truth who believes nothing, than he who believes what is wrong.
                         —Thomas Jefferson, *Notes on the State of Virginia*

I only know when I don't know a thing. . . . wisdom lies in that.
                  —George Macdonald, *The Flight of the Shadow*, Ch. 14

He who would be cured of ignorance must confess it.
                          —Michel de Montaigne, *Essays*, "Of Cripples"

Never think that you already know all. However highly you are appraised, always have the courage to say to yourself—I am ignorant.   —Ivan Petrovich Pavlov,
          "Bequest to the Academic Youth of Soviet Russia," 27 Feb 1936

Ignorance is the mother of research.
          —Laurence J. Peter, compiler, *Peter's Quotations: Ideas for Our Time*

Everybody is ignorant, only on different subjects.   —Will Rogers

I was gratified to be able to answer promptly. I said I don't know.
                                                              —Mark Twain

There was a lot I had never heard of before.
                                          —Kurt Vonnegut, Jr., *Jailbird*

ILLNESS

The best cure for hypochondria is to forget about your body and get interested in someone else's.   —Goodman Ace

Be long sick, that you may be soon hale.   —Anonymous

A healthy body is a guest-chamber for the soul; a sick body is a prison.   —Francis Bacon

For a sick man the world begins at his pillow and ends at the foot of his bed.   —Honoré de Balzac

. . . the drama of sickness. —Saul Bellow, *Humboldt's Gift*

Illness knocks a lot of nonsense out of us; it induces humility, cuts us
down to size . . . When we are a bit scared the salutary effect of
sickness is particularly marked. For only when the . . . gate grows
narrow do some people discover their soul, their God, their life
work. —Dr. Louis E. Bisch

Don't defy the diagnosis, try to defy the verdict. —Norman Cousins

Nothing is more essential in the treatment of serious disease than the
liberation of the patient from panic and foreboding.
—Norman Cousins

The patient must combat the disease along with the physician.
—Hippocrates

Sickness begets chaos, which, through hard work and a touch of
grace, leads to growth and resurrection. —Scott Peck

Illness is the doctor to whom we pay most heed; to kindness, to
knowledge, we make promise only; pain we obey. —Marcel Proust

He who conceals his disease cannot expect to be cured.
—Proverb (Ethiopian)

Illness tells us what we are. —Proverb (Italian)

. . . I was diagnosed with ovarian cancer. Suddenly I had to spend all
my time getting well.
—Gilda Radner, *Gilda Radner—It's Always Something*

Make sickness itself a prayer. —Saint Francis de Sales

I enjoy convalescence. It is the part that makes the illness worthwhile. —George Bernard Shaw, *Back to Methuselah*

'Tis healthy to be sick sometimes. —Henry David Thoreau

I L L S

. . . I cannot help but feel that the ills we knowingly create for others
must most certainly at some point come back to us.
—Doug Cameron,
How to Survive Being Committed to a Mental Hospital

We must make the best of those ills which cannot be avoided.
—Alexander Hamilton, letter to Mrs. Hamilton, 20 Feb 1801

It is some alleviation to ills we cannot cure to speak of them.
—Ovid, *Tristia*

Rather bear those ills we have, / Than fly to others we know not of.
—William Shakespeare, *Hamlet*, Act III, Sc. i

Oh yet we trust that somehow good / Will be the final goal of ill.
—Alfred, Lord Tennyson, *In Memoriam A. H. H.*

IMAGINATION

Imagination is the highest kite one can fly.   —Lauren Bacall

What Homo sapien imagines, he may slowly convert himself to.
—Saul Bellow, *Henderson the Rain King*

Take only your imagination seriously.   —Thomas Berger

What is now proved was once only imagin'd.
—William Blake, *The Marriage of Heaven and Hell*

The primary imagination I hold to be the living power and prime
agent of all human perception, and as a repetition in the finite
mind of the eternal act of creation in the infinite I Am.
—Samuel Taylor Coleridge, *Biographia Literaria*, Ch. 13

We are what and where we are because we have first imagined it . . .
—Donald Curtis

Imagination is more important than knowledge.
—Albert Einstein, *On Science*

Man lives by imagination.   —Havelock Ellis, *Dance of Life*

Everything we can imagine becomes real.   —Robert Fulghum, *Uh-Oh*

Imagination is the one weapon in the war against reality.
—Jules de Gaultier

It's time to start living the life you've imagined.   —Henry James

Were it not for imagination a man would be as happy in the arms of a
chambermaid as of a duchess.
—Samuel Johnson, in James Boswell, *Life of Samuel Johnson*

Imagination is the eye of the soul.   —Joseph Joubert, *Pensées*, No. 42

Generalization is necessary to the advancement of knowledge; but particularity is indispensable to the creations of the imagination.
—Thomas Babington Macaulay, "Milton"

This is where you will win the battle—in the playhouse of your mind.
—Maxwell Maltz

Imagination frames events unknown, / In wild, fantastic shapes of hideous ruin, / And what it fears creates.
—Hannah More, *Balshazzar*, Part II

Everything you can imagine is real.   —Pablo Picasso

Sometimes I feel like a figment of my own imagination. —Lily Tomlin

Imagination is something you do alone.
—Steve Wozniak, Apple Computer co-founder, speech to the Commonwealth Club of California, San Francisco, 27 Feb 1987

IMMORTALITY

I don't want to achieve immortality through my work . . . I want to achieve it through not dying.   —Woody Allen

[Socrates] said there were only two possibilities. Either the soul is immortal or, after death, things would be again as blank as they were before we were born.   —Saul Bellow, *Humboldt's Gift*

For the wages of sin is death, but the gift of God is eternal life through Jesus Christ, our Lord.   —*The Bible* (KJV): Romans 6:23

Immortality will come to such as are fit for it; and he who would be a great soul in future must be a great soul now.
—Ralph Waldo Emerson

The blazing evidence of immortality is our dissatisfaction with any other solution.
—Ralph Waldo Emerson, *Journals*, entry written in July, 1855

Millions long for immortality who do not know what to do with themselves on a rainy Sunday afternoon.
—Susan Ertz, *Anger in the Sky*

The average man does not know what to do with this life, yet wants another which will last forever.   —Anatole France

Life is the childhood of our immortality.

—Johann Wolfgang von Goethe

The belief of immortality is impressed upon all men, and all men act under an impression of it, however they may talk, and though, perhaps, they may be scarcely sensible of it. —Samuel Johnson

There is an awful warmth about my heart like a load of immortality.

—John Keats, letter to J. H. Reynolds, 22 Sep 1818

I believe in the immortality of the soul because I have within me immortal longings. —Helen Keller

Surely God would not have created such a being as man, with an ability to grasp the infinite, to exist only for a day. No, no, man was made for immortality. —Abraham Lincoln

And in the wreck of noble lives / Something immortal still survives.

—Henry Wadsworth Longfellow, "Building of the Ship"

There is no Death! What seems so is transition.

—Henry Wadsworth Longfellow,
The Seaside and the Fireside, "Resignation"

Either the soul is immortal and we shall not die, or it perishes with the flesh, and we shall not know that we are dead. Live, then, as if you were eternal. —André Maurois

Here is the great discovery that awaits us: life is all of a piece. "We are not someday going to be, we are already immortal spirits."

—A. Maude Royden

I have Immortal longings in me.

—William Shakespeare, *Antony and Cleopatra*, Act V, Sc. ii

We feel and know that we are eternal.

—Benedict de Spinoza, *Ethics*, Part V, 23, note

There is only one way to get ready for immortality, and that is to love this life and live it as bravely and faithfully and cheerfully as we can. —Henry Van Dyke

Still seems it strange, that thou shouldst live forever? Is it less strange that thou shouldst live at all?

—Edward Young, *Night Thoughts*, VII

IMPENITENCE

It is not sin that kills the soul, but impenitence.   —Bishop Hall

IMPORTANCE

The most important things in life aren't things.   —Anonymous

Nothing matters very much, and very few things matter at all.
—Arthur James Balfour, First Earl of Balfour, in John Peers,
compiler, *1,001 Logical Laws*, "Balfour's Declaration"

The most important things to do in the world are to get something to
eat, something to drink, and somebody to love you.
—Brandan Behan

Half of the harm that is done in this world Is due to people who want
to feel important.   —T. S. Eliot, "The Cocktail Party"

Rule #1—Don't sweat the small stuff. Rule #2—It's all small stuff.
—Dr. Michael Mantell

There is nothing small in the service of God.   —Saint Francis de Sales

. . . there are no unimportant people.
—George Thomas, former Speaker of the House of Commons,
to Richard Baker, BBC TV, 2 Aug 1981

The IMPOSSIBLE

It's kind of fun to do the impossible.   —Walt Disney

He started to sing as he tackled the thing / That couldn't be done, and
he did it.   —Edgar A. Guest, "It Couldn't Be Done"

All the fun is locking horns with impossibilities.   —Claus Oldenburg

IMPROVEMENT

Everything can be improved.   —C. W. Barron

IMPULSE

Man's chief merit consists in resisting the impulses of his nature.
—Samuel Johnson

Act upon your impulses, but pray that they may be directed by God.
—Emerson Tennent

INACTION

Never do an act of which you doubt the justice or propriety.
—Anonymous

When in doubt, do nothing.
—Anonymous

There are times when the most practical thing is to lie down.
—Saul Bellow, *Humboldt's Gift*

Nobody makes a greater mistake than he who does nothing because
he could only do a little.
—Edmund Burke

The only thing necessary for the triumph of evil is for good men to
do nothing.   —Edmund Burke, letter to William Smith, 9 Jan 1795

I do not believe in a fate that falls on men however they act; but I do
believe in a fate that falls on them unless they act.
—G. K. Chesterton, *Generally Speaking*

To do nothing is in every man's power.
—Samuel Johnson

Activity may lead to evil; but inactivity cannot be led to good.
—Hannah More

Your discovery, as best as I can determine, is that there is an alternative which no one has hit upon. It is that one finding oneself in
one of life's critical situations need not after all respond in one of
the traditional ways. No. One may simply default. Pass. Do as one
pleases, shrug, turn on one's heel and leave. Exit. Why after all
need one act humanly?
—Walker Percy, *The Moviegoer*

One does evil enough when one does nothing good.
—Proverb (German)

When a man has not a good reason for doing a thing, he has one
good reason for letting it alone.
—Sir Walter Scott

Heaven ne'er helps the men who will not act.
—Sophocles, Fragments, no. 288

Between the great things we cannot do and the little things we will
not do, the danger is that we will do nothing.
—H. G. Weaver

INDECISION

Not to decide is to decide. —Harvey Cox

Half the failures in life arise from pulling in one's horse as he is leaping.
  —Julius Charles Hare and Augustus William Hare, *Guesses at Truth*

. . . but in the end I argued myself into solid indecision.
  —Bernard Malamud, *Rembrandt's Hat*, "Man in the Drawer"

Through indecision opportunity is often lost.
  —Publilius Syrus, *Sententioe*, No. 185

. . . I am / At war 'twixt will and will not.
  —William Shakespeare, *Measure for Measure*, Act II, Sc. ii

INDEPENDENCE

I too am a government. —Gustave Courbet

There are worse places to be than on your own.
  —Ernest Hemingway, *Islands in the Stream*

Independence? That's middle-class blasphemy. We are all dependent on one another, every soul of us on earth.
  —George Bernard Shaw, *Pygmalion*

INDISPENSABILITY

A man doesn't begin to attain wisdom until he recognizes that he is no longer indispensable. —Admiral Richard E. Byrd

Make yourself necessary to somebody. Do not make life hard to any.
  —Ralph Waldo Emerson, *The Conduct of Life*,
  "Considerations by the way"

The graveyards are full of indispensable men.
  —Gen. Charles de Gaulle

There is no man but can be dispensed with. —Proverb (French)

None of us who lived close to her perceived that she was the one righteous person without whom, as the saying goes, no city can stand.
Nor the world. —Alexander Solzhenitsyn, *Stories and Prose Poems*,
  "Matryona's House," closing words

There is no indispensable man. The government will not collapse and go to pieces if any one of the gentlemen who are seeking to be entrusted with its guidance should be left at home.

—Woodrow Wilson

The INDIVIDUAL

Every man thinks God is on his side.

—Jean Anouilh

Let each man think himself an act of God, / His mind a thought, his life a breath of God; / And let each try, by great thoughts and good deeds, / To show the most of Heaven he hath in him.

—Philip James Bailey, *Festus*, "Proem"

... I am fearfully and wonderfully made ...

—*The Bible* (KJV): Psalms 139:14

We are all special cases.

—Albert Camus, *The Fall*

Every man is an impossibility until he is born.

—Ralph Waldo Emerson, *Essays, Second Series*, "Experience"

God enters by a private door into every individual.

—Ralph Waldo Emerson, *Essays, First Series*, "Intellect"

No society can ever be so large as one man.

—Ralph Waldo Emerson, *New England Reformers*

The riddle of the age has for each a private solution.

—Ralph Waldo Emerson

It is possible for a single individual to defy the whole might of an unjust empire to save his honor, his religion, his soul, and lay the foundation for that empire's fall or its regeneration.

—Mahatma Gandhi

The individual person is more interesting than people in general; he and not they is the one whom God created in His image.

—André Gide, *Journal*

Every individual has a place to fill in the world, and is important in some respect, whether he chooses to be so or not.

—Nathaniel Hawthorne

He [God] doesn't need me, but He desires me.

—Steve Hawthorne, guest sermon at Hope Chapel, Austin, Texas, 13 Oct 1990

God leads every soul by a separate path.
> —Saint John of the Cross, *Living Flame of Love*

The most intractable problem today is not pollution or technology or war; but the lack of belief that the future is very much in the hands of the individual.
> —Margaret Mead

The race advances only by the extra achievements of the individual. You are the individual.
> —Charles Towne

Whether he was good, bad, or indifferent, he was the Lord's, and nothing that was the Lord's was a thing to be neglected.
> —Mark Twain

Each human being is a more complex structure than any social system to which he belongs.
> —Alfred North Whitehead

Each of us inevitable; / Each of us limitless—each of us with his or her right upon the earth.
> —Walt Whitman, *Salut au Monde*, Sec. 11

INDUSTRY

Hard workers are usually honest; industry lifts them above temptation.
> —Christian Nestell Bovée

Industry need not wish.
> —Benjamin Franklin

It is wonderful how much may be done if we are always doing.
> —Thomas Jefferson, to Martha Jefferson, 5 May 1787

The bird on the wing finds something, the sitting bird nothing.
> —Proverb (Swedish)

If you have great talents, industry will improve them: if you have but moderate abilities, industry will supply their deficiency.
> —Sir Joshua Reynolds, *Discourses on Art*, ii.

INERTIA

Once in motion, to push a cart is easy.
> —Anonymous

Every body perseveres in its state of rest or of uniform motion in a straight line, except in so far as it is compelled to change that state by impressed forces.
> —Isaac Newton, *Principia*, First Law of Motion

. . . once you get up steam, you are carried helplessly along.
—Alexander Solzhenitsyn, *Lenin in Zurich*

INEVITABILITY

There is no good arguing with the inevitable. The only argument
available with an east wind is to put on your overcoat.
—James Russell Lowell, *Democracy and Other Addresses*,
"Democracy," address at Town Hall,
Birmingham, England, 6 Oct 1884

Let us never doubt everything that ought to happen is going to happen. —Harriet Beecher Stowe

Bear the inevitable with dignity. —Streckfuss

INFERIORITY

No one can make you feel inferior without your consent.
—Eleanor Roosevelt, *This Is My Story*

INFINITY

The thirst for the infinite proves the infinite. —Victor Hugo

INFLUENCE

The humblest individual exerts some influence, either for good or
evil, upon others. —Henry Ward Beecher

. . . a fellow can't predict what he will pick up in the form of influence.
—Saul Bellow, *Henderson the Rain King*

It is a mathematical fact that the casting of a pebble from my hand
alters the center of gravity of the universe.
—Thomas Carlyle, *Sartor Resartus*, III, 7

Something rubs off from everything you read, observe, and tinker
with. —R. F. Delderfield, *To Serve Them All My Days*

Our chief want in life is somebody who shall make us do what we
can.
—Ralph Waldo Emerson, *The Conduct of Life*, "Considerations by
the Way"

When one leaf trembles, the whole bough moves.—Proverb (Chinese)

INGRATITUDE

. . . How sharper than a serpent's tooth it is / To have a thankless child!
—William Shakespeare, *King Lear*, Act I, Sc. iv

Ingratitude, thou marble-hearted fiend . . .
—William Shakespeare, *King Lear*, Act I, Sc. iv

If you pick up a starving dog and make him prosperous, he will not
bite you. That is the principal difference between a dog and a man.
—Mark Twain, *Pudd'nhead Wilson*,
"Pudd'nhead Wilson's Calendar"

INHUMANITY

Man's inhumanity to man / Makes countless thousands mourn!
—Robert Burns, "Man was Made to Mourn"

When men are inhuman, take care not to feel towards them as they
do towards other humans.
—Marcus Aurelius Antoninus, *Meditations*

INJURY

The injuries we do and those we suffer are seldom weighed in the
same scales.   —Aesop, *Fables*, "The Partial Judge"

It is better to receive than to do injury.   —Cicero

Slight small injuries, and they will become none at all.
—Thomas Fuller

Requite injury with kindness.   —Lao Tzu

He who injured you was either stronger or weaker. If weaker, spare
him; if stronger, spare yourself.   —Seneca, *De Ira*

There is a noble forgetfulness—that which does not remember
injuries.   —Charles Simmons

INJUSTICE

It is better to suffer injustice than to do it.
—Ralph Waldo Emerson, *Representative Man*, "Plato"

... but it is human to be outraged by injustice, even to the point of
courting destruction!
—Alexander Solzhenitsyn, *The Gulag Archipelago Three*

INNOCENCE

Experience, which destroys innocence, also leads one back to it.
—James Baldwin

Innocence itself sometimes hath need of a mask.   —Proverb (English)

Innocence has nothing to dread.
—Jean Baptiste Racine, *Phèdre*, Act II, Sc. vi

Innocence is ashamed of nothing.   —Jean Jacques Rousseau, *Emile*

Innocence has a friend in heaven.   —Friedrich Schiller

INSOMNIA

Don't count sheep if you can't sleep. Talk to the shepherd.
—Paul Frost

If you can't sleep, rest.   —Robert Watkins

INSPIRATION

A rush of thoughts is the only conceivable prosperity that can
come to us.   —Ralph Waldo Emerson,
Letters and Social Aims, "Inspiration"

We should be taught not to wait for inspiration to start a thing.
Action always generates inspiration. Inspiration seldom generates
action.   —Frank Tibolt

... nothing is more harmful to an artist than to let laziness get the
better of him. One cannot afford to sit and wait for inspiration; she
is a guest who does not visit the lazy but comes to those who call
her.   —Peter Ilyoich Tschaikovski

INSTRUCTIONS

Lose yourself in the song of the instructions, in the precise, detailed
balm of having solved for you that most difficult of problems, what
to do next.   —Donald Barthelme, *Amateurs*

INSULT

It is often better not to see an insult than to avenge it.   —Seneca

INTEGRATION

What we mean by integration is not to be with them [whites] but to
    have what they have.   —Julian Bond

INTEGRITY

There is no better test for man's ultimate integrity than his behavior
    when he is wrong.   —Anonymous

Nothing is at last sacred but the integrity of your own mind.
    —Ralph Waldo Emerson, *Essays, First Series*, "Self-Reliance"

This above all: to thine own self be true, / And it must follow, as the
    night the day, / Thou canst not then be false to any man.
                    —William Shakespeare, *Hamlet*, Act I, Sc. iii

INTELLECT

. . . it is a welcome symptom in an age which is commonly
    denounced as materialistic, that it makes heroes of men whose
    goals lie wholly in the intellectual and moral sphere.
                        —Albert Einstein, *Ideas and Opinions*

We should take care not to make the intellect our god; it has, of
    course, powerful muscles, but no personality.
                        —Albert Einstein, *Out of My Later Years*

There is a limit where the intellect fails and breaks down, and this
    limit is where the questions concerning God and freewill and
    immortality arise.   —Immanuel Kant

An intellectual is someone whose mind watches itself.
                        —Thomas Babington Macaulay

I have wished to understand the hearts of men. I have wished to
    know why the stars shine. And I have tried to apprehend the
    Pythagorean power by which number holds sway above the flux. A
    little of this, but not much, I have achieved.
                —Bertrand Russell, *The Autobiography of Bertrand Russell*

The intellectual is not defined by professional group and type of occupation. Nor are good upbringing and a good family enough in themselves to produce an intellectual. An intellectual is a person whose interest in and preoccupation with the spiritual side of life are insistent and constant and not forced by external circumstances, even flying in the face of them. An intellectual is a person whose thought is nonimitative.
—Alexander Solzhenitsyn, *The Gulag Archipelago Two*

INTELLIGENCE

The true test of intelligence is not how much we know what to do, but how we behave when we don't know what to do.   —John Holt

The intelligent man who is proud of his intelligence is like the condemned man who is proud of his large cell.   —Simone Weil

INTENTIONS

Hell is paved with good intentions.
—Samuel Johnson, in James Boswell, *Life of Samuel Johnson*

INTERDEPENDENCE

No one can make it alone.   —Anonymous

No man is an Island, entire of himself; every man is a piece of the Continent, a part of the main.
—John Donne, *Devotions upon Emergent Occasions*

There is a destiny which makes us brothers; / None goes his way alone; All that we send into the lives of others, / Comes back into our own.
—Edwin Markham, in Charles L. Wallis, editor, *Poems*, "A Creed"

When we know that another depends on us we are spared the despair of living for ourselves alone.   —Rabbi Mervin B. Tomsky

INTEREST

There are no uninteresting things, there are only uninterested people.
—G. K. Chesterton

We are interested in others when they are interested in us.
—Publilius Syrus, *Sententioe*, No. 16

You are only as big as the world you are interested in.   —Roy L. Smith

INTERNATIONAL POLITICS

International affairs will be placed on a better footing when it is
understood that there is no way of punishing a people for the
crimes of its rulers.   —Bernard Berenson

Ours is a world of nuclear giants and ethical infants.
                                               —Gen. Omar Bradley

An appeaser is one who feeds a crocodile—hoping it will eat him last.
                                               —Winston Churchill

More and more, the choice for the world's people is between world
warriors and world citizens.   —Norman Cousins

I firmly believe that the future of civilization is absolutely dependent
upon finding some way of resolving international differences without resorting to war.   —Dwight D. Eisenhower

No nation can be free if it oppresses other nations. —Friedrich Engels

A great empire, like a great cake, is most easily diminished at the
edges.   —Benjamin Franklin

You cannot shake hands with a clenched fist.
                                               —Indira Gandhi, press conference, 1971

I believe that our Great Maker is preparing the world, in His own
good time, to become one nation, speaking one language, and
when armies and navies will be no longer required.
                                               —Ulysses S. Grant

In the field of world policy, I would dedicate this nation to the policy
of a good neighbor.
    —Franklin D. Roosevelt, First Inaugural Address, 4 Mar 1933

We're eyeball to eyeball, and the other fellow just blinked.
    —Dean Rusk, comment in October, 1962, during the Cuban missile
    crisis. Rusk had just been informed that some Soviet ships loaded
    with missiles which were bound for Cuba had turned back.

We live in a Newtonian world of Einsteinian physics ruled by
Frankenstein logic.   —David Russell

... any country that is not careful can be seized.
—Alexander Solzhenitsyn, *The Mortal Danger*

... mutual lack of understanding carries the threat of imminent and violent destruction. —Alexander Solzhenitsyn, *Nobel Lecture*

The same old caveman feeling—greed, envy, violence, and mutual hate, which along the way assumed respectable pseudonyms like class struggle, racial struggle, mass struggle, labor-union struggle— are tearing our world to pieces.
—Alexander Solzhenitsyn, *Nobel Lecture*

Man has unveiled secrets which might have been thought undiscoverable. Much has been achieved in the realm of art, science, literature, and religion. Is all this to end because so few are able to think of man rather than of this or that group of men? —U Thant

The most tragic paradox of our time is to be found in the failure of nation states to recognize the imperative of internationalism.
—Earl Warren

If people behaved in the same way nations do they would all be put in straitjackets. —Tennessee Williams, BBC interview

INVENTION

Nothing is invented and brought to perfection all at once.
—Thomas Cole

Invention is the mother of necessity. —Thorstein Veblen

INVITATIONS

People decline invitations when they are "indisposed" physically, and I wish they would do likewise when they feel indisposed emotionally. A person has no more right to attend a party with a head full of venom than with a throat full of virus. —Sydney J. Harris

INVOLVEMENT

Tell me and I forget. Show me, and I may not remember. Involve me, and I understand. —Proverb (Native American)

— J —

JAZZ

A jazz musician is a juggler who uses harmonics instead of oranges.
—Benny Green, *The Reluctant Art*

Jazz came to America 300 years ago in chains. —Paul Whiteman

JESUS

There is a green hill far away, / Without a city wall, / Where the dear Lord was crucified, / Who died to save us all.
—Cecil Frances Alexander, "There is a Green Hill"

About Jesus we must believe no one but himself.
—Henri Frédéric Amiel

As the Resurrection opened the grave, the Ascension opened heaven.
—Anonymous

Christ died for all men—not just the ones you know and like.
—Anonymous, from a Catholic textbook

Have Jesus—will share. —Anonymous bumper sticker

His blood for my fault; His robe for my blame. —Anonymous

"How much do you love me?" I asked Jesus, and Jesus said, "This much . . ." Then he stretched out his arms and died. —Anonymous

In Jesus, God said yes . . . —Anonymous, from a song

Is Christ being crucified again because of my indifference?
—Anonymous

Jesus Christ dredged me out of myself and has become the foundation of that new person I can see going up every day.—Anonymous

Let Christ stay throughout the meal. Don't dismiss Him with the blessing. —Anonymous

Life is short / Death is sure / Sin the cause / Christ the cure. —Anonymous

Wise Men Still Seek Him.
>—Anonymous, bumper sticker, in Laurel Lee, *Signs of Spring*

Was Christ a man like us? Ah, let us try if we then, too, can be such men as he! —Matthew Arnold

Sickness and death could not stay in the place where Jesus was.
>—Grenville Barber, guest sermon, Hope Chapel, Austin,
>Texas, 7 Mar 1992

Christ leads me through no darker rooms / Than He went through before. —Richard Baxter

Who am I, Jesus, that / You'd call me by name?
>—Margaret Becker, "Who Am I?" (words and music)

For unto us a child is born, unto us a son is given, and the government shall be upon his shoulder; and his name shall be called Wonderful, Counsellor, The Mighty God, The Everlasting Father, The Prince of Peace. —*The Bible* (KJV): Isaiah 9:6

I [John the Baptist], indeed, baptize you with water unto repentance, but he that cometh after me is mightier than I, whose shoes I am not worthy to bear; he shall baptize you with the Holy Spirit, and with fire. —*The Bible* (KJV): Matthew 3:11

. . . This is my beloved Son, in whom I am well pleased.
>—*The Bible* (KJV): Matthew 3:17

Therefore be ye also ready; for in such an hour as ye think not the Son of man cometh. —*The Bible* (KJV): Matthew 24:44

. . . They that are whole have no need of the physician, but they that are sick. I came not to call the righteous, but sinners to repentance.
>—*The Bible* (KJV): Mark 2:7

And when the centurion, who stood facing him, saw that he so cried out, and gave up the spirit, he said, Truly this man was the Son of God. —*The Bible* (KJV): Mark 15:39

And the Word was made flesh, and dwelt among us . . .
>—*The Bible* (KJV): John 1:14

. . . even so must the Son of man be lifted up, that whosoever believeth in him should not perish, but have eternal life.
>—*The Bible* (KJV): John 3:14–15

For God so loved the world, that he gave his only begotten Son, that whosoever believeth in him should not perish, but have everlasting life. —*The Bible* (KJV): John 3:16

I am the door: by me if any man enter in, he shall be saved . . . —*The Bible* (KJV): John 10:9

The thief cometh not but to steal, and to kill, and to destroy; I am come that they might have life, and that they might have it more abundantly. —*The Bible* (KJV): John 10:10

. . . I am the resurrection, and the life; he that believeth in me, though he were dead, yet shall he live. —*The Bible* (KJV): John 11:25

And I, if I be lifted up from the earth, will draw all men unto me. —*The Bible* (KJV): John 12:32

What shall separate us from the love of Christ? Shall tribulation, or distress, or persecution, or famine, or nakedness, or peril, or sword? —*The Bible* (KJV): Romans 8:35

For I am persuaded that neither death, nor life, nor angels, nor principalities, nor powers, nor things present, nor things to come, nor height, nor depth, nor any other creation, shall be able to separate us from the love of God, which is in Christ Jesus, our Lord. —*The Bible* (KJV): Romans 8:38–39

For even Christ pleased not himself . . . —*The Bible* (KJV): Romans 15:3

For ye know the grace of our Lord Jesus Christ, that, though he was rich, yet for your sakes he became poor, that ye through his poverty might be rich. —*The Bible* (KJV): 2 Corinthians 8:9

Jesus Christ, the same yesterday, and today, and forever. —*The Bible* (KJV): Hebrews 13:8

In this was manifested the love of God toward us, that God sent his only begotten Son into the world, that we might live through him. —*The Bible* (KJV): 1 John 4:9

I am Alpha and Omega, the beginning and the ending, saith the Lord. —*The Bible* (KJV): Revelation 1:8

Behold, I stand at the door, and knock; if any man hear my voice, and open the door, I will come in to him, and will sup with him, and he with me. —*The Bible* (KJV): Revelation 3:20

Behold, I come quickly . . . —*The Bible* (KJV): Revelation 22:7

Alexander, Caesar, Charlemagne and I founded empires; but upon what did we rest the creations of our genius? Upon force. Jesus Christ alone founded his empire upon love; and at this hour millions of men would die for him. —Napoleon Bonaparte

If Jesus Christ is not true God, how could he *help* us? If he is not true man, how could he help *us*? —Dietrich Bonhoeffer

. . . Jesus Christ, who by thy death didst take away the sting of death. —*Book of Common Prayer*

When thou hadst overcome the sharpness of death, thou didst open the kingdom of heaven to all believers —*Book of Common Prayer*

Tomb, thou shalt not hold Him longer; / Death is strong but life is stronger; / Stronger than the dark, the light; / Stronger than the wrong, the right; / Faith and hope triumphant say, / "Christ will rise on Easter Day!" —Phillips Brooks

Jesus has never been fussy about whom he mixes with. —Clive Calver, guest sermon, Hope Chapel, Austin, Texas, 4 Oct 1997

If Jesus Christ were to come today, people would not even crucify him. They would ask him to dinner, and hear what he had to say, and make fun of it. —Thomas Carlyle, in D. A. Wilson, *Carlyle at his Zenith* (1927)

Jesu, the very thought of Thee / With sweetness fills the breast. —Rev. Edward Caswall, "Jesu, The Very Thought of Thee," 1849, translated from Latin

Conquering kings their titles take / From the foes they captive make; / Jesu, by a nobler deed From the thousands He hath freed. —John Chandler, "Conquering Kings their Titles Take"

The miracles of Christ were studiously performed in the most unostentatious way. He seemed anxious to veil His majesty under the love with which they were wrought. —William Ellery Channing

Jesus never forced anyone to follow him, and he doesn't expect his followers to use high-pressure tactics to attract disciples.
—Gary R. Collins, *The Magnificent Mind*

There is a fountain filled with blood / Drawn from Immanuel's veins; / And sinners, plunged beneath that flood, / Lose all their guilty stains.
—William Cowper, "There Is a Fountain" (hymn)

Christ beats his drum, but he does not press men; Christ is served with voluntaries.
—John Donne, *Sermons*, No. 39

He [Jesus] is far more precious to us when we have been through trials.
—Sandy Edmonson, *God's Faithfulness in Trials & Testings*

The greatest man in history was the poorest. —Ralph Waldo Emerson

If you are looking for Christ in folks you will not be dwelling on their faults.
—Charles E. Fuller

A man who was completely innocent, [Jesus] offered himself as a sacrifice for the good of others, including his enemies, and became a ransom of the world. It was a perfect act.
—Mahatma Gandhi, *Non-Violence in Peace and War*

Though I cannot claim to be a Christian in the sectarian sense, the example of Jesus suffering is a factor in the composition of my undying faith in non-violence which rules all my actions, worldly and temporal.
—Mahatma Gandhi

It is either Christ or chaos.
—David Lloyd George

Jesus is God spelling himself out in language that man can understand.
—S. D. Gordon

I only know that when Jesus is with a person, that one can endure the deepest suffering and somehow emerge a better and stronger Christian because of it.
—Billy Graham, *Till Armageddon*

. . . the thing that kept Christ on that cross was love, not the nail.
—Billy Graham

What does the divine sufferer [Jesus] demand from us? Only our faith, our love, our grateful praise, our consecrated hearts and lives. Is that too much to ask?
—Billy Graham, *Till Armageddon*

What we think of Christ influences our thinking and controls our
  actions.   —Billy Graham, *World Aflame*

Jesus paid it all, / All to Him I owe; / Sin had left a crimson stain, / He
  washed it white as snow.
                                 —Mrs. E. M. Hall, "Jesus Paid It All" (hymn)

Be that generation that seeks Him.
                         —Steve Hawthorne, guest sermon, Hope Chapel,
                                          Austin, Texas, 21 Mar 1992

It's not what's going to happen, but who's coming.
                         —Steve Hawthorne, about the end times,
                   guest sermon, Hope Chapel, Austin, Texas, 21 Sep 1991

Jesus will brush aside your inabilities.
                         —Steve Hawthorne, guest sermon, Hope Chapel,
                                          Austin, Texas, 3 Dec 1994

Jesus came for the least, the lost, and the last.   —Marilyn Hickey

Certainly, no revolution that has ever taken place in society can be
  compared to that which has been produced by the words of Jesus
  Christ.   —Mark Hopkins

In the beauty of the lilies Christ was born across the sea, / With a glory
  in his bosom that transfigures you and me; / As he died to make men
  holy, let us die to make men free, / While God is marching on.
        —Julia Ward Howe, "Battle Hymn of the Republic" (song)

There is a fountain who is a King.
                         —Dennis Jernigan, "Who Can Satisfy?" (song)

Thou hast conquered, O Galilean.
               —Julian, Latin translation of Theodoret, *Hist. Eccles.* iii 20.

He [Jesus] knew that the old eye-for-eye philosophy would leave
  everyone blind. He did not seek to overcome evil with evil. He
  overcame evil with good. Although crucified by hate, he responded
  with aggressive love. —Martin Luther King, Jr., *The Strength to Love*

When Christ ascended / Triumphantly from star to star / He left the
  gates of Heaven ajar.
                —Henry Wadsworth Longfellow, "Golden Legend"

Be a sinner and sin strongly, but more strongly have faith and rejoice
  in Christ.   —Martin Luther, letter to Malanchthon

Christ designed that the day of his coming should be hid from us,
  that being in suspense, we might be as it were upon the watch.
                                       —Martin Luther

Evil in all its concreteness and personal reality challenged Christ and
  what he stood for, consummating the historic tragedy of the cross.
  This challenge was of the nature of an "everlasting nay" hurled at
  God himself. To this challenge God in Christ responded with an
  "everlasting yea" . . . making an end of sin and its power over man,
  and in the resurrection, triumphing.   —John A. Mackay

There's a / Friend for little children / Above the bright blue sky, / A
  Friend who never changes, / Whose love will never die.
                                       —A. Midlane, hymn

Fight the good fight with all thy might, / Christ is thy strength and
  Christ thy right. / Lay hold on life, and it shall be / Thy joy and
  crown eternally.   —John Monsell, hymn

How sweet the name of Jesus sounds / In a believer's ear!
        —John Newton, *Olney Hymns*, "The Name of Jesus"

Christ is the treasure in my clay pot.
        —Ron Parrish, sermon, Hope Chapel, Austin, Texas, 9 Sep 1995

Jesus had a sinner-friendly attitude.
        —Ron Parrish, sermon, Hope Chapel, Austin, Texas, 19 Nov 1994

Do little things as if they were great, because of the majesty of the
  Lord Jesus Christ who dwells in thee; and do great things as if they
  were little and easy, because of his omnipotence.   —Blaise Pascal

Our spirits are united with Jesus at salvation, but our minds are being
  progressively transformed into his nature.
              —Pat Robertson, *Answers to 200 of Life's Questions*

There is no harm in anybody thinking that Christ is in bread. The
  harm is in the expectation of His presence in gunpowder.
                                       —John Ruskin

Make not Christ a liar in distrusting His promise.
                                       —Samuel Rutherford

There may be flies on you and me,
    But there are no flies on Jesus.   —Salvation Army song (1900)

The idea of Christ is much older than Christianity.
                                                —George Santayana

No one would have been invited to dinner so often as Jesus was
    unless he were interesting and had a sense of humor.
                                                —Charles Schultz

Jesus no doubt fits his teaching into the late-Jewish messianic dogma.
    But he does not think dogmatically. He formulates no doctrine. He
    is far from judging any man's belief by reference to any standard of
    dogmatic correctness. Nowhere does he demand of his hearers that
    they shall sacrifice thinking to believing.   —Albert Schweitzer

It was to a virgin woman that the birth of the Son of God was
    announced. It was to a fallen woman that his resurrection was
    announced.   —Bishop Fulton J. Sheen

What would Jesus do?   —Charles M. Sheldon, *In His Steps* (1899)

O sinner, why don't you answer? Somebody's knocking at your door.
    Answer Jesus.
            —"Somebody's Knocking at Your Door" (Negro spiritual)

I have a great need for Christ; I have a great Christ for my need.
                                                —Charles H. Spurgeon

Jesus was careless of the company he kept.
                    —J. Carter Swaim, *War, Peace, and the Bible*

Jesus Wants Me for a Sunbeam   —Nellie Talbot, title of a hymn

. . . I have never met anybody who was sorry that they asked Jesus
    into their heart.   —Corrie ten Boom, in Pamela Rosewell,
                            The Five Silent Years of Corrie ten Boom

Little Jesus, was Thou shy / Once, and just so small as I? / And what
    did it feel like to be / Out of Heaven, and just like me?
                        —Francis Thompson, "Ex Ore Infantium"

If I give up, he [Jesus] shines through.   —Lewis Timberlake

Unless you accept Him [Jesus], you reject Him.   —Lewis Timberlake

Christ is our Passover! / And we will keep the feast / With the new
   leaven, / The bread of heaven: / All welcome even the least!
                                                    —A. R. Tompson

Try Jesus, you won't regret it, a billboard read.
                                        —Anne Tyler, *Breathing Lessons*

Jesus loves me—this I know,
   For the Bible tells me so.   —Susan Bogert Warner,
                                                   "The Love of Jesus"

All four Gospels agree in giving us a picture of a very definite personality. One is obliged to say, "Here was a man. This could not have
   been invented."   —H. G. Wells

He left His Father's throne above, / (So free, so infinite His grace!)
   / Emptied Himself of all but love, / And bled for Adam's helpless
   race.   —Charles Wesley, "Free Grace"

How else but through a broken heart / May Lord Christ enter in?
   —Oscar Wilde, *The Ballad of Reading Gaol*, Part V, Stanza 14

Jesus Christ will never strong-arm his way into your life.
                                                   —Grady B. Wilson

JOURNALISM

Journalism is literature in a hurry.   —Matthew Arnold

Harmony seldom makes a headline.   —Silas Bent

When a dog bites a man that's not news. If a man bites a dog, that's
   news.
   —John B. Bogart, in Frank M. O'Brien, *The Story of the New York Sun*

News is the first draft of history.   —Benjamin Bradlee

Never pick a fight with anyone who buys ink by the barrel.
   —Jim Brady, 1981, in Norman Augustine, *Augustine's Laws*

A free press can, of course, be good or bad, but, most certainly, without freedom it will never be anything but bad.
                     —Albert Camus, *Resistance, Rebellion and Death*

Acceptance by government of a dissident press is a measure of the
   maturity of a nation.   —William O. Douglas, *An Almanac of Liberty*

Journalism is organized gossip.   —Edward Eggleston

The questions are brutal because research of truth is a kind of surgery.
                                                   —Oriani Fallaci

Journalism is in fact history on the run.
                            —Thomas Griffith, *The Waist-High Culture*

I do not take a single newspaper, nor read one a month, and I feel
    myself infinitely the happier for it.   —Thomas Jefferson

A good newspaper, I suppose, is a nation talking to itself.
                                                   —Arthur Miller

Put it to them briefly, so they will read it; clearly, so they will appreci-
    ate it; picturesquely, so they will remember it; and above all, accu-
    rately, so they will be guided by its light.   —Joseph Pulitzer

All I know is what I read in the papers.   —Will Rogers

Always verify your references.   —Martin Joseph Routh

A good reporter remains a skeptic all his life.   —Jack Smith

The report of my death was an exaggeration.
                            —Mark Twain, cablegram from London to a
                                New York newspaper, 2 Jun 1897

J O Y

Faint not, though the way seem long; / There is joy in each condition.
                                                   —Anonymous

Happiness depends on happenings; joy depends on Christ.
                                                   —Anonymous

The joyfulness of a man prolongeth his day.   —Apocrypha

Joy is more divine than sorrow, for joy is bread and sorrow is medi-
    cine.   —Henry Ward Beecher

The test of your Christian character should be that you are a joy-bear-
    ing agent to the world.   —Henry Ward Beecher

. . . Weeping may endure for a night, but joy cometh in the morning.
                            —*The Bible* (KJV): Psalms 30:5

Joy is the most infallible sign of the presence of God.   —Leon Bloy

The night is past,—joy cometh with the morrow.
                                    —Edward Bulwer-Lytton

There is no beautifier of complexion or form of behavior like the wish
    to scatter joy, and not pain, around us.   —Ralph Waldo Emerson

Joys divided are increased.   —Josiah Gilbert Holland

Joys do not fall to the rich alone; nor has he lived ill of whose birth
    and death no one took note.   —Horace

It is a comely fashion to be glad,— / Joy is the grace we say to God.
                                    —Jean Ingelow, "Dominion"

A thing worth doing is worth doing with joy.   —Thomas A. Langford

Joy is the echo of God's life within us.   —Joseph Marmion, *Orthodoxy*

Great joys, like griefs, are silent.
                        —Shackerly Marmion, *Holland's Leaguer*

A joy that's shared is a joy made double.   —Proverb (English)

If you do not get any joy out of this life, how can you expect to get
    any happiness out of the next?   —Proverb (Hasidic)

Unshared joy is an unlighted candle.   —Proverb (Spanish)

Shared joy is double joy; shared sorrow is half a sorrow.
                                    —Proverb (Swedish)

Joy is not the absence of suffering. It is the presence of God.
                                    —Robert H. Schuller

The joy that isn't shared, I've heard, dies young.
    —Anne Sexton, *The Awful Rowing Toward God*, "Welcome Morning"

. . . joy runs deeper than despair.
                        —Corrie ten Boom, *The Hiding Place*, with
                        John and Elizabeth Sherrill

Joy is a net of love by which we can catch souls.   —Mother Teresa

One filled with joy preaches without preaching.   —Mother Teresa

There is a joy we ought to share.   —Lewis Timberlake

Grief can take care of itself, but to get the full value of a joy you must have somebody to divide it with.
    —Mark Twain, *Following the Equator: A Journey Around the World*

Joy is not in things; it is in us.   —Richard Whately

Joy has no cost.   —Marianne Williamson

JUDGMENT

He hears but half who hears one party only.   —Aeschylus

Good judgment comes from experience, and experience—well, that comes from poor judgment.
    —Aesop, *Fables*, "The Dog and the Shadow"

No accurate thinker will judge another person by what that person's enemies say about him.   —Anonymous

The trouble with most Christians today is that they would rather be on the judgment seat than on the witness stand.   —Anonymous

You should not decide until you have heard what both have to say.
    —Aristophanes, *The Wasps*

The most generous and merciful in judgment upon the faults of others are always the most free from faults themselves.   —Aughey

It is well to open one's mind but only as a preliminary to closing it . . . for the supreme act of judgment and selection.   —Irving Babbitt

The more you judge, the less you love.   —Honoré de Balzac

Excuse me . . . but I reject your definitions of me.
    —Saul Bellow, *Herzog*

Judge not, that ye be not judged.   —*The Bible* (KJV): Matthew 7:1

The books are balanced in heaven, not here.   —Josh Billings

No man can justly censure or condemn another, because indeed no man truly knows another.
    —Sir Thomas Browne, *Religio Medici*, Part ii, Sec. 4

Don't wait for the Last Judgement. It takes place every day.
—Albert Camus, *The Fall*

O mortal men, be wary of how ye judge.   —Dante Alighieri

If . . . it is not in my power to arrive at the knowledge of any truth, I
may at least do what is in my power, namely, suspend judgement . . .
—René Descartes

. . . one could never judge a man without seeing him close, for oneself . . .   —Fyodor Dostoyevsky, *Crime and Punishment*

Judge a tree from its fruit; not from the leaves.   —Euripides

He hath a good judgment that relieth not wholly on his own.
—Thomas Fuller, M. D., *Gnomologia*

You cannot judge a Man till you know his whole Story.
—Thomas Fuller, M. D., *Gnomologia*, No. 5876

How are we justly to determine in a world where there are no innocent ones to judge the guilty?   —Madame de Genlis

Life teaches us to be less severe both with ourselves and others.
—Johann Wolfgang von Goethe

At great cost to Himself, God has made it possible for each of us to
live with Him eternally. Those who reject God's offer of a heavenly
home will be assigned to hell.   —Billy Graham, *Till Armageddon*

Being judgmental and condemning is not one of the gifts of the
Spirit.   —Billy Graham, *Till Armageddon*

But those who chose to reject God during their lifetime on earth will
be separated from him for eternity. This is not God's desire, but
man's own choice. God holds every man accountable for his rejection of Christ.   —Billy Graham, *Till Armageddon*

Don't mind anything that anyone tells you about anyone else. Judge
everyone and everything for yourself.   —Henry James

When the evening of this life comes, we shall be judged on love.
—Saint John of the Cross

As I know more of mankind, I expect less of them, and am ready now
to call a man upon easier terms than I was formerly.
—Samuel Johnson

God himself, sir, does not propose to judge man until the end of his
days. —Samuel Johnson

Judgment is autobiographical. —John A. Kline

Everyone complains of his lack of memory, but nobody of his want of
judgment. —François de La Rochefoucauld, *Maximes*, No. 89

The world is full of pots jeering at kettles.
—François de La Rochefoucauld, *Maximes*

We judge ourselves by what we feel capable of doing, while others
judge us by what we have already done.
—Henry Wadsworth Longfellow, "Kavanagh"

Our duty is to believe that for which we have sufficient evidence, and
to suspend our judgment when we have not. —John Lubbock

I have never for one instant seen clearly within myself; how then
would you have me judge the deeds of others?
—Maurice Maeterlinck, *Pelleas and Melisande*

In men whom men condemn as ill / I find so much of goodness still, /
In men whom men pronounce divine / I find so much of sin and
blot. / I do not dare to draw a line / Between the two, where God
has not. —Joaquin Miller, "Byron," Stanza 1

There is no man so good, who, were he to submit all his thoughts and
actions to the laws, would not deserve hanging ten times in his
life. —Michel de Montaigne, *Essays*, Book III, Ch. 9

We judge ourselves by our motives and others by their actions.
—Dwight Morrow

We are all inclined to judge ourselves by our ideals; others by their
acts. —Harold Nicolson, diary

'Tis with our judgments as our watches, none / Go just alike, yet each
believes his own. —Alexander Pope, *An Essay on Criticism*

God help the sheep when the wolf is judge. —Proverb (Danish)

Whoso judges others condemns himself.   —Proverb (Italian)

You can judge of Hercules' stature by his foot.   —Proverb (Latin)

Don't judge any man until you have walked two moons in his moccasins.   —Proverb (Native American)

God looks at the clean hands, not the full ones.
    —Publilius Syrus, *Moral Sayings*

. . . God is going to judge righteously. . . . what did each one do in relation to what he or she knew to be right of wrong?
    —Pat Robertson, *Answers to 200 of Life's Most Probing Questions*

God will judge people on the basis of what they did in light of what they knew.
    —Pat Robertson, *Answers to 200 of Life's Most Probing Questions*

. . . No one "gets away" with evil. Judgment always comes, only the timing is uncertain.
    —Pat Robertson, *Answers to 200 of Life's Most Probing Questions*

Commonly we say a judgment falls upon a man for something in him we cannot abide.   —John Selden, *Table Talk*, "Judgments"

And how his audit stands who knows, save Heaven?
    —William Shakespeare, *Hamlet*, Act III, Sc. iii

Forbear to judge, for we are sinners all.
    —William Shakespeare, *King Henry VI, Part II*, Act III, Sc. iii

Take each man's censure, but reserve thy judgment.
    —William Shakespeare, *Hamlet*, Act I, Sc. iii

It was wrong to be too pragmatic, to judge people solely by results; it was more humane to judge by intentions.
    —Alexander Solzhenitsyn, *Cancer Ward*

Leave it to eternity to decide.
    —Alexander Solzhenitsyn, *The Oak and the Calf*

. . . We brush aside all scales not our own, as if they were follies or delusions.   —Alexander Solzhenitsyn, *Nobel Lecture*

If you love people, you have no time to judge them.   —Mother Teresa

JUSTICE

Justice delayed is justice denied. —William Gladstone

JUSTIFICATION

I cannot justify. —Saul Bellow, *Herzog*

To do evil a human being must first of all believe that what he's doing is good, or else that it's a well-considered act in conformity with natural law. Fortunately, it is in the nature of the human being to seek a justification for his actions.
—Alexander Solzhenitsyn, *The Gulag Archipelago*

JUSTNESS

. . . God befriend us, as our cause is just!
—William Shakespeare, *King Henry IV, Part I*, Act V, Sc. i

Only the actions of the just smell sweet and blossom in the dust.
—James Shirley

Justness exists, even if few people exist who feel it.
—Alexander Solzhenitsyn

In a just cause the weak will beat the strong.
—Sophocles, *Oedipus at Colonus*

— K —

KEYS

All the keys don't hang at one man's girdle.   —Anonymous

KINDNESS

No act of kindness, no matter how small, is ever wasted.
                    —Aesop, *Fables*, "The Lion and the Mouse"

Life is short and we never have enough time for gladdening the
    hearts of those who travel the way with us. O, be swift to love!
    Make haste to be kind.   —Henri Frédéric Amiel

Be kind to unkind people—they probably need it most.—Anonymous

A kind word is never lost. It keeps going on and on, from one person
    to another, until at last it comes back to you again.   —Anonymous

The kindest word in all the world is the unkind word, unsaid.
                    —Anonymous

There is nothing that needs to be said in an unkind manner.
                    —Hosea Ballou

Shall we make a new rule of life from tonight: always to try to be a lit-
    tle kinder than is necessary?
                    —Sir James Matthew Barrie, *The Little White Bird*

Reason itself, logic, urged you to kneel and give thanks for every
    small sign of true kindness.   —Saul Bellow, *Herzog*

Kindness—a language which the dumb can speak, and the deaf can
    understand.   —Christian Nestell Bovée

Have you had a kindness shown? / Pass it on; / 'Twas not given for
    thee alone, / Pass it on; / Let it travel down the years, / Let it wipe
    another's tears, / Till in Heaven the deed appears— / Pass it on.
                    —Henry Burton, "Pass It On"

If you confer a benefit, never remember it; if you receive one, never
    forget it.   —Chilon

The greatest thing a man can do for his heavenly Father is to be kind
to some of His other children.   —Henry Drummond

In the man whose childhood has known caresses and kindness, there
is always a fiber of memory that can be touched to gentle issues.
                                                   —George Eliot

Kindness is the golden chain by which society is bound together.
                                    —Johann Wolfgang von Goethe

Life is mostly froth and bubble, / Two things stand like stone,
/ Kindness in another's trouble, / Courage in your own.
    —Adam Lindsay Gordon, *Ye Wearie Wayfarer* (1866), "Fytte 8"

Often the only thing a child can remember about an adult in later
years, when he or she is grown, is whether or not that person was
kind.   —Billy Graham, *Till Armageddon*

I expect to pass through this world but once; any good thing therefore that I can do, or any kindness that I can show to my fellow
creature, let me do it now; let me not defer or neglect it, for I shall
not pass this way again.   —Etienne de Grellet

Let me be a little kinder, / Let me be a little blinder / To the faults of
those around me, / Let me praise a little more.
                                        —Edgar A. Guest, "A Creed"

Wise sayings often fall on barren ground; but a kind word is never
thrown away.   —Arthur Helps

Kindness is the sunshine in which virtue grows.
                             —Robert G. Ingersoll, "A Lay Sermon"

Always, Sir, set a high value on spontaneous kindness. He whose
inclination prompts him to cultivate your friendship of his own
accord, will love you more than one whom you have been at pains
to attach to you.   —Samuel Johnson,
                     in James Boswell, *Life of Samuel Johnson*

I have found men more kind than I expected, and less just.
                                                  —Samuel Johnson

Kindness consists in loving people more than they deserve.
                            —Joseph Joubert, *Pensées*, No. 71

Seek to cultivate a buoyant, joyous sense of the crowded kindness of
God in your daily life. —Alexander Maclaren

Let us be kind to one another, for most of us are fighting a hard battle. —Ian Maclaren

Beginning today, treat everyone you meet as if they were going to be
dead by midnight. Extend to them all the care, kindness, and
understanding you can muster, and do it with no thought of any
reward. Your life will never be the same again. —Og Mandino

In this world, you must be a bit too kind in order to be kind enough.
—Pierre Marivaux, *Le Jeu de l'amour et du hasard* (1730)

Kindness, the poetry of the heart. —Aime Martin

Kindness and patience were always called for . . .
—Flannery O'Connor, "The Lame Shall Enter First"

To speak kindly does not hurt the tongue. —Proverb (French)

A kind word never broke anyone's mouth. —Proverb (Irish)

One kind word can warm three winter months. —Proverb (Japanese)

God is merciful to those that are kind. —Proverb (Moroccan)

You can accomplish by kindness what you cannot by force.
—Publilius Syrus

Kindness is more important than wisdom, and the recognition of this
is the beginning of wisdom. —Theodore Isaac Rubin

Oppose kindness to perverseness. The heavy sword will not cut soft
silk; by using sweet words and gentleness you may lead an elephant with a hair. —Saadi

To give pleasure to a single heart by a single kind act is better than a
thousand head-bowings in prayer. —Saadi

Let him that hath done the good office conceal it; let him that hath
received it disclose it. —Seneca

Persistent kindness conquers the ill-disposed.
—Seneca, *De Beneficiis*, Book VII, Sec. 31

A great man shows his greatness by the way he treats little men.
—Thomas Carlyle

Wherever there is a human being there is an opportunity for a kindness.
—Seneca

Yet do I fear thy nature; / It is too full o' the milk of human kindness / To catch the nearest way.
—William Shakespeare, *Macbeth*, Act I, Sc. v

Kindness begets kindness.
—Sophocles, *Ajax*

Men are cruel, but Man is kind.
—Rabindranath Tagore, *Stray Birds*

The highest wisdom is kindness.
—*The Talmud*

Kind words can be short and easy to speak, but their echoes are truly endless.
—Mother Teresa

Let no one ever come to you without leaving better and happier. Be the living expression of God's kindness; kindness in your face, kindness in your eyes, kindness in your smile.
—Mother Teresa

Be kind. Remember everyone you meet is fighting a hard battle.
—T. H. Thompson

If you want to lift yourself up, lift up someone else.
—Booker T. Washington

So many gods, so many creeds, / So many paths that wind and wind, / While just the art of being kind / Is all the sad world needs.
—Ella Wheeler Wilcox, "The World's Need"

I have always depended on the kindness of strangers.
—Tennessee Williams, *A Streetcar Named Desire*, Blanche's final line

That best portion of a good man's life, / His little, nameless, unremembered acts / Of kindness and of love.
—William Wordsworth, "Lines Composed a Few Miles Above Tintern Abbey," 33

KISSING

Kisses kept are wasted;
Love is to be tasted.
—Edmund Vance Cooke

The anatomical juxtaposition of two orbicularis oris muscles in a
state of contraction.   —Dr. Henry Gibbons, definition of a kiss

Lips that taste of tears, they say / Are the best for kissing.
                    —Dorothy Parker, *Enough Rope*, "Threnody"

Dear as remembered kisses after death.
                    —Alfred, Lord Tennyson, *The Princess*, IV

Our spirits rushed together at the touching of the lips.
                              —Alfred, Lord Tennyson

When I was very young, I kissed my first woman, and smoked my
first cigarette on the same day. Believe me, never since have I
wasted any more time on tobacco.   —Arturo Toscanini

KNOTS

To be always ready a man must be able to cut a knot, for everything
cannot be untied.   —Henri Frédéric Amiel

If you can't tie good knots, tie plenty of them.
                    —Anonymous, yachtsman credo

When you come to the end of your rope—tie a knot and hold on.
                              —Anonymous

KNOWLEDGE

If knowledge can create problems, it is not through ignorance that we
can solve them.   —Isaac Asimov

Knowledge is not a shop for profit or sale, but a rich storehouse for
the glory of the Creator, and the relief of men's estate.
                              —Francis Bacon

Knowledge itself is power.
          —Francis Bacon, *Religious Meditations*, "Of Heresies"

I honestly believe it iz better tew know nothing than tew know what
ain't so.   —Josh Billings, *Encyclopedia of Proverbial Philosophy*

The trouble with people is not that they don't know but that they
know so much that ain't so.
          —Josh Billings, *Josh Billings' Encyclopedia of Wit and Wisdom*

... I distrust manifest knowledge.   —Rita Mae Brown,
      in Phillip L. Berman, editor *The Courage of Conviction*

It is a glorious fever, desire to know.

        —Edward Bulwer-Lytton

We owe almost all our knowledge not to those who have agreed, but
   to those who have differed.   —Charles Caleb Colton, *Lacon*

The essence of knowledge is, having it, to apply it; not having it, to
   confess your ignorance.   —Confucius

Real knowledge is to know the extent of one's ignorance. —Confucius

One part of knowledge consists in being ignorant of such things as
   are not worthy to be known.   —Crates

We don't know one millionth of one per cent about anything.
        —Thomas A. Edison

Man has an intense desire for assured knowledge.
      —Albert Einstein, *Ideas and Opinions*

Yet it is equally clear that knowledge of what is does not open the
   door directly to what should be.
      —Albert Einstein, *Ideas and Opinions*

Only so much do I know, as I have lived.
   —Ralph Waldo Emerson, *Nature Addresses*, "The American Scholar"

Knowledge gives a wider choice and more anguish.
   —Samuel C. Florman, *The Existential Pleasures of Engineering*

If you have knowledge, let others light their candles by it.
        —Thomas Fuller

A man could know as much as he had any way to know; it was nonsense to ask more of him.   —John Gardner, *The Resurrection*

And still they gaz'd, and still the wonder grew. / That one small head
   could carry all he knew.
      —Oliver Goldsmith, *The Deserted Village*

The little I know, I owe to my ignorance.   —Sacha Guitry

We are least open to precise knowledge concerning the things we are most vehement about.   —Eric Hoffer, *The Passionate State of Mind*

The best part of our knowledge is that which teaches us where knowledge leaves off and ignorance begins. —Oliver Wendell Holmes, Sr.

One cannot know everything.   —Horace, *Carmina*

It's what a fellow thinks he knows that hurts him.
                    —Frank McKinney ("Kin") Hubbard

If a little knowledge is dangerous, where is the man who has so much as to be out of danger?   —Thomas Henry Huxley, *Science and Culture*,
                    "On Elementary Instruction and Physiology"

There was never an age in which useless knowledge was more important than in our own.   —Cyril Joad

Knowledge is of two kinds. We know a subject ourselves, or we know where we can find information upon it.
     —Samuel Johnson, in James Boswell, *Life of Samuel Johnson*

Knowledge was meant to be shared.   —Louis L'Amour, *Jubal Sackett*

All our knowledge has its origins in our perceptions.
                    —Leonardo da Vinci

I sometimes confuse myself with the little I know.
                    —Bernard Malamud, *The Natural*

Since we cannot know all that is to be known of everything, we ought to know a little about everything.   —Blaise Pascal

From the very beginning of your work, school yourself to severe gradualness in the accumulation of knowledge.
                    —Ivan Petrovich Pavlov,
     "Bequest to the Academic Youth of Soviet Russia," 27 Feb 1936

Knowledge is folly, except grace guide it.   —Proverb (English)

We're drowning in information and starving for knowledge.
                    —Rutherford D. Rogers

It isn't what we don't know that gives us trouble, it's what we know that ain't so.   —Will Rogers

The struggling for knowledge hath a pleasure in it like that of
wrestling with a fine woman.　　　　　　　—George Savile

As we acquire more knowledge, things don't become more compre-
hensible, but more mysterious.　　　　　—Albert Schweitzer

The end of all knowledge should be in virtuous action.
　　　　　　　　　　　　　　　　　—Sir Philip Sidney

All of us were stuck to the surface of a ball incidentally. The planet
was ball-shaped. Nobody knew why we didn't fall off, even though
everybody pretended to kind of understand it.
　　　　　　　　　—Kurt Vonnegut, Jr., *Breakfast of Champions*

. . . most of the world's ills can be traced to the fact that Man's knowledge of himself has not kept pace with his knowledge of the physical world.
　　　　　　　　　—Kurt Vonnegut, Jr., *Welcome to the Monkey House*,
　　　　　　　　　　"Tomorrow and Tomorrow and Tomorrow"

And I remember most of what I know that is good and true and lasting has come not from scholars but from minstrels and gypsies . . .
　　　　　　　　　—Robert James Waller, *Old Songs in a New Cafe*

— L —

LABOR

Labor is the best sauce. —Anonymous

Labor past is pleasant. —Anonymous

He who labors as he prays lifts his heart to God with his hands.
—Saint Bernard of Clairvaux

Industry cannot flourish if labor languish. —Calvin Coolidge

The wealth of a country is its working people.
—Theodor Herzl, *Altneuland*

Labor is no disgrace. —Hesiod

Genius begins beautiful works, but only labor finishes them.
—Joseph Joubert

Thou, O God, dost sell us all good things at the price of labor.
—Leonardo da Vinci, *Notebooks*

Genius may conceive, but patient labor must consummate.
—Horace Mann

It is brought home to you . . . that it is only because miners sweat
their guts out that superior persons can remain superior.
—George Orwell, *The Road to Wigan Pier*, Ch. 2

Temperance and labor are the two best physicians of man.
—Jean Jacques Rousseau

Labor, you know, is prayer. —Bayard Taylor

The fruit derived from labor is the sweetest of all pleasures.
—Luc de Clapiers Vauvenargues

LAND

We do not inherit this land from our ancestors; we borrow it from our
children. —Proverb (Native American—Haida)

LANGUAGE

In language clarity is everything. —Confucius

Language is not only the vehicle of thought, it is a great and efficient
instrument in thinking. —H. Davy

Human language is like a cracked kettle on which we beat out tunes
for bears to dance to, when all the time we are longing to move the
stars to pity. —Gustave Flaubert, *Madame Bovary*

The chief merit of language is clarity, and we know that nothing
detracts so much as do unfamiliar terms.
—Galen, *On the Natural Faculties*

Let's have some new clichés. —Samuel Goldwyn

We never do anything well till we cease to think about the manner of
doing it. This is the reason why it is so difficult for any but natives
to speak a language correctly or idiomatically.
—William Hazlitt, *Sketches and Essays*, "On Prejudice"

Language is the dress of thought. —Samuel Johnson,
The Lives of the Most Eminent English Poets, "Cowley"

To the young, clichés seem freshly minted.
—Bel Kaufman, *Up the Down Staircase*

It is Greek to me. —Proverb (16th century)

The English language is more complex than calculus because numbers don't have nuances.
—Andrew A. Rooney, *Word for Word*, Preface

Many thoughts are so dependent upon the language in which they
are clothed that they would lose half their beauty if otherwise
expressed. —John Ruskin

The language of truth is unvarnished enough. —Seneca, *Epistolae*, 49

England and America are two countries divided by a common language. —George Bernard Shaw

Man's ultimate concern must be expressed symbolically, because
symbolic language alone is capable to express the ultimate.
—Paul Tillich

Great men, like nature, use simple language.
—Luc de Clapiers Vauvenargues

Language, as well as the faculty of speech, was the immediate gift of
God.   —Noah Webster, preface to his dictionary

A language is a dialect with its own army and navy. —Max Weinreich

LATENESS

A little too late is much too late.   —Proverb (German)

LAUGHTER

When people are laughing, they're generally not killing one another.
—Alan Alda

Fools laugh at others; wise men at themselves.   —Anonymous

Laughter is the shortest distance between two people. —Anonymous

Among those whom I like or admire, I can find no common denomi-
nator; but among those whom I love, I can: all of them make me
laugh.   —W. H. Auden, *The Dyer's Hand*

I force myself to laugh at everything, for fear of being compelled to
weep.
—Pierre-Augustin de Beaumarchais, *Le Barbier de Seville*, Act I, Sc. ii

Laffing iz the sensation ov pheeling good all over, and showing it principally in one spot.   —Josh Billings, *Josh Billings' Comical Lexicon*

Always laugh when you can. It is cheap medicine.   —Lord Byron

And if I laugh at any mortal thing, / 'Tis that I may not weep.
—Lord Byron, *Don Juan*, Canto IV, 4

No man who has once heartily and wholly laughed can be altogether
irreclaimably bad. —Thomas Carlyle, *Sartor Resartus*, Book I, Ch. 4

The most wasted of all days is the day one did not laugh.
—Nicolas Chamfort, *Maximes et pensées*

Laughter is the only strategy that has ever worked at all for me when
my world is falling apart.   —Pat Conroy, *The Prince of Tides*, Ch. 7

Once you get people laughing, they're listening and you can tell
them almost anything.   —Herbert Gardner

The man of understanding finds everything laughable.
                                        —Johann Wolfgang von Goethe

Laughter is wholesome. God is not so dull as some people make out.
Did not He make the kitten to chase its tail.   —Heinrich Heine

Laughter is the medicine of the soul.   —Rabbi Bertram Klausner

One must laugh before one is happy or one may die without ever
having laughed at all.   —Jean de La Bruyère, *Les Caractères*

Laughter has no foreign accent.   —Paul B. Lowney

Laugh at yourself before anyone else can.
                        —Elsa Maxwell, NBC-TV interview, 28 Sep 1958

Down deep in His heart God is a comedian who loves to make us
laugh.   —Arthur Miller, *Timebends*

Inject laughter into tense situations to save the day; laughter calms
tempers and soothes jangled nerves.   —Wilferd Peterson

He who laughs, lasts!
                —Mary Pettibone Poole, *A Glass Eye at a Keyhole*
                (1938), "Beggars Can't Be Losers"

He is not laughed at that laughs at himself first.   —Proverb (English)

Laughter can be heard farther than weeping.   —Proverb (Yiddish)

We look before and after, / And pine for what is not: / Our sincerest
laughter / With some pain is fraught; / Our sweetest songs are
those that tell of saddest thought.   —Percy Shelley, "To a Skylark"

What a force is laughter.
                —Alexander Solzhenitsyn, *The Gulag Archipelago Three*

Conversation never sits easier upon us than when we now and then
discharge ourselves in a symphony of laughter, which may not
improperly be called the chorus of conversation.
                                        —Sir Richard Steele

. . . it was her habit to build up laughter out of inadequate materials.
—John Steinbeck, *The Grapes of Wrath*, Ch. 8

A good laugh is sunshine in a house. —William Makepeace Thackeray

Against the assault of laughter nothing can stand.
—Mark Twain, "The Mysterious Stranger"

The human race has only one really effective weapon, and that is laughter. —Mark Twain

A laugh is a smile that bursts. —Mary H. Waldrip

Laugh and the world laughs with you / Weep and you weep alone, / For the sad old earth must borrow its mirth, / But has trouble enough of its own. —Ella Wheeler Wilcox, "Solitude"

Laughter is not at all a bad beginning for a friendship. —Oscar Wilde

If you can make a woman laugh you can do anything with her.
—Nicol Williamson

L A W

People who love sausage and respect the law should never watch either one being made. —Anonymous

Wise men, though all laws were abolished, would lead the same lives.
—Aristophanes

A law is valuable not because it is law, but because there is right in it.
—Henry Ward Beecher

. . . not of the letter, but of the spirit: for the letter killeth, but the spirit giveth life. —*The Bible* (KJV): 2 Corinthians 3:6

Litigant, n. A person about to give up his skin for the hope of retaining his bones. —Ambrose Bierce, *The Devil's Dictionary*

In law nothing is certain but the expense. —Samuel Butler

Agree, for the law is costly.
—William Camden, *Remains Concerning Britain*

We are in bondage to the law so that we may be free. —Cicero

Men do not make laws. They do but discover them.—Calvin Coolidge

One with the law is a majority.
                    —Calvin Coolidge, vice-presidential nomination
                              acceptance speech, Chicago, 27 Jul 1920

It is a secret worth knowing that lawyers rarely go to law.
                                                  —Moses Crowell

They [the poor] have to labor in the face of the majestic equality of
    the law, which forbids the rich as well as the poor to sleep under
    bridges, to beg in the streets, and to steal bread.
                        —Anatole France, *The Red Lilly*, Ch. 7

A jury consists of twelve people chosen to decide who has the better
    lawyer.   —Robert Frost

Every one of us . . . knows better than he practices, and recognizes a
    better law than he obeys.   —James Anthony Froude

Our human laws are but copies, more or less imperfect, of the eternal
    laws, so far as we can read them.   —James Anthony Froude,
                        Short Studies on Great Subjects, "Calvinism"

Law cannot persuade where it cannot punish.   —Thomas Fuller

. . . the true function of a lawyer was to unite parties driven asunder.
                    —Mahatma Gandhi, in C. F. Andrews, editor,
                                Mahatma Gandhi—His Own Story

All laws are an attempt to domesticate the natural ferocity of the
    species.   —John W. Gardner,
                    in *San Francisco Examiner* & *Chronicle*, 3 Jul 1974

A verbal contract isn't worth the paper it's printed on.
                —Samuel Goldwyn, in Alva Johnston, *The Great Goldwyn*

I know of no method to secure the repeal of bad or obnoxious laws so
    effective as their stringent execution.
                        —Ulysses S. Grant, Inaugural Address, 1869

A child who has been taught to respect the laws of God will have lit-
    tle difficulty respecting the laws of men.   —J. Edgar Hoover

It may be true that the law cannot make a man love me, but it can
keep him from lynching me, and I think that's pretty important.
—Martin Luther King, Jr.

The best way to get a bad law repealed is to enforce it strictly.
—Abraham Lincoln

The law was given to drive us to despair over the hopelessness of ever
being able to keep it. —Hal Lindsey

New lords, new laws. —Proverb (16th century)

A lean compromise is better than a fat lawsuit. —Proverb (Italian)

Laws were made that the stronger might not in all things have his
way. —Proverb (Latin)

One lawyer will make work for another. —Proverb (Spanish)

Ignorance of the law excuses no man; not that all men know the law,
but because 'tis an excuse every man will plead, and no man can
tell how to confute him. —John Selden, *Table Talk*, "Law"

There is a higher law than the Constitution.
—W. H. Seward, in the U. S. Senate opposing compromise
on the slavery issue, 11 Mar 1850

Laws are generally found to be nets of such a texture, as the little
creep through, the great break through, and the middlesized are
alone entangled in. —William Shenstone, *Works in Verse and Prose*`

Where is there any book of the law so clear to each man as that written in his heart? —Leo Tolstoy

One listens to one's lawyer prattle on as long as one can stand it and
then signs where indicated. —Alexander Woollcott

LEADERSHIP

A leader is a dealer in hope. —Napoleon Bonaparte, *Maxims*

A leader is best / When people barely know that he exists.
—Witter Bynner

Obedience alone gives the right to command. —Ralph Waldo Emerson

Our chief want in life is somebody who shall make us do what we
can.   —Ralph Waldo Emerson, *The Conduct of Life*,
                                              "Considerations by the Way"

Don't let your constituency capture you.
                   —Gen. John Flynn, speech at Squadron Officer School,
                                       Maxwell AFB, summer, 1977

A prime function of the leader is to keep hope alive.   —John Gardner

A good leader takes a little more than his share of blame, a little less
    than his share of credit.   —Arnold H. Glassgow

The reward of the general is not a bigger tent, but command.
                                       —Oliver Wendell Holmes, Jr.

We tend to select top men for their character and capacity, then over-
    load them according to their willingness.   —Clarence Jones

Find out where the people want to go, then hustle yourself around in
    front of them.   —James Kilpatrick

In the camps we learned to distinguish between good superiors and
    bad. The criterion was simple and infallible: one forbids everything
    that is not specifically permitted, the other permits everything that
    is not specifically forbidden.   —Lev Kopelev, *Ease My Sorrows*

. . . you must know that a superior is not late, but held up, not asleep
    but resting, not wrong, but incorrectly briefed.
                                       —Lev Kopelev, *Ease My Sorrows*

The best of all rulers is but a shadowy presence to his subjects.
                             —Lao Tzu, *Tao Te Ching*, Ch. XVII

When his [the good ruler's] task is accomplished and his work done,
    The people all say, "It happened to us naturally."
                                 —Lao Tzu, *Tao Te Ching*, Ch. XVII

I have to follow them—I am their leader.
                       —Alexandre-Auguste Ledru-Rollin, a leader in
                                     the Revolution of 1848 in France

The final test of a leader is that he leaves behind him in other men
    the conviction and the will to carry on.   —Walter Lippmann,
              column in tribute to Franklin D. Roosevelt, 14 Apr 1945

People buy into the leader before they buy into the vision.
—John C. Maxwell

A leader or a man of action in a crisis almost always acts subconsciously and then thinks of the reasons for his actions.
—Jawaharlal Nehru

Never tell people how to do things. Tell them what to do and they will surprise you with their ingenuity.
—Gen. George S. Patton, *War As I Knew It*

Lead, follow, or get out of the way.
—Laurence J. Peter, *Peter's People*, "Peter's Survival Principle"

If you wish to know what a man is, place him in authority.
—Proverb (Yugoslav)

Uneasy lies the head that wears a crown.
—William Shakespeare, *King Henry IV, Part II*, Act III, Sc. i

A leader should not be a man who arbitrarily imported his own ideas but the essential focal point for a group of people who trusted one another and worked for a common aim.
—Alexander Solzhenitsyn, *Stories and Prose Poems*, "For the Good of the Cause"

A man is led the way he wishes to follow.   —*The Talmud*

A leader can't dash ahead around the bend out of sight.
—Herman Wouk, *The Winds of War*

LEARNING

Learning is not attained by chance, it must be sought for with ardor and attended to with diligence.   —Abigail Adams, 1870

They know enough who know how to learn.
—Henry Adams, *The Education of Henry Adams* (1907)

It is always in season for old men to learn.   —Aeschylus

Do not confine your children to your own learning, for they were born to another time.   —Anonymous

Learn all you can here, and God will teach you the rest in heaven.
—Anonymous

Nothing so much assists learning as writing down what we wish to
    remember.   —Anonymous

What you learn to your cost you remember long.   —Anonymous

What we have to learn to do, we learn by doing.
    —Aristotle, *Nicomachean Ethics*

Disciples do owe their masters only a temporary belief, and a suspen-
    sion of their own judgment till they be fully instructed . . .
    —Francis Bacon

Learning teaches how to carry things in suspense, without prejudice,
    till you resolve it.   —Francis Bacon

It is what we think we know already that often prevents us from
    learning.   —Claude Bernard

Wear your learning, like your watch, in a private pocket: and do not
    merely pull it out and strike it merely to show that you have one.
    —Earl of Chesterfield, letter to his son, 22 Feb 1748

I am always ready to learn, although I do not always like being
    taught.
    —Winston Churchill, House of Commons speech, 4 Nov 1952

Learning without thought is labor lost.   —Confucius

A primary method of learning is to go from the familiar to the unfa-
    miliar.   —Glenn Doman,
    How to Teach Your Baby to Read: The Gentle Revolution

Thoroughly to teach another is the best way to learn for yourself.
    —Tryon Edwards

It is impossible for a man to learn that which he thinks he already
    knows.   —Epictetus, *Discourses*, II

Learning makes a man fit company for himself.
    —Thomas Fuller, M. D., *Gnomologia*, No. 3163

I have never met a man so ignorant that I couldn't learn something
    from him.   —Galileo Galilei

The brighter you are the more you have to learn.   —Don Herold

Sit down before fact as a little child, be prepared to give up every pre-
conceived notion, follow humbly wherever and whatever abysses
nature leads, or you will learn nothing.
—Thomas Henry Huxley, letter to Charles Kingsley, 1860

He who has imagination without learning has wings and no feet.
—Joseph Joubert, *Pensées*

The great art to learn much is to undertake a little at a time.
—John Locke

A man had to learn, it was his nature.   —Bernard Malamud, *The Fixer*

What we learn with pleasure we never forget.   —Alfred Mercier

No man will learn anything at all, / Unless he first will learn humility.
—Owen Meredith, *Vanini*, line 328

Still I am learning.   —Michelangelo

The doer alone learneth.   —Friedrich Nietzsche

Lessons are not given, they are taken.   —Cesare Pavese

The wisest man may always learn something from the humblest
peasant.   —J. Petit-Senn

A learned man has always wealth in himself.
—Phaedrus, *Fables*, Book VI, fable 21

Do not train boys to learning by force and harshness; but direct them
to it by what amuses their minds.   —Plato

Even the whole of life is not sufficient for thorough learning.
—Plautus, *Truculentus*

A little learning is a dangerous thing; /Drink deep, or taste not the
Pierian spring.
—Alexander Pope, *An Essay on Criticism*, lines 215-216

Some people will never learn anything, for this reason, because they
understand everything too soon.
—Alexander Pope, *Thoughts on Various Subjects*

I hear and I forget. I see and I remember. I do and I understand.
—Proverb (Chinese)

Learning is a treasure which follows its owner everywhere.
—Proverb (Chinese)

All things are difficult before they are easy. —Proverb (French)

He who likes cherries soon learns to climb. —Proverb (German)

If you wish to learn the highest truth, you must begin with the alphabet.
—Proverb (Japanese)

There are no national frontiers to learning. —Proverb (Japanese)

In spite of some bad experiences, I'm a firm believer in the trial and error method of learning.
—Andrew A. Rooney, *Pieces of My Mind*, "Directions"

The wisest mind has something yet to learn. —George Santayana

That learning which thou gettest by thy own observation and experience, is far beyond that which thou gettest by precept; as the knowledge of a traveler exceeds that which is got by reading.
—Thomas à Kempis

It's just plain learning something that you didn't know. There is a real aesthetic experience in being dumbfounded. —Lewis Thomas

We hear and apprehend only what we already half know.
—Henry David Thoreau

To be fond of learning is to be near to knowledge.
—Tze-sze, *The Doctrine of the Mean*

From the first I was clamorous to learn . . .
—Eudora Welty, *One Writer's Beginnings*

In order to acquire learning, we must first shake ourselves free of it.
—Alfred North Whitehead

Learning preserves the errors of the past as well as its wisdom.
—Alfred North Whitehead

How empty learning, and how vain is art, but as it mends the life and guides the heart. —Young

L E I S U R E

If you want to get a true estimate of a man, observe what he does
  when he has nothing to do.   —Anonymous

The real problem of your leisure is to keep other people from using it.
                                                              —Anonymous

Absence of occupation is not rest,
  A mind quite vacant is a mind distress'd.
                                    —Hannah Cowley, "Retirement"

What is this life, if full of care, / We have no time to stand and stare?
                        —William Henry Davies, *Songs of Joy*, "Leisure"

No man is obliged to do as much as he can do. A man is to have part
  of his life to himself.   —Samuel Johnson

Leisure in time is like unoccupied floor space in a room.
                                                    —Shu Paihsiang

The time you enjoy wasting is not wasted time.
      —Laurence J. Peter, compiler, *Peter's Quotations*: *Ideas for Our Time*

The time best employed is that which is wasted.   —Proverb (French)

Half our life is spent trying to find something to do with the time we
  have rushed through life trying to save.
                              —Will Rogers, *Autobiography*, Ch. 15

The secret of being miserable is to have leisure to bother about
  whether you are happy or not. The cure for it is occupation.
                                              —George Bernard Shaw

It is well to lie fallow for a while.
      —Martin Farquhar Tupper, *Proverbial Philosophy*, "Of Recreation"

L E N D I N G

Never lend your car to anyone to whom you have given birth.
                                              —Erma Bombeck

Lend only what you can afford to lose.
                              —George Herbert, *Jacula Prudentum*

It is better to give one shilling than lend twenty.   —Proverb (English)

LIBERATION

Women's liberation is the liberation of feminine in the man and the
masculine in the woman. —Corita Kent

LIBERTY

Liberty is always unfinished business.
—American Civil Liberties Union,
title of 36th Annual Report, 1956

Liberty! Equality! Fraternity!
—Anonymous, motto from the French Revolution

Liberty, too, must be limited in order to be possessed.
—Edmund Burke

Liberty is always dangerous, but it is the safest thing we have.
—Harry Emerson Fosdick

Liberty is so much latitude as the powerful choose to accord the
weak. —Judge Learned Hand, speech,
University of Pennsylvania Law School, 21 May 1944

I know not what course others may take; but as for me, give me liberty or give me death.
—Patrick Henry, speech in the Virginia Convention, 23 Mar 1775

Liberty may make mistakes but tyranny is the death of a nation.
—Matteotti

He that would make his own liberty secure must guard even his
enemy from oppression.
—Thomas Paine, *Dissertation on First Principles of Government*

Liberty, when it begins to take root, is a plant of rapid growth.
—George Washington, letter to James Madison, 2 Mar 1788

Liberty is the one thing you can't have unless you give it to others.
—William Allen White

LIBRARIES

I have always imagined that Paradise will be a kind of library.
—Jorge Luis Borges

To add a library to a house is to give that house a soul. —Cicero

A great library contains the diary of the human race. —George Dawson

Over the door of the library in Thebes is the inscription "Medicine for the soul."
—Diodorus Siculus

Libraries can be of indispensable service in lifting the dead weight of poverty and ignorance.
—Francis Keppel

L I F E

Every man's life is a fairy tale, written by God's fingers.
—Hans Christian Andersen

Life is like a bridge—cross over it but don't establish yourself upon it.
—Anonymous

Life is not an answer to a question; it's a mystery in which we participate.
—Anonymous

Life is not to be endured. Life is to be revered.   —Anonymous

No life meaningfully linked to God can be utterly cast down.
—Anonymous

Our lives are a manifestation of what we think about God.
—Anonymous

Youth lives in the future, middle age in the present, and old age in the past.
—Anonymous

Life is a long lesson in humility.
—Sir James Matthew Barrie, *The Little Minister*, III

Life is a dream and death an awakening.   —Beaumelle

God asks no man whether he will accept life. That is not the choice. You must accept it. The only choice is how.
—Henry Ward Beecher, *Life Thoughts*

Let the enemies of life step down.   —Saul Bellow, *Herzog*

My face too blind, my mind too limited, my instincts too narrow. But this intensity, doesn't it mean anything?   —Saul Bellow, *Herzog*

The best and purest human beings, from the beginning of time, have understood that life is sacred.
—Saul Bellow, *Mr. Sammler's Planet*, Ch. 1

Life, you know, is rather like opening a tin of sardines. We are all of
us looking for the key.
—Alan Bennett, *Beyond the Fringe* (1961 revue), "Take a Pew"

. . . For what is your life? It is even a vapor, that appeareth for a little
time, and then vanisheth away.   —*The Bible* (KJV): James 4:14

Life is a grindstone, and whether it grinds a man down or polishes
him up depends on the stuff he's made of.   —Josh Billings

Everything that lives is holy, life delights in life.
—William Blake, "America: A Prophecy"

Death is strong, but Life is stronger . . .
—Phillips Brooks, "An Easter Carol"

I count life just a stuff / To try the soul's strength on . . .
—Robert Browning, *Men and Women*, "In a Balcony"

Every man's life is a plan of God.   —Horace Bushnell

Life is a matter about which we are lost if we reason either too much
or too little.   —Samuel Butler

Life is like playing a violin solo in public and learning the instrument
as one goes on.
—Samuel Butler (1835-1902), speech at the Sumerville
Club, 27 Feb 1895

Life is the art of drawing sufficient conclusions from insufficient
premises.   —Samuel Butler (1835-1902), *Note-books*

To live is like love, all reason is against it, and all healthy instinct for
it.   —Samuel Butler (1835-1902), *Note-books*

I look upon life as a gift from God. I did nothing to earn it. Now that
the time is coming to give it back, I have no right to complain.
—Joyce Cary

Life is a fragment, a moment between two eternities.
—William Ellery Channing

Life is a crucible. We are thrown into it and tried.
—Edwin Hubbel Chapin

Life is fleeting—and therefore endurable.
—Alexander Chase, *Perspectives*

Life is the art of drawing without an eraser.　　—John Christian

What a wonderful life I've had! I only wish I'd realized it sooner.
　　　　　　　　　　　　　　　　　　—Colette

As regards plots I find real life no help at all. Real life seems to have
　no plots.
　　—Dame Ivy Compton-Burnett, in R. Lehmann et al., *Orion I* (1945)

All life connects . . . Nothing happens that is meaningless.
　　　　　　　　　　　—Pat Conroy, *Beach Music*, Ch. 20

Vain, weak-built isthmus, which dost proudly rise / Up between two
　eternities!　　　　　　　　　　　　—Abraham Cowley

Life is made up, not of great sacrifices or duties, but of little things, in
　which smiles and kindness, and small obligations given habitually,
　are what preserve the heart and secure comfort.　　—William Davy

It was curious how life seemed to weave a pattern that was not in the
　least haphazard, as it so often seemed to be.
　　　　　—R. F. Delderfield, *To Serve Them All My Days*

That it will never come again / Is what makes life so sweet.
　　　　　　　　—Emily Dickinson, *Bolts of Melody*

Life had stepped into the place of theory.
　　　　—Fyodor Dostoyevsky, *Crime and Punishment*

. . . what you need more than anything in life is a definite position.
　　　　—Fyodor Dostoyevsky, *Crime and Punishment*

They are not long, the days of wine and roses.
　　　　　—Ernest Dowson, "Vitae Summa Brevis"

Life is infinitely stranger than anything which the mind of man
　could invent.　　　　　　　—Sir Arthur Conan Doyle

For a long time it had seemed to me that life was about to begin—real
　life. But there was always some obstacle in the way, something to
　be got through first, some unfinished business, time still to be
　served, a debt to be paid. Then life would begin. At last it dawned
　on me that these obstacles were my life.　　—Alfred D'Souza

Life is like a game of whist. I don't enjoy the game much; but I like to
　play my cards well, and see what will be the end of it.
　　　　　　　　　　　　　　　　　—George Eliot

Do not be too timid and squeamish about your actions. All life is an
experiment. —Ralph Waldo Emerson, *Journals*

Life itself is . . . a sleep within a sleep. —Ralph Waldo Emerson

One moment of a man's life is a fact so stupendous as to take the lus-
ter out of all fiction. —Ralph Waldo Emerson,
Lectures and Biographical Sketches, "Demonology"

I want you to realize that this whole thing is just a grand adventure.
A fine show. The trick is to play in it and look at it at the same
time. —Edna Ferber, *So Big*

To know life we must detach ourselves from life. —Feuerbach

In three words I can sum up everything I've learned about life. It goes
on. —Robert Frost

Live as you will wish to have lived when you come to die. —Gallert

All life, he had come to understand, was a boring novel.
—John Gardner, *October Light*, Ch. 1

The creature gets sick, his weight grows heavier, he has moments
when he finds himself too weary to go on; yet on he goes, as long
as he lives, on until the end . . .—John Gardner, *October Light*, Ch. 1

Life never presents us with anything which may not be looked upon
as a fresh starting point . . . —André Gide, *The Counterfeiters*

Life is ever / Since man was born, / Licking honey / From a thorn.
—Louis Ginzberg

Daily life is more instructive than the most effective book.
—Johann Wolfgang von Goethe

Life is the childhood of our immortality.
—Johann Wolfgang von Goethe

It has begun to occur to me that life is a stage I'm going through.
—Ellen Goodman

. . . on every important issue life transcends logic and it is folly to
depend on reason alone. —Robert Gordis, *A Faith for Moderns*

. . . what counts in life usually cannot be counted.
                                —Robert Gordis, *A Faith for Moderns*

You notice. And noticing, you live.
                                —John Graves, *From a Limestone Ledge*

Life yields only to the conqueror.   —Dag Hammarskjöld, *Markings*

The time we waste trying to find out what life is all about could be
    spent loving someone and finding out.   —Jack Harris

Ain't it something? Being alive I mean! Ain't it really quite a great
    thing at that?   —Mark Harris, *Bang the Drum Slowly*

The art of life is to know how to enjoy a little and to endure much.
                —William Hazlitt, *Literary Examiner* (English journal),
                                Sep-Dec 1823, "Common Places"

Life is half spent before we know what it is.
                                —George Herbert, *Outlandish Proverbs*

Life is but one continual course of instruction.   —Rowland Hill

The life so short, the craft so long to learn.   —Hippocrates, *Aphorisms*

Life is a romantic business. It is painting a picture, not doing a sum.
        —Oliver Wendell Holmes, Jr., letter to Oswald Ryan, 5 Jun 1911

Life is a great bundle of little things.
        —Oliver Wendell Holmes, Sr., *The Professor at the Breakfast Table*

Life is just one damn thing after another.
                                —Elbert Hubbard, *A Thousand and One Epigrams*

Real life is in love, laughter, and work.   —Elbert Hubbard

Folks, I'm telling you, birthing is hard and dying is mean— so get
    yourself a little loving in between.
                —Langston Hughes, in Arnold Rampersad and David Roessel,
                editors, *The Collected Poems of Langston Hughes*, "Advice"

Life isn't all beer and skittles.
                —Thomas Hughes, *Tom Brown's Schooldays*, Part I, Ch. 2

The great use of life is to spend it for something that will outlast it.
                                —William James

Our life is woven wind. —Joseph Joubert

Life can only be understood backwards; but it must be lived forwards.
—Sören Kierkegaard, *Life*

Oh, how daily life is. —Jules Laforgue

Life is a sexually transmitted disease and there is a 100% mortality
rate. —R. D. Laing

No man is lost while he yet lives. —Louis L'Amour, *The Walking Drum*

We arrive at the various stages of life quite as novices.
—François de La Rochefoucauld

Life is something to do when you can't get to sleep.
—Fran Lebowitz, *Metropolitan Life*

While I thought that I was learning how to live, I have been learning
how to die. —Leonardo da Vinci, *Notebooks*

[Life,] this escalator carrying her from dark into the dark.
—Doris Lessing, *The Memoirs of a Survivor*

I like life. It's something to do. —Sam Levenson

She took walks, and was sensible about shoes and diet. And never did
she feel that she was living. —Sinclair Lewis, *Main Street*, Ch. 1

Life is the gift of God, and is divine. —Henry Wadsworth Longfellow

Ships that pass in the night, and speak each other in passing, / Only a
signal shown and a distant voice in the darkness; / So on the ocean
of life we pass and speak one another, / Only a look and a voice;
then darkness again and a silence.
—Henry Wadsworth Longfellow, *Tales of a Wayside Inn*

Life is meant to be a never-ending education. And when this is fully
appreciated, we are no longer survivors but adventurers.
—David McNally

He . . . blurted, "My goddamn life didn't turn out like I wanted it to."
"Whose does?" she said . . . —Bernard Malamud, *The Natural*

Life is a tragedy full of joy. —Bernard Malamud

The art of living is more like wrestling than dancing.
—Marcus Aurelius Antoninus, *Meditations*

Perform every act in life as if it were your last.
—Marcus Aurelius Antoninus

Thou wilt find rest from vain fancies if thou doest every act in life as though it were thy last.
—Marcus Aurelius Antoninus, *Meditations*, II

What a strange pattern the shuttle of life can weave . . .
—Francis Marion, *Westward the Dream*, Part II, Ch. 14

Life's too damn funny for me to explain.   —Don Marquis

Life is a mission. Every other definition is false, and leads all who accept it astray. Religion, science, philosophy, though still at variance upon many points, all agree in this, that every existence is an aim.   —Mazzini

Life's a voyage that's homeward bound.   —Herman Melville

Life must go on; I forget just why.
—Edna St. Vincent Millay, *Second April*, "Lament"

. . . what thou liv'st / Live well; how long or short permit to Heaven.
—John Milton, *Paradise Lost*, Book XI, 485

Here in the body pent, / Absent from Him I roam, / Yet nightly pitch my moving tent / A day's march nearer home.
—James Montgomery, "At Home in Heaven"

The great business of life is to be, to do, to do without, and to depart.
—John Morley, address on aphorisms, Edinburgh, 1887

Life is like a game of cards. The hand that is dealt you is determinism. The way you play it is free will.   —Jawaharlal Nehru

Looking back, my life seems like one long obstacle race, with me as its chief obstacle.   —Jack Paar

At the point that we give our life [to God], we gain it.
—Ron Parrish, sermon, Hope Chapel, Austin, Texas, 22 Jan 1994

What is laid down, ordered, factual, is never enough to embrace the whole truth; life always spills over the rim of every cup.
—Boris Pasternak

The fever called "living" / Is conquer'd at last.
—Edgar Allan Poe, "For Annie"

Live to explain thy doctrine by thy life. —Matthew Prior

Life is an onion which one peels crying. —Proverb (French)

While there is life, there is hope. —Proverb (Latin)

Life is the greatest bargain; we get it for nothing. —Proverb (Yiddish)

Every day should be passed as if it were to be our last. —Publilius Syrus

The poorest he that is in England hath a life to live as the greatest he.
—Thomas Rainborowe

When people complain of life, it is almost always because they have
asked impossible things from it. —Ernest Renan

As I grow to understand life less and less, I learn to love it more and
more. —Jules Renard

Even when I'm sick and depressed, I love life. —Artur Rubenstein

I long ago came to the conclusion that all life is six to five against.
—Damon Runyon, *Money from Home* (1935), "A Nice Prize"

There is no wealth but life. —John Ruskin, *Unto This Last*

Life is not a spectacle or a feast; it is a predicament.
—George Santayana, *Articles and Essays*

There is no cure for birth and death save to enjoy the interval.
—George Santayana, *Soliloquies in England*, "War Shrines"

In the time of your life, live—so that in that wondrous time you shall
not add to the misery and sorrow of the world, but shall smile to
the infinite delight and mystery of it.
—William Saroyan, "The Time of Your Life"

Life is what happens to us while we are making other plans.
—Allen Saunders, in *Reader's Digest* (Jan 1957), "Quotable Quotes"

Say, what is life? 'Tis to be born / A helpless babe, to greet the light
/ With a sharp wail, as if the morn / Foretold a cloudy noon and
night; / To weep, to sleep, and weep again, / With sunny smiles
between, and then? —J. G. Saxe

Each day is a little life; every waking and rising a little birth, every fresh morning a little youth, every going to rest and sleep a little death.   —Arthur Schopenhauer

The first forty years of life furnish the text, the remaining thirty the commentary.   —Arthur Schopenhauer

The art of living is always to make a good thing out of a bad thing.
                     —E. F. Schumacher, *A Guide for the Perplexed*, Epilogue

By having reverence for life, we enter into a spiritual relation with the world.   —Albert Schweitzer

The man who has become a thinking being feels a compulsion to give to every will-to-live the same reverence for life that he gives to his own.   —Albert Schweitzer

Begin at once to live, and count each separate day as a separate life.
                     —Seneca the Younger, *Moral Letters to Lucilius*, "
                          On the Futility of Planning Ahead"

The web of our life is of a mingled yarn, good and ill together . . .
                     —William Shakespeare, *All's Well that Ends Well*, Act IV, Sc. iii

To each is given a bag of tools, / A shapeless mass and a book of rules, / And each must make, ere life is flown, / A stumbling-block or a stepping-stone. —R. L. Sharpe, "Stumbling-Block or Stepping Stone"

You don't learn to hold your own in the world by standing on guard, but by attacking, and getting well hammered yourself.
                     —George Bernard Shaw, *Getting Married*

Life is God's novel so let him write it.   —Isaac Bashevis Singer

Each person has his special moment of life when he unfolded himself to the fullest, felt to the deepest, and expressed himself to the utmost, to himself and to others.   —Alexander Solzhenitsyn

If so far we have been unable to see clearly or to reflect the eternal lineaments of truth, is it not because we too are still moving towards some end—because we are still alive?
                     —Alexander Solzhenitsyn, *Stories and Prose Poems*, "Reflections"

The essence of life will never be captured by even the greatest of formulas.   —Alexander Solzhenitsyn, *The First Circle*

The most rewarding path of investigation is: "the greatest external resistance in the presence of the least internal resistance."
—Alexander Solzhenitsyn, *The First Circle*

Through His image implanted within me, I share with God a brief terrestrial excursion here on earth. —Rabbi Alexander Alan Steinbach

Everyday life is a stimulating mixture of order and haphazardry. The sun rises and sets on schedule but the wind bloweth where it listeth. —Robert Louis Stevenson, *Virginibus Puerisque*, "Pan's Pipes"

The best things are nearest: breath in your nostrils, light in your eyes, flowers at your feet, duties at your hand, the path of God just before you. —Robert Louis Stevenson

Sit loosely in the saddle of life. —Robert Louis Stevenson

Every human life had its pattern that had to be worked out slowly to its ultimate conclusion. —Irving Stone, *Lust for Life*

God hath given to man a short time here upon earth, and yet upon this short time eternity depends. —Jeremy Taylor

Oh, isn't life a terrible thing, thank God?
—Dylan Thomas, *Under Milk Wood*

It is life near the bone where it is sweetest.
—Henry David Thoreau, *Walden*, "Conclusion"

Love your life, poor as it is. You may perhaps have some pleasant, thrilling, glorious hours, even in a poorhouse. The setting sun is reflected from the windows of the almshouse as brightly as from the rich man's abode.
—Henry David Thoreau, *Walden*, "Conclusion"

My life is like a stroll upon a beach. —Henry David Thoreau,
"A Week on the Concord and Merrimack Rivers"

The faultfinder will find faults even in Paradise. Love your life.
—Henry David Thoreau

Life is a game of whist. From unseen sources / The cards are shuffled, and the hands are dealt. / I do not like the way the cards are shuffled, / But yet I like the game and want to play. —Eugene F. Ware

The confined space I occupy is so minute when compared with the
rest of the universe, where I am not and have no business to be;
and the fraction of time I shall live is so infinitesimal when con-
trasted with eternity, in which I have never been and never shall be
. . . And yet here, in this atom of myself, in this mathematical
point, blood circulates, the brain is active, aspiring to something
too . . .   —Ivan Turgenev, *Fathers and Sons*

How plotless real life was!
                        —Anne Tyler, *Dinner at the Homesick Restaurant*

We never live; we are always in the expectation of living.   —Voltaire

. . . life, by definition, is never still.   —Kurt Vonnegut, Jr., *Bluebeard*

. . . life falls into place only with God.   —H. G. Wells

Our way is not soft grass, it's a mountain path with lots of rocks. But
it goes upward, forward, toward the sun.   —Ruth Westheimer

Life is an offensive, directed against the repetitious mechanism of the
Universe.   —Alfred North Whitehead, *Adventures of Ideas*

Life is ever lord of Death, And Love can never lose its own.
                        —John Greenleaf Whittier, "Snow-Bound"

Life is too important to be taken seriously.   —Oscar Wilde

Life is an unanswered question, but let's still believe in the dignity and
importance of the question.   —Tennessee Williams, *Camino Real*

O joy! that in our embers
Is something that doth live.
                —William Wordsworth, "Intimations of Immortality"

LIGHT

There is not enough darkness in all the world to put out the light of
even one small candle.   —Robert Alden

God's first creature, which was light.
                        —Francis Bacon, *New Atlantis*, Sec. 14

Those who bring sunshine to the lives of others cannot keep it from
themselves.   —Sir James Matthew Barrie

. . . God is light, and in him is no darkness at all.
—*The Bible* (KJV): 1 John 1:5

The light in the world comes principally from two sources,—the sun, and the student's lamp. —Christian Nestell Bovée

It is better to light than to curse the darkness. —Confucius

It's not necessary to blow out your neighbor's light to let your own shine. —M. R. De Haan

The darkness declares the glory of the light.
—T. S. Eliot, *Murder in the Cathedral*

Give light, and the darkness will disappear of itself. —Erasmus

What is to give light must endure burning. —Viktor Frankl

Moonlight is sculpture, sunlight is painting. —Nathaniel Hawthorne

Hail holy light, offspring of Heav'n firstborn!
—John Milton, *Paradise Lost*, Book III

Long is the way / And hard that out of Hell leads up to light.
—John Milton, *Paradise Lost*, Book II, line 432

A tiny spark shines in the dark. —Proverb (French)

When God gives light he gives it for all. —Proverb (Spanish)

God and Nature met in light. —Alfred, Lord Tennyson

L I K E

Like seeks like. —Proverb (French)

L I M I T A T I O N S

The greatest vessel hath but its measure. —Anonymous

Argue for your limitations and sure enough they're yours.
—Richard Bach

Only those who will risk going too far can possibly find out how far one can go. —T. S. Eliot

If you accept your limitations you go beyond them.—Brendan Francis

A good marksman may miss.
>—Thomas Fuller, M. D., *Gnomologia*, No. 163

We have to make peace with our limitations.   —Harold Lindsell

We must learn our limits. We are all something, but none of us are
  everything.   —Blaise Pascal

Don't let what you cannot do interfere with what you can do.
>—John Wooden

Sometimes it is more important to discover what one cannot do, than
  what one can do.   —Lin Yutang

Abraham LINCOLN

Here was a man to hold against the world, / A man to match the
  mountains and the sea.
>—Edwin Markham, "Lincoln, The Man of the People"

His grave a nation's heart shall be,
  His monument a people free.
>—Caroline Mason, "President Lincoln's Grave"

Now he belongs to the ages.   —Edwin M. Stanton,
            upon the death of Abraham Lincoln, 15 Apr 1865

There is no name in all our country's story / So loved as his today:
  / No name which so unites the things of glory / With life's plain,
  common way.   —Robert Whitaker, "Abraham Lincoln"

LISTENING

A good listener is a silent flatterer.   —Anonymous

Though the speaker be a fool, let the hearer be wise.   —Anonymous

Be swift to hear, and with patience give answer.
>—Apocrypha, "Ecclesiasticus"

But people have to be ready to hear, and you have to bide your time.
—Saul Bellow, *More Die of Heartbreak*

Listening, not imitation, may be the sincerest form of flattery.
—Dr. Joyce Brothers

It's just as important to listen to someone with your eyes as it is with your ears.
—Martin Buxbaum

Many a man would rather you heard his story than granted his request.
—Earl of Chesterfield

. . . listen to others, even the dull and ignorant; they too have their story.
—Max Ehrmann, "Desiderata"

A man is already halfway in love with a woman who listens to him.
—Brendan Francis

It takes a great man to make a good listener.
—Arthur Helps

The only way to entertain some folks is to listen to them.
—Frank McKinney ("Kin") Hubbard

Give us grace to listen well.
—John Keble

People will rarely remember your advice, but they will always remember that you listened.
—Cara Lawrence

A good listener is not only popular everywhere, but after a while he knows something.
—Wilson Mizner

Know how to listen, and you will profit even from those who talk badly.
—Plutarch

Listen or your tongue will keep you deaf.
—Proverb (Native American—Blackfoot)

One of the best ways to persuade others is with your ears.
—Dean Rusk

Give every man thine ear, but few thy voice.
—William Shakespeare, *Hamlet*, Act I, Sc. iii

People don't need sex so much as they need to be listened to.
—Jane Wagner

We all know that a sympathetic and intelligent listener not only flatters our vanity, but also frequently enables us to crystallize our own ideas to the best advantage. Why, then, do we so often refuse to perform this service? —Bishop Wilson

Listen so well that you can say what they say. —Tom Zimmermann

LITERATURE

Literature is the question minus the answer. —Roland Barthes

Literature . . . is the rediscovery of childhood.
—George Bataille, *La Littérature et le mal*

Literature is born when something in life goes slightly adrift.
—Simone de Beauvoir, *The Prime of Life*

Literature is the fruit of thinking souls. —Thomas Carlyle

The primary object of a student of literature is to be delighted. His duty is to enjoy himself, his efforts should be directed to developing his faculty of appreciation.
—David Cecil, *The Fine Art of Reading*

Literature is an avenue to glory, ever open for those ingenious men who are deprived of honors or of wealth. —Benjamin Disraeli

The test of literature is, I suppose, whether we ourselves live more intensely for the reading of it . . .
—Elizabeth Drew, *The Modern Novel*,
"Is There a 'Feminine' Fiction?"

Literature is the garden of wisdom. —James Ellis

Literary history and all history is a record of the power of minorities of one. —Ralph Waldo Emerson

Our high respect for a well-read man is praise enough of literature.
—Ralph Waldo Emerson, *Letters and Social Aims*,
"Quotation and Originality"

Literature does not please by moralizing us; it moralizes us because it pleases. —H. W. Garrod

It takes a great deal of history to produce a little literature.
—Henry James, *Life of Nathaniel Hawthorne*

Literature, like a gypsy, to be picturesque, should be a little ragged.
—Douglas William Jerrold, *Literary Men*

Literature is a bad crutch, but a good walking-stick.   —Charles Lamb

Literature is mostly about having sex and not much about having
children; life is the other way round.
—David Lodge, *The British Museum is Falling Down*

Nearly all novels are too long.   —Rose Macaulay, *Potterism*

In literature, as in love, we are astonished at what is chosen by others.
—André Maurois

Literature is news that *stays* news.—Ezra Pound, *ABC of Reading*, Ch. 2

Life without literary studies is death.   —Seneca

But woe to the nation whose literature is cut off by the interposition
of force.   —Alexander Solzhenitsyn, *Nobel Lecture*

[Literature is] the living memory of nations.
—Alexander Solzhenitsyn

The one and only substitute for experience which we have not ourselves had is art, literature. We have been given a miraculous faculty: Despite the differences of language, customs and social
structure we are able to communicate life experience from one
whole nation to another, to communicate a difficult national experience many decades long which the second of the two has never
experienced.   —Alexander Solzhenitsyn, *Nobel Lecture*

Thus, literature, together with language, preserves and protects a
nation's soul.   —Alexander Solzhenitsyn, *Nobel Lecture*

Literature is the daughter of heaven, who descended upon earth to
soften and charm all human ills.   —Bernardin St. Pierre

In literature it is only the wild that attracts us.
—Henry David Thoreau

A classic is something that everybody wants to have read and nobody
wants to read.
—Mark Twain, speech, "The Disappearance of Literature"

To my mind that literature is best and most enduring which is characterized by a noble simplicity.
—Mark Twain, speech, Windsor Hotel, Montreal, 8 Dec 1881

Literature is the immortality of speech.   —Wilmott

LITTLE

Much in little.   —Anonymous

Little drops of water,   little grains of sand, / Make the mighty ocean and the pleasant land. / So the little moments, humble though they be, / Make the mighty ages of eternity.
—Julia A. Carney, "Little Things"

Men live better on little.   —Proverb (Latin)

LOAFING

It is better to have loafed and lost than never to have loafed at all.
—James Thurber

LOGIC

Life eludes logic.   —André Gide

After all, man is a complicated being, why should he be explainable by logic?   —Alexander Solzhenitsyn, *Cancer Ward*

A mind all logic is like a knife all blade. It makes the hand bleed that uses it.   —Rabindranath Tagore, *Stray Birds*

LONELINESS

Wouldn't it be nice if all the people who are lonesome could live in one big dormitory, sleep in beds next to each other, talk, laugh, and keep the lights on as long as they want to?   —Lenny Bruce

The eternal quest of the individual human being is to shatter his loneliness.   —Norman Cousins

The deepest need of man is the need to overcome his separateness, to leave the prison of aloneness.   —Erich Fromm

Once you have lived with another, it is a great torture to have to live alone.   —Carson McCullers, *Ballad of a Sad Cafe*

... we are all terribly alone no matter what people say.
—Bernard Malamud, *The Natural*

Stretch a hand to one unfriended And thy loneliness is ended.
—John Oxenham

Oh lonesome's a bad place / To get crowded into.
—Kenneth Patchen, "Lonesome Boy Blues"

Better be quarreling than lonesome.　　　　　—Proverb (Irish)

The loneliness of the long-distance runner.　　　　—Alan Sillitoe

The soul hardly ever realizes it, but whether he is a believer or not,
his loneliness is really a homesickness for God.
—Hubert van Zeller

LONGING

You could seldom get people to long for what was possible—that was
the cruelty of it.　　　—Saul Bellow, *Mr. Sammler's Planet*, Ch. 6

Besides the pleasure derived from acquired knowledge, there lurks in
the mind of man, and tinged with a shade of sadness, an unsatisfactory longing for something beyond the present, a striving
towards regions yet unknown and unopened.
—Wilhelm von Humboldt

What hidden, hoarded longings there are in all of us.
—John Steinbeck, *Sweet Thursday*, Ch. 27

LOSS

Sometimes the best gain is to lose.　　　　　—George Herbert

In life it is more necessary to lose than to gain. A seed will only ger-
minate if it dies.　　　　　—Boris Pasternak

There are occasions when it is certainly better to lose than to gain.
—Plautus

It is better to lose the saddle than the horse.　　　—Proverb (Italian)

Whatever you lose, reckon of no account.
—Publilius Syrus, *Moral Sayings*

Just think how happy you would be if you lost everything you have
right now, and then got it back again. —Frances Rodman

Looking and not finding is certainly one of the most frustrating ways
to spend time. —Andrew A. Rooney, *Word for Word*

It is not what you have lost, but what you have left that counts.
—Harold Russell

L O V E

Love is a second life . . . —Joseph Addison

Life is short and we have not too much time for gladdening the
hearts of those who are traveling the dark way with us. Oh, be swift
to love! Make haste to be kind! —Henri Frédéric Amiel

Duty makes us do things well, but love makes us do them beautifully.
—Anonymous

I love you not only for what you are, but for what I am when I am
with you. —Anonymous

I love you not only for what you have made of yourself, but for what
you are making of me. —Anonymous

It is not every couple that is a pair. —Anonymous

Love, in fact, can never be deep unless it be pure. —Anonymous

Love is a sweet torment. —Anonymous

Love is a sweet tyrant, because the lover endureth his torments willingly. —Anonymous

Love is like the five loaves and two fishes. It doesn't start to multiply
until you give it away. —Anonymous

Love lightens labor and sweetens sorrow. —Anonymous

Love rules without a sword, / Love binds without a cord. —Anonymous

Lovers' time runs faster than the clock. —Anonymous

Men would be saints if they loved God as they love women.
—Anonymous

Mortal love is but the licking of honey from thorns.
> —Anonymous woman at the court of Eleanor of Aquitaine, 1198,
> in Helen Lawrenson, *Whistling Girl*

The heart that loves is always young. —Anonymous

The test of our love of God is the love we have one for another.
> —Anonymous

To be loved is better than to be famous. —Anonymous

True love is the desire to be encouraging and helpful to others without the thought of recompense. —Anonymous

We must love whomever God has placed in our path. —Anonymous

You only love Jesus as much as the person you love the least.
> —Anonymous

Love is above all else, the gift of oneself.
> —Jean Anouilh, *Ardèle ou la Marguerite*, Act II

Hunger allows no choice / To the citizen or the police; / We must love one another or die. —W. H. Auden, "September 1, 1939"

It is love that asks, that seeks, that knocks, that finds and that is faithful to what it finds. —Saint Augustine

To be beloved, love. —Ausonius, *Epigrams*

Your love has a broken wing if it cannot fly across the sea.
> —Maltbie Davenport Babcock

It is impossible to love and be wise. —Francis Bacon

Love spends his all, and still hath store. —Philip James Bailey, *Festus*

We love because we love. —Honoré de Balzac

Where love is concerned, too much is not even enough.
> —Pierre-Augustin de Beaumarchais

Those have most power to hurt us that we love.
> —Francis Beaumont and John Fletcher,
> *The Maid's Tragedy*, Act V, Sc. iv

Love is ownership. We own whom we love. The universe is God's
because He loves. —Henry Ward Beecher

Love is the wine of existence. —Henry Ward Beecher

A man is only as good as what he loves. —Saul Bellow, *Seize the Day*

Love is the most potent cosmetic . . .
—Saul Bellow, *Mr. Sammler's Planet*, Ch. 1

An exchange occurs between man and woman. Love and thought
complete each other in the human pair, and something like an
exchange of souls takes place, according to the divine plan.
—Saul Bellow, *More Die of Heartbreak*

. . . divine love is not something belonging to God: it is God Himself.
—Henry Bergson

What we love we shall grow to resemble. —Saint Bernard of Clairvaux

. . . for love is strong as death . . .
—*The Bible* (KJV): Song of Solomon 8:6

. . . thou shalt love thy neighbor as thyself.
—*The Bible* (KJV): Matthew 19:19

This is my [Jesus'] commandment, That ye love one another, as I have
loved you. —*The Bible* (KJV): John 15:12

If a man say, I love God, and hateth his brother, he is a liar: for he
that loveth not his brother, whom he hath seen, how can he love
God whom he hath not seen? And this commandment have we
from him, that he who loveth God love his brother also.
—*The Bible* (KJV): 1 John 4:20–21

Love seeketh not itself to please, / Nor for itself hath any care, / But
for another gives its ease, / And builds a Heaven in Hell's despair.
—William Blake, "The Clod and the Pebble"

Who can give law to lovers? Love is a greater law to itself.
—Boethius, *De Consolatione Philosophiae*

Any old woman can love God better than a doctor of theology can.
—Saint Bonaventure

Oh! death will find me, long before I tire / Of watching you . . .
　　　　　　　—Rupert Brooke, "Oh! Death will find me"

An army of lovers shall not fail.　—Rita Mae Brown, "Sappho's Reply"

How do I love thee? Let me count the ways. / I love thee to the depth
　　and breadth and height / My soul can reach . . .
　　　　　—Elizabeth Barrett Browning, *Sonnets from the Portuguese*, #43

Whoso loves believes the impossible.　　—Elizabeth Barrett Browning

Such ever was love's way: to rise, it stoops.
　　　　　　　—Robert Browning, "A Death in the Desert," line 134

Take away love and our world would be a tomb.　—Robert Browning

It is astonishing how little one feels poverty when one loves.
　　　　　　　　　　—Edward Bulwer-Lytton

O, my love's like a red red rose / That's newly sprung in June.
　　　　　—Robert Burns, "My Love is Like a Red Red Rose"

To see her is to love her.　　　　　—Robert Burns, "Bonnie Lesley"

No cord or cable can draw so forcibly, or bind so fast, as love can do
　　with a single thread.　　　　　　　　—Robert Burton

Love! the surviving gift of Heaven, / The choicest sweet of Paradise,
　/ In life's else bitter cup distilled.
　　　　　　　—Thomas Campbell, "Ode to the Memory of Burns"

There are no galley slaves in the royal vessel of divine love—every
　　man works his oar voluntarily.　　　　—Jean Pierre Camus

Love not pleasure; love God. This is the Everlasting Yea, wherein all
　　contradiction is solved . . .　—Thomas Carlyle, *Sartor Resartus*, II, ix

Love is nature's second sun.　　　　—George Chapman, *All Fools*

Love is blind.
　　—Geoffrey Chaucer, *The Canterbury Tales*, "The Merchant's Tale"

The way to love anything is to realize that it might be lost.
　　　　　　　　　　—G. K. Chesterton

Life is too short to be able to love as one should.
　　　　　　　　　　—Christina of Sweden

A man usually falls in love with the woman who asks the kind of
    questions he is able to answer. —Ronald Colman

Love, you know, seeks to make happy rather than to be happy.
    —Ralph Connor

One does not know where love will take you.
    —Pat Conroy, *Beach Music*, Ch. 15

Friendship is love minus sex and plus reason. Love is friendship plus
    sex minus reason. —Mason Cooley

There is no wealth but love. —Marie Corelli

Be of love a little more careful than anything. —e.e. cummings

love did no more begin than love will end . . . —e. e. cummings

O what a heaven is love! O what a hell!
    —Thomas Dekker, *The Honest Whore*, I, i

Love is an egotism of two. —Antoine De La Salle

Gold does not satisfy love; it must be paid in its own coin.
    —Madame Deluzy

I love Mickey Mouse more than any woman I've ever known.
    —Walt Disney, in Walter Wagner, *You Must Remember This*

We are all born for love; it is the principle of existence and its only
    end. —Benjamin Disraeli

Come live with me, and be my love, / And we will some new pleasure
    prove / Of golden sands, and crystal brooks, / With silken lines,
    and silver hooks. —John Donne, "The Bait"

Love built on beauty, soon as beauty, dies.
    —John Donne, *Elegies*, No. 2, "The Anagram," 27

To love someone means to see him as God intended him.
    —Fyodor Dostoyevsky

Her eyes, her lips, her cheeks, her shape, her features, seem to be
    drawn by love's own hand, by love himself in love. —John Dryden

Love is love's reward.   —John Dryden

My love's a noble madness.   —John Dryden, *All for Love*

The pains of love be sweeter far / Than all other pleasures are.
                                                         —John Dryden

The pain of love is the pain of being alive.   —Maureen Duffy, *Wounds*

The love we have in our youth is superficial compared to the love
    that an old man has for his old wife.   —Will Durant

It is a wonderful subduer—this need of love, this hunger of the heart.
                                                        —George Eliot

All mankind love a lover.
            —Ralph Waldo Emerson, *Essays*, *First Series*, "Of Love"

Love that has nothing but beauty to keep it in good health is short-
    lived.   —Erasmus

Love's secret is always to be doing things for God, and not to mind
    because they are such very little ones.   —Frederick William Faber

I don't want to live—I want to love first, and live incidentally.
                                                    —Zelda Fitzgerald

A man is already halfway in love with any woman who listens to
    him.   —Brendan Francis

Love is the only sane and satisfactory answer to the problem of
    human existence.   —Erich Fromm, *The Art of Loving*

Love is an irresistible desire to be irresistibly desired.   —Robert Frost

The strongest evidence of love is sacrifice.   —Caroline Fry

I believe that the sum total of the energy of mankind is not to bring
    us down but to lift us up, and that is the result of the definite, if
    unconscious, working of the law of love. The fact that mankind
    persists shows that the cohesive force is greater than the disruptive
    force, centripetal force greater than centrifugal.—Mahatma Gandhi

To see the universal and all-pervading Spirit of Truth face to face one
    must be able to love the meanest of creation as oneself.
                                                    —Mahatma Gandhi

. . . we have to learn to use that force [love] among all that lives, and in the use of it consists our knowledge of God. Where there is love there is life; hatred leads to destruction.   —Mahatma Gandhi

. . . young people had a right to fall in love as they pleased. It was the most obvious of all lessons of history.
                    —John Gardner, *October Light*, Ch. 1

In love we are all fools alike.   —John Gay

As soon as you cannot keep anything from a woman, you love her.
                    —Paul Geraldy

Love goes without that another may have.   —Rev. J. M. Gibbon

And think not you can direct the course of love, for love, if it finds you worthy, directs your course.   —Kahlil Gibran

Against great advantages in another, there are no means of defending ourselves except love.
          —Johann Wolfgang von Goethe, *Elective Affinities*

Any trifle is enough to entertain two lovers.
                    —Johann Wolfgang von Goethe

Confronted by outstanding merit in another, there is no way of saving one's ego except by love.   —Johann Wolfgang von Goethe

Love concedes in a moment what we can hardly attain by effort after years of toil.   —Johann Wolfgang von Goethe

We are shaped and fashioned by what we love.
                    —Johann Wolfgang von Goethe

We don't get to know anything but what we love.
                    —Johann Wolfgang von Goethe

There is no heaven like mutual love.   —George Granville

As for love—that most passionate of religions—what did anyone really know about it? You did what you had to; that was all.
                    —Judith Guest, *Second Heaven*

None knew thee but to love thee, nor named thee but to praise.
                    —Fitz-Greene Halleck

There is nothing you can do to make God love you more. There is nothing you can do to make God love you less. His love is unconditional, impartial, everlasting, infinite, perfect!
—Richard C. Halverson

And love in the heart wasn't put there to stay; / Love isn't love 'till you give it away. —Oscar Hammerstein II

People need loving the most when they deserve it the least.
—John Harrigan

Love is a hole in the heart. —Ben Hecht

Love is that condition in which the happiness of another person is essential to your own. —Robert Heinlein, *Stranger in a Strange Land*

Love and a cough cannot be hid. —George Herbert

Love makes all hard hearts gentle. —George Herbert

Love rules his kingdom without a sword.
—George Herbert, *Jacula Prudentum*

While faith makes all things possible, it is love that makes all things easy. —Evan Hopkins

The love we give away is the only love we keep.
—Elbert Hubbard, *The Note Book*

The greatest happiness in life is the conviction that we are loved, loved for ourselves, or rather loved in spite of ourselves.
—Victor Hugo

Write me as one that loves his fellow-men.
—James Henry Leigh Hunt, "Abou Ben Adhem and the Angel"

There isn't any formula or method. You learn to love by loving.
—Aldous Huxley

It is hard for the human soul not to love something, and our mind must of necessity be drawn to some kind of affection.
—Saint Jerome, letter to Eustochius

Love is like the measles; we all have to go through it.
—Jerome K. Jerome, *Idle Thoughts on an Idle Fellow*,
"On Being in Love"

It is a beautiful necessity of our nature to love something.
—Douglas William Jerrold

Love doesn't make the world go round—/ Love is what makes the ride worthwhile. —Franklin P. Jones

We should make ourselves loved, for men are only just towards those whom they love. —Joseph Joubert

Where love rules, there is no will to power; and where power predominates, there love is lacking. The one is the shadow of the other.
—Carl Jung

It is not enough to love mankind—you must be able to stand people.
—I. S. Karpunish-Braven, in Alexander Solzhenitsyn,
The Gulag Archipelago Three

My Lord, what love is this that pays so dearly. That I, the guilty one, may go free! —Graham Kendrick, "Amazing Love" (song)

To love another person is to help them love God. —Sören Kierkegaard

Only since I loved is life lovely; only since I loved knew I that I lived.
—Theodor Körner

Love seizes us suddenly, without giving warning, and our disposition or our weakness favors the surprise; one look, one glance, from the fair fixes and determines us. —Jean de La Bruyère

Man, while he loves, is never quite depraved. —Charles Lamb

The heart of him who truly loves is a paradise on earth; he has God in himself, for God is love. —Félicité Lamennais

Loved people are loving people. —Ann Landers

The heart that once has been bathed in love's pure fountain retains the pulse of youth forever. —Walter Savage Landor

He who loves does not dispute: / He who disputes does not love.
—Lao Tzu

There is no disguise which can hide love for long where it exists, or simulate it where it does not.
—François de La Rochefoucauld, *Maximes*

There is only one kind of love, but there are a thousand imitations.
　　　　　　　　　—François de La Rochefoucauld, *Maximes*

Every day should be distinguished by at least one particular act of
　　love.　　　　　　　　　　　　　—Johann Kaspar Lavater

Love doesn't just sit there like a stone; it has to be made, like bread,
　　re-made all the time, made new.
　　　　　　　　　　—Ursula LeGuin, *The Lathe of Heaven*

To love is to find pleasure in the happiness of the person loved.
　　　　　　　　　—Baron Gottfried Wilhelm von Leibnitz

He loved us not because we were lovable but because He is love.
　　　　　　　　　　　—C. S. Lewis, *Membership*

Him that I love, I wish to be / Free— / Even from me.
　　　　　　—Anne Morrow Lindbergh, *The Unicorn* "Even"

Love endures only when the lovers love many things together and
　　not merely each other.　　　　　　　—Walter Lippmann

Love gives itself, but is not bought.
　　　　　　—Henry Wadsworth Longfellow, "Endymion"

Why don't you speak for yourself, John?
　　　　　　　　　—Henry Wadsworth Longfellow,
　　　　　　　　　"The Courtship of Miles Standish"

Two souls with but a single thought, / Two hearts that beat as one.
　　　　　　　—Maria Lovell, "Ingomar the Barbarian"

Those who love are but one step from heaven. —James Russell Lowell

Love lives on, and hath a power to bless when they who loved are
　　hidden in the grave.　　　　　　　　　　—Lowell

. . . But Love can hope where Reason would despair. —Lord Lyttleton

Th' important business of your life is love.　　　—Lord Lyttleton

The love of our neighbor is the only door out of the dungeon of self.
　　　　　　　　　　　　—George Macdonald

. . . If you love somebody, tell them.　　　　　—Rod McKuen

No one has ever loved anyone the way everyone wants to be loved.
—Mignon McLaughlin, *The Neurotic's Notebook*

Love has its roots in sex, but its foliage and flowers are in the pure
light of spirit. —Salvador de Madriaga

Adapt yourself to the environment in which your lot has been cast,
and show true love to the fellow-mortals with whom destiny has
surrounded you. —Marcus Aurelius Antoninus, *Meditations*

In love, as in war, a fortress that parleys is half taken.
—Margaret of Valois

Come live with me, and be my love, / And we will all the pleasures
prove, / That valleys, groves, hills and fields, / Woods or steepy
mountain yields.
—Christopher Marlowe, "The Passionate Shepherd to his Love"

Love cures people—both the ones who give it and the ones who
receive it. —Karl Menninger

Love is the door to eternity. —Thomas Merton

He that would eat of love must eat it where it hangs.
—Edna St. Vincent Millay, *The Harp-Weaver and Other Poems*,
"Never May the Fruit Be Plucked"

Mutual love, the crown of all our bliss. —John Milton

It is not the most lovable individuals who stand more in need of love,
but the most unlovable. —Ashley Montagu

We like someone because. We love someone although.
—Henri de Montherlant

Life! what art thou without love? —E. Moore

There is no surprise more magical than the surprise of being loved. It
is the finger of God on a man's shoulder. —Charles Morgan

Love is the extremely difficult realization that something other than
oneself is real. —Iris Murdoch, "The Sublime and the Good,"
in *Chicago Review*, 1959

. . . but one loves, and when one is on the brink of death, one turns around to look backward, and one says to oneself: "I have often suffered, I have sometimes been wrong, but I have loved."
—Alfred de Musset, *On ne badine pas avec l'amour*

To love is an active verb.
—Ogden Nash, *Many Long Years Ago*, "That Reminds Me"

Love is the greatest of educators.
—Frances Sargent Osgood

The burden becomes light that is shared by love.
—Ovid

with each touch of you i am fresh bread warm and rising.
—Pat Parker, *Movement in Black*, "I Have"

It's God's heart that you walk as people who are loved.
—Ron Parrish, sermon, Hope Chapel, Austin, Texas, 14 May 1994

Two persons who love each other are in a place more holy than the interior of a church.
—William Lyon Phelps

Love is the greatest refreshment in life.
—Pablo Picasso

We all suffer from the preoccupation that there exists . . . in the loved one, perfection.
—Sidney Poitier

Love is not a feeling to be felt, it's an action to be learned.
—John Powell

Be to her virtues very kind; / Be to her faults a little blind.
—Matthew Prior, "An English Padlock"

In the darkest spot on earth / Some love is found.
—Procter

Love lives in cottages as well as in courts.
—Proverb (16th century English proverb)

Love will find a way.
—Proverb (16th century)

Love makes the world go round.
—Proverb (English)

When we cannot get what we love, we must love what is within our reach.
—Proverb (French)

Love rules without rules.
—Proverb (Italian)

Love begets love.　　　　　　　　　　　　—Proverb (Latin)

Love cannot be commanded.　　　　　　　—Proverb (Latin)

He who finds not love finds nothing.　　—Proverb (Spanish)

Love is sweet, but tastes best with bread.　—Proverb (Yiddish)

Love, as much as science, art, and religion, is a mode of cognition.
　　　　—Arnold Rappoport, in Alexander Solzhenitsyn,
　　　　　　　　　　　　　　　　The Gulag Archipelago Three

Women in general want to be loved for what they are and men for
　　what they accomplish.　　　　　　　　—Theodor Reik

Love consists in this: that two solitudes protect and touch and greet
　　each other.　　　　　　　　　　—Rainer Maria Rilke

The time will come when God has assembled a body of people who
　　freely love Him, which will prove beyond any doubt that love is
　　the most powerful force in the universe. With the triumph of love
　　complete, God will then deal with Satan.
　　　—Pat Robertson, *Answers to 200 of Life's Most Probing Questions*

To know her was to love her.　　　　—Samuel Rogers, *Jacqueline*

The giving of love is an education in itself.　　—Eleanor Roosevelt

When love and skill work together expect a miracle.　　—John Ruskin

Physical love is an ephemeral spark designed to kindle in human
　　hearts the flame of a more lasting love.—It is the outer court of the
　　temple.　　　　　　　　　　　　　—Paul Sabatier

Suffering is the true cement of love.　　　　　—Paul Sabatier

Life has taught us that love does not consist in gazing at each other
　　but in looking together in the same direction.
　　　　　　—Antoine de Saint-Exupéry, *Terre des hommes*,
　　　　　　　　　　　translated as *Wind, Sand, and Stars*

God has ordered, that men, being in need of each other, should learn
　　to love each other, and to bear each other's burdens.　—G. A. Sala

To love our neighbor in charity is to love God in man.
　　　　　　　　　　　　　　—Saint Francis de Sales

There is only one happiness in life, to love and be loved.

—George Sand

. . . Love is heaven and claims its own. —Margaret Sangster

. . . the greatest act of love is to pay attention. —Diane Sawyer

In the smallest cottage there is room enough for two lovers.

—Friedrich Schiller

Love shall still be lord of all. —Scott

If you wish to be loved, love. —Seneca

O, that I were a glove upon that hand, / that I might touch that cheek!
—William Shakespeare, *Romeo and Juliet*, Act II, Sc. ii

. . . The course of true love never did run smooth.
—William Shakespeare, *A Midsummer-Night's Dream*, Act I, Sc. i

When love begins to sicken and decay, / It useth an enforced ceremony. / There are no tricks in plain and simple faith.
—William Shakespeare, *Julius Ceasar*, Act IV, Sc. ii

Yet all love is sweet, / Given or returned.
—Percy Shelley, *Prometheus Unbound*, 2, 5, 39

Love is the only weapon we need. —Rev. H. R. L. Sheppard

Love is indestructible, / Its holy flame forever burneth; / From heaven
it came, to heaven returneth.
—Robert Southey, *The Curse of Kehama*, Canto X, Stanza 10

To love her was a liberal education.
—Sir Richard Steele, of Lady Elizabeth Hastings

All the world loves a lover, and a lover loves all the world.
—Anthony Storr, *Solitude: A Return to the Self*

When the satisfaction or the security of another person becomes as
significant to one as one's own satisfaction or security, then the
state of love exists. —Henry Stack Sullivan

To love is to receive a glimpse of heaven. —Karen Sunde

To love deeply in one direction makes us more loving in all others.
—Madame Swetchine

Love's gift cannot be given, it waits to be accepted.
—Rabindranath Tagore, *Fireflies*

While God waits for His temple to be built of love, men bring stones.
—Rabindranath Tagore, *Fireflies*

Take love when love is given. —Sara Teasdale, "Day's Ending"

The greatest pleasure of life is love. —W. Temple

. . . brief is life but love is long.
—Alfred, Lord Tennyson, "The Princess"

'Tis better to have loved and lost / Than never to have love at all.
—Alfred, Lord Tennyson, *In Memoriam A. H. H.*, xxvii

To show great love for God and our neighbor we need not do great
things. It is how much love we put in the doing that makes our
offering something beautiful for God. —Mother Teresa

Love makes fools of us all, big and little.
—William Makepeace Thackeray

When a man is in love with one woman in a family, it is astonishing
how fond he becomes of every person connected with it.
—William Makepeace Thackeray

There is no remedy for love but to love more. —Henry David Thoreau

Love is the strange bewilderment which overtakes one person on
account of another person.
—James Thurber and E. B. White, *Is Sex Necessary?*

The first duty of love is to listen. —Paul Tillich

All, everything that I understand, I understand only because I love.
—Leo Tolstoy, *War and Peace*

Commit no act that is contrary to love. —Leo Tolstoy

. . . she was not only close to him, but . . . he could not now tell
where she ended and he began. —Leo Tolstoy, *Anna Karenina*

We do not love people so much for the good they have done us, as for
the good we have done them. —Leo Tolstoy

Love is a verb. —Sister Mary Tricky

Like anyone in love, she constantly found reasons to mention his
    name.   —Anne Tyler, *Breathing Lessons*

Simply watching her—simply sitting at the kitchen table watching
    her knead a loaf of bread—filled him with contentment.
             —Anne Tyler, *Saint Maybe*, Ch. 10

Money will buy a fine dog, but only love will make him wag his tail.
             —*Ulster* (Northern Ireland) *Post*

A flower cannot blossom without sunshine, and a man cannot live
    without love.   —George P. Upton

Ask the child why it is born; ask the flower why it blossoms; ask the
    sun why it shines. I love you because I must love you.
             —George P. Upton

Love is being stupid together.   —Paul Valéry

. . . for those who love, / Time is not.
        —Henry Van Dyke, "For Katrina's Sun-Dial"

In love and friendship, small, steady payments on a gold basis are
    better than immense promissory notes.   —Henry Van Dyke

The best way to know God is to love many things.
             —Vincent van Gogh

Love conquers all.   —Virgil, *Eclogues*, X.

To love and be loved is to feel the sun from both sides.
    —David Viscott, M. D., *How to Live With Another Person*

Love is where you find it.   —Kurt Vonnegut, Jr., *Slapstick*, Prologue

. . . uncritical love is the only real treasure.
             —Kurt Vonnegut, Jr., *Mother Night*

I think people love each other a little more than they hate each other
    . . . Love has a slim hold on the human corporation, like fifty-one
    per cent, but it's enough.   —Peter de Vries

A man falls in love through his eyes, a woman through her ears.
        —Woodrow Wyatt (Baron Wyatt), *To the Point*

The most wonderful of all things in life, I believe, is the discovery of
another human being with whom one's relationship has a glowing
depth, beauty and joy . . . This inner progressiveness of love
between two human beings is a most marvelous thing, it cannot be
found by looking for it or by passionately wishing for it. It is a sort
of Divine accident. —Hugh Walpole

I love you taller and fatter than the whole universe.
—Brian Alexander Watkins (age 4), said to his parents

Though we cannot think alike, may we not love alike? —John Wesley

Love lights more fires than hate extinguishes.
—Ella Wheeler Wilcox, *Poems of Pleasure* (1888),"Optimism"

To be in love is to surpass oneself.
—Oscar Wilde, *The Picture of Dorian Gray*

The object of love is to serve, not to win. —Woodrow Wilson

Platonic love is love from the neck up. —Thyra Samter Winslow

Love stoops as fondly as he soars. —William Wordsworth,
"On Seeing a Needle Case in the Form of a Harp"

Love before the world did move. —Mary Sidney Wroth

Humble love, and not proud science, keeps the door of heaven.
—Young

L U C K

Luck is not chance— / It's Toil— Fortune's expensive smile / Is earned—.
—Emily Dickinson, "Luck is not chance"

How dare you complain of hard luck if you are strong and well and
whole. —Fletcher

I'm a great believer in luck, and I find the harder I work the more I
have of it. —Thomas Jefferson

The harder you work, the luckier you get. —Gary Player

Don't let good luck fool you or bad luck frighten you.
—Proverb (Russian)

Luck is the residue of design.
>—Branch Rickey, St. Louis Cardinal general manager

We must believe in luck. For how else can we explain the success of
·those we don't like? —Erik Satie

Luck comes to the experienced. —Brian Alexander Watkins (age 10)

L U S T

. . . I say unto you that whosoever looketh on a woman to lust after
her hath committed adultery with her already in his heart.
>—*The Bible* (KJV): Matthew 5:28

I've looked on a lot of women with lust. I've committed adultery in
my heart a number of times. This is something that God recognizes
I will do . . . and God forgives me for it.
>—Jimmy Carter, 1976 *Playboy* interview

L U X U R I E S

Give me the luxuries of life and I will willingly do without the necessities. —Frank Lloyd Wright

L Y I N G

A liar will not be believed, even when he speaks the truth. —Aesop

If lying were a capital crime, / The hangman would work overtime.
>—Anonymous

Falsehood always punishes itself. —Auerbach

Whatever is only almost true is quite false, and among the most dangerous of errors, because being so near truth, it is the more likely to
lead astray. —Henry Ward Beecher

God is not a man, that he should lie . . .
>—*The Bible* (KJV), Numbers 23:19

Parents shouldn't lie to their children—not even when they think it's
for their own good. Even a little lie is dangerous . . . —Pablo Casals

Beware of the half truth. You may have gotten hold of the wrong
half. —Rabbi Seymour L. Essrong

Half the truth is often a great lie.
                    —Benjamin Franklin, *Poor Richard's Almanack*, 1758

It is easy to tell a lie, but hard to tell only one lie.   —Thomas Fuller

You cannot play with falsehood without forfeiting your right to the
    truth, play with cruelty without losing your sensitivity of mind. He
    who wants to keep his garden tidy, doesn't reserve a plot for weeds.
                    —Dag Hammarskjöld

Dare to be true: nothing can need a lie; / A fault, which needs it most,
    grows two thereby.   —George Herbert, *The Church-Porch*

No man has a good enough memory to make a successful liar.
                    —Abraham Lincoln

The trouble with a liar is he can't remember what he said.
                    —Cormac McCarthy, *All the Pretty Horses*, Ch. 4

I do myself a greater injury in lying than I do him of whom I tell a lie.
                    —Michel de Montaigne, *Essays*, "Of Presumption"

One lie must be thatched with another, or it will soon rain through.
                    —Owen

I have seldom known any one who deserted truth in trifles that could
    be trusted in matters of importance.   —William Paley

White lies always introduce others of a darker complexion.
    —William Paley, *The Principles of Moral and Political Philosophy*

Who lies for you will lie against you.   —Proverb (Bosnian)

"They say" is often a great liar.   —Proverb (French)

To tell a falsehood is like the cut of a saber; for though the wound
    may heal, the scar of it will remain.   —Saadi

When my love swears that she is made of truth, I do believe her,
    though I know she lies . . .
                    —William Shakespeare, Sonnet CXXXVIII

Liars ought to have good memories.
                    —Algernon Sidney, *Discourses concerning Government*

A lie never lives to be old.   —Sophocles, *Acrisius*, Fragment 59

He who is false to his fellow-man is also false to his Maker.   —Stahl

The cruelest lies are often told in silence.
—Robert Louis Stevenson, *Virginibus Puerisque,*
"Truth of Intercourse"

If you add to the truth, you subtract from it.   —*The Talmud*

One lie begets another.   —Terence, *Andria*

And he that does one fault at first, / And lies to hide it, makes it two.
—Isaac Watts, *Songs for the Children,* xv, "Against Lying"

Falsehoods not only disagree with truths, but usually quarrel among
themselves.   —Daniel Webster

— M —

MACHINES

Look long on an engine. It is sweet to the eyes.   —MacKnight Black

You can't make anything idiot proof because idiots are so ingenious.
—Ron Burns

The first rule of intelligent tinkering is to save all the parts.
—Paul R. Ehrlich

One machine can do the work of fifty ordinary men. No machine can
do the work of one extraordinary man.
—Elbert Hubbard, *The Philistine*, Vol. xviii

It is only when they go wrong that machines remind you how powerful they are.   —Clive James

You cannot endow even the best machine with initiative; the jolliest
steamroller will not plant flowers.
—Walter Lippmann, *A Preface to Politics* (1914)

The way to get killed around machinery was to take things for
granted.   —Richard McKenna, *The Sand Pebbles*

Gutenberg made everybody a reader. Xerox makes everybody a pub-
lisher.   —Marshall McLuhan

The arithmetical machine produces effects that approach nearer to
thought than all the actions of animals. But it does nothing that
would enable us to attribute will to it, as to the animals.
—Blaise Pascal

Like all country boys they revered machines and understood them.
—Reynolds Price, "The Forseeable Future"

We cannot get grace from gadgets.   —J. B. Priestley

Great engines turn on small pivots.   —Proverb (English)

If it keeps up, man will atrophy all his limbs but the pushbutton finger.
—Frank Lloyd Wright, in *New York Times*, 27 Nov 1955

When I write, I use an Underwood #5 made in 1920. Someone gave
  me an electric typewriter, but there's no use pretending you can
  use machinery that thinks faster than you do. An electric typewriter is ready to go before I have anything to say.
  —Andrew A. Rooney, *And More by Andy Rooney*, Introduction

There is no term comparable to green thumbs to apply to such a
  mechanic, but there should be. For there are men who can look,
  listen, tap, make an adjustment, and a machine works.
  —John Steinbeck, *Cannery Row*

MAJORITY

Nor is the people's judgment always true: / The most may err as
  grossly as the few.   —John Dryden, *Absalom and Achitophel*

A man with God is always in the majority.
  —John Knox, inscription on the Reformation Monument,
  Geneva, Switzerland

The mind of the many is not the mind of God.
  —George Macdonald, *The Flight of the Shadow*

One, on God's side, is a majority.
  —Wendell Phillips, *Speeches*, lecture at Brooklyn,
  New York, 1 Nov 1859

Hain't we got all the fools in town on our side? And ain't that a big
  enough majority in any town?
  —Mark Twain, *The Adventures of Huckleberry Finn*

Whenever you find you are on the side of the majority, it is time to
  pause and reflect.   —Mark Twain

MAKE-UP

You curl your hair and paint your face. Not I: I am curled by the
  wind, painted by the sun.   —Julia de Burgos

Fair Faces need no Paint.
  —Thomas Fuller, M. D., *Gnomologia*, No. 1490

With what hope can we endeavor to persuade the ladies that the time
  spent at the toilet is lost in vanity.   —Samuel Johnson

For whom does the blind man's wife paint herself?
  —Proverb (English)

Let women paint their eyes with tints of chastity.　　—Tertullian

M A L I C E

Malice drinketh up the greater part of its own poison.　　—Socrates

M A N

I am more and more convinced that man is a dangerous creature . . .
　　　　—Abigail Adams, letter to John Adams, 27 Nov 1775

A man without God is like a ship without a rudder.　　—Anonymous

Ten lands are sooner known than one man.　　—Anonymous

Thou hast made us for Thyself, and the heart of man is restless until it
　　finds its rest in Thee.　　　　—Saint Augustine, *Confessions*

Men are like trees: each one must put forth the leaf that is created in
　　him.　　　　—Henry Ward Beecher, in William Drysdale,
　　　　　　　　　　editor, *Proverbs from Plymouth Pulpit*

Man was created a little lower than the angels, and has been getting a
　　little lower ever since.　　　　—Josh Billings

Men are not angels, neither are they brutes.
　　　　—Robert Browning, *Bishop Blougram's Apology*

Man is always on the way.　　—Rudolf Bultmann, "The Future of Man"

Man is in part divine, / A troubled stream from a pure source.
　　　　　　　　—Lord Byron

[Man,] the precious porcelain of human clay.　　—Lord Byron

Man! thou pendulum betwixt a smile and a tear.　　—Lord Byron

Man's unhappiness, as I construe, comes of his greatness; it is because
　　there is an Infinite in him, which with all his cunning he cannot
　　quite bury under the Finite.
　　　　—Thomas Carlyle, *Past and Present*, Book II, Ch. 9

Every man is as Heaven made him, and sometimes a great deal worse.
　　　　—Miguel de Cervantes, *Don Quixote*

Every man is a volume, if you know how to read him.
—William Ellery Channing

Man is a creature of a willful head, / And hardly driven is, but eas'ly led.
—Samuel Daniel, *The Queen's Arcadia*, Act IV, Sc. v

Unless above himself he can / Erect himself, how poor a thing is man!
—Samuel Daniel, "To the Lady Margaret, Countess of Cumberland"

Men are but children of a larger growth.
—John Dryden, *All for Love*, Act IV, Sc. i

A man is a god in ruins.   —Ralph Waldo Emerson

Every man is an impossibility until he is born.
—Ralph Waldo Emerson, *Essays, Second Series*, "Experience"

Man is a piece of the universe made alive.   —Ralph Waldo Emerson

Old boys have their playthings as well as young ones; the difference is
only in the price. —Benjamin Franklin, *Poor Richard's Almanack*,1752

Macho does not prove mucho.   —Zsa Zsa Gabor

Man is creation's masterpiece. But who says so? Man!   —Gavarni

Man is more interesting than men. God made him and not them in
his image. Each one is more precious than all.   —André Gide

Man is greater than a world—than systems of worlds; there is more
mystery in the union of soul with body, than in the creation of the
universe.   —Henry Giles

It is natural to man to regard himself as the final cause of creation.
—Johann Wolfgang von Goethe

Because God is love, He could not completely cast man aside.
—Billy Graham, *World Aflame*

He [man] is both dust of earth and breath of God.
—Billy Graham, *The Hour of Decision*, "Past, Present, and Future"

Man is not an organism; he is an intelligence served by organs.
—W. Hamilton

Man is the only animal that laughs and weeps; for he is the only animal that is struck with the difference between what things are and what they ought to be. —William Hazlitt

Every man is more than just himself; he also represents the unique, the very special and always significant and remarkable point at which the world's phenomena intersect, only once in this way, and never again. —Hermann Hesse

Vaguely at first, then more distinctly, I realized that man is an eternal stranger on this planet. —Eric Hoffer, *First Things, Last Things*

I am mortal, born to love and to suffer. —Friedrich Hölderlin

Man has wants deeper than can be supplied by wealth or nature or domestic affections. His great relations are to his God and to eternity. —Mark Hopkins

Boys'll be boys, and so'll a lot o' middle-aged men.
—Frank McKinney ("Kin") Hubbard,
Abe Martin: Hoss Sense and Nonsense (1926)

Every man is a book in which God himself writes.
—Victor Hugo, *La Vie aux Champs*

The finest fruit earth holds up to its Maker is a finished man.
—Humboldt

Man, biologically considered . . . is simply the most formidable of all beasts of prey, and, indeed, the only one that preys systematically on its own kind. —William James, *Atlantic Monthly*, Dec 1904

Vaster is Man than his works. —Rockwell Kent

Limited in his nature, infinite in his desires, man is a fallen god who remembers the heavens.
—Alphonse de Lamartine, *Méditations poétiques*

Five senses, an incurably abstract intellect, a haphazardly selective memory; a set of preconceptions and assumptions so numerous that I can never examine more than a minority of them—never become even conscious of them all. How much of total reality can such an apparatus let through? —C. S. Lewis, *A Grief Observed*

Man would be otherwise. That is the essence of the specifically
  human.   —Antonio Machado, *Juan de Matrena*

Man must be arched and buttressed from within, else the temple
  wavers to the dust.   —Marcus Aurelius Antoninus

Work, love, and play are the great balance wheels of man's being.
                                           —O. S. Marden

Whoever believes in a man is very foolish.—Marie de France, "Eliduc"

God gave man an upright countenance to survey the heavens, and to
  look upward to the stars.   —Ovid

Man is but a reed, the feeblest thing in nature; but he is a thinking
  reed.   —Blaise Pascal, *Pensées*

[Man,] the glory and the scandal of the universe.   —Blaise Pascal

It takes all sorts to make a world.   —Proverb (17th century)

If Heaven made him—earth can find some use of him.
                                           —Proverb (Chinese)

Man has been lent, not given, to life.   —Publilius Syrus

Gold is Caesar's treasure, man is God's; thy gold hath Caesar's image,
  and thou hast God's.   —Francis Quarles

The more I see of men, the better I like dogs.   —Madame Roland

Man is still the greatest miracle and the greatest problem on this
  earth.   —Gen. David Sarnoff

Wonderful and vast as is the universe, man is greater. The universe
  does not know that it exists; man does. The universe is not free to
  act; man is.   —Martin J. Scott

Every man is odd.
          —William Shakespeare, *Troilus and Cressida*, Act IV, Sc. v

Men should be what they seem.
          —William Shakespeare, *Othello*, Act III, Sc. iii

What a piece of work is man!
—William Shakespeare, *Hamlet*, Act II, Sc. ii

A human being is all hope and impatience.
—Alexander Solzhenitsyn, *The Gulag Archipelago*

Many the wonders but nothing walks stranger than man.
—Sophocles, "Antigone"

Man is a conduit through which heaven flows to earth.
—Rabbi Alexander Alan Steinbach

. . . a man is a very important thing—maybe more important than a
star.   —John Steinbeck, *East of Eden*

Man, unlike any other thing organic or inorganic in the universe,
grows beyond his work, walks up the stairs of his concepts,
emerges ahead of his accomplishments.
—John Steinbeck, *The Grapes of Wrath*, Ch. 14

Man is a complex being: he makes deserts bloom and lakes die.
—Gil Stern

Men may rise on stepping-stones / Of their dead selves to higher
things.   —Alfred, Lord Tennyson, *In Memoriam A. H. H.*

I know of no more encouraging fact than the unquestionable ability
of man to elevate his life by conscious endeavor.
—Henry David Thoreau, *Walden*,
"Where I Lived, and What I Lived For"

Man is but the place where I stand . . .
—Henry David Thoreau, *Journal*, 2 Apr 1852

Man's capacities have never been measured; nor are we to judge of
what he can do by any precedents, so little has been tried.
—Henry David Thoreau, *Walden*, Ch. 1

No man thinks there is much ado about nothing when the ado is
about himself.   —Anthony Trollope

Man is the only animal that blushes. Or needs to.
—Mark Twain, *Following the Equator*, Ch. 27

A man is infinitely more complicated than his thoughts.—Paul Valéry

Tiger got to hunt, / Bird got to fly; / Man got to sit and wonder / "Why, why, why?" / Tiger got to sleep; / Bird got to land; / Man got to tell himself he understand.   —Kurt Vonnegut, Jr., *The Cat's Cradle*

And much it grieved my heart to think / What man has made of man.
—William Wordsworth

Though inland far we be, / Our souls have sight of that immortal sea / Which brought us hither.   —William Wordsworth

MANAGEMENT

Adding manpower to a late project is like getting nine women pregnant in hopes of obtaining a baby in one month.   —Anonymous

Why are we surprised at problems in a world that's run by the kind of people who dominate meetings?   —Alan Harris

In a hierarchy every employee tends to rise to his level of incompetence.
—Laurence J. Peter, *The Peter Principle*

The best executive is the one who has sense enough to pick good men to do what he wants done, and self-restraint enough to keep from meddling with them while they do it.   —Theodore Roosevelt

MANKIND

Everyone in the world is Christ and they are all crucified.
—Sherwood Anderson

All are of the race of God, and have in themselves good.
—Anonymous

There are only the pursued, the pursuing, the busy, and the tired.
—F. Scott Fitzgerald, *The Great Gatsby*

Mankind are earthen jugs with spirits in them.
—Nathaniel Hawthorne,
Passages from the American Notebooks, an 1842 entry

To think ill of mankind, and not wish ill to them, is perhaps the highest wisdom and virtue.   —William Hazlitt, *Characteristics*

If you would love mankind, you should not expect too much of them.   —Helvetius

Mankind has become so much one family that we cannot insure our own prosperity except by insuring that of everyone else.

—Bertrand Russell

The more we realize our minuteness and our impotence in the face of cosmic forces, the more astonishing becomes what human beings have achieved.

—Bertrand Russell

MANNERS

Manners are stronger than laws.

—Alexander Carlile

Good manners are made up of petty sacrifices.

—Ralph Waldo Emerson, *Letters and Social Aims*, "Social Aims"

Savages we call them because their manners differ from ours.

—Benjamin Franklin

The test of good manners is to be patient with bad ones.

—Solomon Ibn Gabiro, *The Choice of Pearls*

They asked Lucman, the Fabulist, From whom did you learn manners? He answered: From the unmannerly.

—Saadi

The great secret, Eliza, is not having bad manners or good manners, but having the same manner for all human souls: in short, behaving as if you were in Heaven, where there are no third-class carriages, and one soul is as good as another.

—George Bernard Shaw, *Pygmalion*

Good manners is the art of making those people easy with whom we converse.

—Jonathan Swift

Suit your manner to the man.

—Terence, *Adelphi*

Good manners and soft words have brought many a difficult thing to pass.

—Sir John Vanbrugh

MARRIAGE

Those marriages generally abound most with love and constancy that are preceded by a long courtship. The passion should strike root and gather strength before marriage be grafted on it.

—Joseph Addison, *The Spectator*

He felt rather vainly sure that he did indeed look very nice, to her
anyhow, and that was all he cared about.
                    —James Agee, *A Death in the Family*

A husband is one who lays down the law to his life and then accepts
all the amendments.   —Anonymous

A perfect wife is one who doesn't expect a perfect husband.
                                        —Anonymous

Every man can rule a shrew save he that has her.   —Anonymous

He who does not honor his wife dishonors himself.   —Anonymous

He who has a good wife can bear any evil.   —Anonymous

One of the chief pleasures of middle age is looking back at the people
you didn't marry.   —Anonymous

I have learned only two things are necessary to keep one's wife
happy. First let her think she is having her own way. Second, let
her have it.   —Antony Armstrong-Jones

I married beneath me—all women do.
                    —Nancy Astor, speech, Oldham, England, 1951

Wives are young men's mistresses; companions for middle age; and
old men's nurses.
            —Francis Bacon, *Essays*, "Of Marriage and Single Life"

Everyone all over the world takes a wife's estimate into account in
forming an opinion of a man.   —Honoré de Balzac

Every man who is high up loves to think that he has done it all himself, and the wife smiles, and lets it go at that.
        —Sir James Matthew Barrie, *What Every Woman Knows*, Act IV

Marriage is our last best chance to grow up.   —Rev. Joseph Barth

'Tis Love alone can make our fetters please.
                    —Aphra Behn, "Love and Marriage"

And the Lord God said, It is not good that the man should be alone; I
will make him an help meet for him.—*The Bible* (KJV): Genesis 2:18

A virtuous woman is a crown to her husband . . .
—The Bible (KJV): Proverbs 12:4

Whoso findeth a wife findeth a good thing, and obtaineth favor of the Lord.
—The Bible (KJV): Proverbs 18:22

. . . What therefore God hath joined together, let not man put asunder.
—The Bible (KJV): Matthew 19:6

To have and to hold from this day forward, for better, for worse, for richer, for poorer, in sickness, and in health, to love and to cherish, till death do us part.
—Book of Common Prayer

Success in marriage is more than finding the right person: it is a matter of being the right person.
—Rabbi B. R. Brickner

Marriage is not just spiritual communion, it is also remembering to take out the trash.
—Dr. Joyce Brothers

The only real argument for marriage is that it remains the best method for getting acquainted.
—Heywood Broun

How much there was of this woman he did not know!
—Pearl S. Buck, *The Good Earth*, Ch. 11

Rarely are marriages wrecked on a big rock of adversity. It is on the small pebbles that they founder.
—Velora Buscher

Marriage is a result of the longing for the deep, deep peace of the double bed after the hurly-burly of the chaise-lounge.
—Mrs. Patrick Campbell (Beatrice Stellar Tanner)

Nobody knows how to manage a wife but a bachelor.
—George Colman (the elder), *The Jealous Wife*, IV

A wife of your own stature is the greatest of all blessings.
—Eugène Delacroix

We meet in society many attractive women whom we would fear to make our wives.
—D'Harleville

Never go to bed mad. Stay up and fight.
—Phyllis Diller, *Phyllis Diller's Housekeeping Hints*

. . . you can never be sure of what has passed between husband and wife or lover and mistress.
—Fyodor Dostoyevsky, *Crime and Punishment*

A sound marriage is not based on complete frankness; it is based on a sensible reticence. —Morris L. Ernst

They err, who say that husbands can't be lovers. —Anne Finch

Keep your eyes wide open before marriage, half shut afterwards.
—Benjamin Franklin

For a wife take the daughter of a good mother. —Thomas Fuller

He knows little who will tell his wife all he knows. —Thomas Fuller

A wife is not to be chosen by the eye only. Choose a wife rather by your ear than your eye.
—Thomas Fuller, M. D., *Gnomologia*, No. 1107

He that speaks ill of his wife dishonors himself.
—Thomas Fuller, M. D., *Gnomologia*

Marriage is a lot like the army, everyone complains, but you'd be surprised at the large number that re-enlist. —James Garner

A wife is a gift bestowed upon a man to reconcile him to the loss of paradise. —Johann Wolfgang von Goethe

Matrimony,—the high sea for which no compass has yet been invented. —Heine

A good wife maketh a good husband. —John Heywood, *Proverbs*

That there is something intrinsically sacred in the marriage contract is evidenced by the fact that all religions, even the most corrupt, always have regarded it as such and surrounded it with religious rites and ceremonies. —K. J. I. Hochban

Marriage itself is not solely an institution for the propagation of children, but is also for the fruition of that richer fellowship God intended when he saw that it was not good for man to live alone.
—George G. Hockman, *Religion in Modern Life*

Of all the home remedies, a good wife is best.
—Frank McKinney ("Kin") Hubbard

He had marveled at how it was that of all the potential pairs on this earth he and she had found each other as unerringly as lock and key. —William Humphrey, "A Heart in Hiding"

Heaven will be no heaven to me if I do not meet my wife there.
—Andrew Jackson

Marriage has many pains, but celibacy has no pleasures.
—Samuel Johnson, *Rasselas*, Ch. 26

One should choose for a wife only such a woman as he would choose for a friend, were she a man. —Joseph Joubert

Marriage, friends, is a lifelong feast; love is no light lunch.
—Garrison Keillor, *We Are Still Married*

Marrying a man is like buying something you've been admiring for a long time in a shop window. You may love it when you get it home, but it doesn't always go with everything else in the house.
—Jean Kerr, *The Snake Has All the Lines*,
"The Ten Worst Things About a Man"

A world of comfort in that one word, wife. —Knowles

The honeymoon is over when he phones to say he'll be late for supper and she's already left a note that it's in the refrigerator.
—Bill Lawrence

Marriage is the learning of someone else's habits.
—Laurel Lee, *Godspeed: Hitchhiking Home*

What counts in making a happy marriage is not so much how compatible you are, but how you deal with incompatibility.
—George Levinger

There's nothing like a good dose of another woman to make a man appreciate his wife. —Clare Booth Luce

Marriages are made in heaven. —John Lyly

A successful marriage requires falling in love many times, always with the same person.
—Mignon McLaughlin, *The Second Neurotic's Notebook*

A happy marriage is a long conversation that always seems too short.
—André Maurois

Marriage is an edifice that must be rebuilt every day. —André Maurois

A man may be a fool and not know it—but not if he is married.
—H. L. Mencken

Often the difference between a successful marriage and a mediocre one consists of leaving about three or four things a day unsaid.
—Harlan Miller

A great marriage is not so much finding the right person as *being* the right person. —Marabel Morgan, *The Total Woman*

At the beginning of a marriage ask yourself whether this woman will be interesting to talk to from now until old age. Everything else in marriage is transitory: most of the time is spent in conversation.
—Friedrich Nietzsche

It is not lack of love but lack of friendship that makes unhappy marriages. —Friedrich Nietzsche

Marriage is a fine and sacred thing if you make it so.
—William Lyon Phelps

All other goods by Fortune's hands are given; / A wife is the peculiar gift of heaven. —Alexander Pope, "January and May"

The secret of happy marriage is simple: Just keep on being as polite to one another as you are to your friends. —Robert Quillen

The ritual of marriage is not simply a social event; it is a crossing of threads in the fabric of fate. Many strands bring the couple and their families together and spin their lives into a fabric that is woven on their children.
—from Portuguese-Jewish wedding ceremony

Marry in haste and repent at leisure. —Proverb (16th century)

A man without a wife is like a vase without flowers.
—Proverb (Cape Verde Islands)

Choose your wife, not at a dance, but in the harvest field.
—Proverb (Czechoslavakian)

In buying a horse and taking a wife, shut your eyes and commend yourself to God. —Proverb (Italian)

He that has a wife has a master.   —Proverb (Scottish)

Marry and grow tame.   —Proverb (Spanish)

A happy marriage is the union of two good forgivers.—Robert Quillen

A good marriage is that in which each appoints the other guardian of
his solitude.   —Rainer Maria Rilke,
letter to Paula Modersohn Becker, 12 Feb 1902

A married couple are well suited when both partners usually feel the
need for a quarrel at the same time.   —Jean Rostand, *Le Mariage*

Marriage simplifies life and complicates the day.   —Jean Rostand

It isn't tying himself to one woman that a man dreads when he
thinks of marrying, it's separating himself from all the others.
—Helen Rowland

Love, the quest; marriage, the conquest; divorce, the inquest.
—Helen Rowland, *A Guide to Men*

It takes two to make a marriage a success and only one to make it a
failure.   —Herbert Samuel

The happiness of married life depends upon making small sacrifices
with readiness and cheerfulness.   —John Selden

Like fingerprints, all marriages are different.   —George Bernard Shaw

A person's character is but half formed till after wedlock.
—Charles Simmons

If they lost the incredible conviction that they can change their wives
or their husbands, marriage would collapse at once.
—Logan Pearsall Smith

By all means marry: If you get a good wife, you'll become happy; if
you get a bad one, you'll become a philosopher.   —Socrates

Teacher, tender comrade, wife, / A fellow-farer true through life.
—Robert Louis Stevenson

[When asked who wore the pants in his house:] I do, and I also wash
and iron them.   —Dennis Thatcher, husband of Margaret Thatcher

My wife is the rest of me. I am the rest of her.   —Lewis Timberlake

My wife makes me better than I am.   —Lewis Timberlake

. . . it is a fact universally acknowledged that a husband is the most ridiculous thing on earth, except for a bachelor.
—Peter de Vries, *Forever Panting*

The world well tried, the sweetest thing in life / Is the unclouded welcome of a wife.   —Nathaniel Parker Willis, "Lady Jane"

MARTYRS

It is the cause, and not the death, that makes the martyr.
—Napoleon Bonaparte

There are daily martyrdoms occurring of more or less self-abnegation, and of which the world knows nothing.   —Edwin Hubbel Chapin

He is no fool who gives what he cannot keep to gain what he cannot lose.   —Jim Elliot, martyred by South American Indians
in the mid 1950's

The tyrant dies and his rule is over; the martyr dies and his rule begins.   —Sören Kierkegaard

It is more difficult, and calls for higher energies of soul, to live a martyr than to die one.   —Horace Mann

MASTERS

He that is master must serve.   —Anonymous

Little is done when every man is master.   —Anonymous

Masters two / Will not do.   —Anonymous

No man can serve two masters . . .   —*The Bible* (KJV): Matthew 6:24

The master sometimes serves, and the servant sometimes is master.
—Cicero, *Pro Rege Deiotaro*

If thou art a master, be sometimes blind; if a servant, sometimes deaf.
—Thomas Fuller

All men would be masters of others, and no man is lord of himself.
—Johann Wolfgang von Goethe

No man is good enough to be another man's master.
—George Bernard Shaw, *Major Barbara*, 3

MATHEMATICS

By studying the masters—not their pupils.
—Niels Henrik Abel, Norwegian mathematician, explaining how
he had become a great mathematician at such a young age

Among mathematicians, the real world is a special case.
—Anonymous

Mathematics is the bell-boy of all sciences. —Anonymous

Mathematics is the door and key to the sciences.
—Roger Bacon, *Opus Majus*

Most geometricians, chemists, mathematicians, and great scientists
submit religion to reason only to discover a problem as unsolvable
as that of squaring a circle. —Honoré de Balzac

We used to think that if we knew one, we knew two, because one and
one are two. We are finding that we must learn a great deal more
about "and." —Sir Arthur Eddington, in Alan L. Mackay,
The Harvest of a Quiet Eye

God does not care about our mathematical difficulties. He integrates
empirically. —Albert Einstein

. . . mathematics . . . affords the exact natural sciences a certain measure of certainty, to which without mathematics they could not
attain. —Albert Einstein, *Ideas and Opinions*

A line is length without breadth. —Euclid, *Elements*

QED — Quod erat demonstrandum.
—Euclid, Greek for "Which was to be proved."
This phrase is used at the end of mathematical proofs.

There is no 'royal road' to geometry.
—Euclid, said to Ptolemy I when this prince asked for an
easier way, in Proclus, *Commentary on Euclid*

Math is the alphabet in which God has written the universe.
—Galileo Galilei

Mathematics is the queen of the sciences.
—Carl Friedrich Gauss, in Sartorius von Walterhausen,
Gauss zum Gedachtniss

About binomial theorem I'm teeming with a lot o' news, / With many
cheerful facts about the square of the hypotenuse. / I'm very good
at integral and differential calculus, / I know the scientific names
of beings animalculous; / In short, in matters vegetable, animal,
and mineral, / I am the very model of a modern Major-General.
—W. S. Gilbert, *The Pirates of Penzance*, I

2 is not equal to 3, not even for large values of 2.   —Grabel's Law

Good mathematics is not how many answers you know, but how you
behave when you don't know the answer.   —H. Hansen

Equations are just the boring part of mathematics. I attempt to see
things in terms of geometry.   —Stephen Hawking

Mathematics is the language of size.
—Lancelot Hogben, *Mathematics for the Million*

Stand firm in your refusal to remain conscious during algebra. In real
life, I assure you, there is no such thing as algebra.
—Fran Lebowitz, *Social Studies*, "Tips for Teens"

The peculiarity of the evidence of mathematical truths is that all the
argument is on one side.   —John Stuart Mill, *On Liberty*

. . . the knowledge of numbers is one of the chief distinctions
between us and the brutes.
—Mary Wortley Montagu, letter to her daughter,
Countess of Bute, 28 Jan 1753

Before a kid learns how to use a computer that can solve mathematical problems, he or she should know how to do arithmetic without
a computer.   —Andrew A. Rooney, *Word for Word*, "Back to Basics"

I'd like to take some calculus, too. I have absolutely no ability in that
direction and not much interest, either, but there's something
going on in mathematics that I don't understand, and I'd like to
find out what it is.   —Andrew A. Rooney, *And More by Andy Rooney*,
"Returning to College"

Numbers are the most certain things we have.
—Andrew A. Rooney, *Word for Word*, "Gaining Entrance"

Numbers tend to give the impression that there's more order in the world than there is.
—Andrew A. Rooney, *Word for Word*, "School Days"

Mathematics, rightly viewed, possesses not only truth, but supreme beauty—a beauty cold and austere, like that of sculpture.
—Bertrand Russell, *Philosophical Essays*, No. 4

Mathematics takes us into the region of absolute necessity, to which not only the actual world, but every possible world, must conform.
—Bertrand Russell, *The Study of Mathematics*

There are no sects in geometry.   —Voltaire

We had tortured circles until they coughed up their secret lives: π.
—Kurt Vonnegut, Jr., *Breakfast of Champions*

A curved line is the loveliest distance between two points.—Mae West

Numbers constitute the only universal language.
—Nathanael West, *Miss Lonely Hearts*

The science of pure mathematics, in its modern developments, may claim to be the most original creation of the human spirit.
—Alfred North Whitehead, *Science and the Modern World* (1925)

MATURITY

Maturity is the art of living in peace with that which we cannot change.   —Anonymous

You grow up the day you have your first real laugh at yourself.
—Ethel Barrymore

Maturity is the capacity to endure uncertainty.   —John Finley

Maturity begins when you feel you are right about something without feeling the need to prove someone else wrong.
—Sydney J. Harris

We have not passed that subtle line between childhood and adulthood until we move from the passive voice to the active voice—that is, until we have stopped saying "It got lost," and say, "I lost it."   —Sydney J. Harris, *On the Contrary*, 7

The turning point in the process of growing up is when you discover the core of strength within you that survives all hurt. —Max Lerner

Growing up is after all only the understanding that one's unique and incredible experience is what everyone shares.   —Doris Lessing

. . . in due time she would fill like a container with substances and experiences. . . . she would become mature, that ideal condition envisaged as the justification of all previous experience, an apex of achievement, inevitable and peculiar to her. This apex is how we see things; it is a biological summit we see: growth, the achievement on the top of the curve of her existence, then a falling away towards death.   —Doris Lessing, *The Memoirs of a Survivor*

A person remains immature, whatever his age, as long as he thinks of himself as an exception to the human race.   —Harry A. Overstreet

That's maturity—when you realize that you've finally arrived at a state of ignorance as profound as your parents.
     —Elizabeth Peters, *The Night of Four Hundred Rabbits*

If you want a place in the sun, you must leave the shade of the family tree.   —Proverb (Native American—Osage)

Maturity consists of no longer being taken in by oneself.
     —Kajetan von Schlaggenberg

The mark of the immature man is that he wants to die nobly for a cause, while the mark of a mature man is that he wants to live humbly for one.   —Wilhelm Stekel

A child becomes an adult when he realizes that he has a right not only to be right but also to be wrong.
     —Thomas Szasz, *The Second Sin*, "Childhood"

One sign of maturity is knowing when to ask for help.
     —Dennis Wholey

MEALS

"Supper's ready" really meant "Somebody loves you."
     —Dr. Richard E. Eby, *Tell Them I Am Coming*, Foreword

All happiness depends upon a leisurely breakfast.   —John Gunther

A man seldom thinks with more earnestness of anything than he does of his dinner.   —Samuel Johnson

Spread the table and contention will cease.   —Proverb (English)

A dinner lubricates business.
—William Scott, in James Boswell, *Life of Samuel Johnson*

Life is uncertain. Eat dessert first. —Ernestine Ulmer

MEANING

Man can only find meaning for his existence in something outside
himself. —Viktor Frankl

In the heart of the God of the universe, each child of his is as necessary to him as the fingers are to the hand.—In the marvelous
design of the universe, not even a sparrow can fall to earth mean-
inglessly . . . —Toyohiko Kagawa, *Meditations on the Cross*

Man—a being in search of meaning. —Plato

Health alone does not suffice. To be happy, to become creative, man
must always be strengthened by faith in the meaning of his own
existence. —Stefan Zweig

MEANNESS

I've met little meanness, wherever I went.
—Reynolds Price, *The Forseeable Future*, "The Face of the Moon"

The MEDIA

One of the things the news media does very well is to make a minority look like a majority. —Anonymous

The most important service rendered by the press is that of educating
people to approach printed matter with distrust.
—Samuel Butler (1835-1902)

It's not the world that's got so much worse but the news coverage
that's got so much better. —G. K. Chesterton

The medium is the message.
—Marshall McLuhan, *Understanding Media*

I don't need the news. If they have a war, I figure someone will tell
me. —Bum Phillips, former NFL coach, *Los Angeles Times*, 1986

MEDICINE

I find the medicine worse than the malady.
> —Francis Beaumont and John Fletcher,
> *The Lover's Progress*, Act III, Sc. ii

Doctors think a lot of patients are cured who have simply quit in disgust. —Don Herold

Medicines are nothing in themselves, if not properly used, but the very hands of the gods, if employed with reason and prudence.
> —Herophilus

To do nothing is also a good remedy. —Hippocrates

Modern science is still trying to produce a tranquilizer more effective than a few kind words. —Douglas Meador

Time is generally the best doctor. —Ovid

I dressed his wounds; God healed him. —Ambroise Paré

Who shall decide when doctors disagree?
> Alexander Pope, *Epistles to Several Persons*, "To Lord Bathurst"

No man is a good physician who has never been sick.—Proverb (Arab)

The surgeon practices on the orphan's head. —Proverb (Arab)

The physician cannot prescribe by letter, he must feel the pulse.
> —Seneca, *Epistuloe ad Lucilium*

Our doctor would never really operate unless it was necessary. He was just that way. If he didn't need the money, he wouldn't lay a hand on you. —Herb Shriner

When you hear hoofbeats, think of horses before zebras.
> —Harley S. Smyth, medical maxim

There are worse occupations in this world than feeling a woman's pulse. —Laurence Sterne, *A Sentimental Journey*, "The Pulse"

A physician is one who pours drugs of which he knows little into a body of which he knows less. —Voltaire

The art of medicine consists of amusing the patient while nature
cures the disease. —Voltaire

Choose your specialist and you choose your disease.
—*The Westminster Gazette*, 18 May 1906

It should be the function of medicine to have people die young as
late as possible. —Ernest L. Wynder

There is a great difference between a good physician and a bad one;
yet very little between a good one and none at all. —Arthur Young

MEDIOCRITY

Some men are born mediocre, some men achieve mediocrity, and
some men have mediocrity thrust upon them.
—Joseph Heller, *Catch 22*

Women want mediocre men, and men are working to become as
mediocre as possible. —Margaret Mead

MEEKNESS

The meek shall inherit the earth—if that's all right with you.
—Anonymous, graffiti

A meek fellow . . . is a real godsend in any gang.
—Alexander Solzhenitsyn, *One Day in the Life of Ivan Denisovich*

MELANCHOLY

All my joys to this are folly, / Naught so sweet as Melancholy.
—Robert Burton, *The Anatomy of Melancholy*

Melancholy is the pleasure of being sad. —Victor Hugo

If you are melancholy for the first time, you will find, upon a little
inquiry, that others have been melancholy many times, and yet are
cheerful now. —Leigh Hunt

MEMBERSHIP

Every uniform corrupts one's character.
—Max Frisch, *Tagebuch* (Diary), 1948

MEMORY

How is it that we remember the least triviality that happens to us,
and yet not remember how often we have recounted it to the same
person?   —Anonymous

God gave us our memories so that we might have roses in December.
—Sir James Matthew Barrie,
Rectoral Address at St. Andrew's, 3 May 1922

The mind's cross-indexing puts the best librarian to shame.
—Sharon Begley, *Newsweek*, 29 Sep 1986, "Memory: Science
Achieves Important New Insights into the Mother of the Muses"

Everybody needs his memories. They keep the wolf of insignificance
from the door.   —Saul Bellow, *Mr. Sammler's Planet*, Ch. 5

A bad memory is the mother of invention.
—Gerald Brenan, *Thoughts in a Dry Season: A Miscellany*, "Life"

Memory is the thing you forget with. —Alexander Chase, *Perspectives*

It is pleasant to recall in happier days the troubles of the past.
—Cicero, *Epistolae and Familiares*

The remembrance of past memory is sweet.   —Cicero, *De Finibus*

Of all the faculties of the mind, memory is the first that flourishes
and the first that dies.   —Charles Caleb Colton

A man should keep his little brain attic stocked with all the furniture
that he is likely to use, and the rest he can put away in the lumber-
room of his library, where he can get it if he wants it.
—Sir Arthur Conan Doyle, *The Adventures of Sherlock Holmes*,
"The Five Orange Pips"

We do not know the true value of our moments until they have
undergone the test of memory.
—Georges Duhamel, *The Heart's Domain*

How sweet to remember the trouble that is past.   —Euripides

Memory believes before knowing remembers.
—William Faulkner, *Light in August*

Unless we remember we cannot understand.   —E. M. Forster

Write injuries in dust, benefits in marble.   —Benjamin Franklin

O Memory! thou fond deceiver.
                    —Oliver Goldsmith, *The Captivity: An Oratorio*, Act I

In a thousand years we shall all forget / The things that trouble us
     now.
                    —Adam Lindsay Gordon, "After the Quarrel"

The number of things I do not remember or maybe never knew or am
     only in the foggiest haze is quite amazing.
                    —Mark Harris, *Bang the Drum Slowly*

'Tis sweet to think on what was hard t' endure.
                    —Robert Herrick, *Satisfaction for the Suffering*

Every man's memory is his private literature.   —Aldous Huxley

You think you have a memory; but it has you!
                    —John Irving, *A Prayer for Owen Meany*

To be able to enjoy one's past life is to live twice.   —Martial, *Epigrams*

Memory inevitably romanticizes, pressing reality to recede like pain.
                    —Arthur Miller, *Timebends*

The brain heals the past like an injury . . .   —Arthur Miller, *Timebends*

Of all liars, the smoothest and most convincing is memory.
                    —Olin Miller

The advantage of a bad memory is that, several times over, one
     enjoys the same good things for the first time.
                    —Friedrich Nietzsche, *Human, All Too Human* (1878)

Memory is a great betrayer.   —Anaïs Nin, letter to Geismar

Memory is a crazy woman who hoards colored rags and throws away
     food.   —Austin O'Malley

I can understand that memory must be selective, else it would choke
     on the glut of experience. What I cannot understand is why it
     selects what it does.   —Virgilia Peterson, *A Matter of Life and Death*

The palest ink is better than the best memory.   —Proverb (Chinese)

Ah! how pleasant it is to remember!   —Proverb (Latin)

I have a remarkable memory; I forget everything. It is wonderfully
    convenient. It is as though the world were constantly renewing
    itself for me.   —Jules Renard

The test of an enjoyment is the remembrance which it leaves behind.
                                                —Jean Paul Richter

Things that were hard to bear are sweet to remember.
                                        —Seneca, *Hercules Furens*

This is the law of benefits between men; the one ought to forget at
    once what was given, and the other ought never to forget what he
    has received.   —Seneca

Own only what you can always carry with you: know languages,
    know countries, know people. Let your memory be your travel bag.
    Use your memory! Use your memory! It is those bitter seeds alone
    which might sprout and grow someday.
            —Alexander Solzhenitsyn, *The Gulag Archipelago*

I've a grand memory for forgetting . . .
                —Robert Louis Stevenson, *Kidnapped*, Ch. 18

Astonishing things can be done with the human memory if you will
    devote it faithfully to one particular line of business.
                        —Mark Twain, *Life on the Mississippi*

It isn't so astonishing, the number of things that I can remember, as
    the number of things I can remember that aren't so. —Mark Twain

Perhaps even these things will some day be pleasant to remember.
                            —Virgil, *Aeneid*, Book I, line 203

What memories for mud to have.
                        —Kurt Vonnegut, Jr., *The Cat's Cradle*

The memory of the just survives in Heaven.
            —William Wordsworth, *The Excursion*, Book VII, line 388

MEN and WOMEN

The woman who is known only through a man is known wrong.
                —Henry Adams, *The Education of Henry Adams* (1907)

When a man becomes familiar with his goddess, she quickly sinks
    into a woman.   —Joseph Addison

Men are nicer to the women they don't marry.   —Anonymous

Women like silent men. They think they're listening.
                            —Marcel Archard, *Quote*, 4 Nov 1956

Instead of getting hard ourselves, women should try and give their
    best qualities—bring them softness, teach them how to cry.
                                                    —Joan Baez

Being a woman is a terribly difficult trade, since it consists principally
    of dealing with men.   —Joseph Conrad

Men's minds are raised to the level of the women with whom they
    associate . . .   —Alexandre Dumas

Venus, thy eternal sway all the race of men obey.   —Euripides

Never try to impress a woman, because if you do she'll expect you to
    keep up to the standard for the rest of your life.   —W. C. Fields

If the heart of a man is deprest with cares, / The mist is dispell'd when
    a woman appears.   —John Gay, *The Beggar's Opera*, Act II, Sc. iii

It's the woman who chooses the man who will choose her.
                                                    —Paul Geraldy

Nothing more surely cultivates and embellishes a man than associa-
    tion with refined and virtuous women.   —William Gladstone

A noble man is led by woman's gentle words.
                            —Johann Wolfgang von Goethe

The most precious possession that ever comes to a man in this world
    is a woman's heart.
            —Josiah Gilbert Holland, *Lessons of Life*, "Perverseness"

Man has his will,—but woman has her way.
                                —Oliver Wendell Holmes, Sr.,
                    The Autocrat of the Breakfast Table, Prologue

A man is as good as he has to be, and a woman is as bad as she dares.
    —Elbert Hubbard, *The Roycroft Dictionary and Book of Epigrams*

If it was woman who put man out of Paradise, it is still woman, and woman only, who can lead him back.
—Elbert Hubbard, *The Roycroft Dictionary and Book of Epigrams*

Women receive the insults of men with tolerance, having been bitten in the nipple by their toothless gums.
—Dilys Laing, *Collected Poems*, "Veterans"

Women who seek to be equal with men lack ambition.
—Timothy Leary

As unto the bow the cord is,/ So unto the man is woman; / Though she bends him she obeys him, / Though she draws him, yet she follows, / Useless each without the other!
—Henry Wadsworth Longfellow, "Hiawatha"

The great fault in women is to desire to be like men.
—Joseph de Maistre

Woman is the Sunday of man; not his repose only, but his joy; the salt of his life.
—Michelet

. . . to hold the body of women in our arms is . . . the one ecstasy granted to the race of men.
—Ayn Rand, *Anthem*

Men and women are like right and left hands: it doesn't make sense not to use both.
—Jeannette Rankin

Even the wisest men make fools of themselves about women, and even the most foolish women are wise about men.
—Theodor Reik

There is on earth no greater treasure or more desirable possession for man, than a woman who truly loves him.
—Sainte-Foi

If woman did turn man out of Paradise, she has done her best ever since to make it up to him.
—Sheldon

Can man be free if woman be a slave?
—Percy Shelley, *The Revolt of Islam*

The voice of woman has been silenced in the state, the church, and the home, but man cannot fulfill his destiny alone, he cannot redeem his race unaided.
—Elizabeth Cady Stanton, speech to the First Women's Rights Convention, 19 Jul 1848

The woman's cause is man's: they rise or sink / Together.
—Alfred, Lord Tennyson, "The Princess"

When a woman dresses up for an occasion, the man should become
the black velvet pillow for the jewel. —John Weitz

Remember Ginger Rogers did everything Fred Astaire did, but she did
it backwards and in high heels. —Faith Whittlesey

Whatever women do they must do twice as well as men to be thought
half as good. Luckily this is not difficult.
—Charlotte Whitton, comment on becoming mayor of Ottawa

What lasting joys the man attend
Who has a polished female friend. —Cornelius Whurr

Why are women . . . so much more interesting to men than men are
to women? —Virginia Woolf, *A Room of One's Own*

MENTAL HOSPITALS

. . . the role people labeled crazy are forced to play once the psychiatric system has a firm hold on them is really that of acquiescent
prisoner. —Anonymous, in Sherry Hirsch, et al., editors,
Madness Network News Reader,
"Processions, Obtrusions, Evacuations"

As to the electro-convulsive-therapy treatments, I like Kesey's tight
comment: "The thing is, no one ever wants another one."
—Anonymous, in Sherry Hirsch, et al., editors,
Madness Network News Reader, "Escape"

. . . I was already able to perceive that only by strictly "normal"
behavior could I ever hope to get out of this place . . . or prevent
my situation from becoming still more unpleasant.
—Anonymous, in Sherry Hirsch, et al., editors,
Madness Network News Reader, "Escape"

Rule: Solitary activity is dangerous, alienating—therefore, reading or
writing are undesirable; any group activity is rehabilitating.
—Anonymous, in Sherry Hirsch, et al., editors,
Madness Network News Reader, "Escape"

The dread Locked Door. —Anonymous, in Sherry Hirsch, et al., editors,
Madness Network News Reader, "Escape"

. . . your behavior record, that unique and precarious ladder to freedom.
—Anonymous, in Sherry Hirsch, et al., editors,
Madness Network News Reader, "Escape"

. . . patients seldom run amuck at mealtime.
—Clifford Beers, *A Mind That Found Itself*

Anyone can find himself suddenly in a mental hospital with more
ease than one likes to imagine . . .
—Doug Cameron,
How to Survive Being Committed to a Mental Hospital

I took my medicine, but I never outgrew my hatred.
—Doug Cameron,
How to Survive Being Committed to a Mental Hospital

. . . merely signing a "voluntary" commitment paper is like confess-
ing to be incompetent to make any future decisions for oneself.
—Doug Cameron,
How to Survive Being Committed to a Mental Hospital

Once in these circumstances [in a psychiatric ward], the policy is
"insane" until proven "sane," even though legally one is entitled
to a trial before being judged.   —Doug Cameron,
How to Survive Being Committed to a Mental Hospital

The main game . . . consists of finding what the doctor wants us to
say or do so that he will be pleased with us and release us from the
hospital.   —Doug Cameron,
How to Survive Being Committed to a Mental Hospital

Two weeks can be a long time to lay on one's back and stare at a light
bulb that never goes out.   —Doug Cameron,
How to Survive Being Committed to a Mental Hospital

We [mental patients] were simply treated so mindlessly, so animal-
istically, that no attempt was made to communicate to us in any
way why we were there or where we were going or what was
about to happen to us. Nothing was explained to us.
—Doug Cameron,
How to Survive Being Committed to a Mental Hospital

The present state of insane persons, confined within this commonwealth, in cages, closets, cellars, stalls, pens! Chained, naked, beaten
with rods, and lashed into obedience.   —Dorothea Lynde Dix,
                              speech to the Legislature of Massachusetts, 1843

. . . every asylum is the question mark in the sentence of civilization.
                              —Samuel A. W. Duffield, *Essays*

[About shock treatments:] Again and again they took to me the
square, lighted room, and increasing the voltage, sent juice to the
center of me where poetry once stirred.   —Janet Gotkin,
                              Too Much Anger, Too Many Tears, with Paul Gotkin

[About shock treatments:] We would go together, victims of our genes,
our dreams, our hurts, and tough stubborn angers, casualties of a vast
clean-up campaign. They would burn it out of us—whatever it was
that made us all possessed, or heavy with the pain of being, or odd
beyond endurance, or "sick." They would set fire to our heads, con-
vulse our poor bodies, befog the brain that screamed and wept and
would not interpret proverbs.   —Janet Gotkin,
                              Too Much Anger, Too Many Tears, with Paul Gotkin

. . . I learned, as time wore on, that you had no choice but to conform
eventually.   —Janet Gotkin,
                              Too Much Anger, Too Many Tears, with Paul Gotkin

When you lived in the closed world of a mental hospital, you learn
quickly not to take any pleasure for granted. You learn the skills of
survival, and the rules of reward and punishment, and the high
comic art of playing the fool.   —Janet Gotkin,
                              Too Much Anger, Too Many Tears, with Paul Gotkin

It is very dangerous to antagonize the influential powers in a mental
hospital; it is unwise to cut off access to what might someday be a
court of appeals.   —Janet and Paul Gotkin,
                              Too Much Anger, Too Many Tears

Bit by bit she regained the distance by which the doctors measured
responsibility: Alone to Her Doctor's Office (100 ft. x 1 hr. sane);
Alone on Front Grounds (200 ft. x 3 hrs. sane); and at last she
applied to go to B ward, where the foot-hour rule would be given
the whole inward sweep of books and pencils and sketch pads.
                              —Hannah Green, *I Never Promised You a Rose Garden*

. . . it was not good form to seem too insistent.
                              —Hannah Green, *I Never Promised You a Rose Garden*

... there was time to wait through, endless time, marked off by meals and sleep, a word or two brushing by, an anger, a story, or the raging delusion of another patient—all experienced disinterestedly and remembered only as part of the frieze of the sick around the walls of the ward.   —Hannah Green, *I Never Promised You a Rose Garden*

The hospital experience can seem—to the acutely psychotic patient— no refuge from paranoia, but its ultimate expression.
—Cara Lawrence, *Both Sides Now*, Aug/Sep 1988

If the majority is insane, the sane must go to the hospital.
—Horace Mann

The first reason mental hospitals came into existence was that we had to have a place for people that just couldn't fit in. They had to go somewhere.   —John Bartlow Martin, *The Pane of Glass*

Mona's lazy days consisted primarily of rising only to shower, eat three meals and play with broken or missing pieces of infantile games.   —LaRita Pryor, *A Lack of Control*

Patients who didn't improve within twelve to eighteen months in the admission wards were sent to the back wards to share the neglect of the chronic patients.
—Susan Sheehan, *Is There No Place on Earth for Me?*

Some of these patients were quiet, and, because they created no problems, they were the patients most often ignored ...
—Susan Sheehan, *Is There No Place on Earth for Me?*

... the locked side of the door.
—Nancy Covert Smith, *Journey Out of Nowhere*

After the hospitalization you feel marked.
—Craig Stafford, *The Walk of the Penguins*

But you do live after the hospital.
—Craig Stafford, *The Walk of the Penguins*

... drugs were used indiscriminately in mental institutions because they made management of asylums much easier: care is often institutionally efficient while less individually concerned. It is difficult to separate behaviors that have a neurological basis from symptoms and side effects induced by medications used to treat these disorders.   —Craig Stafford, *The Walk of the Penguins*

In our drug dazes, the object of existence was simply to pass time.
—Craig Stafford, *The Walk of the Penguins*

The routines of the ward added to the general sense of monotony.
Shifts came and went. Meals were delivered and taken away.
Everything occurred according to schedules. Medications were
passed out at regular intervals. When the medications were ready,
patients queued up in obedient lines to receive little plastic cups
filled with multi-hued pills.
—Craig Stafford, *The Walk of the Penguins*

The struggle is to retain some semblance of dignity.
—Craig Stafford, *The Walk of the Penguins*

I calmed myself down and decided to just wait for whatever happened.   —Mark Vonnegut, *Eden Express*

My only hope was to be polite.   —Mark Vonnegut, *Eden Express*

Once you've been committed to a mental institution you're considered a second-rate citizen from then on and retroactive.
—Mary Jane Ward, *Counterclockwise*

MENTAL ILLNESS

. . . nothing defines the quality of life in a community more clearly
than people who regard themselves, or whom the consensus
chooses to regard, as mentally unwell.   —Renata Adler

The madman who knows that he is mad is close to sanity.
—Juan Ruiz de Alarcón

And so we came forth, and once again beheld the stars.
—Anonymous, closing words of William Styron,
Darkness Visible: A Memoir of Madness

Psychotic episodes are disintegrations which provide an opportunity
for reintegration at new levels.
—Anonymous, in Sherry Hirsch, et al.,
editors, *Madness Network News Reader*, "Odyssey of a Heretic"

Gone is the terror that came hunting for me.
—Anonymous, letter, in Sherry Hirsch, et al.,
editors, *Madness Network News Reader*

I dove into madness and learned how to swim.
—Anonymous, in Sherry Hirsch, et al., editors,
Madness Network News Reader, "The Editors"

Many of the people I've met who've been labeled crazy have been
extraordinarily perceptive, gentle, sensitive, and kind. But often
enough these very qualities get them into trouble. They clog up the
assembly line. —Anonymous, in Sherry Hirsch, et al., editors,
Madness Network News Reader, "The Politics of Insanity is Love"

Now I know how people become "catatonic." This sickening doubt as
to the "right" move holds one paralyzed: the only safe decision is
no decision. —Anonymous, in Sherry Hirsch, et al., editors,
Madness Network News Reader, "Escape"

The neurotic builds castles in the sky. The psychotic lives in them.
The psychiatrist collects the rent. —Anonymous

In our movement, we've had to learn to be patient with sane people,
because we know they're a little slow.
—Anonymous, keynote speech,
Texas Mental Health Consumer caucus, 26 Jan 1991

There is a pane of glass between me and mankind.
—Anonymous, comment of a person with schizophrenia

Those who are insane generally reason correctly, but they reason
from false assumptions and on wrong principles. —Anonymous

No excellent soul is exempt from a mixture of madness. —Aristotle

The world is, for the most part, a collective madhouse, and practically
everyone, however "normal" his facade, is faking sanity.
—Jane Astin

The mind commands the mind to will, and yet, though it be itself, it
minds not. What is this monstrous thing? And why is it?
—Saint Augustine, *The Confessions and Letters of St. Augustine*

Today I had a strange warning. I felt the wind of insanity brush my
mind. —Charles Baudelaire, *Journal*, 23 Jan 1862

Most sane people think that no insane person can reason logically.
But this is not so. —Clifford Beers, *A Mind That Found Itself*

Not a few patients, however, suffering from certain forms of mental
disorder, regain a high degree of insight into their mental condition in what might be termed a flash of divine enlightenment.
—Clifford Beers, *A Mind That Found Itself*

To be on the safe and humane side, let every relative and friend . . .
remember the golden rule, which has never been suspended with
respect to the insane. Go to see them, treat them sanely, write to
them, keep them informed about the home circle; let not your
devotion flag, nor accept any repulse.
—Clifford Beers, *A Mind That Found Itself*

To leave behind what was in reality a hell, and immediately have this
good green earth revealed in more glory than most men ever see it,
was one of the compensating privileges which make me feel that
my suffering was worthwhile.
—Clifford Beers, *A Mind That Found Itself*

Is our species crazy? Plenty of evidence.
—Saul Bellow, *Mr. Sammler's Planet*, Ch. 2

All of us get depressed, and to some extent we all entertain peculiar
thoughts, fears, and fantasies. It is when they get out of proportion, become distorted and highly magnified, and push aside the
rational conscious mind that one is mentally ill.
—Barbara Field Benziger, *The Prison of My Mind*

If I were sick—for instance, if I had cancer—I would still be myself.
How are we going to find the self that was me?
—Barbara Field Benziger, *The Prison of My Mind*

In an effort to understand my illness, I have come to know more
about myself than I might have otherwise.
—Barbara Field Benziger, *The Prison of My Mind*

Every sense hath been o'erstrung, and each frail fiber of the brain
sent forth her thoughts all wild and wide. —Lord Byron

A lot of mental illness is in the mind of the beholder.
—Doug Cameron, Texas Mental Health
Consumer caucus panel discussion, 26 Jan 1991

A mental patient is so without rights, his situation is analogous to
standing in the rain naked. —Doug Cameron,
How to Survive Being Committed to a Mental Hospital

. . . for who is perfect and completely free of mental disturbance?
—Doug Cameron,
How to Survive Being Committed to a Mental Hospital

The real truth of the matter is that what we fear to look at in the mental patient, is ourselves. —Doug Cameron,
How to Survive Being Committed to a Mental Hospital

There nearly always is method in madness. It's what drives men mad, being methodical. —G. K. Chesterton

I have myself been gravely mad, and I can value with greater cause than most the advantages of being sane.
—Morag Coate, *Beyond All Reason*, Prologue

. . . the path I took led to adventures out of the realm of any sober scientist. —Morag Coate, *Beyond All Reason*

In normal life at times of strong emotion, and especially at moments of great fear, we find that we are more keenly aware than usual of the external details of our world . . . In psychotic states, where the fate of the whole universe may be at stake, awareness of material objects and of trivial events can be heightened to an extent that is outside the range of sane experience.
—Morag Coate, *Beyond All Reason*, Prologue

Psychosis opens wide the doors to a world that most people know only through the undercurrent of their dreams.
—Morag Coate, *Beyond All Reason*

. . . the individual is alone. That is the central feature when we penetrate insanity. Not that the world is less with us, but that another world pervades it too, and we, seeing and experiencing life upon a different plane, are cut off from communication with the sane around us. —Morag Coate, *Beyond All Reason*, Prologue

A madman is treated as one absent. —Coke

When a man mistakes his thoughts for persons and things, this is madness. —Samuel Taylor Coleridge

I have reached the conclusion that almost all of us wonder, at least on occasion, about our own mental health.
—Gary R. Collins, *The Magnificent Mind*

Craziness attacks the softest eyes and hamstrings the gentlest flanks.
                    —Pat Conroy, *A Prince of Tides*, Ch. 2

I learned techniques in self-help groups that taught me how to fight
    my own mind.   —Dian Cox, speech

This is a cause that found me.   —Dian Cox, comment as member of a
    mental health consumer panel, Austin State Hospital, 15 Aug 1990

We worked hard as hell to get better.
                —Dian Cox, speech, 1989, about mental illness survivors

I felt a cleaving in my mind / As if my brain had split; / I tried to match
    it, seam by seam, / But could not make them fit. / The thought
    behind I strove to join / Unto the thought before, / But sequence rav-
    eled out of reach / Like balls upon a floor.   —Emily Dickinson

Much madness is divinest sense / To a discerning eye; / Much sense
    the starkest madness. / 'Tis the majority / In this, as all, prevails.
    / Assent, and you are sane; / Demur,—you're straightway dangerous,
    / And handled with a chain.   —Emily Dickinson,
                                        Poems, Part I, No. 11

To be too conscious is an illness—a real thorough-going illness.
                —Fyodor Dostoyevsky, *Notes from Underground*

Great wits are sure to madness near allied, / And thin partitions do
    their bounds divide.
            —John Dryden, *Absalom and Achitophel*, Part I, lines 163-164

There is a pleasure sure / In being mad, which none but madmen
    know!   —John Dryden, *The Spanish Friar*, I, i

I was just sort of moving through time.   —Patty Duke, *Call Me Anna*:
                The Autobiography of Patty Duke, with Kenneth Turan

. . . I went through a very lethargic period . . . I was just sort of getting
    through every night and every day.   —Patty Duke, *Call Me Anna*:
                The Autobiography of Patty Duke, with Kenneth Turan

Great brains (like brightest glass), crack straight; while those of stone
    or wood hold out, and fear not blows.   —Bishop Earle

In the breast of every single man there slumbers a frightful germ of
    madness.   —Feuchtersleben

O this poor brain! ten thousand shapes of fury are whirling there, and reason is no more. —Henry Fielding

"The sooner you 'settle' the sooner you'll be allowed home" was the ruling logic; and "if you can't adapt yourself to living in a mental hospital how do you expect to be able to live 'out in the world'?" How indeed? —Janet Frame, *Faces in the Water*

The bottom of my life had been whisked away; I was falling, falling again. Where would I land?
—Janet Gotkin, *Too Much Anger, Too Many Tears*, with Paul Gotkin

Our infrequent moments of peace and joy were ecstatic and they reminded us of what we struggled for.
—Janet and Paul Gotkin, *Too Much Anger, Too Many Tears*

. . . somewhere in the illness . . . lay a hidden strength.
—Hannah Green, *I Never Promised You a Rose Garden*

. . . she looked out into the congregation on Sunday and wondered if they ever thanked God for the light in their minds, for friends, for cold and pain responsive to the laws of nature, for enough depth of sight into these laws to have expectations, for friends, for the days and nights that follow one another in stately rhythm, for the sparks that fly upward . . .
—Hannah Green, *I Never Promised You a Rose Garden*

. . . this sickness, which everyone shied from and was frightened of, was also an adjustment.
—Hannah Green, *I Never Promised You a Rose Garden*

Always good to have one crazy in the family . . . It takes the pressure off everybody else. —Judith Guest, *Second Heaven*

Insane people easily detect the nonsense of other people.
—Dr. John Hallam

When dealing with the insane, the best method is to pretend to be sane. —Hermann Hesse

Insanity is often the logic of an accurate mind overtaxed.
—Oliver Wendell Holmes, Sr.,
The Autocrat of the Breakfast Table, Ch. 2

I teach that all men are mad. —Horace, *Satires*

Who then is sane? —Horace, *Satires*

They [mental illness survivors] have the right to fail with dignity.
—Nadine Jay, speech, 1988

Walking around on the edge of chaos. —Nadine Jay, speech, 1988

Here I sit—mad as the Hatter—with nothing to do but either become madder and madder or else recover enough of my sanity to be allowed to go back to the life which drove me mad.—Lara Jefferson

. . . wide awake in the middle of a nightmare.
—Lara Jefferson, "These are my Sisters"

. . . he never regarded himself as crazy. The world was.
—Erica Jong, *Fear of Flying*

Neurosis is an inner cleavage—the state of being at war with oneself.
—Carl Jung, *Modern Man in Search of a Soul*

Psychiatrists classify a person as neurotic if he suffers from his problems in living, and a psychotic if he makes others suffer.
—Carl Jung

Lunatics are similar to designated hitters. Often an entire family is crazy, but since an entire family can't go into the hospital, one person is designated as crazy and goes inside.
—Susanna Kaysen, *Girl, Interrupted*

. . . one does not recover from mental illness all at once.
—Elsa Krauch, *A Mind Restored*

Insanity—a perfectly rational adjustment to an insane world.
—R. D. Laing

Madness need not be all breakdown. It may also be break-through. It is potential liberation and renewal as well as enslavement and existential death. —R. D. Laing, *The Politics of Experience*, Ch. 6

Schizophrenic behavior is a special strategy that a person invents in order to live in an unlivable situation.
—R. D. Laing, *The Politics of Experience*

Through the hurt we still love.
—Cara Lawrence, *Both Sides Now* (newsletter), Aug/Sep 1988

To be crazy is not necessarily to writhe in snake pits or converse with imaginary gods. It can sometimes be not knowing what to do in the morning. —Christopher Lehmann-Haupt

Some people had to live with crippled arms, or stammers, or being deaf. She would have to live knowing she was subject to a state of mind she could not own.
—Doris Lessing, *A Man and Two Women*, "To Room 19"

Any breakdown is a breakthrough. —Marshall McLuhan

Insanity consists of building major structures upon foundations which do not exist. —Norman Mailer, speech, 1968

Praised be the gods that made my spirit mad; / Kept me aflame and raw to beauty's touch. —Angela Morgan, "June Rapture"

In individuals insanity is rare, but in groups, parties, nations, and epochs it is the rule. —Friedrich Nietzsche, *Beyond Good and Evil*

Deliriums are dreams not rounded with a sleep. —Jean Paul

We have to lose our minds to come to our senses.
—Dr. Frederick S. Perls

We know that you are mad with much learning.—Petronius, *Satyricon*

. . . I want the world to know that people like me who have returned from the half-world of mental oblivion are not forever contaminated. We have been sick.
—Jim Piersall, *Fear Strikes Out*, with Al Hirschberg

When you look directly at an insane man, all you see is a reflection of your own knowledge that he's insane, which is not to see him at all. To see him you must see what he saw. —Robert Pirsig

The finest minds, like the finest metals, dissolve the easiest.
—Alexander Pope

I don't see no reason to hold it against a man because he went loony once or twice in his lifetime . . . —Katherine Anne Porter, *Noon Wine*

Work and love—these are the basics. Without them there is neurosis.
—Theodor Reik, *Of Love and Lust*

All of us are crazy in one or another way.   —Theodore Isaac Rubin

. . . it is no longer an illness or a passing fit: it is I.
—Jean-Paul Sartre, *Nausea*

It is sometimes pleasant even to act like a madman.   —Seneca

No great genius is free from some tincture of madness.
—Seneca, *De Tranquillitate Animi*

To Bedlam and Part Way Back   —Anne Sexton, title of a book of poetry

Canst thou not minister to a mind diseased, / Pluck from the memory
a rooted sorrow, / Raze out the written troubles of the brain, / And
with some sweet oblivious antidote / Cleanse the stuff'd bosom of
that perilous stuff / Which weighs upon the heart?
—William Shakespeare, *Macbeth*, Act V, Sc. iii

Though this be madness, yet there is method in't.
—William Shakespeare, *Hamlet*, Act II, Sc. ii

We want a few mad people now. See where the sane ones have landed
us.   —George Bernard Shaw, *Saint Joan*

A breakdown is a mental safety valve that comes to our rescue and
temporarily releases us from circumstances too horrible or difficult
to confront immediately.
—Nancy Covert Smith, *Journey Out of Nowhere*

Above all, I was thankful for each day and the ability to function in
it.   —Nancy Covert Smith, *Journey Out of Nowhere*

. . . a breakdown . . . is too enormous a problem to surmount alone.
—Nancy Covert Smith, *Journey Out of Nowhere*

How could all this have happened in a few short hours?
—Nancy Covert Smith, *Journey Out of Nowhere*

The day before me appeared as a blessing rather than a punishment.
—Nancy Covert Smith, *Journey Out of Nowhere*

This was my sickness, the inability to be logical.
—Nancy Covert Smith, *Journey Out of Nowhere*

It cannot be easy to be the parents of children who have been diagnosed as mentally ill.   —Craig Stafford, *The Walk of the Penguins*

It seemed imperative not to show any feelings. Every feeling had
become suspect while in the hospital. After the release I kept emotions tightly controlled to avoid re-institutionalization.
—Craig Stafford, *The Walk of the Penguins*

Once the wheels began churning, I was into craziness over my head.
—Craig Stafford, *The Walk of the Penguins*

It was too nerve-wracking, a shocking spectacle, like seeing an old,
calm friend go insane.   —John Steinbeck, *Travels with Charley*

Emotion turning back on itself, and not leading on to thought or
action, is the element of madness.   —John Sterling

If you talk to God, you are praying; if God talks to you, you have
schizophrenia.   —Thomas Szasz, *The Second Sin*

Insanity is not a distinct and separate empire; our ordinary life bor-
ders upon it, and we cross the frontier in some part of our nature.
—Taine

To have a true idea of man or of life, one must have stood himself on
the brink of suicide, or on the door-sill of insanity, at least once.
—Taine

'Tis a mad world, my masters.   —John Taylor, *Western Voyage*

My life has crept so long on a broken wing
    Thro' cells of madness, haunts of horror and fear,
    That I come to be grateful at last for a little thing.
—Alfred, Lord Tennyson, *Maud*, Part III

. . . both overacuteness of the senses and impaired ability to logically
synthesize incoming stimuli may lie behind many of the delusions
experienced by many schizophrenics.
—Dr. Edwin Torrey, *Surviving Schizophrenia*

. . . most delusions and hallucinations are logical outgrowths of what
the brain is experiencing.   —Dr. Edwin Torrey, *Surviving Schizophrenia*

Most persons with schizophrenia are not dangerous at all.
—Dr. Edwin Torrey, *Surviving Schizophrenia*

To be a mental patient is to be stigmatized, ostracized, socialized, patronized, psychiatrized. —Rae Unzicker, "To be a mental patient"

To be a mental patient is to have everyone controlling your life but you. You're watched by your shrink, your social worker, your friends, your family. And then you're diagnosed as paranoid.
—Rae Unzicker, "To be a mental patient"

To be a mental patient is to live on $82 a month in food stamps, which won't let you buy Kleenex to dry your tears. And to watch your shrink come back to his office from lunch, driving a Mercedes Benz.   —Rae Unzicker, "To be a mental patient"

To be a mental patient is to act glad when you're sad and calm when you're mad.   —Rae Unzicker, "To be a mental patient"

To be a mental patient is to participate in stupid groups that call themselves therapy. Music isn't music, it's therapy; volleyball isn't a sport, it's therapy; sewing is therapy; washing dishes is therapy. Even the air you breathe is therapy, and that's called the "milieu."
—Rae Unzicker, "To be a mental patient"

To be a mental patient is not to die—even if you want to—and not / cry, and not hurt, and not be scared, and not be angry, and not / be vulnerable, and not laugh too loud / —because, if you do, you only prove that you're a mental patient / even if you are not.
—Rae Unzicker, "To be a mental patient"

Madness is to think of too many things in succession too fast, or of one thing too exclusively.   —Voltaire

As well as being one of the worst things that can happen to a human being, schizophrenia can also be one of the richest learning and humanizing experiences life offers. —Mark Vonnegut, *Eden Express*

Colds, ulcers, flu, and cancer are things we get. Schizophrenia is something we are.   —Mark Vonnegut

Well, I thought, last night I paid my dues. I faced death. Now I can stay.   —Mark Vonnegut, *Eden Express*

It happens all the time, I told her, some of us have bad vision, are crippled, have defects, and our reality is a different one, not the correct and ascertainable one, and sometimes it makes us dotty and lonely but it also makes us poets.
—Diane Wakoski, *The East Side Scene*,
"The Birds of Paradise Being Very Plain Birds"

Long ago they lowered insane persons into snake pits; they thought that an experience that might drive a sane person out of his wits might send an insane person back to sanity.
—Mary Jane Ward, *The Snake Pit*

We're all so near the edge, it's a wonder any of us functions at all.
—Bonnie Watkins

If people behaved in the way nations do they would all be put into straightjackets.　　　—Tennessee Williams, BBC Radio interview

Every man has a madness of his own.　　　—Proverb (Yiddish)

M E R C Y

Few men really want justice; what all mankind prays for is mercy.
—Anonymous

O God, be merciful to me a fool.
—Anonymous, quoted by Oliver Wendell Holmes, Jr.

No one thing does human life more need than a kind consideration of the faults of others. Every one sins; everyone needs forbearance. Our own imperfections should teach us to be merciful.
—Henry Ward Beecher

Betwixt the stirrup and the ground / Mercy I asked, mercy I found.
—William Camden, *Remains*,
"Epitaph for a Man Killed Falling from his Horse"

When in doubt, lean to the side of mercy.　　　—Miguel de Cervantes

Mercy surpasses justice.　　　—Geoffrey Chaucer

We hand folks over to God's mercy, and show none ourselves.
—George Eliot, *Adam Bede*, Ch. 42

Being all fashioned of the self-same dust, / Let us be merciful as well as just.　　　—Henry Wadsworth Longfellow,
Tales of a Wayside Inn, "Emma and Eginhard"

The quality of mercy is not strain'd, / It droppeth as the gentle rain from heaven / Upon the place beneath: it is twice blest; / It blesseth him that gives and him that takes . . .
—William Shakespeare, *The Merchant of Venice*, Act IV, Sc. i

. . . me He now delights to spare. —Charles Wesley, "Depth of Mercy"

Jesus weeps and loves me still.   —Charles Wesley, "Depth of Mercy"

MERIT

Beauties in vain their pretty eyes may roll; / Charms strike the sight, but merit wins the soul.   —Alexander Pope, *The Rape of the Lock*

METAPHOR

Metaphor is no argument, though it be sometimes the gunpowder to drive one home, and embed it in the memory.   —Lowell

MIDDLE AGE

You know you've reached middle age when your weightlifting consists merely of standing up.   —Bob Hope

Middle age: the time when a man is always thinking that in a week of two he will feel just as good as ever.
—Don Marquis, in Edward Anthony, *O Rare Don Marquis*

Of middle age the best that can be said is that a middle-aged person has likely learned to have a little fun in spite of his troubles.
—Don Marquis, *The Almost Perfect State* (1927)

Middle age is when it takes longer to rest than to get tired.
—Laurence J. Peter, *Peter's Almanac*, 3 May 1982

Middle age is when work is a lot less fun and fun is a lot more work.
—Laurence J. Peter, *Peter's Almanac*, 4 May 1982

Middle age is when you stop criticizing the older generation and start criticizing the younger one.
—Laurence J. Peter, compiler, *Peter's Quotations*: *Ideas for Our Time*

The MILITARY

Join the army, see the world, meet interesting people, and kill them.
—Anonymous, pacifist slogan, 1970's

Being in the army is like being in the Boy Scouts, except that the Boy Scouts have adult supervision. —Blake Clark

We are all shot through with human imperfections and we shall all fall short of our highest ideals; but if in this loyal brotherhood we find helpful understanding, human sympathy, and affection, then the strong will help make the weakest of us stronger, and together we will find our powers multiplied many times over.
—Gen. Cecil E. Combs, "Loyalty, the Military Touchstone"

Isn't it a shame military doctors couldn't be as good as military sunglasses? —Pat Conroy, *The Great Santini*, Ch. 4

Non-cooperation in military matters should be an essential moral principle for all true scientists . . . —Albert Einstein, 20 Jan 1947, in Nathan and Norden, *Einstein on Peace*

The necessary and wise subordination of the military to civil power must be sustained. —Dwight D. Eisenhower

In military science there is a principle more important than "Forward": it is that the task should be proportionate to the means.
—Alexander Solzhenitsyn, *August 1914*

Lafayette, we are here. —Colonel C. E. Stanton, address, 4 Jul 1917, at the grave of Lafayette in the Picpus Cemetery, Paris

The MIND

The point of having an open mind, like having a open mouth, is to close it on something solid. —G. K. Chesterton

. . . many questions about the mind are beyond the ability of science to answer. —Gary R. Collins, *The Magnificent Mind*

The mind can control its own thinking and this, in turn, can influence behavior. —Gary R. Collins, *The Magnificent Mind*

Tyrants have not yet discovered any chains that can fetter the mind.
—Charles Caleb Colton

My Mind To Me a Kingdom Is. —Edward Dyer, poem title

A house is no home unless it contain food and fire for the mind as well as for the body. —Margaret Fuller

A man's head is his castle. —Joseph Heller, *Something Happened*

The mind grows by what it feeds on. —Josiah Gilbert Holland

The direction of the mind is more important than its progress.
—Joseph Joubert, *Pensées*

The mind is the atmosphere of the soul. —Joseph Joubert, *Pensées*

The heart has its reasons; it's the mind that's suspect.
—Bel Kaufman, *Up the Down Staircase*

A mind, like a home, is furnished by its owner, so if one's life is cold
and bare he can blame none but himself. You have a chance to
select from some pretty elegant furnishings.
—Louis L'Amour, *Bendigo Shafter*

The mind is its own place, and in itself
Can make a Heaven of Hell, a Hell of Heaven.
—John Milton, *Paradise Lost*, Book I, line 254

Within our impure mind the pure one is to be found. —Hui Neng

If you keep your mind sufficiently open people will throw a lot of
rubbish into it. —William A. Orton

Your mind outwears all sorts of things you may set your heart upon;
you can enjoy it when all other things are taken away.
—Katherine Anne Porter, *Old Mortality*

What is this little, agile, precious fire, this fluttering motion which
we call the mind? —Matthew Prior

It does not take a great mind to be a Christian, but it takes all the
mind a man has. —Richard C. Raines

The mind is a strange machine which can combine the materials
offered to it in the most astonishing ways.
—Bertrand Russell, *The Conquest of Happiness*

When the mind is most empty / It is most full.
—Susan Fromberg Schaeffer, *Granite Lady*, "Fortune Cookies"

The mind is the eyesight of the soul. —Friedrich Schiller

A good mind possesses a kingdom. —Seneca, *Thyestes*

For 't is the mind that makes the body rich . . .
—William Shakespeare, *The Taming of the Shrew*, Act IV, Sc. iii

My mind to me an empire is. —Robert Southwell

[The mind's] dynamics transcend the time and space of brain phys-
iology. —Roger Wolcott Sperry

Mind is a kingdom to the man who gathereth his pleasure from ideas.
—Martin Farquhar Tupper

MINISTRY

The world looks at ministers out of the pulpit to know that they
mean in it. —Richard Cecil

As we meet and touch, each day, / The many travelers on our way,
/ Let every such brief contact be / A glorious, helpful minister.
—Susan Coolidge

We are all called to the ministry.
—Ron Parrish, sermon, Hope Chapel, Austin, Texas, 4 Sep 1993

MIRACLES

Miracles are not contrary to nature but only contrary to what we
know about nature. —Saint Augustine

. . . every human being is an unprecedented miracle. —James Baldwin

All we behold is miracle. —William Cowper, *The Task*

There are two ways to live your life. One is as though nothing is a
miracle. The other way is as though everything is a miracle.
—Albert Einstein

I should not be a Christian but for the miracles.
—Blaise Pascal, *Pensées*

Miracles are of all sizes. And if you start believing in little miracles,
you can work up to the bigger ones. —Norman Vincent Peale

Everything is miraculous. It is miraculous that one does not melt in
one's bath. —Pablo Picasso, quoted by Jean Cocteau

It would be a miracle, for example, if I dropped a stone and it rose upwards. But is it no miracle that it falls to the ground?
—Alfred Polgar

Men talk about Bible miracles because there is no miracle in their lives. Cease to gnaw that crust. There is ripe fruit over your head.
—Henry David Thoreau

"What's miraculous about a spider's web?" asked Mrs. Arable. "I don't see why you say a web is a miracle—it's just a web." "Ever try to spin one?" asked Mrs. Dorian.   —E. B. White, *Charlotte's Web*

To me every hour of the light and dark is a miracle, / Every cubic inch of space is a miracle.   —Walt Whitman, "Miracles"

What is a miracle? I know of nothing else but miracles.
—Walt Whitman

MISERY

It is seldom that the miserable can help regarding their misery as a wrong inflicted by those who are less miserable.   —George Eliot

It is difficult to make a man miserable while he feels worthy of himself and claims kindred to the great God who made him.
—Abraham Lincoln, speech, Washington, D. C., 14 Sep 1862

For misery don't blame God. He gives the food but we cook it.
—Bernard Malamud, *The Fixer*

Man is only miserable so far as he thinks himself so.   —Sannazaro

. . . misery acquaints a man with strange bed-fellows.
—William Shakespeare, *The Tempest*, Act II, Sc. ii

MISFORTUNE

In relating our misfortunes, we often feel them lightened.
—Pierre Corneille, *Polyeucte*

We sink to rise.   —Ralph Waldo Emerson

It is well to treasure the memories of past misfortunes; they consitute our bank of fortitude.   —Eric Hoffer

If a man talks of his misfortunes there is something in them that is
   not disagreeable to him . . .
                    —Samuel Johnson, in James Boswell, *Life of Samuel Johnson*

We are all strong enough to endure the misfortunes of others.
                    —François de La Rochefoucauld, *Maximes*

Let us be of good cheer, however, remembering that the misfortunes
   hardest to bear are those which never come.
                                          —James Russell Lowell,
                         speech in Birmingham, England, 6 Oct 1884

Who hath not known ill-fortune, never knew
   Himself, or his own virtue.   —Mallet

Perhaps the school of misfortunes is the very best.   —Mary Masters

She saw shrewdly that the world is quickly bored by the recital of
   misfortune, and willingly avoids the sight of distress.
                    —W. Somerset Maugham, *Moon and Sixpence*

. . . when something is detestable, and yet inevitable, what one must
   do is not merely to endure it—a hard task whatever one may do—
   but find an excuse for loving it. Everything is a matter of points of
   view, and misfortune is often only the sign of a false interpretation
   of life.   —Henri de Montherlant, *Textes sous une occupation*

I never knew any man in my life who could not bear another's misfortunes perfectly like a Christian.
                    —Alexander Pope, *Thoughts of Various Subjects*

Misfortune does not always come to injure.   —Proverb (Italian)

He who falls into the sea will cling even to a snake.
                                          —Proverb (Turkish)

Never find your delight in another's misfortune.   —Publilius Syrus

Contentment with the divine will is the best remedy we can apply to
   misfortune.   —William Temple

Life is thickly sown with thorns, and I know no other remedy than to
   pass quickly through them. The longer we dwell on our misfortunes, the greater is their power to harm us.   —Voltaire

MISSIONARIES

You have the Gospel because missionaries came your way.
—Anonymous

No regrets. No reserve. No retreat.
—Bill Borden, 20th century American missionary to India

He who goes down into the battle of life giving a smile for every frown, a cheery word for every cross one, and lending a helping hand to the unfortunate, is after all, the best of missionaries.
—Miller

You are a sent one.
—Ron Parrish, sermon, Hope Chapel, Austin, Texas, 4 Sep 1993

MISTAKES

A mistake is evidence that someone has tried to do something.
—Anonymous

Wise men learn by other's mistakes, fools by their own.—Anonymous

There is precious instruction to be got by finding we were wrong.
—Thomas Carlyle

Mistakes are often the best teachers.   —James Anthony Froude

Mistakes are the portals of discovery.   —James Joyce

The man who makes no mistakes does not usually make anything.
—William Connor Magee, sermon, 1868

The great virtue of a man lies in his ability to correct his mistakes and continually to make a new man of himself.   —Wang Yang-ming

MODELING

You have to have the kind of body that doesn't need a girdle in order to get to pose in one.   —Carolyn Kenmore

MODERATION

Happy they who steadily pursue a middle course.   —Anonymous

Fortify yourself with moderation; for this is an impregnable fortress.
—Epictetus

Nothing to excess.
—Solon, in Diogenes Laertius, *Lives of Eminent Philosophers*

Moderation in all things.   —Terence, *Andria*

MODESTY

One is proud by nature, modest by necessity.   —Reverdy, *En vrac*

There's a lot to be said for the fellow who doesn't say it himself.
—Maurice Switzer

MONEY

Study how to do the most good and let the pay take care of itself.
—Lymon Abbott

From a bad paymaster get what you can.   —Anonymous

If you want money, ask for advice. If you want advice, ask for money.
—Anonymous, modern fund raising maxim

Not how much of my money will I give to God, but how much of His
money will I keep for myself.   —Anonymous

Money is something you got to make in case you don't die.
—Max Asnas

Money is like muck, not good except it be spread.
—Francis Bacon, *Essays*, "Of Seditions and Troubles"

Money, it turned out, was exactly like sex. You thought of nothing
else if you didn't have it and thought of other things if you did.
—James Baldwin, *Nobody Knows My Name*,
"The Black Boy looks at the White Boy"

If you would know what the Lord God thinks of money, you have
only to look at those to whom it is given.   —Maurice Baring

A nickel ain't worth a dime anymore.   —Yogi Berra, *The Yogi Book*

For the love of money is the root of all evil . . .
—*The Bible* (KJV): 1 Timothy 6:10

Don't trade the very stuff of your life, time, for nothing more than dollars. That's a rotten bargain.
—Rita Mae Brown, in Phillip L. Berman, editor,
The Courage of Conviction

To make three guineas do the work of five. —Burns

To be clever enough to get all that money, one must be stupid enough to want it. —G. K. Chesterton, *The Wisdom of Father Brown*,
"The Paradise of Thieves"

How pleasant it is to have money.
—Arthur Hugh Clough, *Dipsyschus*, Part I

Can anybody remember when the times were not hard, and money not scarce?
—Ralph Waldo Emerson, *Society and Solitude*, "Works and Days"

If you make money your god, it will plague you like the devil.
—Henry Fielding

Beware of little expenses; a small leak will sink a great ship.
—Benjamin Franklin

If you'd know the value of money, go and borrow some.
—Benjamin Franklin, *Poor Richard's Almanack*

. . . some day you will have to give an account for every penny you spent. —Billy Graham

Brother, Can You Spare a Dime?
—E. Y. Harburg, title and refrain of song, 1932

If a man's religion does not affect his use of money, that man's religion is vain. —Hugh Martin

There is nothing so degrading as the constant anxiety about one's means of livelihood . . . Money is like a sixth sense without which you cannot make a complete use of the other five.
—W. Somerset Maugham, *Of Human Bondage*

How to live had started out as an analytical problem of how to place himself so as to intercept the flow of money in the society.
—Arthur Miller, *Timebends*

Give the laborer his wage before his perspiration be dry.

—Mohammed

The two most beautiful words in the English language are "check enclosed."

—Dorothy Parker

And money is not something to go mad about . . . Money is for food and clothes and comfort, and a visit to the pictures. Money is to make happy the lives of children.

—Alan Paton, *Cry, the Beloved Country*

There is nothing at all wrong with having money unless money has you.

—Norman Vincent Peale

Money is a good servant, but a bad master.　　　—Proverb (French)

Nothing is more eloquent than ready money.　　　—Proverb (French)

The price spoils the pleasure.　　　—Proverb (French)

Money in the purse drives away melancholy.　　　—Proverb (German)

When I had money everyone called me brother.　　　—Proverb (Polish)

Gold has wings which carry everywhere except to heaven.

—Proverb (Russian)

If you have money, you are wise and good-looking and can sing well too.

—Proverb (Yiddish)

Less coin, less care . . .　　　—Sir Joshua Reynolds

Once you pass forty, a dime isn't worth bending over to pick up if you drop one.

—Andrew A. Rooney,
A Few Minutes with Andy Rooney, "Bank Names"

Every spending decision is a spiritual decision.　　　—James Ryle

Remember, not one penny can we take with us into the unknown land.

—Seneca

Those who submerge themselves in the desire for money are always in debt.

—Rabbi Nahman ben Simha, the Bratslaver

There are few sorrows, however poignant, in which a good income is of no avail.

—Logan Pearsall Smith, *Afterthoughts*

Money is always there, but the pockets change.   —Gertrude Stein

Nothing that is God's is obtainable by money.   —Tertullian

Look at a man's budget, and you can quickly tell what matters most
to him.   —Henry B. Trimble

When you come right down to it, a man with three children has no
damn right to say that money doesn't matter.
     —Sloan Wilson, *The Man in the Gray Flannel Suit*

MONUMENTS

If you would see his monument look around.
     —Anonymous, inscription on the tomb of Sir Christopher Wren

I would much rather have men ask why I have no statue than why I
have one.   —Cato the Elder, in Plutarch, *Lives*, "Cato," XIX

Here once the embattled farmers stood, / And fired the shot heard
round the world.
     —Ralph Waldo Emerson, hymn sung at
the completion of the Concord Monument

The monuments of the nations are all protests against nothingness
after death; so are statues and inscriptions; so is history.
     —Gen. Lew Wallace

MORALITY

The Devil may also make use of morality.   —Karl Barth

What is moral is what you feel good after and what is immoral is
what you feel bad after. —Ernest Hemingway, *Death in the Afternoon*

Morality is the herd instinct in the individual.
     —Friedrich Nietzsche, *Die fröliche Wissenshaft*

To be rewarded for doing good is to rob goodness of any moral quality. It then becomes good business. It pays to be good. Morality is
not a commercial enterprise.   —Rabbi Levi A. Olan

There are many religions, but there is only one morality.
     —John Ruskin, *Lectures on Art*

Reverence for life affords me my fundamental principle of morality.
—Albert Schweitzer

Morality is always higher than law and we cannot forget this ever.
—Alexander Solzhenitsyn

Man's moral nature is a riddle which only eternity can solve.
—Henry David Thoreau

All sects are different, because they come from men; morality is
everywhere the same, because it comes from God.   —Voltaire

MORNING

I'd like mornings better if they started later.   —Anonymous

The early bird gets the early worm.   —Anonymous

That old saw about the early bird just proves that the worm should
have stayed in bed.   —Robert Heinlein, *Time Enough for Love*

How I have loved this house in the morning before we are all awake
and tangled together like badly cast fishing lines.
—Katherine Anne Porter, *Pale Horse, Pale Rider*

But it's morning. Within my hands is another day. Another day to listen and love and walk and glory. I am here for another day.
—Hugh Prather

There are times when breakfast seems the one thing worth getting up
for . . .   —Peter de Vries, *Forever Panting*

MORTALITY

. . . life itself is brief, and that is what charges the day with such
ridiculous beauty.   —Garrison Keillor, *We Are Still Married*

Treasure each other in the recognition that we do not know how long
we shall have each other.   —Joshua Loth Liebman

Brief life is here our portion; / Brief sorrow, short-lived care.
—James Mason Neale

MOTHERS

. . . the ten thousand little things every day that a woman kept thinking of, on account of children.   —James Agee, *A Death in the Family*

Where there is a mother in the house, matters speed well.
—Bronson Alcott

A Christian mother is the greatest heritage God can give a man.
—Anonymous

Motherhood is a partnership with God.   —Anonymous

Instant availability without continuous presence is probably the best
    role a mother can play.   —Lotte Bailyn

A woman's first child is the man she loves.
—Bazin, *La Mort de petit cheval*

That was a judicious mother who said, "I obey my children for the
    first year of their lives, but ever after I expect them to obey me."
—Henry Ward Beecher

The mother's heart is the child's schoolroom.
—Henry Ward Beecher, *Life Thoughts*

What the mother sings to the cradle goes all the way down to the coffin.
—Henry Ward Beecher, in William Drysdale,
editor, *Proverbs from Plymouth Pulpit*

The sweetest sound to mortals given / Are heard in Mother, Home,
    and Heaven.
—William Goldsmith Brown, "Mother, Home, and Heaven"

A mother is a mother still, / The holiest thing alive.
—Samuel Taylor Coleridge, "The Three Graves"

Educate a man and you educate an individual—educate a woman and
    you educate a family.   —Agnes Cripps

The future of society is in the hands of the mothers. If the world was
    lost through woman, she alone can save it.   —De Beaufort

My mother is a poem I'll never be able to write though everything I
    write is a poem to my mother . . .
—Sharon Doubiago, *Hard Country*, "Mother"

I think my life began with waking up and loving my mother's face.
—George Eliot, *Daniel Deronda*

A mother is not a person to lean on, but a person to make leaning unnecessary.   —Dorothy Canfield Fisher, *Her Son's Wife*

The mother-child relationship is paradoxical and, in a sense, tragic. It requires the most intense love on the mother's side, yet this very love must help the child grow away from the mother, and to become fully independent.   —Erich Fromm, *The Sane Society*

Where yet was ever found a mother, / Who'd give her booby for another?
            —John Gay, *Fables*, "The Mother, the Nurse, and the Fairy"

Richer than I you can never be— I had a mother who read to me.
            —Strickland Gillilan, "The Reading Mother"

What is Home Without a Mother?   —Alice Hawthorne, poem title

. . . no expert is in a position to do for a child what a mother can do.
            —Elaine Hefner

The woman who creates and sustains a home, and under whose hands children grow up to be strong and pure men and woman is a creator second only to God.   —Helen Hunt Jackson

My mother wanted me to be her wings, to fly as she had never quite had the courage to do. I love her for that. I love the fact that she wanted to give birth to her own wings.   —Erica Jong

. . . the heroism of the average mother. Ah! When I think of that broad fact, I gather hope again for poor humanity; and this dark world looks bright . . . because, whatever else it is not full of, it is at least full of mothers.   —Charles Kingsley

In the beginning there was my mother. A shape. A shape and a force, standing in the light. You could see her energy; it was visible in the air. Against any background she stood out . . .   —Marilyn Krysl

No man is poor who has had a godly Mother.   —Abraham Lincoln

The best academy, a mother's knee.
            —James Russell Lowell, "The Academy"

I will go to my home . . . / To Ullinish with its white-hoofed herds, / Where once in childhood I was nourished / On breast-milk of smooth-skinned women.   —Mairi MacLeod,
            "A Complaint About Exile"

The bravest battle that ever was fought; / Shall I tell you where and when? / On the maps of the world you will find it not; / It was fought by the mothers of men.

—Joaquin Miller, "The Bravest Battle"

There is no such thing as a non-working mother.   —Hester Mundis

But children, hark! Your mother would rather, / When you arrived, have been your father.   —Ogden Nash, *Verses From 1929 On*, "A Child's Guide to Parents"

I am my mother's daughter,. . . I am her only novel.
—Marge Piercy, *The Moon Is Always Female*, "My Mother's Novel"

Who takes the child by the hand takes the mother by the heart.
—Proverb (Danish)

In a child's lunch box, a mother's thoughts.   —Proverb (Japanese)

We mothers rock into the heart of the world the melody of peace.
—Nelly Sachs, *The Seeker and Other Poems*, "We Mothers"

No matter how old a mother is she watches her middle-aged children for signs of improvement.
—Florida Scott-Maxwell, *The Measure of My Days*

I have given suck, and know / How tender 't is to love the babe that milks me.   —William Shakespeare, *Macbeth*, Act I, Sc. vii

God could not be everywhere, so therefore he made mothers.
—*The Talmud*

Who ran to help me when I fell, / And would some pretty story tell, / Or kiss the place to make it well? / My mother.
—Ann Taylor, in Jane Taylor, *Original Poems for Infant Minds* (1804), "My Mother"

Mother is the name for God in the lips and hearts of little children.
—William Makepeace Thackeray, *Vanity Fair*, Vol. ii., Ch. 12

A suburban mother's role is to deliver children obstetrically once, and by car forever after.   —Peter de Vries

. . . my mother adorned with flowers whatever shabby house we were forced to live in.   —Alice Walker, *In Search of Our Mothers' Gardens*

The hand that rocks the cradle / Is the hand that rules the world.
—William Ross Wallace, "John o' London's Treasure Trove"

I learned from the age of two or three that any room in our house, at any time of day, was there to be read in, or to be read to. My mother read to me.   —Eudora Welty, *One Writer's Beginnings*

Certainly there she was, in the very centre of that great Cathedral space which was childhood; there she was from the very first.
—Virginia Woolf, *Moments of Being*

MOTIVES

Never judge a man's actions until you know his motives.
—Anonymous

We often do not know ourselves the grounds / On which we act, though plain to others. —Bertolt Brecht, *Roundheads and Peakheads*

Man knows so little about his fellows. In his eyes all men or women act upon what he believes would motivate him if we were mad enough to do what that other man or woman is doing.
—William Faulkner, *Light in August*

The spirit from which we act is the principal matter.
—Johann Wolfgang von Goethe

A man's acts are usually right, but his reasons seldom are.
—Elbert Hubbard

In the motive lies the good or ill.   —Samuel Johnson

We would often be ashamed of our finest actions if the world understood all the motives which produced them.
—François de La Rochefoucauld, *Maximes*, No. 409

Real motives, however seemingly apparent, are still hidden.
—Alfred Mercier

. . . you must not expect to find that people understand what they do.
—John Steinbeck, *East of Eden*

We are not only to look at the action, but at the reason of it.
—Stillingfleet

Man sees your actions, but God your motives.   —Thomas à Kempis

MOURNING

They truly mourn, that mourn without a witness.   —Baron

Mourn if you must, but don't stop fighting.
                    —Alexander Solzhenitsyn, *The Oak and the Calf*

MOVEMENTS

All movements go too far.   —Bertrand Russell, *Unpopular Essays*

MOVIES

A film is a petrified fountain of thought.   —Jean Cocteau

Movies are the art form most like man's imagination.
                              —Francis Ford Coppola

Photography is truth. The cinema is truth 24 times a second.
                    —Jean-Luc Godard, *Le Petit Soldat* (1960 film)

You ain't heard nothin' yet, folks.
                    —Al Jolson, remark in the first talking film,
                              The Jazz Singer, Jul 1927

The cinema, like the detective story, makes it possible to experience
    without danger, all the excitement, passion and desirousness
    which must be suppressed in a humanitarian ordering of society.
                              —Carl Jung

Good movies make you care, make you believe in possibilities again.
            —Pauline Kael, *Going Steady*, "Movies as Opera"

The words "Kiss Kiss Bang Bang," which I saw on an Italian movie
    poster, are perhaps the briefest statement imaginable of the basic
    appeal of movies.   —Pauline Kael

We may be reaching the end of the era in which individual movies
    meant something to people. In the new era, movies may just mean
    a barrage of images.   —Pauline Kael

Hollywood's a place where they'll pay you a thousand dollars for a
    kiss, and fifty cents for your soul.
        —Marilyn Monroe, in John Robert Colombo, *Popcorn in Paradise*

Cinema is a matter of what is in the frame and what is out.
—Martin Scorscese, film director

In good films, there is always a directness that entirely frees us from the itch to interpret.   —Susan Sontag, *Evergreen Review*, Dec 1964, "Against Interpretation"

The motion picture is the people's Art.
—Adela Rogers St. Johns, *Love, Laughter, and Tears*

[About the movies:] Well, I git enough of sorrow. I like to git away from it.   —John Steinbeck, *The Grapes of Wrath*, Ch. 23

The great thing about the movies . . . is—you're giving people little . . . tiny pieces of time . . . that they never forget.   —Jimmy Stewart

M U S I C

Music, the greatest good that mortals know, / And all of heaven we have below.   —Joseph Addison, "A Song for St. Cecilia's Day"

The music teacher came twice each week to bridge the awful gap between Dorothy and Chopin.   —George Ade

Oboe—an ill woodwind that nobody blows good.   —Anonymous

Please do not shoot the pianist. He is doing his best.
—Anonymous sign, in Oscar Wilde, *Impressions of America*, "Leadville"

Those who hear not the music think the dancers mad. —Anonymous

Music is the best means we have of digesting time.   —W. H. Auden

Music washes away from the soul the dust of every-day life.
—Auerbach

The grand object of music is to touch the heart.   —Karl Bach

Rugged the breast that music cannot tame.
—John Codrington Bampfylde, sonnet

Is there a heart that music cannot melt?
—Beattie, *The Minstrel*, Book I, Stanza 56

There are two golden rules for an orchestra: start together and finish
  together. The public doesn't give a damn what goes on in between.
                                    —Sir Thomas Beecham, in Harold Atkins
                                    and Archie Newman, *Beecham Stories*

Men think God is destroying them because he is tuning them. The
  violinist screws up the key till the tense cord sounds the concert
  pitch; but it is not to break it, but to use it tunefully, that he
  stretches the string upon the musical rack.   —Henry Ward Beecher

Music is the mediation between the intellect and the sensuous life.
                                    —Ludwig van Beethoven, quoted by Bettine Brentano in a
                                    letter to Johann Wolfgang von Goethe

I must play the instrument I've got.   —Saul Bellow, *Herzog*

Fiddle, n. An instrument to tickle human ears by friction of a horse's
  tail on the entrails of a cat.   —Ambrose Bierce

We are all strings in the concert of His joy.   —Jacob Boehme

Who hears music, feels his solitude / Peopled at once.
                                    —Robert Browning, "Balaustion's Adventure"

Music, once admitted into the soul, becomes a sort of spirit, and
  never dies.   —Edward Bulwer-Lytton

There is music in all things, if men had ears.   —Lord Byron

Music is well said to be the speech of the angels.   —Thomas Carlyle

Music has Charms to soothe a savage Breast.
                                    —William Congreve, *The Mourning Bride, a Tragedy*

That's where rock 'n roll is really at. Driving around in a car with the
  radio on.   —Jeffrey Connolly, rock musician

Music is the arithmetic of sounds as optics is the geometry of light.
                                    —Claude Debussy

Music is but wild sounds civilized into time and tune.
                                    —Thomas Fuller

. . . there are chords in every human heart. If we only knew how to
  strike the right chord, we would bring out the music.
                                    —Mahatma Gandhi, *Harijan*, 27 May 1939

Music stands in much closer connection with pure sensation than
any of the other arts. —Helmholtz

Music expresses that which cannot be said and on which it is impossible to be silent. —Victor Hugo

Classical music is th' kind that we keep thinkin'll turn into a tune.
—Frank McKinney ("Kin") Hubbard

People think the Beatles know what's going on. We don't. We're just
doing it. —John Lennon

Music is not a science any more than poetry is. It is a sublime
instinct, like genius of all kinds. —Ouida

Music is an invisible dance, as dancing is a silent music. —Jean Paul

Twelve Highlanders and a bagpipe make a rebellion.
—Proverb (Scottish)

It is in learning music that many youthful hearts learn love. —Ricard

You cannot play the piano well unless you are singing within you.
—Artur Rubinstein

People who have memorized your songs—how can you not love
them? —Todd Rundgren, rock musician

Not without design does God write the music of our lives.
—John Ruskin

The notes I handle no better than many pianists. But the pauses
between the notes—ah, that is where the art resides.
—Artur Schnabel

The sonatas of Mozart are unique; they are too easy for children, and
too difficult for artists. —Artur Schnabel

Too many pieces of music finish too long after the end.
—Igor Stravinsky

Conductors must give unmistakable and suggestive signals to the
orchestra, not choreography to the audience. —George Szell

The still, sad music of humanity. —William Wordsworth

The MYSTERIOUS

The most beautiful experience we can have is the mysterious.
—Albert Einstein, *Ideas and Opinions*

. . . science and speculation pass into mystery at last.
—William Mountford

The ultimate gift of a conscious life is a sense of the mystery that
  encompasses it.   —Lewis Mumford, *The Conduct of Life*

A genuine faith resolves the mystery of life by the mystery of God.
—Reinhold Niebuhr

We have come to see how great is the unexplored.
—Ayn Rand, *Anthem*

As soon as man does not take his existence for granted, but beholds it
  as something unfathomably mysterious, thought begins.
—Albert Schweitzer, *The Teaching of Reverence for Life*

With all your science can you tell how it is, and whence it is, that
  light comes into the soul?
—Henry David Thoreau, *Journal*, 16 Jul 1851

MYTHS

A myth is a religion in which no one any longer believes.
—James K. Feibleman, *Understanding Philosophy*

— N —

NAIVETE

Dare to be naive.

—R. Buckminster Fuller

NAKEDNESS

The first undressing of two lovers is a most special event.
—Saul Bellow, *More Die of Heartbreak*

The nakedness of woman is the work of God. —William Blake

Her gentle limbs did she undress, / And lay down in her loveliness.
—Samuel Taylor Coleridge, *Christabel*, Part I, Stanza 24

a pretty girl who naked is
is worth a million statues. —e. e. cummings, *Collected Poems*

Man is the sole animal whose nudity offends his own companions,
and the only one who, in his natural actions, withdraws and hides
himself from his own kind. —Michel de Montaigne

NAMES

A nickname is the heaviest stone the devil can throw at a man.
—William Hazlitt, *Sketches and Essays*

What's in a name? that which we call a rose / By any other name
would smell as sweet.
—William Shakespeare, *Romeo and Juliet*, Act II, Sc. ii

NATIONALITY

Every man loves and admires his own country because it produced
him. —Edward Bulwer-Lytton

Nationality isn't soul . . .
—Bernard Malamud, *Rembrandt's Hat*, "Man in the Drawer"

NATURE

Nature, to be commanded, must be obeyed.
—Francis Bacon, *Novum Organum*

The emotion felt by a man in the presence of nature certainly counts for something in the origin of religions.
—Henry Bergson, *The Two Sources of Morality and Religion*

Nature speaks to us in detail, and . . . only through detail can we find her grand design.
—J. Bronowski and Bruce Mazlish, *The Western Intellectual Tradition*

Nature's mighty law is change.
—Robert Burns, "Let Not Women E'er Complain"

Nature is but a name for an effect, / Whose cause is God.
—William Cowper, *The Task*, Book VI, "The Winter Walk at Noon"

Nature is the art of God.   —Dante Alighieri, *De Monarchia*, Book I

It is an outcome of faith that nature—as she is perceptible to our five senses—takes the character of such a well formulated puzzle.
—Albert Einstein, *Out of My Later Years*

In the woods is perpetual youth.   —Ralph Waldo Emerson

Nature is too thin a screen; the glory of the omnipresent God bursts through everywhere.   —Ralph Waldo Emerson

All Nature wears one universal grin.
—Henry Fielding, *Tom Thumb the Great*, Act I, Sc. i

Nature is the living, visible garment of God.
—Johann Wolfgang von Goethe

Nature loves to hide.   —Heraclitus

Nature loves simplicity.   —Johannes Kepler

The old Lakota was wise. He knew that man's heart away from nature becomes hard; he knew that lack of respect for growing, living things soon led to lack of respect for humans too.
—Chief Luther Standing Bear

All nature is but art, unknown to thee; / All chance, direction, which thou canst not see; / All discord, harmony not understood; / All partial evil, universal good.   —Alexander Pope, *An Essay on Man*

Nature abhors a vacuum.—François Rabelais, *Gargantua and Pantagruel*

In nature's infinite book of secrecy / A little I can read.
—William Shakespeare, *Antony and Cleopatra*, Act I, Sc. ii

One touch of nature makes the whole world kin . . .
—William Shakespeare, *Troilus and Cressida*, Act III, Sc. iii

But nothing is all black in nature.
—Alexander Solzhenitsyn, *Victory Celebrations*

A stern discipline pervades all nature, which is a little cruel that it
may be very kind.   —Spenser

A butterfly flitting from flower to flower ever remains mine,
I lose the one that is netted by me.   —Rabindranath Tagore, *Fireflies*

Men argue, nature acts.   —Voltaire

NECESSITY

Necessity is a hard nurse, but she raises strong children.
—Anonymous

Necessity makes even cowards brave.   —Anonymous

Necessity has no law.   —Saint Augustine, *Soliloquia Animae ad Deum*

Necessity urges desperate measures.
—Miguel de Cervantes, *Don Quixote*, Book III, Ch. xxiii

Necessity makes an honest man a knave.
—Daniel Defoe, *Serious Reflections of Robinson Crusoe*

Man must have bread and butter, but he must also have something to
lift his heart.   —Farouk El Baz

Necessity does everything well.
—Ralph Waldo Emerson, *Essays, Second Series*, "Gifts"

We do what we must, and call it by the best names.
—Ralph Waldo Emerson, *The Conduct of Life*,
"Considerations by the Way"

Necessity never made a good bargain.
—Benjamin Franklin, *Poor Richard's Almanack*, 1735

And yet the true creator is necessity, which is the mother of our
  invention. —Plato, *The Republic*

Necessity, that excellent master, hath taught me many things.
                                    —Pliny the Younger

Necessity breaks iron. —Proverb (German)

What is necessary is never a risk. —Cardinal de Retz, *Mémoires*

Necessity makes even the timid brave.
                    —Sallust, *Bellum Catilinoe*, Ch. 58

Everything that happens, happens of necessity.
                                —Arthur Schopenhauer

When it is necessary, one learns to do what one has never done
  before. —Janice Jordan Shefelman, *A Paradise Called Texas*

NEEDS

The greatest need of youth is money; of middle age is time, of old age
  is energy. —Anonymous

Danger levels man and brute, and all are fellows in their need.
                                    —Lord Byron

We all need to think we belong to other people.
              —Linda Donelson, speech, Jun 1988, Dallas, Texas

We act as though comfort and luxury were the chief requirements of
  life, when all that we need to make us really happy is something to
  be enthusiastic about. —Charles Kingsley

One of the oldest human needs is having someone to wonder where
  you are when you don't come home at night. —Margaret Mead

. . . our three basic human needs (self-worth, intimacy with others,
  and intimacy with God).
        —Frank B. Minirth and Paul D. Meier, *Happiness is a Choice*

All men need something to poetize and idealize their life a little—
  something which they value for more than its use, and which is a
  symbol of their emancipation from the mere materialism and
  drudgery of daily life. —Theodore Parker

Need teaches a plan.   —Proverb (Irish)

... a man can safely sacrifice a great deal as long as he clings to the
   essential.   —Alexander Solzhenitsyn, *The Gulag Archipelago Three*

How quickly a zek [a prisoner] gets cheeky—or, putting it in literary
   language, how quickly a man's requirements grow.
                 —Alexander Solzhenitsyn, *The Gulag Archipelago Three*

Heaven's eternal wisdom has decreed, that man should ever stand in
   need of man.   —Theocritus

NEGOTIATION

To jaw-jaw is always better than to war-war.
         —Winston Churchill, speech at the White House, 26 June 1954

Let us never negotiate out of fear. But let us never fear to negotiate.
               —John F. Kennedy, Inaugural Address, 20 Jan 1961

NEIGHBORS

... thou shalt love thy neighbor as thyself.
                        —*The Bible* (KJV): Leviticus 19:18

We make our friends; we make our enemies; but God makes our next-
   door neighbor.   —G. K. Chesterton

A man's neighbor is everyone that needs help.   —J. C. Geikie

Let me be a little meeker / With the brother that is weaker, / Let me
   think more of my neighbor / And a little less of me.
                             —Edgar A. Guest, "A Creed"

Love your neighbor, yet pull not down your hedge.
                    —George Herbert, *Jacula Prudentum*

When your neighbor's wall is on fire, it becomes your business.
                                      —Horace, *Epistles*

A good neighbor doubles the value of a house.   —Proverb (German)

No one likes the house next door to look worse or a lot better than
   his own.   —Andrew A. Rooney, *Pieces of My Mind*, "Neighbors"

NETWORKS

You never know the power of the network of another person.
—Bob Keith, speech at a Community Support Program conference,
Austin, Texas, 20 May 1988

NEUTRALITY

Neutral men are the devil's allies.   —Edwin Hubbel Chapin

Isaac NEWTON

I do not know what I may appear to the world, but to myself I seem
to have been only like a boy playing on the sea-shore, and divert-
ing myself in now and then finding a smoother pebble or a prettier
shell than ordinary, whilst the great ocean of truth lay undiscov-
ered before me.
—Isaac Newton, in Brewster's *Memoirs of Newton*, II. xxvii.

If I have seen further it is by standing on the shoulders of giants.
—Isaac Newton, letter to Robert Hooke, 5 Feb 1676

Nature and Nature's laws lay hid in night: / God said, Let Newton be!
and all was light.
—Alexander Pope, "Epitaph Intended for Sir Isaac Newton"

NIGHT

. . . the unexplainable nighthawks you found in any fair-sized town.
—James Agee, *A Death in the Family*

Blessed to us is the night, for it reveals the stars.   —Anonymous

He who wants to enjoy the glory of the sunrise must live through the
night.   —Anonymous

Night is the mother of thoughts. —John Florio, *Florio His Firste Fruites*

I have been one acquainted with the night.
—Robert Frost, *West-Running Brook*, "Acquainted with the Night"

There is a budding morrow in midnight.   —John Keats

The night is a good counselor.   —Proverb (French)

NOBLENESS

Are not our noblest feelings as it were the poems of our will.
—Honoré de Balzac

Every noble work is at first impossible. —Thomas Carlyle

I count this thing to be grandly true: / That a noble deed is a step
toward God. —Josiah Gilbert Holland, "Gradatim"

Be noble! and the nobleness that lies / In other men, sleeping, but
never dead, / Will rise in majesty to meet thine own.
—James Russell Lowell, Sonnet IV

They are never alone that are accompanied with noble thoughts.
—Sir Philip Sidney, *Arcadia*

Accost whoever you may meet with noble feeling; perhaps what is
noble will begin to stir in him. —J. Trojan

NONCONFORMITY

Whoso would be a man must be a nonconformist.
—Ralph Waldo Emerson, *Essays, First Series*, "Self-Reliance"

Two roads diverged in a wood, and I—/ I took the one less traveled by,
/ And that has made all the difference.
—Robert Frost, "The Road Not Taken"

Commandment Number One of any truly civilized society is this: Let
people be different. —David Grayson

It isn't fair that there's pressure exerted on those who choose to live
on the edges of the bell-shaped curve of normal.
—Laurel Lee, *Godspeed: Hitchhiking Home*

If a man does not keep pace with his companions, perhaps it is because
he hears a different drummer. Let him step to the music he hears,
however measured or far away.
—Henry David Thoreau, *Walden*, "Conclusion"

NON-COOPERATION

Behind my non-cooperation there is always the keenest desire to
cooperate on the slightest pretext even with the worst of opponents. To me, a very imperfect mortal, ever in need of God's grace,
no one is beyond redemption. —Mahatma Gandhi

There is, however, one other human right which is infrequently mentioned but which seems to be destined to become very important: this is the right, or the duty, of the individual to abstain from cooperating in activities which he considers wrong or pernicious.
—Albert Einstein, *Ideas and Opinions*

In my humble opinion, non-cooperation with evil is as much a duty as is cooperation with good. But in the past, non-cooperation has been deliberately expressed in violence to the evildoer. I am endeavoring to show my countrymen that violent non-cooperation only multiplies evil and that evil can only be sustained by violence. Withdrawal of support of evil requires complete abstention from violence. Non-violence implies voluntary submission to the penalty for non-cooperation with evil.
—Mahatma Gandhi, defense against charge of sedition,
23 Mar 1922

This is in essence the principle of nonviolent non-cooperation. It follows therefore that it must have its root in love. Its object should not be to punish the opponent or to inflict injury upon him. Even while non-cooperating with him, we must make him feel that in us he has a friend and we should try to reach his heart by rendering him humanitarian service whenever possible.
—Mahatma Gandhi

NON-VIOLENCE

That's all non-violence is—organized love.   —Joan Baez, *Daybreak*

The point of nonviolence is to build a floor, a strong new floor, beneath which we can no longer sink. A platform which stands a few feet above napalm, torture, exploitation, poison gas, A and H bombs, the works.   —Joan Baez, *Daybreak*

We're not really pacifists, we're nonviolent soldiers.   —Joan Baez

A non-violent revolution is not a programme of seizure of power. It is a programme of transformation of relationships, ending in a peaceful transfer of power.
—Mahatma Gandhi, *Non-Violence in Peace and War*

Belief in non-violence is based on the assumption that human nature in the essence is one and therefore unfailingly responds to the advances of love . . .   —Mahatma Gandhi

If blood be shed, let it be our blood. Cultivate the quiet courage of
dying without killing. For man lives freely only by his readiness to
die, if need be, at the hands of his brother, never by killing him.
—Mahatma Gandhi

I have no secret methods. I know no diplomacy save that of truth. I
have no weapon but non-violence.   —Mahatma Gandhi

I wanted to avoid violence. Non-violence is the first article of my
faith. It is also the last article of my creed.   —Mahatma Gandhi,
speech at Shahi Bag, 18 Mar 1922, in *Young India*, 23 Mar 1922

It is no non-violence if we merely love those that love us. It is non-
violence only when we love those that hate us. —Mahatma Gandhi

Non-violence implies voluntary submission to the penalty for non-
cooperation with evil.   —Mahatma Gandhi

Non-violence is a weapon of the strong.   —Mahatma Gandhi

Non-violence . . . is the only thing that the atom bomb cannot
destroy. I did not move a muscle when I first heard that the atom
bomb had wiped out Hiroshima. On the contrary, I said to myself,
Unless now the world adopts non-violence, it will spell certain suicide for mankind.
—Mahatma Gandhi, speech at New Delhi, 24 Sep 1946

Non-violence should never be used as a shield for cowardice. It is a
weapon for the brave.   —Mahatma Gandhi

The strength to kill is not essential for self-defense; one ought to have
the strength to die. When a man is fully ready to die, he will not
even desire to offer violence. Indeed, I may put it down as a self-
evident proposition that the desire to kill is in inverse proportion
to the desire to die. And history is replete with instances of men
who by dying with courage and compassion on their lips converted
the hearts of their violent opponents.   —Mahatma Gandhi

We have to make truth and non-violence not matters for mere individual practice but for practice by groups and communities and
nations. That at any rate is my dream. I shall live and die in trying
to realize it. My faith helps me to discover new truths every day.
—Mahatma Gandhi

What is wanted is a deliberate giving up of violence out of strength.
—Mahatma Gandhi

At the center of non-violence stands the principle of love.
—Martin Luther King, Jr.

Non-violence is a powerful and just weapon. It is a weapon unique in
history, which cuts without wounding and ennobles the man who
wields it. It is a sword that heals.   —Martin Luther King, Jr.

The modern choice is between non-violence or non-existence.
—Martin Luther King, Jr.

Dying is more honorable than killing.—Seneca, *Epistuloe and Lucilium*

Let yourself be killed, but do not kill.   —*The Talmud*

. . . active nonviolence is an appropriate personal response to the
challenges of the Nuclear Age.   —Gerard A. Vanderhaar,
Christians and Nonviolence in the Nuclear Age, Introduction

NORMALITY

The only normal people are the ones you don't know very well.
—Joe Ancis

Why be normal?   —Anonymous, bumper sticker

NOSTALGIA

Nostalgia isn't what it used to be.   —Peter de Vries

NURTURING

Nurturing one another is what it's all about, and this generation has a
long way to go before we love too much.   —Marianne Williamson

— O —

OBEDIENCE

... We ought to obey God rather than men.
—*The Bible* (KJV): The Acts 5:29

For as by one man's disobedience many were made sinners, so by the obedience of one shall many be made righteous.
—*The Bible* (KJV): Romans 5:19

Children, obey your parents in the Lord: for this is right.
—*The Bible* (KJV): Ephesians 6:1

Let thy child's first lesson be obedience, and the second will be what thou wilt. —Benjamin Franklin, *Poor Richard's Almanack*

God does not call us to be successful, but to be obedient.
—Billy Graham, *Till Armageddon*

I find that doing the will of God leaves me no time for disputing His plans. —George Macdonald, *Marquis of Lossie*, Ch. 72

Obedience is yielded more readily to one who commands gently.
—Seneca, *De Clementia*, Book I, Sec. 24

Learn to obey before you command.
—Solon, in Diogenes Laertius, *Lives of Eminent Philosophers*

He obeyed, mostly out of exhaustion. —Anne Tyler, *Breathing Lessons*

OBJECTIONS

Nothing will ever be attempted, if all possible objections must be first overcome. —Samuel Johnson, *Rasselas*, Ch. 6

OBJECTIVITY

Don't ask the barber whether you need a haircut. —Daniel Greenberg

It is difficult to see the picture when you are inside the frame.
—R. S. Trapp

OBSCURITY

Little fishes slip through nets, but great fishes are taken.

—Anonymous

It often happens that those of whom we speak least on earth are best known in heaven. —Nicolas Caussin

I am afraid of losing my obscurity. Genuineness only thrives in the dark. Like celery. —Aldous Huxley, *Those Barren Leaves*

OFFENSE

When any one has offended me, I try to raise my soul so high that the offense cannot reach it. —René Descartes

It is just as much an offense to take offense as it is to give offense.

—Ken Keyes

OPINIONS

The horror of our history has purged me of opinions.
—John Barth, *Lost in the Funhouse*, "Night-Sea Journey"

Men get opinions as boys learn to spell, / By iteration chiefly . . .
—Elizabeth Barrett Browning, *Aurora Leigh*, Book VI

He that complies against his will, / Is of his own opinion still, / Which he may adhere to, yet disown, / For reasons to himself best known.
—Samuel Butler (bapt. 1612, d. 1680), *Hudibras*

Every new opinion, at its starting, is precisely in a minority of one.
—Thomas Carlyle,
On Heroes and Hero-Worship, and the Heroic in History, II

If you must tell me your opinions, tell me what you believe in. I have plenty of doubts of my own. —Johann Wolfgang von Goethe

Those who never retract their opinions love themselves more than they love truth. —Joseph Joubert, *Pensées*

Men are never so good or so bad as their opinions.
—James Mackintosh,
Dissertation on the Progress of Ethical Philosophy

Where there is much desire to learn, there of necessity will be much
    arguing, much writing, many opinions; for opinion in good men is
    but knowledge in the making.   —John Milton, *Areopagitica*

My opinion, my conviction, gains infinitely in strength and success,
    the moment a second mind has adopted it.   —Novalis

This world belongs to the man who is wise enough to change his
    mind in the presence of facts.   —Roy L. Smith

You're sincere, but in order not to upset your views you avoid talking
    with people who think differently. You pick your thoughts from
    conversations with people like yourself, from books written by
    people like yourself. In physics they call it resonance. You start out
    with modest opinions, but they match and build each other up to a
    scale . . .   —Alexander Solzhenitsyn, *The First Circle*

. . . one person with their mind made up can shove a lot of folks
    aroun'!   —John Steinbeck, *The Grapes of Wrath*, Ch. 16

So many men, so many opinions.   —Terence, *Phormio*

Do not interfere when your opinion is not sought.
          —Thomas à Kempis

It is difference of opinion that makes horse races.
          —Mark Twain, *Pudd'nhead Wilson*,
          "Pudd'nhead Wilson's Calendar"

OPPORTUNITY

Every day gives you another chance.   —Anonymous

Sail while the breeze blows, wind and tide wait for no man.
          —Anonymous

While you wait for great things, the door to little ones may close.
          —Anonymous

A man must make his opportunity, as oft as find it.
        —Francis Bacon, *Advancement of Learning*, Bk. II

A wise man will make more opportunities than he finds.
        —Francis Bacon, *Essays*, "Of Ceremonies and Respects"

Opportunity makes a thief.
        —Francis Bacon, letter to the Earl of Essex, 1598

When God shuts a door he opens a window.
—Hugh Casson and Joyce Grenfell, *Nanny Says*

When one door is shut, another opens.　　—Miguel de Cervantes

Opportunity does not knock; it presents itself when you beat down the door.　　—Kyle Chandler

Not only strike while the iron is hot, but make it hot by striking.
—Oliver Cromwell

The secret of success in life is for a man to be ready for his opportunity when it comes.　　—Benjamin Disraeli

Seek not for fresher founts afar, / Just drop your bucket where you are.
—Sam Walter Foss

Make hay while the sun shines.　　—John Heywood, *Proverbs*

We are confronted with insurmountable opportunities.
—Walt Kelly, from his cartoon comic strip "Pogo"

Often God has to shut a door in our face, so that he can subsequently open the door through which He wants us to go.
—Catherine Marshall, *A Man Called Peter*, Ch. 2

This chance will stand before you only once. —Sandra Day O'Connor

Pluck with quick hand the fruit that passes.　　—Ovid

Strike while the iron is hot.　　—Proverb (14th century)

The opportunity of a lifetime is seldom so labeled.
—Proverb (American)

God's best gift to us is not things, but opportunities.
—Alice W. Rollins

. . . let not advantage slip.　—William Shakespeare, *Venus and Adonis*

There is a tide in the affairs of men / Which, taken at the flood, leads on to fortune; / Omitted, all the voyage of their life / Is bound in shallows and in miseries. / On such a full sea are we now afloat; / And we must take the current when it serves, / Or lose our ventures.
—William Shakespeare, *Julius Caesar*, Act IV, Sc. iii

Opportunities are seldom labeled. —John A. Shedd, *Salt from My Attic*

We are all faced with a series of great opportunities brilliantly disguised as impossible situations. —Charles P. Swindoll

The hour is ripe, and yonder lies the way. —Virgil, *Aeneid*

OPTIMISM

There are nettles everywhere, / But smooth green grasses are more common still. / The blue of heaven is larger than the cloud.
—Elizabeth Barrett Browning

I am an optimist. It does not seem too much use being anything else.
—Winston Churchill

The worst doesn't usually happen.   —Elizabeth Croman, 16 Jan 1991

Speak the affirmative; emphasize your choice by utter ignoring of all that you reject. —Ralph Waldo Emerson

The habit of looking on the best side of every event is worth more than a thousand a year. —Samuel Johnson

Some people are always grumbling that roses have thorns; I am thankful that thorns have roses. —Alphonse Karr

The lowest ebb is the turn of the tide.—Henry Wadsworth Longfellow

When things come to the worst, they generally mend.
—Susanna Moodie

She wanted to believe that tomorrow, or at least the day after, life, such a battle at best, was going to be better.
—Katherine Anne Porter, *Noon Wine*

In this the best of all possible worlds . . . all is for the best.
—Voltaire, *Candide*

Say you are well, or all is well with you, / And God shall hear your words and make them true. —Ella Wheeler Wilcox

ORDER

Order is a lovely thing; / On disarray it lays its wing, / Teaching simplicity to sing. —Anna H. Branch

Order is heaven's first law. —Alexander Pope

A place for everything, and everything in its place.
—Samuel Smiles, *Thrift*, Ch. 5

The ORDINARY

Consciously cultivate the ordinary. —Walker Percy

ORIGINALITY

Originality is the act of forgetting where you read it. —Anonymous

There is nothing original; all is reflected light. —Honoré de Balzac

There is nothing new but what is forgotten. —Madamoiselle Bertine

Is there any thing whereof it may be said, See, this is new? . . .
—*The Bible* (KJV): Ecclesiastes 1:10

There is not a thought in our heads which hasn't been worn shiny by
other brains. —Henry S. Haskins, *Meditations in Wall Street*

They will say that you are on the wrong road, if it is your own.
—Antonio Porchia

What a good thing Adam had. When he said a good thing, he knew
nobody had said it before. —Mark Twain, *Notebooks*

ORNAMENTATION

For loveliness / Needs not the foreign aid of ornament, / But is when
unadorned adorned the most. —Francis Thomson

OTHERS

It is some comfort to the wretched to have others to share in their
woe. —Anonymous

We are on earth to do good to others. What the others are here for, I
don't know. —W. H. Auden

We are born not for ourselves alone. —Cicero

Only a life lived for others is the life worth while.
—Albert Einstein, "Defining Success"

Other men are lenses through which we read our own minds.
—Ralph Waldo Emerson

Always think in terms of what the other person wants.
—James van Fleet

It is well to remember that the entire universe, with one trifling exception, is composed of others.   —John Andrew Holmes

Try to forget our cares and our maladies, and contribute, as we can, to the cheerfulness of each other.   —Samuel Johnson

The best way to cheer yourself is to try to cheer somebody else up.
—Mark Twain

You probably wouldn't worry about what people think of you if you could know how seldom they do.   —Oscar Wilde

— P —

PACE

Always do one thing less than you think you can do.
—Bernard Baruch

What is done well is done quickly enough.
—Augustus Caesar, in Suetonius, *Lives of the Caesars*

Adopt the pace of nature; her secret is patience.
—Ralph Waldo Emerson

If they try to rush me, I always say, "I've only got one other speed,
and it's slower." —Glenn Ford

Slow and steady wins the race.
—Robert Lloyd, *The Hare and the Tortoise*

Wisely, and slow; they stumble that run fast.
—William Shakespeare, *Romeo and Juliet*, Act II, Sc. iii

For fast-acting relief try slowing down. —Lily Tomlin

The lazy man gets round the sun as quickly as the busy one.
—R. T. Wombat

Life is a marathon, not a sprint. —Tom Zimmermann

PACIFISM

I am an absolute pacifist . . . It is an instinctive feeling. It is a feeling
that possesses me, because the murder of men is disgusting.
—Albert Einstein, interview with Paul Hutchinson
in *Christian Century*, 28 Aug 1929

My pacifism is not based on any intellectual theory but on a deep
antipathy to every form of cruelty and hatred.
—Albert Einstein, comment on the outbreak of World War I

PAIN

There is advantage in the wisdom won from pain.
—Aeschylus, *Eumenides*

Learn the lesson of your own pain. —Anonymous

When the head aches, all the members share the pain.
—Miguel de Cervantes, *Don Quixote*

Faint is the bliss, that never past thro' pain.
—Colley Cibber, *Love in a Riddle*, Act III, Sc. ii

God can use a sensitive Christian to be a rich blessing in the life of
one who knows pain and sorrow. —Billy Graham, *Till Armageddon*

Out of pain and problems have come the sweetest songs, the most
poignant poems, the most gripping stories.
—Billy Graham, *Till Armageddon*

The least pain in our little finger gives us more pain and uneasiness
than the destruction of millions of our fellow beings.
—William Hazlitt, *The Edinburg Review* (Scottish),
Oct 1829, "American Literature—Dr. Channing"

Pain and disease awaken us to convictions which are necessary to our
moral condition. —Samuel Johnson

Those who do not feel pain seldom think that it is felt.
—Samuel Johnson, *The Rambler*

There is a pleasure that is born of pain. —Owen Meredith

Be patient and tough; someday this pain will be useful to you. —Ovid

The measure of a man is not whether he has pain, for this all men
must have in common. The measure of a man is what gives him
pain. —Rabbi Jack Riemer

Joy shared is joy doubled; pain shared is pain divided. —Rückert

It seemed to me a matter of course that we should all take our share
of the burden of pain which lies upon the world.
—Albert Schweitzer

. . . one fire burns out another's burning. One pain is lessen'd by
another's anguish.
—William Shakespeare, *Romeo and Juliet*, Act I, Sc. ii

Nearly everyone has his box of secret pain . . .
—John Steinbeck, *East of Eden*

Nothing begins, and nothing ends, / That is not paid for with moan; / For we are born in other's pain, / And perish in our own.
—Francis Thompson, "Daisy"

Sooner or later, even the sharpest pain became flattened.
—Anne Tyler, *Breathing Lessons*

PAINTING

Not a day without a line.   —Apelles, proverbial from Pliny the Elder, *Natural History*, XXXV, 36

It's so good and so terrible to attack a blank canvas.   —Paul Cézanne

Few people can look at a painting longer than it takes to peel an orange and eat it.   —Sir Kenneth Clark

Painting is the intermediate between a thought and a thing.
—Samuel Taylor Coleridge

In painting you must give the idea of the true by means of the false.
—Edgar Dégas

One always has to spoil a picture a little bit, in order to finish it.
—Eugène Delacroix

The mind paints before the brush.   —James Ellis

A painter told me that nobody could draw a tree without in some sort becoming a tree.   —Ralph Waldo Emerson, *Essays*, "History"

I think sculpture and painting have an effect to teach us manners and abolish hurry.   —Ralph Waldo Emerson

There are three things I have always loved, and never understood—painting, music, women.   —Bernard le Bovier de Fontenelle

I shut my eyes in order to see.   —Paul Gauguin

That which probably hears more stupidities than anything else in the world is a painting in a museum.
—Edmond and Jules de Goncourt, *Idées et sensations*

Life is painting a picture, not doing a sum.
>—Oliver Wendell Holmes, Jr.

Every new painting is like throwing myself into the water without knowing how to swim. —Édouard Manet

I paint as I feel like painting; to hell with all their studies.
>—Édouard Manet

[In Fauve painting] it is as though the natural world were transposed into another key. —Denis Mathews, *Fauvism*

Picture making is a mixture of creation and craft. The artist goes to his work under the stimulus of some excitement which has been filtered through his own temperament. His temperament, of course, has been itself conditioned by the period in which he lives, the culture and taste with which he is surrounded, the purpose which his art will serve, and the technical means available for him to express himself. —Denis Mathews, *Fauvism*

Everyone wants to understand painting. Why don't they try to understand the singing of birds? People love the night, a flower, everything which surrounds them without trying to understand them. But painting—that they must understand. —Pablo Picasso

I understand my own pictures best six months after I have done them. —Pablo Picasso

When I am finished painting, I paint again for relaxation.
>—Pablo Picasso, in Francoise Gilot, *Life with Picasso*

[Matisse painted] not as a pastime, but as a way of embracing life.
>—John Russell

The artist finds a greater pleasure in painting than in having completed the picture. —Seneca, *Letters to Lucilius*

... a canvas that I have covered is worth more than a blank canvas. My pretensions go no further; that is my right to paint, my reason for painting. —Irving Stone, *Lust for Life*

A painter should not paint what he sees, but what will be seen.
>—Paul Valéry

I have walked this earth for 30 years, and, out of gratitude, want to
leave some souvenir.
—Vincent van Gogh, in Jan Julsker, editor, *Van Gogh's Diary*

Good painting is like good cooking; it can be tasted, but not
explained.
—Maurice de Vlaminck

[Van Gogh was] a man who did not seek to seize or hold a kingdom
but to give one away.
—Robert Wallace

A painting can do something for your spirit that nothing else can.
—Reva Yares

PARADISE

The bird of paradise alights only upon the hand that does not grasp.
—John Berry, *Flight of White Crows*

Having mourned your sin, for outward Eden lost, find paradise
within.
—John Dryden

The wonder is what you can make a paradise out of. —Eva Hoffman

Paradise is here or nowhere: you must take your joy with you or you
will never find it.
—O. S. Marden

One path leads to paradise, but a thousand to hell.
—Proverb (Yiddish)

PARDON

Pardon is granted to necessity. —Cicero, *De Officiis*

God will pardon me: that is his business. —Heinrich Heine

We pardon to the extent that we love.
—François de La Rochefoucauld, *Maximes*

The very best men stand in need of pardon. —Proverb (English)

Virtue pardons the wicked, as the sandal-tree perfumes the axe which
strikes it.
—Saadi

I pardon him, as God shall pardon me.
—William Shakespeare, *King Richard II*, Act V, Sc. iii

Pardon, not wrath, is God's best attribute.
  —Bayard Taylor, "The Temptation of Hassan Ben Kaled," Stanza 11

Know all and you will pardon all.
                    —Thomas à Kempis, *The Imitation of Christ*

PARENTING

One didn't issue instructions to comets. Grown children did what
  they had to do, and parents could only grit their teeth and watch
  and pray for them to get through it.   —Lisa Alther, *Kinflicks*

If you don't firmly program your children's minds with truth, someone else will do so with half-truth, untruth, and unimportant
  truth.   —Anonymous

No man ever really finds out what he believes in until he begins to
  instruct his children.   —Anonymous

The best inheritance a parent can give his children is—a few minutes
  of his time each day.   —Anonymous

Train up a child in the way he should go: and when he is old, he will
  not depart from it.   —*The Bible* (KJV): Proverbs 22:6

Train up a child in the way he should go and walk there yourself once
  in a while.   —Josh Billings

Parents are not quite interested in justice, they are interested in quiet.
                                                    —Bill Cosby

The best way to raise one child is to have two.   —Marcelene Cox

Religious words have value to the child only as experience in the
  home gives them meaning.   —John Drescher

Respect the child. Be not too much his parent. Trespass not on his
  solitude.   —Ralph Waldo Emerson,
                        Lectures and Biographical Sketches, "Education"

Let your children go if you want to keep them.   —Malcolm Forbes

Teach your child to hold his tongue; he'll learn fast enough to speak.
        —Benjamin Franklin, *Poor Richard's Almanack*, 1734

Your children are not your children.   —Kahlil Gibran

You are the bows from which your children as living arrows are sent
   forth.   —Kahlil Gibran, *The Prophet*, "On Children"

We can't form our children on our own concepts; we must take them
   and love them as God gives them to us.
                    —Johann Wolfgang von Goethe, *Hermann and Dorothea*

Where parents do too much for their children, the children will not
   do much for themselves.   —Elbert Hubbard, *The Note Book*

The instruction received at the mother's knee, and the paternal
   lessons, together with the pious and sweet souvenirs of the fireside,
   are never entirely effaced from the soul.   —Lamennais

A torn jacket is soon mended; but hard words bruise the heart of a
   child.   —Henry Wadsworth Longfellow

Children aren't happy with nothing to ignore, / And that's what parents were created for.
                    —Ogden Nash, *Many Long Years Ago*, "The Parent"

What a relief it is when you find that you've actually brought up a
   reasonable and civilized human being.
                    —Philip, Duke of Edinburgh, in Peter Lane, *Our Future King*

Don't limit a child to your own learning, for he was born in another
   time.   —Rabinnical saying

Romance fails us and so do friendships, but the relationship of parent
   and child, less noisy than all others, remains indelible and indestructible, the strongest relationship on earth.
                    —Theodor Reik, *Of Love and Lust*

If a child tells you a lie, tell him that he has told a lie, but don't call
   him a liar. If you define him as a liar, you break down his confidence in his own character.   —Jean Paul Richter

Before I got married I had six theories about bringing up children.
   Now I have six children—and no theories.   —Lord Rochester

Whatever you would have your children become, strive to exhibit in
   your own lives and conversation.   —Lydia Sigourney

Was it Gorky who said: "If your children are no better than you are, you have fathered in vain, indeed you have lived in vain."
—Alexander Solzhenitsyn, *Cancer Ward*

The more people have studied different methods of bringing up children the more they have come to the conclusion that what good mothers and fathers instinctively feel like doing for their babies is usually best after all. —Dr. Benjamin Spock

You know more than you think you do.
—Dr. Benjamin Spock, *Baby and Child Care*, opening words

It's clear that most American children suffer too much mother and too little father. —Gloria Steinem

Making the decision to have a child—it's momentous. It is to decide forever to have your heart go walking outside your body.
—Elizabeth Stone

It is better to keep children to their duty by sense of honor and by kindness than by fear. —Terence

[Cartoon caption:] I never really rallied after the birth of my first child. —James Thurber, *Thurber & Company*

Parenthood remains the greatest single preserve of the amateur.
—Alvin Toffler

[About parenting:] . . . all that tedium, broken up by little spurts of high drama. —Anne Tyler, *Saint Maybe*, Ch. 10

Who of us is mature enough for offspring before the offspring themselves arrive? The value of marriage is not that adults produce children but that children produce adults.
—Peter de Vries, *Tunnel of Love*

The time not to become a father is eighteen years before a war.
—E. B. White

Schoolmasters and parents exist to be grown out of.
—John Wolfenden

PARTING

Every parting is a form of death, as every reunion is a type of heaven.
—Tryon Edwards

In every parting there is an image of death.
                                    —George Eliot, *Scenes of Clerical Life*

Only in the agony of parting do we look into the depths of love.
                                    —George Eliot

To part is to die a little.   —Proverb (French)

God be with you till we meet again.
                                    —Jeremiah Eames Rankin, "Mizpah"

Good night, good night! Parting is such sweet sorrow.
                                    —William Shakespeare, *Romeo and Juliet*, Act II, Sc. ii

P A S S I O N

There exists a passion for comprehension, just as there exists a passion for music. That passion is rather common in children, but gets lost in most people later on. Without this passion there would be neither mathematics nor natural science.   —Albert Einstein

A man in a passion rides a mad horse.
                                    —Benjamin Franklin, *Poor Richard's Almanack*, 1749

Nothing great in the world was ever accomplished without passion.
                                    —G. W. F. Hegel, *Philosophy of History*

The ruling passion, be it what it will, / The ruling passion conquers reason still.
                                    —Alexander Pope, *Epistles to Several Persons*, "To Lord Bathurst"

Three passions, simple but overwhelmingly strong, have governed my life: the longing for love, the search for knowledge, and the unbearable pity for the suffering of mankind.
                                    —Bertrand Russell, *Autobiography*, Vol. 2, Ch. 3

The passions are the winds which fill the sails of the vessel; they sink it at times, but without them it would be impossible to make way.
                                    —Voltaire

P A S T

Even God cannot change the past.   —Agathon

Study the past, if you would divine the future.   —Confucius, *Analects*

Fret not over the irretrievable, but ever act as if thy life were just
   begun.   —Johann Wolfgang von Goethe

Yesterday is in the books, dead and buried.
              —Mark Harris, *Bang the Drum Slowly*

Though the past haunt me as a spirit, I do not ask to forget.
            —Felicia Dorothea Browne Hemans

The mill cannot grind with water that's past.
           —George Herbert, *Jacula Prudentum*

. . . what is past is gone and I don't have to drag it along with me . . .
      —Joyce Rebeta-Burditt, *The Cracker Factory*

Everyone is the child of his past.   —Edna G. Rostow

I tell you the past is a bucket of ashes.
          —Carl Sandburg, *Cornhuskers*, "Prairie"

Those who cannot remember the past are condemned to repeat it.
              —George Santayana,
   The Life of Reason: Reason in Common Sense, Vol. 1, Ch. 12

Does one come to enjoy even the hardships that help make one the
   person one is? Or is it that the past becomes a legend to be remembered with laughter?   —Mary Sarton

What's gone and what's past help / Should be past grief . . .
     —William Shakespeare, *The Winter's Tale*, Act III, Sc. ii

. . . what's past is prologue . . .
       —William Shakespeare, *The Tempest*, Act II, Sc. i

. . . they don't sell tickets to the past.
         —Alexander Solzhenitsyn, *The First Circle*

The past was a dream wasn't it? And who ever remembers dreams?
           —Ivan Turgenev, *Fathers and Sons*

Each has his past shut in him like the leaves of a book known to him
   by his heart; and his friends can only read the title.
           —Virginia Woolf, *Jacob's Room*

PATIENCE

Patience is a stout horse, but it will tire at last.   —Anonymous

There is no road too long to the man who advances deliberately and without undue haste; there are no honors too distant to the man who prepares himself for them with patience.　　—Anonymous

The secret of patience . . . to do something else in the meantime.
　　　　　　　　　　　　　　　　　　　　　　—Anonymous

My brethren, count it all joy when ye fall into diverse temptations; knowing this, that the trying of our faith worketh patience.
　　　　　　　　　　　　　　—*The Bible* (KJV): James 1:2–3

. . . the patience of Job . . .　　　　　—*The Bible* (KJV): James 5:11

Patience, n. A minor form of despair, disguised as a virtue.
　　　　　　　　　　　　　　　　　　　—Ambrose Bierce

But the waiting time, my brothers, / Is the hardest time of all.
　　　—Sarah Doudney, *Psalms of Life*, "The Hardest Time of All"

He that can have patience can have what he will.
　　　　　　　　　　　　　　　　　—Benjamin Franklin

Never cut what you can untie.　　　　　　—Joseph Joubert

Let us, then, be up and doing, / With a heart for any fate; / Still achieving, still pursuing, / Learn to labor and to wait.
　　　　　　—Henry Wadsworth Longfellow, "A Psalm of Life"

Patience comes to him who waits.　　　　　—Dane Marshall

With time and patience the mulberry leaf becomes a silk gown.
　　　　　　　　　　　　　　　　　—Proverb (Chinese)

A beggar must be prepared to wait.　　—Proverb (West African)

Patience is bitter, but its fruit is sweet. —Jean Jacques Rousseau, *Émile*

Only those who have the patience to do simple things perfectly will acquire the skill to do difficult things easily.　　—Friedrich Schiller

How poor are they that have not patience! What wounds did ever heal but by degrees?　—William Shakespeare, *Othello*, Act II, Sc. iii

. . . though patience be a tired mare, yet she will plod.
　　　　　—William Shakespeare, *King Henry V*, Act II, Sc. i

For endurance is a mighty charm, / And patience giveth many things.
—*The Testament of Joseph*, II. 7

Patience is the art of hoping.
—Luc de Clapiers Vauvenargues, *Maximes*

It's hard to wait for grapes, Daddy.
—Brian Alexander Watkins (age 2),
while waiting for grapes to be peeled

You lose a little but gain a lot by being patient.
—Brian Alexander Watkins (age 10)

PATRIOTISM

Our country! In her intercourse with foreign nations, may she always be in the right; but our country, right or wrong.
—Stephen Decatur, toast given at Norfolk, April 1816

Ay, tear her tattered ensign down! / Long has it waved on high, / And many an eye has danced to see / That banner in the sky.
—Oliver Wendell Holmes, Sr.

Patriotism is the last refuge of a scoundrel.
—Samuel Johnson, in James Boswell, *Life of Samuel Johnson*

Intellectually I know that America is no better than any other country; emotionally I know she is better than every other country.
—Sinclair Lewis, interview, Berlin, 29 Dec 1930

. . . if you love your country why is it necessary to hate other countries?
—Arthur Miller, *Incident at Vichy*

Breathes there the man, with soul so dead, / Who never to himself hath said, / This is my own, my native land!   —Sir Walter Scott

PEACE

Wearily the sentry moves / Muttering the one word: "Peace."
—Richard Aldington, "Picket"

Hard to dislike a chap who likes you, isn't it? Well, there's your peace plan.
—Anonymous

Nobody loves peace more than a soldier.
—Anonymous

Teach peace. —Anonymous, bumper sticker, 1988

Wage peace. —Anonymous, bumper sticker, 1989

War is costly. Peace is priceless. —Anonymous, bumper sticker

If you do not find peace in yourself you will never find it anywhere else. —Paula A. Bendry

And he shall judge among the nations, and shall rebuke many people: and they shall beat their swords into plowshares, and their spears into pruning hooks: nation shall not lift up sword against nation, neither shall they learn war any more.
—*The Bible* (KJV): Isaiah 2:4

Peace I leave with you, my peace I give unto you: not as the world giveth, give I unto you. Let not your heart be troubled, neither let it be afraid. —*The Bible* (KJV): John 14:27

Sweet Prince, the arts of peace are great, / And no less glorious than those of war. —William Blake, *King Edward the Third*

Give peace in our time, O Lord. —*The Book of Common Prayer*

Glory be to God on high, / and on earth peace, good will towards men. —*The Book of Common Prayer*

If the human race wishes to have a prolonged and indefinite period of material prosperity, they have only got to behave in a peaceful and helpful way toward one another, and science will do for them all they wish and more than they dream. —Winston Churchill

Let wars yield to peace . . . —Cicero, *De Officiis* I. xxii. 82

War is an invention of the human mind. The human mind can invent peace with justice. —Norman Cousins, *Who Speaks for Man?*

In His will is our peace. —Dante Alighieri

Peace is knowing that God cannot fail.
—Sandy Edmonson, *God's Faithfulness in Trials & Testings*

Peace cannot be kept by force. It can only be achieved by understanding.
—Albert Einstein

I think that people want peace so much that one of these days government had better get out of the way and let them have it.
—Dwight D. Eisenhower, broadcast discussion, Aug 1959

But the real and lasting victories are those of peace, and not of war.
—Ralph Waldo Emerson, *The Conduct of Life*, "Worship"

The god of Victory is said to be one-handed, but Peace gives victory to both sides.   —Ralph Waldo Emerson, *Journals*

Peace is not something you *wish* for; it's something you *make*, something you *are*, and something you give *away*!   —Robert Fulghum,
All I Really Need to Know I Learned in Kindergarten

There never was a time when, in my opinion, some way could not be found to prevent the drawing of the sword.   —Ulysses S. Grant

Far from the madding crowd's ignoble strife.
—Thomas Gray, *Elegy Written in a Country Churchyard*

Make peace with what is.   —Judith Guest, *Errands*, Ch. 38

Peace is such a precious jewel that I would give anything for it but truth.   —Matthew Henry

One sword keeps another in the sheath.
—George Herbert, *Jacula Prudentum*, No. 725

Let peace begin with me.   —Janice Jackson Miller

Peace hath her victories / No less renowned than War.
—John Milton, sonnet, "To the Lord General Cromwell, May 1652"

Peace is the masterpiece of reason.   —J. Müller

We are not a postwar generation, but a pre-peace generation. Jesus is coming.   —Corrie ten Boom

First keep the peace within yourself, then you can also bring peace to others.   —Thomas à Kempis

Since wars begin in the minds of men, it is in the minds of men that the defenses of peace must be constructed.   —UNESCO Constitution

Let him who desires peace, prepare for war.   —Vegitius, *De re mil*

Peace hath higher tests of manhood / Than battle ever knew.
—John Greenleaf Whittier, "The Hero"

Peace is ever the final aim of war. —Wieland

A little known folk song ends with an important truth: "Peace in the world or the world in pieces." —Rabbi Amiel Wohl

P E O P L E

How could you know what people—individuals—were really doing!
—Saul Bellow, *Mr. Sammler's Planet*, Ch. 3

There are two kinds of people, those who finish what they start and so on. —Robert Byrne

Everyone is as God made him, and often a great deal worse.
—Miguel de Cervantes, *Don Quixote*

In spite of everything, I still believe people are really good at heart.
—Anne Frank

Treat people as if they were what they ought to be and you help them to become what they are capable of being.
—Johann Wolfgang von Goethe

Never give up on anybody. —Hubert Humphrey

People are like vines . . . We are born and we grow. Like vines, people also need a tree to cling to, to give them support.
—Elizabeth Kata, *A Patch of Blue*

Common-looking people are the best in the world: that is the reason the Lord makes so many of them. —Abraham Lincoln, in John Hay, *Letters of John Hay and Extracts from His Diary*

. . . people are always turning out to be tougher than I think they are.
—Larry McMurtry, *The Last Picture Show*, Ch. 14

. . . where does one person end and another person begin?
—Iris Murdoch

It takes all sorts to make a world. —Proverb (17th century)

There's nought so queer as folk. —Proverb (English)

When I look at the world I'm pessimistic, but when I look at people I
    am optimistic.   —Carl Rogers

Apparently, he thought, there were people in this world who simply
    never came clear . . . In the end you had to accept that the day
    would never arrive when you finally understood what they were all
    about. For some reason, this made him supremely happy.
                                    —Anne Tyler, *Saint Maybe*, Ch. 10

PERCEPTION

A fool sees not the same tree that a wise man sees.
                    —William Blake, *The Marriage of Heaven and Hell*

As a man is, so he sees.   —William Blake

. . . our own perception always seems the truth.   —Richard Fritz

Each one sees what he carries in his heart.
                                    —Johann Wolfgang von Goethe

What we see depends mainly on what we look for.   —John Lubbock

We don't see things as they are, we see them as we are.   —Anaïs Nin

Every act of perception has an emotional coloring.
                        —Alexander Solzhenitsyn, *The First Circle*

The older you get, the more you learn to see what you've been taught
    to see. When you're a kid, you see what's there.   —Steven Wright

PERFECTION

It is true that we shall not be able to reach perfection, but in our
    struggle toward it we shall strengthen our characters and give sta-
    bility to our ideas, so that, whilst ever advancing calmly in the
    same direction, we shall be rendered capable of applying the facul-
    ties with which we have been gifted to the best possible account.
                                                    —Confucius

PERILS

Great perils have this beauty, that they bring to light the fraternity of
    strangers.   —Victor Hugo, *Les Misérables*

PERSECUTION

When Hitler attacked the Jews I was not a Jew, therefore, I was not concerned. And when Hitler attacked the Catholics, I was not a Catholic, and therefore, I was not concerned. And when Hitler attacked the unions and the industrialists, I was not a member of the unions and I was not concerned. Then, Hitler attacked me and the Protestant church—and there was nobody left to be concerned.
—Martin Miemöller

PERSEVERANCE

God is with those who persevere. —Anonymous

Today's mighty oak is just yesterday's little nut that held its ground.
—Anonymous

Genius, that power which dazzles mortal eyes, / Is oft but perseverance in disguise. —Henry W. Austin, "Perseverance Conquers All"

. . . the best way out is always through.
—Robert Frost, *North of Boston*, "Servant to Servants"

It matters if you just don't give up. —Stephen Hawking

Press on! a better fate awaits thee. —Victor Hugo

As long as a man stays alive he can't tell what chances will pop up next. But a dead man signs no checks.
—Bernard Malamud, *The Fixer*

Patient perseverance in well doing is infinitely harder than a sudden and impulsive self-sacrifice. —Horace Mann

Fall seven times, stand up eight. —Proverb (Japanese)

If there is no wind, row. —Proverb (Latin)

By perseverance the snail reached the Ark. —Charles H. Spurgeon

'Taint no use to sit and whine / 'Cause the fish ain't on your line; / Bait your hook an' keep on tryin', / Keep a-goin'!
—Frank L. Stanton, "Keep A-goin'"

When you get into a tight place and everything goes against you, till it seems as though you could not hold on a minute longer, never give up then, for that is just the place and time that the tide will turn.   —Harriet Beecher Stowe

PERSISTENCE

Persistent people begin their success where others end in failure.
                                        —Edward Eggleston

PERSONALITY

It may be that even if half consciously, we choose our personalities to maintain a certain saving balance in the family's little universe.
                                        —Arthur Miller, *Timebends*

PERSPECTIVE

It has, I believe, been often remarked that a hen is only an egg's way of making another egg.
                    —Samuel Butler (1835-1902), *Life and Habit*, Ch. 8

Life is eating us up. We shall all be fables presently. Keep cool: it will be all one a hundred years hence.
                    —Ralph Waldo Emerson, *Representative Men*, "Montaigne"

Men in the game are blind to what men looking on see clearly.
                                        —Proverb (Chinese)

PERSUASION

Men are so made that they can resist sound argument, and yet yield to a glance.   —Honoré de Balzac

If you would convince others, seem open to conviction yourself.
                    —Earl of Chesterfield, letter to his son, 22 Feb 1748

We are less convinced by what we hear than by what we see.
                                        —Herodotus

There is a holy, mistaken zeal in politics, as well as religion. By persuading others we convince ourselves. —Junius, letter, 19 Dec 1769

If you would win a man to your cause, first convince him that you are his sincere friend.   —Abraham Lincoln

Yet hold it more humane, more heav'nly, first, / By winning words to conquer willing hearts, / And make persuasion do the work of fear.
—John Milton

We are in general more easily convinced by reasons that we have discovered ourselves, than by those suggested to us by others.
—Blaise Pascal, *Pensées*

Would you persuade, speak of interest, not of reason.
—Proverb (American)

The best cause requires a good pleader.
—Proverb (Dutch)

One of the best ways to persuade others is by listening to them.
—Dean Rusk

PHILOSOPHY

The philosophy of one century is the common sense of the next.
—Henry Ward Beecher

If the East loves infinity, the West delights in boundaries.
—Ralph Waldo Emerson

. . . an existentialist, a man who defines the whole universe by the fact that he happens to be in it.
—John Gardner, *October Light*, Ch. 6

You do what you have to do in life, when you form a philosophy that you can't talk yourself out of . . .   —Constantine Karamanlis

. . . a little philosophy carries a man from God, but a great deal brings him back again.   —Bathsua Makin,
     "An Essay to Revive the Ancient Education of Gentlewomen"

Science is what you know, philosophy is what you don't know.
—Bertrand Russell

I've developed a new philosophy . . . I only dread one day at a time.
—Charles Schulz, spoken by Charlie Brown in cartoon strip *Peanuts*

Philosophy does not regard pedigree; she did not receive Plato as a noble, but she made him so.   —Seneca

There are more things in heaven and earth, Horatio, / Than are dreamt of in your philosophy.   —William Shakespeare, *Hamlet*, Act I, Sc. v

PHOTOGRAPHY

Pictures are wasted unless the motive power which impelled you to
action is strong and stirring.   —Berenice Abbott

I have never forgotten a picture that I ever made.
                                —Margaret Bourke-White

Utter truth is essential, and that is what stirs me when I look through
the camera.   —Margaret Bourke-White

Photography is like fencing. You must keep your distance, wait, and
then thrust.   —Henry Cartier-Bresson

Pictures should never be posed. They are 'revealed' so must be
accepted as they are. Left alone.   —Henry Cartier-Bresson

Instantaneity is photography.   —Edgar Dégas

A photograph is a portrait painted by the sun.   —Dupins

Good photography is unpretentious.   —Walker Evans

. . . pay attention to everything within the field of view.
                    —Andreas Feininger, *Photographic Seeing*

Photography is for me the simultaneous recognition in a fraction of a
second of the significance of an event, as well as of a precise formal
organization (i.e. composition) which brings that event to life.
                    —Helmut Gernsheim, *Creative Photography*

Photography is the only "language" understood in all parts of the
world, and, bridging all nations and cultures, it links the family of
man.   —Helmut Gernsheim, *Creative Photography*

The danger lies in unconventional experiments signaling for a general license to do as they please, and pass off sloppy workmanship
as creative intention.   —Helmut Gernsheim, *Creative Photography*

Each shot ought to surprise.   —David A. Hamby, letter, 16 Nov 1976

The whole area should be active.
                    —David A. Hamby, letter, 16 Nov 1976

The camera is an instrument that teaches people how to see without
a camera.   —Dorothea Lange

The camera has its own kind of consciousness; in the lens the Garden of Eden itself would become ever so slightly too perfect.
—Arthur Miller, *Timebends*

The photographer is like the cod, which produces a million eggs in order that one may reach maturity.　　　—George Bernard Shaw

There is a terrible truthfulness about photography that sometimes makes a thing look ridiculous.　　　—George Bernard Shaw

A photograph comes into being, as it is seen, all at once.
—Susan Sontag

A photograph is not only an image . . . it is also a trace, something directly stencilled off the real, like a footprint or a death mask.
—Susan Sontag

Instead of just recording reality, photographs have become the norm for the way things appear to us, thereby changing the very idea of reality and of realism.　　　—Susan Sontag

The highest vocation of photography is to explain man to man.
—Susan Sontag

Every other artist begins with a blank canvas, a piece of paper . . . the photographer begins with the finished product. —Edward Steichen

Photography records the gamut of feelings written on the human face; the beauty of the earth and skies that man has inherited; and the wealth and confusion man has created. It is a major force in explaining man to man.　　　—Edward Steichen

I photograph to find out what something looks like photographed.
—Garry Winograd, in Susan Sontag, *On Photography*

PITY

One cannot weep for the entire world, it is beyond human strength. One must choose.　　　—Jean Anouilh

He best can pity who has felt the woe. —John Gay, *The Captives*, II. ii.

Not being untutored in suffering, I learn to pity those in affliction.
—Virgil

PLANNING

A good plan today is better than a perfect plan tomorrow.
—Anonymous

Take time to be quick.
—Anonymous

Make no little plans; they have no magic to stir men's blood.
—Daniel H. Burnham, in Charles Moore, *Daniel H. Burnham*

The best laid schemes o' mice an' men / Gang aft a-gley.
—Robert Burns, "To a Mouse"

Before beginning, prepare carefully.
—Cicero

The time to repair the roof is when the sun is shining.
—John F. Kennedy, State of the Union Message, 11 Jan 1962

I wonder if we climb to heaven over the ruins of many cherished
schemes.
—Laurel Lee, *Godspeed: Hitchhiking Home*

Plans can be like a winged horse, but their execution plods along
pulling carts.
—Laurel Lee, *Godspeed: Hitchhiking Home*

Measure thrice before you cut once.
—Proverb (Italian)

If you want to give God a good laugh, tell him your plans.
—Proverb (Yiddish)

It's a bad plan that can't be changed.
—Publilius Syrus, *Moral Sayings*

PLAY

In our play we reveal what kind of people we are.
—Ovid

Work consists of whatever a body is obliged to do . . . Play consists of
whatever a body is not obliged to do.
—Mark Twain, *The Adventures of Tom Sawyer*

PLEASING

He labors in vain who studies to please everybody.
—Anonymous

I cannot give you the formula for success, but I can give you the formula for failure, which is—try to please everybody.
—Herbert Bayard Swope

PLEASURE

Mingle your cares with pleasure now and then.
—Dionysius Cato, *Disticha de Moribus*, Book III, No. 7

Sweet is pleasure after pain. —John Dryden, "Alexander's Feast"

Many a man thinks he is buying pleasure, when he is really selling
  himself a slave to it. —Benjamin Franklin

Rare indulgence produces greater pleasure. —Juvenal

To look forward to pleasure is also a pleasure.
—Gotthold Ephraim Lessing

Toil and pleasure, in their natures opposite, are yet linked together in
  a kind of necessary connection. —Livy

Our pleasures and our discontents,
  Are rounds by which we may ascend.
—Henry Wadsworth Longfellow

PLUCK

A pound of pluck is worth a ton of luck.
—James A. Garfield, in Thomas A. Bailey, *Presidential Greatness*:
    The Image and the Man from George Washington to the Present

POETRY

God has made me his poem.
—Lee Alvord, "Poetry—What's It All About?"

Poetry is the stuff in books that doesn't quite reach the margins.
—Anonymous, from a child's essay

It is a sad fact about our culture that a poet can earn much more
  money writing or talking about his art than he can by practicing it.
—W. H. Auden, *The Dyer's Hand and Other Essays*, Foreward

Poetry is the only art people haven't learned to consume like soup.
—W. H. Auden

The author of haiku should be absent, and only the haiku present.
—Anne Bancroft

Each man has his own batch of poems.   —Saul Bellow, *Herzog*

Prose is when all the lines except the last go on to the end. Poetry is
  when some of them fall short of it.
        —Jeremy Bentham, in M. St. J. Packe, *Life of John Stuart Mill*

Poetry is the impish attempt to paint the color of the wind.
        —Maxwell Bodenheim, in Ben Hecht, *Winkelberg* (play)

Poetry is life distilled.
        —Gwendolyn Brooks, in Brian Lanker, *I Dream a World*

Poetry is man's rebellion against being what he is.
        —James Branch Cabell

If you cannot be a poet, be the poem.   —David Carradine

The success of the poem is determined not by how much the poet felt
  in writing it, but by how much the reader feels in reading it.
        —John Ciardi

There is a pleasure in poetic pains
  Which only poets know. —William Cowper, *The Task*, "Timepiece"

The poet lights the light and fades away. But the light goes on and
  on.   —Emily Dickinson

A poet is a painter of the soul.   —Isaac D'Israeli

Genuine poetry can communicate before it is understood. —T. S. Eliot

The finest poetry was first experience.
        —Ralph Waldo Emerson, *Representative Men*, "Shakespeare"

We all write poems; it is simply that poets are the ones who write in
  words.   —John Fowles, *The French Lieutenant's Woman*, Ch. 19

Poetry is a way of taking life by the throat.
    —Robert Frost, in E. S. Sergeant, *Robert Frost: the Trial by Existence*

Writing free verse is like playing tennis with the net down.
        —Robert Frost, speech at the Milton Academy,
        Massachusetts, 17 May 1935

Poetry is the language in which man explores his own amazement.
—Christopher Fry

But the life of poetry lies in fresh relationships between words, in the spontaneous fusion of hitherto unrelated words.
—Marie Gilchrist, *Writing Poetry*, Ch. 1

If there's no money in poetry, neither is there poetry in money.
—Robert Graves,
speech at London School of Economics, 6 Dec 1963

To be a poet is a condition rather than a profession.   —Robert Graves

Thoughts that breathe and words that burn.   —Gray, *Progress of Poesy*

Poetry is emotion put into measure.   —Thomas Hardy,
quoted by his wife Emma in *Life of Thomas Hardy*

Science sees signs; Poetry, the thing signified.   —Hare

And take back ill-polished stanzas to the anvil.   —Horace

A good poet is someone who manages, in a lifetime of standing out in thunderstorms, to be struck by lightning five or six times.
—Randell Jarrell

For a good poet's made as well as born.   —Ben Jonson,
"To the Memory of My Beloved, Mr. William Shakespeare"

If poetry comes not as naturally as the leaves to a tree, it had better not come at all.   —John Keats, letter to John Taylor, 27 Feb 1818

Poetry should be great and unobtrusive, a thing which enters into one's soul, and does not startle or amaze us with itself, but with its subject.   —John Keats, in Sidney Colvin, *Life of Keats*

[Of one of his poems:] God and I both knew what it meant once; now God alone knows.   —Friedrich Klopstock

I can't understand these chaps who go around American universities explaining how they write poems: it's like going round explaining how you sleep with your wife.   —Philip Larkin

Perhaps no person can be a poet, or can even enjoy poetry, without a certain unsoundness of mind.   —Thomas Babington Macaulay

A poem should not mean / But be.
　　　　　—Archibald MacLeish, *Streets in the Moon*, "Ars Poetica"

Poetry is what Milton saw when he went blind.　　　—Don Marquis

Publishing a volume of poetry is like dropping a rose petal down the
　　Grand Canyon and waiting for the echo.
　　　　　—Don Marquis, *The Sun Dial*

Most people ignore most poetry because most poetry ignores most
　　people.　　　　　—Adrian Mitchell

[Poems are] imaginary gardens with real toads in them.
　　　　　—Marianne Moore, in Helen Bevington,
　　　　　When Found, Make a Verse Of

The courage of the poet is to keep ajar the door that leads to madness.
　　　　　—Christopher Morley, *Inward Ho*

Poets utter great and wise things which they do not themselves
　　understand.　　　　　—Plato

Truth shines the brighter, clad in verse.　　　—Alexander Pope

Poetry is a perfectly reasonable means of overcoming chaos.
　　　　　—I. A. Richards

The office of poetry is not to make us think accurately, but feel truly.
　　　　　—Frederick W. Robertson

Poetry is the exquisite expression of exquisite impressions.
　　　　　—Joseph Roux

In most men there exists a poet who died young, whom the man sur-
　　vived.　　　　　—Charles Augustin Sainte-Beuve

I've written some poetry I don't understand myself.　—Carl Sandburg

Poetry is an echo asking a shadow to dance.　　　—Carl Sandburg

A poet is a nightingale, who sits in the darkness and sings to cheer its
　　own solitude with sweet sounds.　　　　　—Percy Shelley

Poetry lifts the veil from the hidden beauty of the world, and makes
　　familiar objects be as if they were not familiar.
　　　　　—Percy Shelley, "A Defence of Poetry"

The poet speaks to all men of that other life of theirs that they have
smothered and forgotten.   —Edith Sitwell, *Rhyme and Reason*

A poet cannot be a Party member . . . without paying the price.
—Alexander Solzhenitsyn, *The Oak and the Calf*

Poetry is the mathematics of writing and closely kin to music.
—John Steinbeck

A poet looks at the world as a man looks at a woman.
—Wallace Stevens, *Opus Posthumous*, "Adagia"

The poet makes silk dresses out of worms.
—Wallace Stevens, *Opus Poshumous*

A good poem is a contribution to reality. The world is never the same
once a good poem has been added to it.
—Dylan Thomas, *On Poetry*, "Quite Early One Morning"

The works of great poets have never been read by mankind, for only
great poets can read them.   —Henry David Thoreau, *Walden*

The poet . . . may be used as a barometer, but let us not forget that he
is also part of the weather. —Lionel Trilling, *The Liberal Imagination*

Poetry is the overflowing of the soul.   —Tuckerman

Poetry says more in fewer words than prose.   —Voltaire

The poem . . . is a little myth of man's capacity of making life meaningful. And in the end, the poem is not a thing we see—it is, rather,
a light by which we may see—and what we see is life.
—Robert Penn Warren, in *Saturday Review*, 22 Mar 1958

Love the earth and sun and animals, / Despise riches, give alms to
everyone that asks, / Stand up for the stupid and crazy, / Devote
your income and labor to others... / And your very flesh shall be a
great poem.   —Walt Whitman

To have great poets, there must be great audiences too.
—Walt Whitman, *Notes Left Over*, "Ventures on an Old Theme"

A poet can survive everything but a misprint.
—Oscar Wilde, *The Children of the Poets*

Poetry is the language of feeling.   —William Winter

POLITENESS

Anyone can be polite to a king. It takes a gentleman to be polite to a
beggar. —Anonymous

Politeness is benevolence in small things. —Anonymous

Politeness is better than logic. You can often persuade when you cannot convince. —Josh Billings

Now as to politeness . . . I would venture to call it benevolence in trifles.
—Lord Chatham

Politeness is the flower of humanity. —Joseph Joubert

Politeness costs little and yields much. —Mademoiselle de Lambert

With hat in hand one gets on in the world. —Proverb (German)

Politeness goes far, yet costs nothing. —Samuel Smiles

Politeness is the art of choosing among one's real thoughts.
—Abel Stevens, *Life of Mme. de Staël*, Ch. 4

POLITICS

Politics is like roller skating. You go partly where you want to go, and
partly where the damn things take you. —Henry Fountain Ashurst

The American people did not send us here to bicker.
—George Bush, State of the Union speech, 31 Jan 1990

Politics is the art of the possible. —R. A. Butler, *The Art of the Possible*

A politician thinks of the next election; a statesman, of the next generation. —James Freeman Clarke

I would rather be right than be President.
—Henry Clay, when Preston, of Kentucky, advised Clay that
his advocacy of the Missouri Compromise of 1850
would injure his chances for the Presidency

Political parties serve to keep each other in check, one keenly watching the other. —Henry Clay

The middle of the road is where the white line is—and that's the
worst place to drive.   —Robert Frost

He serves his party best who serves the country best.
                          —Rutherford B. Hayes, speech, 5 Mar 1877

Nothing is politically right which is morally wrong.
                                              —Abraham Lincoln

Politics isn't in my nature.   —Bernard Malamud, *The Fixer*

For the political world, I have come to believe, is fundamentally
beyond anyone's control, yet we all go on as though it were a kind
of vehicle that only needs a change of drivers in order to steer it
away from its frequent hair-raising visits to the edge of the cliff.
                                        —Arthur Miller, *Timebends*

Any party which takes credit for the rain must not be surprised if its
opponents blame it for the drought.
                          —Dwight W. Morrow, campaign speech, Oct 1930

Politics is the science of exigencies.   —Theodore Parker

The best thing about this group of candidates is that only one of
them can win.   —Will Rogers

The Republicans have their splits right after election and Democrats
have theirs just before an election.
                          —Will Rogers, syndicated column, 29 Dec 1930

Those of us who don't have a party affiliation ought to be able to register under the heading "Confused."
          —Andrew A. Rooney, *And More by Andy Rooney*, Introduction

In politics if you want anything said, ask a man. If you want anything
done, ask a woman.   —Margaret Thatcher

You may have to fight a battle more than once to win it.
                                          —Margaret Thatcher

A statesman is a politician who has been dead ten or fifteen years.
                                              —Harry S. Truman

P O S S E S S I O N S

Lord, what do we have in our hands but what You gave us?
                                              —Anonymous

You can't have anything unless you let go of it.   —Anonymous

. . . give me neither poverty nor riches; feed me with food convenient
for me.   —*The Bible* (KJV): Proverbs 30:8

For we brought nothing into this world, and it is certain we can carry
nothing out.   —*The Bible* (KJV): 1 Timothy 6:7

There are only two families in the world, my old grandmother used
to say, the Haves and the Have-nots.
     —Miguel de Cervantes, *Don Quixote*

Our possessions don't own us any more, because we don't possess
them.
     —Dan Davis, sermon, Hope Chapel, Austin, Texas, 6 Oct 1991

We are made loveless by our possessions.   —Elizabeth of Thuringia

The possession of a great many things, even the best of things, tends
to blind one to the real value of anything.   —Holbrook Jackson

Lives based on having are less free than lives based either on doing or
on being.   —William James

To have what we want is riches; but to be able to do without is power.
     —George Macdonald

O grant me, Heaven, a middle state, / Neither too humble nor too
great; More than enough, for nature's ends, / With something left
to treat my friends.   —David Mallet, "Imitation of Horace"

If there is to be any peace it will come through being, not having.
     —Henry Miller

"All this shall pass away." Then why not enjoy the few days we have?
All we possess is just loaned to us.
     —Alfred Armand Montapert, *Distilled Wisdom*

An object in possession seldom retains the same charm that it had in
pursuit.   —Pliny the Younger, *Letters*, Book II

He has enough who is content.   —Proverb (French)

The best things in life aren't things.   —Raven

"You're a boat owner, Pete," Cass said. "You know how it feels."
"I sure do. They say the two happiest days in a man's life are the
day he buys his boat and the day he sells it," Pete said.
—Luanne Rice, *Blue Moon*

It is preoccupation with possession, more than anything else, that
prevents men from living freely and nobly.
—Bertrand Russell, *Principles of Social Reconstruction*

How could there be any question of acquiring or possessing, when
the one thing needful for a man is to become—to be at last, and to
die in the fullness of his being.
—Antoine de Saint-Exupéry, *The Wisdom of the Sands*

When in doubt, do without. —Viscount Herbert Louis Samuel

No possession is gratifying without a companion. —Seneca

Don't let your possessions possess you. —M. R. Siemens

And keep as few things as possible, so that you don't have to fear for
them. Give them up without a struggle—because otherwise the
humiliation will poison your heart. They will take them away from
you in a fight, and trying to hold onto your property will only
leave you with a bloodied mouth . . . But by owning things and
trembling about their fate aren't you forfeiting the rare opportunity of observing and understanding?
—Alexander Solzhenitsyn, *The Gulag Archipelago*

. . . people don't know what they are striving for. They waste themselves in senseless thrashing around for the sake of a handful of
goods and die without realizing their spiritual wealth.
—Alexander Solzhenitsyn, *The First Circle*

The bird in a forest can perch but on one bough, / And this should be
the wise man's pattern. —Tso Ssu

You can't have everything. Where would you put it?
—Stephen Wright

POSSIBILITIES

I've never met a person, I don't care what his condition, in whom I
could not see possibilities. —Preston Bradley

Every man believes that he has a greater possibility.

—Ralph Waldo Emerson

A possibility is a hint from God. —Sören Kierkegaard

There is not a human life so poor and small as not to hold many a
divine possibility. —James Martineau

P O V E R T Y

A man without money is a bow without an arrow. —Anonymous

Poverty is an anomaly to rich people. It is very difficult to make out
why people who want dinner do not ring the bell.

—Walter Bagehot, *Literary Studies*, 2

Anyone who has ever struggled with poverty knows how extremely
expensive it is to be poor. —James Baldwin, *Nobody Knows My Name*

He that hath pity upon the poor lendeth unto the Lord; and that
which he hath given will he pay him again.

—*The Bible* (KJV): Proverbs 19:17

. . . Blessed be ye poor: for yours is the kingdom of God.

—*The Bible* (KJV): Luke 6:20

Thousands upon thousands are yearly brought into a state of real
poverty by their great anxiety not to be thought poor.

—William Cobbett

To be poor and independent is very nearly an impossibility.

—William Cobbett, *Advice to Young Men*

The poor are only they who feel poor. —Ralph Waldo Emerson

Poverty is no vice, but an inconvenience.

—John Florio, *Florio's Second Fruites*

Poverty is not a shame, but the being ashamed of it is.

—Thomas Fuller

The poor never have enough for themselves . . . but always have
enough to give away. —Joseph F. Girzone, *Joshua*, Ch. 5

God oft hath a great share in a little house.

—George Herbert, *Jacula Prudentum*

Poverty is no sin.   —George Herbert, *Jacula Prudentum*

And when you're poor, you grow up fast.
 —Billie Holiday, *Lady Sings the Blues*, with William Dufty, Ch. 1

Have the courage to appear poor and you disarm poverty of its
 sharpest sting.   —Anna Jameson

This Administration here and now declares unconditional war on
 poverty in America.
  —Lyndon B. Johnson, State of the Union Message, 8 Jan 1964

A great provision for the poor is the true test of civilization.
       —Samuel Johnson

This mournful truth is ev'rywhere confess'd, / Slow rises worth by
 poverty depress'd.   —Samuel Johnson, "London"

The travelers with empty pockets will sing even in the robber's face.
      —Juvenal, *Satires*

The trouble with being poor is that it takes up all your time.
      —Willem de Kooning

Few save the poor feel for the poor.   —Letitia Elizabeth Landon,
     The Easter Gift (1832), "The Widow's Mite"

The poor too often turn away unheard, / From hearts that shut
 against them with a sound / That will be heard in heaven.
    —Henry Wadsworth Longfellow

There is many a good man to be found under a shabby hat.
      —Proverb (Chinese)

Poverty is no disgrace.   —Proverb (German)

He is poor who does not feel content.   —Proverb (Japanese)

No one is poor but he who thinks himself so. —Proverb (Portuguese)

Poverty is no disgrace, but no honor either.   —Proverb (Yiddish)

Not he who has little, but he who wishes more, is poor.   —Seneca

Poverty is no disgrace to a man, but it is confoundly inconvenient.
—Sydney Smith, *Wit and Wisdom of Rev. Sydney Smith*

None is so wretched as the poor man who maintains the semblance
of wealth.   —Charles H. Spurgeon

There seems to me a great many blessings which come from true
poverty and I should be sorry to be deprived of them.
—Saint Teresa of Ávila, "Spiritual Relations"

I've never been poor, only broke. Being poor is a frame of mind.
Being broke is only a temporary situation.   —Mike Todd

Poor maids have more lovers than husbands.   —John Webster

Who, being loved, is poor?   —Oscar Wilde

Lord of himself, though not of lands, / And having nothing, yet hath
all.   —Sir Henry Wotton, "The Character of a Happy Life"

P O W E R

Power tends to corrupt, and absolute power corrupts absolutely.
—Lord Acton, letter to Mandell Creighton, 5 Apr 1887

The desire of power in excess caused the angels to fall.
—Francis Bacon

There is more power in the open hand than in the clenched fist.
—Herbert N. Casson

Power will intoxicate the best hearts, as wine the strongest heads. No
man is wise enough, nor good enough to be trusted with unlimited
power.   —Charles Caleb Colton

Let not thy will roar when thy power can but whisper.
—Thomas Fuller, M. D.

The sole advantage of power is that you can do more good.
—Baltasar Gracián, *The Art of Wordly Wisdom*

Now when I bore people at a party they think it's their fault.
—Henry Kissinger

Power is the great aphrodisiac.
—Henry Kissinger, in *New York Times*, 19 Jan 1971

A partnership with the powerful is never safe.
—Phaedrus, *Fables*, Book I

Unlimited power is apt to corrupt the minds of those who possess it.
—William Pitt, speech, House of Lords, 9 Jan 1770

He who pays the piper can call the tunes.
—John Ray, *English Proverbs* (1670)

Excess of power intoxicates.　　　　　—Madame de Remusat

It is impossible to reign innocently.
—Louis de Saint-Just, speech, 1793

He who has great power should use it lightly.　　—Seneca, *Troades*

You only have power over people so long as you don't take everything away from them. But when you've robbed a man of everything he's no longer in your power—he's free again.
—Alexander Solzhenitsyn, *The First Circle*, Ch. 17

Whatever God wants from you, He will give you the power to do.
—Lewis Timberlake

We have, I fear, confused power with greatness.
—Stewart L. Udall, commencement address,
Dartmouth College, 13 June 1965

POWERLESSNESS

At times it is strangely sedative to know the extent of your own pow-
erlessness.　　　　　—Erica Jong, *Fear of Flying*

PRACTICALITY

A mariner must have his eye upon rocks and sands, as well as upon
the North Star.　　　　　—Thomas Fuller

A barley-corn is better than a diamond to a cock.
—Thomas Fuller, M. D., *Gnomologia*

If everybody contemplates the infinite instead of fixing the drains,
many of us will die of cholera.　　　　　—John Rich

PRACTICE

Repetition is the mother of skill.　　　　　—Anonymous

Skill to do comes by doing.
>—Ralph Waldo Emerson, *Society and Solitude*, "Old Age"

Practice yourself, for heaven's sake, in little things; and thence to greater. —Epictetus, *Discourses*, Ch. xv.

All things are difficult before they are easy.
>—Thomas Fuller, M. D., *Gnomologia*

Knowledge is a treasure, but practice is the key to it.
>—Thomas Fuller, M. D., *Gnomologia*, No. 3139

We never do anything well till we cease to think about the manner of doing it. —William Hazlitt, *Sketches and Essays*, "On Prejudice"

What we hope ever to do with ease, we must learn first to do with diligence. —Samuel Johnson

Everything is difficult at first. —Proverb (Chinese)

Practice makes perfect. —Proverb (German)

Practice is the best of all instructors.
>—Publilius Syrus, *Sententioe*, No. 439

A juggler's skill hath been long years alearning.
>—Martin Farquhar Tupper

P R A I S E

If you would reap praise you must sow the seeds: gentle words and useful deeds. —Anonymous

Neither praise nor dispraise thyself; thy actions serve the turn.
>—Anonymous

Let us now praise famous men, and our fathers that begat us.
>—Apocrypha, "Ecclesiasticus," 44, 1

Let another praise thee, and not thine own mouth . . .
>—*The Bible* (KJV): Proverbs 27:2

Every potter praises his own pot. —H. G. Bohn

Judicious praise is to children what the sun is to flowers.
>—Christian Nestell Bovée

Watch how a man takes praise and there you have the measure of
him.   —Thomas Burke

Tell a man he is brave, and you help him to become so.
   —Thomas Carlyle

Praise the bridge that carried you over.
   —George Colman (the younger)

One thing scientists have discovered is that often-praised children
become more intelligent than often-blamed ones. There's a creative element in praise.   —Thomas Dreier

Praise God even when you don't understand what He is doing.
   —Henry Jackson

Praise God, from whom all blessings flow; / Praise Him, all creatures
here below; / Praise Him above, ye heavenly host: / Praise Father,
Son, and Holy Ghost.
   —Thomas Ken, "Morning and Evening Hymn"

Refusal of praise is a desire to be praised twice.
   —François de La Rochefoucauld, *Maximes*

Men are not to be judged by their looks, habits, and appearances but
by the character of their lives and conversations, and by their
works. It is better to be praised by one's own works than by the
words of another.   —L'Estrange

The trouble with most of us is that we would rather be ruined by
praise than saved by criticism.   —Norman Vincent Peale

Praise makes good men better and bad men worse.
   —Proverb (17th century)

Rest satisfied with doing well, and leave others to talk of you as they
will.   —Pythagoras

Every man praises his own wares.   —John Ray, *English Proverbs* (1670)

You done splendid.   —Casey Stengel

Try praising your wife, even if it does frighten her at first.
   —William Ashley Sunday

The sweetest of all sounds is praise.   —Xenophon

The love of praise, howe'er concealed by art, / Reigns more or less,
and glows in ev'ry heart.   —Edward Young

(About) PRAYER

It is strange that while praying, we seldom ask for a change of character, but always a change of circumstances.   —Anonymous

None can pray well but he who lives well.   —Anonymous

Pray for a good harvest, but keep on hoeing.   —Anonymous

When praying, do not give God instructions—report for duty!
—Anonymous

When the outlook is bad, try the uplook.   —Anonymous

Prayer is the spirit speaking truth to Truth.   —Philip James Bailey

It is not well for a man to pray cream and live skim milk.
—Henry Ward Beecher, in William Drysdale,
editor, *Proverbs from Plymouth Pulpit*

Pray devoutly, but hammer stoutly.   —W. G. Benham

The wish for prayer is a prayer in itself.
—Georges Bernanos, *Diary of a Country Priest*, Ch. 2

If you begin to live life looking for the God that is all around you,
every moment becomes a prayer.   —Frank Bianco

. . . What things soever ye desire, when ye pray, believe that ye
receive them, and ye shall have them.—*The Bible* (KJV): Mark 11:24

If ye shall ask anything in my name, I will do it.
—*The Bible* (KJV): John 14:14

Be careful for nothing; but in everything by prayer and supplication
with thanksgiving let your requests be made known unto God.
—*The Bible* (KJV): Philippians 4:6

Pray without ceasing.   —*The Bible* (KJV): 1 Thessalonians 5:17

Confess your faults one to another, and pray one for another, that ye
may be healed. The effectual fervent prayer of a righteous man
availeth much.   —*The Bible* (KJV): James 5:16

A prayer, in its simplest definition, is merely a wish turned heaven-
ward. —Phillips Brooks

Do not pray for easy lives. Pray to be stronger men! Do not pray for
tasks equal to your powers. Prayer is not conquering God's reluctance, but taking hold of God's willingness. —Phillips Brooks

Pray for powers equal to your tasks. —Phillips Brooks, *Sermons*

Only in prayer do we achieve that complete and harmonious assembly of body, mind, and spirit which gives the frail human reed its
unshakable strength. —Alexis Carrel

Hurry is the death of prayer. —Samuel Chadwick

He prayeth best, who loveth best / All things both great and small;
/ For the dear God loveth us, / He made and loveth all.
—Samuel Taylor Coleridge, *The Rime of the Ancient Mariner*

Prayer makes the Christian's armor bright; / And Satan trembles
when he sees / The weakest saint upon his knees.
—William Cowper, *Olney Hymns*

Keep praying, but be thankful that God's answers are wiser than your
prayers! —William Culbertson

I throw myself down in my chamber, and I call in and invite God and
his angels thither, and when they are there, I neglect God and his
angels, for the noise of a fly, for the rattling of a coach, for the
whining of a door. —John Donne

To pray is to desire; but it is to desire what God would have us desire.
—François Fénelon, *Advice Concerning Prayer*

God answers prayer in His own way, not ours. —Mahatma Gandhi

Prayer is not asking. It is a longing of the soul. It is daily admission of
one's weakness . . . It is better in prayer to have a heart without
words than words without a heart. —Mahatma Gandhi

Heaven is full of answers to prayer for which no one ever bothered to
ask. —Billy Graham, *Till Armageddon*

I have lived to thank God that all my prayers have not been
answered. —Jean Ingelow

I pray hard, work hard and leave the rest to God.
—Florence Griffith Joyner, Olympic track star

You should pray to have a sound mind in a sound body.
—Juvenal, Satires

The course of prayer who knows? —John Keble

Prayer does not change God, but it changes him who prays.
—Sören Kierkegaard

We never can long continue to dislike people for whom we pray.
—H. L. Sidney Lear

A single grateful thought raised to heaven is the most perfect prayer.
—Gotthold Ephraim Lessing, Minna von Barnhelm, II, vii

Pray hardest when it is hardest to pray. —Martin Luther

If you don't hear His voice so let Him hear yours. When prayers go up
blessings descend. —Bernard Malamud, The Fixer

God warms his hands at man's heart when he prays.
—John Masefield, Widow in the Bye Street, Part vi

Who rises from prayer a better man, his prayer is answered.
—George Meredith, The Ordeal of Richard Feverel, Ch. 12

Spread out your petition before God, and then say, "Thy will, not
mine, be done." The sweetest lesson I have learned in God's school
is to let the Lord choose for me. —Dwight L. Moody

Did not God / Sometimes withhold in mercy what we ask, / We
should be ruined at our own request.
—Hannah More, Sacred Dramas (1782), "Moses in the Bulrushes"

In prayer we see the issues; by prayer we are moved to act.
—Roy Neehall

What God sends is better than what men ask for.—Proverb (Croation)

He who prays for his neighbor will be heard for himself.
—Proverb (Hebrew)

Call on God, but row away from the rocks. —Proverb (Indian)

Pray to God, but row for the shore.   —Proverb (Russian)

Prayer is not an argument with God to persuade him to move things our way, but an exercise by which we are enabled by his Spirit to move ourselves his way.   —Leonard Ravenhill

The answer to our prayer may be the echo of our resolve.
     —Viscount Herbert Louis Samuel

Though God knows all our needs, prayer is necessary for the cleansing and enlightenment of the soul.
     —John Sergieff of Constadt, *My Life in Christ*

There is no prayer so blessed as the prayer which asks for nothing.
     —O. J. Simon, *Faith and Experience*

Our prayers should be for blessings in general, for God knows best what is good for us.   —Socrates

Pray as if everything depended upon God and work as if everything depended upon man.   —Francis Cardinal Spellman

Let us never forget that right living is a necessary condition for the person who prays.
     —Lehman Strauss, *Sense and Nonsense About Prayer*

The true purpose is not to obtain the things we want from God but rather to make us content with the things He wants us to have.
     —Lehman Strauss, *Sense and Nonsense About Prayer*

When we are praying in the Holy Spirit, we will not be trying to talk God into doing something He does not want to do, but rather we will be yielding to the Holy Spirit, who knows what is best for us.
     —Lehman Strauss, *Sense and Nonsense About Prayer*

More and more the distinction between prayer and the rest of life seemed to be vanishing for Betsie.
     —Corrie ten Boom, of her sister, *The Hiding Place*,
     with John and Elizabeth Sherrill

More things are wrought by prayer / Than this world dreams of . . .
   —Alfred, Lord Tennyson, *Idylls of the King*, "The Passing of Arthur"

Don't pray what happens to you; pray to use what happens to you.
     —Lewis Timberlake

The secret of prayer is not getting what you want done in heaven; it's getting what heaven wants done on earth.   —Lewis Timberlake

You don't just pray for those you like.   —Lewis Timberlake

Prayer moves the hand which moves the world.   —J. A. Wallace

If laser beams can cut through mountains, why should we doubt the power of prayer?   —William Arthur Ward

Proceed with much prayer, and your way will be made plain.
        —John Wesley

P R A Y E R S

Matthew, Mark, Luke, and John, The bed be blest that I lie on. / Four angels round my head, / One to watch, and one to pray, / And two to bear my soul away.   —Thomas Ady, "A Candle in the Dark"

Kingdom of God, come. Will of God, be done.
        —Anonymous, quoted by Ron Parrish, sermon, Hope Chapel,
        Austin, Texas, 15 May 1993, based on "The Lord's Prayer"

Lord, help me to remember that nothing is going to happen to me today that you and I together can't handle.   —Anonymous

O Lord, I ain't what I wanna be, O Lord, I ain't what I oughta be, and O Lord, I ain't what I gonna be, but thanks, Lord, I ain't what I used to be.   —Anonymous, "Prayer of a Long-Dead Slave"

Give me chastity and continence, but not just now.
        —Saint Augustine, *Confessions*

Lord, I confess I am not what I ought to be, but I thank you, Lord, that I'm not what I used to be.   —Maxie Dunnan

Guard us, guide us, keep us, feed us, / For we have no help but Thee.
        —James Edmeston

I am going out on Thy path. God be behind me, God be before, God be in my footsteps.   —Gaelic prayer

Good morning, God, I love You! What are You up to today? I want to be part of it.   —Norman Grubb

God, give me hills to climb, / And strength for climbing!
        —Arthur Guiterman, "Hills"

Night is drawing nigh—For all that has been—Thanks! To all that
    shall be—Yes!   —Dag Hammarskjöld, *Markings*

[On the night he was robbed:] I thank Thee first because I was never
    robbed before; second, because although they took my purse they
    did not take my life; third, although they took my all, it was not
    much; and fourth, because it was I who was robbed and not I who
    robbed.   —Matthew Henry

Here stand I. I can do no other. God help me. Amen.
        —Martin Luther, speech at the Diet of Worms, 18 Apr 1521

Lord, grant that I may always desire more than I can accomplish.
                                                    —Michelangelo

What in me is dark, / Illumine; what is low, raise and support; / That
    to the height of this great argument / I may assert Eternal
    Providence, / And justify the ways of God to men.
                                    —John Milton, *Paradise Lost*

Those things, good Lord, that we pray for, give us also the grace to
    labor for.   —Thomas More

I am only a spark: / Make me a fire.   —Amado Nervo

Now I lay me down to take my sleep, / I pray thee, Lord, my soul to
    keep; / If I should die before I wake, / I pray thee, Lord, my soul to
    take.   —*New England Primer* (1814)

God, give us the grace to accept with serenity the things that cannot
    be changed; / Give us the courage to change the things which
    should be changed; / Give us the wisdom to distinguish the one
    from the other.
            —Reinhold Niebuhr, often called the "Serenity Prayer,"
                in Richard Wightman Fox, *Reinhold Niebuhr*, Ch. 12.
                Prayer said to have been first published in 1951.

Lord, make me a vessel for you from which others might drink.
    —Ron Parrish, sermon, Hope Chapel, Austin, Texas, 9 Sep 1995

Lord, reform Thy world, beginning with me.
                —Franklin D. Roosevelt, quoting a Chinese Christian

Lord, save all the elect, and then elect some more.
                                            —Charles H. Spurgeon

The greatest prayer anyone can pray is, "Thy will be done."
—Lehman Strauss, *Sense and Nonsense About Prayer*

PREACHERS

Good preachers give their hearers fruit, not flowers.
—Angelina Maria Lorraine Collins,
Mrs. Ben Darby or *The Weal and Woe of Social Life*

The test of a preacher is that his congregation goes away saying, not "What a lovely sermon," but "I will do something about it."
—Saint Francis de Sales

PREACHING

Every man is a priest, even involuntarily; his conduct is an unspoken sermon, which is forever preaching to others.
—Henri Frédéric Amiel

Never preach beyond your experience.   —Anonymous

"He preaches well that lives well," quoth Sancho, "that's all the divinity I can understand."   —Miguel de Cervantes

Goodness that preaches undoes itself.
—Ralph Waldo Emerson, *Journals*

None preaches better than the ant, and she says nothing.
—Benjamin Franklin

Truth from his lips prevail'd with double sway, / And fools, who came to scoff, remain'd to pray.   —Oliver Goldsmith, *The Deserted Village*

Practice yourself what you preach.   —Plautus

PREJUDICE

Acquaintance softens prejudice.   —Aesop

. . . God hath showed me [Peter] that I should not call any man common or unclean.   —*The Bible* (KJV): Acts 10:28

Prejudice, n. A vagrant opinion without visible means of support.
—Ambrose Bierce

We hate some persons because we do not know them; and will not know them because we hate them.   —Charles Caleb Colton

He had only one eye, and the popular prejudice runs in favor of two.
—Charles Dickens

Prejudice is the child of ignorance.
—William Hazlitt, *Sketches and Essays*, "On Prejudice"

There is a tendency to judge a race, a nation, or a distinct group by its least worthy members. —Eric Hoffer, *The True Believer*

My parents gave us a fantastic sense of security and worth. By the time the bigots got around to telling us we were nobody, we already knew we were somebody. —Florynce R. Kennedy

Clearly much that seemed valid seemed so only because he had been taught it from earliest youth.
—W. Somerset Maugham, *Of Human Bondage*

A great many people think they are thinking when they are really rearranging their prejudices. —Edward R. Murrow

The first problem for all of us, men and women, is not to learn, but to unlearn. —Gloria Steinem

It is never too late to give up our prejudices. —Henry David Thoreau

You can't hold a man down without staying down with him.
—Booker T. Washington

PREORDINATION

Whatever befalls thee was preordained for thee from eternity.
—Marcus Aurelius Antoninus, *Meditations*

PREPARATION

The will to succeed is important, but what's even more important is the will to prepare. —Bobby Knight

PRESENCE

A good presence is a letter of recommendation. —Anonymous

The PRESENT

Live in to-day, but not for to-day. —Anonymous

This isn't just any day. —Anonymous

Yesterday's the past and tomorrow's the future, but today is a gift.
That's why it's call the PRESENT.   —Anonymous

One of the illusions of life is that the present hour is not the critical
decisive hour. Write it on your heart that every day is the best day
of the year. He only is right who owns the day, and no one owns
the day who allows it to be invaded by worry, fret and anxiety.
Finish every day, and be done with it. You have done what you
could.   —Ralph Waldo Emerson

You can only understand the present age when it is past. —Han Suyin

Seize the present day, trusting the morrow as little as you can.
                                    —Horace, *Odes*

Learn that the present hour alone is man's.
                    —Samuel Johnson, *Irene*, Act III, Sc. ii

Now is the time for all good men to come to.   —Walt Kelly

Quickly seize the moment: only the present is thine.
                                —Theodor Körner

The present is great with the future.   —Gottfried Wilhelm Leibniz

Trust no future, howe'er pleasant! / Let the dead Past bury its dead!
/ Act, act in the living present! / Heart within, and God o'erhead!
            —Henry Wadsworth Longfellow, "A Psalm of Life"

Let others praise ancient times; I am glad that I was born in these.
                                        —Ovid

No time like the present.   —Mary de la Riviere Manley, *The Lost Lover*

Use the present moment.   —Proverb (German)

Oh, seize the instant time; you never will / With waters once passed
by impel the mill.   —Trench

PRETENSE

Do we really know anybody? Who does not wear one face to hide
another?   —Francis Marion, *Westward the Dream*

The world is full of people who are very clever at seeming much
smarter than they really are.   —Kurt Vonnegut, Jr., *Slapstick*

We are what we pretend to be.
—Kurt Vonnegut, Jr., *Mother Night*, Preface

PREVENTION

An ounce of prevention is worth a pound of cure. —Proverb (English)

PRIDE

Temper is what gets most of us into trouble. Pride is what keeps us
there.   —Anonymous

Pride goeth before destruction, and an haughty spirit before a fall.
—*The Bible* (KJV): Proverbs 16:18

The proud will sooner lose than ask their way.   —Charles Churchill

Though pride is not a virtue, it is the parent of many virtues.
—Churton Collins

Pride had rather go out of the way than go behind.   —Thomas Fuller

Pride, perceiving humility honorable, often borrows her cloak.
—Thomas Fuller

Pride will have a fall.   —Proverb (16th century)

Pride grows in the human heart like lard on a pig.
—Alexander Solzhenitsyn, *The Gulag Archipelago*

Be not proud of race, face, place, or grace.   —Charles H. Spurgeon

PRINCIPLES

His principles were curious, but such as they were they governed his
actions.   —Bertrand Russell, about himself, *The Future of Science*

PRIORITIES

God first; / Others second; / I am third.   —Anonymous

The laundress washeth her own smock first.   —Anonymous

. . . in all the world only one thing really mattered, to do the will of
the one she followed and loved, no matter what it involved or cost.
—Hannah Hurnard, *Hinds' Feet on High Places*

Live near to God, and so all things will appear to you little in comparison with eternal realities. —Robert Murray McCheyne

Let temporal things serve thy use, but the eternal be the object of thy desire. —Thomas à Kempis

PRISON

Whatever you hold in contempt is your jailer. —Brendan Francis

A jailer is as much a prisoner as his prisoner.
—Mahatma Gandhi, in the foreword to his
Correspondence with the Government, 1942-1944

Two men look out through the same bars: / One sees the mud, and one the stars. —Frederick Langbridge, *A Cluster of Quiet Thoughts*

Stone walls do not a prison make, / Nor iron bars a cage.
—Richard Lovelace, "To Althea, from Prison"

If you ever get twenty-five years for nothing, if you find yourself wearing four number patches on your clothes, holding your hands permanently behind your back, submitting to searches morning and evening, working until you are utterly exhausted, dragged into the cooler whenever someone denounces you, trodden deeper and deeper into the ground—from the hole you're in, the fine words of the great humanists will sound like the chatter of the well-fed and free. —Alexander Solzhenitsyn, *The Gulag Archipelago Three*

Let all of us who shared the prison soup meet again in better times!
—Alexander Solzhenitsyn, *Prisoners*

Submissiveness to fate, the total abdication of your own will in the shaping of your life, the recognition that it was impossible to guess the best and the worst ahead of time but that it was easy to take a step you would reproach yourself for—all this freed the prisoner from any bondage, made him calmer, and even ennobled him.
—Alexander Solzhenitsyn, *The Gulag Archipelago*

The events were trivial, but for the first time in my life I learned to look at them through a magnifying glass.
—Alexander Solzhenitsyn, *The Gulag Archipelago*

They should have a heart, but all they think about is output.
—Alexander Solzhenitsyn, *One Day in the Life of Ivan Denisovich*

When one is already on the edge of the grave, why not resist?
—Alexander Solzhenitsyn, *The Gulag Archipelago*

If England treats her criminals the way she has treated me, she doesn't deserve to have any.
—Oscar Wilde

PRIVACY

The ideal man is his own best friend and takes delight in privacy.
—Aristotle

Give me, kind heav'n, a private station, / A mind serene for contemplation.
—John Gay, *Fables*, "The Vulture, the Sparrow, and Other Birds"

We're all torn between the desire for privacy and the fear of loneliness.
—Andrew A. Rooney, *Word for Word*,
"Being with People, Being Without"

PROBLEMS / SOLUTIONS

Glance at the problems, but gaze at Jesus.
—Anonymous

My first rule was to accept nothing as true which I did not clearly recognize to be so; to accept nothing more than what was presented to my mind so clearly and distinctly that I could have no occasion to doubt it. The second rule was to divide each problem or difficulty into as many parts as possible. The third rule was to commence my reflections with objects which were the simplest and easiest to understand, and rise thence, little by little, to knowledge of the most complex. The fourth rule was to make enumerations so complete, and reviews so general, that I should be certain to have omitted nothing.
—René Descartes

We must know that as His children, He's going to allow problems even when we are in the center of His will.
—Sandy Edmonson, *God's Faithfulness in Trials & Testings*

I am more important than my problems.
—José Ferrer

A problem adequately stated is a problem well on its way to being solved.
—R. Buckminster Fuller

Problems worthy of attack prove their worth by hitting back.
—Piet Hein, *Grooks*, "Problems"

A good problem statement often includes what is known, what is unknown, and what is sought. —Edward Hodnett

Every man born of woman has problems.
—Elizabeth Kata, *A Patch of Blue*

A problem well stated is a problem half solved. —Charles F. Kettering

Problems are to the mind what exercise is to the muscles, they toughen and make strong. —Norman Vincent Peale

There is eternal simplicity to a solution once it has been discovered!
—Alexander Solzhenitsyn, *The Gulag Archipelago*

PROCRASTINATION

By the streets of "By and By" one arrives at the house of "Never."
—Miguel de Cervantes

Putting off an easy thing makes it hard, and putting off a hard one makes it impossible. —George H. Lorimer

Procrastination is the thief of time.
—Edward Young, *Night Thoughts*, "Night 1"

PROFIT

If you mean to profit, learn to please. —Winston Churchill

PROGRESS

All innovation is accomplished by lazy people who were tired of doing things the hard way. —Anonymous

Acorns were good till bread was found.
—Francis Bacon, *Colours of Good and Evil*, 6

Progress, man's distinctive mark alone, / Not God's, and not the beasts': God is, they are, / Man partly is and wholly hopes to be.
—Robert Browning, *Dramatis Personae*,
"A Death in the Desert," line 586

The march of the human mind is slow.
—Edmund Burke, speech, 22 Mar 1775

We sometimes think that progress is illusory, and that the devices and
  gadgets which became indispensable to civilized men in the last 500
  years are only a self-propagating accumulation of idle luxuries. But
  this has not been the purpose in the minds of scientists and techni-
  cians, nor has it been the true effect of these inventions on human
  society. The purpose and the effect has been to liberate men from the
  exhausting drudgeries of earning their living, in order to give them
  the opportunity to live. From Leonardo to Franklin, the inventor has
  wanted to give, and has succeeded in giving, more and more . . .
  which was once the monopoly of princes.
    —J. Bronowski and Bruce Mazlish, *The Western Intellectual Tradition*

All progress is based upon a universal innate desire of every organism
  to live beyond its means.   —Samuel Butler (1835-1902), *Note-books*

Men love newfangleness.
    —Geoffrey Chaucer, *The Canterbury Tales*, "The Squire's Tale"

. . . we will hope that future historians will explain the morbid symptoms of present-day society as the childhood ailments of an aspiring humanity, due entirely to the excessive speed at which
  civilization was advancing.   —Albert Einstein, *Ideas and Opinions*

Invention breeds invention.   —Ralph Waldo Emerson

Our way lies not in human ingenuity, but in a return to God.
                                              —Billy Graham

Progress,—the stride of God!   —Victor Hugo

Is it progress if a cannibal uses a fork?
                          —Stanislaw J. Lec, *Unkempt Thoughts*

Not enjoyment, and not sorrow, / Is our destined end or way; / But to
  act, that each to-morrow / Brings us farther than to-day.
                —Henry Wadsworth Longfellow, "A Psalm of Life"

Why build these cities glorious / If man unbuilded goes? / In vain we
  build the world, unless / The builder also grows.
                          —Edwin Markham, "Man-Making" (1920)

Modern man is the victim of the very instruments he values most.
  Every gain in power, every mastery of natural forces, every scientific addition to knowledge, has proved potentially dangerous,
  because it has not been accompanied by equal gains in self-under-
  standing and self-discipline.   —Lewis Mumford

Not to go back, is somewhat to advance.
—Alexander Pope, *Epistles and Satires of Horace Imitated*

The more we realize our minuteness and our impotence in the face of cosmic forces, the more astonishing becomes what human beings have achieved. —Bertrand Russell, *New Hopes for a Changing World*

The reasonable man adapts himself to the world; the unreasonable one persists in trying to adapt the world to himself. Therefore all progress depends on the unreasonable man.
—George Bernard Shaw, *Man and Superman*,
"The Revolutionist's Handbook"

All progress has resulted from people who took unpopular positions.
—Adlai Stevenson, speech, Princeton University, 22 Mar 1954

. . . men may rise on stepping-stones / On their dead selves to higher things. —Alfred, Lord Tennyson, *In Memoriam A. H. H.*

We are never as modern, as far ahead of the past as we like to think we are. —Kurt Vonnegut, Jr., *Mother Night*

Civilization advances by extending the number of important operations which we can perform without thinking about them.
—Alfred North Whitehead, *An Introduction to Mathematics*

And, step by step, since time began, I see the steady gain of man.
—John Greenleaf Whittier, "The Chapel of the Hermits"

If it keeps up, man will atrophy all his limbs but the push-button finger.
—Frank Lloyd Wright

PROMISES

A promise should be given with caution and kept with care.
—Anonymous

The woods are lovely, dark and deep. / But I have promises to keep, / And miles to go before I sleep, / And miles to go before I sleep.
—Robert Frost, *New Hampshire*,
"Stopping by Woods on a Snowy Evening," last stanza

In the land of promise a man may die of hunger. —Proverb (Dutch)

Promise little and do much; and receive every man cheerfully.
—Proverb (Jewish)

He who is the most slow in making a promise is the most faithful in
the performance of it. —Jean Jacques Rousseau

PROPAGANDA

Every occasion had its propaganda . . . You had a desire, a view, a line,
and you disseminated it. —Saul Bellow, *Mr. Sammler's Planet*, Ch. 2

Unfortunately, propaganda works. —Andrew A. Rooney

PROPERTY

Great is the good fortune of a state in which the citizens have a moderate and sufficient property. —Aristotle

I do not own an inch of land, / But all I see is mine.
—Lucy Larcom, "A Strip of Blue"

We are all great landed proprietors, if we only knew it. What we lack
is not land, but the power to enjoy it. Moreover, this great inheritance has the additional advantage that it entails no labor, requires
no management. The landlord has the trouble, but the landscape
belongs to everyone who has eyes to see it. —John Lubbock

Lord of himself, though not of lands; / And having nothing, yet hath
all. —Sir Henry Wotton, "The Character of a Happy Life"

PROPHECY / PROPHETS

. . . A prophet is not without honor, save in his own country, and in
his own house. —*The Bible* (KJV): Matthew 13:57

The best of prophets of the future is the past. —Lord Byron

The best way to predict the future is to invent it. —Alan Kay

PROSPERITY

As many suffer from too much as too little. —Christian Nestell Bovée

Put not your trust in prosperity. —Claudian, *In Rufinum*

When prosperity comes, do not use all of it. —Confucius

The problem of poverty is to remain physically alive. The problem of
prosperity is to remain spiritually alive. —Rabbi Herbert E. Drooz

In a small house God has His corner, in a big house He has to stand in the hall. —Proverb (Swedish)

Prosperity is the touchstone of virtue; for it is less difficult to bear misfortunes than to remain uncorrupted by pleasure. —Tacitus

PROTESTING

Sometimes a scream is better than a thesis. —Ralph Waldo Emerson

The lady protests too much, methinks.
—William Shakespeare, *Hamlet*, Act III, Sc. ii

If you want a symbolic gesture, don't burn the flag, wash it.
—Norman Thomas

PROVERBS

Proverbs are potted wisdom. —Charles Buxton

Proverbs are short sentences drawn from long experience.
—Miguel de Cervantes

A proverb is no proverb to you till life has illustrated it. —John Keats

The study of proverbs may be more instructive and comprehensive than the most elaborate scheme of philosophy. —Motherwell

The wisdom of nations lies in their proverbs, which are brief and pithy. —William Penn

A proverb is the child of experience. —Proverb (English)

[A proverb is] the wisdom of many and the wit of one.
—Lord John Russell

Patch grief with proverbs . . .
—William Shakespeare, *Much Ado About Nothing*, Act V, Sc. i

PROVIDENCE

Accept the place the divine providence has found for you.
—Ralph Waldo Emerson, *Essays, First Series*, "Self-Reliance"

Tie your camel up as best you can, and then trust it to Providence.
—Mohammed

Begin to weave and God will give the thread. —Proverb (German)

God gives, but man must open his hand. —Proverb (German)

God gives no linen, but flax to spin. —Proverb (German)

God gives the milk but not the pail. —Proverb (German)

For a web begun, God sends thread. —Proverb (Italian)

God gave teeth; He will give bread. —Proverb (Lithuanian)

God builds the nest of the blind bird. —Proverb (Turkish)

That which is not allotted the hand cannot reach; what is allotted
you will find wherever you may be. —Saadi

I know not where His islands lift / Their fronded palms in air; / I only
know I cannot drift / Beyond His love and care.
—John Greenleaf Whittier, "The Eternal Goodness"

I firmly believe in divine Providence. Without belief in Providence I
think I should go crazy. Without God the earth would be a maze
without a clue. —Woodrow Wilson

PRUDENCE

Do not count your chickens before they are hatched.
—Aesop, "The Milkmaid and her Pail"

Milk the cow, but don't pull off the udder. —Anonymous

Never cackle till your egg is laid. —Anonymous

Better a tooth out than always aching. —Thomas Fuller

Whose house is of glass, must not throw stones at another.
—George Herbert

The dog's kennel is not the place to keep a sausage.
—Proverb (Danish)

Although it rains, throw not away your watering pot.
—Proverb (English)

Milk the cow which is near. —Proverb (Greek)

Have more strings to thy bow than one. —Proverb (Latin)

Don't call a wolf to help you against the dogs. —Proverb (Russian)

Don't throw away the old bucket until you know whether the new
one holds water. —Proverb (Swedish)

He who has far to ride spares his horse. —Jean Baptiste Racine

Always take an extra quarter to the laundry room. —Wes Smith

PSYCHIATRY

A psychiatrist is a fellow who asks a lot of expensive questions your
wife asks for nothing. —Joey Adams

Psychiatry is the care of the id by the odd. —Anonymous

The psychiatrist must become a fellow traveler with his patient.
—R. D. Laing

PSYCHOANALYSIS

Psychoanalysis makes quite simple people feel they're complex.
—S. N. Behrman

Psychoanalysis is confession without absolution. —G. K. Chesterton

Look into the depths of your own soul and learn first to know yourself, then you will understand why this illness was bound to come
upon you and perhaps you will thenceforth avoid falling ill.
—Sigmund Freud

The four-letter word for psychotherapy is Talk. —Eric Hodgins

Fortunately [psycho]analysis is not the only way to resolve inner conflicts. Life itself still remains a very effective therapist.
—Karen Horney, *Our Inner Conflicts* (1945)

Analysis does not take into account the creative products of neurotic
desires. —Anaïs Nin, *The Diary of Anaïs Nin*, Vol. II

Frequently psychiatrists place no great stock in any of that religious
mumbo-jumbo talk. Instead, they prefer to further confuse
patients with lofty talk of Freudian, Jungian or personal analysis.
—LaRita Pryor, *A Lack of Control*

PSYCHOLOGY

Behavioral psychology is the science of pulling habits out of rats.
—Douglas Busch

Too many individuals in this field [psychology] fall into the trap of confusing the labeling of an illness with really understanding it.
—Richard I. Evans

The brain is viewed as an appendage of the genital glands.
—Carl Jung, on Freud's theory of sexuality

Both the Freudian and the Platonic metaphors emphasize the considerable independence of and tension among the constituent parts of the psyche, a point that characterizes the human condition.
—Carl Sagan, *The Dragons of Eden*

PUNCTUALITY

A Man consumes the Time you make him Wait
In thinking of your Faults—so don't be late!   —Arthur Guiterman

Unfaithfulness in the keeping of an appointment is an act of clear dishonesty. You may as well borrow a person's money as his time.
—Horace Mann

He was always late on principle, his principle being that punctuality is the thief of time.   —Oscar Wilde

PUNISHMENT

The public has more interest in the punishment of an injury than he who receives it.   —Cato the Elder

Distrust all men in whom the impulse to punish is powerful.
—Friedrich Nietzsche

It's quite enough to show a well-beaten dog the whip.
—Alexander Solzhenitsyn, *The Gulag Archipelago*

PURITY

Who can say, I have made my heart clean, I am pure from my sin?
—*The Bible* (KJV): Proverbs 20:9

Long lotus, short lotus, / Cook it for a welcome, / Be ready with bells
and drums / For the pure-hearted girl.
—from an old Chinese poem, in Elizabeth Kata, *A Patch of Blue*

PURPOSE

For the cause that lacks assistance, / For the wrong that needs resistance. / For the Future in the distance, / And the good that I can do.
—George Linnaueus Banks, "Daisies in the Grass, What I Live For"

Preservation for what? —Saul Bellow, *Humboldt's Gift*

Do not dare to live without some clear intention toward which your
living shall be bent. Mean to be something with all your might.
—Phillips Brooks

I think we're here for each other. —Carol Burnett

The purpose of life is a life of purpose. —Robert Byrne

Live for something. —Thomas Chalmers

The only true happiness comes from squandering ourselves for a purpose. —William Cowper

Strange is our situation here upon the earth. Each of us comes for a
short visit, not knowing why, yet sometimes seeming to divine a
purpose. —Albert Einstein, from "My Credo,"
for the German League of Human Rights, 1932

What do we live for, if it is not to make life less difficult to each to
other? —George Eliot, *Middlemarch*

Man is not born to solve the problems of the universe, but to find out
where the problems begin, and then to take his stand within the
limits of the intelligible. —Johann Wolfgang von Goethe

A sense of purpose and the opportunity to contribute to others—
these are as vital to total health as are adequate nutrition and rest.
—H. A. Holle

The human heart refuses to believe in a universe without a purpose.
—Immanuel Kant

Nature fits all her children with something to do.
—Lowell, *A Fable for Critics*

Life is a great gift, and as we reach years of discretion, most of us naturally ask ourselves what should be the main object of our existence. —John Lubbock

If we have our own *why* of life, we shall get along with almost any *how*. —Friedrich Nietzsche, *Twilight of the Idols* (1888), "Maxims and Missiles"

We are here to add what we can to, not to get what we can from life. —Sir William Osler

There is no circumstance, no trouble, no testing, that can ever touch me until, first of all, it has gone past God and past Christ, right through to me. If it has come that far, it has come with a great purpose, which I may not understand at the moment. —Alan Redpath

A great preservative against angry and mutinous thoughts, and all impatience and quarreling, is to have some great business and interest in your mind, which, like a sponge shall suck up your attention and keep you from brooding over what displeases you. —Joseph Rickaby

Nothing contributes so much to tranquilize the mind as a steady purpose—a point on which the soul may fix its intellectual eye. —Mary Wollstone Shelley

Each soul must accomplish its task, or it would not have been sent here. —Isaac Bashevis Singer, *The Slave*

More men fail through lack of purpose than through lack of talent. —Billy Sunday

Bind together your spare hours by the cord of some definite purpose. —W. M. Taylor

I knew my life had been given back for a purpose. —Corrie ten Boom, *Tramp for the Lord*, with Jamie Buckingham

God has something only you can do. —Lewis Timberlake

Everyone is unique. Compare not yourself with anyone else lest you spoil God's curriculum. —Baal Shem Tov

We are here to help each other get through this thing, whatever it is. —Mark Vonnegut, from a 1985 letter to his father, Kurt Vonnegut, Jr. This quote appears on the fly page of Kurt Vonnegut, Jr., *Bluebeard*

God made me so that I might find Him. —Robert Watkins

He who governed the world before I was born shall take care of it like-wise when I am dead. My part is to improve the present moment.
—John Wesley

— Q —

QUALITY

Good things cost less than bad ones.
—Proverb (Italian)

QUARRELING

A little explained, a little endured, a little forgiven, the quarrel is
cured.
—Anonymous

Those who remember that we must come to an end in this world,
their quarrels cease at once.
—Buddhist saying

God turns His back on those who quarrel among themselves.
—Mahatma Gandhi

Persons unmask their evilest qualities when they do quarrel.
—George Herbert

Quarrels would not last so long, if the fault lay all on one side.
—François de La Rochefoucauld, *Maximes*

When two quarrel both are to blame.
—Proverb (Dutch)

Better be quarreling than lonesome.
—Proverb (Irish)

The second word makes the fray.
—Proverb (Japanese)

Beware of entrance into a quarrel.
—Proverb (Persian)

In quarreling, the truth is always lost.
—Publilius Syrus

I say, when there are spats, kiss and make up before the day is done.
—Randolph Ray

The test of a man or woman's breeding is how they behave in a quarrel.
—George Bernard Shaw, *The Philanderer*

I won't quarrel with my bread and butter.
—Jonathan Swift, *Polite Conversation*, Dialogue 1

There is no such test of a man's superiority of character as in the well-
conducting of an unavoidable quarrel.
—Sir Henry Taylor

QUESTIONS

The first key to wisdom is assiduous and frequent questioning . . . For
by doubting we come to inquiry, and by inquiry we arrive at truth.
—Peter Abelard, *Yes and No*

He who nothing questions, nothings learns.　　　　—Anonymous

A prudent question is one-half of wisdom.　　　　—Francis Bacon

If you ask me a question I don't know, I'm not going to answer.
—Yogi Berra, *The Yogi Book*, to the press

Every sentence I utter must be understood not as an affirmation, but
as a question.　　　　　　　　　　　　　　　—Niels Bohr

Examinations are formidable even to the best prepared, for the greatest fool may ask more than the wisest man can answer.
—Charles Caleb Colton, *Lacon*

The important thing is not to stop questioning.　　—Albert Einstein

The riddle of the age has for each a private solution.
—Ralph Waldo Emerson, *The Conduct of Life*, "Fate"

Our object in life should be to accumulate a great number of grand
questions to be asked and resolved in eternity . . .　　　—Foster

If you wish a wise answer, you must put a rational question.
—Johann Wolfgang von Goethe

I keep six honest serving-men / (They taught me all I knew); / Their
names are What and Why and When / And How and Where and
Who.　　　—Rudyard Kipling, *Just-So Stories*, "The Elephant's Child"

You are your own best teacher. My advice is to question all things.
Seek for answers, and when you find what seems to be an answer,
question that, too.　　　　　—Louis L'Amour, *The Walking Drum*

The only questions that really matter are the ones you ask yourself.
—Ursula K. LeGuin, in *The Writer*, 1992

I had a thousand questions to ask God; but when I met Him they all
fled and didn't seem to matter.　—Christopher Morley, *Inward Ho!*,
"I had a thousand questions . . . "

Southerners ask intimate questions in the way monkeys groom each other for lice, not to pry but to make you feel cared for.
—Reynolds Price, *The Tongues of Angels*, Ch. 1

It is not every question that deserves an answer.
—Publilius Syrus, *Maxims*

By nature's kindly disposition most questions which it is beyond a man's power to answer do not occur to him at all.
—George Santayana

But Doc had one mental habit he could not get over. When anyone asked a question, Doc thought he wanted to know the answer.
—John Steinbeck, *Cannery Row*

No man really becomes a fool until he stops asking questions.
—Charles P. Steinmetz

. . . plain question and plain answer make the shortest road out of most perplexities.   —Mark Twain, *Life on the Mississippi*

The "silly question" is the first intimation of some totally new development.   —Alfred North Whitehead

QUIET

How sweet delight a quiet life affords.   —Drummond

He has the gift of quiet.   —John Le Carré

'Tis the quiet people that do the work.   —Proverb (Italian)

Quiet minds cannot be perplexed or frightened, but go on in fortune or misfortune at their own private pace, like a clock in a thunder storm.   —Robert Louis Stevenson

QUITTING

Some things are best mended by a break.
—Edith Wharton, *The Custom of the Country* (1913)

QUOTATIONS

Collect as pearls the words of the wise and virtuous.   —Abd-El-Kader

Platitudes are among the most useful things in the world for those
    who know how to use them, for truth is not the worse for being
    obvious, undeniable, or familiar.   —Anonymous

Write a wise saying and your name will live forever.   —Anonymous

How these curiosities would be quite forgott, did not such idle fel-
    lowes as I am putt them downe.   —John Aubrey

I really didn't say everything I said.   —Yogi Berra, *The Yogi Book*

Where you find / Bright passages strike your mind, / And which per-
    haps you may have reason / To think on at another season,—
    / Take them down in black and white.
                —John Byrom, "Hint to a Young Person"

The majority of those who put together collections of verses or epi-
    grams resemble those who eat cherries or oysters: they begin by
    choosing the best and end by eating everything.
              —Nicolas Chamfort, *Maximes et pensées*

Collecting quotations seems a similar occupation to the one prac-
    ticed by those birds and animals who pick up shiny pebbles, pieces
    of glass and paper to line their nests and burrows. They discard
    one, pick up another, apparently at random, but all with a particu-
    lar spot in mind. The result is a living place that conforms to their
    own sensibility and shape.   —James Charlton

The quotations when engraved upon the memory give you good
    thoughts. They also make you anxious to read the authors and
    look for more.   —Winston Churchill

There are gems of thought that are ageless and eternal.   —Cicero

What is an epigram? A dwarfish whole,
    Its body brevity, and wit its soul.
             —Samuel Taylor Coleridge, "An Epigram"

Quotation brings to many people one of the intensest joys of living.
            —Bernard Darwin, in the introduction to
        Oxford Dictionary of Quotations, Second Edition

Pithy sentences are like sharp nails which force truth upon our memory.
                  —Denis Diderot

Nurture your mind with great thoughts.   —Benjamin Disraeli

The wisdom of the wise and the experience of the ages are perpetu-
ated by quotations. —Benjamin Disraeli

A book which hath been culled from the flowers of all books.
—George Eliot

By necessity, by proclivity,— and by delight, we all quote.
—Ralph Waldo Emerson, *Letters and Social Aims,*
"Quotation and Originality"

Next to the originator of a good sentence is the first quoter of it.
—Ralph Waldo Emerson, *Letters and Social Aims,*
"Quotation and Originality"

But I find that two seemingly conflicting thoughts which have made
it to proverb or aphorism status can be, and usually are, in the
ambivalence of life, both true. —Robert I. Fitzhenry

. . . sayings resonate with significance.—Dag Hammarskjöld, *Markings*

He is a benefactor of mankind who contracts the great rules of life
into short sentences, that may be easily impressed on the memory,
and so recur habitually to the mind. —Samuel Johnson

There are single thoughts that contain the essence of a whole volume, single sentences that have the beauties of a large work.
—Joseph Joubert

We believe the quotation itself is more important than the person
who said it. —Marjorie P. Katz and Jean S. Arbeiter, compilers,
Pegs to Hang Ideas On, p. xvii

The truest sayings are paradoxical. —Lao Tzu

Though old the thought and oft exprest, / 'Tis his at last who says it
best. —James Russell Lowell, *Under the Willows and Other Poems,*
"For an Autograph"

Maxims are the condensed good sense of nations.
—James Mackintosh

Often we were rescued by that ever-present help in trouble, the
beloved benefactor known only as "Anonymous."
—Frank S. Mead, compiler,
The Encyclopedia of Religious Quotations, Preface

We recognize the epigram when uttered or printed just as swiftly as
  we recognize beauty in a woman, yet rarely can we describe either.
                              —G. F. Monkshood, *Woman and the Wits*, Preface

To be amused by what you read—that is the great spring of happy
  quotations.   —C. E. Montague

I quote others only the better to express myself.
                                    —Michel de Montaigne, *Essays*

A good aphorism is too hard for the tooth of time . . .
              —Friedrich Nietzsche, *Miscellaneous Maxims and Opinions*

I might repeat to myself, slowly and soothingly, a list of quotations
  beautiful from minds profound; if I can remember any of the damn
  things.   —Dorothy Parker, *The Little Hour*

An inveterate quote plucker is what I have become.
      —Elaine Partnow, *The Quotable Woman from Eve to 1799*, Preface

There are plenty of maxims in the world; all that remains is to apply
  them.   —Blaise Pascal, *Pensées*

A book that furnishes no quotations is . . . no book—it is a plaything.
                  —Thomas Love Peacock, *Crotchet Castle*, Ch. 9

The maxims of men disclose their hearts.   —Proverb (French)

Almost every wise saying has an opposite one, no less wise, to balance it.
        —George Santayana, *The Life of Reason: Reason in Common Sense*

Precepts or maxims are of great weight; and a few useful ones at hand
  do more toward a happy life than whole volumes that we know not
  where to find.   —Seneca

Whatever is well said by another, is mine.   —Seneca

If you hear a wise sentence or an apt phrase, commit it to your memory.
                                              —Sir Henry Sidney

When someone has the wit to coin a useful phrase, it ought to be
  acclaimed and broadcast or it will perish.   —Jack Smith

A short saying often carries much wisdom.   —Sophocles

If these little sparks of holy fire which I have thus heaped together do not give life to your prepared and already enkindled spirit, yet they will sometimes help to entertain a thought, to actuate a passion, to employ and hallow a fancy. —Jeremy Taylor

Colors fade, temples crumble, empires fall, but wise words endure.
—Edward Thorndike

I am a gatherer and disposer of other men's stuff. —Wasson

An epigram often flashes light into regions where reason shines dimly. —E. P. Whipple

A thought embodied and embrained in fit words walks the earth a living being. —E. P. Whipple

Those who have had experience with type are aware of its satanic persistence towards error . . .
—Frank J. Wilstach, *A Dictionary of Similes*, Preface

If the quality be good, the quantity is of little account . . .
—James Wood, compiler,
The Nuttall Dictionary of Quotations, Preface

. . . though the truth and worth of the sayings are nowise dependent on their authorship, it is well to know who those were that felt the burden they express, and found relief in uttering them.
—James Wood, compiler,
The Nuttall Dictionary of Quotations, Preface

— R —

RACE

There are no "white" or "colored" signs on the foxholes or graveyards
of battle. —John F. Kennedy,
message to Congress on civil rights, 19 Jun 1963

We do not want the men of another color for our brothers-in-law, but
we do want them for our brothers. —Booker T. Washington

RACISM

Whatever the color of a man's skin, we are all mankind. So every
denial of freedom, of equal opportunity for a livelihood, or for an
education, diminishes me. —Everett McKinley Dirksen

At the heart of racism is the religious assertion that God made a creative mistake when He brought some people into being.
—Friedrich Otto Hertz

The conviction that all men are equal by reason of their natural dignity has been generally accepted. Hence racial discrimination can
no longer be justified. —Pope John XXIII

RAIN

Into each life some rain must fall,
Some days must be dark and dreary.
—Henry Wadsworth Longfellow, "The Rainy Day"

Vexed sailors curse the rain for which shepherds prayed in vain.
—Waller

RAW MATERIALS

There was never a good knife made of bad steel. —Anonymous

Rotten wood cannot be carved. —Confucius

READING

I am a part of all I have read. —John Kieran

I took a course in speed reading, learning to read straight down the
middle of the page, and was able to read *War and Peace* in twenty
minutes. It's about Russia. —Woody Allen

What good is all this reading if you can't use it in a crunch? All I
asked was a small mental profit. —Saul Bellow, *Humboldt's Gift*

Children are made readers on the laps of their parents.
—Emilie Buchwald, speech, 1994

Never read anything until not to have read it has bothered you for
some time. —Samuel Butler

Choose an author as you choose a friend.
—Wentworth Dillon, "Essay on Translated Verse"

Many times the reading of a book has made the future of a man.
—Ralph Waldo Emerson

There is creative reading as well as creative writing.
—Ralph Waldo Emerson

'Tis the good reader that makes the good book.
—Ralph Waldo Emerson, *Society and Solitude*, "Success"

We often read with as much talent as we write.
—Ralph Waldo Emerson

The end of reading is not more books but more life.
—Holbrook Jackson

A man ought to read just as inclination leads him, for what he reads
as a task will do him little good.
—Samuel Johnson, in James Boswell, *Life of Samuel Johnson*

Read the book you do honestly feel a wish and curiosity to read.
—Samuel Johnson

I want to point the way to something that should forever lure them,
when the TV set is broken and the movie is over and the school
bell has rung for the last time.
—Bel Kaufman, *Up the Down Staircase*

. . . we must read, not only for what we read but for what it makes us
think. —Louis L'Amour, *The Warrior's Path*

What is reading but silent conversation?
>—Walter Savage Landor, *Imaginary Conversations*,
>"Aristotle and Callisthenes"

Some people read only because they are too lazy to think.
>—G. C. Lichtenberg

Reading furnishes us only with the materials of knowledge; it is thinking makes what we read ours.
>—John Locke, "An Essay Concerning Human Understanding"

Resolve to edge in a little reading every day, if it is but a single sentence. If you gain fifteen minutes a day, it will make itself felt at the end of a year. —Horace Mann

The pleasure of all reading is doubled when one lives with another who shares the same books. —Katherine Mansfield, *Letters*

. . . he formed the most delightful habit in the world, the habit of reading. —W. Somerset Maugham, *Of Human Bondage*

No entertainment is so cheap as reading, nor any pleasure so lasting.
>—Mary Wortley Montagu, letter to her daughter,
>Countess of Bute, 28 Jan 1753

I don't want to review books any more. It cuts in too much on my reading.
>—Dorothy Parker, *Constant Reader*,
>"A Good Novel, and a Great Story," 4 Feb 1928

There's something special about people who are interested in the printed word. They are a species all their own—learned, kind, knowledgeable and human. —Nathan Pine

. . . who read as naturally and constantly as ponies crop grass, and with much the same kind of pleasure . . .
>—Katherine Anne Porter, *Old Mortality*

Choose an author as you choose a friend.
>—Earl of Roscommon, "Essay on Translated Verse"

But we read, and usually we believe; good, bad, or indifferent, any string of English words holds our attention . . .
>—J. D. Salinger, *Seymour an Introduction*

Give me a bed and a book and I am happy. —Logan Pearsall Smith

People say that life is the thing, but I prefer reading.
—Logan Pearsall Smith, *Afterthoughts*, "Myself"

Employ your time in improving yourself by other men's writings so
that you shall come easily by what others have labored hard for.
—Socrates

Reading is to the mind what exercise is to the body.
—Sir Richard Steele

How many a man has dated a new era in his life from the reading of a
book! —Henry David Thoreau, *Walden*, "Reading"

Read the best books first, or you may not have a chance to read them
at all. —Henry David Thoreau

A classic is something that everybody wants to have read and nobody
wants to read. —Mark Twain, speech,
"The Disappearance of Literature," New York, 20 Nov 1900

What do people do that don't read?
—Brian Alexander Watkins (age 12)

Reading is the work of the alert mind, is demanding, and under ideal
conditions produces finally a sort of ecstasy. This gives the experience of reading a sublimity and power unequaled by any other
form of communication. —E. B. White

Just a little every day   That's the way Children learn to read and
write Bit by bit and mite by mite. —Ella Wheeler Wilcox

A good reader is nearly as rare as a good writer. —Willmott

The wise man reads both books and life itself. —Lin Yutang

REALITY

Cloquet hated reality but realized it was still the only place to get a
good steak. —Woody Allen

What men perceive as real is real in its consequences.
—Anonymous, sociological axiom

I like reality. It tastes of bread. —Jean Anouilh, *Catch as Catch Can*

It's goodbye to reality when love sets in.
—Saul Bellow, *More Die of Heartbreak*

What could possibly be more fantastic than reality?
—Ashleigh Brilliant

Reality is merely an illusion, albeit it a very persistent one.
—Albert Einstein

. . . human kind cannot bear very much reality.
—T. S. Eliot, *Four Quarters*, "Burnt Norton"

Dreams are real while they last. Can we say more of life?
—Havelock Ellis

. . . the central problem of the modern age, the quest for a meaningful image of reality. This problem has ruled the destinies of painting in our time. It has, likewise, been the goad of modern
literature, philosophy, and science.   —Hans L. C. Jaffé

Reality is something you rise above.   —Liza Minelli

What is reality anyway? Nothin' but a collective hunch.
—Jane Wagner, *The Search for Signs of Intelligent Life in the Universe*

R E A S O N

Reason is a light that God has kindled in the soul.   —Aristotle

Reason is itself a matter of faith. It is an act of faith to assert that our
thoughts have any relation to reality at all.
—G. K. Chesterton, *Orthodoxy*, "The Suicide of Thought"

Reason is our Soul's left hand, Faith her right, / By these we reach
divinity.   —John Donne, "To the Countess of Bedford"

If you will not hear Reason, she will surely rap your knuckles.
—Benjamin Franklin, *Poor Richard's Almanack*, 1758

I do not feel obliged to believe that the same God who has endowed
us with sense, reason and intellect has intended us to forego their
use.   —Galileo Galilei

Reason is one thing and faith is another and reason can as little be
made a substitute for faith, as faith can be made a substitute for
reason.   —John Henry Newman, *Discourse to Mixed Congregations*

All reasoning ends in an appeal to self-evidence. —Coventry Patmore

Say first, of God above or man below, / What can we reason but from
what we know? —Alexander Pope

Most of our so-called reasoning consists in finding arguments for
going on believing as we already do.
—James Harvey Robinson, *The Mind in the Making*

Nothing has an uglier look to us than reason, when it is not on our
side. —George Savile

Passion and prejudice govern the world, only under the name of reason. —John Wesley

R E A S O N S

A man's acts are usually right, but his reasons seldom are.
—Elbert Hubbard

A man always has two reasons for doing anything—a good reason
and the real reason. —J. P. Morgan

We are generally more convinced by the reasons we discover on our
own than by those given to us by others. —Marcel Proust

R E C O G N I T I O N

. . . men want recognition of their work, to help them believe in
themselves. —Dorothy Miller Richardson, *Pilgrimage*, Vol. IV, Ch. 9

R E F U S A L

It is kindness immediately to refuse what you intend to deny.
—Publilius Syrus, *Maxims*

The prompter the refusal, the less the disappointment.
—Publilius Syrus, *Moral Sayings*

R E G I M E N

The one thing more difficult than following a regimen is not imposing it on others. —Marcel Proust

R E G R E T

Never regret. If it's good, it's wonderful. If it's bad, it's experience.
—Victoria Holt, *The Black Opal*

R E L A T I O N S H I P S

A relationship is what happens between two people who are waiting
for something better to come along. —Anonymous

Don't smother each other. No one can grow in the shade.
—Leo F. Buscaglia

Let there be spaces in your togetherness. —Kahlil Gibran, *The Prophet*

Life and death in a relationship depend on attitudes.
—Laurel Lee, *Godspeed: Hitchhiking Home*

Reinforce the stitch that ties us, and I will do the same for you.
—Doris Scherin

I never was attached to that great sect, / Whose doctrine is that each
one should select / Out of the crowd a mistress or a friend, / And all
the rest, though fair and wise, commend, / To cold oblivion.
—Percy Shelley, "Epipsychidion"

The planks in the foundation of a good relationship are added one at
a time. —Kathleen Watkins, 28 Jan 1994

R E L I G I O N

Many have quarreled about religion that never practiced it.
—Anonymous

We use religion like a trolley-car—we ride on it only while it is going
our way. —Anonymous

Sects differ more in name than tenets. —Honoré de Balzac

All God's religions . . . have not been able to put mankind back
together again. —John Cage

It has often been said, very truly, that religion is the thing that makes
the ordinary man extraordinary; it is an equally important truth
that religion is the thing that makes the extraordinary man feel
ordinary. —G. K. Chesterton

It is the test of a good religion whether you can joke about it.
—G. K. Chesterton

Let your religion be less of a theory and more of a love affair.
—G. K. Chesterton

Men will wrangle for religion; write for it; fight for it; anything but—
live for it.   —Charles Caleb Colton, *Lacon*

"Sensible men are all of the same religion." "And pray what is that?"
inquired the prince. "Sensible men never tell."
—Benjamin Disraeli, *Endymion*

. . . a person who is religiously enlightened appears to me to be one
who has, to the best of his ability, liberated himself from the fetters
of his selfish desires and is preoccupied with thoughts, feelings,
and aspirations to which he clings because of their superpersonal
value.   —Albert Einstein, *Ideas and Opinions*

But mere thinking cannot give us a sense of the ultimate and fundamental ends. To make clear these fundamental ends and valua-
tions, and to set them fast in the emotional life of the individual,
seems to me precisely the most important function which religion
has to perform in the social life of man. And if one asks whence
derives the authority of such fundamental ends, since they cannot
be stated and justified merely by reason, one can only answer: they
exist in a healthy society as powerful traditions, which act upon
the conduct and aspirations and judgments of the individuals;
they are there, that is, as something living, without its being necessary to find justification for their existence. They come into being
not through demonstration but through revelation, through the
medium of powerful personalities.
—Albert Einstein, *Ideas and Opinions*

My religion consists of a humble admiration of the illimitable superior spirit who reveals himself in the slight details we are able to
perceive with our frail and feeble minds. That deeply emotional
conviction of the presence of a superior reasoning power, which is
revealed in the incomprehensible universe, forms my idea of God.
—Albert Einstein

Science without religion is lame, religion without science is blind.
—Albert Einstein,
Science, Philosophy and Religion: A Symposium, Ch. 13

Be short in all religious exercises. Better leave the people longing
than loathing.   —Nathaniel Emmons

Here is my Creed. I believe in one God, creator of the Universe. That
he governs it by his Providence. That he ought to be worshiped.
That the most acceptable service we render him is doing good to
his other children. That the soul of Man is immortal, and will be
treated with justice in another life respecting its conduct in this.
              —Benjamin Franklin, letter to Ezra Stiles, 9 Mar 1790

If men are so wicked with religion, what would they be without it?
                                       —Benjamin Franklin

In reality there are as many religions as there are individuals.
                         —Mahatma Gandhi, *Hind Swaraj*, Ch. 2

Religion is not what is grasped by the brain, but a heart grasp.
                                        —Mahatma Gandhi

Your daily life is your temple and your religion.   —Kahlil Gibran

Many people have just enough natural religion to make them
immune to the real thing.   —Billy Graham, *World Aflame*

Much of the philosophy of religious education has been based upon a
false premise, and perhaps many have missed the essence of
Christian experience, having had religious training take its place.
                                            —Billy Graham

Religion is a disease, but it is a noble disease.   —Heraclitus

That part of a man's religion which is convenient, that he'll never
drop.   —Aloysius Horn

Primitive societies without religion have never been found.
                              —William Howells, *The Heathens*

Religion is caught, not taught.   —William R. Inge

The day that this country ceases to be free for irreligion, it will cease
to be free for religion.
              —Robert H. Jackson, opinion in Zerach vs. Clausor, 1952

. . . for it is from our lives and not from our words, that our religion
must be read.   —Thomas Jefferson, letter to John Adams

In thirty years I have treated many patients. Among all my patients in the second half of life, every one of them fell ill because he had lost that which the living religions of every age had given their followers, and none of them was really healed who did not regain his religious outlook. —Carl Jung

Religion's greatest task is to destroy the myth that accumulation of wealth and the achievement of comfort are the chief vocations of man. —Rabbi Arnold Kaiman

Some theologians say that the history of religion is the story of man's search for God. That is only half the truth. It also is the history of the search of God for man. —Rabbi Isaac Klein

Every sect is a moral check on its neighbor. Competition is as wholesome in religion as in commerce. —Walter Savage Landor

Churches come and go, but there has ever been but one religion. The only religion is conscience in action. —Henry Demarest Lloyd

It is in the area of feeling that religion enters the heart and is expressed by man. —Edgar F. Magnin

We must respect the other fellow's religion . . . to the extent that we respect his theory that his wife is beautiful.
—H. L. Mencken, *Minority Report*

Man is certainly stark mad; he cannot make a flea, and yet he will be making gods by the dozens. —Michel de Montaigne, *Essays*

Religion is a multicolored lantern. Everyone looks through a particular color, but the candle is always there. —Mohammed Naguib

Every religion is good that teaches man to be good. —Thomas Paine

My country is the world, and my religion is to do good.
—Thomas Paine, *The Rights of Man*

Religion is nothing else but love of God and man.
—William Penn, *Some Fruits of Solitude*

Religion is the hospital of the souls that the world has wounded.
—J. Petit-Senn

The broad-minded see the truth in different religions; the narrow-minded see only the differences. —Proverb (Chinese)

A woman without religion is as a flower without scent.
—Proverb (German)

A man without religion is like a horse without a bridle.
—Proverb (Latin)

Religions tend to disappear with man's good fortune.
—Raymond Queneau, *Une Histoire Modèle*

Religion is not a popular error; it is a great instinctive truth, sensed by the people, expressed by the people.   —Ernest Renan, *Les Apôtres*

According to the orthodox Christian's Bible, all religions do not lead to God.   —Fritz Ridenour, *So What's the Difference*, Introduction

There is obviously a great human need for religion because life seems to be such a mystery.
—Andrew A. Rooney, *Word for Word*, "School Prayer"

The lovers of God have no religion but God alone.
—Jalluddin Rumi, in Dag Hammarskjöld, *Markings*

Men of sense are really all of one religion. But men of sense never tell what it is.   —Earl of Shaftesbury

There is only one religion, though there are a hundred versions of it.
—George Bernard Shaw, *Arms and the Man*, Preface

To learn the worth of a man's religion, do business with him.
—John Lancaster Spalding

We have just enough religion to make us hate, but not enough to make us love one another.
—Jonathan Swift, *Thoughts of Various Subjects*

A religion without mystery must be a religion without God.
—Jeremy Taylor

It is a mistake to assume that God is interested only, or even chiefly, in religion.
—William Temple, Archbishop of Canterbury, in R. V. C. Bodley, *In Search of Serenity*, Ch. 12

There are many faiths, but the spirit is one, in me, in you, and in every man.   —Leo Tolstoy

The ultimate verification of our religion consists of the changed lives
to which it can point and for which it is responsible.
—David Elton Trueblood

Systems of faith are different, but God is one.   —Vemana

. . . the reverence I felt for the holiness of life is not ever likely to be
entirely at home in organized religion.
—Eudora Welty, *One Writer's Beginnings*

There is nothing more unnatural to religion than contentions about
it.   —Benjamin Whichcote, *Sermons*

Religion is what the individual does with his own solitariness.
—Alfred North Whitehead, *Religion in the Making*

Religion is the fashionable substitute for belief.   —Oscar Wilde

R E M E D I E S

The remedy is worse than the disease.
—Francis Bacon, *Essays*, "Of Seditions and Troubles"

Extreme remedies are very appropriate for extreme diseases.
—Hippocrates, *Aphorisms*

The hole and the patch should be commensurate. —Thomas Jefferson

Desperate diseases must have desperate remedies.   —Proverb (Latin)

There are some remedies worse than the disease.
—Publilius Syrus, *Moral Sayings*

Our remedies oft in ourselves do lie / Which we ascribe to heaven . . .
—William Shakespeare, *All's Well That Ends Well*, Act I, Sc. i

R E P A I R

If it ain't broke, don't fix it.   —Bert Lance, *Nation's Business*

I soon knew that I could fix things better than he, with his tendency
to storm a mechanical problem in the hope that by sheer righteous
determination it would yield to him.   —Arthur Miller, *Timebends*

We need someone who specialized in fixing things that are too small
to bother with.
—Andrew A. Rooney, *Word for Word*, "Mending Molehills"

REPENTANCE

True repentance is to cease from sin. —Saint Ambrose

. . . Repent ye: for the kingdom of heaven is at hand.
—*The Bible* (KJV): Matthew 3:2

. . . but, except ye repent, ye shall all likewise perish.
—*The Bible* (KJV): Luke 13:3

Most people repent of their sins by thanking God they ain't so wicked
as their neighbor. —Josh Billings

Repentance was perhaps best defined by a small girl: It's to be sorry
enough to quit. —C. H. Kilmer, *The New Illustrator*

To do so no more is the truest repentance. —Martin Luther

He who is sorry for having sinned is almost innocent. —Seneca

REPROACH

The sting of a reproach is the truth of it. —Benjamin Franklin

Reprove your friend in secret and praise him openly.
—Leonardo da Vinci

REPUTATION

Glass, china, and reputation are easily cracked, and never well
mended. —Anonymous

A good name is rather to be chosen than great riches, and loving
favor rather than silver and gold. —*The Bible* (KJV): Proverbs 22:1

The art of being able to make good use of moderate abilities wins
esteem, and often acquires more reputation than actual brilliancy.
—François de La Rochefoucauld

If I take care of my character, my reputation will take care of itself.
—Dwight L. Moody

If you want people to think well of you, do not speak well of yourself.
—Blaise Pascal, *Pensées*

The reputation of a thousand years may be determined by the conduct of one hour. —Proverb (Japanese)

RESEARCH

The only possible interpretation of any research whatever in the
"social sciences" is: Some do, some don't.   —Anonymous

Research is the process of going up alleys to see if they are blind.
                                                  —Marston Bates

Basic research is what I'm doing when I don't know what I'm doing.
                                                  —Wernher von Braun

There is only one proved method of assisting the advancement of
pure science—that of picking men of genius, backing them heavily,
and leaving them to direct themselves.
    —James Bryant Conant, letter to *New York Times*, 13 Aug 1945

I think and think for months and years. Ninety-nine times, the conclusion is false. The hundredth time I am right.   —Albert Einstein

Scientific research? Only when not at the cost of ethics—and first of
all, those of the researchers themselves.   —Alexander Solzhenitsyn

RESIGNATION

Once they've skinned you, there's no point in grieving over the wool.
                                                  —Anonymous

A man must take the fat with the lean.   —Charles Dickens

Where there is no choice, we do well to make no difficulty.
                            —George Macdonald, *Sir Gibble*, XI.

He that cannot get bacon must be content with cabbage.
                                                  —Proverb (Danish)

Gnaw the bone which is fallen to thy lot.   —Proverb (Hebrew)

Things without all remedy /Should be without regard; what's done is
done.   —William Shakespeare, *Macbeth*, Act III, Sc. ii

RESISTANCE

Indeed, one perfect resister is enough to win the battle of Right
against Wrong.   —Mahatma Gandhi

RESOLVE

But we are mostly what we are, and the turtle stretching toward delicious buds on high does not lighten his carapace by his resolve.
—Arthur Miller, *Timebends*

RESPECT

The respect of those you respect is worth more than the applause of the multitude.
—Anonymous

This is the final test of a gentleman: his respect for those who can be of no possible service to him.
—William Lyon Helps

When we feel that we are not sufficiently respected, we should ask ourselves whether we are living as we should.
—Alexander Solzhenitsyn, *The Gulag Archipelago Three*

RESPONSIBILITY

The buck stops here.
—Anonymous,
motto mounted on the desk of President Harry S. Truman

Responsibility educates.
—Wendell Phillips

If you can't stand the heat, get out of the kitchen.
—Harry Vaughn, in *Time*, 28 Apr 1952,
often quoted by President Harry S. Truman

REST

Unless we find repose within ourselves, it is vain to seek it elsewhere.
—Hosea Ballou

It is no disgrace to rest a bit.
—Gene Fowler

"O stay," the maiden said, "and rest / Thy weary head against this breast!"
—Henry Wadsworth Longfellow, *Excelsior*

Take rest; a field that has rested gives a bountiful crop.
—Ovid

You will soon break the bow if you keep it always stretched.
—Phaedrus, *Fables*, Book III, fable 14

Rest is the sweet sauce of labor.
—Plutarch

Men tire themselves in pursuit of rest.
—Laurence Sterne

RESTLESSNESS

Man's restlessness makes him strive.
—Johann Wolfgang von Goethe, *Faust*

RESURRECTION

. . . Christ, being raised from the dead, dieth no more; death hath no more dominion over him.   —*The Bible* (KJV): Romans 6:9

Our Lord has written the promise of the resurrection, not in books alone, but in every leaf in springtime.   —Martin Luther

What reason have atheists for saying that we cannot rise again? Which is the more difficult—to be born, or to rise again? That what has never been, should be, or that what has been should be again? Is it more difficult to come into being than to return to it?
—Blaise Pascal, *Pensées*

RETIREMENT

Retire? I'm going to stay in show business until I'm the only one left.
—George Burns (1896-1996), at age 90

A retired husband is often a wife's full-time job.   —Ella Harris

REVENGE

The best way to get even is to forget.   —Anonymous

There is no revenge so complete as forgiveness.   —Josh Billings

He that returns a good for evil obtains the victory.
—Thomas Fuller, M. D., *Gnomologia*, No. 2268

An eye for an eye makes the whole world blind.   —Mahatma Gandhi

Living well is the best revenge.   —George Herbert, *Jacula Prudentum*

The only people with whom you should try to get even are those who have helped you.   —Mae Maloo

Revenge, at first though sweet, bitter erelong back on itself recoils.
—John Milton

REWARDS

As for me, prizes mean nothing. My prize is my work.
—Katharine Hepburn, in Charles Higham, *Kate*

There is yet something remaining for the dead, and some far better
thing for the good than for the evil. —Plato, *Phaedo*

RICHES

Remember that moderate riches will carry you; if you have more, you
must carry them . . . —Anonymous

The rich never want kindred. —Anonymous

Labor not to be rich: cease from thine own wisdom.
—*The Bible* (KJV): Proverbs 23:4

. . . he that maketh haste to be rich shall not be innocent.
—*The Bible* (KJV): Proverbs 28:20

. . . It is easier for a camel to go through the eye of a needle, than for a
rich man to enter into the kingdom of God.
—*The Bible* (KJV): Matthew 19:24

The best condition in life is not to be so rich as to be envied nor so
poor as to be damned. —Josh Billings

Of all the riches that we hug, of all the pleasures that we enjoy, we
can carry no more out of this world than out of a dream.
—James Bonnell

He is rich who wishes no more than he has. —Cicero

There is nothing wrong with men possessing riches. The wrong
comes when riches possess men. —Billy Graham

You're rich if you've had a meal today. —Billy Graham

Being rich and thin isn't everything.
—Garrison Keillor, *We Are Still Married*

As riches and honor forsake a man, we discover him to be a fool, but
nobody could find it out in his prosperity. —Jean de La Bruyère

A short cut to riches is to subtract from our desires.
—Petrarch, *Epistolae de Rebus Familiaribus*

We may see the small value God has for riches by the people he gives
    them to.   —Alexander Pope, *Thoughts on Various Subjects*

He is rich who owes nothing.   —Proverb (Hungarian)

He is rich enough who wants nothing.   —Proverb (Latin)

The wretchedness of being rich is that you live with rich people.
    —Logan Pearsall Smith, *Afterthoughts*, 4, "In the World"

To suppose, as we all suppose, that we could be rich and not behave
    as the rich behave, is like supposing that we could drink all day
    and keep absolutely sober.
        —Logan Pearsall Smith, *Afterthoughts*, "In the World"

Who is rich? He who rejoices in his portion.   —*The Talmud*

The RIDICULOUS

There is only one step from the sublime to the ridiculous.
    —Napoleon Bonaparte, to De Pradt, Polish Ambassador, after the
    retreat from Moscow in 1812, in De Pradt, *Histoire de l'Ambassade
    dans le Grand-duché de Varsovie en 1812*

RIGHT and WRONG

There is no right way to do a wrong thing.   —Anonymous

You had to be a crank to insist on being right.
    —Saul Bellow, *Mr. Sammler's Planet*, Ch. 1

Distinction between virtuous and vicious actions has been engraven
    by the Lord in the heart of every man.   —John Calvin

I leave this rule for others when I'm dead, / Be always sure you are
    right—then go ahead.   —Davy Crockett, *Autobiography*

I beseech you, in the bowels of Christ, think it possible you may be
    mistaken.
        —Oliver Cromwell, letter to the General Assembly
        of the Church of Scotland, 3 Aug 1650

The first duty of man is to take none of the principles of conduct
    upon trust; to do nothing without a clear and individual convic-
    tion that it is right to be done.
        —William Godwin, *An Enquiry Concerning Political Justice*

None but a fool is always right. —Hare

The right act is far less than the right-thinking mind. —Hindu saying

Two things strike me dumb: the infinite starry heavens, and the sense
of right and wrong in man. —Immanuel Kant

Let us have faith that right makes might, and in that faith let us to
the end dare to do our duty as we understand it.
—Abraham Lincoln, closing words of address at
Cooper Institute, New York City, 27 Feb 1860

My concern is not whether God is on our side; my great concern is to
be on God's side, for God is always right. —Abraham Lincoln

With malice toward none; with charity for all; with firmness in the
right, as God gives us to see the right.
—Abraham Lincoln, Second Inaugural Address, 4 Mar 1865

If it is not right, do not do it; if it is not true, do not say it.
—Marcus Aurelius Antoninus

Do what you ought, come what may.
—Thomas May, *Sanford and Merton*

For modes of faith, let graceless zealots fight; / His can't be wrong
whose life is in the right. —Alexander Pope, *An Essay on Man*

A man should never be ashamed to own he has been in the wrong,
which is but saying, in other words, that he is wiser today than he
was yesterday. —Alexander Pope, *Miscellanies*

Whatever is, is right. —Alexander Pope, *An Essay on Man*

Human beings are perhaps never more frightening than when they
are convinced beyond doubt that they are right.
—Laurens van der Post

Everybody is a bit right. —Rosenstock-Huessy

Do right and leave the results with God. —Talmadge

Always do right—this will gratify some people and astonish the rest.
—Mark Twain, message to Young People's Society,
Greenpoint Presbyterian Church, Brooklyn, New York, 16 Feb 1901

RIGHTS

I disapprove of what you say, but I will defend to the death your right
to say it. —Anonymous, often attributed to Voltaire

We hold these truths to be self-evident, that all men are created equal;
they are endowed by their creator with certain unalienable rights;
that among these are life, liberty, and the pursuit of happiness.
—Declaration of Independence

Give to every other human being every right that you claim for yourself. —Robert G. Ingersoll, *Limitations of Toleration*

... every man on the planet / Has just as much right as yourself to
the road. —John Boyle O'Reilly, "The Rainbow's Treasure"

The greatest right in the world is the right to be wrong.
—Harry Weinberger

RISK

He is not worthy of the honeycomb / That shuns the hive because the
bees have stings. —Anonymous

A wise man doesn't trust all his eggs to one basket.
—Miguel de Cervantes, *Don Quixote*

Those who'll play with cats must expect to be scratched.
—Miguel de Cervantes, *Don Quixote*

In skating over thin ice our safety is in our speed.
—Ralph Waldo Emerson, *Essays, First Series*, "Prudence"

Hang not all on one nail. —Proverb (German)

Far better it is to dare mighty things, to win glorious triumphs, even
though checkered by failure, than to take rank with those poor
spirits who neither enjoy much nor suffer much, because they live
in the great twilight that knows not victory nor defeat.
—Theodore Roosevelt

Remember, you can't steal second if you don't take your foot off first.
—Mike Todd

Risk is a part of God's game, alike for men and nations.
—George E. Woodberry

ROBUSTNESS

. . . there was an honesty inherent in bulkiness if it is just the right
amount. —Don DeLillo, *White Noise*

The reason fat people are happy is that the nerves are well protected.
—Luciano Pavarotti

I see no objection to stoutness, in moderation.
—W. S. Gilbert, *Iolanthe*, I

ROLES

For some must follow, and some command,
Though all are made of clay!
—Henry Wadsworth Longfellow, "Kéramos"

It makes people nervous for one to step out of one's role.
—Walker Percy, *Lancelot*

Art thou anvil, be patient; art thou hammer, strike hard.
—Proverb (German)

. . . everyone must play his role.
—Anne Tyler, *Dinner at the Homesick Restaurant*

ROMANCE

In a great romance, each person basically plays a part that the other
really likes. —Elizabeth Ashley, in *The San Francisco Chronicle,* 1982

The average man is more interested in a woman who is interested in
him than he is in a woman with beautiful legs. —Marlene Dietrich

You see an awful lot of smart guys with dumb women, but you hardly
ever see a smart woman with a dumb guy. —Erica Jong

Romance might not last, but it was something while it did.
—Larry McMurtry, *The Last Picture Show*, Ch. 15

With a dame all you needed was a beginning.
—Bernard Malamud, *The Assistant*

ROUTINE

There is comfort in routine. —John Steinbeck, *Sweet Thursday*, Ch. 16

ROWING

Everyone must row with the oars he has. —Proverb (English)

ROYALTY

A cat may look at a king. —John Heywood, *Proverbs*

RUDENESS

Rudeness is the weak man's imitation of strength.
—Eric Hoffer, *The Passionate State of Mind*

RUMOR

A rumor is about as hard to unspread as butter. —Anonymous

In every ear it spread, on every tongue it grew. —Alexander Pope

Rumor travels faster, but it don't stay put as long as Truth.
—Will Rogers, *The Illiterate Digest*, "Politics Getting Ready to Jell"

RUSSIA

. . . that there is a special Russian asset, which is the belief that Russia
is the homeland of the deeper and sincerer emotions.
—Saul Bellow, *More Die of Heartbreak*

I cannot forecast to you the action of Russia. It is a riddle wrapped in
a mystery inside an enigma.
—Winston Churchill, broadcast, Oct 1939

Russia has two generals in whom she can confide—Generals Janvier
and Février [January and February]. —Emperor Nicholas I of Russia

— S —

The SABBATH

. . . it is lawful to do well on the sabbath days.
—*The Bible* (KJV): Matthew 12:12

And he [Jesus] said unto them, The sabbath was made for man, and
not man for the sabbath.   —*The Bible* (KJV): Mark 2:27

. . . Which of you shall have an ass or an ox fallen into a pit, and will
not straightway pull him out on the sabbath day?
—*The Bible* (KJV): Luke 14:5

SADNESS

The ground of all great thoughts is sadness.   —Philip James Bailey

Joy and sadness come by turns.   —Walker Percy, *The Moviegoer*

Though sad at heart, to sing joyfully.   —Christine de Pisan

SAFETY

It's an old adage that the way to be safe is never to be secure . . . Each
one of us requires the spur of insecurity to force us to do our best.
—Harold W. Dodds

A ship in harbor is safe, but that is not what ships are built for.
—John A. Shedd, *Salt from My Attic*

SAILING

I'm not afraid of storms, for I am learning how to sail my ship.
—Louisa May Alcott

A smooth sea never made a skillful sailor.   —Anonymous

In a calm sea every man is a pilot.   —Anonymous

In order to realize the worth of the anchor, we need to feel the stress
of the storm.   —Anonymous

There is no trick to being a captain as long as the sea is quiet.
—Benjamin I

Skillful pilots gain their reputation from storms and tempests.
—Epicurus

The winds and the waves are always on the side of the ablest naviga-
tors.   —Edward Gibbon, *Decline and Fall of the Roman Empire*, 68

Being in a ship is being in a jail, with the chance of being drowned.
—Samuel Johnson, in James Boswell, *Life of Samuel Johnson*

Any port in a storm.   —Proverb (18th century Scottish)

Little boats must keep the shore, larger boats may venture more.
—Proverb (English)

If the wind will not serve, take to the oars.   —Proverb (Latin)

Anyone can hold the helm when the sea is calm.   —Publilius Syrus

A great pilot can sail even if his canvas is rent.
—Seneca, *Moral Letters to Lucilius*, "On Conquering the Conqueror"

SAINTS

The only thing different between sinners and saints is one is forgiven
and the other ain't.   —George Jones

The wonderful thing about saints is that they were human . . . Still
they went on doggedly blundering toward heaven.
—Phyllis McGinley

We are content to place a statue of Francis of Assisi in the middle of
the birdbath and let the whole business of the saints go at that.
—C. Kiler Myers

A saint is a person who does almost everything any other decent person does, only somewhat better and with a totally different
motive.   —Coventry Patmore

They are not all saints who use holy water.   —Proverb (English)

Saints can spring from any soil.   —John Steinbeck, *East of Eden*

The saints are the sinners who keep on trying.

—Robert Louis Stevenson

SALVATION

God predestines every man to be saved. The devil predestines every man to be damned. Man has the casting vote. —Anonymous

He who created us without our help will not save us without our consent. —Saint Augustine

Salvation is the first day of eternity. —John Ballard

If a Savior leaves you as you are, from what has He saved you?

—Rev. Denny Brake

. . . if thou shalt confess with thy mouth the Lord Jesus, and shalt believe in thine heart that God hath raised him from the dead, thou shalt be saved. —*The Bible* (KJV): Romans 10:9

I have a life that was changed. —Ray Boltz, from a song

Salvation is seeing that the universe is good, and becoming a part of that goodness. —Arthur G. Clutton-Brock

I haven't yet to this day gotten over my salvation. —David Crain

Salvation includes an ongoing transformation in your life.
—Steve Hawthorne, guest sermon,
Hope Chapel, Austin, Texas, 12 Mar 1994

The best that can be said of you is that you got saved.
—Steve Hawthorne, guest sermon,
Hope Chapel, Austin, Texas, 12 Mar 1994

There's much more for me included in Christ's salvation than merely a paid ticket to heaven. There is victory over present circumstances if I am willing to accept it.
—Matilda Nordtvedt, *Living Beyond Depression*

I have a new heritage.
—Ron Parrish, sermon, Hope Chapel, Austin, Texas, 10 Dec 1994

Fiction, however pious, cannot save. —Rich Pedersen, guest sermon,
Hope Chapel, Austin, Texas, 1 Sep 1990

SANITY

I don't really trust a sane person. You can never depend on them.
—Lyle Alzado, NFL defensive lineman, *The Washington Post*, 1984

Part of being sane is being a little bit crazy.　　　　—Janet Long

He who can simulate sanity will be sane.　—Ovid, *Remediorum Amoris*

Sanity is a cozy lie.　　　　　　　　　　—Susan Sontag

SARCASM

Sarcasm I now see to be, in general, the language of the devil.
—Thomas Carlyle, *Sartor Resartus*, ii, 4

SATISFACTION

He is rich that is satisfied.　　　—Thomas Fuller, M. D., *Gnomologia*

He is well paid, that is well satisfied.
—William Shakespeare, *The Merchant of Venice*, Act IV, Sc. i

SCARCITY

We never know the worth of water till the well is dry.
—Thomas Fuller, M. D., *Gnomolologia*, 5451

SCHOLARSHIP

The office of the scholar is to cheer, to raise, and to guide men by
showing them facts amidst appearances.
—Ralph Waldo Emerson, *Nature Addresses*, "The American Scholar"

Don't appear so scholarly, pray. Humanize your talk, and speak to be
understood. Do you think a Greek name gives more weight to your
reasons?　　　　—Molière, *The Critique of the School for Wives*

A scholar knows no boredom.　　　—Jean Paul Richter, *Hesparus*

Scholars are wont to sell their birthright for a mess of learning.
—Henry David Thoreau,
A Week on the Concord and Merrimack Rivers, "Sunday"

SCIENCE

The theist is persuaded that while nothing that contradicts science is
likely to be true, still nothing that stops with science can be the
whole truth.   —Gordon W. Allport, *The Individual and His Religion*

Handy guide to modern science: If it's green or it wriggles, it's biology. If it stinks, it's chemistry. If it doesn't work, it's physics.
                                                                —Anonymous

The scientist explains everything except himself.   —Anonymous

Give me a firm spot on which to stand, and I will move the earth.
                            —Archimedes, on the principle of the lever,
                                    in Pappus of Alexandria, *Collectio*

We all know we fall. Newton's discovery was that the moon falls,
too—and by the same rule that we do.
—Isaac Asimov, *Isaac Asimov's Book of Science and Nature Quotations*,
                    compiled by Isaac Asimov and Jason A. Shulman

From Euclid to Newton there were straight lines. The modern age
analyzes the wavers.   —Saul Bellow, *Seize the Day*

The true worth of an experimenter consists in his pursuing not only
what he seeks in his experiment, but also what he did not seek.
                                                    —Claude Bernard

. . . Newtonian and Galilean physics . . . supplied the model of society
as an artificial construction, made up of individual atoms of
humanity. But it had left unanswered the basic question: the
nature of the fundamental building block—man.
—J. Bronowski and Bruce Mazlish, *The Western Intellectual Tradition*

. . . the physical sciences have found that their fundamental entities
and axioms are a great deal less obvious than was hoped.
—J. Bronowski and Bruce Mazlish, *The Western Intellectual Tradition*

We are a scientific civilization. That means a civilization in which
knowledge and its integrity are crucial. Science is only a Latin word
for knowledge . . . Knowledge is our destiny.
                    —J. Bronowski, in Carl Sagan, *The Dragons of Eden*

To pursue science is not to disparage the things of the spirit. In fact,
to pursue science rightly is to furnish a framework on which the
spirit may rise. —Vannevar Bush, speech at Massachusetts Institute
                                        of Technology, 5 Oct 1953

If science tends to thicken the crust of ice on which, as it were, we are skating, it is all right. It if tries to find, or professes to have found, the solid ground at the bottom of the water, it is all wrong.
—Samuel Butler (1835-1902)

There is something in man which your science cannot satisfy.
—Thomas Carlyle

Science is wonderfully equipped to answer the question "How?" but it gets terribly confused when you ask the question "Why?"
—Erwin Chargraff, Professor of Biological Chemistry, Columbia University, Columbia Forum, summer, 1969

As soon as questions of will or decision arise, human science is at a loss.
—Noam Chomsky

Science bestowed immense new powers on man, and at the same time, created conditions which were largely beyond his comprehension.
—Winston Churchill

. . . the scientific trilogy: observation, hypothesis, experiment.
—Morag Coate

Science really creates wealth and opportunity which did not exist before. Whereas the old order was based on competition, the new order of science makes possible, for the first time, a cooperative creative effort in which every one is the gainer and no one the loser . . .
—Karl Taylor Compton, speech, "The Social Implication of Scientific Discovery," 1938

The stumbling way in which even the ablest of the scientists in every generation have had to fight through thickets of erroneous observations, misleading generalizations, inadequate formulation, and unconscious prejudice is rarely appreciated by those who obtain their scientific knowledge from textbooks. —James Bryant Conant

Good science is almost always so very simple. *After* it has been done by someone else, of course.
—L. L. Larison Cudmore, *The Center of Life*

In science the credit goes to the man who convinces the world, not to the man to whom the idea first occurred.
—Francis Darwin, Galton Lecture to Eugenics Society, 1914

Not only will atomic power be released, but someday we will harness
the rise and fall of the tides and imprison the rays of the sun.
—Thomas A. Edison, newspaper interview, 23 Aug 1921

There will one day spring from the brain of science a machine or
force so fearful in its potentialities, so absolutely terrifying that
even man, the fighter, who will dare torture and death in order to
inflict torture and death, will be appalled, and so abandon war forever. What man's mind can create, man's character can control.
—Thomas A. Edison

As to science, we may well define it for our purpose as "methodical
thinking directed toward finding regulative connections between
our sensual experiences."   —Albert Einstein, *Ideas and Opinions*

Every serious scientific worker is painfully conscious of this involun-
tary relegation to an ever-narrowing sphere of knowledge, which
threatens to deprive the investigator of his broad horizon and
degrades him to the level of a mechanic.
—Albert Einstein, *Ideas and Opinions*

Concern for man himself and his fate must always form the chief
interest of all technical endeavors, concern for the great unsolved
problems of the organization of labor and the distribution of
goods—in order that the creations of our mind shall be a blessing
and not a curse to mankind. Never forget this in the midst of your
diagrams and equations.   —Albert Einstein

Science can only ascertain what is, but not what should be, and outside of its domain value judgments of all kinds remain necessary.
—Albert Einstein, *Out of My Later Years*

Science is an attempt to make the chaotic diversity of our sense-expe-
rience correspond to a logically uniform system of thought.
—Albert Einstein, *Out of My Later Years*

The grand aim of all science is to cover the greatest number of empirical facts by logical deduction from the smallest number of
hypotheses.   —Albert Einstein

The scientist finds his reward in what Henri Poincaré calls the joy of
comprehension, and not in the possibilities of application to
which any discovery may lead.
—Albert Einstein, from the "Epilogue" to Planck,
Where is Science Going? (1932)

We scientists, whose tragic destination has been to help in making
the methods of annihilation more gruesome and more effective,
must consider it our solemn and transcendent duty to do all in our
power in preventing these weapons from being used for the brutal
purpose for which they were invented.
—Albert Einstein, *Ideas and Opinions*

Modern man worships at the temple of science, but science tells him
only what is possible, not what is right.   —Milton S. Eisenhower

Science does not know its debt to imagination.
—Ralph Waldo Emerson

There is not a piece of science, but its flank may be turned tomorrow.
—Ralph Waldo Emerson

Religion needs science, to protect it from religion's greatest danger,
superstition.   —Edgar J. Goodspeed, *Four Pillars of Democracy*

Science is the knowledge of consequences and the dependence of one
fact on another.   —Thomas Hobbes, *Leviathan*

Science books are letters from God, telling how He runs His universe.
—Toyohiko Kagawa

There is nothing in science which teaches the origin of anything at
all.   —Lord Kelvin

I am sorry to say that there is too much point to the wisecrack that
life is extinct on other planets because their scientists were more
advanced than ours.   —John F. Kennedy

The means by which we live have outdistanced the ends for which we
live. Our scientific power has outrun our spiritual power. We have
guided missiles and misguided men.
—Martin Luther King, Jr., *Strength to Love*

Though many have tried, no one has ever yet explained away the
decisive fact that science, which can do so much, cannot decide
what it ought to do.   —Joseph Wood Krutch

Science is the systematic classification of experience.
—George Henry Lewes

We especially need imagination in science. It is not all mathematics, nor all logic, but it is somewhat beauty and poetry.
—Maria Mitchell, in Phebe Mitchell Kendall, editor, *Maria Mitchell, Life, Letters, and Journals* (1896)

Science tends to develop natural virtues which are basically Christian—humility, patience, perseverance, honesty and integrity.
—Joseph F. Mulligan

To every action there is always opposed an equal action.
—Isaac Newton, *Principia Mathematica*, third law of motion

. . . the human heart has a hidden want which science cannot supply.
—Sir William Osler

In the field of observation, chance favors only the prepared minds.
—Louis Pasteur

What is needed in the present plight of mankind is not more science but a change of heart that shall move mankind to devote to constructive and peaceful purposes . . .
—Ralph Barton Perry, *The Humanity of Man*

A new scientific truth does not triumph by convincing its opponents and making them see the light, but rather because its opponents eventually die, and a new generation grows up that is familiar with it.
—Max Planck, *Scientific Autobiography*

Science is built of facts the way a house is built of bricks; but an accumulation of facts is nor more science than a pile of bricks is a house.
—Henry Poincaré, *La Science et l'hypothèse*

The simplest schoolboy is now familiar with truths for which Archimedes would have given his life.
—Ernest Renan, *Souvenirs d'enfance et de jeunesse*

All science is either physics or stamp collecting. —Lord E. Rutherford

Science is the key which unlocks the storehouses of nature.
—Viscount Herbert Louis Samuel

How could science be an enemy of religion when God commanded man to be a scientist the day He told him to rule the earth and subject it?
—Bishop Fulton J. Sheen, *The Life of All Living*

The modern man, finding that Humanism and Sex both fail to satisfy, seeks his happiness in Science . . . But Science fails too, for it is something more than a knowledge of matter the soul craves.
—Bishop Fulton J. Sheen, *The Eternal Galilean*

If God exists He must be manifest somehow in matter, and His ways are what science is discovering.
—Edmund W. Sinnott, *The Biology of the Spirit*

. . . scientists have made no clear effort to become an important, independently active force of mankind. Whole congresses at a time, they back away from the suffering of others; it is more comfortable to stay within the bounds of science.
—Alexander Solzhenitsyn, *Nobel Lecture*

Nature is neutral. Man has wrested from nature the power to make the world a desert or to make the deserts bloom. There is no evil in atoms; only in men's souls.
—Adlai Stevenson, speech, Hartford, Connecticut, 18 Sep 1952

It is rather pedantic to say that science never explains anything, but it is true to say that its explanations are never in terms of purpose.
—Arthur Thompson, *Science and Religion*

Our western science is a child of moral virtues; and it must now become the father of further moral virtues if its extraordinary material triumphs in our time are not to bring human history to an abrupt, unpleasant and discreditable end.   —Arnold J. Toynbee

We have not the reverent feeling for the rainbow that the savage has, because we know how it is made. We have lost as much as we gained by prying into that matter.   —Mark Twain

True science teaches, above all, to doubt and to be ignorant.
—Miguel de Unamuno, *The Tragic Sense of Life*

"Science" means simply the aggregate of all the recipes that are always successful. All the rest is literature.   —Paul Valéry, *Moralitiés*

I find it as difficult to understand a scientist who does not acknowledge the presence of a superior rationality behind the existence of the universe as it is to comprehend a theologian who would deny the advances of science. And there is certainly no scientific reason why God cannot retain the same position in our modern world that he held before we began probing his creation with telescope and cyclotron.   —Wernher von Braun

A physicist is an atom's way of knowing about atoms. —George Wald

An ounce of application is worth a ton of abstraction.
—Booker T. Washington

SCRATCHING

I have a simple philosophy. Fill what's empty, empty what's full, and scratch where it itches.
—Alice Roosevelt Longworth, in Peter Passell and Leonard Ross, *The Best*

Scratching is one of nature's sweetest gratifications, and nearest at hand.   —Michel de Montaigne

'Neath tile or thatch / That man is rich / Who has a scratch / For every itch.   —Ogden Nash, *Many Long Years Ago*, "Taboo to Boot"

One bliss for which / There is no match / Is when you itch / To up and scratch.   —Ogden Nash, *Many Long Years Ago*, "Taboo to Boot"

SCRIPTURES

Scriptures, n. The sacred books of our holy religion, as distinguished from the false and profane writings on which other faiths are based.   —Ambrose Bierce

SCULPTURE

It is well with me only when I have a chisel in my hand.
—Michelangelo

SEASONS

In the midst of winter, I finally learned that there was in me an invincible summer.   —Albert Camus, *Summer*, "Return to Tipasa"

If Winter comes, can Spring be far behind?
—Percy Shelley, "Ode to the West Wind"

SECRETS

A secret is something I tell to only one person at a time.   —Anonymous

A talebearer revealeth secrets: but he that is of a faithful spirit concealeth the matter.   —*The Bible* (KJV): Proverbs 11:13

For there is nothing covered, that shall not be revealed; neither hid, that shall not be known. Therefore, whatsoever ye have spoken in darkness shall be heard in the light; and that which ye have spoken in the ear in closets shall be proclaimed upon the housetops.
—*The Bible* (KJV): Luke 12:2–3

Three may keep a secret if two of them are dead.
—Benjamin Franklin, *Poor Richard's Almanack*, 1735

Another person's secret is like another person's money, you are not so careful with it as you are of your own.   —Edgar Watson Howe

Nothing weighs more than a secret.
—Jean de La Fontaine, *Les Femmes et le Secret*

How can we expect another to guard our secret if we have not been able to guard it ourselves?
—François de La Rochefoucauld, *Maximes*

Which of us is other than a secret to all but God!
—George Macdonald, *The Flight of the Shadow*, Ch. 1

The truth of a man is first and foremost what he hides.
—André Malraux

Nothing is so burdensome as a secret.   —Proverb (French)

A secret is seldom safe in more than one breast.   —Jonathan Swift

Shy and unready men are great betrayers of secrets, for there are few wants more urgent for the moment than the want of something to say.   —Sir Henry Taylor, *The Statesman*

It's no damn fun to keep the truth from people.
—Sloan Wilson, *The Man in the Gray Flannel Suit*

SECURITY

Who is to guard the guards themselves?   —Juvenal, *Satires*, VI

There is no security on this earth. There is only opportunity.
—Gen. Douglas MacArthur

True security lies not in the things one has, but in the things one can do without.   —Og Mandino

SEED

The cosmic secrecy of seed.
—Anonymous, phrase from the movie *Cross Creek*

I throw fresh seeds out. Who knows what survives?
—Charles Baudelaire, "The Ruined Garden"

Anything that you have is seed that God has given you.
—Dan Davis, sermon, Hope Chapel, Austin, Texas, 6 Oct 1991

The seed dies into a new life, and so does man.   —George Macdonald

SEEKING

Seek that which may be found.   —Anonymous

. . . seek, and ye shall find . . .   —*The Bible* (KJV): Matthew 7:7

A man is not old as long as he is seeking something.   —Jean Rostand

Look, and you will find it—what is unsought will go undetected.
—Sophocles

SELF

Forgetfulness of self is remembrance of God.   —Bayazid Al-Bistami

The disease we all have and that we have to fight against all our lives
is . . . the disease of self . . .
—Sherwood Anderson, in Howard Mumford Jones,
editor, *Letters of Sherwood Anderson*

Each bird loves to hear himself sing.   —Anonymous

Every ass loves to hear himself bray.   —Anonymous

Nobody calls himself rogue.   —Anonymous

Self is the greatest burden I have to carry.   —Anonymous

What lies behind us or before us are tiny matters compared with what
lies in us.   —Anonymous

What you are is God's gift to you. What you become is your gift to
God.   —Anonymous

Great pressure is brought to bear to make us undervalue ourselves.
On the other hand, civilization teaches that each of us is an inestimable prize. There are, then, these two preparations: one for life
and the other for death. Therefore we value and are ashamed to
value ourselves.   —Saul Bellow, *Dangling Man*

The heavy weight of selfhood.   —Saul Bellow, *Humboldt's Gift*

You have, like the external world, your own phenomena inside.
                    —Saul Bellow, *Humboldt's Gift*

Deliver me, O Lord, from that evil, myself.   —Brooks

Lord deliver me from myself.   —Sir Thomas Browne, *Religio Medici*

We carry within us the wonders we seek without us.
                    —Sir Thomas Browne, *Religio Medici*

When the fight begins within himself, / A man's worth something.
                    —Robert Browning, *Bishop Blougram's Apology*

Over the times thou hast no power . . . Solely over one man thou
hast quite absolute power. Him redeem and make honest.
                    —Thomas Carlyle

Love not what you are, but what you may become.
                    —Miguel de Cervantes

One may understand the cosmos, but never the ego; the self is more
distant than any star.   —G. K. Chesterton, *Orthodoxy*

We are all serving a life-sentence in the dungeon of self.
                    —Cyril Connolly, *The Unquiet Grave*

To be nobody but yourself—in a world which is doing its best, night
and day, to make you everybody else—means to fight the hardest
battle which any human being can fight, and never stop fighting.
                    —e. e. cummings

The ultimate mystery is one's own self.   —Sammy Davis, Jr.

I'd like to lose interest in myself . . .   —Don DeLillo, *White Noise*

Be thine own palace, or the world's thy jail.   —John Donne

We are apt to believe what the world believes about us. —George Eliot

What lies behind us and what lies before us are small compared to
what lies within us.
—Ralph Waldo Emerson, *Essays*, *First Series*, "Intellect"

Do we know what we look like? Not really. —Walker Evans

Men are not against you; they are merely for themselves.
—Gene Fowler, *Skyline*

Self-love is in fact religious awe in the presence of the mystery of life
represented in oneself. —John Gardner, *The Resurrection*

When we come to the end of ourselves, we come to the beginning of
God. —Billy Graham, *Till Armageddon*

The longest journey
Is the journey inwards. —Dag Hammarskjöld, *Markings*

What other dungeon is so dark as one's own heart! What jailer so
inexorable as one's self!
—Nathaniel Hawthorne, *The House of the Seven Gables*

There is nothing noble about being superior to some other man. The
true nobility is in being superior to your previous self.
—Hindu saying

It is thus with most of us; we are what other people say we are. We
know ourselves chiefly by hearsay. —Eric Hoffer

What you do when you don't have to, determines what you will be
when you can no longer help it. —Rudyard Kipling

All of the significant battles are waged within the self.
—Sheldon Kopp

He who knows others is wise. He who knows himself is enlightened.
—Lao Tzu

Not in the clamor of the crowded street, / Not in the shouts and plau-
dits of the throng, / But in ourselves, are triumph and defeat.
—Henry Wadsworth Longfellow, "The Poets"

I am bigger than anything that can happen to me.
—Charles F. Lummis

The world is as good as you are. You've got to learn to like yourself
first. I'm a little screwed up, but I'm beautiful. —Steve McQueen

Look within. Within is the fountain of good, and it will ever bubble
up, if thou wilt ever dig. —Marcus Aurelius Antoninus

I think Dostoevsky was right, that every human being must have a
point at which he stands against the culture, where he says, this is
me and the damned world can go to hell. —Rollo May

It was not really possible to understand oneself, let alone another
human being. —Arthur Miller, *Timebends*

I have never seen a greater monster or miracle in the world than
myself. —Michel de Montaigne

May God defend me from myself. —Michel de Montaigne, *Essays*

A man can stand a lot as long as he can stand himself. He can live
without hope, without friends, without books, even without
music, as long as he can listen to his own thoughts. —Axel Munthe

Every bird thinks its own nest beautiful. —Proverb (Italian)

What you think of yourself is much more important than what others think of you. —Proverb (Latin)

Change yourself, and your fortune will change too.
—Proverb (Portugeuse)

There is nothing else anything like so interesting to ourselves as ourselves. —James Harvey Robinson

Know thyself, for through thyself only thou canst know God.
—John Ruskin

Promote yourself but do not demote another. —Israel Salanter

I am my own heaven and hell! —Friedrich Schiller, *Die Rauber*

Put your ear down close to your soul and listen hard. —Anne Sexton

. . . which can say more / Than this rich praise, that you alone are you.
—William Shakespeare, Sonnet LXXXIV

Better keep yourself clean and bright: you are the window through
which you see the world. —George Bernard Shaw

Each of us makes his own weather, determines the color of the skies
in the emotional universe which he inhabits.
—Bishop Fulton J. Sheen

I am a frail vessel full of errors.
—Alexander Solzhenitsyn, *The First Circle*

We cease loving ourselves if no one loves us. —Madame de Staël

In every part and corner of our life, to lose oneself is to be gainer; for
to forget oneself is to be happy.
—Robert Louis Stevenson, "Old Mortality"

Always there remains portions of our heart into which no one is able
to enter, invite them as we may. —Mary Dixon Thayer

For a man needs only to be turned around once with his eyes shut in
this world to be lost . . . not 'til we are lost . . . do we begin to find
ourselves. —Henry David Thoreau, *Walden*

The labor of self-love is a heavy one indeed . . . As long as you set
yourself up as a little god to which you must be loyal, how can you
hope to find inward peace. —A. W. Tozer

Good breeding consists in concealing how much we think of ourselves and how little we think of the other person.
—Mark Twain, *Notebooks*

Self is the only prison that can ever bind the soul.
—Henry Van Dyke, *The Prisoner and the Angel*

I've got at least one tiny corner of the universe I can make just the
way I want it . . . —Kurt Vonnegut, Jr., *Welcome to the Monkey House*,
"The Kid Nobody Could Handle"

Trying to define yourself is like trying to bite your own teeth.
—Alan Watts

The final mystery is oneself. —Oscar Wilde

I can't do anything about the state of the world, but I can put my
own life in order. —Sloan Wilson, *The Man in the Gray Flannel Suit*

SELF-ASSERTION

You don't learn to hold your own in the world by standing on guard,
but by attacking, and getting well-hammered yourself.
—George Bernard Shaw, *Getting Married*

SELF-CENTEREDNESS

It was prettily devised of Aesop, "The fly sat upon the axletree of the
chariot-wheel and said, what a dust do I raise."
—Francis Bacon, *Essays*, "Of Vain-Glory"

He was like the cock who thought the sun had risen to hear him
crow. —George Eliot, *Adam Bede*, Ch. 33

The least pain in our little finger gives us more concern and uneasiness, than the destruction of millions of our fellow-beings.
—William Hazlitt, *Works*, Vol. X

Conceit is just as natural a thing to human minds as a center is to a
circle. —Oliver Wendell Holmes, Sr.

A man is in general better pleased when he has a good dinner upon
his table, than when his wife talks Greek.
—Samuel Johnson, *Johnsonian Miscellanies*,
Vol. II, edited by G. B. Hill

God sends no one away empty except those who are full of themselves. —Dwight L. Moody

Self-praise is no recommendation. —Proverb (17th century)

When a man is all wrapped up in himself he makes a pretty small
package. —John Ruskin

If it goes well with you, then all is well.
—Alexander Solzhenitsyn, *The Gulag Archipelago Three*

SELF-CONSCIOUSNESS

He that has a big nose thinks everyone speaks of it.
—Proverb (Scottish)

SELF-EXAMINATION

O wad some power the giftie gie us, / To see ourselves as others see us!
—Robert Burns, "To a Louse"

Nothing will make us so charitable and tender to the faults of others, as, by self-examination, thoroughly to know our own.
—François Fénelon

The examined life is no picnic. —Robert Fulghum,
All I Really Need to Know I Learned in Kindergarten

Learn what you are and be such. —Pindar, *Odes*

Know then thyself, presume not God to scan; / The proper study of mankind is man. —Alexander Pope, *An Essay on Man*

Go to your bosom; / Knock there, and ask your heart what it doth know . . . —William Shakespeare, *Measure for Measure*, Act II, Sc. ii

. . . we know what we are, but know not what we may be.
—William Shakespeare, *Hamlet*, Act IV, Sc. v

The unexamined life is not worth living. —Socrates, in Plato's *Apology*

You will never be an inwardly religious and devout man unless you pass over in silence the shortcomings of your fellow men, and diligently examine your own weaknesses. —Thomas à Kempis

SELF-IMPROVEMENT

Begin to be now what you will be hereafter. —Saint Jerome

The greatest responsibility entrusted to man is that of developing himself. —William Ross

Every man is capable of being something better than he is.
—Roy L. Smith

SELF-INDULGENCE

My most serious character flaw is that I don't deny myself much.
—Andrew A. Rooney, *Word for Word*

SELF-INTEREST

It is not from the benevolence of the butcher, the brewer, or the baker that we expect our dinner, but from their regard to their own interest. —Adam Smith, *The Wealth of Nations*

SELFISHNESS

Selfishness is that detestable vice which no one will forgive in others, and no one is without in himself. —Henry Ward Beecher

A man is called selfish, not for pursuing his own good, but for neglecting his neighbor's. —Richard Whately

SELF-MASTERY

Conquer yourself rather than the world. —René Descartes

He is great enough who is his own master. —Joseph Hall

The mastery of nature is vainly believed to be an adequate substitute for self-mastery. —Reinhold Niebuhr

Let him who would move the world, first move himself. —Socrates

Lord of himself, though not of lands, / And having nothing, yet hath all. —Sir Henry Wotton, "The Character of a Happy Life"

SELF-PRESERVATION

Any fish will fight. —Saul Bellow, *Mr. Sammler's Planet*, Ch. 2

To preserve his life, should a man pay everything that gives it color, scent and excitement? —Alexander Solzhenitsyn, *Cancer Ward*

SELF-SACRIFICE

Self-preservation is the first law of nature, but self-sacrifice is the highest rule of grace. —Anonymous

Greater love hath no man than this, that a man lay down his life for his friends. —*The Bible* (KJV): John 15:13

You must give some time to your fellow men. Even if it's a little thing, do something for others—something for which you get no pay but the privilege of doing it. —Albert Schweitzer

The SENSES

The ear tends to be lazy, craves the familiar and is shocked by the unexpected; the eye on the other hand, tends to be impatient, craves the novel and is bored by repetition.
—W. H. Auden, *The Dyer's Hand*

The eye likes novelty, but the ear craves familiarity.   —W. H. Auden

I shall hear in heaven.   —Ludwig van Beethoven, on his deafness

The sweetest sounds to mortals given / Are heard in Mother, Home,
    and Heaven.
                —William Goldsmith Brown, "Mother, Home, and Heaven"

Men are born with two eyes, but with one tongue, in order that they
    should see twice as much as they say.
                            —Charles Caleb Colton, *Lacon*

None so deaf as he that will not hear.
                    —Matthew Henry, *Commentaries*, "Psalm 58"

Men trust their ears less than their eyes.   —Herodotus, *Histories*

To the man whose senses are alive and alert there is not even the
    need to stir from one's threshold.   —Henry Miller

The eyes believe themselves; the ears believe other people.
                                —Proverb (German)

I'm quite deaf now; such a comfort.   —Evelyn Waugh

SERMONS

You preach a better sermon with your life than with your lips.
                                —Oliver Goldsmith

I'd rather see a sermon than hear one any day; / I'd rather one should
    walk with me than merely tell the way.   —Edgar A. Guest

Every time you walk a mile to church and carry a Bible with you, you
    preach a sermon a mile long.   —Dwight L. Moody

Few sinners are saved after the first twenty minutes of a sermon.
                                —Mark Twain

SERVANTS

. . . a true servant of God is someone who helps another succeed.
                        —Billy Graham, *Till Armageddon*

Servant of God, well done.   —John Milton, *Paradise Lost*

. . . servanthood is the very highest calling.
  —Pamela Rosewell, *The Five Silent Years of Corrie ten Boom*

The cook was a good cook, as cooks go; and as good cooks go, she
 went. —Saki, *Reginald*, "Reginald on Besetting Sins"

Every good servant does not all commands; / No bond but to do just
 ones. —William Shakespeare, *Cymbeline*, Act V, Sc. i

S E R V I C E

In Christian service the branches that bear the most fruit hang the
 lowest. —Anonymous

Service is the rent we pay for the space we occupy. —Anonymous

What is serving God? 'Tis doing good to man. —Anonymous

All service ranks the same with God— / With God, whose puppets,
 best and worst, / Are we: there is no last nor first.
  —Robert Browning, *Pippa Passes*, Epilogue

A man should be encouraged to do what the Maker of him has
 intended by the making of him, according as the gifts have been
 bestowed on him for that purpose. —Thomas Carlyle

We can't do everything for everyone everywhere, but we can do
 something for someone somewhere. —Richard L. Evans

The great fact is, that life is a service. The only question is, "Whom
 will we serve?" —Frederick William Faber

It is possible to be so active in the service of Christ as to forget to love
 him. —P. T. Forsyth

The most acceptable service of God is doing good to man.
  —Benjamin Franklin, *Autobiography*, Ch. 1

There is no better armor against the shafts of death than to be busied
 in God's service. —Thomas Fuller

The noblest service comes from nameless hands, / And the best servant does his work unseen.
  —Oliver Wendell Holmes, Sr., *The Poet at the Breakfast Table*

Have thy tools ready; God will find thee work. —Charles Kingsley

What is it to serve God and to do His will? Nothing else than to show mercy to our neighbor. For it is our own neighbor who needs our service; God in heaven needs it not. —Martin Luther

Help me to live for others / That I may live like Thee. —C. D. Meigs

They also serve who only stand and wait.
—John Milton, "On His Blindness"

God has created me to do him some definite service; he has committed some work to me which he has not committed to another. I have my mission—I never may know it in this life, but I shall be told it in the next. —John Henry Newman

They serve God well, who serve his creatures.
—Caroline Norton, *The Lady of La Garaye*

Do what you can, with what you have, where you are.
—Theodore Roosevelt

I don't know what your destiny will be, but one thing I do know: the only ones among you who will be really happy are those who have sought and found how to serve. —Albert Schweitzer

I can more easily see our Lord sweeping the streets of London, than issuing edicts from its cathedral. —Dick Sheppard

There are no little jobs in the Kingdom of God. —Lewis Timberlake

Joy can be real life only if people look upon their life as service, and have a definite object in life outside themselves and their personal happiness. —Leo Tolstoy

No one has learned the meaning of living until he has surrendered his ego to the service of his fellow man. —W. Beran Wolfe

Small service is true service while it lasts; / Of humblest friends, bright creature! scorn not one; / The daisy, by the shadow that it casts, / Protects the lingering dew-drop from the sun.
—William Wordsworth

S E X

Sex alleviates tension. Love causes it. —Woody Allen

Sex is the great amateur art. —David Cort

It doesn't matter what you do in the bedroom as long as you don't do it in the street and frighten the horses.
—Beatrice Stella Campbell, in Daphne Fielding,
Duchess of Jermyn Street, Ch. 2

. . . sex is one of the great wonders and glories of life.
—Morag Coate, *Beyond All Reason*

To remain virtuous, a man has only to combat his own desires; a woman must resist her own inclinations and the continual attack of man.
—De Latena

There is a tendency to think of sex as something degrading; it is not, it is magnificent, an enormous privilege, but because of that the rules are tremendously strict and severe.
—Francis Devas

The sexual embrace can only be compared with music and with prayer.
—Havelock Ellis, *Essays on Love and Virtue*, "On Life and Sex"

There may be some things better than sex, and some may be worse. But there is nothing exactly like it.
—W. C. Fields

The best kind of sex education is life in a loving family.
—Rosemary Haughton

Sex cannot be contained within a definition of physical pleasure, it cannot be understood as merely itself for it has stood for too long as a profound connection between human beings.
—Elizabeth Janeway, *Between Myth and Morning*

Nobody will ever win the battle of the sexes. There's too much fraternizing with the enemy.
—Henry Kissinger

Most mothers think that to keep young people away from love-making it is enough never to speak of it in their presence.
—Marie Madeleine de La Fayette, *The Princess of Clèves*, First Part

Whatever else can be said about sex, it cannot be called a dignified performance.
—Helen Lawrenson

One antidote for sexual truancy lies in simply teaching youth the wonder, the miracle, the reverence for the creation of life itself. Life is a divine creation. You don't take chances with creation.
—Levenson

How alike are the groans of love to those of the dying.
—Malcolm Lowry, *Under the Volcano*

Whoever named it necking was a poor judge of anatomy.
—Groucho Marx

The sexual impulse is God-given, and it must be God-guided.
—James Earl Massey

Neither sex, without some fertilization of the complementary characters of the other, is capable of the highest reaches of human
endeavor.
—H. L. Mencken, *In Defense of Women* , "The Feminine Mind"

Aren't women prudes if they don't and prostitutes if they do?
—Kate Millett, speech, Women's Writer's Conference,
Los Angeles, 22 Mar 1975

Contraceptives should be used on all conceivable occasions.
—Spike Milligan, *The Last Goon Show of All*

Whether a pretty woman grants or withholds her favors, she always
likes to be asked for them.   —Ovid, *Ars Amatoria*

Sexuality throws no light upon love, but only through love can we
learn to understand sexuality.   —Rosenstock-Huessy

Answering questions is a major part of sex education. Two rules cover
the ground. First, always give a truthful answer to a question; sec-
ondly, regard sex knowledge as exactly like any other knowledge.
—Bertrand Russell

The total amount of undesired sex endured by woman is probably
greater in marriage than in prostitution.
—Bertrand Russell, *Marriage and Morals*

As I grow older and older / And totter towards the tomb, / I find I care
less and less / Who goes to bed with whom.
—Dorothy Sayers, "That's Why I Never Read Modern Novels"

I told my girl friend that unless she expressed her feelings and told
me what she liked I wouldn't be able to please her, so she said, "Get
off me."   —Garry Shandling

The purpose of sexual intercourse is to get it over with as long as possible.   —Steven Max Singer

[He] told us about one of Plato's dialogues, in which an old man is asked how it felt not to be excited by sex anymore. The old man replies that it was like being allowed to dismount from a wild horse.　　　　　　　　　　　　—Kurt Vonnegut, Jr., *Deadeye Dick*

SHADOW

There is no sun without shadow, and it is essential to know the night.　　　　　　　　　　　　　　　　　　—Albert Camus

Thus shadow owes its birth to light.
　　　　　　　　—John Gay, "The Persian, Sun, and Cloud"

Even a single hair casts its shadow.　　　—Publilius Syrus, *Moral Sayings*

William SHAKESPEARE

Shakespeare was a dramatist of note; / He lived by writing things to quote.　　　　　　　　　　　　　　　　　　—H. C. Bunner

He was not of an age, but for all time!
　　　　—Ben Jonson, "To the Memory of William Shakespeare"

Now we sit through Shakespeare to recognize the quotations.
　　　　　　　　　　　　　　　　　　—Orson Welles

SHARING

Take that which God has given you and share it.　　—Stephen F. Olford

SHOES

I can tell where my own shoe pinches me.　　　—Miguel de Cervantes

High heels were invented by a woman who had been kissed on the forehead.　　　　　　　　　　　　　　—Christopher Morley

Don't throw away the old shoes till you've got new ones.
　　　　　　　　　　　　　　　　　　—Proverb (Dutch)

A handsome shoe often pinches the foot.　　　　—Proverb (French)

Doctor Luther's shoes don't fit every village priest.
　　　　　　　　　　　　　　　　　　—Proverb (German)

One shoe does not fit every foot.　　　　　　—Proverb (Italian)

The wearer knows best where the shoe hurts.   —Proverb (Portuguese)

SHOW BUSINESS

There's No Business Like Show Business
> —Irving Berlin, title of song from the
> musical comedy *Annie Get Your Gun*

Show business is like sex. When it's wonderful, it's wonderful. But
when it isn't very good, it's still all right.   —Max Wall

SIGNIFICANCE

Not even a sparrow falls to earth unheeded.   —Anonymous

The dream of man's heart . . . is that life may complete in significant
pattern.   —Saul Bellow, *Herzog*

There is nothing insignificant—nothing.   —Samuel Taylor Coleridge

Whatever you do will be insignificant, but it is very important that
you do it.   —Mahatma Gandhi

Consider, sir, how insignificant this will appear a twelve-month
hence. —Samuel Johnson, in James Boswell, *Life of Samuel Johnson*

Significance is sweet . . .   —Ivan Turgenev, *Fathers and Sons*

It's necessary to be slightly underemployed if you are to do something significant.   —James Watson

SILENCE

Silence is one of the hardest arguments to refute.   —Josh Billings

Speech is silver, silence is golden.   —Thomas Carlyle

. . . silence [can] be the most eloquent form of lying.
> —Pat Conroy, *The Prince of Tides*

Go placidly amid the noise and haste, and remember what peace
there may be in silence.   —Max Ehrman, "Desiderata"

The temple of our purest thoughts is silence.   —Sarah J. Hale

Well-timed silence is the purest speech.   —Alan Harris

Silence is one great art of conversation.   —William Hazlitt

Silence gives consent.   —Proverb (14th century)

Silence is also speech.   —Proverb (Yiddish)

A word is worth one coin; silence is worth two.   —*The Talmud*

Well timed silence hath more eloquence than speech.
—Martin Farquhar Tupper

SIMPLICITY

Simplicity is truth's most becoming garb.   —Anonymous

Unless a man is simple, he cannot recognize God, the Simple One.
—Bengali song

Less is more.   —Robert Browning, "Andrea del Sarto"

Everything should be as simple as possible, but no simpler.
—Albert Einstein

I believe that a simple and unassuming manner of life is best for
everyone, best for both the body and the mind.   —Albert Einstein

Joshua chose the simple life . . . because it gave him the freedom to
expand the breadth of his inner life.
—Joseph F. Girzone, *Joshua*, Ch. 13

The ability to simplify means to eliminate the unnecessary so that
the necessary may speak.   —Hans Hofmann

Simplicity of manner is the last attainment. Men are very long afraid
of being natural, from the dread of seeming ordinary.   —Jeffrey

Sometimes you have to gag on fancy before you can appreciate plain . . .
—Jan Karon, *At Home in Mitford*, Ch. 13

Realize thy Simple Self, Embrace thy Original Nature.
—Lao Tzu, *Tao Te Ching*, XIX

A simple life is its own reward.   —George Santayana

Live simply, that others might simply live.   —Elizabeth Seaton

Pray God, keep us simple.   —William Makepeace Thackeray

I love a life whose plot is simple.   —Henry David Thoreau,
          A Week on the Concord and Merrimack Rivers, "Sunday"

Our life is frittered away be detail . . . Simplify, simplify.
                    —Henry David Thoreau, *Walden*,
          "Where I Lived, and What I Lived For"

Simplicity is making the journey of this life with just baggage
     enough.   —Charles Dudley Warner

Seek simplicity; and distrust it.
          —Alfred North Whitehead, *The Concept of Nature*

Besides the noble art of getting things done, there is the noble art of
     leaving things undone. The wisdom of life consists in the elimina-
     tion of non-essentials.   —Lin Yutang

S I N

If you do not want the fruits of sin, stay out of sin's orchard.
                    —Anonymous

. . . for there is no man which sinneth not . . .
          —*The Bible* (KJV): 2 Chronicles 6:36

. . . He that is without sin among you, let him first cast a stone at her.
          —*The Bible* (KJV): John 8:7

Keep yourself from opportunity and God will keep you from sins.
                    —Jacob Cats

No one has leave to sin.   —Cicero

He said he was against it.   —Calvin Coolidge, when asked what
                    a clergyman said who preached on sin

O sin, what hast thou done to this fair earth!   —Dana

The knowledge of sin is the beginning of salvation.   —Epicurus

A man who has broken with his past feels a different man. He will not
     feel it a shame to confess his past wrongs, for the simple reason
     that these wrongs do not touch him at all.   —Mahatma Gandhi

Man must choose either of the two courses, the upward or the downward; but as he has the brute in him, he will more easily choose the downward course than the upward, especially when the downward course is presented to him in a beautiful garb. Man easily capitulates when sin is presented in the garb of virtue.
—Mahatma Gandhi

Sin is whatever obscures the soul.
—André Gide, *La Symphonie pastorale*

Suppose someone should offer me a plateful of crumbs after I had eaten a T-bone steak. I would say, "No, thank you. I am already satisfied." Christian, that is the secret—you can be so filled with the things of Christ, so enamored with the things of God that you do not have time for the sinful pleasures of the world. —Billy Graham

The Bible does not teach that sin is completely eradicated from the Christian in this life, but it does teach that sin shall no longer reign over you.   —Billy Graham, *World Aflame*

The Bible teaches that all sin begins with sinful thinking.
—Billy Graham

The only thing He forgets is our sins. —Billy Graham, *Till Armageddon*

It is right to hate sin, but not to hate the sinner.
—Giovanni Guareschi, *The Little World of Don Camillo*

Sin has many tools, but a lie is the handle which fits them all.
—Oliver Wendell Holmes, Sr., *The Autocrat of the Breakfast Table*

Men are punished by their sins, not for them.
—Elbert Hubbard, *The Philistine*, Vol. xi

Sin has always been an ugly word, but it has been made so in a new sense over the last half-century. It has been made not ugly but passé. People are no longer sinful, they are only immature or underprivileged or frightened or, more particularly, sick.
—Phyllis McGinley

Original sin is that thing about man which makes him capable of conceiving of his own perfection and incapable of achieving it.
—Reinhold Niebuhr

Love the offender, yet detest the offense.   —Alexander Pope

Adam ate the apple, and our teeth still ache.   —Proverb (Hungarian)

I hate the sin, but I love the sinner.
>—Thomas Buchanan Read, "What a Word May Do"

There is a way from every point in a circle to the center; from the far-thest error there is a way back to God Himself.   —Rückert

Some psychological and sociological conditioning occurs in every man's life and this affects the decisions he makes. But we must resist the modern concept that all sin can be explained merely on the basis of conditioning.   —Francis A. Schaeffer

Sin is a state of mind, not an outward act.   —Sewell

I am a man / More sinn'd against than sinning.
>—William Shakespeare, *King Lear*, Act III, Sc. ii

To create the world cost God nothing; to save it from sin cost His Life Blood.   —Bishop Fulton J. Sheen

It was the sinner that Christ came to help.
>—Charles M. Sheldon, *In His Steps*

. . . every little boy thinks he invented sin.
>—John Steinbeck, *East of Eden*

SINCERITY

However much we may distrust men's sincerity, we always believe they speak to us more sincerely than to others.
>—François de La Rochefoucauld

SINGING

A bird does not sing because it has an answer. It sings because it has a song.   —Anglund

He who sings drives away sorrow.   —Anonymous

Never take from any man his song.   —Anonymous

Those who wish to sing will always find a song.   —Anonymous

O sing unto the Lord a new song: sing unto the Lord, all the earth.
>—*The Bible* (KJV): Psalms 96:1

Oh, give us the man who sings at his work.   —Thomas Carlyle

Families without songs are unhappy families.   —Pat Conroy

A song will outlive all sermons in the memory.   —Henry Giles

Regard your voice as capital in the bank . . . Sing on your interest and
   your voice will last.   —Lauritz Melchior

Let every bird sing its own song.   —Proverb (Danish)

Our sincerest laughter / With some pain is fraught; / Our sweetest
   songs are those that tell of saddest thought.
                              —Percy Shelley, "To a Skylark"

Birds sing on a bare bough; / O, believer, canst not thou?
                           —Charles H. Spurgeon, "Salt-Cellars"

SKEPTICISM

Skepticism is slow suicide.   —Ralph Waldo Emerson

I am too much of a skeptic to deny the possibility of anything.
   —Thomas Henry Huxley, letter to Herbert Spencer, 22 Mar 1886

Skepticism and faith are no less necessary. Skepticism, riddling the
   faith of yesterday, prepared the way for the faith of tomorrow.
                              —Romain Rolland

SLANDER

A slander is like a hornet; if you cannot kill it dead at first blow, better
   not strike at it.   —Josh Billings

When you are stung by slanderous tongues, comfort yourself with
   this thought: it is not the worst fruits that are gnawed by wasps.
                              —G. A. Bürger

A generous confession disarms slander.
                  —Thomas Fuller, M. D., *Gnomologia*, No. 126

SLAVERY

The chains of a slave are broken the moment he considers himself a
   free man.   —Mahatma Gandhi

Death is a slave's freedom.
> —Nikki Giovanni, at the funeral of Martin Luther King, Jr., 1968

"A house divided against itself cannot stand." I believe this government cannot endure permanently half-slave and half-free.
> —Abraham Lincoln, speech, Springfield, 1858

If slavery is not wrong, nothing is wrong.
> —Abraham Lincoln, letter to A. G. Hodges, 4 Apr 1864

Whenever I hear anyone arguing for slavery, I feel a strong impulse to see it tried on him personally.
> —Abraham Lincoln, speech, 17 Mar 1865

Where slavery is, there liberty cannot be; and where liberty is, there slavery cannot be.
> —Abraham Lincoln

Men! whose boast it is that ye / Come of fathers brave and free, / If there breathe on earth a slave, / Are ye truly free and brave?
> —James Russell Lowell, "Stanzas on Freedom"

Am I not a man and brother?
> —Josiah Wedgwood, inscription on the seal
> of the Anti-Slavery Society of London, circa 1770

S L E E P

Heaven trims our lamps while we sleep.
> —Bronson Alcott, *Table Talk*, "Sleep"

The fate of the worm refutes the pretended ethical teaching of the proverb, which assumes to illustrate the advantage of early rising and does so by showing how dangerous it is.
> —Thomas Bailey Aldrich, *Ponkapog Papers*,
> "Asides: Writers and Talkers"

Sleep is the poor man's treasure.
> —Anonymous

Care-charming Sleep, thou easer of all woes, Brother of Death.
> —Francis Beaumont and John Fletcher, *Valentinian*

Sleeping is very underrated.
> —Suzy Becker, *All I Need to Know I Learned From My Cat*

Yet a little sleep, a little slumber, a little folding of the hands to sleep.
> —*The Bible* (KJV): Proverbs 6:10

The sleep of a laboring man is sweet . . .
—*The Bible* (KJV): Ecclesiastes 5:12

It is nought good a sleeping hound to wake.
—Geoffrey Chaucer, *Troilus and Criseyde*

Oh, Sleep! it is a gentle thing, / Beloved from pole to pole.
—Samuel Taylor Coleridge, *The Rime of the Ancient Mariner*

A sleeping child gives me the impression of a traveler in a very far country.
—Ralph Waldo Emerson

There will be sleeping enough in the grave.
—Benjamin Franklin, *Poor Richard's Almanack*, 1758

Whenever life gets to be too much for me, I have a hard time keeping my eyes open. Sleeping is cheaper and safer than drinking. It keeps you from saying or doing things you'll regret later, and though you may have nightmares, you won't wake up with a hangover. I recommend it wholeheartedly.
—Elizabeth Forsythe Hailey, *Joanna's Husband and David's Wife*

To carry care to bed is to sleep with a pack on your back.
—Thomas Chandler Haliburton

That we are not much sicker and much madder than we are is due exclusively to that most blessed and blessing of natural graces, sleep.
—Aldous Huxley, *Theme and Variations*

Something attempted, something done, / Has earned a night's repose.
—Henry Wadsworth Longfellow, "The Village Blacksmith"

Sleep . . . peace of the soul, who puttest care to flight.
—Ovid

Thank God for sleep! And when you cannot sleep, still thank Him that you live to lie awake.
—John Oxenham

Let sleeping dogs lie.
—Proverb (14th century)

The night rinses what the day hath soaped.
—Proverb (Swiss)

Put off thy cares with thy clothes; so shall thy rest strengthen thy labor, and so thy labor sweeten thy rest.
—Francis Quarles

Sleep is to a man what winding up is to a clock.

—Arthur Schopenhauer

. . . he that sleeps feels not the toothache.
—William Shakespeare, *Cymbeline*, Act V, Sc. iv

O sleep, O gentle sleep! Nature's soft nurse . . .
—William Shakespeare, *King Henry IV, Part II*, Act III, Sc. i

. . . Sleep that knits up the ravell'd sleave of care, / The death of each day's life, sore labor's bath, / Balm of hurt minds, great nature's second course, / Chief nourisher in life's feast.
—William Shakespeare, *Macbeth*, Act II, Sc. ii

To sleep: perchance to dream.
—William Shakespeare, *Hamlet*, Act III, Sc. i

That sweet sleep which medicines all pain.
—Percy Shelley, *Julian and Maddalo*, line 498

Maybe it's because I sleep slow.   —Jack Teagarden, jazz trombonist, when asked why he liked to sleep long periods

I've always thought sleep was a wonderful invention. Not that being awake isn't nice too, of course. But when I get up in the morning, I think, boy, only fourteen more hours and I can be back to sleep again . . . And I never dream, because it distracts my mind from pure sleeping . . .   —Anne Tyler, *If Morning Ever Comes*

Providence has given us hope and sleep as a compensation for the many cares of life.   —Voltaire

Is sleep a mating with oneself?
—Freiherr von Friedrich Leopold von Hardenberg

SLIGHTS

If slighted, slight the slight, and love the slighter.   —Anonymous

SMELLS

The woman one loves always smells good.   —Rémy de Gourmont

. . . the blisses of scented proximity.   —Peter de Vries, *Forever Panting*

SMILES

All people smile in the same language.   —Anonymous

A smile is a light in the window indicating that the heart is home.
                                                          —Anonymous

A smile is God's cosmetic.   —Anonymous

Learn to greet your friends with a smile; they carry too many frowns
     in their own hearts to be bothered with yours.   —Mary Ayer

Sometimes your joy is the source of your smile, but sometimes your
     smile can be the source of your joy.   —Thich Nhat Hanh

Smiles are the language of love.
               —Julius Charles Hare and Augustus William Hare

They gave each other a smile with a future in it.   —Ring Lardner

A warm smile is the universal language of kindness.
                                            —William Arthur Ward

SOARING

One can never consent to creep when one feels an impulse to soar.
                                                    —Helen Keller

SOCIETY

On the attraction between man and woman society is based . . .
                                                         —Bartol

In human society the warmth is mainly at the bottom.
                                            —Noel Jack Counihan

Is it not a terrible thing to be forced by society to do things which all
     of us as individuals regard as abominable crimes?
                              —Albert Einstein, *Ideas and Opinions*

I claim that human mind or human society is not divided into water-
     tight compartments called social, political and religious. All act
     and react upon one another.   —Mahatma Gandhi

I must try to live in society and yet remain untouched by its pitfalls.
                                            —Mahatma Gandhi

What can you say about a society that says that God is dead and Elvis is alive?
—Irv Kupcinet

SOLDIERS

Here rests in honored glory an American soldier known but to God.
—Anonymous, inscription on Tomb of the Unknown Soldier, Arlington National Cemetery

And the soldiers likewise demanded of him [John the Baptist], saying, And what shall we do? And he said unto them, Do violence to no man, neither accuse any falsely; and be content with your wages.
—*The Bible* (KJV): Luke 3:14

Soldiers generally win battles; generals generally get credit for them.
—Napoleon Bonaparte, to Gaspard Gourgaud at St. Helena

Soldiers in peace are like chimneys in summer.
—Lord Burleigh

Never in the field of human conflict was so much owed by so many to so few.
—Winston Churchill, speech, House of Commons, 20 Aug 1940, on the role of the Royal Air Force in the Battle of Britain

Let the soldier yield to the civilian.
—Cicero, *Orationes Philippicae*

There are no atheists in the foxholes.
—William T. Cummings, *Sermons on Bataan*, Mar 1942

Eh-oh, my little brother, / They rigged you up in state, / In khaki coat and gun to tote, / But you never could learn to hate.
—Martin Feinstein, "In Memoriam"

Old soldiers never die, / They just fade away.
—J. Foley, "Old Soldiers Never Die" (1920 song), perhaps a folk song from the First World War, popularized by Gen. Douglas MacArthur in a speech to U. S. Congress, 19 Apr 1951

For it's Tommy this, an' Tommy that, an' "Chuck him out, the brute!" / But it's "Savior of 'is country" when the guns begin to shoot.
—Rudyard Kipling, *Barrack-Room Ballads*, "Tommy"

How Ya Gonna Keep 'Em Down on the Farm (After they've seen Paree)
—Sam M. Lewis and Joe Young, title and refrain of 1919 song with music by Walter Donaldson

An old warrior is never in haste to strike the blow. —Pietro Metastasio

Our God and soldiers we alike adore / Ev'n at the brink of danger; not before: / After deliverance, both alike requited, / Our God's forgotten, and our soldiers slighted.   —Francis Quarles, *Emblems*

There are soldiers of the ploughshare as well as soldiers of the sword.
                    —John Ruskin

Who will remember, passing through this Gate / The unheroic Dead who fed the guns? / Who shall absolve the foulness of their fate— / Those doomed, conscripted unvictorious ones?
                    —Siegfried Sassoon, *The Heart's Journey*,
                    "On Passing the New Menin Gate"

We [soldiers] are like cloaks,—one thinks of us only when it rains.
                    —Maurice Saxe

Soldier, rest! thy warfare o'er, / Sleep the sleep that knows not breaking; / Dream of battled fields no more, / Days of danger, nights of waking.   —Sir Walter Scott, "The Lady of the Lake"

If one is a professional soldier, it is part of one's job to die sooner or later.   —Alexander Solzhenitsyn, *August 1914*

Theirs is not to reason why, / Theirs is but to do and die.
          —Alfred, Lord Tennyson, "The Charge of the Light Brigade"

It is not a fair deal to take a man from a farm or a factory, clap a tin hat on his head, and then shoot him if his nerve fails.
          —Ernest Thurtle, speech, House of Commons, in support of a
                    bill to abolish the death penalty for desertion

The existence of the soldier, next to capital punishment, is the most grievous vestige of barbarism which survives among men.
          —Alfred de Vigny, *Servitude et grandeur militaires*

If there were no warriors, there would be no wars.   —Robert Watkins

SOLITUDE

Conversation enriches the understanding, but solitude is the school of genius.   —Anonymous

He never is alone that is accompanied with noble thoughts.
          —Francis Beaumont and John Fletcher, *Love's Cure*

A man alone is either a saint or a devil.   —Robert Burton

If from society we learn to live, / 'Tis solitude should teach us how to
   die; / It hath no flatterers.   —Lord Byron, *Childe Harold's Pilgrimage*

Amid all your duties, keep some hours to yourself.   —Margaret Fuller

Jesus but people got weird when they lived alone.
                                   —Judith Guest, *Second Heaven*

In solitude all great thoughts are born.   —Moses Harvey

By all means use sometimes to be alone. Salute thyself; see what thy
   soul doth wear.   —George Herbert

I have a house where I go / When there's too many people, / I have a
   house where I go / Where no one can be; / I have a house where I
   go, / Where nobody says anything—so / There is no one but me.
              —A. A. Milne, *Now We Are Six*, "Solitude"

The great virtue of being alone is that your mind can go its own way.
              —Andrew A. Rooney, *Word for Word*,
              "Being With People, Being Without"

Fond as we are of our loved ones, there comes at times during their
   absence an unexplained peace.   —Anne Shaw

I never found the companion that was so companionable as solitude.
                          —Henry David Thoreau

Alexander SOLZHENITSYN

Tell me what you think of Ivan Denisovich and I'll tell you who you
   are.
     —*Novy Mir*, about the novel *One Day in the Life of Ivan Denisovich*,
                          by Alexander Solzhenitsyn

Precisely in that refusal to go beyond the daily mundane facts is the
   novel's [*One Day in the Life of Ivan Denisovich*] great power; by carefully sticking to those facts, by his macabre humor, by his irony
   and understated sense of horror, Solzhenitsyn gives an even greater
   reality to the cruelty of the camps, to the systematic criminality of
   the Soviet system, than a shriller voice would . . .
     —Abraham Rothberg, *Aleksandr Solzhenitsyn, The Major Novels*

Ultimately . . . Solzhenitsyn is a moral writer, not a political one.
> —Abraham Rothberg, *Aleksandr Solzhenitsyn, The Major Novels*

I am neither a political scientist nor a politician. I am simply an artist who is distressed by the painfully clear events and crises of today.
> —Alexander Solzhenitsyn, *The Mortal Danger*

My work! Year after year you'll mature with me, / Year in, year out, you'll tramp dusty convict roads. / The day will break when you'll warm more blood than only mine, / When not only I will be seized by your shivers.
> —Alexander Solzhenitsyn, in David Burg and
> George Feifer, *Solzhenitsyn, A Biography*

SORROW

Two in distress make sorrow less. — Anonymous

There is something pleasurable in calm remembrance of a past sorrow. — Cicero, *Ad Familiares*

The path of sorrow, and that path alone, / Leads to the land where sorrow is unknown. — William Cowper

Be careful before leaving someone in a sorrowing situation. Say a word of prayer with them and share even a brief word of encouragement from the Scriptures. — Billy Graham, *Till Armageddon*

Sorrows when shared are less burdensome, though joys divided are increased. — Josiah Gilbert Holland

But a heart which trusts in God's goodness is armed against sorrow.
> —Hrosvitha of Gandersheim, *Gallicanus*, Part I

Sorrow is a fruit; God does not allow it to grow on a branch that is too weak to bear it. — Victor Hugo

She had the feeling that somehow, in the very far-off places, perhaps even in far-off ages, there would be a meaning found to all sorrow and an answer too fair and wonderful to be as yet understood.
> —Hannah Hurnard, *Hinds' Feet on High Places*

We could never learn to be brave and patient, if there were only joy in the world. — Helen Keller

Believe me, every man has his secret sorrows which the world knows not; and oftentimes we call a man cold when he is only sad.
—Henry Wadsworth Longfellow

Joy takes far away from us thoughts of our action; sorrow it is that awakens the soul.   —Marguerite of Valois, *Memoirs*

Great sorrow makes sacred the sufferer.   —Owen Meredith

Earth hath no sorrow that Heaven cannot heal.
—Thomas Moore, "Come, Ye Disconsolate"

But sorrow is better than fear. For fear impoverishes always, while sorrow may enrich.   —Alan Paton, *Cry, the Beloved Country*

Sorrow seems sent for our instruction, as we darken the cages of birds when we teach them to sing.   —Jean Paul

Sorrows remembered sweeten present joy.
—Robert Pollok, *The Course of Time*

We cannot prevent the birds of sorrow from flying over our heads, but we can refuse to let them build their nests in our hair.
—Proverb (Chinese)

Great sorrows are dumb.   —Proverb (Italian)

I shall drink with joy the cup of sorrow because my Beloved is the cup-bearer.   —Saadi

Sorrow and joy have the same Lord.
—Charles Reign Scoville, "Christ is King"

Light griefs do speak, while sorrow's tongue is bound.   —Seneca

There is a sweet joy that comes to us through sorrow.
—Charles H. Spurgeon

O Sorrow, wilt thou live with me / No casual mistress, but a wife?
—Alfred, Lord Tennyson, *In Memoriam A. H. H.*

'Tis held that sorrow makes us wise.
—Alfred, Lord Tennyson, *In Memoriam A. H. H.*

There is a joy in sorrow which none but a mourner can know.
—Martin Farquhar Tupper

That each sorrow has its purpose, / By the sorrowing oft unguessed, / But as sure as the sun brings morning, / Whatever is—is best.
— Ella Wheeler Wilcox

Where there is sorrow, there is holy ground.   —Oscar Wilde

S O U L

What church could compete with the fireworks of the pure soul?
—Ray Bradbury, *The Illustrated Man*, "The Fire Balloons"

Earth changes, but thy soul and God stand sure.
—Robert Browning, *Dramatis Personae*, "Rabbi ben Ezra," Stanza 27

For the sword outwears its sheath, / And the soul wears out the breast.   —Lord Byron, "So We'll Go No More a-Roving"

The body,—that is dust; the soul,—it is a bud of eternity.
—Nathanael Culverwel

'Tis not the fairest form that holds / The mildest, purest soul within; 'Tis not the richest plant that holds / The sweetest fragrance in. —Dawes

It is one soul which animates all men.   —Ralph Waldo Emerson

The one thing in the world, of value, is the active soul.
—Ralph Waldo Emerson

Whether or not the philosophers care to admit that we have a soul, it seems obvious that we are equipped with something or other which generates dreams and ideals, and which sets up values.
—John Erskine

The principal thing in this world is to keep one's soul aloft.
—Gustave Flaubert

Out of the night that covers me, / Black as the pit from pole to pole, / I thank whatever gods may be, / For my unconquerable soul.
—William Ernest Henley, "Invictus"

The human soul develops up to the time of death.   —Hippocrates

It was in the recognition that there is in each man a final essence, that is to say an immortal soul which only God can judge, that a limit was set upon the dominion of men over men.
—Walter Lippmann

The wealth of the soul is the only true wealth.   —Lucian, *Dialogues*

Nowhere can man find a quieter or more untroubled retreat than in
    his own soul.   —Marcus Aurelius Antoninus, *Meditations*

And every man decideth / The way his soul shall go.—John Oxenham

God trusts every one with the care of his own soul.
                                    —Proverb (Scottish)

. . . the human soul, beaten down, overwhelmed, faced by complete
    failure and ruin, can still rise up against unbearable odds and tri-
    umph.   —Harold Russell

The soul, too has her virginity and must bleed a little before bearing
    fruit.   —George Santayana

Every subject's duty is the king's; but every subject's soul is his own.
          —William Shakespeare, *King Henry V*, Act IV, Sc. i

It is well, it is well with my soul.
          —Horatio G. Spafford, "It is Well With My Soul" (hymn)

Each elect soul . . . possesses God directly and finds in that unique
    possession the fulfillment of his own individuality.
          —Pierre Teilhard de Chardin, *Christianity and Evolution*,
              "Note on the Physical Union Between the Humanity of
    Christ and the Faithful in the Course of Their Sanctification"

. . . a man has to think of his soul before everything else.
                          —Leo Tolstoy, *Anna Karenina*

Soul of my soul! Life that dwells within me! Many-named mystery
    that I name my ego, my self, my being!
                          —Albert Verwey, *Cor Cordium*

Re-examine all you have been told. Dismiss what insults your Soul.
                          —Walt Whitman

S P A C E

One small step for [a] man, one giant leap for mankind.
          —Neil Armstrong, as he stepped on the moon's surface

I just don't think the moon is going to be an adequate substitute for
    the fact that we haven't addressed ourselves to clearing up the
    slums.   —Kenneth B. Clark

There is hopeful symbolism in the fact that flags do not wave in a
    vacuum.   —Arthur C. Clarke

In curved Einsteinian space we are at all times, technically, looking at
    the back of our own head.   —Guy Davenport

The world would be a safer place, / If someone had a plan, / Before
    exploring outer space, / To find the inner man.
                        —E. Y. Harburg, *Rhymes for the Irreverent*

Space is the stature of God.   —Joseph Joubert

Space, like Switzerland, should be neutral.
    —Andrew A. Rooney, *Word for Word*, "Annexing the Moon"

The scientific theory I like best is that the rings of Saturn are com-
    posed entirely of lost airline luggage.   —Mike Russell

We can lick gravity, but sometimes the paperwork is overwhelming.
                            —Wernher von Braun

SPECIALIZATION

Learn to limit yourself, to content yourself with some definite thing,
    and some definite work; dare to be what you are, and learn to
    resign with a good grace all that you are not, and to believe in your
    own individuality.   —Henri Frédéric Amiel

The shoemaker makes a good shoe because he makes nothing else.
                        —Ralph Waldo Emerson

The same man cannot well be skilled / In everything; each has his
    special excellence.   —Euripides, "Rhesus"

Do that for which nature has suited you . . .
    —Cassandra Fedele, letter to Alessandra Scala

Specialization is for insects!   —Robert Heinlein, *Time Enough for Love*,
                "Notes from the Diary of Lazarus Long"

A man may have intelligence enough to excel in a particular thing
    and lecture on it, and yet not have sense enough to know he ought
    to be silent on some other subject of which he has but a slight
    knowledge; if such an illustrious man ventures beyond the bounds
    of his capacity, he loses his way and talks like a fool.
                        —Jean de La Bruyère

You specialize in something until one day it is specializing in you.
—Arthur Miller

The trouble with specialists is that they tend to think in grooves.
—Elaine Morgan, *The Descent of Woman*, Ch. 1

If you want to succeed, limit yourself.
—Charles Augustin Sainte-Beuve

SPEECH

He is a good orator who convinces himself. —Anonymous

No speech can be entirely bad if it is short. —Anonymous

Do not speak harshly to anyone; for those who are spoken to will
answer you in the same way. —Buddhist saying

An after-dinner speech should be like a lady's dress—long enough to
cover the subject and short enough to be interesting.
—R. A. Butler, speech, Anglo-Jewish Association dinner,
Dorchester Hotel, 1 Jun 1957

I have never been hurt by anything I didn't say. —Calvin Coolidge

One of the lessons of history is that nothing is often a good thing to
do and always a clever thing to say. —Will Durant

An orator or author is never successful till he has learned to make his
words smaller than his ideas. —Ralph Waldo Emerson

The music that can deepest reach, / And cure all ill, is cordial speech.
—Ralph Waldo Emerson

We should ask ourselves three questions before we speak: Is it true? Is
it kind? Does it glorify Christ? —Billy Graham

Speak clearly, if you speak at all; / Carve every word before you let it
fall. —Oliver Wendell Holmes, Sr., "A Rhymed Lesson"

The flowering moments of the mind / Drop half their petals in our
speech. —Oliver Wendell Holmes, Sr.

When you have well thought out your subject, words will come spontaneously. —Horace, *De Arte Poetica*

The human brain starts working at the moment you are born and
    never stops until you stand up to speak in public.   —George Jessel

It is better to debate a question without settling it, than to settle it
    without debate.   —Joseph Joubert

My heavens! I've been talking prose for the last forty years without
    knowing it.   —Molière, *Le Bourgeois Gentilhomme*

Only begin, and you will become eloquent of yourself.
                           —Ovid, *Ars Amatoria*

Speeches cannot be made long enough for the speakers, nor short
    enough for the hearers.   —James Perry

Much of delivery is the natural and unconscious bodily expression of
    the emotions.   —Philodemus

Speech is a mirror of the soul: as a man speaks, so he is.
             —Publilius Syrus, *Moral Sayings*

My basic rule is to speak slowly and simply so that my audience has
    an opportunity to follow and think about what I am saying.
                    —Margaret Chase Smith

No phrase can convey the idea of surprise so vividly as opening the
    eyes and raising the eyebrows. A shrug of the shoulders would lose
    much by translation into words.   —Herbert Spencer

In oratory, the greatest art is to conceal art.   —Jonathan Swift

Speech is the golden harvest that followeth the flowering of thought.
                 —Martin Farquhar Tupper

It usually takes more than three weeks to prepare a good impromptu
    speech.   —Mark Twain

The right word may be effective, but no word was ever as effective as
    a rightly timed pause.   —Mark Twain

We cannot always oblige, but we can always speak obligingly.
                             —Voltaire

Surely whoever speaks to me in the right voice, him or her shall I fol-
    low.   —Walt Whitman

What can be said at all can be said clearly . . .
> —Ludwig Wittgenstein, *Tractatus Logico-philosophicus*, Preface

SPEED

There is more to life than increasing its speed.   —Mahatma Gandhi

We must check our speed. We bring up our children too fast, we work too fast, we dissipate too fast, we eat too fast, live too fast, and consequently, always ahead of time, we die too fast.
> —"How to Keep Well," *Harper's Monthly*, Dec 1856

Speed provides the one genuinely modern pleasure.
> —Aldous Huxley, *Music at Night*, "Wanted, a New Pleasure"

SPIRIT

Everyone has, inside himself . . . what shall I call it? A piece of good news! Everyone is . . . a very great, very important character.
> —Ugo Betti, *The Burnt Flower-bed*, II

The life is more than meat, and the body is more than raiment.
> —*The Bible* (KJV): Luke 12:23

If matter mute and inanimate, though changed by the forces of Nature into a multitude of forms, can never die, will the spirit of man suffer annihilation when it has paid a brief visit, like a royal guest, to this tenement of clay?
> —William Jennings Bryan, *The Prince of Peace*

Man's unhappiness, as I construe, comes of his greatness; it is because there is an Infinite in him, which with all his cunning he cannot quite bury under the Finite.   —Thomas Carlyle, *Sartor Resartus*

Unrest of spirit is a mark of life.
> —Karl Menninger, *This Week*, 16 Oct 1958

The spirit needs several sorts of food of which knowledge is only one.
> —John Ruskin, *Stones of Venice*

. . . some kind of clean, pure feeling does live within us, existing apart from all our convictions.
> —Alexander Solzhenitsyn, *The Gulag Archipelago*

I don't care what they say with their mouths—everybody knows that
   something is eternal. And it ain't houses and it ain't names, and it
   ain't earth, and it ain't even the stars—everybody knows in their
   bones that something is eternal, and that something has to do
   with human beings . . . There's something way down deep that's
   eternal about every human being.   —Thornton Wilder

Man never made any material as resilient as the human spirit.
                                                    —Bern Williams

S P I R I T U A L I T Y

Spirituality leaps where science cannot yet follow, because science
   must always test and measure, and much of reality and human
   experience is immeasurable.   —Starhawk, *The Spiral Dance*

S P O R T S

Sport develops not character, but characters.
               —Anonymous, in James A. Michener, *Sports in America*

In America it is sport that is the opiate of the masses.
                          —Russell Baker, *New York Times*, 3 Oct 1967

Nobody roots for Goliath.   —Wilt Chamberlain

Interest and proficiency in almost any one activity—swimming, boat-
   ing, fishing, skiing, skating—breed interest in many more. Once
   someone discovers the delight of mastering one skill, however
   slightly, he is likely to try out not just one more, but a whole
   ensemble.   —Margaret Mead, *A Way of Seeing*

S P O R T S M A N S H I P

For when the One Great Scorer comes / To write against your name,
   / He marks—not that you won or lost— / But how you played the
   Game.   —Grantland Rice, *Only the Brave*, "Alumnus Football"

S P R I N G

One swallow does not make a spring.
                             —Aristotle, *Nichomachean Ethics*, I

In the spring a young man's fancy lightly turns to thoughts of love.
                          —Alfred, Lord Tennyson, "Locksley Hall"

S T A R S

A mountain shames a molehill until they are both humbled by the stars.   —Anonymous

Astronomy is to look in the sky and see the stars. Astrology is to look up and see lions and crabs and other spooky creatures.
                                    —Anonymous, a child's definition

Over rough paths to the stars.   —Anonymous

To the stars through difficulties. —Anonymous, state motto of Kansas

Overhead without any fuss the stars were going out.
                                            —Arthur C. Clarke

If the stars should appear one night in a thousand years, how would men believe and adore.   —Ralph Waldo Emerson

We are all in the gutter, but some of us are looking at the stars.
                    —Oscar Wilde, *Lady Windermere's Fan*, Act III

I have loved the stars too fondly to be fearful of the night.
                                            —Sarah Williams

S T A T E

The state is made for man, not man for the state.
                            —Albert Einstein, *The World As I See It*,
                            "The Disarmament Conference of 1932"

S T E W A R D S H I P

Stewardship is what a man does after he says, "I believe."
                                            —W. H. Greever

S T R A N G E N E S S

All the world is queer save thee and me, and even thou art a little queer. —Robert Owen, to his business partner, William Allen, 1828

S T R A N G E R S

Everyone's quick to blame the alien.
                            —Aeschylus, *The Suppliant Maidens*

A stranger is a friend I haven't met yet.   —Anonymous

The heart of a stranger beats the same as a friend.   —Anonymous

How can we be strangers if we both believe in God?
    —Bernard Malamud, *Rembrandt's Hat*, "The Silver Crown"

STRENGTH

Be sure that God
    Ne'er dooms to waste the strength he deigns impart.
                    —Robert Browning, *Paracelsus*, Part 1

Strength does not come from physical capacity. It comes from an
    indomitable will.   —Mahatma Gandhi

The problem of life is not to make life easier, but to make men
    stronger.   —David Starr Jordan

Strong people make as many mistakes as weak people. The difference
    is that strong people admit them, laugh at them, learn from them.
    That is how they became strong.   —Richard J. Needham

That which does not kill me makes me stronger.
        —Friedrich Nietzsche, *Twilight of the Idols* (1888),
                    "Maxims and Missiles"

Dwell not upon thy weariness, thy strength shall be according to the
    measure of thy desire.   —Proverb (Arab)

Some people think it's holding on that makes one strong. Sometimes
    it's letting go.   —Sylvia Robinson

A strong man never loses his head in defeat or despondency.
        —Alexander Solzhenitsyn, *Lenin in Zurich*

STRESS

Only when we have enough mental stress to force us to see our own
    bankruptcy of power, do we trust in God, and only when we trust
    in God can we make a contribution which will not collapse.
                    —Kenneth L. Pike

STRIVING

The upright, honest-hearted man / Who strives to do the best he can,
    / Need never fear the church's ban / Or hell's damnation.
                    —Robert Burns

Who strives always to the utmost, him can we save.
—Johann Wolfgang von Goethe, *Faust*

You are not responsible for being down, but you are responsible for getting up.
—Rev. Jesse Jackson

. . . Striving to better, oft we mar what's well.
—William Shakespeare, *King Lear*, Act I, Sc. iv

Who does the best his circumstance allows, / Does well, acts nobly; angels could no more.   —Edward Young, *Night Thoughts*, "Night 2"

STUDIES

To study the abnormal is the best way of understanding the normal.
—William James

I will study and get ready, and perhaps my chance will come.
—Abraham Lincoln

As turning the logs will make a dull fire burn, so changes of studies a dull brain.
—Henry Wadsworth Longfellow

You have to study a great deal to know a little.
—Montesquieu, *Pensées et fragments inedits*

STYLE

Style is the dress of thoughts.
—Earl of Chesterfield

Fashions fade, style is eternal.
—Yves Saint Laurent

SUBORDINATES

Mistrust a subordinate who never finds fault with his superior.
—Churton Collins

SUBURBIA

. . . the whole sprawling paraphernalia of suburban childhood.
—Sylvia Plath, *The Bell Jar*

Suburbia is where the developer bulldozes out the trees, then names the streets after them.
—Bill Vaughn

SUCCESS

Eighty percent of success is showing up.
—Woody Allen, in Thomas J. Peters and
Robert H. Waterman, *In Search of Excellence*

. . . success is failure turned inside out.
—Anonymous, from a poem entitled "Don't Quit"

The toughest thing about success is that you've got to keep on being
a success. —Irving Berlin

It takes twenty years to make an overnight success. —Eddie Cantor

Success is having to worry about every damn thing in the world,
except money. —Johnny Cash

Success is going from failure to failure without loss of enthusiasm.
—Winston Churchill

Success is counted sweetest / By those who ne'er succeed.
—Emily Dickinson, *Poems*, "Success is counted sweetest"

The secret of success is constancy of purpose. —Benjamin Disraeli

Nothing succeeds like success. —Alexandre Dumas, *Ange Pitou*

Try not to become a man of success but rather try to become a man of
value. —Albert Einstein

Success has ruined many a man.
—Benjamin Franklin, *Poor Richard's Almanack*, 1752

Most successes are built on failures. —Charles Gow

[Success is] to retire at the end of the day with the satisfaction of
knowing that today, you did good work, bettered someone's life,
and look forward to arising in the morning to do it again, and
again, and again. —Chip Greenstein

To go about your work with pleasure, to greet others with a word of
encouragement, to be happy in the present and confident in the
future; this is to have achieved some measure of success in living.
—Edwin Osgood Grover

Young man, the secret of my success is that at an early age I discovered I was not God. —Oliver Wendell Holmes, Jr., reply to a reporter's question on his ninetieth birthday

'Tis man's to fight, but Heaven's to give success. —Homer, *Iliad*

A successful man cannot realize how hard an unsuccessful man finds life. —Edgar Watson Howe

Every successful man I have heard of has done the best he could with conditions as he found them, and not waited until next year for better. —Edgar Watson Howe

The moral flabbiness born of the exclusive worship of the bitch-goddess SUCCESS. That—with the squalid cash interpretation put on the word success—is our national disease.
—William James, letter to H. G. Wells, 11 Sep 1906

People rarely succeed at anything unless they have fun doing it.
—François de La Rochefoucauld

Nothing succeeds like the appearance of success. —Christopher Lasch

Success is not the result of spontaneous combustion. You must set yourself on fire. —Reggie Leach

To succeed in the world, we must be foolish in appearance, but really wise. —Montesquieu

Success is how high you bounce after you hit bottom.
—Gen. George S. Patton

If you visualize a failure, you tend to create the conditions that produce failure. Visualize—believe—and thank God in advance.
—Norman Vincent Peale

He who undertakes too much seldom succeeds. —Proverb (Dutch)

"It has always seemed strange to me," said Doc. "The things we admire in men, kindness and generosity, openness, honesty, understanding and feeling are the concomitants of failure in our system. And those traits we detest, sharpness, greed, acquisitiveness, meanness, egotism and self-interest are the traits of success. And while men admire the quality of the first they love the produce of the second." —John Steinbeck, *Cannery Row*

The man is a success who has lived well, laughed often and loved
much . . . who leaves the world better than he found it, whether by
an improved poppy, a perfect poem, or a rescued soul . . . who
looked for the best in others and gave the best he had.
—Robert Louis Stevenson

Nothing succeeds so well as success. —Talleyrand

There's no deodorant like success. —Elizabeth Taylor

Not to the swift, the race: / Not to the strong, the fight: / Not to the
righteous, perfect grace: / Not to the wise, the light. / But often fal-
tering feet / Come surest to the goal; / And they who walk in darkness meet / The sunrise of the soul. —Henry Van Dyke, "Reliance"

I have learned that success is to be measured not so much by the position that one has reached in life as by the obstacles which he has
overcome while trying to succeed. —Booker T. Washington

An honest try is better than success. —Brian Alexander Watkins (age 9)

Success often costs more than it is worth. —E. Wigglesworth

High station in life is earned by the gallantry with which appalling
experiences are survived with grace. —Tennessee Williams, *Memoirs*

SUFFERING

There is not in earth a spectacle more worthy than a great man superior to his sufferings. —Joseph Addison

By suffering comes wisdom. —Aeschylus

We learn from the things we suffer. —Aesop

Do not despise your situation; in it you must act, suffer, and conquer.
From every point on earth we are equally near to heaven and to the
infinite. —Henri Frédéric Amiel

Do you know what makes man the most suffering of all creatures? It
is that he has one foot in the finite and the other in the infinite,
and that he is torn between the two worlds. —Anonymous

Out of suffering come the strongest souls. God's wounded often make
his best soldiers. —Anonymous

Blessed art Thou, Lord, who giveth suffering / As a divine remedy for our impurities. —Charles Baudelaire, "Les Fleurs du mal"

Suffering is the main condition of the artistic experience.
—Samuel Beckett

Suffering is part of the divine idea. —Henry Ward Beecher

For I reckon that the sufferings of this present time are not worthy to be compared with the glory which shall be revealed in us.
—*The Bible* (KJV): Romans 8:18

It is better to suffer once than to be in perpetual apprehension.
—Julius Caesar

Suffering gives us no special rights. —Albert Camus, *Carnets*

Pain is inevitable. Suffering is optional.
—M. Kathleen Casey, in Karen Casey and
Martha Vanceburg, *The Promise of a New Day*

He who suffers, remembers. —Cicero

The only cure for suffering is to face it head on, grasp it round the neck, and use it. —Mary Craig

There is nothing special about your suffering.
—Dan Davis, sermon, Hope Chapel, Austin, Texas, 15 Sep 1991

He deposes Doom / Who hath suffered him.
—Emily Dickinson, poem, 1862

Pain and suffering are always inevitable for a large intelligence and a deep heart. —Fyodor Dostoyevsky, *Crime and Punishment*

We enjoy suffering, at least in small doses . . . It makes us feel alert, wide awake. And of course it gives happiness definition.
—John Gardner, *October Light*, Ch. 4

Pain and suffering are the dark strands through the tapestry of your life, providing the shadows that give depth and dimension to the masterpiece God is fashioning within you.
—Joseph F. Girzone, *Joshua in the Holy Land*, Ch. 17

In a very real sense, the suffering of this world was created by man himself. —Billy Graham, *Till Armageddon*

It takes suffering to widen the soul.   —Billy Graham, *Till Armageddon*

Sometimes the greatest sermon is silence! A suffering person does not
need a lecture—he needs a listener.
—Billy Graham, *Till Armageddon*

The word of God teaches that Christians suffer in order that they
might glorify God in their lives.   —Billy Graham

Those who have suffered make the best comforters.
—Billy Graham, *Till Armageddon*

We must never minimize the suffering of another. Scripture's mandate to us is, "weep with them that weep." (Romans 12:15, KJV)
—Billy Graham, *Till Armageddon*

. . . you have no corner on suffering.
—Hannah Green, *I Never Promised You a Rose Garden*

It is the crushed grape that gives out the blood-red wine: it is the suffering soul that breathes the sweetest melodies.   —Gail Hamilton

If suffering is accepted and lived through, not fought and refused,
then it is completed and becomes transmuted. It is absorbed, and
having accomplished its work, it ceases to exist as suffering, and
becomes part of our growing self.
—E. Graham Howe and L. Le Mesurier

If you suffer, thank God!—it is a sure sign that you are alive.
—Elbert Hubbard, *A Thousand and One Epigrams*

Although the world is full of suffering, it is full also of the overcoming of it.   —Helen Keller, *Optimism*

I know that God is not going to willfully hurt us. Why there is suffering is the business of the Lord, but He never seems to give us more
than we can bear.   —Martin Luther King, Sr.

The way of surviving is to find meaning in suffering.
—Laurel Lee, *Signs of Spring*

The great thing with unhappy times is to take them bit by bit, hour
by hour, like an illness. It is seldom the present, the exact present,
that is unbearable.   —C. S. Lewis

Know how sublime a thing it is
    To suffer and be strong.   —Henry Wadsworth Longfellow,
          in *Knickerbocker* (magazine), Jan 1839, "The Light of Stars"

We have two lives, . . ., the life we learn with and the life we live after
    that. Suffering is what brings us toward happiness.
            —Bernard Malamud, *The Natural*

Suffering is nature's way of indicating a mistaken attitude or way of
    behavior, and to the nonegocentric person every moment of suffer-
    ing is the opportunity for growth. People should rejoice in suffer-
    ing, strange as it sounds, for this is a sign of the availability of
    energy to transform their characters.   —Rollo May

There is nothing the body suffers that the soul may not profit by.
        —George Meredith, *Diana of the Crossways*

In extreme youth, in our most humiliating sorrow, we think we are
    alone. When we are older we find that others have suffered too.
            —Suzanne Moarny

We must learn to suffer what we cannot evade.
            —Michel de Montaigne

Only suffering draws / The inner heart of song, and can elicit / The
    perfumes of the soul.   —Lewis Morris

Never to have suffered would have been never to have been blessed.
            —Edgar Allan Poe

We are healed of a suffering only by experiencing it to the full.
        —Marcel Proust, *Remembrance of Things Past*

We must learn from life how to suffer it.   —Proverb (French)

Sufferings are lessons.   —Proverb (Greek)

There are only two remedies for the suffering of the soul: hope and
    patience.   —Proverb (Greek)

The burden of suffering seems a tombstone hung about our necks,
    while in reality it is only the weight which is necessary to keep
    down the diver while he is hunting for pearls.   —Jean Paul Richter

For there are . . . sufferings which have no tongues.   —Percy Shelley

. . . the inexorable lesson of centuries: suffering must be borne; there is no way out. —Alexander Solzhenitsyn, *August 1914*

To have suffered . . . sets a keen edge on what remains of the agreeable. This is a great truth and has to be learned in the fire.
—Robert Louis Stevenson

You're down now . . . it doesn't matter. What does matter is to taste your own ashes. —John Updike, *Couples*

Being myself no stranger to suffering, I have learned to relieve the suffering of others. —Virgil

Clergymen and people who use phrases without wisdom sometimes talk of suffering as a mystery. It is really a revelation.
—Oscar Wilde, *De Profundis*

To become the spectator of one's own life is to escape the suffering of life. —Oscar Wilde

SUFFICIENCY

Let him who has enough ask for nothing more. —Horace

SUICIDE

We must not pluck death from the Maker's hand.
—Philip James Bailey

. . . many a suicide might be averted if the person contemplating it could find the proper assistance when such a crisis impends.
—Clifford Beers, *A Mind That Found Itself*

The children were the only brake that stopped me from killing myself. —Barbara Field Benziger, *The Prison of My Mind*

Our time is fixed, and all our days are number'd; / How long, how short, we know not:—this we know, / Duty requires we calmly wait the summons, / Nor dare to stir till Heaven shall give permission.
—Robert Blair, *The Grave*

It is a brave act of valor to condemn death; but where life is more terrible than death, it is then the truest valor to dare to live.
—Sir Thomas Browne

'Tis more brave / To live, than to die. —Edward Bulwer-Lytton

The strangest whim has seized me . . . After all I think I will not hang
myself today. —G. K. Chesterton, *A Ballade of Suicide*

The divinity who rules within us, forbids us to leave this world without his command. —Cicero, *Tusculanarum Disputationum*

Eventually I reached a pitch where I might even have been suicidal,
except that I feared death more than I feared myself.
—Morag Coate, *Beyond All Reason*

Suicide is the worst form of murder, because it leaves no opportunity
for repentance. —Churton Collins

Fool! I mean not that poor-souled piece of heroism, self-slaughter.
Oh, no; the miserablest day we live there's many a better thing to
do than die. —George Daley

Suicide is not a remedy. —James A. Garfield

I take it that no man is educated who has never dallied with the
thought of suicide. —William James

It was easy enough to kill yourself in a fit of despair. It was easy
enough to play the martyr. It was harder to do nothing. To endure
your life. To wait. —Erica Jong, *Fear of Flying*, Ch. 17

Keep it a question. It's not really an answer.
—Peter McWilliams, "The Question of Suicide"

Many suicidal people speak in coded messages. —Marv Miller

Never challenge a suicidal person. —Marv Miller

Suicide is a drastic form of communication. —Marv Miller

Nor love thy life, nor hate; but what thou liv'st / Live well; how long
or short permit to Heaven. —John Milton, *Paradise Lost*

Suicide is never God's will.
—Frank B. Minirth and Paul D. Meier, *Happiness is a Choice*

The thought of suicide is a great consolation: by means of it one gets
successfully through many a bad night.
—Friedrich Nietzsche, *Beyond Good and Evil*

Razors pain you; / Rivers are damp; / Acids stain you; / And drugs
    cause cramp. / Guns aren't lawful; / Nooses give; / Gas smells
    awful; / You might as well live.
                —Dorothy Parker, *Not So Deep as a Well*, "Résumé"

But when it came right down to it, the skin of my wrist looked so
    white and defenseless that I couldn't do it.
                —Sylvia Plath, *The Bell Jar*

The trouble with jumping was that if you didn't pick the right num-
    ber of stories, you might still be alive when you hit bottom.
                —Sylvia Plath, *The Bell Jar*

Man is a prisoner who has no right to open the door of his prison and
    run away . . . A man should wait, and not take his own life until
    God summons him.   —Plato, *Dialogues*

A man should live if only to satisfy his curiosity.   —Proverb (Yiddish)

We ought not to quit our post without the permission of Him who
    commands; the post of man is life.   —Pythagoras

I did not, however, commit suicide, because I wished to know more
    about mathematics.
        —Bertrand Russell, *The Autobiography of Bertrand Russell*

Sometimes even to live is an act of courage.
                —Seneca, *Letters to Lucilius*

To be or not to be, that is the question . . .
                —William Shakespeare, *Hamlet*, Act III, Sc. i

It was deeply a part of Lee's kindness and understanding that man's
    right to kill himself is inviolable, but sometimes a friend can make
    it unnecessary.   —John Steinbeck, *Cannery Row*

[Suicide] takes some doing, with maybe pain and maybe hell.
                —John Steinbeck, *East of Eden*

SUMMER

Do what we can, summer will have its flies.
        —Ralph Waldo Emerson, *Essays, First Series*, "Prudence"

The SUN

Speak not against the sun.

—Anonymous

There is always sunshine, only we must do our part: we must move
into it.

—Clara Louise Burnham

The sun, with all those planets revolving around it and dependent
upon it, can still ripen a bunch of grapes as if it had nothing else in
the universe to do.

—Galileo Galilei

The sun is new each day.

—Heraclitus

Keep your face to the sunshine and you cannot see the shadow.

—Helen Keller

The sun shines upon all alike.

—Proverb (English)

SUNDAY

Sunday clears away the rust of the whole week.

—Joseph Addison, *The Spectator*, No. 112, 9 Jul 1711

SUPERSTITION

A superstition is a premature explanation that overstays its time.

—George Iles

Superstition is idolatry.

—Rabbi Daniel Jeremy Silver

SURRENDER

Surrender one hair, and you'll end up beardless.

—Alexander Solzhenitsyn, *The Oak and the Calf*

SURVIVAL

Survival is triumph enough.

—Harry Crews

But just get through this day. That's all you have to do.

—Alexander Dolgun, *Alexander Dolgun's Story*

I am ignorant and impotent and yet, somehow or other, here I am,
unhappy, no doubt, profoundly dissatisfied . . . In spite of everything I survive.

—Aldous Huxley

. . . a great devotee of the Gospel of Getting On.
—George Bernard Shaw, *Mrs. Warren's Profession*, Act IV

I survived. —Emmanuel Joseph Sieyes, asked what he had done during the French Revolution

How can they say my life isn't a success? Have I not for more than sixty years got enough to eat and escaped being eaten?
—Logan Pearsall Smith

A fish does not campaign against fisheries—it only tries to slip through the mesh.
—Alexander Solzhenitsyn, *The Gulag Archipelago Three*

We have ourselves to save. —Alexander Solzhenitsyn, *Prussian Nights*

To survive the day is triumph enough for the walking wounded among the great many of us. —Studs Terkel

I guess everybody who isn't dead yet is a survivor.
—Kurt Vonnegut, Jr., *Galapágos*

SUSPICION

Caesar's wife must be above suspicion.
—Julius Caesar, in Plutarch, *Life of Caesar*

SYMBOLS

Unable to grasp God's essence, we seek help in words, in names, in animal forms, in figures, . . ., in trees and flowers, summits and sources. —*Maxims of Tyre*

Symbols are the poetry of a people's soul. —Rabbi M. Robert Syme

SYMPATHY

Needs there groan a world in anguish just to teach us sympathy?
—Robert Browning

Three-fourths of the people you will meet tomorrow are hungering and thirsting for sympathy. Give it to them, and they will love you.
—Dale Carnegie

The less we parade our misfortunes, the more sympathy we command. —O. Dewey

Those who do not feel pain seldom think that it is felt.
—Samuel Johnson

To ease another's heartache is to forget one's own.—Abraham Lincoln

He jests at scars that never felt a wound.
—William Shakespeare, *Romeo and Juliet*, Act II, Sc. ii

When you're cold, don't expect sympathy from someone who's
warm.
—Alexander Solzhenitsyn, *One Day in the Life of Ivan Denisovich*

Everybody in the world ought to be sorry for everybody else. We all
have our little private hell. —Bettina von Hutten, *The Halo*

— T —

TACT

Tact is the intelligence of the heart. —Anonymous

Be sure, when you think you are being extremely tactful, that you are not in reality running away from something you ought to face.
—Sir Frank Medlicott

In the battle of existence, Talent is the punch; Tact is the clever foot-work. —Wilson Mizner

I've learned *never* to ask a woman if she's pregnant. —Robert Watkins

TALENT

Mediocrity knows nothing higher than itself, but talent instantly rec-ognizes genius. —Sir Arthur Conan Doyle, *The Valley of Fear*

Hide not your talents, they for use were made. What's a Sun-dial in the shade? —Benjamin Franklin, *Poor Richard's Almanack*, 1750

The world is always ready to receive talent with open arms.
—Oliver Wendell Holmes, Sr.

At that point in life where your talent meets the needs of the world, that is where God wants you to be. —Albert Schweitzer

Every man loves what he is good at.
—Thomas Shadwell, *A True Widow*

Talent is always conscious of its own abundance, and does not object to sharing. —Alexander Solzhenitsyn

TALES

The tale runs as it pleases the teller. —Anonymous

What is so tedious as a twice-told tale? —Homer

. . . believe not every tale. —Proverb (Jewish)

I cannot tell how the truth may be; I say the tale as 'twas said to me.
—Sir Walter Scott

An honest tale speeds best being plainly told.
—William Shakespeare, *King Richard III*, Act IV, Sc. iv

TALK

When men speak ill of thee, live so as nobody may believe them.
—Anonymous

I know that after all is said and done, more is said than done.
—Rita Mae Brown, *In Her Day*

There are some silent people who are more interesting than the best talkers.
—Benjamin Disraeli

Who talks much, must talk in vain.
—John Gay

He who talks much cannot always talk well.
—Goldoni

The thoughtless are rarely wordless.
—Howard W. Newton

Easier said than done.
—Proverb (15th century)

Talk does not cook rice.
—Proverb (Chinese)

Don't speak unless you can improve on the silence.
—Proverb (Spanish)

. . . all of us talk faster than we listen.
—Andrew A. Rooney, *A Few Minutes with Andy Rooney*, Preface

. . . even the most sublimely accomplished non-stop talker can't consistently please.
—J. D. Salinger, *Seymour an Introduction*

Have more than thou showest, / Speak less than thou knowest.
—William Shakespeare, *King Lear*, Act I, Sc. iv

Never speak loudly to one another unless the house is on fire.
—H. W. Thompson, *Body, Boots and Britches*

People have to talk about something just to keep their voice boxes in working order, so they'll have good voice boxes in case there's ever anything really meaningful to say.
—Kurt Vonnegut, Jr., *The Cat's Cradle*

... talk, not sex, constitutes most of the intercourse between a man
and his wife.   —Herman Wouk, *The Winds of War*

TASKS

Give me a task too big, too hard for human hands, then I shall come
at length to lean on Thee, and leaning, find my strength.
—W. H. Fowler

I long to accomplish a great and noble task, but it is my chief duty to
accomplish humble tasks as though they were great and noble. The
world is moved along, not only by the mighty shoves of its heroes,
but also by the aggregate of the tiny pushes of each honest worker.
—Helen Keller

Father, I beg of Thee a little task / To dignify my days, 'tis all I ask.
—Edna St. Vincent Millay

TASTE

Such and so various are the tastes of men.
—Akenside, *Pleasures of the Imagination*, Book III, line 567

Every man according to his taste.   —Proverb (French)

He who has not tasted bitter does not know what sweet is.
—Proverb (German)

A taste is enough.   —Proverb (Greek)

There is no disputing between tastes.   —Proverb (Latin)

To taste the sea all one needs is one gulp.
—Alexander Solzhenitsyn, *The Gulag Archipelago Two*, Introduction

Different strokes for different folks.   —Emlem Tunnell

TAXATION

The art of taxation consists in so plucking the goose as to obtain the
largest possible amount of feathers with the smallest possible
amount of hissing.   —Jean Baptiste Colbert

Taxation without representation is tyranny.   —James Otis

TEACHING

A teacher affects eternity; he can never tell where his influence stops.
—Henry Adams, *The Education of Henry Adams* (1907)

The true teacher defends his pupils against his own personal influence. —Bronson Alcott, "Orphic Sayings"

To know how to suggest is the great art of teaching.
—Henri Frédéric Amiel,
The Private Journal of Henri Frédéric Amiel, 16 Nov 1864

A teacher should work with the grain of a child. —Anonymous

A wise teacher makes learning a joy. —Anonymous

If we succeed in giving the love of learning, the learning is sure to come. —Anonymous

Teaching others teacheth yourself. —Anonymous

Garden work consists much more in uprooting weeds than in planting seed. This applies also to teaching. —Auerbach

Attempt to teach the young but little at a time; this will be easier to impart, easier to receive, and surer to be retained.
—Hosea Ballou

The teacher is like the candle, it lights others in consuming itself.
—Hosea Ballou

I am quite sure that in the hereafter she will take me by the hand and lead me to my proper seat.
—Bernard Baruch, on one of his early teachers

Teaching is not a lost art, but the regard for it is a lost tradition.
—Jacques Barzun

You can teach a student a lesson for a day; but if you can teach him to learn by creating curiosity, he will continue the learning process as long as he lives. —Clay P. Bedford

Precise knowledge is the only true knowledge, and he who does not teach exactly, does not teach at all. —Henry Ward Beecher

Any subject can be effectively taught in some intellectually honest
form to any child at any stage of development.   —Jerome Bruner,
The Process of Education, Ch. 3

The best teacher is the one who suggests rather than dogmatizes, and
inspires his listener with the wish to teach himself.
—Edward Bulwer-Lytton

Of all the excellent teachers of college English whom I have known I
have never discovered one who knew precisely what he was doing.
Therein have lain their power and their charm. —Mary Ellen Chase

And gladly would he learn and gladly teach.
—Geoffrey Chaucer, *Canterbury Tales*, Prologue

The authority of those who teach is often an obstacle to those who
want to learn.   —Cicero

Give a man a fish, and you feed him for a day. Teach a man to fish,
and you feed him for a lifetime.   —Confucius

In teaching there should be no class distinctions.   —Confucius

One can do anything, anything at all . . . if provided with a passionate and gifted teacher.   —Pat Conroy, *Beach Music*, Ch. 28

We loved the doctrine for the teacher's sake.
—Daniel Defoe, *Character of the Late Dr. Annesley*

Every spring he vowed to quit teaching school, and every summer he
missed his pupils and searched for them on the streets.
—Annie Dillard, *The Annie Dillard Reader*, "The Living"

We teach more by what we are than by what we teach. —Will Durant

If you would thoroughly know anything, teach it to others.
—Tryon Edwards

Teaching should be such that what is offered is perceived as a valuable gift and not as a hard duty.
—Albert Einstein, *Ideas and Opinions*

Knowledge exists to be imparted.   —Ralph Waldo Emerson

The whole art of teaching is only the art of awakening the natural curiosity of young minds for the purpose of satisfying it afterwards.
—Anatole France, *The Crime of Sylvestre Bonnard*

Good teaching is one-fourth preparation and three-fourths theatre . . .
—Gail Godwin, *The Odd Woman*

A teacher who can arouse a feeling for one single good action, for one single good poem, accomplishes more than he who fills our memory with rows and rows of natural objects, classified with name and form.   —Johann Wolfgang von Goethe, *Elective Affinities*

There is nothing more frightful than for a teacher to know only what his scholars are intended to know. —Johann Wolfgang von Goethe

Uncursed by doubt, our earliest creed we take; / We love the precepts for the teacher's sake.   —Oliver Wendell Holmes, Sr.

Everything I learn about teaching I learn from bad students.
—John Holt

Whatever you teach, be brief; what is quickly said, the mind readily receives and faithfully retains, everything superfluous runs over as from a full vessel.   —Horace

The question mark is the teacher's badge.   —Herman H. Horne

The object of teaching a child is to enable him to get along without his teacher.   —Elbert Hubbard

The teacher is one who makes two ideas grow where only one grew before.   —Elbert Hubbard

I would have all the professors in colleges, all the teachers in schools of every kind, including those in Sunday schools, agree that they would teach only what they know, that they would not palm off guesses as demonstrated truths.
—Robert G. Ingersoll, *What I Want for Christmas*

You cannot, by all the lecturing in the world, enable a man to make a shoe.   —Samuel Johnson

To teach is to learn twice.   —Joseph Joubert, *Pensées et lettres*

. . . good teachers, like Tolstoy's happy families, are alike everywhere.
—Bel Kaufman, *Up the Down Staircase*, Introduction

A teacher should, above all things, first induce a desire in the pupil
for the acquisition he wishes to impart.   —Horace Mann

A teacher who is attempting to teach without inspiring the pupil
with a desire to learn is hammering on a cold iron. —Horace Mann

In teaching it is the message and not the content that is the message . . .
the drawing out, not the pumping in.   —Ashley Montagu

Never help a child with a task at which he feels he can succeed.
          —Maria Montessori

Teachers can change lives with just the right mixture of chalk and
challenges.   —Joyce A. Myers

A master can tell you what he expects of you. A teacher, however,
awakens your own expectation.   —Patricia Neal

Imparting knowledge is only lighting other men's candles at our
lamp, without depriving ourselves of any flame.   —Jane Porter

We math teachers should emphasize "stop and think" instead of
"rush and do."   —Vera Preston, 4 Jun 1994

Who teaches, often learns himself.   —Proverb (Italian)

We learn by teaching.   —Proverb (Latin)

The useful type of successful teacher is one whose main interest is the
children, not the subject.   —Sir Walter Raleigh, *Letters*

The true aim of everyone who aspires to be a teacher should be, not
to impart his own opinions, but to kindle minds.
          —Frederick W. Robertson

Great teachers are usually a little crazy.
          —Andrew A. Rooney, *Word for Word*, "School Days"

Most of us end up with no more than five or six people who remember us. Teachers have thousands of people who remember them for the rest of their lives.
          —Andrew A. Rooney, *Word for Word*, "School Days"

The teacher who knows the most about a subject isn't necessarily the
one who can teach it best.
          —Andrew A. Rooney, *Word for Word*, "School Days"

For every person wishing to teach there are thirty not wanting to be
   taught.   —Walter Carruthers Sellar and Robert Julian Yeatman,
                                           And Now All This, Introduction

Men learn while they teach.   —Seneca

We shouldn't teach great books; we should teach a love of reading.
                                         —B. F. Skinner, in Richard I. Evans,
                                         B. F. Skinner: The Man and His Ideas

Shall I describe the happiness it gave me to go into the classroom and
   pick up the chalk? . . . It seemed to me the supreme, heartbreaking
   happiness to enter a classroom carrying a register as that bell rang,
   and start a lesson with the mysterious air of one about to unfold
   wonders.   —Alexander Solzhenitsyn, *The Gulag Archipelago Three*

First teach a person to the point of his limitations and then—pfft!—
   break the limitation. When you teach your son, you teach your
   son's son.   —*The Talmud*

The best learning I had came from teaching.
         —Corrie ten Boom, *In My Father's House*, with C. C. Carlson

Delightful task! to rear the tender thought, / To teach the young idea
   how to shoot.   —James Thomson, *The Seasons*, "Spring"

The art of teaching is the art of assisting discovery. —Mark Van Doren

The mediocre teacher tells. The good teacher explains. The superior
   teacher demonstrates. The great teacher inspires.
                                         —William Arthur Ward

It matters not the subject taught, nor all the books on all the shelves,
   / What matters most, yes most of all, is what the teachers are themselves.   —John Wooden

When God is our teacher, we come to think alike.   —Xenophon

Parents create life. Teachers help make it worthwhile.
                                         —Rabbi Leonard Zion

T E A R S

They are not long, the weeping and the laughter. / Love and desire and
   hate; / I think they have no portion in us after / We pass the gate.
                         —Ernest Dowson, "Vitae Summa Brevis"

Tears hinder sorrow from becoming despair. —Leigh Hunt

Tears may soothe the wounds they cannot heal. —Thomas Paine

Lofty mountains are full of springs; great hearts are full of tears.
—Joseph Roux

Tears, idle tears, I know not what they mean, / Tears from the depth of some divine despair. —Alfred, Lord Tennyson, "The Princess"

Tears are the silent language of grief. —Voltaire

Please, Lord, teach us to laugh again; but, God, don't ever let us forget that we cried. —Bill Wilson, co-founder of Alcoholics Anonymous

TECHNOLOGY

Any sufficiently advanced technology is indistinguishable from magic. —Arthur C. Clarke, *The Lost Worlds of 2001*

All about us the sense of disenchantment with technology appears to be growing. No one . . . can ignore the fall of the engineer from the dizzying heights he once occupied. . . . with the coming of the environmental crisis, our relationship to society has changed. We cannot . . . pretend that . . . a hundred space spectaculars can restore things to what they were.
—Samuel C. Florman, *The Existential Pleasures of Engineering*

. . . it is clear that our survival and the salvaging of our environment are dependent on more technology, not less.
—Samuel C. Florman, *The Existential Pleasures of Engineering*

There is scarcely a technical issue for which you cannot find expert witnesses of differing opinions.
—Samuel C. Florman, *The Existential Pleasures of Engineering*

Humanity is acquiring the right technology for all the wrong reasons.
—R. Buckminster Fuller

We should now give some real thought to the possibility of reforming our technology in the directions of smallness, simplicity, and non-violence. —E. F. Schumacher

The TELEPHONE

Just because you're home, you don't have to answer the phone.
—Suzy Becker, *All I Need to Know I Learned From My Cat*

. . . a bell summoning us to the sacrifice.
—Ambrose Bierce, about the telephone

TELEVISION

If a man watches three football games in a row, he should be declared
   legally dead. —Erma Bombeck, on "Donahue,"
   television talk show, 22 May 1986

The primary danger of the television screen lies not so much in the
   behavior it produces as the behavior it prevents—the talks, the
   games, the family activities and the arguments through which
   much of the child's learning takes place and his character is
   formed. —Urie Bronfenbrenner

[Television is] chewing gum for the eyes.
—John Mason Brown, interview with
James B. Simpson, 28 Jul 1955

[Television] is a medium of entertainment which permits millions of
   people to listen to the same joke at the same time, and yet remain
   lonesome. —T. S. Eliot

Television has changed the American child from an irresistible force
   to an immovable object. —Laurence J. Peter

No matter what critics say, it's hard to believe that a television program which keeps four children quiet for an hour can be all bad.
—Beryl Pfizer

I hate television. I hate it as much as peanuts. But I can't stop eating
   peanuts. —Orson Welles

TEMPERANCE

Abstinence is easier than temperance. —Seneca

TEMPTATION

He who avoids the temptation avoids the sin. —Anonymous

Unless you have never been tempted, don't pass judgment on someone who has yielded. —Anonymous

Watch and pray, that ye enter not into temptation: the spirit indeed
   is willing, but the flesh is weak. —The Bible (KJV): Matthew 26:41

... God is faithful, who will not suffer you to be tempted above that ye are able; but will with the temptation also make a way to escape, that ye may be able to bear it.
—*The Bible* (KJV): 1 Corinthians 10:13

[You] don't leave the chicken to watch the feed.
—Pat Conroy, *The Great Santini*

The Woman tempted me—and tempts me still! Lord God, I pray You that she ever will! —Edmund Vance Cooke, "Adam"

Better shun the bait than struggle in the snare. —John Dryden

No man is matriculated to the art of life till he has been well tempted.
—George Eliot

An open door may tempt a saint. —Thomas Fuller, M. D., *Gnomologia*

Many a dangerous temptation comes to us in fine gay colors, that are but skin-deep. —Matthew Henry

Temptations hurt not, though they have access; Satan o'ercomes none but by willingness. —Robert Herrick, *Hesperides*

Those Saints, which God loves best, / The Devil tempts not least.
—Robert Herrick, "Temptation"

Honest bread is very well—it's the butter that makes the temptation.
—Douglas William Jerrold, *The Catspaw*, Act III

Satan now is wiser than of yore, / And tempts by making rich, not making poor. —Alexander Pope

Opportunity makes the thief. —Proverb (13th century)

Lock your door and preserve your neighbor's honor.
—Proverb (Spanish)

How oft the sight of means to do ill deeds / Makes deeds ill done!
—William Shakespeare, *King John*, Act IV, Sc. ii

'T is one thing to be tempted, . . . / Another thing to fall.
—William Shakespeare, *Measure for Measure*, Act II, Sc. i

He who has no mind to trade with the Devil should be so wise as to keep from his shop. —South

There are several good protections against temptations, but the surest is cowardice.   —Mark Twain, *Following the Equator*, "Pudd'nhead Wilson's New Calendar"

TESTIMONY

Testimony is showing your scars and telling how Jesus healed you.
                     —Warren Walden, in his testimony at Hope Chapel, Austin, Texas, 13 Jun 1992

TESTING

Even though it's a time of testing for us, it's a time of glorifying Him in a way that the smooth places in our lives could never do.
                     —Sandy Edmonson, *God's Faithfulness in Trials & Testings*

It may be difficult to understand why a test comes our way, but we must never forget that the test is accomplishing refining and purification.   —Billy Graham, *Till Armageddon*

God does not offer us a way out of the testings of life. He offers us a way through, and that makes all the difference.   —W. T. Purkiser

THANKFULNESS

If you can't be thankful for what you receive, be thankful for what you escape.   —Anonymous

Look up on high, and thank the God of all.   —Geoffrey Chaucer

I thank You God for most this amazing day: / for the leaping greenly spirits of trees and a blue true dream of sky; / and for everything-which is natural which is infinite which is yes . . . —e. e. cummings

And let us give thanks for Someone to thank.   —Gerhard E. Frost

Thank God when he oppresses you, and again when he releases you.
                     —Johann Wolfgang von Goethe

When any calamity has been suffered the first thing to be remembered is how much has been escaped.   —Samuel Johnson

Let never day nor night unhallow'd pass, / But still remember what the Lord hath done.
                     —William Shakespeare, *King Henry VI, Part II*, Act II, Sc. i

It has seemed to me fit and proper that the gifts of God should be
solemnly, reverently, and gratefully acknowledged with one heart
and one voice by the whole American people. I do, therefore,
invite my fellow citizens . . . to set apart and observe the last
Thursday of November next as a day of thanksgiving and praise to
our beneficent Father who dwelleth in the heavens.

—Abraham Lincoln

I murmured because I had no shoes, until I met a man who had no
feet.   —Proverb (Persian)

The THEATER

All the difference in the world between the movies and the thrill I get
out of a play at the theater. Ay, yes! Like fooling around with paper
dolls when you could be playing with a real live baby.

—Edna Ferber, *So Big*

One's roused by this, another finds that fit: / Each loves the play for
what he brings to it.

—Johann Wolfgang von Goethe, *Faust*, Part I,
"Prelude to the Theatre"

The truth is you don't like the theater except the times when you're
in a room by yourself putting the play on paper.

—Dashiell Hammett, to Lillian Hellman

We do not go [to the theater], like our ancestors, to escape from the
pressure of reality, so much as to confirm our experiences of it.

—Charles Lamb, *Essays of Elia*,
"On the Artificial Comedy of the Last Century"

Coming to New York and not going to the theater is like going to bed
with a beautiful woman and not making love.   —Gregory Nunn

My soul, sit thou a patient looker-on; / Judge not the play before the
play is done: / Her plot hath many changes; every day Speaks a
new scene; the last act crowns the play. —Francis Quarles, *Emblems*

Not to go to the theater is like making one's toilet without a mirror.

—Arthur Schopenhauer, *Parerga and Paralipomena*,
"Further Psychological Observations"

All the world's a stage / And all the men and women merely players.

—William Shakespeare, *As You Like It*, Act II, Sc. vii

Play out the play . . .
> —William Shakespeare, *King Henry IV, Part I*, Act II, Sc. iv

. . . the play's the thing / Wherein I'll catch the conscience of the king.
> —William Shakespeare, *Hamlet*, Act II, Sc. ii

As long as more people will pay admission to a theater to see a naked body than to see a naked brain, the drama will languish.
> —George Bernard Shaw

THEOLOGY

Men are better than their theology.
> —Ralph Waldo Emerson, *Essays*, "Compensation"

My theology, briefly, is that the universe was dictated but not signed.
> —Christopher Morley

Your theology is what you are when the talking stops and the action starts.
> —Colin Morris

THEORY

Grey is the color of all theory.   —Johann Wolfgang von Goethe

A theory must be tempered with reality.   —Jawaharlal Nehru

Theory helps us bear our ignorance of facts.
> —George Santayana, *The Sense of Beauty*

THERAPY

The greatest healing therapy is friendship and love.
> —Hubert Humphrey

Words of comfort, skillfully administered, are the oldest therapy known to man.   —Louis Nizer

There is no better therapy than understanding.
> —Jim Piersall, *Fear Strikes Out*, with Al Hirshberg

The personality of the therapist is the most important human element in the therapeutic process.   —Thomas Tyndall

THOUGHT

To be free from evil thoughts is God's greatest gift.   —Aeschylus

One does not see his thought distinctly till it is reflected in the image
of another's.   —Alcott

Be careful of your thoughts—they may break into words at any time.
                                                            —Anonymous

Make not your thoughts your prison.   —Anonymous

Your thoughts are a machine you can learn to operate. —Anonymous

Every pure thought is a glimpse of God.   —Bartol

It is a joy to be choked with thought.   —Saul Bellow, *Herzog*

The manner in which one single ray of light, one single precious
hint, will clarify and energize the whole mental life of him who
receives it, is among the most wonderful and heavenly of intellectual phenomena.   —Arnold Bennett

I think that I think, therefore I think that I am.
                —Ambrose Bierce (paraphrase of René Descartes,
                                "I think, therefore I am.")

You can't lay down laws for what people think and hope.
                          —Maeve Binchy, *Circle of Friends*

The busiest of living agents are certain dead men's thoughts.
                                        —Christian Nestell Bovée

First doubt, then inquire, then discover. This has been the process
with all our great thinkers.   —H. T. Buckle, *History of Civilization*

What we think, we become.   —Buddha

Man, whose body is fragile as a jar, should make his thoughts firm as
a fortress.   —Buddhist saying

You think too much, Boss.
                —Michael Cacoyannis, *Zorba the Greek* (screenplay)

Thought once awakened does not again slumber.   —Thomas Carlyle

No fathers or mothers think their own children ugly; and this self-
deceit is yet stronger with respect to the offspring of the mind.
                                            —Miguel de Cervantes

We are no more responsible for the evil thoughts that pass through our minds than a scarecrow for the birds which fly over the seed-plot he has to guard. The sole responsibility in each case is to prevent them from settling. —Churton Collins, *Maxims and Reflections*

The quality of our lives is closely related to the quality of our thinking. —Gary R. Collins, *The Magnificent Mind*

It is nonsense to say there is not enough time to be fully informed . . . Time given to thought is the greatest timesaver of all.
—Norman Cousins

The highest possible stage in moral culture is when we recognize that we ought to control our thoughts.
—Charles Darwin, *The Descent of Man*, 4

Impromptu thoughts are mental wild-flowers.
—Marie de Vichy-Chamrond Deffand

I think, therefore I am. —René Descartes, *Discourse of Method*

Nurture your mind with great thoughts; to believe in the heroic makes heroes. —Benjamin Disraeli

Beware when the great God lets loose a thinker on this planet.
—Ralph Waldo Emerson, *Essays*, *First Series*, "Circles"

Great men are they who see that spiritual is stronger than any material force, that thought rules the world.
—Ralph Waldo Emerson, *Letters and Social Aims*,
"Progress of Culture," an address given 18 Jul 1867

Life consists in what a man is thinking all day.
—Ralph Waldo Emerson, *Journals*

Look sharply after your thoughts. They come unlooked for, like a new bird seen on your trees, and, if you turn to your usual task, disappear; and you shall never find that perception again; never, I say— but perhaps years, ages, and I know not what events and worlds may lie between you and its return. —Ralph Waldo Emerson

Our best thoughts come from others. —Ralph Waldo Emerson

So far as a man thinks, he is free.
—Ralph Waldo Emerson, *Conduct of Life*, "Fate"

The soul of God is poured into the world through the thoughts of
    men.   —Ralph Waldo Emerson

Thought is the seed of action.   —Ralph Waldo Emerson

Thought is action in rehearsal.   —Sigmund Freud

It's true of all of us . . . We think too much.
        —John Gardner, *October Light*, Ch. 4

The fundamental fact about the Greek was that he had to use his
    mind. The ancient priests had said, "Thus far and no further. We
    set the limits of thought." The Greeks said, "All things are to be
    examined and called into question. There are no limits set on
    thought."   —Edith Hamilton, *The Greek Way*

Never be afraid to sit awhile and think.
        —Lorraine Hansberry, *A Raisin in the Sun*, Act III

Every man has special thoughts of his own, rivaling the best litera-
    ture of any nation.   —Henry S. Haskins

A thought must tell at once, or not at all.
        —William Hazlitt, *Characteristics*

The glow of one warm thought is to me worth more than money.
        —Thomas Jefferson, *Writings*, Vol. iv

The essence of life consists in thinking, and being conscious of one's
    soul.   —Joseph Joubert

Vigilantly guard your mind against erroneous and destructive
    thought as you would guard your house against burglars and assas-
    sins.   —Grenville Kleiser

You talk to yourself all the time, be careful what you say. Negative
    images are destructive.   —William Lantz

Think wrongly, if you please, but in all cases think for yourself.
        —Doris Lessing

Thoughts have no sex.   —Clare Booth Luce

Thoughts are not subject to duty.
        —Martin Luther, *On worldly authority,*
    to what extent one requires to be obedient to it (1523)

Your life is what your thoughts make it. —Marcus Aurelius Antoninus

We lift ourselves by our own thought; we climb upon our vision of
ourselves.   —O. S. Marden

A man can stand a lot as long as he can stand himself. He can live
without hope, without friends, without books, even without
music, as long as he can listen to his own thoughts. —Axel Munthe

Sometimes I sits and thinks and sometimes I just sits.
                                              —Leroy "Satchel" Paige

What we picture ourselves to be, we become.   —Paul Parker

By thought I embrace the universal.   —Blaise Pascal

We can all do good deeds, but very few of us can think good
thoughts.   —Cesare Pavese

Change your thoughts and you change your world.
                                              —Norman Vincent Peale

Thinking is the talking of the soul with itself.   —Plato

We become what we contemplate.   —Plato, *Ion*

Thought is free.   —Proverb (14th century)

Act quickly, think slowly.   —Proverb (Greek)

That man is best who considers everything for himself.
                                                      —Proverb (Greek)

Speak as the many, think as the few.   —Proverb (Latin)

We only think when we are confronted with a problem.
                                                      —Proverb (Persian)

To live thy better, let thy worst thoughts die.   —Sir Walter Raleigh

We find it hard to believe that other people's thoughts are as silly as
our own, but they probably are.   —James Harvey Robinson

A delicate thought is a flower of the mind.   —Rollin

A man may dwell so long upon a thought that it may take him prisoner.   —George Savile

The thought that you must carry all the time, like a big sign hanging over the stage of your living is this: I am going to keep my thinking and my attitude calm and cheerful right now.
                                                    —John Schindler, M. D.

Make not your thoughts your prisons . . .
                    —William Shakespeare, *Antony and Cleopatra*, Act I, Sc. ii

Thoughts are but dreams till their effects be tried.
                              —William Shakespeare, *The Rape of Lucrece*

They are never alone that are accompanied with noble thoughts.
                              —Sir Philip Sidney, *The Arcadia*, Book I

Your thoughts are making you.   —Bishop Steere

Everyone who lives any semblance of an inner life thinks more nobly and profoundly than he speaks.   —Robert Louis Stevenson

To have ideas is to gather flowers; to think is to weave them into garlands.   —Madame Swetchine

A penny for your thought.   —Jonathan Swift

I have no riches but my thoughts, / Yet these are wealth enough for me.   —Sara Teasdale, *Long Songs*, "Riches"

All the past of Time reveals / A bridal dawn of thunder-peals, / Whenever Thought hath wedded Fact.   —Alfred, Lord Tennyson

Associate reverently, as much as you can, with your loftiest thoughts.
                                              —Henry David Thoreau

He is the rich man, and enjoys the fruit of his riches, who summer and winter forever can find delight in his own thoughts.
                                              —Henry David Thoreau

Let a man strive to purify his thoughts. What a man thinketh, that is he.   —*The Upanishads*

They can because they think they can.   —Virgil, *Aeneid*

We are where our thoughts have taken us.   —William Webb

Guard well thy thoughts: our thoughts are heard in heaven. —Young

THRIFT

Thrift is a great revenue.   —Cicero

How great, my friends, is the virtue of living upon a little!   —Horace

Resolve not to be poor; whatever you have, spend less.
                        —Samuel Johnson, letter to James Boswell

I believe that thrift is essential to well-ordered living.
                                    —John D. Rockefeller, Jr.

TIME

Catch, then, O catch the transient hour; / Improve each moment as it
flies; / Life's a short summer—man a flower— / He dies—alas! how
soon he dies.   —Anonymous

The Lord wants our precious time, not our spare time. —Anonymous

Time was invented so everything wouldn't happen at once.
                                    —Anonymous

The greatest sacrifice is the sacrifice of time.   —Antiphon

Let him who would enjoy a good future waste none of his present.
                                    —Roger Babson

Time is a dressmaker specializing in alterations.   —Faith Baldwin

Tom Seaver: Yogi, what time is it? Yogi Berra: You mean now?

This is the day which the Lord hath made; we will rejoice and be glad
in it.   —*The Bible* (KJV): Psalms 118:24

. . . one day is with the Lord as a thousand years, and a thousand
years as one day.   —*The Bible* (KJV): 2 Peter 3:8

He said "What's time? Leave Now for dogs and apes! Man has forever."   —Robert Browning, "A Grammarian's Funeral," line 83

Now five years is nothing in man's life except when he is very young
and very old . . .   —Pearl S. Buck, *The Good Earth*, Ch. 30

You will never "find" time for anything. If you want time you must
   take it.   —Charles Buxton

Sometimes I wish life had a fast-forward button.   —Dan Chopin

Time is the great physician.   —Benjamin Disraeli

Time goes, you say? Ah no! Alas, Time stays, we go.
          —Henry Austin Dobson, *Proverbs in Porcelain*,
                    "The Paradox of Time"

I have measured out my life with coffee spoons.
         —T. S. Eliot, "The Love Song of J. Alfred Prufrock"

The years teach much which the days never know.
     —Ralph Waldo Emerson, *Essays*, *Second Series*, "Experience"

This time, like all times, is a very good one, if we but know what to do
   with it.   —Ralph Waldo Emerson

What a day may bring, a day may take away.   —Thomas Fuller

Time flies like an arrow. Fruit flies like a banana.   —Lisa Grossman

Time is a circus, always packing up and moving away.   —Ben Hecht

When you feel how depressingly / Slowly you climb, / It's well to
   remember that / Things Take Time.   —Piet Hein, Grooks, "T.T.T."

Almost all human affairs are tedious. Everything is too long. Visits,
   dinners, concerts, plays, speeches, pleadings, essays, sermons, are
   too long. Pleasure and business labor equally under this defect, or,
   as I should rather say, this fatal super-abundance.   —Arthur Helps

By time and toil we sever / What strength and rage could never.
                    —Jean de La Fontaine, *Fables*

No one ever regarded the first of January with indifference.
                        —Charles Lamb

Every evening brings us nearer God.   —Martin Luther

The darkest hour has only sixty minutes.   —Morris Mandel

Each day provides its own gifts.   —Martial, *Epigrams*

Time has been given only for us to exchange each year of our life
with the remembrance of truth. —Saint Martin

God has so arranged the chronometry of our spirits, that there shall
be thousands of silent moments between the striking hours.
—James Martineau

But at my back I always hear Time's wingèd chariot hurrying near.
—Andrew Marvell, "To His Coy Mistress"

It is astonishing what a lot of odd minutes one can catch during the
day, if one really sets about it. —Dinah Maria Mulock

We crucify ourselves between two thieves: regret for yesterday and
fear of tomorrow. —Fulton Oursler

It is distrust of God to be troubled about what is to come; impatience
against God to be troubled with what is present; and anger at God
to be troubled for what is past. —Simon Patrick

The mystery lies in the here and now. The mystery is: What is one to
do with oneself? As you get older you begin to realize the trick time
is playing, and that unless you do something about it, the passage
of time is nothing but the encroachment of the horrible banality of
the past on the pure future. The past devours the future like a tape
recorder, converting pure possibility into banality. The present is
the tape head, the mouth of time.   Then where is the mystery and
why bother kicking through the ashes?   Because there is a clue in
the past. —Walker Percy, *Lancelot*

Time is the wisest counselor. —Pericles

Seize time by the forelock. —Pittacus of Mytilene

It seems no more than right that men should seize time by the forelock, for the rude old fellow, sooner or later, pulls all their hair out.
—George D. Prentice, *Prenticeana*

In theory one is aware that the earth revolves, but in practice one
does not perceive it, the ground upon which one treads seems not
to move, and one can live undisturbed. So it is with Time in one's
life. —Marcel Proust, *The Past Recaptured*

To-day me, to-morrow thee. —Proverb (13th century)

The day is short and the work is long. —Proverb (15th century)

Time and tide wait for no man. —Proverb (16th century)

The evening crowns the day. —Proverb (17th century)

Every day in thy life is a leaf in thy history. —Proverb (Arab)

The dogs bark, but the caravans move on. —Proverb (Arab)

Good things take time. —Proverb (Dutch)

There is no mortar that time will not loose. —Proverb (French)

Long is not forever. —Proverb (German)

Long as the day may be the night comes at last. —Proverb (Irish)

Time gives good advice. —Proverb (Maltese)

Every day is a messenger of God. —Proverb (Russian)

. . . but the longest day hath its evening. —Sir Walter Raleigh

The past and future are veiled; but the past wears the widow's veil,
the future, the virgin's. —Jean Paul Richter

Every day is a little life; every waking and rising a little birth; every
going to rest and sleep a little death.
—Arthur Schopenhauer, *Our Relation to Ourselves*

If God adds another day to our life, let us receive it gladly.
—Seneca, *Epistles*

One should count each day a separate life. —Seneca

Time heals what reason cannot. —Seneca, *Agamemnon*

Come what come may,
Time and the hour runs through the roughest day.
—William Shakespeare, *Macbeth*, Act I, Sc. iii

My day is my epoch. —Alexander Solzhenitsyn, *The Gulag Archipelago*

There is a law of time, a law of oblivion: glory to the dead; life to the
living. —Alexander Solzhenitsyn, *The First Circle*

You today; me tomorrow. —Alexander Solzhenitsyn,
The *Gulag Archipelago*

Gentle time will heal our sorrows. —Sophocles, *Electra*

Time eases all things. —Sophocles, *Oedipus Rex*

What we love to do we find time to do. —John Lancaster Spalding

Every dog must have his day. —Jonathan Swift

The butterfly counts not months but moments, and has time enough.
—Rabindranath Tagore, *Fireflies*

Enjoy the blessings of this day, if God sends them; and the evils of it
bear patiently and sweetly: for this day only is ours, we are dead to
yesterday, and we are not yet born to the morrow.
—Jeremy Taylor

A day may sink or save a realm. —Alfred, Lord Tennyson

Time is but the stream I go a-fishing in.
—Henry David Thoreau, *Walden*,
"Where I Lived, and What I Lived For"

Time will pass and I shall regard this, too, with indifference.
—Leo Tolstoy, *Anna Karenina*

. . . life is too short to do the whole. —Vincent van Gogh

Time was given us like jewels to spend, and it's the ultimate sacrilege
to wish it away. —Sloan Wilson, *The Man in the Gray Flannel Suit*

A man he seems of cheerful yesterdays / And confident to-morrows.
—William Wordsworth

Some hours weigh against a whole lifetime.
—Herman Wouk, *The Winds of War*

How swift the shuttle flies, that weaves thy shroud!
—Edward Young, *Night Thoughts*, "Night 4"

TIMIDITY

Remember the old saying, "Faint heart ne'er won fair lady."
—Miguel de Cervantes, *Don Quixote*, II, iii, 10

Women do not fancy timid men. —Madame Deluzy

Faint hearts fair ladies never win.   —William Elterton, *Britain's Ida*

. . . it's possible to let love fly by like a cloud in a windy sky if one is too timid, or perhaps unable to believe he is entitled to good fortune.   —Bernard Malamud, *The Fixer*

Who timidly requests invites refusal.   —Seneca, *Hippolytus*

TODAY

Today is the first day of the rest of our life.
            —Charles Dederich, founder of Synanon anti-heroin centers

Happy the man, and happy he alone, / He who can call to-day his own; He who, secure within, can say, / Tomorrow do thy worst, for I have lived to-day.
            —John Dryden, *Sylvae*, translation of Horace's *Odes*, III

TOLERANCE

If you would have a hen lay, you must bear with her cackling.
                                —Anonymous

Has not God borne with you these many years? Be ye tolerant to others.
                                —Hosea Ballou

Let every man come to God in his own way.   —Henry Ward Beecher

The best creed we can have is charity toward the creeds of others.
                                —Josh Billings

No man can justly censure or condemn another, because indeed no man truly knows another.
                        —Sir Thomas Browne, *Religio Medici*, Part II

. . . every dog is allowed one bite.
                        —R. F. Delderfield, *To Serve Them All My Days*

If thou would'st be borne with, then bear with others.
                                —Thomas Fuller

The golden rule of conduct . . . is mutual toleration, seeing that we will never all think alike and we shall always see Truth in fragment and from different angles of vision.   —Mahatma Gandhi

I let everyone follow his own bent, that I may be free to follow mine.
—Johann Wolfgang von Goethe

Error of opinion may be tolerated when reason is left free to combat
  it.   —Thomas Jefferson, First Inaugural Address, 4 Mar 1801

It has been my fortune to love in general those men most who have
  thought most differently from me, on subjects wherein others pardon no discordance. I think I have no more right to be angry with
  a man, whose reason has followed up a process different from what
  mine has, and is satisfied with the result, than with one who has
  gone to Venice while I am at Siena, and who writes to me that he
  likes the place.   —Walter Savage Landor

Tolerance is the positive and cordial effort to understand another's
  beliefs, practices and habits without necessarily sharing or accepting them.   —Joshua Loth Liebman

If thou wouldst bear thy neighbor's faults, cast thine eyes upon thine
  own.   —Molinos

Live and let live.   —Proverb (Dutch)

Be not angry that you cannot make others as you wish them to be,
  since you cannot make yourself as you wish to be.
                                              —Thomas à Kempis

TOMORROW

Tomorrow never comes.   —Anonymous

Tomorrow is a new day.   —Proverb (16th century)

The TONGUE

The blow of a whip raises a welt, but a blow of the tongue crushes
  bones.   —Apocrypha, "Ecclesiasticus," 28, 17

Many have fallen by the edge of the sword: but not so many as have
  fallen by the tongue.   —Apocrypha, "Ecclesiasticus," 28, 18

... the tongue is a little member, and boasteth great things. Behold,
  how great a matter a little fire kindleth! —*The Bible* (KJV): James 3:5

But the tongue can no man tame; it is an unruly evil, full of deadly
  poison.   —*The Bible* (KJV): James 3:8

Be slow of tongue and quick of eye. —Miguel de Cervantes

Out of some little thing, too free a tongue
  Can make an outrageous wrangle. —Euripides, *Andromache*

A sharp tongue cuts itself. —Alan Harris

Never trust your tongue when your heart is bitter. —Samuel J. Hurwitt

A sharp tongue is the only edge-tool that grows keener with constant
  use. —Washington Irving

It is a gude tongue that says nae ill. —Proverb (Scottish)

Men govern nothing with more difficulty than their tongues . . .
  —Benedict de Spinoza

TONGUES

Spiritual language is no substitute for spiritual maturity.
  —Ron Parrish, sermon, Hope Chapel, Austin, Texas, 24 Jul 1993

There is validity in talking in tongues, but it's not a criteria for spirituality.
  —Ron Parrish, sermon, Hope Chapel, Austin, Texas, 24 Jul 1993

TOOLS

The implements to him who can handle them.
  —Napoleon Bonaparte, in Thomas Carlyle, *On Heroes, Hero-
  Worship, and the Heroic in History* (1841), "The Hero as King"

A workman who wants to do his work well must first prepare his
  tools. —Confucius

A bad workman quarrels with his tools.
  —George Herbert, *Outlandish Proverbs*

In this world a man must either be anvil or hammer.
  —Henry Wadsworth Longfellow, *Hyperion*, IV, vii

If the only tool you have is a hammer, you tend to see every problem
  as a nail. —Abraham Maslow

The nail that sticks out is hammered down. —Proverb (Japanese)

Finding the tool is often half the battle.
>—Andrew A. Rooney, *Word for Word*, "Carpentry for Ladies"

T O Y S

Old boys have their playthings as well as young ones; the difference is only in price. —Benjamin Franklin,
>*Poor Richard's Almanack*, 1752

War toys are not just noise and games that little boys play.
>—Jeanne-Marie Houston, "War Toys" (song)

T R A D E S

A smith becomes a smith by working at the forge. —Anonymous

He is a poor smith who cannot bear smoke. —Anonymous

When it comes to getting things done, we need fewer architects and more brick layers. —Colleen C. Barrett

Each honest calling, each walk of life, has its own elite, its own aristocracy based upon excellence of performance. —James Bryant Conant

He that hath a trade hath an estate. —Benjamin Franklin

Love the little trade which thou hast learned, and be content therewith. —Marcus Aurelius Antoninus

Who has a trade may go anywhere. —Proverb (Spanish)

T R A D I T I O N

[Tradition] is the democracy of the dead. —G. K. Chesterton

The dead govern the living. —Auguste Comte, *Catechisme positiviste*

Sometimes tradition is a way of keeping going.
>—Maxine Kumin, *The Designated Heir*, Ch. 6

T R A F F I C

Traffic signals in New York are just rough guidelines.
>—David Letterman

T R A G E D Y

A tragic life is romantic when it happens to somebody else.
—Charles Schulz, a line by his character Sally in
the comic strip "Peanuts"

The tragedy of life is what dies inside a man while he lives.
—Albert Schweitzer

T R A N Q U I L I T Y

Back of tranquility lies always conquered unhappiness.
—David Grayson

It is tranquil people who accomplish much.   —Henry David Thoreau

T R A N S F O R M A T I O N

. . . unless you made your life a turning point, there was no reason for
existing.   —Saul Bellow, *More Die of Heartbreak*

T R A N S L A T I O N

Interpreter, n. One who enables two persons of different languages to
understand each other by repeating to each what it would have
been to the interpreter's advantage for the other to have said.
—Ambrose Bierce, *The Devil's Dictionary*

Translation from one language to another is like viewing a piece of
tapestry on the wrong side where though the figures are distin-
guishable yet there are so many ends and threads that the beauty
and exactness of the work is obscured.   —Miguel de Cervantes

As a true translator you will take care not to translate word for word.
—Horace

An idea does not pass from one language to another without change.
—Miguel de Unamuno, *Tragic Sense of Life*

T R A V E L

If you don't care where you are, you ain't lost.   —Anonymous

If you don't know where you're going, any road will take you there.
—Anonymous

Make short the miles with talk and smiles.   —Anonymous

You must be content sometimes with rough roads.   —Anonymous

We're lost, but we're making good time!
> —Yogi Berra, *The Yogi Book*, to his family on the way
> to his Hall of Fame induction ceremony, 1972

You've got to be very careful if you don't know where you are going
'cause you might not get there.   —Yogi Berra, *The Yogi Book*

Men travel faster now, but I do not know if they go to better things.
> —Willa Cather, *Death Comes for the Archbishop*

The end is nothing, / The road is all.
> —Willa Cather, "Song of the Lark"

Travel teaches toleration.
> —Benjamin Disraeli, *Contarini Fleming*, Part V, Ch. 7

If an ass goes traveling, he'll not come home a horse.
> —Thomas Fuller, M. D., *Gnomologia*, No. 2668

Go West, young man, and grow up with the country.
> —Horace Greeley, *Hints toward Reform*

Never go on trips with anyone you do not love.
> —Ernest Hemingway, *A Moveable Feast*

A good traveler has no fixed plans and is not intent on arriving.
> —Lao Tzu

The only people who ever get anyplace interesting are the people that
get lost.   —Jerome Lawrence and Robert E. Lee,
> *The Night Thoreau Spent in Jail*

When lost, I look for gas stations for counsel.
> —Laurel Lee, *Godspeed: Hitchhiking Home*

. . . a man leaves much when he leaves his own country.
> —Cormac McCarthy, *All the Pretty Horses*, Ch. 4

They say money kinda melts when you take it across a border.
> —Larry McMurtry, *The Last Picture Show*, Ch. 15

It is a long lane that has no turning.   —Proverb (Arab)

He who is outside his door already has a hard part of his journey
    behind him.   —Proverb (Dutch)

Who wishes to travel far spares his steed.   —Proverb (French)

What is the use of running when we are not on the right road?
                                      —Proverb (German)

Two shorten the road.   —Proverb (Irish)

Better ask than lose your way.   —Proverb (Italian)

Good company on the road is the shortest cut.   —Proverb (Italian)

You can't drive straight on a twisting lane.   —Proverb (Russian)

No matter how far you have gone on a wrong road, turn back.
                                   —Proverb (Turkish)

No road is long with good company.   —Proverb (Turkish)

An agreeable companion on a journey is as good as a carriage.
                      —Publilius Syrus, *Moral Sayings*

A rolling stone gathers no moss.   —Publilius Syrus, *Maxims*

I never was lost. I was bewildered right bad once for as much as a
    week, but not lost.   —Elizabeth Madox Roberts, *The Great Meadow*

Go west, young man.
              —John Babsone Lane Soule, article in the *Terra Haute*
                                   (Indiana) *Express*

The more I see of other countries the more I love my own.
                                    —Madame de Staël

It took Doc longer to go places than other people. He didn't drive fast
    and he stopped and ate hamburgers very often.
                          —John Steinbeck, *Cannery Row*

Travel is glamorous only in retrospect.   —Paul Theroux

Short cuts make long delays.   —J. R. R. Tolkien

TREASON

Treason doth never prosper: what's the reason? For if it prosper, none dare call it treason.   —Sir John Harington, *Epigrams*, "Of Treason"

TREES

A forest is in an acorn.   —Anonymous

The boughs that bear the most hang lowest.   —Anonymous

The tree is no sooner down than everyone runs for his hatchet.
                                                                  —Anonymous

The groves were God's first temples.
                                —William Cullen Bryant, "A Forest Hymn"

I like trees because they seem more resigned to the way they have to live than other things do.   —Willa Cather, *O Pioneers!*, Part II, Ch. 8

Large streams from little fountains flow, / Tall oaks from little acorns grow.   —David Everett, "Lines Written for a School Declamation"

He that plants trees loves others besides himself.
                                        —Thomas Fuller, M. D., *Gnomologia*

The tree doth not withdraw its shade, even from the woodcutter.
                                                           —*The Hitopadesa*

It would be as silly as to carry sticks into the forest.   —Horace

I think that I shall never see / A poem as lovely as a tree.
                                                    —Joyce Kilmer, "Trees"

Poems are made by fools like me, / But only God can make a tree.
                                                    —Joyce Kilmer, "Trees"

He who plants a tree / Plants a hope.   —Lucy Larcom

A tree is known by its fruit.   —Proverb (14th century)

Little strokes fell great oaks.   —Proverb (16th century)

A tree falls the way it leans.   —Proverb (Bulgarian)

A society grows great when old men plant trees whose shade they know they shall never see.   —Proverb (Greek)

The forest is the poor man's overcoat. —Proverb (New England)

As the forest grew, so the ax handle grew with it. —Proverb (Russian)

The tree falls not at the first stroke. —John Ray

Except during the nine months before he draws his first breath, no
man manages his affairs as well as a tree does.
—George Bernard Shaw

A forest doesn't weep over one tree.
—Alexander Solzhenitsyn, *Prisoners*

He that planteth a tree is the servant of God, / He provideth a kindness for many generations, / And faces that he hath not seen shall
bless him. —Henry Van Dyke, "The Friendly Trees"

TRIALS

Reckon any matter of trial to thee among thy gains. —T. Adam

The gem cannot be polished without friction, nor man perfected
without trials. —Confucius

When God wants to make a man, he puts him into some storm.
—Lettie Cowman

Thank you Lord that this has a purpose. You're going to teach me
something of your greatness in this that I would never have known
otherwise.—Sandy Edmonson, *God's Faithfulness in Trials* & *Testings*

Every moment of my life I realize that God is putting me on my trial.
—Mahatma Gandhi

. . . Not only are we comforted in our trials, but our trials can equip us
to comfort others. —Billy Graham, *Till Armageddon*

As sure as ever God puts His children in the furnace, He will be in the
furnace with them. —Charles H. Spurgeon, *Privileges of Trial*

Trials teach us what we are. —Charles H. Spurgeon

TRIBULATION

. . . we must through much tribulation enter into the kingdom of
God. —*The Bible* (KJV): The Acts 14:22

TRIFLES

Small things are what make great things possible.　　—Anonymous

Trifles, trifles are what matter!
> —Fyodor Dostoyevsky, *Crime and Punishment*

For the want of a nail the shoe was lost, / For the want of a shoe the
horse was lost, / For the want of a horse the rider was lost, / For the
want of a rider the battle was lost, / For the want of a battle the
kingdom was lost— / And all for the want of a horseshoe-nail.
> —Benjamin Franklin, *Poor Richard's Almanack*, 1758, an
elaboration of lines from George Herbert's *Jacula Prudentum*

O Diamond! Diamond! thou little knowest the mischief done!
> —Isaac Newton, when his dog knocked over a candle, burning
papers developed over several years

What dire offence from am'rous causes springs, / What mighty con-
tests rise from trivial things. —Alexander Pope, *The Rape of the Lock*

Man shows his character best in trifles.　　—Arthur Schopenhauer

Be master of your petty annoyances and conserve your energies for
the big, worthwhile things. It isn't the mountain ahead that wears
you out—it's the grain of sand in your shoe.　　—Robert Service

A horse! a horse! my kingdom for a horse!
> —William Shakespeare, *King Richard III*, Act V, Sc. iv

Cracks make caves collapse.
> —Alexander Solzhenitsyn, *The Gulag Archipelago Three*

The TRINITY

Tell me how it is that in this room there are three candles and but one
light, and I will explain to you the mode of the divine existence.
> —John Wesley

TROUBLE

All things work for good for those who love God. Romans 8:28. Not
some things or most things but all things; so praise Him even in
your troubles.　　—Anonymous

In every trouble, there's a blessing.　　—Anonymous

The more you talk about your troubles, the harder it is to find somebody who will listen.   —Anonymous

The really happy man is the one who can enjoy the scenery even
when he has to take a detour.   —Anonymous

Nobody knows the trouble I've seen, / Nobody knows but Jesus.
                                    —Anonymous, black spiritual

The art of living lies less in eliminating our troubles than in growing
with them.   —Bernard Baruch

Troubles are often the tools by which God fashions us for better
things.   —Henry Ward Beecher, in William Drysdale,
                                    Proverbs from Plymouth Pulpit

. . . call upon me [God] in the day of trouble: I will deliver thee, and
thou shalt glorify me.   —*The Bible* (KJV): Psalms 50:15

People need trouble—a little frustration to sharpen the spirit on,
toughen it. Artists do, I don't mean you need to live in a rathole or
gutter, but you do have to learn fortitude, endurance. Only vegetables are happy.
          —William Faulkner, *Selected Letters of William Faulkner*

I have had many troubles in my life, but the worst of them never
came.   —James A. Garfield

. . . I'm not going to lie down and let trouble walk over me.
                                            —Ellen Glasgow

Trouble is only opportunity in work clothes.   —Henry J. Kaiser

Only the dead have no troubles.   —Leonard Louis Levinson

Everybody's got their troubles.
          —Dorothy Parker, *The Portable Dorothy Parker*, "Big Blonde"

When an elephant is in trouble, even a frog will kick him.
                                            —Proverb (Hindu)

No one can say of his house, "There is no trouble here."
                                            —Proverb (Oriental)

If trouble comes, make use of it too.   —Proverb (Russian)

Light troubles speak; the weighty are struck dumb.

—Seneca, *Hippolytus*

Trouble is a part of your life, and if you don't share it, you don't give
the person who loves you enough chance to love you enough.

—Dinah Shore

It is usually not so much the greatness of our trouble as the littleness
of our spirit which makes us complain. —Jeremy Taylor

No man is without his load of trouble. —Thomas à Kempis

We shall all of us die, so why grudge a little trouble?
—Leo Tolstoy, *The Death of Ivan Ilych and Other Stories*,
"The Death of Ivan Ilych"

When bad things happened—the usual accidents, illnesses, jogs in
the established pattern—Bee treated them with eye-rolling good
humor, as if they were the stuff of situation comedy.
—Anne Tyler, *Saint Maybe*, Ch. 1

TRUST

It is an equal failing to trust everybody, and to trust nobody.
—Anonymous

The willingness to trust others even when you know you may be
taken advantage of is the cornerstone of becoming civilized.
—O. A. Battista

Some trust in chariots, and some in horses: but we will remember the
name of the Lord our God. —*The Bible* (KJV): Psalms 20:7

Put not your trust in princes . . . —*The Bible* (KJV): Psalms 146:3

Trust in the Lord with all thine heart; and lean not unto thine own
understanding. —*The Bible* (KJV): Proverbs 3:5

The man who trusts men will make fewer mistakes than he who dis-
trusts them. —Camillo Cavour

When we trust our brother, whom we have seen, we are learning to
trust God, whom we have not seen. —James Freeman Clarke

You may be deceived if you trust too much, but you will live in torment if you do not trust enough. —Frank Crane

Trust ivrybody—but cut th' cards.
—Finley Peter Dunne, *Mr. Dooley's Philosophy*

Trust men and they will be true to you; treat them greatly, and they will show themselves great.
—Ralph Waldo Emerson, *Essays, First Series*, "Prudence"

People whom we trust tend to become trustworthy.
—Rabbi Solomon B. Freehof

Always to distrust is an error, as well as always to trust.
—Johann Wolfgang von Goethe

God provides for him that trusteth.
—George Herbert, *Outlandish Proverbs*

It is better to suffer wrong than to do it, and happier to be sometimes cheated than not to trust.
—Samuel Johnson, *The Rambler* (an English journal), 18 Dec 1750

Trust as little as you can to report, and examine all you can by your own senses.
—Samuel Johnson

To be trusted is a greater compliment than to be loved.
—George Macdonald, *Marquis of Lossie*, Ch. 4

Trust in Allah, but tie your camel.
—Proverb (Arab)

Don't trust your brother, trust your own bad eye. —Proverb (Russian)

I would rather be the man who bought the Brooklyn Bridge than the man who sold it.
—Will Rogers

Love all, trust a few, / Do wrong to none . . .
—William Shakespeare, *All's Well That Ends Well*, Act I, Sc. i

Why should I trust you? We haven't drunk from the same bowl of soup.
—Alexander Solzhenitsyn, *Cancer Ward*

The soul and spirit that animates and keeps up society is mutual trust.
—South

Trust one who has tried.
—Virgil

Few things help an individual more than to place responsibility upon him, and to let him know that you trust him.—Booker T. Washington

We have a saying in the movement that you can't trust anybody over
    thirty.   —Jack Weinberg, in *San Francisco Chronicle*, 15 Nov 1964

TRUTH

Simple are the words of truth.   —Aeschylus

The truth is not always what we want to hear.   —Anonymous

Truth, by whomsoever spoken, comes from God.   —Anonymous

Truth may languish, but can never perish.   —Anonymous

Truth needs no crutches; / If it limps it's a lie.   —Anonymous

When you tell the truth you do not have to remember what you said.
    —Anonymous

The first wrote, Wine is the strongest. The second wrote, The king is
    strongest. The third wrote, Women are strongest: but above all
    things Truth beareth away the victory.
    —Apocrypha, "1 Esdras," 3, 10

Great is Truth, and mighty above all things.
    —Apocrypha, "1 Esdras," 4, 41

If you live your life in truth, the truth will out.
    —John Astin, in Patty Duke, *Call Me Anna*, with Kenneth Turan

And ye shall know the truth, and the truth shall make you free.
    —*The Bible* (KJV): John 8:32

All things to all men only fools will tell, / Truth profits none but
    those that use it well.   —J. S. Blackie

A truth that's told with bad intent / Beats all the lies you can invent.
    —William Blake, "Auguries of Innocence"

Error is created; truth is eternal.   —William Blake

The seal of truth is simplicity.   —Boerhaave

Sow truth, if thou the truth wouldst reap: / Who sows the false shall
    reap the vain.
    —Horatius Bonar, "He Liveth Long Who Liveth Well"

Truth, like the sun, submits to be obscured; but, like the sun, only for
a time. —Christian Nestell Bovée

Truth exists, only falsehood has to be invented.
—Georges Braque, *Pensées sur l'art*

Truth is error burned up. —Norman O. Brown

Truth is within ourselves. —Robert Browning, *Paracelsus*

Truth is the shattered mirror strewn / In myriad bits; while each
believes his little bit the whole to own. —Robert Burton

'Tis strange—but true; for truth is always strange,— Stranger than fiction. —Lord Byron, *Don Juan*, Canto XIV, 101

The fewer the voices on the side of truth, the more distinct and
strong must be your own. —William Ellery Channing

Every man seeks the truth, but God only knows who has found it.
—Earl of Chesterfield, *Letters*, 21 Sep 1747

He who begins by loving Christianity better than Truth will proceed
by loving his own sect or church better than Christianity, and end
in loving himself better than all.
—Samuel Taylor Coleridge, *Aids to Reflection*,
"Moral and Religious Aphorisms"

Truth is a river that is always splitting up into arms that reunite.
Islanded between the arms, the inhabitants argue for a lifetime as
to which is the main river. —Cyril Connolly

The world is now too dangerous for anything but the truth, too small
for anything but brotherhood. —Arthur Powell Davies

There is nothing so strong or safe in an emergency of life as the simple truth. —Charles Dickens

We swallow whole-heartedly any lie that flatters us, but we sip reluc-
tantly at any truth we find harsh.
—Denis Diderot, *Le Neveu de Rameau*

. . . truth shines brightest thro' the plainest dress.
—Wentworth Dillon, *Essay on Translated Verse*

If you are out to describe the truth, leave elegance to the tailor.
—Albert Einstein

. . . the desire for truth must take precedence over all other desires.
—Albert Einstein, *Ideas and Opinions*

The greatest homage we can pay to truth is to use it.
—Ralph Waldo Emerson

The highest compact we can make with our fellow is,—Let there be truth between us two forevermore.
—Ralph Waldo Emerson, *The Conduct of Life*, "Behavior"

We are of different opinions at different hours, but we always may be said at heart to be on the side of truth.   —Ralph Waldo Emerson

Wherever the truth is injured, defend it.
—Ralph Waldo Emerson, *Journals*

You need not fear to handle the truth roughly. She is no invalid.
—Ralph Waldo Emerson

The ultimate aim of the human mind, in all its efforts, is to become acquainted with Truth.
—Eliza Farnham, *Eliza and Her Era*, Part I, Ch. 1

From the physician and lawyer keep not the truth hidden.
—John Florio, *Firste Fruites*

All truth is not to be told at all times.
—Thomas Fuller, M. D., *Gnomologia*, No. 567

Craft must have clothes, but truth loves to go naked.
—Thomas Fuller, M. D., *Gnomologia*, No. 1200

Truth is the daughter of God.   —Thomas Fuller, M. D., *Gnomologia*

Truth makes the Devil blush.   —Thomas Fuller, M. D., *Gnomologia*

Truth in the end shall prevail.   —Ulpian Fulwell, *Ars Adulandi*

I believe in what Max Muller said years ago, namely, that truth needed to be repeated as long as there were men who disbelieved it.
—Mahatma Gandhi

To see the universal and all-pervading Spirit of Truth face to face one
must be able to love the meanest of creatures as oneself.
—Mahatma Gandhi

Truth never damages a cause that is just.
—Mahatma Gandhi, *Non-Violence in Peace and War*

Say not, "I have found the truth," but rather, "I have found a truth."
—Kahlil Gibran, *The Prophet*, "On Self-Knowledge"

Believe those who are seeking the truth; doubt those who find it.
—André Gide, *So Be It*

Let there be truth between us.   —Johann Wolfgang von Goethe

If you tell the truth, you have infinite power supporting you; but if
not, you have infinite power against you.   —Charles Gordon

What is true is what you can't help believing.
—Oliver Wendell Holmes, Jr.

It is the customary fate of new truths to begin as heresies and end as
superstitions.   —Thomas Henry Huxley, *Science and Culture*,
"The Coming of Age of the Origin of Species"

Time, whose tooth gnaws away everything else, is powerless against
truth.   —Thomas Henry Huxley

The man who finds a truth lights a torch.
—Robert G. Ingersoll, *The Truth*

We have to live today by what truth we can get today and be ready
tomorrow to call it falsehood.   —William James

You have no business with consequences; you are to tell the truth.
—Samuel Johnson

It takes few words to tell the truth.
—Chief Joseph of the Nez Percé (Native American)

Truth does less good in the world than its appearances do harm.
—François de La Rochefoucauld

Say the truth and shame the devil.   —Hugh Latimer, *Sermons*

Absolute truth belongs to Thee alone.   —Gotthold Ephraim Lessing

It is said that truth is often eclipsed but never extinguished. —Livy

Who dares / To say that he alone has found the truth?
　　　　　　　　　　　　　　—Henry Wadsworth Longfellow

Peace, if possible, but the truth at any rate. —Martin Luther

Man has no nobler function than to defend the truth.
　　　　　　　　　　—Ruth McKenney, letter to George Seldes

One should accept the truth from whatever source it proceeds.
　　　　　　　　　　　　　　　　　—Maimonides

You need not tell all the truth, unless to those who have a right to
　　know it; but let all you tell be truth. —Horace Mann

Man with his burning soul / Has but an hour of breath / To build a
　　ship of Truth / In which his soul may sail— / Sail on the sea of
　　death./ For death takes toll / Of beauty, courage, youth, / Of all but
　　Truth. —John Masefield, "Truth"

Tradition and conscience are the two wings given to the human soul
　　to reach the truth. —Giuseppe Mazzini

Hard are the ways of truth, and rough to walk.
　　　　　　　　　　—John Milton, *Paradise Regained*, Book I

Let her [Truth] and Falsehood grapple; who ever knew Truth put to
　　the worse in a free and open encounter?—John Milton, *Areopagitica*

A lie has speed, but truth has endurance. —Edgar J. Mohn

Some folks never handle the truth without scratching it.
　　　　　　　　　　　　　　　　—Austin O'Malley

We arrive at truth, not by reason only, but also by the heart.
　　　　　　　　　　　　　　—Blaise Pascal, *Pensées*

. . . the unarmed power of naked truth. —Boris Pasternak

Truth often suffers more by the heat of its defenders, than from the
　　argument of its opposers. —William Penn

Truth needs not many words. —Proverb (16th century)

Better suffer for truth than prosper by falsehood. —Proverb (Danish)

Time trieth truth.   —Proverb (English)

Socrates is dear to me, but truth is dearer still.   —Proverb (Latin)

Truth will out.   —Proverb (Latin)

The man who speaks the truth is always at ease. —Proverb (Persian)

All else will pass, but the truth will remain.   —Proverb (Russian)

One word of truth outweighs the world.
  —Proverb (Russian), in Alexander Solzhenitsyn, *Nobel Lecture*

Truth rests with God alone, and a little bit with me.
           —Proverb (Yiddish)

Every truth passes through three stages before it is recognized. In the
 first it is ridiculed, in the second it is opposed, in the third it is
 regarded as self-evident.   —Arthur Schopenhauer

The language of truth is simple.   —Seneca, *Ad Lucilium*, XLIX

Truth hath a quiet breast.
    —William Shakespeare, *King Richard II*, Act I, Sc. iii

. . . truth is truth to the end of reckoning.
    —William Shakespeare, *Measure for Measure*, Act V, Sc. I

All great truths begin as blasphemies.
      —George Bernard Shaw, *Annajanska*

If you will be guided by me, you will make little account of Socrates,
 and much more of truth.   —Socrates, in Plato, *Phoedo*

Even the most broad-minded of us can embrace only that part of
 truth into which our own snout has blundered.
    —Alexander Solzhenitsyn, *The Gulag Archipelago*

No one can bar the road to truth, and to advance its cause I am prepared to accept even death.
    —Alexander Solzhenitsyn, "Letter to the Fourth Congress
        of Soviet Writers," 16 May 1967

The trouble is, my boy's growing up, he's clever and he asks about
 everything. How ought I bring him up? Should I burden him with
 the whole truth?   —Alexander Solzhenitsyn, *Cancer Ward*

Truth must be told—and things must change! If words are not about
real things and do not cause things to happen, what is the good of
them?   —Alexander Solzhenitsyn, *The Gulag Archipelago Three*

The truth is always the strongest argument.   —Sophocles, *Phoedra*

The truth is ever best.   —Sophocles, *Antigone*

. . . in darkness God's truth shines most clear.
                —Corrie ten Boom, *The Hiding Place*, with
                              John and Elizabeth Sherrill

Between whom there is hearty truth, there is love.
                              —Henry David Thoreau

Truth burns up error.   —Sojourner Truth

When in doubt, tell the truth.   —Mark Twain, *Pudd'nhead Wilson*,
                        "Pudd'nhead Wilson's Calendar"

He who seeks truth should be of no country.   —Voltaire

Love truth, and pardon error.   —Voltaire

Truth is not a crystal that you can stash away in your pocket; it is an
infinite liquid into which you fall.   —Robert von Musil

It is one thing to wish to have truth on your side, and another to
wish sincerely to be on the side of truth.
                —Richard Whately, *On the Love of Truth*

Everything that is true is God's word, whoever may have said it.
                              —Ulrich Zwingli

TYRANNY

Tyrants have not yet discovered any chains that can fetter the mind.
                              —Charles Caleb Colton

Nature has left this tincture in the blood, / That all men would be
tyrants if they could.   —Daniel Defoe, *The Kentish Petition*

It's no use making peace with tyranny.
                —John Gardner, *October Light*, Ch. 4

Resistance to tyrants is obedience to God.   —Thomas Jefferson

O! it is excellent / To have a giant's strength; but it is tyrannous / To
   use it like a giant.
                              —William Shakespeare, *Measure for Measure*, Act II, Sc. ii

'Tis time to fear when tyrants seem to kiss.
                              —William Shakespeare, *Pericles*, Act I, Sc. ii

The most tyrannical governments are those which make crimes of
   opinions, for everyone has an inalienable right to his thoughts.
                              —Benedict de Spinoza, *Theologico-Political Treatise*, Ch. 18

— U —

U N C E R T A I N T Y

Unrest and uncertainty are our lot.
—Johann Wolfgang von Goethe, letter to
Sophie von La Roche, 1774

The only thing that makes life possible is permanent, intolerable
uncertainty, not knowing what comes next.   —Ursula LeGuin

U N D E R S T A N D I N G

A man only understands what is akin to some things already in his
mind.   —Henri Frédéric Amiel

I shall light a candle of understanding in thine heart, which shall not
be put out.   —Apocrypha, "2 Esdras," 14, 25

It's taken all my life to understand that it is not necessary to understand everything.   —René Coty

A man hears only what he understands.
—Johann Wolfgang von Goethe

. . . he understands who loves.   —Kabir

The well fed does not understand the lean.   —Proverb (Irish)

A man used to riding in a car cannot understand a pedestrian.
—Alexander Solzhenitsyn, *The Oak and the Calf*

No one can develop freely in this world and find a full life without
feeling understood by at least one person.   —Paul Tournier

U N I Q U E N E S S

You have a place to fill in the world, one no one else can fill. You are
important in God's plan whether you want to believe it or not.
—Anonymous

No one can bring to God what you can.
—Steve Hawthorne, guest sermon, Hope Chapel,
Austin, Texas, 11 Jan 1991

Every man is more than just himself; he also represents the unique, the very special and always significant and remarkable point at which the world's phenomena intersect, only once in this way and never again. —Herman Hesse

God gives you something only you can do. —Lewis Timberlake

The UNITED NATIONS

The United Nations was set up not to get us to heaven, but only to save us from hell. —Winston Churchill

... The real victim is the future.
—Dag Hammarskjöld, on efforts to discredit the United Nations

Let us make this floor the last battlefield.
—Gen. Carlos P. Romulo, said as Philippine ambassador to the United Nations in an address to its founding session

UNITY

All for one, and one for all. —Alexandre Dumas, *The Three Musketeers*

We must indeed all hang together, or, most assuredly, we shall all hang separately.
—Benjamin Franklin, remark to John Hancock at the signing of the Declaration of Independence, 4 Jul 1776

All your strength is in your union, All your danger is in discord; / Therefore be at peace henceforward, / And as brothers live together. —Henry Wadsworth Longfellow, "Hiawatha"

Union gives strength to the humble. —Publilius Syrus

Even weak men when united are powerful. —Friedrich Schiller

UNIVERSALITY

In every man there is something of all men. —G. C. Lichtenberg

The UNIVERSE

I cannot believe that the inscrutable universe turns on an axis of suffering; surely the strange beauty of the world must somewhere rest on pure joy. —Louise Bogan, letter to John Hall Wheelock

I don't pretend to understand the universe—it's a great deal bigger than I am . . . People ought to be modester.
—Thomas Carlyle, in D. A. Wilson and D. Wilson MacArthur, *Carlyle in Old Age* (1934)

The Universe is but one vast symbol of God.   —Thomas Carlyle

Whether or not it is clear to you, no doubt the universe is unfolding as it should.   —Max Ehrmann, "Desiderata"

. . . the universe is the property of every individual in it.
—Ralph Waldo Emerson

The universe begins to look more like a great thought than a great machine.   —Sir James Jeans, *The Mysterious Universe*, Ch. 5

The universe can best be pictured as consisting of pure thought, the thought of what for want of a better word we must describe as a mathematical thinker.
—Sir James Jeans, Rede Memorial lecture, Cambridge, 4 Nov 1930

The universe does not make sense without God.   —E. Stanley Jones

If the universe is so bad, or even half so bad, how on earth did human beings ever come to attribute it to the activity of a wise and good Creator?   —C. S. Lewis

The universe is full of magical things, patiently waiting for our wits to grow sharper.   —Eden Phillpotts, *A Shadow Passes*

Only God understands the universe.   —Proverb (German)

The universe is a thought of God.   —Friedrich Schiller

. . . something is afoot in the universe, something that looks like gestation and birth.   —Pierre Teilhard de Chardin

The universe is like a safe to which there is a combination—but the combination is locked up in the safe.   —Peter de Vries

The UNKNOWN

Rare indeed is the person who is neutral about the unknown.
—Anonymous

The difference between what the most and the least learned people know is inexpressibly trivial in relation to that which is unknown.
—Albert Einstein

UNSELFISHNESS

Real unselfishness consists in sharing the interests of others.
—George Santayana

USE

The used key is always bright.
—Benjamin Franklin, *Poor Richard's Almanack*, 1739

. . . I never was one to get upset about a few scratches on a motor vehicle, it is meant to be used, not saved.
—Garrison Keillor, *We Are Still Married*

Keep a thing seven years and you will find a use for it.
—Proverb (German)

The plow that works is always shiny.   —Proverb (Greek)

Even the prettiest shoe makes a sorry hat.   —Proverb (Japanese)

USELESSNESS

No one is useless in this world who lightens the burden of it to anyone else.   —Charles Dickens

. . . no man is useless while he has a friend. —Robert Louis Stevenson

— V —

VANITY

. . . vanity of vanities; all is vanity.   —*The Bible* (KJV): Ecclesiastes 1:2

But thou didst trust in thine own beauty.
—*The Bible* (KJV): Ezekiel 16:15

Vanity plays lurid tricks with our memory.
—Joseph Conrad, *Lord Jim* (1900)

Vanity is the greatest of all flatterers. —François de La Rochefoucauld

Dear to girls' hearts is their own beauty. —Ovid, *De Medicamine Faciei*

Vanity is often the unseen spur.   —William Makepeace Thackeray

VARIETY

Variety's the very spice of life,
   That gives it all its flavor.
—William Cowper, *The Task*, Book II, "The Timepiece"

VEGETARIANISM

Meat is murder.   —Anonymous, bumper sticker

Respect animals; don't eat them.   —Anonymous, bumper sticker

A vegetarian is a person who won't eat anything that can have children.   —David Brenner

I have always eaten animal flesh with a somewhat guilty conscience.
—Albert Einstein, Einstein Archive 60-058, Aug 1953

VICES

Vices are their own punishment.
—Aesop, *Fables*, "Avaricious and Envious"

Avoid dishonest gain; no price can recompense the pang of vice.
—Anonymous

If we tread our vices under our feet, we make of them a ladder by
which to rise to higher things.   —Saint Augustine, *Sermo*, clxxvii.

This is the essential evil of vice: it debases a man.
                                    —Edwin Hubbel Chapin

Search others for their virtues, thyself for thy vices.
                          —Benjamin Franklin, *Poor Richard's Almanack*, 1738

As virtue is its own reward, so vice is its own punishment.
                          —Thomas Fuller, M. D., *Gnomologia*, No. 743

When our vices leave us, we flatter ourselves with the credit of having
left them.   —François de La Rochefoucauld, *Maximes*

Spare the person but lash the vice.   —Martial

He that can apprehend and consider vice with all her baits and seeming pleasures, and yet abstain, and yet distinguish and prefer that
which is truly better, he is the true warfaring Christian.
                                    —John Milton, *Areopagitica*

Be at peace with men, at war with their vices.   —Proverb (Latin)

Men love their vices and hate them at the same time.   —Seneca

VICTIMIZATION

To be a complete victim may be another source of power.
                                    —Iris Murdoch, *The Unicorn*

VICTORY

The victor belongs to the spoils.   —F. Scott Fitzgerald

On the day of victory no one is tired.   —Proverb (Arab)

Great is the victory that is gained without bloodshed.
                                    —Proverb (Spanish)

There is no pain in the wound received in the moment of victory.
                                    —Publilius Syrus, *Moral Sayings*

The first step on the way to victory is to recognize the enemy.
                                    —Corrie ten Boom

V I G O R

Vigor is contagious; and whatever makes us either think or feel
strongly adds to our power and enlarges our field of action.
—Ralph Waldo Emerson

V I L L A I N S

. . . one may smile, and smile, and be a villain.
—William Shakespeare, *Hamlet*, Act I, Sc. v

V I O L E N C E

Violence begets violence. —Anonymous

He who achieves power by violence does not truly become lord or
master. —Saint Thomas Aquinas

Violence is the last refuge of the incompetent.
—Isaac Asimov, *Foundation*

The only thing that's been a worse flop than the organization of non-
violence has been the organization of violence.
—Joan Baez, *Daybreak*, "What Would You Do If?"

Treachery and violence are spears pointed at both ends.
—Emile Brontë, *Wuthering Heights*, Ch. 17

Where violence reigns, reason is weak. —Nicolas Chamfort

One of the great meanings of the Cross was the deliberate repudia-
tion by Christ of violence as a means of overcoming evil.
—Executive Body of London Yearly Meeting [Quakers], Sep 1914

. . . I am an uncompromising opponent of violent methods even to
serve the noblest of causes . . .
—Mahatma Gandhi, in *Young India*, 11 Dec 1924

Nothing good ever comes of violence. —Martin Luther

Suppose that men kill thee, cut thee in pieces, curse thee, what can
these things do to prevent thy mind from remaining pure, wise,
sober, just? —Marcus Aurelius Antoninus

You can almost be certain that the man who commits violent crimes
has been treated violently as a child. —Karl Menninger

Nothing that is violent is permanent.   —Proverb (16th century)

Power exercised with violence has seldom been of long duration . . .
    —Seneca

These violent delights have violent ends / And in their triumph die,
  like fire and powder, / Which as thy kiss consume . . .
    —William Shakespeare, *Romeo and Juliet*, Act II, Sc. vi

What can literature do against the pitiless onslaught of naked violence? Let us not forget that violence does not and cannot flourish
  by itself; it is inevitably intertwined with lying . . . It [violence]
  does not always or necessarily go straight for the gullet; usually it
  demands only allegiance to the lie . . .
The simple act of an ordinary courageous man is not to take part, not
  to support lies! Let that come into the world and even reign over it,
  but not through me. Writers and artists can do more: they can van-
  quish lies! . . . Lies can stand up against much in the world, but not
  against art.   —Alexander Solzhenitsyn, *Nobel Lecture*

God, in His wisdom, has so linked the whole human family together
  that any violence done at one end of the chain is felt throughout
  its length.   —Elizabeth Cady Stanton, speech to the First
    Women's Rights Convention, 19 Jul 1848

I am obliged to renounce violence, and abstain from it altogether.
    —Leo Tolstoy

VIRGINITY

Virginity is not honored simply because it is virginity, but because it
  is consecrated of God.   —Augustine of Hippo

VIRTUE

The virtue which we appreciate we to some extent appropriate.
    —Anonymous

Virtue is the safest helmet.
    —Anonymous, motto of The Golden Hind,
    whose captain was Francis Drake

Virtue is the strongest shield.   —Anonymous

Virtue which parleys is near a surrender. —Anonymous

Virtue is like a rich stone, best plain set.
—Francis Bacon, *Essays*, "Of Beauty"

Many wish not so much to be virtuous, as to seem to be. —Cicero

Virtue is its own reward. —Cicero, *De Finibus*, Book II

Virtue, though in rags, will keep me warm.
—John Dryden, *Imitation of Horace*

Try not to be a person of success, but rather a person of virtue.
—Albert Einstein

There is no sanctuary of virtue like home. —E. Everett

Is virtue raised by culture, or self-sown? —Horace, *Epistles*, I

Virtue consists in fleeing vice. —Horace, *Epistles*, I

He that would have his virtue published, is not the servant of virtue,
but glory. —Ben Jonson

Wisdom is knowing what to do next; virtue is doing it.
—David Starr Jordan, *The Philosophy of Despair*

Virtue treads paths that end not in the grave. —James Russell Lowell

When you can't have anything else, you can have virtue.
—Don Marquis

The strength of a man's virtue should not be measured by his special
exertions, but by his habitual acts. —Blaise Pascal

The most virtuous of all men is he that contents himself with being
virtuous without seeking to appear so. —Plato

He who dies for virtue does not perish. —Plautus, *Captivi*

Know then this truth, enough for man to know, "Virtue alone is happiness below." —Alexander Pope, *An Essay on Man*

Virtue never dwells alone; it always has neighbors.
—Proverb (Chinese)

Beauty without virtue is a rose without scent. —Proverb (Danish)

Virtue is a sure anchor. —Proverb (Latin)

Virtue survives death. —Proverb (Latin)

Virtue unites man with God. —Proverb (Latin)

The virtue of man is, in a word, the great proof of God.
—Ernest Renan

The glory of wealth and of beauty is fleeting and frail; virtue is illustrious and everlasting. —Sallust

Virtue, though clothed in a beggar's garb, commands respect.
—Friedrich Schiller

We are born to lose and to perish, to hope and to fear, to vex ourselves and others; and there is no antidote against a common calamity but virtue; for the foundation of true joy is in the conscience. —Seneca

Virtue unrewarded is doubly beautiful. —Seume

Assume a virtue, if you have it not.
—William Shakespeare, *Hamlet*, Act III, Sc. iv

Virtue consists, not in abstaining from vice, but in not desiring it.
—George Bernard Shaw

I am no herald to inquire of men's pedigrees; it sufficeth me if I know their virtues. —Sir Philip Sidney

We have been fortunate enough to live at a time when virtue, though it does not triumph, is nonetheless not always tormented by attack dogs. Beaten down, sickly, virtue has now been allowed to enter in all its tatters and sit in the corner, as long as it doesn't raise its voice. —Alexander Solzhenitsyn, *The Gulag Archipelago*

We must not forget that our vocation is to practice virtue that men are won to it; it is possible to be morally upright repulsively.
—William Temple

Heaven made virtue; man, the appearance. —Voltaire

Few men have virtue to withstand the highest bidder.
—George Washington

VISION

Better one-eyed than stone-blind.   —Anonymous

In the land of the blind, the one-eyed is king.
—Apostolius, *Paroemiae*, VII, xxiii

Sight is the noblest sense of man.   —Albrecht Dürer

One of the most wonderful things in nature is a glance of the eye; it
transcends speech; it is the bodily symbol of identity.
—Ralph Waldo Emerson

The sky is the daily bread of the eyes.
—Ralph Waldo Emerson, *Journals*

In the country of the blind the one-eyed man is king.
—Erasmus, *Adages*

None so blind as those who won't see.   —John Heywood, *Proverbs*

Women's glances express what they dare not speak.   —Alphonse Karr

True vision is always twofold. It involves emotional comprehension
as well as physical perception. Yet how rarely we have either. We
generally only glance at an object long enough to tag it with a
name.   —Ross Parmenter, *The Plant in My Window*, "The Pothook"

It is my eyes which see, and the sight of my eyes grants beauty to the
earth.   —Ayn Rand, *Anthem*

One single glance will conquer all descriptions.
—Martin Farquhar Tupper

To see is to forget the name of the thing one sees.
—Paul Valéry, *Selected Writings*

VISIONS

Nowhere does the Bible say that anyone was seeking a vision when it
came. They just happened without their seeking it.
—Kenneth Hagin, *How You Can Be Led by the Spirit of God*

VISITS

A short visit is best and that not too often. —Proverb (Irish)

VOICE

The voice is a second face. —Gérard Bauër, *Carnets inédits*

Like music on the waters is thy sweet voice to me. —Lord Byron

Her voice was ever soft, / Gentle, and low, an excellent thing in
woman. —William Shakespeare, *King Lear*, Act V, Sc. iii

VOID

That there should absolutely be nothing at all is utterly impossible.
The mind, let it stretch its conceptions ever so far, can never so
much as bring itself to conceive of a state of perfect nothing.
—Jonathan Edwards

VOTING

There no longer can be anyone too poor to vote.
—Lyndon B. Johnson, upon signing the 24th amendment,
which banned the poll tax in federal elections

The ballot is stronger than the bullet.
—Abraham Lincoln, speech, 1856

America is a land where a citizen will cross the ocean to fight for
democracy—and won't cross the street to vote in a national election. —Bill Vaughan

VOWS

The vow that binds too strictly snaps itself. —Anonymous

VULGARITY

... vulgarity has no nation. —Arthur Miller, *Incident at Vichy*

VULNERABILITY

Everyone is, in his own way, vulnerable. —Anonymous

To be is to be vulnerable. —Norman O. Brown

— W —

WAITING

He [God] never comes to those who do not wait.
—Frederick William Faber

How wonderful it is that nobody need wait a single moment before
starting to improve the world.   —Anne Frank

We wait always for something that does not come.
—Ernest Hemingway, *Islands in the Stream*

He who waits for a roast duck to fly into his mouth must wait for a
very, very long time.   —Proverb (Chinese)

Once a man would spend a week patiently waiting if he missed a
stage coach, but now he rages if he misses the first section of a
revolving door.   —Simeon Strunsky

WALKING

We make the path by walking.   —Robert Bly, *Iron John*, Preface

Road's in front o' me, / Nothin' to do but walk.   —Langston Hughes

If you are seeking creative ideas, go out walking. Angels whisper to a
man when he goes for a walk.   —Raymond Inmon

It is good walking when one hath his horse in hand.   —John Lyly

Walking is good for the soul.   —Andrew A. Rooney, *Word for Word*,
"Walking with Horse in Hand"

Walking is the favorite sport of the good and wise.
—A. L. Rowse, *The Use of History*

WALLS

The wall must go.
—Anonymous, chant in the streets of Berlin, 11 Nov 1989, as the
wall was being torn down

Something there is that doesn't love a wall, / That wants it down.
—Robert Frost, "Mending Wall"

People are lonely because they build walls instead of bridges.
—Joseph Fort Newton

. . . maybe it is only by banging our heads against it that we can bring this accursed wall down.
—Alexander Solzhenitsyn, *The Gulag Archipelago Three*

W A N T S

If you don't get everything you want, think of the things you don't get that you don't want.
—Anonymous

Poverty wants some things, luxury many things, and avarice all things.
—Anonymous

I want, I want.
—Saul Bellow, *Henderson the Rain King*

Necessities are few, but our wants are endless.   —Benjamin Franklin

Constantly choose rather to want less, than to have more.
—Thomas à Kempis

W A R

The Spartans do not inquire how many the enemy are, but where they are.
—Agis II, King of Sparta

Federals—respect my father's corpse.
—Anonymous, penciled note on the body of a Confederate officer at the Battle of Shiloh, according to a Union officer, *The Civil War in Song & Story*

Good kings never make war, but for the sake of peace. —Anonymous

The price of pride is high, and paid by the young.
—Anonymous, inscription on the German memorial at Alamein

There will be more wars until men grow brave enough to stop them.
—Anonymous

They shall not pass.—Anonymous, slogan used by French army at the defense of Verdun in 1916, variously attributed to Marshal Pétain and to Gen. Robert Nivelle

Too many dead, not enough tears.
  —Anonymous, line delivered by the character Coleen McMurphy
         in the TV series *China Beach*

War is a blunt instrument.
              —Anonymous

War is the science of destruction.
              —Anonymous

Even in waging war, cherish the spirit of peace-maker; that, by conquering those whom you attack, you may lead them back to the
advantages of peace.
           —Saint Augustine

O God of love, / O King of peace, / Make wars throughout the world
to cease.
            —Henry W. Baber

In peace the sons bury their fathers and in war the fathers bury their
sons.
            —Francis Bacon

It takes twenty years or more of peace to make a man; it takes only
twenty seconds of war to destroy him.
        —King Baudouin I, of Belgium

Let us determine to die here, and we will conquer. There is Jackson
standing like a stone wall. Rally behind the Virginians.
  —Gen. Bernard Elliott Bee, at the First Battle of Bull Run, 1861

It is not merely cruelty that leads men to love war, it is excitement.
    —Henry Ward Beecher, in William Drysdale, editor,
          Proverbs from Plymouth Pulpit

All quiet along the Potomac they say / Except now and then a stray
picket Is shot as he walks on his beat, to and fro, / By a rifleman hid
in the thicket.
     —Ethel Lynn Beers, "All Quiet Along the Potomac,"
          in *Harper's Magazine*, 1861

All quiet along the Potomac to-night, / No sound save the rush of the
river, While soft falls the dew on the face of the dead— / The
picket's off duty forever.
     —Ethel Lynn Beers, "All Quiet Along the Potomac,"
          in *Harper's Magazine*, 1861

Certain blood will be given for half certain reasons, as in all wars.
        —Saul Bellow, *Dangling Man*

It you start to take Vienna—take Vienna. —Napoleon Bonaparte

War is the business of barbarians.   —Napoleon Bonaparte

. . . someday we'll remember so much we'll build the biggest god-
    damn steamshovel in history and dig the biggest grave of all time
    and shove war in and cover it up.   —Ray Bradbury, *Fahrenheit 451*

And to him war was a thing like earth and sky and water and why it
    was no one knew but only that it was.
                          —Pearl S. Buck, *The Good Earth*, Ch. 31

There are no warlike peoples—just warlike leaders.   —Ralph Bunche

War never leaves where it found a nation.
                    —Edmund Burke, *Letters on a Regicide Peace*

God is usually on the side of the big squadrons against the small.
                     —Comte de Bussy-Rabutin,
                letter to Comte de Limoges, 18 Oct 1677

Christianity has not failed. It is simply that nations have failed to try
    it. There would be no war in a God-directed world.
                      —Admiral Richard E. Byrd

A thousand years scarce serves to form a State; an hour may lay it in
    the dust.   —Lord Byron

I came, I saw, I conquered.
              —Julius Caesar, after victory at Zela, 47 B.C.

What millions died—that Caesar might be great!
              —Thomas Campbell, *Pleasures of Hopes*

A battle is a terrible conjugation of the verb to kill: I kill, thou killest,
    he kills, we kill, they kill, all kill.   —Thomas Carlyle

War will never yield but to the principles of universal justice and
    love, and these have no sure root but in the religion of Jesus Christ.
                    —William Ellery Channing

Earth will grow worse till men redeem it, / And wars more evil, ere all
    wars cease.   —G. K. Chesterton, "A Song of Defeat"

One is left with the horrible feeling now that war settles *nothing*; that
    to *win* a war is as disastrous as to lose one!
                —Agatha Christie, *An Autobiography*

[In war] the latest refinements of science are linked with the cruelties
  of the Stone Age.
> —Winston Churchill, speech, London, 26 Mar 1942

Boys are the cash of war.
> —John Ciardi, *This Strangest Thing*, "New Year's Eve"

Laws are silent in time of war.
> —Cicero, *Pro Milone*

The only excuse for war is that we may live in peace unharmed.
> —Cicero, *De Officiis*, Book I

War should be undertaken in such a way as to show that its only
  object is peace.
> —Cicero, *De Officiis*, Book I

War is a series of catastrophes which result in victory.
> —Georges Clemenceau

And blood in torrents pours in vain—always in vain, / For war breeds
  war again.
> —John Davidson, "War Song"

The world will never have lasting peace so long as men reserve for
  war the finest human qualities.
> —John Foster Dulles

How many deaths will it take 'til he knows / That too many people
  have died?
> —Bob Dylan, "Blowin' in the Wind" (song)

How vile and despicable war seems to me! I would rather be hacked to
  pieces than take part in such an abominable business.
> —Albert Einstein

I appeal to all men and women, whether they be eminent or humble,
  to declare that they will refuse to give any further assistance to war
  or the preparation of war.   —Albert Einstein, in a statement to the
> War Resistors International, Lyons, 1931

I believe serious progress [in the abolition of war] can be achieved
  only when men become organized on an international scale and
  refuse, as a body, to enter military or war service.
> —Albert Einstein, statement in *Jugendtribüne*, 17 Apr 1931

I don't know what will be used in the next world war, but the fourth
  will be fought with stones.
> —Albert Einstein

To my mind, to kill in war is not a whit better than to commit ordinary murder.
> —Albert Einstein, *Ideas and Opinions*

I firmly believe that the future of civilization is absolutely dependent
upon finding some way of resolving international differences without resorting to war. —Dwight D. Eisenhower

I hate war as only a soldier who has lived it can, only as one who has
seen its brutality, its futility, its stupidity. —Dwight D. Eisenhower

War, to sane men at the present day, begins to look like an epidemic
insanity, breaking out here and there like the cholera or influenza,
infecting men's brains instead of their bowels.
—Ralph Waldo Emerson, *Miscellanies*, "War"

War is sweet to those who do not fight.
—Gerard Bidier Erasmus, *Adagia*

All wars are civil wars, because all men are brothers . . . Each one owes
infinitely more to the human race than to the particular country in
which he was born. —François Fénelon

The blood of a nation ought never to be shed except for its own
preservation in the utmost extremity.
—François Fénelon, *Télémaque*, Book XIII

My center is giving way, my right is retreating. Situation excellent. I
shall attack.
—Marshal Ferdinand Foch, message to Joffre,
Sep 1914, in Aston, *Biography of Foch*

I renounce war for its consequences, for the lies it lives on and propa-
gates, for the undying hatred it arouses, for the dictatorships it
puts in the place of democracy, for the starvation that stalks after
it. I renounce war and never again, directly or indirectly, will I
sanction or support it. —Harry Emerson Fosdick

The tragedy of war is that it uses man's best to do man's worst.
—Harry Emerson Fosdick

I have bin [sic] in one battle, and that satisfied me with war and I
would beg to be excused next time.
—Habun R. Foster, Confederate soldier from Virginia, 26 Jul 1862

Men love war because it allows them to look serious. Because it is the
only thing that stops women from laughing at them.
—John Fowles, *The Magus*

There never was a good war or a bad peace.
>   —Benjamin Franklin, letter to Josiah Quincy, 11 Sep 1783

God is always with the strongest battalions.
>   —Frederick the Great, letter to the
>   Duchess Luise Dorothea von Gotha, 9 May 1760

. . . every man has a right over his own life and war destroys lives that
were full of promise; it forces the individual into situations that
shame his manhood, obliging him to murder fellow men, against
his will . . .   —Sigmund Freud, letter to Albert Einstein, Sep 1932

Either man is obsolete or war is.
>   —R. Buckminster Fuller, *I Seem To be a Verb*

I believe all war to be wholly wrong.
>   —Mahatma Gandhi, *Harijanz*, 18 Aug 1940

War with all its glorification of brute force is essentially a degrading
thing.   —Mahatma Gandhi, *Indian Opinion*, 12 Feb 1910

You cannot stop big wars if you carry on little wars yourselves.
>   —Mahatma Gandhi

How sweet war is to such as know it not.   —George Gascoigne, *Posies*

What if someone gave a war & Nobody came? Life would ring the
bells of Ecstasy and Forever be Itself again.
>   —Allen Ginsberg, *Fall of America*, "Graffiti"

All wars are wars among thieves who are too cowardly to fight and
who therefore induce the young manhood of the whole world to
do the fighting for them.   —Emma Goldman, 1917

He who fights and runs away, / May live to fight another day; / But he
who is in battle slain / Can never rise and fight again.
>   —Oliver Goldsmith

I have never advocated war except as a means of peace.
>   —Ulysses S. Grant

War determines not who is right but who is left.
>   —Rabbi Sidney Greenberg

War is death's feast.   —George Herbert, *Jacula Prudentum*

War will cease when men refuse to fight. —F. Hansen

Yes, quaint and curious war is! / You shoot a fellow down / You'd treat
if met where any bar is, / Or help to half-a-crown.
—Thomas Hardy, "The Man He Killed"

Those who are at war with others are not at peace with themselves.
—William Hazlitt

Frankly, I'd like to see government get out of war altogether and leave
the whole field to private industry. —Joseph Heller, *Catch-22*

There was only one catch and that was Catch-22, which specified
that a concern for one's own safety in the face of dangers that were
real and immediate was the process of a rational mind.
—Joseph Heller, *Catch-22*

. . . never think that war, no matter how necessary, nor how justified,
is not a crime. Ask the infantry and ask the dead.
—Ernest Hemingway

When war begins, then hell openeth.
—George Herbert, *Jacula Prudentum*

In peace sons bury fathers, but war violates the order of nature, and
fathers bury sons. —Herodotus, *Histories*

We should wage war not to win war, but to win peace.
—Paul Hoffman

It is not right to exult over slain men. —Homer, *Odyssey*

Older men declare war. But it is youth that must fight and die.
—Herbert Hoover, speech at the Republican national convention,
Chicago, 27 Jun 1944

Man is unique in organizing the mass murder of his own species.
—Aldous Huxley

What is absurd and monstrous about war is that men who have no
personal quarrel should be trained to murder one another in cold
blood. —Aldous Huxley

The object of war is to survive it. —John Irving

So far war has been the only force that can discipline a whole community, and until an equivalent discipline is organized, I believe
that war must have its way.   —William James

The first casualty when war comes is truth.
                    —Hiram Johnson, speech in the U. S. Senate, 1917

In modern warfare there are no victors; there are only survivors.
                    —Lyndon B. Johnson

Among the calamities of war may justly be numbered the diminution
of the love of truth.   —Samuel Johnson, *The Idler*

I have not yet begun to fight.
                    —John Paul Jones, reply to a surrender ultimatum, as
                    his ship Bonhomme Richard was sinking, 23 Sep 1779

No state at war with another state should engage in hostilities of such
a kind as to render mutual confidence impossible when peace will
have been made.   —Immanuel Kant

I look upon the whole world as my fatherland, and every war has to
me the horror of a family feud.   —Helen Keller

Mankind must put an end to war, or war will put an end to mankind.
                    —John F. Kennedy, United Nations address, 25 Sep 1961

People have not been horrified by war to a sufficient extent . . . War
will exist until that distant day when the conscientious objector
enjoys the same reputation and prestige as the warrior does today.
                    —John F. Kennedy

If I live, I mean to spend the rest of my life working for perpetual
peace. I have seen war and faced artillery and know what an outrage it is against simple men.
                    —Thomas Kettle, killed during World War I at the Somme

Everything, everything in war is barbaric . . . But the worst barbarity
of war is that it forces men collectively to commit acts against
which individually they would revolt with their whole being.
                    —Ellen Key, *War, Peace, and the Future*

War is a poor chisel to carve out tomorrows. —Martin Luther King, Jr.

The slaying of multitudes should be mourned with sorrow. A victory should be celebrated with the funeral rite.
>—Lao Tzu, *The Character of Tao*

To delight in conquest is to delight in slaughter.
>—Lao Tzu

There is no such thing as an inevitable war. If war comes it will be from failure of human wisdom.
>—Bonar Law, speech, Jul 1914

God ordered otherwise.
>—Gen. Robert E. Lee, General Orders No. 5, 7 May 1863, on why the Confederates lost at Chancellorsville

He has lost his left arm, but I have lost my right.
>—Gen. Robert E. Lee, on hearing of Gen. Stonewall Jackson's death at Chancellorsville, 4 May 1863

It is well that war is so terrible, or we should grow too fond of it.
>—Gen. Robert E. Lee, on seeing a Federal charge repulsed at Fredericksburg, Dec 1862

What a cruel thing is war: to separate and destroy families and friends; and mar the purest joys and happiness God has granted us in this world: to fill our hearts with hatred instead of love for our neighbors, and to devastate the fair face of this beautiful world.
>—Gen. Robert E. Lee, letter to his wife, 25 Dec 1862

He had grown up in a country run by politicians who sent the pilots to man the bombers to kill the babies to make the world safer for children to grow up in.
>—Ursula LeGuin, *The Lathe of Heaven*

Military glory—that attractive rainbow that rises in showers of blood, that serpent's eye that charms to destroy.
>—Abraham Lincoln, speech against the war with Mexico, U. S. House of Representatives, 12 Jan 1848

Ez fer war, I call it murder— / There you hev it plain an' flat; / I don't want to go no furder   Than my Testyment fer that.
>—James Russell Lowell, *The Biglow Papers*, Series I

Ninepence a day fer killin' folks comes kind o' low fer murder.
>—James Russell Lowell, *The Biglow Papers*, Series I

We kind o' thought Christ went agin war an' pillage.
>—James Russell Lowell, *The Biglow Papers*, Series I

I know war as few other men now living know it, and nothing to me
is more revolting. I have long advocated its complete abolition, as
its very destructiveness on both friend and foe has rendered it useless as a method of settling international affairs.
—Gen. Douglas MacArthur, address to Congress, 19 Apr 1951

I shall return.
—Gen. Douglas MacArthur, to his fellow officers when he departed
from the Philippine Islands for Australia, 11 Mar 1942

Nuts! —Gen. Anthony C. McAuliffe, answer to a German demand for
surrender at Bastogne, Belgium, 22 Dec 1944

War should never be entered upon until every agency of peace has
failed.   —William McKinley, Inaugural Address, 4 Mar 1897

In Flanders fields the poppies blow / Between the crosses, row on row.
—John Macrae, "In Flanders Fields"

Accurst be he that first invented war.
—Christopher Marlowe, *Tamburlaine the Great*, Act II, Sc. iv

Any government has as much of a duty to avoid war as a ship's captain has to avoid a shipwreck.   —Guy de Maupassant

War is only an invention, not a biological necessity. —Margaret Mead

In the long run all battles are lost, and so are all wars.
—H. L. Mencken

And this I hate—not men, nor flag nor race, / But only War with its
wild grinning face.   —Joseph Dana Miller

For what can war but endless war still breed?
—John Milton, Sonnet XV, "On the Lord
General Fairfax at the siege of Colchester"

Every war is a national misfortune.
—Helmuth von Moltke, speech, 1880

There will be no veterans of World War III.
—Walter Mondale, speech, 5 Sep 1984

War hath no fury like a non-combatant.
—C. E. Montague, *Disenchantment*

War is a specific product of civilization.   —Lewis Mumford

Anyone who isn't confused doesn't really understand the situation.
                    —Edward R. Murrow, about the Vietnam War

Make love not war.   —Howard Nemerov

Before we become too arrogant with the most deadly of the seven
    deadly sins, the sin of pride, let us remember that the two great
    wars of this century, wars which cost twenty million dead, were
    fought between Christian nations praying to the same God.
                    —Richard M. Nixon

The only true solution would be a convention under which all the
    governments would bind themselves to defend collectively any
    country that was attacked.   —Alfred Nobel

Men killed, and died, because they were embarrassed not to.
                    —Tim O'Brien, *The Things They Carried*

My subject is War, and the pity of War. The Poetry is in the pity.
                    —Wilfred Owen

Red lips are not so red / As the stained stones kissed by the English
    dead.   —Wilfred Owen, *Poems*, "Greater Loved"

And war—the worst form of evil!   —Theodore Parker

Can anything be more ridiculous than that a man has a right to kill
    men because he dwells on the other side of the water, and because
    his prince has a quarrel with mine, although I have none with
    him?   —Blaise Pascal

Don't cheer, boys; the poor devils are dying.
                    —Captain John Woodward Philip, said on the
                    Battleship Texas about the burning Spanish ship
                    Vizcaya during the Battle of Santiago, 4 Jul 1898

The theory of war as an apt and proportionate means of solving inter-
    national conflicts is now out of date.   —Pope Pius XII

In time of war the devil makes more room in hell.—Proverb (German)

The devil invented war and fools practice it.   —Proverb (Greek)

War begun—hell unchained.   —Proverb (Italian)

Sweet is war to those who have never experienced it.—Proverb (Latin)

When the flag is unfurled, all reason is in the trumpet.
—Proverb (Ukrainian)

One more such victory, and we are undone.
—King Pyrrhus of Epirus, after fighting the Romans
at Asculum, 279 B.C.

War is, after all, the universal perversion . . . war stories, the pornography of war.
—John Rae, *The Custard Boys*

As a woman I can't go to war, and I refuse to send anyone else.
—Jeannette Rankin, in Hannah Josephson,
Jeannette Rankin: First Lady in Congress

You can no more win a war than you can win an earthquake.
—Jeannette Rankin, in Hannah Josephson,
Jeannette Rankin: First Lady in Congress

He that preaches war is the devil's chaplain.
—John Ray, *English Proverbs* (1670)

To-day we have naming of parts. Yesterday / We had daily cleaning.
And tomorrow morning, / We shall have what to do after firing.
But to-day, / To-day we have naming of parts.
—Henry Reed, "Naming of Parts" (1946)

All Quiet on the Western Front.
—Erich Maria Remarque, title of translation of his 1929 novel *Im
Western nichts Neues* (Nothing New in the West)

You can't say civilization don't advance . . . for in every war they kill
you a new way.   —Will Rogers, *The Autobiography of Will Rogers*

Love of my country does not demand that I shall hate and slay those
noble and faithful souls who also love theirs.   —Romain Rolland

Everyone hates war, everyone says.
—Andrew A. Rooney, *Word for Word*, "Explaining It All for You"

Sooner or later the world will have to return to the good old days
when we fought wars and killed people the old-fashioned way, one
at a time.   —Andrew A. Rooney, *Word for Word*,
"The One-Man, One Gun Conference"

Don't hit at all if it is honorably possible to avoid hitting; but never
hit soft! —Theodore Roosevelt

War is not an adventure. It is a disease.
—Antoine de Saint-Exupéry, *Flight to Arras*

It is always easy to begin a war, but very difficult to stop one. —Sallust

Sometime they'll give a war and nobody will come.
—Carl Sandburg, "The People, Yes"

When the rich wage war it is the poor who die. —Jean-Paul Sartre

Who will remember, passing through this gate, / The unheroic dead
who fed the guns? / Who shall absolve the foulness of their fate—
/ Those doomed, conscripted, unvictorious ones.
—Siegfried Sassoon, "On Passing the New Menin Gate"

War is not healthy for children and other living things.
—Lorraine Schneider

Women's rights, men's rights—human rights—all are threatened by
the everpresent specter of war so destructive now of human material and moral values as to render victory indistinguishable from
defeat.
—Rosika Schwimmer, speech, Centennial Celebration
of Seneca Falls Convention of Woman's Rights, Jul 1948

. . . that devil's madness—War.
—Robert William Service, *Ballads of a Bohemian*, "Michael"

O war! thou son of Hell!
—William Shakespeare, *King Henry VI, Part II*, Act V, Sc. ii

They there may dig each other's graves, / And call the sad work glory.
—Percy Shelley, "Battlefields"

I am tired and sick of war. Its glory is all moonshine. It is only those
who have neither fired a shot nor heard the shrieks and groans of
the wounded who cry aloud for blood, more vengeance, more des-
olation. War is hell. —Gen. William Tecumseh Sherman

There's many a boy here today who looks on war as all glory, but,
boys, it is all hell.—Gen. William Tecumseh Sherman, speech, 1880

War at best is barbarism. —Gen. William Tecumseh Sherman

You cannot qualify war in harsher terms than I will. War is cruelty, and you cannot refine it.
> —Gen. William Tecumseh Sherman, *Memoirs*

Any fool can bomb a train, but just try sorting out the mess.
> —Alexander Solzhenitsyn, *Stories and Prose Poems*,
> "An Incident at Krechetovka Station"

A whole week, a single campaign, a month, a week, even a day was far more than enough to cut a company or platoon to ribbons or cripple a man for life: it needed only a quarter of an hour.
> —Alexander Solzhenitsyn, *August 1914*

It takes a fool to rush off to war!
> —Alexander Solzhenitsyn, *The Gulag Archipelago*

Only a magician can fix a head on a body, but any fool can lop it off.
> —Alexander Solzhenitsyn, *Cancer Ward*

Whither and to what end will we . . . be moving? To beat the enemy over the head with a club—even cavemen knew that.
> —Alexander Solzhenitsyn, *The Gulag Archipelago Two*

War loves to seek its victims in the young.
> —Sophocles

It must be a hard thing to kill a man you don't know and don't hate.
> —John Steinbeck, *East of Eden*

War under modern conditions is bereft of even that dubious logic it may have had in the past.
> —Adlai Stevenson

War, that mad game the world so loves to play.
> —Jonathan Swift, "Ode to Sir William Temple"

How mad it is to summon grim death by means of war!
> —Tibillus, *Elegies*

We have met here to fight against war. The truth is that one may not and should not in any circumstances or under any pretext kill his fellow man.
> —Leo Tolstoy, speech, Swedish Government
> Congress Peace Conference, 1909

If we do not abolish war on this earth, then surely one day war will abolish us from the earth.
> —Harry S. Truman, speech, Independence, Missouri, 1966

Vice stirs up war; virtue fights. —Luc de Clapiers Vauvenargues

War! horrible war! —Virgil

War is the greatest of all crimes; and yet there is no aggressor who
    does not color his crime with the pretext of justice.
                        —Voltaire, *The Ignorant Philosopher*

Oh woe be to orders that marched my love away.
        —"The Wars of Germany," words and music traditional

Nothing except a battle lost can be half so melancholy as a battle
    won.
                    —Arthur Wellesley, 1st Duke of Wellington,
                        military dispatch from Waterloo, 1815

Take my word for it: If you had seen but one day of war you would
    pray to Almighty God that you might never see such again.
                    —Arthur Wellesley, 1st Duke of Wellington

As long as war is regarded as wicked, it will always have its fascina-
    tion. When it is looked upon as vulgar, it will cease to be popular.
                    —Oscar Wilde, "The Critic as Artist"

. . . a war always ends. —Herman Wouk, *The Winds of War*

Strange, isn't it, that warfare has come down to fencing with compli-
    cated toys that only a few seedy scholars can make or understand.
                    —Herman Wouk, *The Winds of War*

W A S T E

Willful waste brings woeful want. —Thomas Fuller

Waste not, want not. —Thomas Hardy

W A T E R

A drowning man will catch at a straw. —Anonymous

Vast is the mighty ocean, but drops have made it vast. —Anonymous

God brings men into deep waters, not to drown them, but to cleanse
    them. —Aughey

Water, water, everywhere, / Nor any drop to drink.
—Samuel Taylor Coleridge, *Rime of the Ancient Mariner*

We never know the worth of water till the well is dry.
—Thomas Fuller, M. D., *Gnomologia*, No. 5451

All know that the drop merges into the ocean but few know that the ocean merges into the drop.
—Kabir

He who has access to the fountain does not go to the water-pot.
—Leonardo da Vinci

The lowest ebb is the turn of the tide.—Henry Wadsworth Longfellow

The mill cannot grind with the water that has passed.
—O. S. Marden, *Conquest of Worry*

Whitewashing the pump won't make the water pure.
—Dwight L. Moody

Still waters runs deep.
—Proverb (14th century)

When you drink the water, remember the spring. —Proverb (Chinese)

Smooth runs the waters where the brook is deep . . .
—William Shakespeare, *King Henry VI, Part II*, Act III, Sc. i

A drop in the ocean has no fear of a hurricane.
—Alexander Solzhenitsyn, *Stories and Prose Poems*,
"A Storm in the Mountains"

It's not the sea that drowns you—it's the puddle.
—Alexander Solzhenitsyn, *The First Circle*

One may explain water, but the mouth will not become wet.—Takuan

Water which is too pure has no fish.
—Ts'ai Ken T'an

WEAKNESS

God appoints our graces to be nurses to other men's weaknesses.
—Henry Ward Beecher

. . . let the weak say, I am strong.
—*The Bible* (KJV): Joel 3:10

The weak have one weapon: the errors of those who think they are
strong. —Georges Bidault

WEALTH

Wealth is the test of a man's character. —Anonymous

. . . the monotonous beauty of wealth. —Judith Guest, *Ordinary People*

It is great wealth to a man to live frugally with a contented mind.
—Lucretius

Great wealth, great care. —Proverb (Dutch)

The greatest wealth is contentment with a little. —Proverb (English)

Reports of wealth or worth are best halved—and then halved again.
—Proverb (Spanish)

The advantages of wealth are greatly exaggerated. —Leland Stanford

WEAPONS

A bayonet is a weapon with a worker at both ends.
—Anonymous, British pacifist slogan, 1940

Stick by your guns, but don't fire.
—Anonymous, line from the movie *Now, Voyage* (1942)

Now we are all sons of bitches.
—Kenneth Bainbridge, American nuclear physicist,
remark after directing the first atomic test, 1945

I am become death—the shatterer of worlds.
—*Bhagavad-Gita*, recited by J. Robert Oppenheimer at
A-bomb test, Alamogordo, New Mexico, 16 Jul 1945

The way to win an atomic war is to make certain it never starts.
—Gen. Omar Bradley

I am proud of the fact that I never invented weapons to kill.
—Thomas A. Edison, *New York Times*, 8 Jun 1915

Arms are instruments of ill omen, not the instruments of the gentleman. When one is compelled to use them, it is best to do so without relish. —Lao Tzu, *Tao Te Ching*, Ch. XXXI

There will one day spring from the brain of science a machine or force so fearful in its potentialities, so absolutely terrifying, that even man, the fighter . . . will be appalled, and so abandon war forever. What man's mind can create, man's character can control.
—Thomas A. Edison, newspaper interview, 22 Aug 1921

The release of atom power has changed everything except our way of thinking . . . the solution to this problem lies in the heart of mankind. If only I had known, I should have become a watchmaker.
—Albert Einstein

Every gun that is made, every warship launched, every rocket fired signifies, in the final sense, a theft from those who hunger and are not fed, those who are cold and are not clothed. This world in arms is not spending money alone. It is spending the sweat of its laborers, the genius of its scientists, the hopes of its children.
—Dwight D. Eisenhower, speech, American Society of Newspaper Editors, 16 Apr 1953

We have perfected our weapons but failed to perfect the men who use them.
—Billy Graham, *World Aflame*

Covenants without swords are but words.
—Thomas Hobbes

. . . savage bears agree among themselves, but man without remorse beats out the deadly sword on the accursed anvil.
—Juvenal

In the future, if nuclear weapons are unleashed there will be no front and no rear.
—Nikita Kruschchev

As the bomb fell over Hiroshima and exploded, we saw an entire city disappear. I wrote in my log the words: "My God, what have we done?"
—Captain Robert Lewis, co-pilot of the B-29 "Enola Gay"

We knew the world would not be the same.
—J. Robert Oppenheimer, after first atomic test

Son, never pick up a gun unless you're starving, you or some of your kin . . . Unless somebody you love is hungry.
—Reynolds Price, "The Forseeable Future"

Never give a child a sword.
—Proverb (Latin)

A weapon is an enemy even to its owner.
—Proverb (Turkish)

W E A T H E R

Everybody talks about the weather, but nobody does anything about it.
　　—Charles Dudley Warner, editorial, *Hartford Courant*, 24 Aug 1897

W E A V I N G

The dark threads are as needful in the Weaver's skillful hand,
　As the threads of gold and silver in the pattern He has planned.
　　　　—Anonymous, "The Divine Weaver"

W I C K E D N E S S

Better be poor than wicked. 　　　　　　　　　—Anonymous

God bears with the wicked, but not forever. 　　—Miguel de Cervantes

To see and listen to the wicked is already the beginning of wickedness.
　　　　　　　　　　　—Confucius

Few men are wantonly wicked.
　　　　—Mahatma Gandhi, in *Young India*, 7 Jul 1927

One may detest the wickedness of a brother without hating him.
　　　　　　　　—Mahatma Gandhi

. . . wickedness is its own punishment. 　　　　—Francis Quarles

Do good even to the wicked; it is as well to shut a dog's mouth with a
　crumb. 　　　　　　　　　—Saadi, *Gulistan*

God preserves the wicked to give them time to repent.
　　—Comtesse de Sophie Rostopchine Ségur, *Un Bon Petit Diable*

I never wonder to see men wicked, but I often wonder to see them
　not ashamed. 　　—Jonathan Swift, *Thoughts on Various Subjects*

W I L L

What is the highest secret of victory and peace? To will what God
　wills, and strike a league with destiny. 　　—William R. Alger

Good is the will of the Lord. 　　　　　　　—Anonymous

You may fetter my leg, but Zeus himself cannot get the better of my
　free will. 　　　　　　　—Epictetus, *Discourses*

Where your will is ready, your feet are light.
—George Herbert, *Jacula Prudentum*

God's will sufficeth me.   —Mary of France (1496-1533), motto

All will be as God wills.   —Proverb (Gaelic)

What God wills, I will.   —Proverb (Italian)

When the will is prompt, the legs are light.   —Proverb (Italian)

If it is God's will, a broomstick can shoot.   —Proverb (Yiddish)

Every day you must find in yourself the will to put one foot in front
of the other . . .   —Alexander Solzhenitsyn, *The Oak and the Calf*

His will is our hiding place.   —Corrie ten Boom, *The Hiding Place*,
with John and Elizabeth Sherrill

WILLINGNESS

When a man's
Willing and eager, God joins in.   —Aeschylus

If you agree to carry a calf, they'll make you carry the cow.
—Anonymous

A good horse should be seldom spurred.
—Thomas Fuller, M. D., *Gnomologia*, No. 156

All lay load on the willing horse. —Thomas Fuller, M. D., *Gnomologia*

Spur not a willing horse.   —Proverb (German)

The one who pulls is the one they urge on.
—Alexander Solzhenitsyn, *The Gulag Archipelago Two*

WIND

I cannot explain the wind, but I can hoist a sail.   —Anonymous

WINNING

You have deeply ventured; / But all must do so who would greatly win.
—Lord Byron, *Marino Faliero*, I. ii.

Fields are won by those who believe in winning.
—Thomas Wentworth Higginson, *Americanism in Literature*

Winning is overemphasized. The only time it is really important is in surgery and war. —Al McGuire

When you win, nothing hurts. —Joe Namath

He who does not hope to win has already lost. —Jose Joaquin Olmedo

WINTER

I like winter because I can stay indoors without feeling guilty.
—Teressa Skelton

WISDOM

It is a profitable thing, if one is wise, to seem foolish.
—Aeschylus, *Prometheus Bound*

A learned man is a tank; a wiser man is a spring. —William R. Alger

Knowledge becomes wisdom only after it has been put to practical use. —Anonymous

Wisdom is a good purchase, though we pay dear for it. —Anonymous

A fool sees not the same tree that a wise man sees.
—William Blake, *The Marriage of Heaven and Hell*

As a solid rock is not shaken by the wind, so the wise man does not waver before blame or praise. —Buddhist saying

There is often wisdom under a shabby cloak. —Statius Caecilius

Wise men learn more from fools than fools from wise men.
—Cato the Elder

Be wiser than other people if you can, but do not tell them so.
—Earl of Chesterfield, letter to his son, 19 Nov 1745

Common sense, in an uncommon degree, is what the world calls wisdom. —Samuel Taylor Coleridge

Knowledge is proud that he has learned so much; / Wisdom is humble that he knows no more.
>—William Cowper, *The Task*, "The Winter Walk at Noon"

The fool wonders, the wise man asks. —Benjamin Disraeli

Before God we are all equally wise—equally foolish.
>—Albert Einstein, speech, Sorbonne, Paris

Go where he will, the wise man is at home.
>—Ralph Waldo Emerson, *Woodnotes*, Part iii.

Men are wiser than they know. —Ralph Waldo Emerson

The invariable mark of wisdom is to see the miraculous in the common.
>—Ralph Waldo Emerson,
>*Nature, Addresses, and Lectures*, "Prospects"

Knowledge is a process of piling up facts; wisdom lies in their simplification. —Martin H. Fischer

Wisdom was not at the top of the graduate-school mountain, but there at the sandpile at Sunday School. —Robert Fulghum,
>*All I Really Need to Know I Learned in Kindergarten*

Not to know certain things is a great part of wisdom. —Hugo Grotius

Do not grudge / To pick out treasures from an earthen pot. / The worst speaks something good. —George Herbert, *The Church-Porch*

He dares to be a fool, and that is the first step in the direction of wisdom. —James Gibbons Huneker

The art of being wise is the art of knowing what to overlook.
>—William James, *The Principles of Psychology*

It is a great folly to wish to be wise all alone.
>—François de La Rochefoucauld

It is easier to be wise on behalf of others than to be so for ourselves.
>—François de La Rochefoucauld, *Maximes*

Ripe in wisdom was he, but patient, and simple, and childlike.
>—Henry Wadsworth Longfellow, *Evangeline*

For only by unlearning Wisdom comes.
>—James Russell Lowell, *The Parting of the Ways*, Stanza 8

Knowledge comes by taking things apart. But wisdom comes by putting things together.
>—John A. Morrison

No man is wise enough by himself.
>—Plautus, *Miles Gloriosus*

No one is wise at all times.
>—Pliny the Elder, *Historia Naturalis*, Book VII, Ch. 41

No man is born wise.
>—Proverb (17th century)

The beginning of wisdom is to call things by their right names.
>—Proverb (Chinese)

A hint suffices for a wise man.
>—Proverb (French)

There exists a tie of kindred between all wise people.
>—Proverb (Greek)

Seek wisdom, not knowledge. Knowledge is of the past. Wisdom is of the future.
>—Proverb (Lumbee, Native American)

He bids fair to grow wise who has discovered that he is not so.
>—Publilius Syrus

It is not wise to be wiser than is necessary.
>—Philippe Quinault, *Armide*

Knowledge, to become Wisdom, needs Judgment.
>—Viscount Herbert Louis Samuel

The fool doth think he is wise, but the wise man knows himself to be a fool.
>—William Shakespeare, *As You Like It*, Act V, Sc. i

The beginning of wisdom is the definition of terms.
>—Socrates

A man should never be ashamed to own that he has been in the wrong, which is but saying, in other words, that he is wiser today than he was yesterday.
>—Jonathan Swift, *Thoughts on Various Subjects*

Knowledge comes, but wisdom lingers.
>—Alfred, Lord Tennyson, "Locksley Hall"

A word to the wise is sufficient.   —Terence

Wisdom is not high IQ. It is the best use of knowledge.
                                          —Lewis Timberlake

Wisdom is ofttimes nearer when we stoop / Than when we soar.
                              —William Wordsworth, *The Excursion*

The wise man reads both books and life itself.
                              —Lin Yutang, *The Importance of Living*

WISHES

We would often be sorry if our wishes were gratified.   —Aesop

If wishes were fishes, beggars would drink.   —Dane Marshall

If wishes were horses, beggars would ride.
                              —John Ray, *English Proverbs* (1670)

Few have all they need, none all they wish.   —Robert Southwell

WIT

The more wit you have, the more good nature you must show, to
   induce people to pardon your superiority, for that is no easy matter.
                                          —Earl of Chesterfield

Wit is salt of conversation, not the food.
                              —William Hazlitt, *Lectures on English Comic Writers*

WITNESSING

People can see when you've got good news.
                              —Grenville Barber, guest sermon, Hope Chapel,
                                          Austin, Texas, 7 Mar 1992

Let the redeemed of the Lord say so, whom he hath redeemed from
   the hand of the enemy.   —*The Bible* (KJV): Psalms 107:2

The way from God to a human heart is through a human heart.
                                          —S. D. Gordon

Witnessing is not a spare-time occupation or a once-a-week activity. It
   must be a quality of life. You don't go witnessing, you are a witness.
                                          —Dan Greene

What we have to share that's most powerful is what God has done for us. —Ron Parrish, sermon, Hope Chapel, Austin, Texas, 9 Sep 1995

Witnessing is one beggar telling another beggar where to find food.
—Lewis Timberlake

WOE

W'en you see a man in woe, / Walk right up and say 'hullo'; / Say "hullo" and "how d'ye do. / How's the world a-usin' you?"
—Sam Walter Foss, "Hullo"

Out of my great woe I make my little song.
—Heinrich Heine, "Aus meinen grossen Schmerzen"

Alas! by some degree of woe we every bliss must gain.
—Lord Lyttleton

By telling our woes we often assuage them.   —Proverb (French)

As night to stars, woe lustre gives to man.
—Edward Young, *Night Thoughts*, "Night 9"

WOMAN

The whisper of a beautiful woman can be heard farther than the loudest call of duty.   —Anonymous

Women are God's special creation—beautiful and foolish. Beautiful so that men would love them; foolish so that they would love men.
—Anonymous

Not she with trait'rous kiss her Savior stung, / Not she denied him with unholy tongue; / She, while apostles shrank, could danger brave, / Last at his cross and earliest at his grave.
—Eaton S. Barrett, "Woman"

One is not born a woman, one becomes one.
—Simone de Beauvoir, *The Second Sex*

Miss, n. A title which we brand unmarried women to indicate that they are in the market.   —Ambrose Bierce, *The Devil's Dictionary*

Next to God we are indebted to women, first for life itself, and then for making it worth having.   —Christian Nestell Bovée

If you get a fine woman, you get the finest thing on earth.
—Elaine Francis Burton, *What of the Woman?*

... it wasn't a woman who betrayed Jesus with a kiss.
—Catherine Carswell, *The Savage Pilgrimage*

A woman's advice has little value, but he who won't take it is a fool.
—Miguel de Cervantes, *Don Quixote*, Part II, Ch. 7

What is bettre than wisedoom? Womman. And what is bettre than a good womman? Nothyng.   —Geoffrey Chaucer, *Tale of Malibee*

... she seemed too friendly to be thought a beauty ...
—John Cheever, *Oh What a Paradise It Seems*

Her gentle limbs did she undress, and lay down in her loveliness.
—Samuel Taylor Coleridge, "Christabel"

O woman shapely as a swan. —Padraic Colum, *I Shall Not Die for Thee*

Woman is the most moral element in all humanity. —Auguste Comte

Woman is the masterpiece.   —Confucius

A lady is one who never shows her underwear unintentionally.
—Lillian Day, *Kiss and Tell*

There are few young women in existence who have not the power of fascinating, if they choose to exert it.   —Benjamin Disraeli

I'm not denyin' the women are foolish: God Almighty made 'em to match the men.   —George Eliot, *Adam Bede*, Ch. 53

A sufficient measure of civilization is the influence of good women.
—Ralph Waldo Emerson, *Society and Solitude*, "Civilization"

I did but see her passing by / And yet I love her till I die.
—Thomas Ford

Woman, I hold, is the personification of self-sacrifice, but unfortunately today she does not realize what a tremendous advantage she has over man. As Tolstoy used to say, they are laboring under the hypnotic influence of man. If they would realize the strength of non-violence they would not consent to be called the weaker sex.
—Mahatma Gandhi

It is, as it were, born in maidens that they should wish to please
everything that has eyes. —Salomon Gessner

There is Nothing Like a Dame. —Oscar Hammerstein II, title of a song
from the musical play *South Pacific*, music by Richard Rodgers

Women are the poetry of the world, in the same sense as the stars are
the poetry of heaven. —Hargrave

[Woman,] the crown of creation. —Herder

Nature is in earnest when she makes a woman.
—Oliver Wendell Holmes, Sr.,
The Autocrat of the Breakfast Table, Ch. 12

She moves a goddess, and she looks a queen. —Homer

Whoever embarks with women embarks with a storm; but they are
themselves the safety boats. —Arsene Houssaye

When a woman is talking to you, listen to what she says with her
eyes. —Victor Hugo

There is only one attribute that all charming women possess in common—an expressive, responsive face. —Peter Joray

Without woman the beginning of our life would be helpless, the middle without pleasure, and the end void of consolation.
—Victor de Jouy, *Sylla*

Some women'll stay in a man's memory if they once walked down a
street. —Rudyard Kipling, *Traffics and Discoveries*

The deep sea can be fathomed, but who knows the heart of a woman?
—Louis L'Amour, *The Walking Drum*

Nature meant woman to be her masterpiece.
—Gotthold Ephraim Lessing, *Emilia Galotti*, Act V, Sc. vii

Modesty in woman is a virtue most deserving, since we do all we can
to cure her of it. —Lingrée

She was not fair, / Nor beautiful;—those words express her not. / But,
oh, her looks had something excellent, / That wants a name!
—Henry Wadsworth Longfellow, *Hyperion*, Book III

When she had passed, it seemed like the ceasing of exquisite music.
—Henry Wadsworth Longfellow, *Evangeline*, Part I

Earth's noblest thing, a Woman perfected. —James Russell Lowell, *Irene*

But if God had wanted us to think just with our wombs, why did He
give us a brain? —Clare Booth Luce, in *Life*, 16 Oct 1970

A woman's best protection is a little money of her own.
—Clare Booth Luce

When you educate a man you educate an individual; when you edu-
cate a woman you educate a whole family.
—Dr. Charles D. McIver, speech,
North Carolina College for Women

Disguise our bondage as we will, / Tis woman, woman, rules us still.
—Thomas Moore, *Miscellaneous Poems*, "Sovereign Woman"

But all ladies think they weigh too much.
—Ogden Nash, *Verses From 1929 On*, "Curl Up and Diet"

Oh woman! lovely woman! nature made thee / To temper man; we
had been brutes without you; / Angels are painted fair to look like
you; / There's in you all that we believe of heaven, / Amazing
brightness, purity, and truth, / Eternal joy, and everlasting love.
—Thomas Otway, *Venice Preserved*, Act I, Sc. i

Whether they give or refuse, women are glad to have been asked.
—Ovid, *Ars Amatoria*

As long as she is wise and good, a girl has sufficient dowry.
—Plautus, *Aulularia*

The woman who has the best perfume is she who has none.
—Plautus, *Mostellaria*

If to her share some female errors fall / Look on her face, and you'll forget 'em all. —Alexander Pope, *The Rape of the Lock*, Canto II, line 17

Woman! thou loveliest gift that here below / Man can receive, or
Providence bestow. —Praed

We ask four things from a woman—that virtue dwell in her heart,
modesty in her forehead, sweetness in her mouth, and labor in her
hands. —Proverb (Chinese)

A maid that laughs is half taken. —Proverb (English)

I've always found it much more dangerous to fool with a man's mistress than his wife. —Harold Robbins, *The Inheritors*

O, woman! In our hours of ease, / Uncertain, coy, and hard to please, / And variable as the shade / By the light quivering aspen made; When pain and anguish wring the brow, / A ministering angel thou! —Sir Walter Scott, *Marmion*, Canto VI, Stanza 30

Kindness in women, not their beauteous looks, / Shall win my love. —William Shakespeare, *The Taming of the Shrew*, Act IV, Sc. ii

Who is't can read a woman? —William Shakespeare, *Cymbeline*, Act V, Sc. v

. . . one can judge a civilization by the way its treats its women. —Helen Foster Snow, *Woman in Modern China*, "Bound Feet and Straw Sandals"

. . . we had eyes only for the women. —Alexander Solzhenitsyn, *The Gulag Archipelago Three*

A simple maiden in her flower, / Is worth a hundred coats of arms. —Alfred, Lord Tennyson

Women add zest to the unlicensed hours. —Allen D. Thomas

. . . women are the pivot round which the world turns. —Leo Tolstoy, *Anna Karenina*

Women were the ones that held the reins, it emerged. —Anne Tyler, *Saint Maybe*, Ch. 1

People call me a feminist whenever I express sentiments that differentiate me from a doormat or a prostitute. —Rebecca West, in *The Clairion* (1913)

If woman lost us Eden, such / As she alone restore it. —John Greenleaf Whittier, "Among the Hills"

WONDER

Wonder—which is the seed of knowledge. —Francis Bacon, *Advancement of Learning*

Wonder is the basis of worship.
—Thomas Carlyle, *Sartor Resartus*, Book I, Ch. 10

Men love to wonder, and that is the seed of science.
—Ralph Waldo Emerson

Wonder rather than doubt is the root of knowledge.
—Abraham Joshua Heschel

Two things fill my mind with ever-increasing wonder and awe . . . the starry heavens above me and the moral law within me.
—Immanuel Kant, *Critique of Practical Reason*, Conclusion

It is man's destiny to ponder on the riddle of existence and, as a byproduct of his wonderment, to create a new life on this earth.
—Charles F. Kettering

To be surprised, to wonder, is to begin to understand.
—Jose Ortega y Gasset, *The Revolt of the Masses*

There is no other start to philosophy but wonder.   —Plato, *Theaetetus*

Wonder is the beginning of wisdom.   —Proverb (Greek)

A child said What is the grass? fetching it to one with full hands.
/ How could I answer the child? I do not know what it is any more than he.   —Walt Whitman, *Leaves of Grass*, "Song of Myself"

WONDERS

The more we learn about the wonders of our universe, the more clearly we are going to perceive the hand of God.   —Frank Borman

The world will never starve for want of wonders.   —G. K. Chesterton

WORDS

With our aptness for phrasemaking, we sometimes mesmerize ourselves into assuming that since we have cleverly labeled something, we have somehow magically solved the problem it presents.
—Louis L. Allen

Soft words win hard hearts.   —Anonymous

All words are pegs to hang ideas on.
—Henry Ward Beecher, in William Drysdale, editor,
Proverbs from Plymouth Pulpit, "Human Mind"

And I'm convinced that knowing the names of things braces people
up. —Saul Bellow, *Mr. Sammler's Planet*, Ch. 3

Pleasant words are as an honeycomb, sweet to the soul, and health to
the bones. —*The Bible* (KJV): Proverbs 16:24

Some of mankind's most terrible misdeeds have been committed
under the spell of certain magic words or phrases.
—James Bryant Conant

A word and a stone cannot be called back.
—Thomas Fuller, M. D., *Gnomologia*

Eschew fine words as you would rouge; love simple ones as you would
native roses on your cheek. —Hare

Words are such a playground! —Maureen Herring

A word once uttered can never be recalled. —Horace

Thanks to words, we have been able to rise above the brutes, and
thanks to words, we have often sunk to the level of the demons.
—Aldous Huxley, *Adonis and the Alphabet*

How many people make themselves abstract to appear profound! The
greatest part of abstract terms are shadows that hide a vacuum.
—Joseph Joubert

Words, like glasses, obscure everything they do not make clear.
—Joseph Joubert

Words are, of course, the most powerful drug used by mankind.
—Rudyard Kipling, speech, 14 Feb 1923

I am a Bear of Very Little Brain, and long words Bother me.
—A. A. Milne, *Winnie-the-Pooh*, Ch. 4

Words have a longer life than deeds. —Pindar

We don't sufficiently consider that words are deeds.
—Proverb (French)

Words do not make flour. —Proverb (Italian)

O! many a shaft, at random sent, / Finds mark the archer little meant; / And many a word, at random spoken, / May soothe or wound a heart that's broken.
> —Sir Walter Scott, *The Lord of the Isles*, Canto V, Stanza 18

The knowledge of words is the gate of scholarship. —Wilson

WORK

It is work which gives flavor to life.
> —Henri Frédéric Amiel, *The Private Journal of Henri Frédéric Amiel*

As is the workman so is the work. —Anonymous

A work ill done must be done twice. —Anonymous

Believe in yourself—you are marvelously endowed. Believe in your job—all honest work is sacred. —Anonymous

Everybody wants to harvest, but nobody wants to plow.
> —Anonymous

Every man's work is a portrait of himself. —Anonymous

Everything comes to him who waits, if he works while he waits.
> —Anonymous

Hard work is like shaving; the longer you put it off, the harder and tougher it becomes. —Anonymous

Interest will begin a hard work. Grit will continue it. But only love makes a man endure to the end. —Anonymous

It's always been and always will be the same in the world: the horse does the work and the coachman is tipped. —Anonymous

Mind your work, and God will find you wages. —Anonymous

Most of this world's useful work is done by people who are pressed for time, or are tired, or don't feel well. —Anonymous

No man is born into the world whose work is not born with him.
> —Anonymous

Not to oversee workmen is to leave them your purse open.
> —Anonymous

People forget how fast you did a job but they remember how well you did it.   —Anonymous

Plaster thick, / Some will stick.   —Anonymous

Too many people are ready to carry the stool when the piano needs to be moved.   —Anonymous

Workers find a thousand joys / The idle never do.   —Anonymous

The way to tell if your job is done: if you're alive, you've got a job.
—Richard Bach

Nothing is really work unless you would rather be doing something else.   —Sir James Matthew Barrie

You just can't be miserable as long as you are properly and enjoyably busy; there is no room for misery . . . Work is the best wonder drug ever devised by God.   —Dr. Orlando Battista

As a remedy against all ills—poverty, sickness, and melancholy—only one thing is absolutely necessary: a liking for work.
—Charles Baudelaire

The use of the head abridges the labor of the hands.
—Henry Ward Beecher

To work is to pray.   —Saint Benedict of Nursia, motto

. . . if any would not work, neither should he eat.
—*The Bible* (KJV): 2 Thessalonians 3:10

Hasten slowly, and without losing heart, put your work twenty times upon the anvil.   —Nicolas Boileau

Occupation is the scythe of time.   —Napoleon Bonaparte

Hard workers are usually honest, for industry lifts them above temptation.   —Christian Nestell Bovée

To have meaningful work is a tremendous happiness.
—Rita Mae Brown

Let us be content to work / To do the things we can, and not presume / To fret because it's little.   —Elizabeth Barrett Browning

Blessed is he who has found his work; let him ask no other blessedness.
—Thomas Carlyle, *Past and Present*, Book III

Every noble work is at first impossible.   —Thomas Carlyle

It is the first of all problems for a man to find out what kind of work
he is to do in this universe.   —Thomas Carlyle

. . . There is always hope in a man who actually and earnestly works.
—Thomas Carlyle

The work an unknown good man has done is like a vein of water
flowing hidden underground, secretly making the ground green.
—Thomas Carlyle

Work makes a callus against grief.   —Cicero

Honor lies in honest toil.   —Grover Cleveland

There is no truer and more abiding happiness than the knowledge
that one is free to go on doing, day by day, the best work one can
do, . . . , and that this work is absorbed by a steady market and thus
supports one's own life . . . Perfect freedom is reserved for the man
who lives by his own work and in that work does what he wants to
do.   —R. G. Collingwood, *Speculum Mentis*

When you are laboring for others let it be with the same zeal as if it
were for yourself.   —Confucius

I don't like work—no man does—but I like what is in the work—the
chance to find yourself.   —Joseph Conrad, *Heart of Darkness*

God gave man work, not to burden him, but to bless him, and useful
work, willingly, cheerfully, effectively done, has always been the
finest expression of the human spirit.   —Walter R. Courtenay

The worker is far more important to our Lord than the work.
—Lettie Cowman

We work not only to produce but to give value to time.
—Eugène Delacroix

The reward for work well done is more work to do. —Monroe E. Dodd

I never did a day's work in my life—it was all fun.—Thomas A. Edison

How do I work? I grope. —Albert Einstein

. . . one does people the best service by giving them some elevating
work to do and thus indirectly elevating them.
—Albert Einstein, *Ideas and Opinions*

A good solid bit of work lasts. —George Eliot

You must love your work and not always be looking over the edge of
it wanting your play to begin. —George Eliot

Every man's task is his life-preserver.
—Ralph Waldo Emerson, *The Conduct of Life*, "Worship"

If a man write a better book, preach a better sermon, or make a better
mouse-trap than his neighbor, tho' he build his house in the
woods, the world will make a beaten path to his door.
—Ralph Waldo Emerson

The reward of a thing well done, is to have done it.
—Ralph Waldo Emerson, *Essays, Second Series*,
"Nominalist and Realist"

What is there of the divine in a load of brick? What . . . in a barber
shop? . . . Much. All. —Ralph Waldo Emerson, *Journal*, 18 Jul 1834

Work and acquire, and thou hast chained the wheel of chance.
—Ralph Waldo Emerson, *Essays, First Series*, "Self-Reliance"

To the worker, God himself lends aid. —Euripides, *Hippolytus*

If people really liked to work, we'd still be plowing the land with
sticks and transporting goods on our backs. —William Feather

We all have ambivalent feelings toward work . . . We try to avoid it,
and yet we seem to require it for our emotional well-being.
—Samuel C. Florman, *The Existential Pleasures of Engineering*

Work is the meat of life, pleasure the dessert. —B. C. Forbes

Nothing is particularly hard if you divide it into small jobs.
—Henry Ford

At the working man's house hunger looks in, but dares not enter.
—Benjamin Franklin, *Poor Richard's Almanack*

The eye of the master will do more work than both his hands.
—Benjamin Franklin, *Poor Richard's Almanack*, 1758

No other technique for the conduct of life attaches the individual so
firmly to reality as laying emphasis on work; for his work at least
gives him a secure place in a portion of reality, in the human community.   —Sigmund Freud

By working faithfully eight hours a day, you may eventually get to be
a boss and work twelve hours a day.   —Robert Frost

Work is love made visible.   —Kahlil Gibran

Do thine own task, and be therewith content.
—Johann Wolfgang von Goethe

To love what you do and feel that it matters—how could anything be
more fun.   —Katherine Graham

Lift where you stand.   —Edward Everett Hale

Much good work is lost for lack of a little more.   —Edward Harriman

No life can be dreary when work is delight.   —F. R. Havergal

... happy because he does something well and does it every day.
—Ernest Hemingway, *Islands in the Stream*

... the carapace of work that he had built for his protection.
—Ernest Hemingway, *Islands in the Stream*

Good workmen are seldom rich.—George Herbert, *Outlandish Proverbs*

Work is the means of living, but it is not living.
—Josiah Gilbert Holland

O sweet solace of labor.   —Horace, *Odes*

We work to become, not to acquire.   —Elbert Hubbard

Every child should be taught that useful work is worship and that
intelligent labor is the highest form of prayer.
—Robert G. Ingersoll, "How to Reform Mankind"

I like work: it fascinates me. I can sit and look at it for hours.
—Jerome K. Jerome, *Three Men in a Boat*, Ch. 15

Few enterprises of great labor or hazard would be undertaken if we
had not the power of magnifying the advantages we expect from
them. —Samuel Johnson

When your work speaks for itself, don't interrupt it. —Henry J. Kaiser

Amateurs hope. Professionals work. —Garson Kanin

Thank God every morning when you get up that you have something
to do that day which must be done whether you like it or not.
—Charles Kingsley

No longer diverted by other emotions, I work the way a cow grazes.
—Kathè Kollwitz, *Kathè Kollwitz: Diaries and Letters*

By the work one knows the workman.
—Jean de La Fontaine, *Fables*, "The Hornets and the Bees"

To be successful, the first thing to do is fall in love with your work.
—Sister Mary Lauretta

If I had eight hours to chop down a tree, I'd spend six sharpening my
ax. —Abraham Lincoln

And so we plough along, as the fly said to the ox.
—Henry Wadsworth Longfellow

His brow is wet with honest sweat, / He earns whate'er he can, / And
looks the whole world in the face, / For he owes not any man.
—Henry Wadsworth Longfellow, "The Village Blacksmith"

It takes less time to do a thing right, than it does to explain why you
did it wrong. —Henry Wadsworth Longfellow

Let us, then, be up and doing, / With a heart for any fate; / Still
achieving, still pursuing, / Learn to labor and to wait.
—Henry Wadsworth Longfellow, *A Song of Life*

No man is born into the world whose work / Is not born with him;
there is always work, / And tools to work withal, for those who
will. —James Russell Lowell, *A Glance Behind the Curtain*

A dairymaid can milk cows to the glory of God. —Martin Luther

We must respect the work we do. / A slipshod method never pays— / It may get by, but in our minds It makes a scar that always stays.
—Rebecca McCann, "Cheerful Cherub"

When you work for the thing you believe in / You're rich though the whole way is rough— / But work that is simply for money / Will never quite pay you enough. —Rebecca McCann, "Cheerful Cherub"

Work should never make me weary / If I'm really meant to do it, / But it soon becomes exhausting / If it's greed that drives me to it.
—Rebecca McCann, "Cheerful Cherub"

A man's work is his dilemma: his job is his bondage, but it also gives him a fair share of his identity and keeps him from being a bystander in somebody else's world. —Melvin Maddocks

Capitalize on something you like to do. —Marchant

In the morning, when thou art sluggish at rousing thee, let this thought be present: "I am rising to a man's work."
—Marcus Aurelius Antoninus, *Meditations*

Every one who has labored honestly in the past has aided to place knowledge and comfort within the reach of a constantly increasing number. —O. S. Marden, *Pushing to the Front*

The workman still is greater than his work. —Menander

I go on working for the same reason that a hen goes on laying eggs.
—H. L. Mencken

. . . people who work sitting down get paid more than people who work standing up.
—Ogden Nash, *Many Long Years Ago*, "Will Consider Situation"

Work expands to fill the time available for its completion.
—C. Northcote Parkinson, Parkinson's Law (1962)

Whenever it is any way possible, every boy and girl should choose as his life work some occupation which he should like to do anyhow, even if he did not need the money. —William Lyon Phelps

Work, ah! that talisman to guard one against one's self. —Praed

If you could once make up your mind never to undertake more work . . .
than you can carry on calmly, quietly, without hurry or flurry . . . and
if the instant you feel yourself growing nervous and . . . out of breath,
you would stop and take a breath, you would find this simple com-
mon-sense rule doing for you what no prayers or tears could ever
accomplish.　　　　　　　　　　　　　　　　—Elizabeth Prentiss

The day is short and the work is long.　　　—Proverb (15th century)

One person can thread a needle better than two.
　　　　　　　　　　　　　　　　—Proverb (American Negro)

Do it well, that thou may'st not do it twice.　　—Proverb (English)

Think of ease, but work on.　　　　　　　　—Proverb (English)

The work will teach you how to do it.　　　　—Proverb (Estonian)

Work is worship.　　　　　　　　　　　　　—Proverb (French)

Work is our business; its success is God's.　　—Proverb (German)

The work praises the man.　　　　　　　　　　—Proverb (Irish)

Soon enough, if well enough.　　　　　　　　—Proverb (Latin)

A job is what we do for money; work is what we do for love.
　　　　　　　　　　　　　　　　　　　—Marysarah Quinn

Relax yourself from one job by doing a different one.
　　　　—Ernest Renan, inaugural lecture, Còllege de France, 1857

Far and away the best prize that life offers is the chance to work hard
at work worth doing.　　　—Theodore Roosevelt, Labor Day address,
　　　　　　　　　　　　　　　　　　Syracuse, New York, 7 Sep 1903

The highest reward for man's toil is not what he gets for it but what
he becomes by it.　　　　　　　　　　　　　　　—John Ruskin

One's work is never so bad as it appears on bad days, nor so good as it
appears on good days.
　　　　—Bertrand Russell, *The Autobiography of Bertrand Russell*

Work is not man's punishment. It is his reward and his strength, his
glory and his pleasure.　　　　　　　　　　　　—George Sand

I have never seen a man who could do real work except under the stimulus of encouragement and enthusiasm and the approval of the people for whom he is working.　　—Charles Schwab

I have yet to find the man, however exalted his station, who did not do better work and put forth greater effort under a spirit of approval, than under of a spirit of criticism.　　—Charles Schwab

All work that is worth anything is done in faith.
　　—Albert Schweitzer, *Out of My Life and Thought*

Lay hold of today's task, and you will not depend so much upon tomorrow's.　　—Seneca, *Epistuloe ad Lucilium*

When I was a young man I observed that nine out of ten things I did were failures. I didn't want to be a failure, so I did ten times more work.　　—George Bernard Shaw

The test of a vocation is the love of the drudgery it involves.
　　—Logan Pearsall Smith, *Afterthoughts*, "Art and Letters"

It was a funny thing how time flew when you were working.
　　—Alexander Solzhenitsyn, *One Day in the Life of Ivan Denisovich*

I know what pleasure is, for I have done good work.
　　—Robert Louis Stevenson

Integrate what you believe into every single area of your life. Take your heart to work and ask the most and best of everybody else. Don't let your special character and values, the secret that you know and no one else does, the truth—don't let that get swallowed up by the great chewing complacency.　　—Meryl Streep

God's work done in God's way will never lack God's supplies.
　　—J. Hudson Taylor

Many people mistake our work, for our vocation is the love of Jesus.
　　—Mother Teresa, from the documentary film *Mother Teresa*

In our zeal to make a living we have forgotten to make a life.
　　—Lewis Timberlake

You can employ men and hire hands to work for you, but you must win their hearts to have them work with you.　　—Tiorio

... it is the work and not the reward that is precious.
—Leo Tolstoy, *Anna Karenina*

The less important you are on the table of organization, the more you'll be missed if you don't show up for work.
—Bill Vaughan, "Vaughan's Rule of Corporate Life,"
in Paul Dickson, compiler, *The Official Rules*

That's true enough, said Candide, but we must go and work in the garden.
—Voltaire, *Candide*

Work spares us from three evils: boredom, vice, and need.
—Voltaire, *Candide*

Out of the strain of the Doing, / Into the peace of the Done.
—Julia Louise Mathilda Woodruff, "Harvest Home"

W O R K S

Your actions in passing, pass not away, for every good work is a grain of seed for eternal life.
—Saint Bernard of Clairvaux

... He that believeth on me, the works that I do shall he do also ...
—*The Bible* (KJV): John 14:12

But be ye doers of the word, and not hearers only, deceiving your own selves.
—*The Bible* (KJV): James 1:22

What doth it profit, my brethren, though a man say he hath faith, and have not works? Can faith save him?
—*The Bible* (KJV): James 2:14

... faith without works is dead ...
—*The Bible* (KJV): James 2:20

... by works a man is justified, and not by faith only.
—*The Bible* (KJV): James 2:24

Every man is the son of his own works.
—Miguel de Cervantes, *Don Quixote*

You never will be saved by works; but let us tell you most solemnly that you never will be saved without works.
—T. L. Cuyler

You are not saved by works; you are saved to work.
—Lewis Timberlake

The WORLD

Isn't it wonderful to have such a beautiful world to suffer in?
—Anonymous

No cradle for an emperor's child was ever prepared with so much
magnificence as this world has been made for man. But it is only
his cradle. —Henry Ward Beecher, in William Drysdale, editor,
Proverbs from Plymouth Pulpit

The world is God's workshop for making men in.
—Henry Ward Beecher, in William Drysdale, editor,
Proverbs from Plymouth Pulpit, "Manhood"

To see a World in a Grain of Sand, / And a Heaven in a Wild Flower, /
Hold Infinity in the palm of your hand, / And Eternity in an hour.
—William Blake, "Auguries of Innocence"

All isn't well with the world. —Ray Bradbury, *Fahrenheit 451*

Who knows but the world may end to-night.
—Robert Browning, *The Last Ride Together*

This world, after all our science and sciences, is still a miracle; wonderful, inscrutable, magical and more, to whosoever will think of
it. —Thomas Carlyle, *On Heroes,
Hero-Worship, and the Heroic in History* (1841)

If we can't turn the world around we can at least bolster the victims.
—Liz Carpenter

The world is not made for the prosperous alone, nor for the strong.
—George William Curtis

To me it seems as if when God conceived the world, that was Poetry;
He formed it, and that was Sculpture; He colored it, and that was
Painting; He peopled it with living beings, and that was the grand,
divine, eternal Drama. —Charlotte Cushman

How can this world, which is so beautiful, include so much horror?
—Eugène Delacroix

With all its sham, drudgery and broken dreams, it is still a beautiful
world. —Max Ehrman, "Desiderata"

The world is a beautiful place to be born into if you don't mind some
people dying all the time or maybe only starving some of the time
which isn't half so bad if it isn't you.
—Lawrence Ferlinghetti, *Pictures of the Gone World*

It's a funny old world—a man's lucky if he gets out of it alive.
—W. C. Fields, *You're Telling Me* (movie)

If you think the world is all wrong, remember that it contains people
like you. —Mahatma Gandhi

I believe that our Great Maker is preparing the world, in His own
good time, to become one nation, speaking one language, and
when armies and navies will be no longer required.
—Ulysses S. Grant

The world is charged with the grandeur of God.
—Gerard Manley Hopkins, "God's Grandeur"

For every man the world is as fresh as it was at the first day, and as full
of untold novelties for him who has the eyes to see them.
—Thomas Henry Huxley

This world, where much is to be done and little to be known.
—Samuel Johnson, *Prayers and Meditations*

As the world is wearie of me so am I of it. —John Knox

The new electronic interdependence recreates the world in the image
of a global village. —Marshall McLuhan, *The Gutenberg Galaxy*

The world, dear Agnes, is a strange affair. —Molière, *L'Ecole des fem*

The unrest of this weary world is its unvoiced cry after God.—Munger

You can't measure the whole world with your own yardstick.
—Proverb (Yiddish)

Half the world does not know how the other half lives.
—François Rabelais, *Pantagruel*

A wonder it must be, that there should be any man found stupid as to
persuade himself that this most beautiful world could be produced
by the fortuitous concourse of atoms. —John Ray

The world that we're living in / Is mighty hard to beat; / You get a thorn with every rose— / But ain't the roses sweet.
—James Whitcomb Riley

A world is to be fought for, sung, and built: Love must imagine the world.
—Muriel Rukeyser

. . . the whole world of loneliness, poverty, and pain make a mockery of what human life should be.
—Bertrand Russell, *The Autobiography of Bertrand Russell*

The world that we must seek is a world in which the creative spirit is alive, in which life is an adventure full of joy and hope, based rather upon the impulse to construct than upon the desire to retain what we possess or to seize what is possessed by others. It must be a world in which affection has free play, in which love is purged of the instinct for domination, in which cruelty and envy have been dispelled by happiness and the unfettered development of all the instincts that build up life and fill it with mental delights. Such a world is possible; it waits only for men to wish to create it.
—Bertrand Russell, *Roads to Freedom*

A man's feet should be planted in his country, but his eyes should survey the world.
—George Santayana

You should live in the world so as it may hang about you like a loose garment.
—George Savile

Why, then the world's mine oyster, / Which I with sword will open.
—William Shakespeare, *The Merry Wives of Windsor*, Act II, Sc. ii

The world is too dangerous for anything but the truth and too small for anything but brotherhood.
—Adlai Stevenson

The World is so full of a number of things, / I'm sure we should all be as happy as kings.
—Robert Louis Stevenson, *A Child's Garden of Verses*, XXIV, "Happy Thought"

The only true method of action in this world is to be in it, but not of it.
—Madame Swetchine

The world is a looking glass and gives to every man the reflection of his own face.
—William Makepeace Thackeray

Dear Lord, what a madhouse the world is!
—Leo Tolstoy, *Anna Karenina*

All is for the best in the best of possible worlds.
>—Voltaire, *Candide*, Ch. 1

This world is a comedy to those that think, a tragedy to those that
feel.
>—Horace Walpole, letter to Anne, Countess of Upper Ossory, 1776

The world is too much with us; late and soon, / Getting and spending, we lay waste our powers. —William Wordsworth, *Miscellaneous*
>*Sonnets*, Part I, xxxiii., "To Sleep"

WORRY

And which of you with taking thought can add to his stature one
cubit?
>—*The Bible* (KJV): Luke 12:25

When I look back on all these worries I remember the story of the old
man who said on his deathbed that he had a lot of trouble in his
life, most of which never happened.
>—Winston Churchill

Worry never robs tomorrow of its sorrow; it only saps today of its
strength.
>—A. J. Cronin

Worry is interest paid on trouble before it falls due. —William R. Inge

How much pain have cost us the evils which never happened.
>—Thomas Jefferson, *Writings*, Vol. xvi

I'll worry about that tomorrow, if it happens.
>—Al Leighton, 7 Aug 1990

My daddy used to tell me not to chew on somethin that was eatin
you.
>—Cormac McCarthy, *All the Pretty Horses*, Ch. 4

Worries go down better with soup than without. —Proverb (Jewish)

Worry gives a small thing a big shadow. —Proverb (Swedish)

If you love God, you never have to worry again.
>—Phillip Daniel Watkins (age 7)

WORSHIP

Worship is transcendent wonder.
>—Thomas Carlyle, *On Heroes and Hero-Worship, and the Heroic in*
>*History* (1841), I, "The Hero as Divinity"

There must be some great truth underlying the instinct for worship.
—Sir Oliver Joseph Lodge

He who carves the Buddha never worships him.   —Proverb (Chinese)

To worship rightly is to love each other, each smile a hymn, each
kindly deed a prayer.   —John Greenleaf Whittier

WRITING

After being turned down by numerous publishers, he had decided to
write for posterity.   —George Ade, *Fables in Slang*

It's not a college degree that makes a writer. The great thing is to have
a story to tell.   —Polly Adler

A blank page is God's way of showing you how hard it is to be God.
—Anonymous

A writer is a person who can't resist raping an innocent piece of
paper.   —Anonymous

What is spoken flies, what is written remains.   —Anonymous

I write with experiences in mind, but I don't write about them, I write
out of them.   —John Ashberry

Reading maketh a full man; conference a ready man; and writing an
exact man.   —Francis Bacon, *Essays*, "Of Studies"

Writing is nothing more than a guided dream.
—Jorge Luis Borges, *Dr. Brodie's Report*, Preface

Tell a good story. And let it bring your characters to a different place
(in soul and/or body) than where they started out.
—Catherine Breslin

Beneath the rule of men entirely great, / The pen is mightier than the
sword.   —Edward Bulwer-Lytton (1803-1873), *Richelieu*

In books, it is the chief of all perfections to be plain and brief.—Butler

Every word written is a victory against death.   —Michael Butor

A drop of ink may make a million think.   —Lord Byron

Those who write clearly have readers; those who write obscurely have commentators. —Albert Camus

Talent, and genius as well, is like a grain of pearl sand shifting about in the creative mind. A valued tormentor. —Truman Capote

To me, the greatest pleasure of writing is not what it's about, but the inner music the words make.
—Truman Capote, in *McCall's*, Nov 1967

Writing has laws of perspective, of light and shade, just as painting does, or music. —Truman Capote

Most of the basic material a writer works with is acquired before the age of fifteen. —Willa Cather

The pen is the tongue of the mind.
—Miguel de Cervantes, *Don Quixote*

Speak your dialogue out loud. If it sounds like the way people talk, then write it down. —Tom Clancy

I am convinced that all writers are optimists whether they concede the point or not . . . How otherwise could any human being sit down to a pile of blank sheets and decide to write, say two hundred thousand words on a given theme? —Thomas Costain

Who often reads, will sometimes wish to write.
—George Crabbe, *Tales*, xi, "Edward Shore"

Writing is a holy chore. —Harlan Ellison

Talent alone cannot make a writer. There must be a man behind the book. —Ralph Waldo Emerson

If you would be a reader, read; if a writer, write.—Epictetus, *Discourses*

Everything goes by the board: honor, pride, decency . . . to get the book written. If a writer has to rob his mother, he will not hesitate; the "Ode on a Grecian Urn" is worth any number of old ladies.
—William Faulkner

It is the writer's privilege to help man endure by lifting his heart.
—William Faulkner, speech upon receiving the Nobel Prize, 10 Dec 1950

Writing is easy; all you do is sit staring at a blank sheet of paper until the drops of blood form on your forehead. —Gene Fowler

I publish a piece in order to kill it, so that I won't have to fool around with it any longer. —William Gass

The most beautiful things are those that madness prompts and reason writes. —André Gide, *Journal*

The difference between prose and poetry is that prose is written all the way across the page, and poetry is written only half way across. —Laura Glover

If any man wishes to write in a clear style, let him first be clear in his thoughts. —Johann Wolfgang von Goethe

If they didn't pay me [to write], I'd do it for nothing. —Laurel Goldman

Writing is a form of therapy; how do all those who do not write, compose, or paint manage to escape the melancholia, the panic and fear which is inherent in the human condition? —Graham Greene

Writing is putting one's obsessions in order. —Jean Grenier

Everything that a painter did or that a writer wrote was a part of his training and preparation for what he was to do. —Ernest Hemingway, *Islands in the Stream*

We are all apprentices in a craft where no one ever becomes a master. —Ernest Hemingway

Money to a writer is time to write. —Frank Herbert

A writer and nothing else: a man alone in a room with the English language, trying to get human feelings right. —John K. Hutchens

Great writers leave us not just their works, but a way of looking at things. —Elizabeth Janeway

By writing, you learn to write. —Samuel Johnson

The only end of writing is to enable the readers better to enjoy life, or better to endure it. —Samuel Johnson, *A Free Inquiry*

While an author is yet living, we estimate his powers by his worst
performance; and when he is dead, we rate him by his best.
—Samuel Johnson

Everyone has talent. What is rare is the courage to follow the talent
to the dark place where it leads.   —Erica Jong

I don't like to write, but I love to have written.   —Michael Kanin

When my sonnet was rejected, I exclaimed, "Damn the age; I will
write for Antiquity!"   —Charles Lamb, letter to B. W. Proctor

How can you write if you can't cry?   —Ring Lardner

I try to leave out the parts that people skip.   —Elmore Leonard

When once the itch of literature comes over a man, nothing can cure
it but the scratching of a pen. —Samuel Lover, *Handy Andy*, Ch. 36

Tell a story! Don't try to impress your reader with style or vocabulary
or neatly turned phrases. Tell the story first!   —Anne McCaffrey

The writer must hew the phantom rock.
—Carson McCullers, *The Mortgaged Heart*,
"Who Has Seen the Wind?"

But I begin to think the chief difficulty in writing a book must be to
keep out what does not belong to it.
—George Macdonald, *The Flight of the Shadow*, Ch. 1

Writers don't have lifestyles. They sit in little rooms and write.
—Norman Mailer

You can't be a serious writer of fiction unless you believe the story
you are telling.
—Norman Mailer, Sean Abbott interview,
"Mailer Goes to the Mountain," *At Random*, Spring-Summer 1997

I think I did pretty well, considering I started out with nothing but a
bunch of blank paper.   —Steve Martin

I write in order to attain that feeling of tension relieved and function
achieved which a cow enjoys on giving milk.   —H. L. Mencken

A person who publishes a book appears willfully in public with his
pants down.   —Edna St. Vincent Millay

Writing, like life itself, is a voyage of discovery. —Henry Miller

Never write up your diary on the day itself, for it takes longer than that to know what happened. —Christopher Morley

An author departs; he does not die. —Dinah Maria Mulock

Authors of all races, be they Greeks, Romans, Teutons, or Celts, / Can't seem just to say anything is the thing it is but have to go out of their way to say that it is like something else.
  —Ogden Nash, *Verses From 1929 On*, "Very Like a Whale"

I needed to live, but I also needed to record what I lived. —Anïas Nin

I can't write five words but that I change seven. —Dorothy Parker

. . . The principle, axiomatic in literature: that to know when one's self is interested, is the first condition of interesting other people.
  —Walter Pater, *Marius the Epicurean*

A good title should be like a good metaphor: it should intrigue without being too baffling or too obvious. —Walker Percy

Just get it down on paper, and then we'll see what to do with it.
  —Maxwell Perkins, advice to Marcia Davenport

Word by word the book is made. —Proverb (French)

Writing is the only profession where no one considers you ridiculous if you earn no money. —Jules Renard

Fundamentally, all writing is about the same thing: it's about dying, about the brief flicker of time we have here, and the frustrations that it creates. —Mordecai Richler

Anyone should be very suspicious of a sentence he's written that can't be read aloud easily.
  —Andrew A. Rooney, *A Few Minutes with Andy Rooney*, Preface

The only reason for being a professional writer is that you just can't help it. —Leo Rosten

Whatever may be our natural talents, the art of writing is not acquired all at once. —Jean Jacques Rousseau

The universe is made of stories, not of atoms.
—Muriel Rukeyser, *The Speed of Darkness*, "The Speed of Darkness"

A pure style in writing results from the rejection of everything super-fluous. —Albertine Adrienne Necker de Saussure

Long sentences in a short composition are like large rooms in a little house. —William Shenstone

Biting my truant pen, beating myself for spite: / "Fool!" said my Muse to me, "look in thy heart and write."
—Sir Philip Sidney, *Astrophel and Stella*, Sonnet 1

A good writer is basically a story-teller, not a scholar or a redeemer of mankind. —Isaac Bashevis Singer

The waste basket is a writer's best friend. —Isaac Bashevis Singer

What I like in a good author is not what he says, but what he whis-pers. —Logan Pearsall Smith, *Afterthoughts*, "All Trivia"

There's nothing to writing. All you do is sit down at a typewriter and open a vein. —Red Smith

In our age, when technology is gaining control over life, when mater-ial well-being is considered the most important goal, when the influence of religion has been weakened everywhere in the world, a special responsibility lies upon the writer.
—Alexander Solzhenitsyn

A good writer always works at the impossible. —John Steinbeck

In utter loneliness a writer tries to explain the inexplicable.
—John Steinbeck

One does not consider style, because style is. —Robert Stone

You can only write about what bites you.
—Tom Stoppard, in *The Observer*, 1984

The two most engaging powers of an author are to make new things familiar, and familiar things new. —William Makepeace Thackeray

Writing . . . is practically the only activity a person can do that is not competitive. —Paul Theroux

As to the adjective: when in doubt, strike it out.
—Mark Twain, *Pudd'nhead Wilson*, Ch. 11

The difference between the almost right word and the right word is really a large matter—'tis the difference between the lightning bug and lightning.
—Mark Twain, *The Art of Authorship*

All styles are good except the tedious kind.
—Voltaire, *L'Enfant prodigue* (1738 edition), Preface

The adjective is the enemy of the noun.
—Voltaire

You can never correct your work well until you have forgotten it.
—Voltaire

The art of writing is the art of applying the seat of the pants to the seat of the chair.
—Mary Heaton Vorse

All morning I worked on the proof of one of my poems, and I took out a comma; in the afternoon I put it back.
—Oscar Wilde

Why did I write? Because I found life unsatisfactory.
—Tennessee Williams

WRONGS

They hurt themselves that wrong others.
—Anonymous

He who wrongs one threatens many.
—Publilius Syrus

— Y —

YIELDING

Oaks may fall when reeds stand the storm.
—Thomas Fuller, M. D., *Gnomologia*, No. 3692

I bend but do not break.
—Jean de La Fontaine, *Fables*, Book I, "The Oak and the Reed"

Bowed down then preserved; / Bent then straight; / Hollow then full; / Worn then new; / A little then benefited; / A lot then perplexed.
—Lao Tzu, *Tao Te Ching*, Ch. XXII

A storm breaks trees. It only bends grass.
—Alexander Solzhenitsyn, *Cancer Ward*

Yield to God.
—Virgil

YOUTH

In case you're worried about what's going to become of the younger generation, it's going to grow up and start worrying about the younger generation.
—Roger Allen

Few, if any, survive their teens. Most surrender to the vague but murderous pressure of adult conformity.
—Maya Angelou, *I Know Why the Caged Bird Sings*

Youth is easily deceived because it is quick to hope.
—Aristotle, *Rhetoric*

It is good for a man that he bear the yoke in his youth.
—*The Bible* (KJV): Lamentations 3:27

The young do not know enough to be prudent, and therefore they attempt the impossible, and achieve it, generation after generation.
—Pearl S. Buck

. . . you are a man still young, so to say, in your first youth and so put intellect above everything . . .
—Fyodor Dostoyevsky, *Crime and Punishment*

Girls we love for what they are; young men for what they promise to
   be.   —Johann Wolfgang von Goethe

No young man believes he shall ever die.
        —William Hazlitt, "On the Feeling of Immortality in Youth"

What is more enchanting than the voices of young people when you
   can't hear what they say?   —Samuel Johnson

Be gentle with the young.   —Juvenal, *Satires*

Youth is happy because it has the ability to see beauty. Anyone who
   keeps the ability to see beauty never grows old.   —Franz Kafka

When you're a little kid, your heart is open and tender and a harsh
   word can go straight in and become part of your life.
                —Garrison Keillor, *We Are Still Married*

A boy's will is the wind's will, / And the thoughts of youth are long,
   long thoughts.   —Henry Wadsworth Longfellow, "My Lost Youth"

. . . it was good that God kept the truths of life from the young as
   they were starting out or else they'd have no heart to start at all.
           —Cormac McCarthy, *All the Pretty Horses*, Ch. 4

"We've all got to be young once," said Mr. Thompson. "It's like the
   measles, it breaks out all over you, and you're a nuisance to yourself and everybody else, but it don't last, and it usually don't leave
   no ill effects."   —Katherine Anne Porter, *Noon Wine*

There is a strong disposition in youth, from which some individuals
   never escape, to suppose that everyone else is having a more enjoyable time than we are ourselves.
           —Anthony Powell, *A Buyer's Market*, Ch. 4

Youth lives on hopes, old age on remembrance.   —Proverb (French)

It's all that the young can do for the old, to shock them and keep
   them up to date.
        —George Bernard Shaw, *Fanny's First Play*, "Induction"

Don't laugh at a youth for his affectations; he is only trying on one
   face after another until he finds his own.
            —Logan Pearsall Smith, *Afterthoughts*

The denunciation of the young is a necessary part of the hygiene of older people, and greatly assists the circulation of their blood.
—Logan Pearsall Smith, *More Trivia*, "Last Words"

... the peak age when the ear of experience had already ripened and yet the stem of energy is still strong.
—Alexander Solzhenitsyn, *Cancer Ward*

The youth gets together his materials to build a bridge to the moon, or, perchance, a palace or temple on the earth, and, at length, the middle-aged man concludes to build a woodshed with them.
—Henry David Thoreau, *Journal*, 14 Jul 1852

Youth must have its fling.
—Leo Tolstoy, *The Death of Ivan Ilych and Other Stories*, "The Death of Ivan Ilych"

The deepest definition of youth is life as yet untouched by tragedy.
—Alfred North Whitehead, *Adventures of Ideas*

— Z —

Z E A L

Press bravely onward! not in vain / Your generous trust in human-kind; / The good which bloodshed could not gain / Your peaceful zeal shall find.
  —John Greenleaf Whittier, *To the Reformers of England*, Stanza 13

INDEX

THOSE MOST QUOTED